Best Practices in School Psychology

Best Practices in School Psychology

Edited by

Alex Thomas
Port Clinton City Schools
Port Clinton, Ohio

Jeff Grimes
Iowa Department of Public Instruction
Des Moines, Iowa

The National Association of School Psychologists
Kent, Ohio

First Printing: 1985
Second Printing: 1986

Published by The National Association of School Psychologists
Kent, Ohio

ISBN 0-932955-00-2

Printed in the United States of America

Acknowledgements

The editors wish to thank Carol Kelly and Susan Vess for their assistance in reviewing drafts of all manuscripts. In addition, we are indebted to Dan Reschly, George Batsche, David Hanson, Mary St. Cyr, and Judy Fulwider for their efforts in this project.

Although we realize that *Best Practices in School Psychology* does not necessarily represent the universe of current knowledge for the respective topics, we fervently hope it will provide a valuable professional resource.

Alex Thomas
Jeff Grimes

From NASP Publications Policy Handbook

The content of this document reflects the ideas and positions of the authors. The responsibility lies solely with the authors and does not necessarily reflect the position or ideas of the National Association of School Psychologists.

Contents

16. **Best Practices in Vocational Assessment for Handicapped Students**
    Thomas Hohenshil, Edward Levinson and Kathy Heer 215

17. **Best Practices in Neuropsychological Assessment**
    George Hynd and Jeff Snow 229

18. **Best Practices in Procedural Safeguards**
    Michael Kabler 237

19. **Best Practices in Dealing with Discipline Referrals**
    Howard Knoff 251

20. **Best Practices in Parent Training**
    Jack Kramer 263

21. **Best Practices in Evaluating Educational Programs**
    Charles Maher and Louis Kruger 275

22. **Best Practices in Working with Severely and Profoundly Handicapped Children**
    Christopher Matey 285

23. **Best Practices in Computer Applications**
    C. Sue McCullough 301

24. **Best Practices in Interviewing**
    James Murphy 311

25. **Best Practices in Working with Families of Handicapped Children**
    Joseph Murray 321

26. **Best Practices in Working with Community Agencies**
    Jeanne Plas and Blanche Williams 331

27. **Best Practices in Organizing Professional Support Groups**
    Jack Presbury and Harriet Cobb 341

28. **Best Practices: Adaptive Behavior**
    Daniel Reschly 351

29. **Best Practices in Assessment of Visually Handicapped Students**
    Greg Robinson 369

30. **Best Practices in Report Writing**
    Gary Ross-Reynolds 381

31. **Best Practices in Counseling Senior High School Students**
    Marcia Shaffer 393

Appendices

Ordering Information
Available in January, 1985
Price for BEST PRACTICES IN SCHOOL PSYCHOLOGY is $20.00

Name _____

Mailing Address _____

_____

Enclose check and send to: NASP Publications, 10 Overland Drive, Stratford, CT 06497

BEST PRACTICES IN THE ASSESSMENT OF CHILDREN'S PERSONALITY

David W. Barnett
University of Cincinnati

Karl B. Zucker
Indiana State University

OVERVIEW

Personality assessment has been controversial for some time. The field is often represented by one of several schools of thought leading to the development of seemingly different methods of personality appraisal, with none completely escaping criticism.

Yet children today are as complex as ever, and despite numerous problems, the assessment of personal and social functioning has much to offer. No other domain of assessment is as integrative in that it requires the psychologist to consider the subjective experience, personal goals, skills, motivations of the client and significant others in terms of the deeper meanings of adjustment. Nor does any other domain come closer to the priorities that should be established when intervening in the lives of children. The focus should be on the most significant sources of life satisfaction and the most complete view of the child. This chapter includes a review of the major issues and a contemporary overview of personality assessment along with suggested practices.

Brief History/Background

Personality assessment has played an integral role in the practice of psychology almost as long as psychology has been practiced as a profession. The early history of personality assessment is largely the history of projective techniques, although objective personality tests had their beginnings at about the same time (Magary, 1967). As early as 1909, Jung was lecturing on the word association method at Clark Univerity (Goodstein & Lanyon, 1971). In 1921 the Rorschach test was published, and in 1935, the Thematic Apperception Test (Morgan & Murray, 1935).

Interest in the study of personality grew rapidly along with the fields of clinical and school psychology during the 1940s and 1950s. In the 1960s, when anything that had been "established" was challenged, when the behavioral model attracted many psychologists, when humanists questioned the need for testing, and when published research raised serious questions regarding validity, personality assessment, and especially the use of projective techniques, began to fall out of favor (Cleveland, 1976). Interest in other approaches, such as objective tests of personality, rating scales, and systematic behavioral observations, had already been increasing. It appeared to many that if personality assessment were to survive — and even this was hotly debated — these other approaches would have to be the procedures of the future.

But many psychologists who were interested in personality assessment never saw a conflict between the use of projective techniques or other methods. Rather, they advocated an integration of all types of assessment procedures within the framework of an idiographic approach (Klopfer, 1970). This process is still favored by many experienced school and clinical psychologists (Conti, 1983; Falk, 1981; Knoff, 1983a; Weiner, 1983) and is an approach to assessment described in the present chapter.

A Contemporary Overview

The idiographic method of personality assessment acquired many adherents during the years when personality assessment was experiencing its greatest popularity. Not only has this continued to be the preferred approach, but the state of our knowledge today, with much credit due to critics, enables one to use assessment methods in a conservative, but effective manner. An emphasis should be on procedural safeguards, an inherent part of the method. Stated in contemporary language, using currently accepted concepts, the model recommended in this chapter can be described as follows: Learning about people through personality assessment is a matter of drawing reasonable inferences from the careful study of behavior samples, including test responses. Both the idiographic approach and the N=1 research model are important. First, one generates hypotheses from available data and tests them until sufficient internal verification is obtained to warrant confidence in their acceptance. Next these hypotheses must be evaluated not only in terms of their potential for accounting for the varied data, but also their potential for making consistent predictions and suggesting interventions. The results from these predictions and interventions serve as further validity checks. Single-case research designs imply that behavior is continuously assessed, as are the effects of well defined interventions (Kazdin, 1982).

Personality "is a hypothetical construct designed to bring order and consistency to the explanation of an individual's behavior" (Monte, 1977, p. 26). Personality assessment does not give a direct answer to the question of whether the child is "disturbed"; instead the result should be a clearer understanding of how the child functions and why. It is from this better understanding of the child's functioning that the psychologist must judge if the child fits the criteria of disturbance under consideration, whether those of PL 94-

142 or any others. This is a judgment which a psychologist must make after careful study and thought, taking into account the personality assessment results.

BASIC CONSIDERATIONS

Professional Preparation

Since personality assessment is a complex process, no single course can be expected to prepare a person adequately for it. Foundation courses, especially in personality theory and emotional disturbance; coursework and practica in psychoeducational interventions; and formal coursework in personality assessment should precede and be integrated into supervised experience in assessment, normally gained through practica and internships.

Procedural Safeguards for Reducing Clinical Assessment Error

The nature of clinical assessment errors deserve consideration. The discussion should go beyond the reliability and validity of tests, interviews, and observations, which have received attention for their psychometric characteristics. The validity issue, so often used as a reason for excluding personality tests, especially projectives, from the assessment process becomes less problematic when the idiographic approach is understood. Knoff (1983b) reminds us that the validation process is a broader issue and should include test batteries, judgment, and corresponding decisions. The most serious errors probably stem from inadequate conceptualizations, theoretical biases, and the selection of goals for treatment based upon inadequate tools (McDermott, 1981; Nay, 1979). For example, different theoretical frameworks for understanding aggressive behaviors can imply very different assessment techniques and treatments, only some of which may have established validity. Other errors involve overgeneralizing from a relatively small sample of behavior and perceiving consistencies in behavior due to bias or limited information. Therefore, the importance of building in safeguards needs to be stressed. A review of some of the important ones follows.

Decisions about techniques should be based on a consideration of the information needed. Tests and techniques should be evaluated as sources of information, each with its own possible bias and error. The analysis of test responses should be within the contexts of contemporary theory and recent research, especially if older instruments are used. Choices about personality constructs, processes, and sources of information can be guided, at least in part, by the research in the area of psychosocial change. Assessments include the identification of healthy, constructive mechanisms as well as barriers to adjustment. Professional and ethical safeguards also need to be incorporated. These include mutually agreed upon goals for assessment, and logic and validity checks to confirm findings, whenever possible, with the client and significant others.

Another practical way to reduce the chance for error is to implement formal problem solving procedures. It may be important to withhold prior assumptions about the causes of a particular problem in order to reduce the possible influence of preconceptions as in applying a "favorite" theory or the undue influence that a particular score or observation may have. Based on information obtained during assessment, unique hypotheses about individuals are made, and are carefully checked through available means. "To the extent that hypotheses are confirmed

and consistent observations follow from the constructed model, the process is validated" (Maloney & Ward, 1976, p. 74). In addition to the focus on the person referred, the process of assessment also includes a consideration of the referral agent, factors that led to the referral, the possible sources and causes of the problems, constraints operating against problem definition and resolution, availability of resources to assess and to plan interventions, and the social and political context (Sloves, Docherty, & Schneider, 1979).

BEST PRACTICES

*Using Many and Varied
Sources of Information*

Data for the personality assessment procedure should be obtained from a number of sources including interviews, observations, rating scales, review of school records and developmental/social histories, and tests. Since many of these topics are covered in other chapters in this volume, the following section will emphasize the interpretation of data from personality tests.

Interviews. In contrast to other assessment methods, formal treatment of the interview has been relatively neglected. Interviews provide an opportunity for obtaining information that is unlikely to be gathered from tests. They provide a mechanism for problem identification and clarification through an examination of consistencies and contrasts of the perceptions of parents, teachers, the child, and other involved individuals. Peterson (1968) describes the first step of the interview as a "scanning operation," involving an inquiry into the nature and circumstances of the problem. This is followed by "extended inquiry," requiring a "detailed and individualized study of the clients and others most centrally involved" (p. 120). Interviews should begin with a problem-oriented focus. However decisions may be made to broaden the scope of the interview to help assess facets of psychological constructs (e.g., motivation, locus of control or related beliefs about change) important to the planning of interventions. Interviews are also useful for the evaluation of psychoeducational interventions from multiple viewpoints. Non-test based information such as family history, structure, and values; living conditions; interests; skills; aspirations; avocations; and unusual or stressful life circumstances may be important.

Interviews must be evaluated for accuracy. "Reliability, validity, and decisional utility" of interviews require scrutiny similar to that of other assessment methods (Peterson, 1968, p. 13). Anastasi (1982) warns that "an interview may lead to wrong decisions because important data were not elicited or because given data were inadequately or incorrectly interpreted" (pp. 610-611). Since interviews are subject to theoretical and conceptual biases, a recommended plan is to initially base interviews on a behavioral model (Morganstern & Telvin, 1981; Nay, 1979). Safeguards involve comparing reports from different sources such as the parents, teachers, and children. But even when there are inconsistencies, insights can be gained. For example, a parent may report unusual talents that a child denies and the teacher has not witnessed. The discrepancy may be important, but more information is needed to help determine if the child is being modest or reluctant to demonstrate the skills, if the parent perceives the child unrealistically, or if the characteristics of the setting interfere with the expression of the talents.

Observations. Observational techniques are invaluable for (a) helping to establish target behaviors, (b) defining the significant aspects of situations in which the behaviors occur, (c) serving as an indication of the completeness of information, and (d) similar to interviews and all other techniques, assessing facets of psychological constructs. The assessment of covert or private phenomena through self-observation and recording is also important (Roberts & Nelson, 1984). Thoughts, feelings, and sensations all may be targets for self-monitoring. Karoly (1981) provides recommendations for assessing self-management in children.

Skill in systematic behavioral observation should be acquired by every assessor of personality. It is important to observe a referred child in a variety of settings with different people, and at different times. Likewise, observational data noted during test administration are extremely important. In a broad sense, all of the data discussed in this chapter are observational data, from the way a child interacts with peers on the playground to the way he/she interacts during testing, to specific responses given during testing, to interview and rating information provided by others about the child. The decisions related to observations are similar to those involved in the selection of test instruments. Observers are guided by implicit or explicit beliefs that focus attention on certain behaviors or features of the setting.

Observational techniques often have unknown statistical properties and may be invalid and biased. As a safeguard, the outcomes of the interviews related to problem identification and clarification should be incorporated into the plans for at least the initial observations. Behaviors that provide confirming as well as disconfirming evidence of problems should be evaluated. Formal observations can be based on maladaptive behavior in part, but they should also include emerging but often variable adaptive or coping skills, the analysis of learning processes such as attention and problem solving behavior, and the evaluation of setting or learning contexts. Another important view is the child's analysis of the problem behavior and the corresponding degree that self-observation and self-management can be taught.

Rating scales. There are several types of rating scales, many of which are best thought of as adjuncts to observational data and interviews. Parents, teachers, and clients may be asked to rate the presence, absence, or degree of behavior; the behaviors of significant others; and aspects of situations. The use of rating scales does not eliminate the measurement or theoretical problems associated with psychological tests. While usually reliable in one or more respects (e.g., internal consistency, temporal stability), findings may vary according to the raters, instruments selected, or both, and it may be difficult to determine exactly what is being measured (Edelbrock, 1983), thereby making interpretation an issue. Often it is useful to examine individual items that do not achieve overall statistical significance on a scale but may be important. For example, a person may rate an area such as social isolation in an extreme manner, or report unusual fears, but overall may appear well-adjusted because of the way in which the scale is constructed. The items should not be ignored and can be addressed in interviews and through observations. Although the limitations of rating scales must be understood, they are useful because of their economy and versatility. It is important to examine systematically how a child is viewed from differing perspectives.

Goh and Fuller (1983) note that no single rating scale is used by a majority of school psychologists, but there appears to be a growing trend in the use of these instruments. Two are described for illustration purposes. The Burks' Behavior Rating Scale (Burks, 1977) is comprised of 110 items which may be filled out by parent(s), teacher(s), or both in a brief amount of time. Information is provided on how the rater describes the child on nineteen personality related dimensions. In contrast, the Personality Inventory for Children (Lachar, 1982) is a longer inventory (a choice can be made to give 131, 280, 420 or 600 items depending on the purpose) to be rated by parent(s). The manual and related research require careful study and some of the individual subscales (e.g., psychosis) and particularly the preschool scales could be potentially abused. When scale scores are elevated, an item by item analysis, interviews, and observations may prevent the incorrect assignment of the labels associated with the scales.

Review of School Records and Developmental and Social History. Much can be learned from school records, ranging from factual information to possible attitudes of school personnel toward the child and family. They may provide information pertaining to academic progress or retention, attendance, prior test results, disciplinary actions, extracurriculr activities, and notations of other events, all of which yield a context for assessing school and community functioning. Especially valuable may be the assessment of significant changes over long time periods.

Projective techniques. In terms of time spent in data collection, the information obtained from projective techniques can be rewarding. Important issues affecting children interpersonally and intrapersonally can be identified (Conti, 1983). An understanding of how they perceive themselves and their peers, teachers, school, and family can frequently be obtained, as well as a sense of their personal needs, creative capacities, and hidden resources (Knoff, 1983a).

Projective test data, along with all other data gathered as a part of the personality assessment process, should be viewed as information which may add to the total understanding of the examinee. All the data must be used for generating hypotheses, which are then studied, evaluated, and rejected or supported. If the hypotheses are finally supported, the related information must be integrated into as comprehensive an understanding of the examinee as possible and should lead to recommendations for psychoeducational intervention.

As an example, if on the Bender Gestalt test the child copied the figures much smaller than they actually appear, this would be one bit of information to be included with all other data gathered in the personality assessment process. A likely hypothesis would be that the child may tend to be somewhat constricted, shy, inhibited, and/or reserved (Koppitz, 1964). At this point this would be merely another hypothesis among many others to be tested. If no other supporting data emerged, this finding would be better viewed as an isolated instance and the hypothesis should be rejected. On the other hand, if data were found to support this inference, the examiner could start to refine the emerging impression of the child. Since situational factors are known to affect behavior to a marked degree, questions such as if this behavior manifests itself in other settings and to what extent, could be addressed.

Any of the available data might suggest answers, but for illustrative purposes, the discussion will focus on how other projective data might be used. The examiner might look at the size of the Human Figure Drawing. If also small, evidence is available from two test situations. Is this a reflection of how the child functions in most test situations? To what degree? How about non-test situations? Obviously, non-test data must be examined to answer this question. Perhaps the child feels inadequate and functions in a constricted manner in most school related activities, but not in other settings. Many possible explanations for this would be explored, and the recommendations for interventions made accordingly.

Scores derived from projective tests should be used in the same manner. For example, many use the Koppitz systems for scoring the Bender-Gestalt and Human Figure Drawings (Koppitz, 1964, 1968). If a child being tested had three of Koppitz' (1968) emotional indicators on the Human Figure Drawing, this suggests the hypothesis of the presence of emotional adjustment problems. The examiner must keep in mind, though, that when scientists test hypotheses, they sometimes end up being rejected. Much more data would be needed before determining that a serious social/emotional/behavioral problem exists and what recommendations need to be made.

With this general understanding of how *any* data from projective techniques can be used, specific comments can be made about some of the different projective techniques. Although some of these techniques seem extremely simple, without formal instruction and supervised experience, it is difficult to acquire the hypothesis-generating, hypothesis-testing, verification, and inference-drawing skills which are the keys to personality assessment. Moreover, some of these techniques are *not* so simple.

1. *Picture-story tests.* These tests essentially involve showing a series of pictures and asking subjects to make up a story about what is happening in each picture. Subjects are asked to include thoughts about what led up to the situation, how any characters in the story might be thinking or feeling, and how it turns out. The tests vary according to the number of pictures, their content and structure, and according to whether there is a formal scoring system recommended by the authors or by others who did research with the test. Regardless of these

variations, many psychologists select approximately ten pictures and analyze the stories clinically. Common themes are identified, and then hypothesis testing procedures are initiated in order to help determine to what extent these themes represent how the subject typically perceives adults, children, fathers, male authority figures, mothers, female authority figures, and his/herself. Perceptions of certain situations, such as if the subject perceives the environment as generally hostile and threatening or warm and supportive, may be ascertained. If a formal scoring system is thought to help in this analysis, the scores are treated as additional data to be used for generating hypotheses, as illustrated in the example using Koppitz emotional indicators.

The tests which may be used in this way include the Thematic Apperception Test (Murray, 1971), the Children's Apperception Test (Bellak & Bellak, 1974), the Michigan Picture Test-Revised (Hutt, 1980), Tasks of Emotional Development (Cohen & Weil, 1971), the School Apperception Method (Solomon & Starr, 1968), and the Roberts Apperception Test for Children (McArthur & Roberts, 1982). Although these techniques lack good psychometric properties, the clinician is more interested in qualitative information, and these techniques are likely to supply such data (Obrzut & Cummings, 1983).

2. *Projective drawings.* Despite scathing criticisms of these techniques (Martin, 1983; Peterson & Batsche, 1983), projective drawings are widely used (Goh & Fuller, 1983), but as a part of a larger battery and within a problem-solving framework (Falk, 1981; Koppitz, 1983). They can be administered quickly and often provide a rich source of hypotheses about the examinee (Koppitz, 1983). Through Koppitz' work more research on Human Figure Drawings (HFD) applicable to children ages 5-12 is available for

generating hypotheses than is the case for the other drawing techniques (Koppitz, 1968). She has provided group data to show that certain features of HFDs, such as small or large size, certain distortions, and some omissions, are more commonly associated with children who tend to be, for example, shy, aggressive, or anxious. How a child draws a human figure *may* be a behavioral expression of some important perception of self and/or others or of an attitude or feeling which influences behavior, at least the behavior of drawing a human figure.

There are many statements in the projective drawing literature which should be considered very cautiously, if at all, because of their questionable validity. Although certain features of houses and trees, for example, may reflect something significant about one person's personality, they may not have the same meaning for other people. Hypotheses generated about any given individual must be as readily rejected as accepted, depending upon the other data gathered.

A brief inquiry or discussion with the examinee about the drawing after it is completed often adds helpful insights. Lengthy inquiry, however, such as that suggested by Machover (1949), may be counterproductive. As such, a brief projective technique is converted into a lengthy, time-consuming procedure, and the additional information frequently does not justify the time spent obtaining it.

3. *Sentence Completion Technique.* This technique involves administering a list of sentence stems to be completed by the subject. The preferred method of administration usually is for the examiner to read the stems to the subject and record his/her responses verbatim. Many children who are not responsive on less structured verbal tasks, such as picture-story tests, provide substantially more information on sentence completion tests.

Sometimes they seem pleased to have a chance to express some of their concerns directly. A discussion of sentence completion tests can be found in Rabin and Zlotogorski (1981). Specific tests offer different items and suggestions for analysis, including a variety of approaches to scoring.

In interpreting the results from sentence completion tests, common themes and individual responses which reveal something especially significant for understanding the child should be identified. Of course, no response can necessarily be taken at face value. Each theme or individual response can only be used to generate hypotheses to be explored through other available data. If, for example, a child completed a stem which started with "I hate" by saying "my stepmother," although one hypothesis would be that the statement was true, other possible hypotheses might be that (a) the child wants to create that impression for the examiner, (b) the child is being negative that day, (c) he/she is angry at the step-mother for the moment but normally gets along quite well with her, or (d) this has become a practiced response so that the child always says this but doesn't really feel that way about the stepmother.

Sentence completion techniques are particularly susceptible to conscious manipulation on the part of the examinees. They can say what they want to say, for their private reasons, and it doesn't always have to be the truth. Additionally, they may fail to respond for many different reasons, such as constriction, negativism, fear, or reluctance to comment on very personal and private matters. In order to use this technique effectively, as with all other personality techniques, the psychologist must be alert to a myriad of possible explanations for the data obtained, while keeping in mind the aforementioned cautions.

4. *Bender Visual-Motor Gestalt Test.*

This technique provides an interesting sample of perceptual-motor, as well as personality functioning. It involves having the child copy nine designs. Developmental norms provided by Koppitz (1964, 1975) can help the examiner decide whether errors and distortions suggest more than average difficulty with this task. If so, this information, when combined with other data, may help in understanding some perceptual-motor functioning factors which may be contributing to the student's learning problems. Personality factors, however, also affect how people copy designs. A conscientious student, for example, who does everything carefully and neatly, will probably do an excellent job. Even so, the size he/she draws them and how they are organized on the paper provide insights into the student's work habits. Some students, for example, copy the designs well, but scatter them randomly over the paper, while others organize them in a systematic fashion. These observations provide behavioral data which can help the examiner learn how the student goes about other assignments. Sources of hypotheses regarding personality functioning as it affects Bender performance may be found in Koppitz (1964, 1975), Clawson (1962), Murstein (1965), and Hutt (1977). Hutt also suggests other ways to administer the test for obtaining more data.

An interesting issue to consider, when problems with both emotional adjustment and visual-motor perception are suggested as is often the case, is which one of these is primary and which is secondary. Both views have support. Koppitz (1964) takes the position that the emotional problems are secondary, often a result of the "frustration and frequent failure in school and at home" (p. 124). Hutt (1977), on the other hand, argues that "emotional disturbance can be causative of disturbance in the perceptual-motoric area" (p. 31).

5. *Rorschach Technique.* This technique requires extensive training before it can be used safely and effectively. For those who have had such formal training, it can be a significant source for hypotheses regarding personality functioning. A great deal of myth surrounds the Rorschach, such as that it takes hours to give and then leads to mostly invalid, speculative, and useless information such as that the child has a castration complex. In a brief introduction, Exner and Martin (1983) describe a contemporary approach to the Rorschach which should help dispel these misunderstandings. They give examples of how the Rorschach should be used, and the types of insights that can be gained. Referred children can often complete it in 30-40 minutes, although more time will be needed for scoring and interpretation. Nevertheless, the time may be well spent in terms of shedding light on some difficult issues. An examination of the three volumes of Exner's Comprehensive System is needed to gain an appreciation of the type of data generated and the related research (Exner, 1974, 1978; Exner & Weiner, 1982).

6. *Miscellaneous.* There are many other projective techniques that have been found to be helpful by some psychologists. Space allows for brief mention of only a few. The Word Association Method can sometimes suggest areas of special sensitivity for the examinee. A brief explanation of how the method can be used is given in Rabin and Zlotogorski (1981). Adlerian psychologists and others sometimes find Early Recollections useful, especially for revealing something about an individual's subjective view of life and sometimes his/her central values. Articles by Mosak (1958), and Manaster and Perryman (1974) serve as good introductions to this technique. Some school psychologists have developed proficiency with the Hand Test, particularly in exploring aggression and acting out behaviors

(Bricklin, Piotrowski, & Wagner, 1981). The Paired Hands Test is instructive for learning about a person's perceptions of other people and his/her interpretation of social situations (Zucker & Barnett, 1977). Conti (1983) emphasizes the importance of attending to these two factors.

Objective Techniques. Objective scales are another potential source of useful hypotheses. From most widely used to least are: self-concept scales, the Minnesota Multiphasic Personality Inventory, the California Test of Personality, the Sixteen Personality Factor Questionnaire, and the Children's Personality Questionnaire (Goh & Fuller, 1983). Others used by school psychologists are the High School Personality Questionnaire and the California Psychological Inventory. Also, there are many specialized scales which measure a particular dimension of interest, such as locus of control or anxiety.

To use objective techniques properly, the examiner must become familiar with not only the information in the manual, but also further research involving the instrument. For some, such as the MMPI, a considerable amount of background is required in order to derive full value from them.

Additionally, there are a number of practical points to keep in mind. (a) In the final analysis, any score derived from the instrument or any other behavior observed such as the response to a single item, will have to be thought of as a possible hypothesis about the examinee and then treated like any other hypothesis in the assessment process. (b) Examinees may not necessarily respond truthfully to these instruments. Whether they did in any given instance must be judged by the examiner. Sometimes a "Lie" scale can help in making that judgment. (c) If the examiner judges that the subject did not respond accurately, he/she must be sensitive to any possible explanations for this. Such explanations might include a wish to make the results come out a certain way in order to convey a desired impression to the examiner, negativism, fear of acknowledging certain self-perceptions, embarrassment, or maybe lack of self-insight. Regarding this last point, the fact that some people are more introspective and less defensive than others, so that there are wide individual differences with respect to accuracy of self-perceptions, is sometimes overlooked by examiners analyzing the results of objective personality tests.

Even though it is suspected that accuracy has been distorted, for one reason or another, this does not mean that the results have no value. If the examiner can understand *why* the examinee responded in that manner, a potentially helpful insight about the person has been obtained. Moreover, if the examinee honestly reported self-perceptions, even if they are highly discrepant in terms of other information about the subject, these too constitute important data. Again, the data gathered from all other sources must be integrated in the final analysis, but it should be kept in mind that self-perceptions are necessary for a complete and useful understanding of any individual's functioning. Objective personality tests, being self-reports, are an important source of that information.

Guidelines for Thinking about People in Necessarily Complex Ways

Assessment should focus on enhancing the probability that hypotheses lead to constructs, insights, and plans for helping people. The following guidelines are recommended.

Assess for Psychosocial Change
1. When assessing personality, the psychologist should keep in mind the major trends that stem from ecological, psychosocial/situational, and cognitive behavioral assessment and intervention. The ecological approach implies the study of small groups, including families, and the social and physical environment of children (Hobbs, 1979). Psychosocial/ psychosituational assessment stresses the importance of sets of skills necessary for adaptation to specific settings or across similar settings, and implies that skill deficits are often reversible to a large degree (Ellett & Bersoff, 1976; Peterson, 1968). The fact that situational factors have an important influence on behavior, so that any individual may act quite differently as situations change, must not be overlooked (Mischel, 1977). The most recent trend, the cognitive-behavioral, has contributed renewed sanction to the study of private phenomena and subjective experience and includes the functional analysis of the client's thinking processes, inventory of cognitive skills, and imaginal and fantasy experiences as they apply to personal adjustment and social behavior (Kendall & Hollon, 1981). The unit of analysis for psychosocial change is the "continuous reciprocal interaction between cognitive, behavioral, and environmental determinants" (Bandura, 1977). Mischel (1973) suggests five "person variables" that serve as guides: (a) the individual's competencies to construct (generate) diverse behaviors under appropriate conditions, (b) the encoding or categorizing of events, (c) expectancies about outcomes, (d) the subjective values of different outcomes, and (e) self-regulatory systems and plans (p. 265). The last point, related to self-control, has received the most attention recently (Karoly & Kanfer, 1982).

A related trend emphasizes direct client participation (Peterson, 1968; Mischel, 1977). Assessments may include children's perceptions of their relationship to the problem, subsuming levels of self-understanding and self-analysis of the problem (Nelson & Evans, 1977) and corresponding beliefs about change (Bandura, 1981).

2. Positive aspects of functioning should be assessed, an infrequent suggestion by psychologists. Hobbs (1966) commented that there is an extensive literature on anxiety, guilt and dread, but little that is well developed on joy. That "a child should know joy" was one of twelve points considered to be significant in working with emotionally disturbed children. Research strongly suggests that social and symbolic play may be developed through intervention, and that play is instrumental in social and cognitive growth (Rubin & Pepler, 1980). Play and peer relationships or friendships for older children should be important points of assessment (Rubin & Ross, 1982).

3. The psychologist must keep in mind that significant information may be overlooked through the use of traditional assessment techniques. For example, it is often important to assess emerging skills, such as socially appropriate behaviors that may be in the formative stages, may be rare or intermittent, or may be elicited only during experimental procedures.

4. The potential use of validated interventions to guide assessments represents a major departure from tradition. Assessment techniques often attempt to establish the dimensions and severity of pathology. While it is necessary to reliably measure maladaptive behaviors, it is more important to consider the degree of possible change in behaviors that may result from psychoeducational interventions and from factors related to implementing the plans. Researched interventions may suggest evidence of the modifiability of behaviors considered troublesome. For example, enuresis is found on many scales used to establish psychopathology. However successful treatment for enuresis, perhaps the most widely researched

problem behavior, is often relatively brief. Assessments influenced by validated interventions should also establish important guidelines for evaluating learning contexts as, for example, special programs for the emotionally disturbed child.

Other Considerations

5. The order of presentation of tests in a battery may be an important point. Many examiners neglect the possible influence of taking one test on the responses to the next test presented. Mangold (1982) demonstrated the differential effects of doing a Kinetic Family Drawing after either the WISC-R or Rorschach: the drawings after the WISC-R looked less disturbed.

6. A thorough personality assessment should account for internal as well as external behavioral phenomena, even when they may not appear to be linked. In doing so, levels of personality and mechanisms of control should always be kept in mind. For example, if a child demonstrates a proclivity for making up stories about violence, an attempt should be made to account for this, even if the child has never been observed to act violently. Self-awareness may need to be assessed. A child viewed by others and him/herself as non-aggressive might daydream frequently about blowing up the school and other violent fantasies. A good brief overview of how the concept of levels of personality may be addressed in personality assessment can be found in Klopfer (1981).

7. The issue brought up in the discussion of the Bender-Gestalt regarding the possibility of emotional factors affecting perceptual-motor behavior, as well as the reverse, should be kept in mind in regard to all types of psychological functioning, for example, emotional, social, cognitive, perceptual, and motoric. Any facet of human functioning can be affected by any other. This was a major

reason for describing personality assessment as integrative earlier in this chapter.

8. Psychologists attempting to integrate data from many diverse sources into one comprehensive, meaningful, and relevant personality description might feel overwhelmed at first by the amount of data obtained. At the same time, they must be confronted with the possibility that gaps may still exist and information may remain undiscovered. They should realize that organizing data involves ordering inferences in terms of importance and, as a final outcome, disregarding some which are deemed relatively unimportant. These decisions involve professional judgments, a responsibility which assessors assume. "What all clinical assessors must do, whatever their approach, is first to monitor the extent of inference involved in getting from client responses to personality description and behavioral predictions, and second, to limit themselves to conclusions that can be justified on the basis of sound concepts or solid empirical data" (Weiner, 1983, p. 452).

9. The functioning of a disturbed child is often like that of a "normal" child in many respects. Both, for example, may have similar problems and conflicts, but the differences may lie in how they cope with them. Therefore, clearcut differences in test data should not ordinarily be expected anymore than differences in other behaviors would be. Simple test signs or formulae cannot be a substitute for careful thinking about each case.

Minority Issues

The assessment of personality with minorities has not received sufficient attention (Pettigrew, 1964). A Thematic Apperception Test depicting Blacks (Thompson, 1949) was developed, but interest has been limited. Other modifications with a specific ethnic emphasis show promise (Bailey & Green, 1977).

All of the usual difficulties are con-

founded by cross-cultural issues including personal and sociocultural variables: language, cognitive style, limited opportunities, diverse adaptive and coping mechanisms, and prejudice. Controversies exist with respect to problem identification, especially to the degree problems can or should be attributed to social, political, or individual factors. For example, individual interventions may not be sufficient when problems stem from more profound economic or social concerns. In addition to possibly considering broad-based interventions, the points raised in this chapter are thought to be pertinent although shifts in emphasis are important. Barriers to interracial assessment may be addressed by (a) establishing a position of advocacy, (b) enlisting the aid of professionals and community members of the same ethnic background as the client to help "anchor" the cultural appropriateness of assessments (e.g., Savage & Adair, 1980), and (c) focusing on behavioral assessment (Turner & Jones, 1982). Recent research in the area of cognitive style and attributional processes may ultimately have special utility for ethnic minorities. The most serious errors perhaps occur at the conceptual level and a number of professional resources are available to help provide needed background (see, e.g., Jones, 1980; White, 1984).

With respect to formal tests, when ethnic differences are reported, they are sometimes significant (Jones, 1978). Differences do not necessarily connote cultural bias, but can lead to biased decisions and may be misleading if not properly interpreted. The formal analysis of bias in personality measures has recently received attention (Reynolds, Plake, & Harding, 1983).

Differences are not always found. Yando, Seitz, and Zigler (1979) studied six constructs (creativity, self-confidence, dependency, curiosity, frustration threshold, and autonomy) with the result that socioeconomic status was more predictive of behavior than ethnic differences in the first four constructs. The superior performances did *not* always belong to advantaged groups.

Interracial acceptance is another related topic (Barnett, 1982); the Paired Hands Test (Zucker & Barnett, 1977) may be a valuable aid in that a series of biracial stimuli are interpreted along a friendliness-hostility continuum.

SUMMARY

It is not difficult to critique personality assessment. The challenge is in using the information provided while not building in errors and unnecessary or harmful constructs. An important consideration is that tests are usually developed for a specific purpose, and the purpose of the authors may or may not match the needs of the psychologists offering services. Personality assessment techniques do *not*, by themselves, present adequate guidelines for assessment. They may be based on a personality theory, a model of psychopathology, or empirical relationships between items or between items and behaviors. Constructs may be neglected, and they do not necessarily focus on change. While a great deal is known about personality development and behavior, personality processes, and psychopathology, research has been, with few exceptions, only tangentially related to personality appraisal. The future of personality assessment is an important one, and professional psychologists are only beginning to find ways of incorporating developments into practice. The most important points are to implement procedural safeguards as a part of an intensive case study and to base assessments, to the extent possible, on research related to psychosocial change.

REFERENCES

Anastasi, A. (1982). *Psychological testing* (5th ed.). New York: Macmillan.

Bailey, B. E., & Green, J. (1977). Black thematic apperception test stimulus material. *Journal of Personality Assessment, 41,* 25-30.

Bandura, A. (1977). *Social learning theory.* Englewood Cliffs, NJ: Prentice-Hall.

Bandura, A. (1981). Self-referent thought: A developmental analysis of self-efficacy. In J. H. Flavell & L. Ross (Eds.), *Social cognitive development: Frontiers and possible futures* (pp 200-239). New York: Cambridge Universit, Press.

Barnett, D. (1982). Some issues and findings related to interracial acceptance. *Psychological Reports, 51,* 27-37.

Bellak, L., & Bellak, S. S. (1974). *Children's apperception test.* Larchmont, NY: C. P. S.

Bricklin, B., Piotrowski, Z. A., & Wagner, E. E. (1981). *The hand test.* Springfield, IL: Thomas.

Burks, H. F. (1977). *Burks' behavior rating scales.* Los Angeles: Western Psychological Services.

Clawson, A. (1962). *The Bender visual motor gestalt test for children: A manual.* Los Angeles: Western Psychological Services.

Cleveland, S. E. (1976). Reflections of the rise and fall of psychodiagnostics. *Professional Psychology, 7,* 309-318.

Cohen, H., & Weil, G. P. (1971). *Tasks of emotional development test.* Lexington, MA: Heath.

Conti, A. P. (1983). Implementing interventions from projective findings: Suggestions for school psychologists. *School Psychology Review, 12,* 435-439.

Edelbrock, C. (1983). Problems and issues in using rating scales to assess child personality and psychopathology. *School Psychology Review, 12,* 293-299.

Ellett, C. D., & Bersoff, D. N. (1976). An integrated approach to the psychosituational assessment of behavior. *Professional Psychology, 7,* 485-494.

Exner, J. E. (1974). *The Rorschach: A comprehensive system* (Vol. 1). New York: Wiley.

Exner, J. E. (1978). *The Rorschach: A comprehensive system* (Vol. 2). New York: Wiley.

Exner, J. E., & Martin, L. S. (1983). The Rorschach: A history and description of the comprehensive system. *School Psychology Review, 12,* 407-413.

Exner, J. E., & Weiner, I. B. (1982). *The Rorschach: A comprehensive system* (Vol. 3). New York: Wiley.

Falk, J. D. (1981). Understanding children's art: An analysis of the literature. *Journal of Personality Assessment, 45,* 465-472.

Goh, D. S., & Fuller, G. B. (1983). Current practices in the assessment of personality and behavior by school psychologists. *School Psychology Review, 12,* 240-243.

Goodstein, L. D., & Lanyon, R. I. (Eds.). (1971). *Readings in personality assessment* (pp. 19-35). New York: Wiley.

Hobbs, N. (1966). Helping disturbed children: Psychological and ecological strategies. *American Psychologist, 21* 1105-1115.

Hobbs, N. (1979). *Helping disturbed children: Psychological and ecological strategies, II; Project Re-ed, twenty years later.* Nashville, TN: Center for the Study of Families and Children, Vanderbilt Institute for Public Policy Studies, Vanderbilt University.

Hutt, M. L. (1977). *The Hutt adaptation of the Bender gestalt test* (3rd ed.). New York: Grune & Stratton.

Hutt, M. L. (1980). *The Michigan picture test-revised.* New York: Grune & Stratton.

Jones, E. E. (1978). Black-white personality differences: another look. *Journal of Personality Assessment, 42,* 244-252.

Jones, R. L. (1980). *Black psychology* (2nd ed.). New York: Harper & Row.

Karoly, P. (1981). Self-management problems in children. In E. J. Mash & L. G. Terdal (Eds.), *Behavioral assessment of childhood disorders* (pp. 79-126). New York: Guilford.

Karoly, P., & Kanfer, F. H. (Eds.). (1982). *Self-management and behavior change: From theory to practice.* New York: Pergamon.

Kazdin, A. E. (1982). *Single-case research designs: Methods for clinical and applied settings.* New York: Oxford University Press.

Kendall, P. C., & Hollon, S. D. (Eds.). (1981). *Assessment strategies for cognitive behavioral interventions.* New York: Academic Press.

Klopfer, W. G. (1970). Editorial. *Journal of Projective Techniques and Personality Assessment, 34,* p. 444.

Klopfer, W. G. (1981). Integration of projective techniques in a case study. In A. I. Rabin (Ed.), *Assessment with projective techniques* (pp. 233-263). New York: Springer.

Knoff, H. M. (1983a). Personality assessment in the schools: Issues and procedures for school psychologists. *School Psychology Review, 12,* 391-398.

Knoff, H. M. (1983b). Justifying projective/personality assessment in school psychology: A response to Batsche and Peterson. *School Psychology Review, 12,* 446-451.

Koppitz, E. M. (1964). *The Bender gestalt test for young children* (Vol. 1). New York: Grune & Stratton.

Koppitz, E. M. (1968). *Psychological evaluation of children's human figure drawings.* New York: Grune & Stratton.

Koppitz, E. M. (1975). *The Bender gestalt test for young children* (Vol. 2). New York: Grune & Stratton.

Koppitz, E. M. (1983). Projective drawings with children and adolescents. *School Psychology Review, 12,* 421-427.

Lachar, D. (1982). *Personality inventory for children (PIC) revised format manual supplement.* Los Angeles: Western Psychological Services.

McArthur, D. S., & Roberts, G. E. (1982). *Roberts apperception test for children.* Los Angeles: Western Psychological Services.

McDermott, P. A. (1981). Sources of error in the psychoeducational diagnosis of children. *Journal of School Psychology, 19,* 31-44.

Machover, K. (1949). *Personality projection in the drawings of a human figure.* Springfield, IL: Thomas.

Magary, J. F. (Ed.). (1967). *School psychological services.* Englewood Cliffs, NJ: Prentice-Hall.

Maloney, M. P., & Ward, M. P. (1976). *Psychological assessment: A conceptual approach.* New York: Oxford University Press.

Manaster, G. J., & Perryman, T. B. (1974). Early recollections and occupational choice. *Journal of Individual Psychology, 30,* 232-237.

Mangold, J. (1982). *A study of the primary process in children's kinetic family drawings as a function of pre-drawing activity.* Unpublished doctoral dissertation, Indiana State University, Terre Haute.

Martin, R. P. (1983, October). Ethics column. *The School Psychologist* (APA Division of School Psychology Newsletter), *38* (1), 6.

Mischel, W. (1973). Toward a cognitive social learning reconceptualization of personality. *Psychological Review, 80,* 252-283.

Mischel, W. (1977). On the future of personality measurement. *American Psychologist, 32,* 246-254.

Monte, C. F. (1977). *Beneath the mask: An introduction to theories of personality.* New York: Praeger.

Morgan, C. D., & Murray, H. A. (1935). A method for investigating fantasies: The TAT. *Archives of Neurology & Psychiatry, 34,* 289-306.

Morganstern, K. P., & Tevlin, H. E. (1981). Behavioral interviewing. In M. Hersen & A. S. Bellack (Eds.), *Behavioral assessment* (pp. 71-100). New York: Pergamon.

Mosak, H. H. (1958). Early recollections as a projective technique. *Journal of Projective Techniques, 22,* 302-311.

Murray, H. A. (1971). *Thematic apperception test manual.* Cambridge: Harvard University.

Murstein, B. I. (Ed.). (1965). *Handbook of projective techniques.* New York: Basic Books.

Nay, W. R. (1979). *Multimethod clinical assessment.* New York: Gardner.

Nelson, R. O., & Evans, I. M. (1977). Assessment of child behavior problems. In A. R. Ciminero, K. S. Calhoun, & H. E. Adams (Eds.), *Handbook of behavioral assessment* (pp. 603-639). New York: Wiley.

Obrzut, J. E., & Cummings, J. A. (1983). The projective approach to personality assessment: An analysis of thematic picture techniques. *School Psychology Review, 12,* 414-420.

Peterson, D. R. (1968). *The clinical study of social behavior.* New York: Appleton-Century-Crofts.

Peterson, D. W., & Batsche, G. M. (1983). School psychology and projective assessment: A growing incompatibility. *School Psychology Review, 12,* 440-445.

Pettigrew, T. F. (1964). Negro American personality: Why isn't more known? *The Journal of Social Issues, 20,* 4-23.

Rabin, A. I., & Zlotogorski, Z. (1981). Completion methods: Word association, sentence and story completion. In A. I. Rabin (Ed.), *Assessment with projective techniques* (pp. 121-149). New York: Springer.

Reynolds, C. R., Plake, B. S., & Harding, R. E. (1983). Item bias in the assessment of children's anxiety: Race and sex interaction on items of the revised children's manifest anxiety scale. *Journal of Psychoeducational Assessment, 1* (1), 17-24.

Roberts, R. N., & Nelson, R. O. (1984). Assessment issues and strategies in cognitive behavior therapy with children. In A. W. Meyers & W. E. Craighead (Eds.), *Cognitive behavior therapy with children* (pp. 99-128). New York: Plenum.

Rubin, K. H., & Pepler, D. J. (1980). The relationship of child's play to social-cognitive growth and development. In H. C. Foot, A. J. Chapman, & J. R. Smith (Eds.), *Friendships and social relations in children* (pp. 209-233). Chichester, Great Britain: Wiley.

Rubin, K. H., & Ross, H. S. (Eds.). (1982). *Peer relationships and social skills in children.* New York: Springer-Verlag.

Savage, J. E., & Adair, A. V. (1980). Testing minorities: Developing more culturally relevant assessment systems. In R. L. Jones (Ed.), *Black psychology* (2nd ed.) (pp. 196-215). New York: Harper & Row.

Sloves, R. E., Docherty, E. M., & Schneider, K. C. (1979). A scientific problem-solving model of psychological assessment. *Professional Psychology, 10,* 28-35.

Solomon, I. L., & Starr, B. D. (1968). *School apperception method.* New York: Springer.

Thompson, C. E. (1949). *Thematic apperception test: Thompson modification.* Cambridge, MA: Harvard University Press.

Turner, S. M., & Jones, R. T. (Eds.). (1982). *Behavior modification in black populations: Psychosocial issues and empirical findings.* New York: Plenum.

Weiner, I. B. (1983). The future of psychodiagnostics revisited. *Journal of Personality Assessment, 47,* 451-459.

White, J. L. (1984). *The psychology of blacks: An Afro-American perspective.* Englewood Cliffs, NJ: Prentice-Hall.

Yando, R., Seitz, V., & Zigler, E. (1979). *Intellectual and personality characteristics: social class and ethnic-group differences.* Hillsdale, NJ: Earlbaum.

Zucker, K. B., & Barnett, D. W. (1977). *The paired hands test.* Dallas: McCarron-Dial Systems.

ANNOTATED BIBLIOGRAPHY

Barnett, D. W. (1983). *Nondiscriminatory multifactored assessment: A sourcebook.* (pp. 44-68; 85-103). New York: Human Sciences Press. A chapter on personality assessment provides a more in depth discussion of why personality assessment represents a major context, points of view regarding the alleged decline of personality assessment, and important theoretical issues as viewed by different schools of thought including that of social learning theory (e.g., Bandura, Mischel). A second section deals with practical issues.

Knoff, H. M. (Ed.). (1983). Projective/personality assessment in the schools [Special issue]. *School Psychology Review, 12,* (4).
This issue presents current practices and issues involving projective techniques from a school psychology perspective. A commentary section highlights the controversy which surrounds the use of projective techniques by offering two articles, one pro and one con.

Martin, R. P. (Ed.). (1983). Personality assessment: The rating scale approach [Special issue]. *School Psychology Review, 12* (3).
Newer rating scales applicable to the school setting, responded to primarily by parents, teachers, or significant others, and related issues are the foci of this special issue.

Rabin, A. I. (Ed.). (1981). *Assessment with projective techniques.* New York: Springer.
A contemporary survey of major projective techniques which can also serve as a broad general introduction. Several chapters deal with pragmatic and theoretical issues. Chapter 8, by Walter Klopfer, provides a good discussion of how to integrate findings from projective techniques with data from other sources.

Weiner, I. B. (1983). The future of psychodiagnosis revisited. *Journal of Personality Assessment, 47,* 451-459.
An optimistic prediction for the future of personality assessment based on "convergence among theoretical perspectives . . . during the last decade." survey data, and new directions in professional practice made by a recent president of the Society for Personality Assessment.

BEST PRACTICES IN RURAL SCHOOL PSYCHOLOGY

A. Jerry Benson
James Madison University

OVERVIEW

Much of the literature on rural education and rural school psychology issues reads like a good news-bad news joke. Some of the very factors that serve as enhancers for the development of quality psychological and educational practices in rural areas are also, at times, inhibitors to such practice. This phenomena derives from the fact that what we call *the* "rural" setting actually is an ambiguous label reflecting the great diversity that exists in needs, resources, economics, politics, and other factors. A chapter on "best practices" further muddies the water by assuming the ability to accurately define successes and then generalize such practices in the heterogeneity of rural settings.

This chapter is then intended to provoke thought rather than offer solutions. Its purpose is to generate discussion and ideas among persons currently practicing in rural areas, training programs who are preparing practitioners for rural areas, and persons in administrative or supervisory positions dealing with rural education and mental health.

Historical Perspective

In the last three to five years there has been a burgeoning interest in services offered in rural communities among school psychologists, mental health professionals, and educators. Rural communities are perceived as a new frontier with a realization that the practice of psychology and the implementation of educational services in rural areas is different than that which occurs in urban settings.

Fagan (1981) offers a good chronology of the development of psychological services in rural school districts. Noting the close association of rural school psychology development and developments in special education, he delineates these phases: (1) the early practice of school psychology in urban school systems and urban-based child development clinics as the only alternative for rural consumers; (2) the itinerant model of psychologists from urban centers, university programs or state departments of education coming to the rural site; and (3) finally with the passage of P.L. 94-142, the trend of rural systems hiring their own school psychologists or participating in regional programs. Each phase has introduced new problems for the practitioner and the consumer.

Concurrent with the growth in numbers of rural school psychologists, urban-rural, environmental, and cultural differences have assumed greater prominence in the conceptualization and investigation of delivery of educational and psychological services in recent years. Sher (1983) indicates at least four reasons for this renewed interest. First, *demographic and economic* changes have stimulated refocusing upon rural services. Since the early 1970's, there has been a significant shift of residences from urban to rural areas. President Carter's *Rural and Small Towns Policy Statement*, in 1979, noted that rural areas were gaining population at a rate 40% higher than metropolitan areas. As of 1980, nearly two thirds of all school districts, one half of all public schools, and one third of all teachers in the United States were serving predominately rural constituencies (National Center for Educational Statistics, 1980). This urban-to-rural shift in population patterns has created more of a voice, both politically and economically, for rural education.

Political and legal pressures have been another reason for the renewed interest. P.L. 94-142 has had an enormous impact on the growth of special education and related services in rural areas (Helge, 1980). The recent Pawley versus Bailey case in West Virginia (No. 74-1268, West Virginia Circuit Court, Kanawha County, 1982) is exemplary of the rising pressures for equal educational opportunities for rural areas. Other political trends toward decentralization and defederalization of education and human services have also fueled the fires of interest and concern for rural education.

One of the more promising reasons for renewed interest has been renewed *respect for rural education models.* Rural schools are now being seen as exemplary in their school-community relations, their participatory forms of local control, and their informal familial approach (Sher, 1983). Sher (1981) notes the relative success of rural schools in teaching the basics, after controlling for intelligence and social class. Researchers (Cyr, 1959; Barker & Gump, 1964; Sher, 1981) have shown that students in rural schools are found to (a) participate more in extra curricular activities, (b) more likely be club members and officers, (c) take more courses with greater variety, and (d) form closer, more lasting relationships than their urban counterparts.

Rural schools are also being seen as *natural laboratories for innovative practices.* Although much of this innovation has come out of necessity, educational researchers and program planners are looking closely at practices such as individualized instruction, smaller pupil-teacher ratios, one teacher teaching multiple grades, cross-aged grouping and tutoring, and the fuller utilization of the community as a learning resource.

The growth of interest groups for rural education is also reflected within our own profession. Special rural interest groups have emerged in the National Association of School Psychologists, Division 27 (community psychology) and Division 16 (school psychology) of the American Psychological Association, and the American Education Research Association. Likewise, projects such as the American Council on Rural Special Education (ACRES, Murray State University), the National Rural Research and Personnel Preparation Project (Murray State University), and the University of Indiana Rural Preparation Program indicate the growth in the investigation and conceptualization of service delivery for rural areas. The importance of recognizing urban-rural differences and efforts to resolve service delivery issues seems to have been formally sanctioned.

Uniqueness of Rural School Psychology

The current literature suggests that the practice of school psychology is different in rural versus urban settings. Flax, Wagenfield, Ivens and Weiss (1978) have documented characteristics of rural communities that affect the provision of mental health services and suggest that attention must be paid to the sociological context in providing these services. Trenary (1978, 1980), Hamblin (1981), and Benson, Bischoff and Boland (1983) have identified a number of issues common to rural school psychology practice. Consistent findings in these surveys denote the following issues as unique: (a) lack of alternative programs and services for special needs children; (b) heavy caseloads; (c) limited access to fellow psychologists for informal consultation; (d) limited community services (such as counseling, and parent education services); (e) limited availability of continuing education programs; (f) lack of administrative and consumer understanding of the school psychologists' role; and (g) work conditions such as, travel and inadequate space.

Hughes and Clark (1981) and Hamblin (1981) found that school psychologists working in either rural or non-rural settings had comparable levels of graduate school training and preferred their present manner of professional functioning as seen in high job satisfaction. Hughes and Clark also noted a greater role diversity reported by rural school psychologists in their sample, which seems to contradict other findings and popularized thought on the matter.

It appears then that rural school psychologists can self-identify themselves and issues they feel unique to their practice on a consistent basis. However, to address these issues as if they are a given in all rural settings would be presumptious and probably not productive. The uniqueness of rural practice, and the resulting issues, is more likely derived from the mixture of the nature of the sociological context, the perceived needs of all participants, and the subsequent exchange of resources. Thus, an understanding and appreciation of the rural context is primary to effective practices.

BASIC CONSIDERATIONS

If one spends time with farmers, one often hears them talking about getting "a feel for the lay of the land." This is important, for the wrong crop planted in an inappropriate field for the type of soil, drainage, federal subsidies, or the inappropriate plowing, terracing or insecticiding may have dire effects on the anticipated product. The following discussion of the rural context and political realities is offered as stimuli to aid the reader in assessing the "lay of the land" prior to tilling the psychological and educational intervention soil.

The Rural Context

In introducing this chapter two major, underlying questions have been posed: "What is rural?" and "Is the practice of school psychology actually different in rural settings than urban settings?" School psychologists have often maintained that the application of psychology in educational settings requires an understanding of the unique quality and set of circumstances that exists in the educational system. It seems only natural then that this same assumption should be applied to the practice of school psychology in rural settings, i.e., the need to understand the rural context.

In looking at the question "What is rural?", a modification of an old adage comes to mind: "Ruralness, like beauty, lies in the eyes of the beholder." The images conjured up by the word "rural" vary enormously from community to community. The term "rural," even though common characteristics are recognized in the literature, obscures the diversity that is inherent in the rural context. It would be more accurate to speak of rural America as having multiple definitions. While this type of multiple definition more accurately reflects the rural context, the lack of a precise definition of rural is at least one reason that rural education has been largely ignored in recent years (Nachtigal, 1982). Lacking clear criteria for differentiating between rural and urban, public policy has too often viewed education as a generic process which operates under the "one best system" model. This has typically meant indiscriminately applying techniques of urban practice to rural settings.

How then do we deal with the juxtiposition of diversity and the need for common definition in light of public policy? Nachtigal (1982, p. 270) offers a summary of the common characteristics generally thought to discriminate between rural and urban settings. These characteristics are shown in Figure 1. Although some common characteristics tend to be shared among rural communities, differences in degrees do exist and appear to be related to "(a) the availability of economic resources, (b) cultural priorities of the local community, (c) commonality of the purpose, and (d) political efficacy" (Nachtigal, 1982, p. 271). Nachtigal, by analyzing the characteristics of rural communities offered in the literature, suggests that a taxonomy of rural America naturally demarks three categories: the Rural Poor; traditional Middle-America; and Communities in Transition.

The first category, the Rural Poor, is described by lower median income, lower level of educational development, and lower level of political power. The economic and political power tends to be concentrated and often lies outside of the community. Within these rural communities, the more basic socio-economic problems need to be resolved first before major interventions in the provision of educational or psychological services can be initiated.

The second category, traditional Middle-America, is best characterized by the Midwest farm community where solid family lifestyle, the Puritan work ethic, and commitment to education are evident. Power structures in these communities are relatively open and political participation is broadbased. The commitment of these communities to education creates an environment where ideas can serve as a catalyst for action.

The third category, Communities in Transition, is best seen as a community

Figure 1.
Rural/Urban Differences

Rural ——————————————————————————————————— Urban

Personal/tightly linked .... Impersonal/loosely coupled

Generalists .... Specialists

Homogeneous .... Heterogeneous

Nonbureaucratic .... Bureaucratic

Verbal communication .... Written memos

Who said it .... What's said

Time measured by seasons .... Time measured by time clock

Traditional values .... Liberal values

Entrepreneur .... Corporate labor force

Make do/respond to environment .... Rational planning to control environment

Self-sufficiency .... Leave problem solving to experts

Poorer (spendable income) .... Richer (spendable income)

Less formal education .... More formal education

Smaller/less density .... Larger/greater density shifting from "old-timers to new-comers." The social structure of these communities is often in a state of flux with conflict between the old established inhabitants and the influx of outsiders who bring new or different ideas. Schools in these communities often serve as the focal point of conflict between two different value systems, different demands for services, and different ideas. In these communities, consensus building must be the top priority. Thus, the diversity of rural communities in economy, social-cultural values, and attitudes indicates the importance of assessing community social dynamics in deciding how best to provide educational and psychological services in rural schools.

Generalizations about rural communities must be approached with caution. Though diversity is the norm in describing the rural context, it is still useful to look at some of the common characteristics of rural areas and investigate their relationship to the provision of psychological services. First, rural areas are often defined by their geographic characteristics. They are less dense, with fewer people in a large physical area. This tends to produce transportation problems. Rural areas are also characterized by a scarcity of services. Within rural communities one finds many professionals serving in generalist roles to fulfill the needs of the community. Looking at the rural economy, the tax base for services in general, and mental health and human services specifically, tends to be limited. This limitation is also reflected in the work opportunities or employment levels in rural communities.

Despite differences in economy and geography, rural communities are often highlighted by close family ties and mistrust of outsiders. Since many of the professionals providing mental health and human services in rural settings are outsiders, this further exacerbates the difficulty of obtaining acceptance both for the professional and the programs that one would like to implement in rural settings. Correspondingly, there is a very heavy emphasis on the self-help ethos. Many of the problems faced by families in rural settings are kept within the family, with the assumption that the family system can deal with the problem without intervention from the outside.

This closeness of family also spills over into a closeness of the community and is reflected in community unity and community pride. Although there may be as many diversities and subcultures as there are in urban settings, they are often transcended when the local community perceives intervention as being initiated by outside forces and community control as being lost. The school system often serves as the one institution with which the community aligns and defines itself.

In summary, it is important to reemphasize the need for understanding the priority needs and available resources in the community in relation to the goals of the educational system and psychological services. The application of the "one best system" approach to all educational programs serves to remove control from the local community, thus inherently promoting conflict between the educational or psychological programs and local values.

BEST PRACTICES

Political Realities

Inherent in the political reality of rural schools appears to be a tension between the fundamental promise of local control versus the need for promulgating national culture (Dunn, 1983). Dunn has called this educational control issue the continued playing out of Jeffersonian populism versus Hamiltonian centralized philosophies of government. Much of the early development of education in America followed the Jeffersonian model of political power resting in the hands of decentralized communities. However, as the nation began to urbanize and as much of education became standardized after World War II, a system run by the centralized urban elite, Hamiltonian philosophy, began to take shape. Bit by bit, the rights and responsibilities of local school boards gave way to the rights and responsibilities of state educational agencies.

The state education agencies are now entrusted with creating a uniform system of education. They have garnished the power of certificating people who practice in educational systems, standardized the curriculum content and requirements of educational systems, and even impringed upon the decisions made about physical facilities (Dunn, 1983). This, in many ways, has made the role of the local board of education perfunctory. Conflict arises from the fact that the local school is seen as the rallying point for continuing community control by the local citizenry. In many rural communities, the school is the center of daily life. It serves both as the monitor of each child's development within that community, and as an affirmation of membership in the community by each citizen. In other words, the school not only serves an educational function for the children of the community, but it also serves an educational and entertainment function for the community as a whole. It takes on many characteristics of being the self-image of the community. An often complicating factor is that the local school district may be the largest employer within the community, thus exerting significant economic control. Therefore, control of their local school is literally a matter of life and death for the community. This has direct implications for the planning and implementing of educational programs in the local school that may be perceived as threatening the homeostasis of the community.

Another point of built-in tension contributing to the political climate is that of consolidation. Proponents for centralized, consolidated school systems often note the poor cost-effectiveness of providing numerous educational programs in rural schools. They often question the quality of these numerous programs and, instead, offer the promise of higher quality and better services through consolidation. On the other hand, the bulk of small rural schools seems to meet the need of their constituencies reasonably well. In a study of small rural schools in the United States, Dunn and Carlson (1981) found that about 75% of the community respondents expressed contentment with factors ranging from student achievement to drug and alcohol control to teacher quality in their school system. The study noted that the rural people speak with pride about the family feeling that exists in their schools, about the individual attention given to their children's needs and about the commitment of community resources. In this period of a national feeling of distress about the quality of public schooling, as elucidated in the "A Nation at Risk" report (National Commission on Excellence in Education, 1983), this level of satisfaction must cause one to question the overall benefits of consolidation and centralization.

Finally, the purpose, or the goals, of the school is another point of political conflict. The Hamiltonian philosophy would hold that the purpose of the educational system is to transmit national cultural values and serve as a system of identifying those who could advance and make useful contributions in the centralized elite aristocracy. This, of course, could translate within a local community as education promoting a road out of the community, and thus opening the potential for conflict between the values being taught within the educational system and those of the community. Sher (1983, p. 282), in looking at the politics of rural school reform, notes that one of the greatest obstacles to reform is that "children across rural America live in a society that is not particularly concerned about or committed to helping them reach their full potential as workers, as citizens or human beings." He states that improving the lives and futures of rural youth is not a national priority. Therefore rural education is treated with indifference by both the public and private sector. An obstacle to reform, then, is the lack of serious respect for the integrity and intrinsic worth of rural people and rural communities.

What are the implications of this built-in tension for school psychologists practicing in rural areas? First, there has to be recognition of and appreciation for the tension that exists between the need for centralized, standardized education and the need for local community control. There has to be greater attention paid to the *process* by which educational reforms are planned and implemented as this has direct ramifications to the locus of control issues. And, most importantly, there has to be the respect for the intrinsic worth of the rural people and the rural community.

Appreciation of potential value conflicts in a rural setting should aid the school psychologist in serving in an enabling role. Heightening the constituents' awareness of the issues involved and the different perspectives of the issues would enhance working toward community concensus. This also includes an examination of the values of the community versus the values of the practitioner. Many rural practitioners lament the lack of responsiveness of their system to, what seems to them as evident, change. Organizational psychologists have delineated reasons for resistance to change (Watson, 1966). Effective practice will require more facilitation of others' self-analysis and participation, and less ego involvement by the school psychologist in leading the way.

Issues and Practices

In discussing potential practices for school psychologists in rural areas, one needs to keep in mind the basic considerations of the rural context, the community's values and needs, sources of potential conflict, and an awareness of self in this context. This discussion will focus on the issues identified as important by rural practitioners: service delivery, recruitment of staff, retention of staff, training and technology (Trenary, 1978, 1981; Benson et al, 1983), and potentially effective practices. This section is not a complete compilation of rural practices, nor does it propose effectiveness without consideration of the specific ecological context. In reviewing these practices and thinking of their application in a particular setting, just remember this old quote: "Whatever you've decided to do, you can find someone who'll advise against it."

Service Delivery

Many of the unique issues of rural school psychology practice noted earlier can be included under the rubric of service delivery: lack of alternative programs for special needs children, sparse population dilemma, lack of community resources, travel, and the impact of community attitudes and values on the services offered. In looking at the first two of these issues, we can note that the establishment of collaborative service delivery models such as intermediate education units and interagency models have constituted a direct assault on the problem of getting special services to those in need. However, there are many situations where even these practices cannot adequately serve the needs due to the sparsity of population.

Providing services in sparsely populated rural areas has caused us to rethink the least restrictive alternative model. Burrello and Sage (1979) offer a comprehensive four-dimensional model for service delivery for handicapped children in rural areas. This model expands the classic Reynolds framework to include delivery options of non-categorical resource room, full-time teacher/consultant to regular education, itinerant teacher/consultant, itinerant home trainer, parent trainer with supportive services, and telecommunications. Decisions on placement then have to involve consideration of severity, population density/number of cases, and location of services. In rural settings the issues are not always ones of specific diagnosis and concern over selecting the least restrictive setting from many options. The issues are more often those of evaluating trade-offs and deciding among alternatives, none of which can be considered optimal but hopefully will suffice.

Another approach to service delivery in rural ares is the use of interagency collaborative models (Hughes & Clark, 1981; Benson, Canfield & Hanson, 1981). The formation of interagency councils and human development teams sanctions the drawing of resources from many agencies to focus on specific children or issues. The rural community offers the accessibility of people and agencies for such activities. Recently, the author was involved in organizing a coalition of representatives from the school system, a university, the mental health system, the public health department, the community services board, the social services department, and the local hospital to plan a community effort on prevention of mental retardation and developmental disabilities.

The use of paraprofessionals is another resource for the rural practitioner. One project, implemented in a rural sparsely populated county in West Virginia, involved the use of school bus drivers as paraprofessional social workers/counselors for potential dropouts. The school bus drivers were chosen as a delivery mechanism because of their availability to the school system and their knowledge of and accessibility to the cultural, social context of the potential dropout's life. Some districts in California use paraprofessionals to help implement the recomendations of the school psychologists such as implementing specific behavior management programs or individual curricula intervention in support of the regular teacher. Finally, educators and psychologists need to look at the home-based resources for the child. Examples would include parent as primary teacher, supplementing this with consultation via telecommunications, itinerant visits of professionals, and occasional temporary residential placement.

The issue of community attitudes and values has been addressed throughout this chapter. One of the toughest components of this issue for the entering school psychologist, who is usually an outsider, is that of assimilation. In addition to recognizing and appreciating the local mores, the rural practitioner must become an active part of the community. Taking part in community activities such as Lions Club, PTA, Boy Scout pancake suppers, helps alleviate misconceptions both of the practitioner as a person by the community, and of the community and residents by the practitioner. Also, assimilation into the school community is not automatic. School psychologists are likely to find themselves as one of the most educated persons on the staff or in the community. Engaging in activities that do more to boost one's ego than to build up the team effort often leads to isolation and little support.

Recruitment

Delivery systems are important, support systems are vital and formal politics have major impact. Yet *people* actually have to make the delivery system work. Thus, the individual school psychologist can be viewed as the key to the quality of psychological services in the rural school. This obviously places a heavy emphasis upon the recruitment process. At the same time, difficulty in recruiting and retaining mental health professionals is a pervasive problem in rural areas (MITRE, 1979; Helge & Marrs, 1981). A National Rural Research and Personnel Preparation project study (Helge, 1980) found that of the 75 rural school districts surveyed, almost two thirds (64%) reported recruitment problems and almost one half (48%) reported retention problems as critical areas of difficulty in implementing P.L. 94-142.

In analyzing the recruitment dimensions with rural educators, Sher (1983) delineates three types of potential employees: (a) *homebodies* — individuals who grew up in rural areas and understand the rural community; (b) *flashes in the pan* — individuals assigned to rural areas involuntarily or as a stepping-stone who may, at best, inspire thought or innovation and, at worst, be psychologically detached from the community; and (c) *transplants* — individuals who move to rural areas voluntarily, because a spouse is transferred, or urban life is rejected, and may contribute talents uncommon to the local area. Each type yields different motivation or personal needs to be met in the job. Addressing these characteristics in recruitment dictates the need for efforts at the preservice level, such as enticing existing rural educators or psychological professionals to expand their compentencies into the area of school psychology.

Issues of employment conditions and compensation must also be addressed in enhancing recruitment efforts. Realistic expectations for travel and caseload must be negotiated by the school psychologist at the initiation of employment. Research (Hughes & Clark, 1981) indicates the potential for broad role expansion in rural areas which is a plus in employment con-

ditions. The feelings of professional isolation may be addressed by local school districts including provisions for professional development and adequate supervision/consultation in the school psychologist's contract. Finally, the variability within states and regions on school psychologists' salaries warrants discussion by the State Department of Education (SEA) and local districts. If rural districts want quality services comparable to others in their state, they will have to equally, if not over, compensate monetarily.

Retention

Closely related to the issue of recruitment is that of retention. Additional considerations include staff development, professional burn-out and isolation. According to the staff development literature in education and business, 15-25% of an employee's time should be spent in staff development experiences (Helge, 1981). Yet, Helge found many rural school districts had no formalized staff development program and they readily acknowledged the linkage between inadequate staff development programs and staff retention problems. Regional, state and national school psychology meetings, workshops and conventions are viable models of professional development. The weekend or summer university-based seminars also provide a chance for two-way professional exchange, as well as socialization opportunities. National associations such as NASP provide continuing professional development programs through audio and/or videotapes.

Peer consultation offers another professional development and support system. The Iowa Department of Public Instruction produces paperback monographs on best practices in many areas of the school psychologists' role and disseminates them to all practitioners within the state (Grimes, 1983). Alaska, because of its vastness of territory, uses a combination of tele-conferencing and statewide computer linkages for a system of peer consultation and support. At the local level the school psychologist might formulate study groups or consultation opportunities. These could include professionals from agencies such as the mental health center, vocational rehabilitation, and the juvenile courts.

Bina (1981), in reviewing the research on burn-out and attrition in rural areas, notes the relationship between teacher retention and teacher morale. One of the factors most often identified as precipitating low morale was the low frequency of supervision. Creative methods of *appropriate* supervision and peer consultation should be pursued by the rural administrator. A clear distinction must be made between supervision as related to line-staff hierarchies within the system and supervision related to professional consultation.

Personal isolation, or "culture shock," is another major reason for practitioners leaving rural practice. Sher (1983) and Benson et al (1981) recommend that rural practitioners take cultural holidays to nearby larger, urban settings. To help mollify personal isolation, many rural school districts offer dual appointments for married couples. Also, belonging and sharing help circumvent the feelings of personal and professional isolation. Taking an active part in national, state, and regional professional groups and sharing your successes and concerns with others via state newsletters are isolation-prevention activities.

Training

The training of school psychologists to practice in rural settings encompasses issues of preservice and professional development programs. Hughes and Clark (1981) recommend the preservice training of school psychologists at a generalist level introducing counseling, clinical, community and organizational psychology skills and theory, in addition to educational and developmental psychology. It seems imperative that the preservice training for school psychologists heading for rural areas include sufficient "survival orientation," that is, exposure to the realities of rural communities and rural practice. Benson, et al (1983) found that the majority of practicing rural school psychologists had no specialized coursework to prepare them for rural practice nor had they completed practica or internships in rural settings.

The issue of continuing professional development has previously been addressed. However, this reminder is offered: creative planning by the individual rural school psychologist is the key to effective professional development.

Technology

Perhaps some of the most fertile ground for innovation in the practice of school psychology, and education in general, in rural areas lies with technological advancements. The potential for expanded services via technology pertains to all the issues of rural practice that have been delineated: service delivery, professional development, isolation, and peer consultation.

In the area of service delivery the use of telecommunications in working with professionals or paraprofessionals in remote areas was previously mentioned. Imagine the potential for inservice programs and consultation between the school psychologist and teachers spread over wide distances when the presentation of theoretical constructs and the modeling of specific techniques can be accomplished through videotape systems. The follow-up could then include conference calling among those teachers who share common concerns or face similar problems, complemented by direct contact of the itinerant school psychologist. The reverse of this process holds promise in providing the school psychologist video input of classroom environments, specific children, or even tapes of faculty meetings, discussions, or parent meetings for review and consultative follow-up.

This model of training and consultation holds great promise when, as Burrello and Sage (1979) point out, we move further down the continuum of school-based interventions and look toward home-based interventions using parents or paraprofessionals as the primary intervener. One could conceivably approach a parent education class or support group for parents of handicapped children using a slightly modified approach.

Much of the technology and logistics of this approach have been demonstrated through projects such as those providing higher education to teachers of remote areas (Hagstrom, 1983; WVCOGS, 1977) and providing professional development to school psychologists (Grimes, 1983). In the higher education projects, a locally selected coordinator monitored viewing of presentations originating from a central campus or location and facilitated group discussions via teleconference hookups with the featured speaker or other class locations. These projects found that the face-to-face contact with the instructor was primary to the building of the sense of community or groupness (Hagstrom, 1983). Naisbitt (1982) has warned of the futility of attempting teleconferencing in such a "high-touch" society oriented to face-to-face meetings. Thus, the careful attention to the "high-touch" component of a "high-tech" intervention becomes imperative.

Remoteness for school professionals and students is also reduced through such projects as "Dial-an-Author" and "Computer Chronicles" programs which offer Alaskan children a link with nationally known authors and other students through audioconference and computer hookups. The Dial-a-Consultant program was initiated by the West Virginia School Psychologists Association as an attempt to combat the rural remoteness of the state and enhance the quality of psychological services provided in the schools. The Association asked members to indicate areas of expertise on which they were willing to consult with others. The information was then compiled and distributed to all school districts.

Finally, Heath (1983) has brought to us an awareness of computer programs such as bulletin board and data bases and their potential for school psychologists. A bulletin board offers the computer user the opportunity to leave messages which others may access through their computer. Linking of school psychologists, university-based persons, and others via computers and modems (using the existing telephone system) is a cost-effective and fast method of sharing ideas and people resources. Likewise, data bases are "like a great shopping mall with over 5,000 stores. These stores are places of information, e.g., *PSYCINFO, ERIC,* etc." (Heath, 1983, p.1). This allows even the school psychologist in the remotest area to keep up-to-date with the latest research and literature. All rural practitioners placing their ideas and successful practices in such a data base or bulletin board would instantly make an effort such as this chapter obsolete.

The financing of such programs may seem insurmountable, but the major cost comes in the initial acquisition of the hardware. Here are two ideas how rural practitioners have faced this issue. Barnhardt and Barnhardt (1983), in Alaska, have suggested "giving" this idea away to your local legislators and then piggybacking on their system. "Audio (and computer) conferencing systems designed to facilitate legislator's interactions with their constituents during a legislative session can also serve the needs of children, teachers, and school psychologists in rural schools" (p. 274-275). Others (Bear and Lancaster, 1983) have seized upon the wave of "high-tech" being introduced in public school programs to obtain state funding for computer hardware, software and also address the "high-tech" versus "high-touch" issues. Through programs such as "Providing for Success Through Computer Education and Development of Social Responsibility," they are not only introducing computers into the instructional and management areas of education, but are also using the opportunity to develop affective education programs.

SUMMARY

The effectiveness of the practice of school psychology in rural areas appears to depend upon an understanding of the *social context*, the *individual* behind the school psychology role, and the *transaction* that occurs within the setting. "Rural" is defined in terms of the diversity of multiple realities, each of which carries important sociological and philosophical aspects that impinge upon the work of the school psychologist. An appreciation for the rural context then is primary to best practices in the rural area, and the brief introduction of salient aspects of that context presented here was designed to provoke thought and discussion.

Secondly, using the unique issues identified by school psychology practitioners in rural areas, a discussion of the issues and practices was offered. These issues included service delivery, recruitment of staff, retention of staff, training and technology. Again, this sharing of practices and ideas was intended not to offer specific programs for ready adoption in various locales, but rather to stimulate thought

and encourage the continued sharing of ideas.

In conclusion, the practice of school psychology in rural areas is a challenging and demanding task. The lack of specialization by professionals and the lack of resources is both at times a hinderance to providing services and a door opening to the opportunity for role expansion by the school psychologist. The essential difference may lie in you, the rural practitioner.

REFERENCES

Barker, R. G., & Gump, P. V. *Big School, Small School.* Stanford, Calif.: Stanford University Press, 1964.

Barnhardt, R., & Barnhardt, C. Chipping away at rural school problems: The Alaskan experience with educational technology. *Phi Delta Kappan*, 1983, *64(4)*, 274-278.

Benson, A. J., Canfield, J., & Hanson, D. P. Rural school psychology: The need for networking. Communique (NASP), Jan.-Feb., 1981, *9(5)*, pp. 1, 3.

Bina, M. J. Teacher morale in rural areas: Implications for administrators regarding teacher burn-out and attrition. *NRP: National Rural Research and Personnel Preparation Project Newsletter*, 1981, *3(1)*, p. 2-3.

Burrello, L. C., & Sage, D. D. *Leadership and Change in Special Education.* Englewood Cliffs, N. J.: Prentice-Hall, 1979.

Cyr, F. *Catskill Area Project in Small School Design.* Oneonta, N. Y.: State University Teachers College, 1959.

Dunn, F. Good government vs. self-government: Educational control in rural America. *Phi Delta Kappan*, 1983, *65(4)*, 252-256.

Dunn, F., & Carsen, W. S. *Small rural schools in the United States: A statistical profile.* Small Schools Project, Department of Education, Dartmouth College: Hanover, N. H., 1981.

Fagan, T. School psychology in rural areas: Problems and promising developments. *National Rural Research and Personnel Preparation Project*, 1981, *3(1)*, 6-7.

Flax, J., Wagenfield, M., Ivens, R., & Weiss, R. *Mental health and rural America: An overview and annotated bibliography.* NIMH, Washington, D. C., 1978.

Hagstrom, D. A. Teaching in Alaska. *Phi Delta Kappan*, 1983, *65(4)*, 276-277.

Hamblin, A. *Current practices of rural and non-rural school psychologists.* Unpublished doctoral dissertation, Rutgers the State University of N. J., 1981.

Heath, C. Research for the school psychologist or find in seconds what you couldn't find in weeks. *NASP CTASP Newsletter*, 1983, Sept., 1.

Helge, D. I. *A national comparative study regarding rural special education delivery systems before and after passage of PL 94-142.* Murray, Kentucky: Center for Innovation and Development, Murray State Univ., 1980.

Helge, D. I. *Individualizing staff development in rural school districts to enhance services for all children, including the handicapped.* Murray State University, Murray, Kentucky: National Rural Project, 1981.

Helge, D. I., & Marrs, L. W. *Personnel recruitment and retention in rural America.* Murray, Kentucky: Center for Innovation and Development, Murray State University, 1981.

Hughes, J., & Clark, R. Differences between urban and rural school psychology: Training implications. *Psychology in the Schools*, 1981, *18*, 191-196.

MITRE Corporation. *Research directions for rural mental health.* Published in collaboration with NIMH. Available from MITRE Corp., Metrek Div., 1820 Dolly Madison Blvd., McLean, Virginia.

Nachtigal, P. M. (ed.). *Rural education: In search of a better way.* Boulder, Colorado: Westview Press, 1982.

National Center for Education Statistics. *Statistics of local public school systems.* Washington, D.C.: U.S. Government Printing Office, 1980.

National Commission on Excellence in Education. *A Nation at Risk.* U.S. Government Printing Office, Washington, D. C., 1983.

Sher, J. P. (ed.). *Rural education in urbanized nations: Issues and innovations.* Boulder, Colo: Westview Press, 1981.

Sher, J. P. Education's ugly duckling: Rural schools in urban nations. *Phi Delta Kappan*, 1983, *65(4)*, 257-262.

The Carter Administration. *Small community and rural development policy.* Washington, D. C.: U.S. Government Printing Office, 1979.

Trenary, D. S. Report of the commitee on school psychology in rural areas. *The School Psychologist*, 1978, *33(2)*, 3.

Trenary, D. S. The unique problems of rural school psychologists. *The School Psychologist*, 1980, *23*, 13.

Watson, G. Resistance to change. In Bennis, Benne, & Chin (eds.), *The Planning of Change.* New York: Holt, Reinhardt & Winston, 1969 (2nd ed.).

ANNOTATED BIBLIOGRAPHY

As previously noted, the literature specifically on the practice of school psychology in rural settings is sparse. This comes primarily from the fact that this is a growing area of research and theoretical interest. Therefore, much of the existing and new materials come through presentation, newsletters and personal contacts. Rather than recommend specific citations from the author's reference list with a fuller description of each, the author would advise interested readers to become involved in the developing and sharing of new ideas in rural practice by joining some of the following associations:

American Council on Rural Special Education (ACRES), Box 2470 University Station, Murray State University, Murray, Kentucky, 42071. ACRES offers a newsletter, papers of interest and presents an annual National Rural Special Education Conference.

Rural School Psychology Special Interest Group of the National Association of School Psychologists (NASP). Randy King, 8030 MacKenzie Road, Affton, MO 63123.
Through this special interest group, NASP has sponsored preliminary survey research in the area and supports the networking of rural practitioners. Special meetings are held at each annual NASP Convention. Publications appear in the *Communique* and as special documents prepared by the Assistance to States Committee.

Committee on School Psychology in Rural Areas of Division 16 of the American Psychological Association. Tom Oakland, Past Pres. Div. 16, 252 Ed. B., Ed. Psych. Dept., University of Texas, Austin, TX 78712.
Networking of interested persons is supported and publication in the Division 16 Newsletter.

Association for Rural Mental Health. Gail Gladding, University of Wisconsin-Madison, Continuing Education in Mental Health, 414 Lowell Hall, 610 Langdon Street, Madison, Wisconsin, 53706.
Association provides a newsletter and a Summer Study program in Madison.

BEST PRACTICES IN ASSESSMENT OF
SOCIAL SKILLS AND PEER INTERACTION

M. Patricia Brockman
Meyer Children's Rehabilitation Institute
University of Nebraska Medical Center

OVERVIEW

The social competence of children is an important area of study which has received increasing attention and scientific interest in the past decade (Wine, 1981). Social skills, usually conceptualized as a part of the broader construct of social competence, have been defined as "those responses which within a given situation prove effective, or in other words, maximize the probability of producing, maintaining, or enhancing positive effects for the interactor" (Foster & Ritchey, 1979, p. 626).

The importance of social skills has been repeatedly underscored in the literature. There is increasing evidence that children's friendships serve important, if not essential, functions and that children without friends are at risk in terms of later peer relationships (Asher & Taylor, 1981) and in other areas of development such as academic achievement (Walker and Hops, 1976). Researchers and educators have attempted to establish methods of identifying children who have difficulties relating to peers and to develop strategies for remediating these deficient skills. This chapter will focus on issues related to the assessment of social skills and peer interactions in children.

Within recent years, there has been much innovation in the area of social skills assessment with children (Van Hasselt, Hersen, Whitehill, & Bellack, 1979). This represents an important new assessment strategy for school psychologists to incorporate into their existing repertoire of evaluation skills. The over-use of traditional testing methods such as intellectual assessments has often been challenged because of their limited usefulness and fairness for some referral problems. In addition, legal mandates such as PL 94-142 have provided an impetus for the school psychologist to include varied methods of evaluation in their work with children. By including social skills assessment instead of or as an adjunct to more traditional methods of evaluation, school psychologists may more successfully address the needs of the children they serve.

The purpose of this chapter is to provide an overview of the area of social skills assessment to acquaint school psychologists with its usefulness and importance. Various methods of assessing social skills and peer interactions will be presented and critically reviewed in terms of their potential contributions to the evaluation process. Such a review will hopefully encourage more school psychologists to address this important area of development in their assessments and interventions with children.

BASIC CONSIDERATIONS

Importance of Development of Social Skills

Children's interactions with their peers provide unique and important contributions to the development of social competence (Asher, 1978). Children who lack friends are more likely to be deficient in a variety of social skills such as cooperation, communication of needs, and responding positively to peers (Gottman,

Gonso, & Rasmussen, 1975). These children often show delays in cognitive development (Strain, Cooke, & Apolloni, 1976), impaired academic performance (Cartledge & Milburn, 1978), school maladjustment (Gronlund & Anderson, 1963), and frequently drop out of school (Ullmann, 1957). Socially isolated children are also more likely to have serious adjustment problems later in life (Cowen, Pederson, Babigian, Izzo, & Trost, 1973). Low social status in childhood has been found to be related to a variety of undesirable life events including delinquency (Roff, Sells, & Golden, 1972), suicide (Stengel, 1971) and bad conduct discharges from the military (Roff, 1961). While these studies are correlational in nature and therefore cannot provide a causal link between early social difficulties and problems in school and adulthood, they strongly suggest that children with poor social interaction skills are at risk for continuing difficulties (See Gresham, 1981a for review).

The assessment of social skills is particularly essential with handicapped children because skills in this area often differentiate between severe and mild delays in functioning (Morris & Dolker, 1974) and are critical in determining the extent to which handicapped individuals are rejected by their nonhandicapped peers. Over the past 30 years, a plethora of research has shown that handicapped students are poorly accepted by their peers (Gresham, 1981b). Studies conducted on the social status of mentally retarded (Ballard, Corman, Gottlieb, & Kaufman, 1977), physically handicapped (Force, 1956), learning disabled (Siperstein, Bopp, & Bak, 1978), and emotionally disturbed/behaviorally disordered (Morgan, 1977) children have generally found the handicapped children to be significantly lower in sociometric status than their nonhandicapped peers. These findings have important implications for the mainstreaming of handicapped or special needs

students. Because a particularly important outcome of mainstreaming is the extent to which handicapped children are accepted by the peer group, social skills assessment needs to be included in the evaluation process before a responsible decision can be made concerning placement of special needs students. Placement of handicapped children in regular classroom programs without providing them with the social skills necessary for peer acceptance may result in increased social isolation and a more restrictive social environment (Gresham, 1982a). Thus, although mainstreaming has largely been an attempt to place children in their least restrictive environment, the opposite effect may result if specific attention is not provided to the area of social skills.

Definition and Conceptualization of Social Skills

There are several different definitions in the literature reflecting various dimensions of the social skills construct. Most definitions of social skills fall into one of three basic categories: (a) sociometric, (b) behavioral, and (c) competence-correlates (Gresham, 1982a).

Sociometric Definition. The sociometric definition has been proposed by researchers who focus on social status or the degree of acceptance/rejection by the peer group as a global measure of a child's level of social skill (Asher & Hymel, 1981). The assumption is that children who are well accepted by their peers are thought to be more socially competent than children who are less well accepted or are rejected. This definition is especially useful in terms of predictive validity because sociometric status in childhood has been correlated with numerous long-term social behavior and adjustment measures (Asher, Oden, & Gottman, 1977). However, being a fairly global conception of social skills, the sociometric definition has limited practical utility (Foster & Ritchey, 1979) because it conveys little or no information about the specific behaviors that are effective in interpersonal interactions.

Behavioral Definition. Within a behavioral framework, social skills have been defined as "the complex ability to emit behaviors that are positively reinforced or negatively reinforced and not emit behaviors which are punished or extinguished by others" (Libet & Lewinsohn, 1973, p. 304). Although this orientation is very useful in the development of social skills intervention programs, individual behavioral components have varied depending on the specific child behaviors, antecedents, and consequences identified in a functional analysis of the behavior.

Support for the behavioral definition can be found in the social skills literature that suggests correlations between rates of giving positive social reinforcement and positive social status and between rates of negative social behaviors and negative social status (Hartrup, Glazer, & Charlesworth, 1967). A variety of behaviors have been targeted in social skills treatment programs; however, few of these behaviors were selected because they had been systematically validated for their ability to differentiate between socially competent and less competent children (Green & Forehand, 1980).

Competence-correlates Definition. In their definition of social skills, Asher and Taylor (1981) included the element of social validation, that is, the identification and selection of relevant skills on the basis of their relationship to an independent criterion of social competence. This competence-correlates definition is seen as a synthesis of the sociometric and behavioral definitions into a socially valid definition (Gresham, 1982c). For this reason, the competence-correlates definition

is presently viewed as the most useful conceptualization of social skills.

Gresham (1981a) viewed social skills difficulties along three dimensions: (a) skill deficits, (b) performance deficits, and (c) self-control deficits. Skill or acquisition deficits are based upon the child's knowledge or performance of the skill and are said to occur when the child does not know how to perform the skill or has never been observed to perform it. Treatment usually involves techniques such as social modeling, behavioral rehearsal, and coaching. Interactional problems are labeled performance deficits when the child has been observed performing the social skill(s), but not at an acceptable rate. Treatment is usually focused on the child's motivation through the systematic arrangement of antecedents and/or consequences in the environment. Self-control deficits are said to occur when the child lacks the behavioral control to inhibit the disruptive, aggressive, or impulsive responses that interfere with the acquisition or performance of the appropriate social behavior. Self-control deficits have been remediated using cognitive behavior modification procedures such as relaxation training, self-instruction, self-monitoring, and self-reinforcement.

Given the diversity of these definitions, it follows that social skills assessment will not involve a singular process. The following section will include a summary of some of the major assessment techniques including purpose, basic procedure, and advantages and disadvantages. Such a review is meant to facilitate future use of these assessment tools by school psychologists who recognize the importance of social skills in the overall development of children.

BEST PRACTICES

The assessment of social skills in the school environment can be useful for a

number of reasons, including the identification of children with interactional problems, the placement/classification of special needs students, the evaluation of social
skills intervention programs, and the determination of factors related to social
skills deficits in school-age children. Due
to the complexity of defining and conceptualizing social skills and the diversity of
functions for which social skills assessment has been used, educators and researchers have employed a variety of assessment tools. Despite this fact, there are
three general categories of social skills
assessment which are most commonly
used: (a) sociometric measures, (b) parent
and teacher behavior rating scales, and
(c) naturalistic observtions. The key to
successful social skills assessment is that:
(a) it involves more than one evaluation
tool, (b) it is conducted with more than
one informant, and (c) skills are assessed
across a variety of situations to ensure
valid results. Each of the various methods
of social skills assessment presented in the
following section make a unique and important contribution to the overall evaluation of the child's level of social functioning.

Sociometrics

Sociometric assessment was developed to measure the degree of attraction/
acceptance or rejection among members
of a group and includes a number of different types of instruments. Among the
sociometric measures, the peer nomination and peer rating techniques are the
most common. There is evidence that these
two different procedures tap different
aspects of sociometric status. Gresham
(1981c) has suggested that peer nominations produce a global measure of a student's popularity or friendship status
whereas peer rating scales generally yield
a global measure of a child's likability or
overall acceptance in the peer group.

Peer Nomination. The most common
method for measuring peer acceptance is
the peer nomination or partial-rank-order
technique developed by Moreno (1934). In
this technique, children are asked to nominate their classmates according to certain criteria, such as, desirability as work
or play partners. These nominations can
be either limited or unlimited choices, that
is, the instructions can specify that the
child nominate all the children in the class
that meet the criteria or limit the choices
to three or four classmates. The criteria
can be positive, such as, "Who would you
like to play with?" and "Name three children you especially like" or negative, for
example, "Name three children you don't
especially like" and "Who would you *not*
like to work with if you had to complete
some school work?" When using peer nominations, it has been helpful to present
each student with a list of his/her classmates to ensure that no one is temporarily
forgotten.

A child's score is determined by divid-
ing the total number of nominations s/he
receives by the number of students in the
class who participated. Because there is
considerable sex bias in sociometric assessment in elementary age children, only
nominations from same sex peers should
be included in a child's score. When positive criteria are used, a child with a high
score is assumed to have more social status or to be more popular. When negative
questions have been presented, a child
with a large number of nominations is
seen as rejected by the group. Research
findings indicate that positive and negative criteria tap different aspects of peer
relationships (Moore & Updegraff, 1964)
and by using both in sociometric assessment, children can potentially be identified as accepted, rejected, or neglected.

One of the advantages of using sociometric nominations with children in elementary grades is the stability of the measure over time (Busk, Ford, & Schulman,

1973). Two cautions should be noted when negative criteria and/or limited choices are used in peer nominations. When employing negative criteria to determine socially rejected children, users should guard against the possible damaging effect those nominations might have on peer relationships. It should also be noted that when the number of nominations made by each child is limited to three or four, this may diminish the sensitivity and utility of the peer nomination scores as outcome measures.

Peer Rating Scales. When using the rating scale sociometric (Roistacher, 1974), the child rates each of his/her classmates on a 1-to-3 or 1-to-5 Likert-type scale according to some specified criteria. Examples include the degree to which the rater would like to play games or work on a class project with each classmate. For students in the early elementary grades, Singleton and Asher (1977) also included faces ranging from a frown to a smile to help communicate the meaning of the numbers on the scale.

A child's score is determined by averaging the ratings s/he received from his/her classmates. As with peer nominations, only ratings from same sex peers should be used when sex bias is present (Singleton & Asher, 1977).

One advantage of this sociometric technique over peer nomination is that it provides information concerning relationships between each group member as opposed to only those nominated, thus permitting a more detailed analysis of individual peer relationships. Research has also indicated that the scores obtained from the peer rating method have higher test-retest reliability (Thompson & Powell, 1951). In addition, ratings of acceptance by classmates obtained when using peer ratings may be more realistic outcome measures than ratings of popularity obtained when using the peer nomination

technique (Gresham, 1982b).

In conclusion, sociometric assessment generally yields global measures of a child's popularity or acceptance in the peer group. Although this cannot be relied upon as a sole measure of social skill level, these assessments provide useful information to educators and researchers concerning a child's social status. As such, these techniques can be used to produce outcome measures that are considered socially valid. Of the two sociometric methods discussed, peer rating is probably more useful in assessing social skills.

Parent/Teacher Rating Scales and Checklists

Parent and teacher ratings are an important part of the multifactored assessment strategy employed when evaluating children's social skills. These individuals spend a great deal of time with the children and therefore can generally provide useful information regarding a child's social behavior and status (Greenwood, Walker, & Hops, 1977). Rating scales and checklists may be used as diagnostic tools to pinpoint behavioral objectives and to assess treatment effects. Individual items can be stated in global terms to obtain information about a child's social status or worded specifically to help identify particular behaviors in need of remediation. Teacher ratings have been found to be quite useful in identifying students with low social status (Bolstad & Johnson, 1977) and tend to correlate highly with sociometrics (Pekarik, Prinz, Liebert, Weintraub, & Neale, 1976). As treatment outcome measures, they can be used by: (a) comparing scores to the pre-intervention rating(s) provided by the parent or teacher, (b) comparing scores to any normative criterion that might be available, or (c) comparing scores to the level of an untreated control group. However, when assessing treatment outcomes, ratings are not likely to be sensitive to small or subtle changes in behavior, especially with untrained or minimally trained observers (Weinrott, 1977).

There are several behavioral checklists commonly used in school settings to distinguish students with behavioral difficulties from children without problems that also have been used in social skills assessment. They include, but are not limited to: the Walker Problem Identification Behavior Checklist (Walker, 1976), the Devereaux Elementary School Behavior Rating Scale (Spivack & Swift, 1967), the Behavior Problem Checklist (Quay & Peterson, 1967), the Burks Behavior Rating Scale (Burks, 1977), and the Personality Inventory for Children Revised (Lachar, 1982). Although social behaviors are included on these scales, the instruments were not specifically designed to provide an organized classification of children with social skills deficits.

There are only a few rating scales that have been devised solely for the purpose of assessing children's social skills. In the CORBEH Programs for socially withdrawn and aggressive children, teacher rating scales comprised the second part in a trilevel assessment strategy (Walker, Hops, & Greenwood, 1981). The rating scales are contained in procedural manuals for teacher-consultants who have prime responsibility for assessment and intervention (Greenwood, Todd, Walker, & Hops, 1978; Hops, Fleischman, Guild, Paine, Street, Walker, & Greenwood, 1978; Walker, Street, Garrett, Crossen, Hops & Greenwood, 1978). Each of these scales also provides a characteristic behavioral profile of the children. The CORBEH materials are suggested for use with preschoolers and students in the early primary grades.

The Social Behavior Assessment (SBA) (Stephens, 1980) is a teacher rating scale designed to measure specific social skills that are important for successful adjust-ment in school activities. The SBA consists of 136 social behaviors arranged under 30 subcategories further grouped into four domains: (a) environmental behaviors, (b) interpersonal behaviors, (c) self-related behaviors, and (d) task-related behaviors. Parents and/or teachers are asked to estimate the rate of some or all of the social behaviors on a scale from zero to three. Although the SBA is a relatively new scale, it has shown promise as a reliable instrument (test-retest $r = .89$; interrater $r = .76 - .97$) and possesses adequate content validity (Stephens, 1980). The SBA was designed to be used with a broader age range than the social skills rating scales developed by the CORBEH researchers. Another useful feature of the SBA is that it can be used in conjunction with *Social Skills in the Classroom* (Stephens, 1978), a procedural manual for teaching each of the social skills included in the rating scale.

Naturalistic Observations

Behavioral observations have been used most frequently in the identification of students with social deficits and in the evaluation of social skills intervention programs. This method of assessing children's social skills possess the most face validity because it involves systematic recording of the child's social behavior in the natural environment (e.g., playground, cafeteria, classroom) at the time of its actual occurrence. Direct observation may be most appropriate for measuring the reciprocal process of social interaction, especially when a dyadic observation system is employed. A dyadic system provides a measure of the antecedent and consequent events that are the immediate determinants of a child's social behavior.

Observation procedures may involve a variety of recording techniques, such as frequency, duration, time-sampling, or interval systems. The specific observational method will vary depending upon the purpose for the assessment, the sophistication of the observor, the amount of training required for reliable use of the system, and practical utility of the system in applied settings. In an educational setting, assessment requirements can sometimes be satisfied by simple frequency count of one or two social behaviors. This can easily be recorded by minimally trained personnel (Hops, 1981).

Direct and systematic observation can be most effectively used as the final stage of the social skills assessment process to verify the findings of less costly and less direct screening/referral measures such as teacher/parent ratings or peer sociometrics. This increases the cost-efficiency of the evaluation process and is similar to the "behavioral assessment funnel" described by Hawkins (1979) in which assessment moves from a broad focus involving peer and adult ratings to a more narrow focus involving direct observation of specific behaviors in the natural setting.

A significant advantage of behavioral observation is the direct relationship that exists between assessment and treatment procedures designed to correct the problem. The primary goal of assessment is to identify the child's deficits so that appropriate treatment can be planned and implemented; however, there is a major stumbling block to achieving this relatively simple goal. As was discussed earlier, it has not yet been established which social skills are necessary for normal social functioning because there is no agreement on a set of external criteria for social competence (Anderson & Messick, 1974). Behaviors recorded during naturalistic observations should be selected because of their discriminant validity with reference to an established measure of social status (Gottman et al., 1975). This would increase the social validity of the assessment and pinpoint behaviors for intervention that are more likely to affect a child's social status with his/her peers.

Behavioral observations can be specifically designed to assess the amount of time a child is interacting with his/her peers as well as the type (e.g., positive or negative) of social behavior in which s/he engages. Behavioral indices of social skills have included: percentage of total time with peers, number of avoidance responses, or frequency of interactions. To obtain measures that are more qualitative in nature, behaviors should be selected that have high correlations with significant criteria such as social maladjustment, popularity, or acceptance. Examples of qualitative behaviors have included: withdrawal; positive or negative reinforcement such as positive attention and approval, disapproval and criticism; frequency of positive or negative peer and teacher interactions such as compliance or noncompliance, disruptive behavior, ignoring, cooperative play, and aggression. Other less frequently used measures have included nurturance, friendliness, positive and negative visibility, and support.

Several systematic observation systems have been developed for recording the social interactions of children. These systems can be easily learned and provide sufficient data for identifying children in need of treatment, for selecting an appropriate intervention, or for evaluating the effect of the intervention. Examples include the Consultant Social Interaction Code (CSIC) from the PEERS program for socially withdrawn primary grade children (Hops et al., 1978), the SAMPLE Observation System (SOS) for identifying socially withdrawn preschoolers (Greenwood et al., 1978), and the Consultant Interval Recording System (CIRS) from the RECESS Program for socially negative-aggressive elementary school children (Walker et al., 1978). Each was developed for use by teacher-consultants with minimal training. The procedural manuals describing each system contain normative data for preschoolers through students in grade three to assist with decision making and evaluation processes.

Naturalistic observation offers many advantages. Data are generally easy to interpret to those directly involved in the intervention process and on-line staff can usually be taught to collect their own data instead of relying on nonparticipant experts (Hops, 1981). Another advantage of naturalistic observation is that the obtained data is not as dependent upon memory, judgment, or perception of other persons as are parent/teacher ratings or peer sociometrics. It also permits an assessment of the larger environmental context including such factors as availability of space, types of on-going activities, and degree of adult-imposed structure, all of which have been shown to be related to the social interactions of children.

Although behavioral observation is one of the most important elements to include in the assessment of social skills, some potential concerns need to be addressed. There is a tendency for observer drift and bias to affect the reliability and validity of the data collected. Other possible problems include the complexity of the observational system, the behaviors to be coded, and the nature of observer training and reliability assessment (Cunningham & Tharp, 1981). Finally, naturalistic observations are less useful when low frequency events are important determinants of social status. For these reasons, naturalistic observation should be seen as an important component in the assessment process, but one that also has some limitations. It is recommended that behavioral observations be conducted to verify the findings of more global and less costly assessment procedures and to provide a more direct measure of the behaviors in the settings where they occur. This type of assessment will provide more definitive information regarding behaviors to be targeted for treatment.

Behavioral role plays have been widely used in social skills assessment. Because performances in these contrived situations typically show low correlations with social skills exhibited in naturalistic settings, their use is generally not recommended for social skills assessments conducted in the schools. Although behavioral role playing can be an effective treatment tool, especially for children with acquisition deficits, the use of this technique as an assessment tool should be limited to differentiating children with skill versus performance deficits.

SUMMARY

The evaluation of social competence is one of the most influential recent developments relevant to the evaluation of preschool and school-age children, especially disadvantaged and handicapped students. Although the development of appropriate social skills has been acknowledged as important, many school psychologists have not yet incorporated social skills assessment methodologies in their work with children.

There are various dimensions and conceptualizations of social skills in the literature, each reflecting different dimensions of a very complex construct. The variety of assessment methods also reflects these different dimensions. It is suggested that to provide a socially valid and economically feasible assessment of a child's social status and behavior, a combination of various methodologies is needed.

Peer ratings, the sociometric method that is generally preferred, provides a global and socially valid measure of the child's acceptance by the peer group. Behavior checklists, preferably specifically designed to assess social skills such as the Social Behavior Assessment (Stephens, 1980), provide more information about the particular behaviors that may be targeted for treatment. These two methods are seen as very useful in the initial or referral stages of an overall social skills assessment strategy. Once it has been determined that a problem exists, parent or teacher interviews can be conducted to further delineate behaviors of concern as well as situational variables that may be important to remedition of problem areas. Finally, behavioral observations conducted in the setting(s) where the problem behaviors are occurring can provide the most direct assessment that can lead to the selection of appropriate treatment strategies that hopefully will improve the child's social behavior and status among his/her peers.

REFERENCES

Anderson, S., & Messick, S. (1974). Social competency in young children. *Developmental Psychology, 10*, 282-293.

Asher, S. R. (1978). Children's peer relations. In M. E. Lamb (Ed.), *Social and Personality Development* (pp. 91-113). New York: Holt, Rinehart, & Winston.

Asher, S. R., & Hymel, S. (1981). Children's social competence in peer relations: Sociometric and behavioral assessment. In J. D. Wine & M. D. Syme (Eds.), *Social Competence.* New York: Guilford Press.

Asher, S. R., Oden, S. L., & Gottman, J. M. (1977). Children's friendships in school settings. In L. G. Katz (Ed.), *Current Topics in Early Childhood Education* (Vol. 1). Norwood, NJ: Ablex.

Asher, S. R., & Taylor, A. R. (1981). The social outcomes of mainstreaming: Sociometric assessment and beyond. *Exceptional Education Quarterly, 1*, 13-30.

Ballard, M., Corman, L., Gottlieb, J., & Kaufman, M. J. (1977). Improving the social status of mainstreamed retarded children. *Journal of Educational Psychology, 69*, 605-611.

Bolstad, O. D., & Johnson, S. M. (1977). The relationship between teacher's assessment of students and students' actual behavior in the classroom. *Child Development, 48*, 570-578.

Burks, H. F. (1977). *Burks Behavior Rating Scales Manual.* Los Angeles, CA: Western Psychological Services.

Busk, P. L., Ford, R. C., & Schulman, J. L. (1973). Stability of sociometric responses in classrooms. *Journal of Genetic Psychology, 123*, 69-84.

Cartledge, G., & Milburn, J. F. (1978). The case for teaching social skills in the classroom: A review. *Review of Educational Research, 48*, 133-156.

Cowen, E. L., Pederson, A., Babigian, H., Izzo, L. D., & Trost, M. A. (1973). Long-term follow-up of early detected vulnerable children. *Journal of Consulting and Clinical Psychology, 41*, 438-446.

Cunningham, T. R., & Tharp, R. G. (1981). The influence of settings on accuracy and reliability of behavioral observation. *Behavioral Assessment, 3*, 67-87.

Force, D. G. (1956). Social status of physically handicapped children. *Exceptional Children, 23*, 104-107.

Foster, S. L., & Ritchey, W. L. (1979). Issues in the assessment of social competence in children. *Journal of Applied Behavior Analysis, 12*, 625-638.

Gottman, J., Gonso, J., & Rasmussen, B. (1975). Social interaction, social competence, and friendship in children. *Child Development, 46*, 709-718.

Green, K. D., & Forehand, R. (1980). Assessment of children's social skills: A review of methods. *Journal of Behavioral Assessment, 2*, 143-159.

Greenwood, C. R., Todd, N. M., Walker, H. M., & Hops, H. (1978). *Social Assessment Manual for Preschool Level (SAMPLE).* Eugene, OR: Center at Oregon for Research in the Behavioral Education of the Handicapped, University of Oregon.

Greenwood, C. R., Walker, H. M., & Hops, H. (1977). Issues in social interaction/withdrawal assessment. *Exceptional Children, 43*, 490-499.

Gresham, F. M. (1981a). Assessment of children's social skills. *Journal of School Psychology, 19*, 120-133.

Gresham, F. M. (1981b). Social skills training with handicapped children: A review. *Review of Educational Research, 51*, 139-176.

Gresham, F. M. (1982a). Misguided mainstreaming: The case for social skills training with handicapped children. *Exceptional Children, 48*, 422-433.

Gresham, F. M. (1982b). *Social Skills: Principles, procedures, and practices.* Des Moines, Iowa: Department of Public Instruction, 1-35.

Gresham, F. M. (1982c). Social validity in the assessment of children's social skills: Establishing standards for social competency. In F. M. Gresham, *Social Skills: Principles, procedures, and practices.* Des Moines, IA: Department of Public Instruction.

Gronlund, H., & Anderson, L. (1963). Personality characteristics of socially accepted, socially neglected, and socially rejected junior high school pupils. In J. Seiderman (Ed.), *Educating for Mental Health.* New York: Crowell.

Hartup, W. W., Glazer, J. A., Charlesworth, R. (1967). Peer reinforcement and sociometric status. *Child Development, 38,* 1017-1024.

Hawkins, R. P. (1979). The functions of assessment: Implications for selection and development of devices for assessing repertoires in clinical, educational, and other settings. *Journal of Applied Behavior Analysis, 12,* 501-516.

Hops, H. (1981). Behavioral assessment of exceptional children's social development. *Exceptional Education Quarterly, 1,* 31-43.

Hops, H., Fleischman, D. H., Guild, J., Paine, S., Street, A., Walker, H. M., & Greenwood, C. R. (1978). *Program for Establishing Effective Relationship Skills (PEERS): Consultant Manual.* Eugene, OR: Center at Oregon for Research in the Behavioral Education of the Handicapped. University of Oregon.

Lachar, D. (1982). *Personality Inventory for Children (PIC): Revised format manual and supplement.* Los Angeles, CA: Western Psychological Services.

Libet, J. M., & Lewinsohn, P. M. (1973). Concept of social skill with special reference to the behavior of depressed persons. *Journal of Consulting and Clinical Psychology, 40,* 304-312.

Moore, S. G., & Updegraff, R. (1964). Sociometric status of preschool children to age, sex, nurturance giving, and dependency. *Child Development, 35,* 519-524.

Moreno, J. L. (1934). *Who shall survive? A New Approach to the Problem of Human Interrelations* (Monograph No. 58). Washington, D.C.: Nervous and Mental Disease Publishing Co.

Morgan, S. R. (1977). A descriptive analysis of maladaptive behavior in socially rejected children. *Behavioral Disorders, 3,* 23-30.

Morris, R. J., & Dolker, M. (1974). Developing cooperative play in socially rejected retarded children. *Mental Retardation, 12,* 24-27.

Pekarik, E. G., Prinz, R. J., Liebert, D. E., Weintraub, S., & Neale, J. M. (1976). The pupil evaluation inventory: A sociometric technique for assessing children's social behavior. *Journal of Abnormal Child Psychology, 4,* 83-97.

Quay, H. C., & Peterson, D. R. (1967). *Manual for the Behavior Problem Checklist.* Champaign, IL: University of Illinois.

Roff, M. (1961). Childhood social interactions and young adult bad conduct. *Journal of Abnormal Psychology, 63,* 333-337.

Roff, M., Sells, S. B., & Golden, M. M. (1972). *Social Adjustment and Personality Development in Children.* Minneapolis: University of Minnesota Press.

Roistacher, R. C. (1974). A microeconomic model of sociometric choice. *Sociometry, 37,* 219-228.

Singleton, L. C., and Asher, S. R. (1977). Peer preferences and social interaction among third-grade children in an integrated school district. *Journal of Educational Psychology, 69,* 330-336.

Siperstein, G. N., Bopp, M. J., & Bak, J. J. (1978). Social status of learning disabled children. *Journal of Learning Disabilities, 11,* 98-102.

Spivack, G., & Swift, M. (1967). *Devereux Elementary School Behavior Rating Scale Manual.* Deven, PA: Devereux Foundation.

Stengel, E. (1971). *Suicide and Attempted Suicide.* Middlesex: Penguin.

Stephens, T. M. (1978). *Social Skills in the Classroom.* Columbus, OH: Cedars Press.

Stephens, T. M. (1980). *Social Behavior Assessment.* Columbus, OH: Cedars Press.

Strain, P. S., Cooke, T. P., & Apolloni, T. (1976). *Teaching Exceptional Children: Assessing and modifying social behavior.* New York: Plenum.

Thompson, G. G., & Powell, M. (1951). An investigation of the rating-scale approach to the measurement of social status. *Educational and Psychological Measurement, 11,* 440-455.

Ullmann, C. A. (1957). Teachers, peers, and tests are predictors of adjustment. *Journal of Educational Psychology, 48,* 257-267.

Van Hasselt, V. B., Hersen, M., Whitehill, M. B., & Bellack, A. S. (1979). Social skill assessment and training for children: An evaluative review. *Behaviour Research and Therapy, 17,* 413-437.

Walker, H. M. (1976). *Walker Problem Behavior Identification Checklist Manual.* Los Angeles, CA: Western Psychological Services.

Walker, H. M., & Hops, H. (1976). Increasing academic achievement by reinforcing direct academic performance and/or facilitating nonacademic responses. *Journal of Educational Psychology, 68,* 218-225.

Walker, H. M., Hops, H., Greenwood, C. R. (1981). RECESS: Research and development of a behavior management package for remediating social aggression in the school setting. In P. S. Strain (Ed.), *The Utilization of Classroom Peers as Behavior Change Agents.* New York: Plenum.

Walker, H. M., Street, A., Garrett, B., Crossen, J., Hops, H., & Greenwood, C. R. (1978). *Reprogramming Environmental Contingencies for Effective Social Skills (RECESS): Consultants manual.* Eugene, OR: Center at Oregon for Research in the Behavioral Education of the Handicapped, University of Oregon.

Weinrott, M. R. (1977). Improving the validity of global ratings. *Journal of Abnormal Child Psychology, 5,* 187-198.

Wine, J. D. (1981). From defect to competence models. In J. D. Wine and M. D. Syme (Eds.), *Social Competence.* New York: Guilford Press.

ANNOTATED BIBLIOGRAPHY

Lamb, M. E. (Ed.) (1978). *Social and personality development.* New York: Holt, Rinehart, & Winston.
This edited volume provides a broad-based background of social development in children. Chapters are written by major contributors to the field of child development who represent a variety of theoretical perspectives. The importance of family and peer relationships and moral development are examples of topics included in this volume.

Gresham, F. M. (1982). *Social skills: Principles, procedures, and practices.* Des Moines, Iowa: Department of Public Instruction.
This is an excellent resource including a collection of published and unpublished articles by Dr. Gresham providing an overview of the area of social skills as well as specific concerns about assessment and training. The social needs of handicapped children and how this relates to mainstreaming are also addressed in a couple of the papers.

Hops, H., Fleischman, D. H., Guild, J., Paine, S., Street, A., Walker, H. M., & Greenwood, C. R. (1978). *Program for establishing effective relationship skills (PEERS): Consultant manual.* Eugene, OR: Center at Oregon for Research in the Behavioral Education of the Handicapped. University of Oregon, 1978.

This manual describes a set of procedures for modifying the behavior of children in the primary grades who have low levels of social involvement with their peers. This resource provides a well written overview of the topic of social withdrawal in children, assessment/screening procedures and instruments, intervention techniques, and procedures for maintaining skill development. The assessment and treatment package has been thoroughly tested in experimental and regular classroom settings.

Walker, H. M., Street, A., Garrett, B., Crossen, J., Hops, H., & Greenwood, C. R. (1978). *Reprogramming environmental contingencies for effective social skills (RECESS): Consultant manual.* Eugene, OR: Center at Oregon for Research in the Behavioral Education of the Handicapped, University of Oregon.
This is a comprehensive treatment manual describing a social skills intervention for socially negative/aggressive children in the primary grades. The goal of the treatment is to reduce the frequency of socially inappropriate behavior, while teaching a pattern of constructive social behavior that will facilitate social-emotional development. Included are background information, introductory and screening materials, complete descriptions of playground treatment procedures, and assessment and evaluation instruments. Specific procedures are also provided for the fading of treatment procedures and extend the program effects to the classroom.

Wine, J. D., & Smye, M. D. (Eds.). (1981). *Social competence.* New York: Guilford Press.
This volume is divided in four basic components. Part I provides broad perspectives on the social competence construct, including historical background, conceptual models, and critical reviews. Part II presents work on the assessment and enhancement of social competence of children. Part III focuses on institutionalized psychiatric populations. In Part IV a social interaction approach to social skills training is contrasted with an assertiveness model.

BEST PRACTICES FOR WORKING WITH SINGLE-PARENT AND STEPFAMILIES

Cindy I. Carlson
The University of Texas at Austin

OVERVIEW

There are three major family forms in the United States: the intact nuclear family, the single-parent family, and the stepfamily. It is predicted that by 1990 only 56% of children under 18 years of age will live with both natural parents. As many as 50% of all children will live with one parent only and up to 15% will reside in stepfamilies (Glick, 1979). We can expect one in three white children and three of four black children to spend at least part of their childhood in a single-parent home (Children's Defense Fund, 1982). In any classroom, one of every six children is likely to be a stepchild (Prosen & Farmer, 1982).

Family disruption is related to academic and behavior problems in school. Children from separated families, according to teacher's reports, are more likely to require disciplinary action than children in low conflict, intact families (Zill & Peterson, 1982). Boys appear to be at particular risk for short- and long-term school problems associated with marital dissolution (Guidabaldi, Cleminshaw, Perry & McLonghlin, 1983; Hetherington, Cox & Cox, 1979a; 1979b). Although the evidence is preliminary, girls find remarriage the more stressful adjustment (Santrock, Warshak, Lindbergh, & Meadows, 1982).

It has been demonstrated that the family roles and organizational structures of the intact, single-parent, and stepparent families are distinct from one another and place unique adjustment demands upon children. It is the goal of this chapter to provide school psychologists with a conceptual framework for understanding the contrasting dynamics of intact, single-parent and stepparent family systems from which children's school problems can be understood and effectively treated. Following clarification of the conceptual distinctions, best practice alternatives and guidelines for assessment and intervention across system levels are provided.

BASIC CONSIDERATIONS

Defining Single-Parent and Stepparent Families

In working with single-parent and stepfamilies several biases are commonly encountered:

1. Single-parent and stepfamilies represent homogeneous entities such that the problems and treatment of each family type are easily categorized.

2. Single-parent and stepfamilies are less effective than intact families in the socialization of children.

The myth of homogeneity is the focus of the following discussion.

Single-Parent Variations and Emotional Tasks

A single-parent family is one in which someone raises children alone without the household presence of a second parent or parent substitute (Weiss, 1979a). Within this definition many variations exist which are differentiated primarily by the route to single-parenthood.

Divorce or marital separation is the most common antecedent (70%) of the single-parent household. Two characteristics are particularly salient to this single-parent subtype: (a) the divorce adjustment process and (b) the post-divorce co-parental relationship. The process of divorce is an acknowledged stressor for all family members and is almost universally accompanied by emotional reactions of anger, grief, guilt and self-doubt (Wallerstein, & Kelly, 1980). It is beyond the scope of this chapter to consider in depth the long- and short-term impact of divorce on parents and their children; however, interventions with post-divorce single-parent families cannot be separated from the successful resolution of the divorce process by family members. Key research findings (Hetherington, Cox & Cox, 1982; Kurdek, 1981; Wallerstein & Kelley, 1980) follow:

1. Deterioration of child and parent functioning in response to divorce is most pronounced in the first two years;

2. Seventy-five percent of children and parents have resumed pre-divorce levels of functioning two years post-divorce;

3. Children's developmental status, social-cognitive ability, and sex influence their divorce adjustment;

4. Level of parental hostility pre- and post-divorce, visitation by the noncustodial parent, authoritative parenting by the custodial parent, open discussion with children about divorce-related concerns, and minimal depletion of financial resources all mediate children's divorce adjustment.

The continuation of a co-parental relationship (at least legally) and the nature of that relationship is the second dimension which contributes to the variability of post-divorce single-parent families. Durst (1981) identified five distinct types of post-divorce families based upon the co-parental relationship: mother and nonparent father; mother and friend father; mother and restricted father; timesharing parents; and co-parents. Actual co-parenting arrangements did not necessarily conform to legal custody decisions.

Emotional tasks facing the post-

divorce single-parent family include overcoming grief and anger regarding the loss of an intact family unit and renegotiating the relationships altered by family dissolution. This single-parent family variation is particularly vulnerable to continued inter-parental conflict, resentment toward the noncustodial parent for either too much or too little involvement, and the placement of children in the middle of parental battles.

Death of a spouse is the cause of 14% of single-parent households (Weiss, 1979a). The psychological issues faced by this single-parent family vary considerably from those faced by the post-divorce family. The primary emotional response to death is grief. In contrast to frequent attempts by family members to cover up feelings in divorce, the emotional response to death is likely to be an open, shared experience with considerable intra- and extra-familial support. While post-divorce single-parents frequently suffer lowered sexual self-esteem and compensate with dating, widows continue their marital commitment for an extended period of time. Children who lose a parent are often caught up in an overly cohesive family unit and idealization of the dead parent, whereas children of divorce are often caught between their parents' negative emotional expressions and become victims of parental distance. Thus death of a parent encourages a centripetal movement in the family while divorce fosters a centrifugal movement. Both have potentially negative consequences for children if reactions are extreme or chronic.

The final major single-parent family subtype is the never-married parent. This group constitutes 10% of single-parent families and presents yet another form of psychological adjustment. The unmarried single-parent family is noteworthy for its vulnerability. In no other parenting circumstance are children so easily blamed for the future life difficulties encountered by the parent. This increases risk of maltreatment. For many unmarried single-parents, the birth of a child disrupts education or career aspirations which are never recovered (Clapp & Raab, 1978). While fewer than half of divorced single-parents receive child support, almost no unmarried single-parent receives support from the father (Coletta, 1979). The financial vulnerability of the single, unmarried parent increases the likelihood of significant emotional and financial dependence upon parents — a situation exacerbated with teenage parenting (Furstenberg & Crawford, 1978). Conflict in parenting, lack of role clarity, and cut-off adolescent development are endemic when the young, unmarried single-parent remains with the family of origin (LaBarre, 1972; Rosen, Benson & Stack 1982; Smith, 1975). Children in unmarried single-parent homes may experience lowered self-esteem and cognitive development resulting from the typically cut-off relationship with the father (Biller, 1974; Shinn, 1978).

While divorced, widowed and never-married single-parents represent the major variations in households, the additional factors of sex and race differentiate single-parents. Single fathers constitute a small minority (3%) of single-parent households. Research on single fathers is limited; the consensus, however, is that less economic stress and ambivalence about working is experienced. Greater importance is attached to fulfilling personal needs, and single fathers are more likely to obtain help with child care and household tasks. They are as likely as single mothers to feel stressed by the logistics of managing home, children and work, and more likely to lack knowledge of normal child development (Mendes, 1976; Fry & Thiessen, 1981).

Race is an additional factor which differentiates single-parent families. Black families comprise the greatest proportion of the single-parent population. Recent research indicates that compared to Caucasians, greater variety exists in black single-parent family structures with extended (relatives in the home), augmented (nonrelatives in the home), and parent-surrogate (nonrelative assumes parental role) arrangements common. Positive child outcomes in the black single-parent family are associated with continued involvement by the absent parent or parental substitutes provided by the community and kinship network (Bass, Wyatt, & Powell, 1982). In contrast with both Black and Caucasian populations, the vast majority of Mexican-American children (81%) are raised in intact families due to a low divorce rate (Staples & Mirando, 1980). The close-knit, extended Hispanic family structure is expected to serve the "human service" role for single-parents.

Stepparent Family Variations and Emotional Tasks

A stepparent family is created by the marriage or living together in a committed relationship of two persons, one or both of whom have children (adapted from Crohn, Sager, Brown, Rodstein, & Walker, 1982). Katz and Stein (1983) identify four types of stepfamily units each with unique adjustment tasks:

Type I: A previously married woman with children marrying a man with no children. In Type I families the primary issue is how great a parent role is to be played by the stepfather. The mother may seek to limit the stepfather role either to protect her relationship with the children or to protect him from the stress of child rearing. The stepfather may also limit his involvement with his stepchildren reflecting lack of confidence in parenting ability or the ambiguity of his role. Child discipline is a key focal area for parental role limit setting.

Type II: A previously married man with children marrying a woman with no children. Type II stepfamilies, like Type I families, face the "how much to be a parent" issue; however, the issue is exacerbated for the stepmother. Since women in our society are socialized to be the primary caretakers of children, the stepmother faces greater social and self-expectations of parental role involvement while suffering the greatest negative success expectations in the "wicked stepmother" myth (Visher & Visher, 1979). Stepchildren significantly contribute to the stepmother's parenting difficulty by using non-compliance as a means of preserving loyalty to their biological parents. Child management problems are common in Type II families with stepmother and child alternatively the target of the father's anger.

Type III: A remarriage where both spouses have children from previous marriages. The Type III family has been immortalized on television with "The Brady Bunch". One need only briefly recall this series to recognize that the Type III stepfamily is likely to be the most stressful for all family members yet it possesses great strength. Only within the blended stepfamily system do all members experience the contrasts between biological and stepfamily bonds, creating a common empathic ground. Yet blending two pre-existing families results in many potentially competing groups and values. Tension is reduced when stepsiblings are close in age. A particularly difficult blended-family arrangement is created when one parent has custody of their children but the other parent's children are visitors. Stepparents whose natural children reside elsewhere often find themselves feeling guilty and resentful of the time they are asked to spend with stepchildren. Breakdown over emotional issues in the Type III stepfamily are characterized by clearly demarcated battle boundaries which conform to pre-existing household membership.

Type IV: A single-parent with children whose ex-spouse has remarried. The Type IV stepfamily represents a convergence of the single-parent and stepfamily system. This family type is vulnerable to both real and imagined loss of involvement with the former family unit by the remarried spouse and vulnerable to resentment by the new spouse of the family's financial and emotional obligations to the previous family unit.

Contrasting the Single-Parent and Stepparent Family Systems

Whereas the focus of the preceeding discussion defining single-parent and step-families was on variability, the focus of the following discussion is the common problems faced by these family types as a result of their unique structures. Since problems facing the stepfamily are eased or exacerbated by the adequacy of resolution by the single-parent family of its developmental demands and structural transformations, discussion of the stepfamily builds upon that of the single-parent family system. The discussion adopts a family systems perspective and school psychologists are urged to become familiar with this framework (Carter & McGoldrick, 1980; Kantor & Lehr, 1975; Minuchin, 1974).

Single-Parent Family System

Single-parent households are notable for the necessity of accomplishing the same functions or roles as the nuclear family with fewer role participants. The absence of a partner in the single-parent family creates a vacuum for the fulfillment of emotional intimacy, seriously undermines the parental echelon, and substantially increases the role allocation of the custodial parent. The single-parent family, therefore, is highly vulnerable to role strain.

A second major vulnerability of the single-parent (female-headed) family is economic (Coletta, 1979). The response of the majority of single-parents (70%) to economic decline is full-time employment (Richman & Smith, 1983). Employment strains the family roles of child care, child socialization, and housekeeping. Child care arrangements present the single-parent with several particularly aversive choices — financial burden (organized day care programs), emotional indebtedness (friends or relatives), or guilt and anxiety (child responsible for own welfare).

When there is considerable strain experienced by family members from roles essential to the family's survival, companionship roles (recreation, therapeutic, sexual) are the first to be abandoned (Rollins & Galligan, 1978). Paradoxically, companionship roles contribute the most to family satisfaction. In the single-parent family, roles essential to family survival supersede the enactment of enrichment roles so helpful to children's optimal development and school functioning.

The "undermanned" structure of the single-parent family suggests that chilren are automatically at developmental risk. A note of caution is essential. Research consistently finds children reared in conflict-ridden intact homes to be more poorly adjusted than children in well-functioning single-parent homes (Rutter & Garmezy, 1983). The well-functioning single-parent family, however, requires an alteration of roles and structure to permit adequate "manning" of the system.

Internal Family Restructuring

One possible adaptation to task overload in the single-parent family is to alter family roles. Within the single-parent family, children, out of necessity, are called upon to assume responsibilities of the absent spouse-parent. Children are likely to be expected to "do their share" of the housekeeping. Older children also become responsible for the care of younger siblings or for their own care before or after school. Demanding additional maturity of children often encourages single-parents to give children new rights and authority. The single-parent is more likely to consult their children before making decisions, to share their worries with children, and to rely upon their children for companionship (Weiss, 1979b).

There are potential costs and benefits associated with the "role-sharing" common in single-parent families. On the positive side, children who are capable of assuming more responsible family roles develop greater competence, capacity for independent functioning, and emotional sensitivity in comparison with their intact family peers (Weiss, 1979b). Potential risks to the child are incurred when family role demands exceed the developmental capabilities of the child or preclude the child from meeting his or her needs for security and nurturance. Children who are required to suppress their need for more involved parenting are likely to signal their distress indirectly through constant quarrels with parents, acting out or failing academically in school, or becoming overly invested in their family role as evidenced by peer disinterest, excessive worry about adult concerns, or "parental child" behavior (Minuchin, 1974).

Critical to the success of role-sharing within the single-parent family is the clarity of the boundary between the parent and child subsystems. Role strain, the absence of a co-parent, guilt, and the traditional socialization of fathers as the authoritative parent all contribute the difficulties experienced by single-parents, particularly mothers, in establishing a clear, authoritative relationship with their children. The problem is particularly acute in single mother-male child interactions. Patterson (1982) eloquently describes the coercive cycle which is established by mothers who are simultaneously over-involved and inadequately forceful with their children. In the coercive cycle the child misbehaves, the mother reprimands at a low level of intensity, the child's misbehavior escalates, wears down the mother who gives in to the child which strongly reinforces the misbehavior. The coercive cycle is broken only with the establishment of clear behavioral contingencies and an adequately intense parental response to child misbehavior. The traditional nurturing role of mothers appears to conflict with the authoritative and often punitive stance required for the management of tempermentally difficult or stressed children.

External Family Restructuring

Single-parents also meet their role responsibilities by using external supports. Three types of social support network structures have been identified as common responses to single-parenthood: the family of origin network, the extended network, and the conjugal network (McLanahan, Wedemeyer & Adelberg, 1981). Of particular concern to the psychologist is a fourth type of adaptation — the failure to establish a social support network (Wahler, 1980). The implications for single-parents and their children of each of these social support networks is examined.

One way to adapt to single-parenthood is to reunite with one's family of origin either psychologically, physically, or in some functional relationship. The advantage of this form of support to both parent and child is the economic and emotional security provided and the sharing of the parental role with someone who also shares an emotional investment in the child. The disadvantages of the family of origin network lie within the intergenerational relationships. Relying upon one's family origin demands reciprocal loyalty which isolates the single-parent from community supports, discourages intimate relationships, and delays passage through

adult developmental stages (Mendes, 1979). Sharing the parental role with one's parents has additional risks. The "related substitute" parent (Mendes, 1979), particularly if a grandmother, may become involved in a parental authority struggle and gradual "deskilling" of the single-parent. This struggle often culminates in the "related substitute" parent emerging as the "real" parent. The struggle between parent and grandparent produces an unmanageable, dictatorial child (Dell & Appelbaum, 1977). The success of the family of origin social support network depends, therefore, on the clarity of boundaries and roles in the extended family.

Developing an extended network based upon friendship ties is a second form of single-parent adaptation. This type of network is characterized by having many different persons to call upon for distinctly different kinds of support. This form of external support permits the single-parent the greatest latitude for individual development. An extended network, however, is less secure, more transient, and based upon relationships of exchange versus obligation. For some children, the complexity, the instability, the numerous adjustments required, and the greater adult focus of this network are inadequate to their developmental needs.

Re-establishing a conjugal family form is a third coping alternative. This network is characterized by the presence of a key spouse-equivalent. The spouse-equivalent may be the ex-spouse with whom the parent has maintained a close relationship or a person with whom the parent has a significant dating relationship. This form of adaptation provides both parents and children with security and role support while limiting the intensity of a marital relationship. One problem associated with this network is the possible lack of commitment by the spouse-equivalent to the children. In the most extreme situations children are physically or sexually abused by the spouse-equivalent. Frequent adjustments to a series of spouse-equivalents presents a second potential problem of this network. When the key spouse-equivalent figure remains the ex-spouse, the child's post-divorce adjustment is prolonged either by keeping alive reconciliation fantasies or embroiling the child in negative emotional interactions.

A final choice available to single-parents is to become the "sole executive" of their family, avoiding reliance upon external support. Choosing social isolation is most likely when the single-parent does not have the personal resource capability to develop an extended network and has a conflictual relationship with the family of origin. The problems associated with this form of adaptation are task overload, intensification of the parent-child relationship which increases the likelihood of aversive interaction patterns, and inadequate resources for family survival. Children in isolated single-parent families are at high risk for child abuse (Wahler, 1980).

The "insular" parent presents a formidable challenge to the school psychologist. "Insular" parents typically demonstrate overt compliance but covert non-compliance to interventions from outside the family. A friendship intervention approach is recommended to offset resistance (Wahler, 1980).

Stepparent Family Systems

Stepparent families, unlike single-parent families, represent adequately "manned" family systems. Remarriage is expected to alleviate the task overload and role-strain inherent in single-parent households. It provides parents greater ease in fulfilling family enrichment roles and children greater freedom to accomplish individual developmental tasks. From this perspective stepfamilies appear similar to intact families. The stepfamily system, however, is significantly more complex. Varying numbers of households typically comprise the system. Roles and relationships within the stepfamily are multiple and poorly defined by social norms. Clarifying household boundaries and role relationships are the major stepfamily tasks imposed by the structure of this family system.

Stepfamilies are characterized by a high level of interaction outside the household and by regular shifts in family membership with children's visitation schedules. As in all family systems, boundary pathologies can occur. The boundaries between households may be too open and cooperative. Ex-spouses, for example, may remain emotionally involved with one another and undermine the stabilization of the remarried couple. In this situation, children, hoping for a reconciliation, commonly develop school problems to keep their biological parents involved with one another and to limit commitment to the step-parent.

Stepfamilies also operate "as if" they were nuclear families and establish boundaries between households which are too rigid. In these stepfamilies the importance of the other household(s) is denigrated or denied. Parents often scapegoat the non-custodial household for any child problems and threaten to end visitation. Children in these stepfamilies experience intense loyalty conflicts, confusion, loss, and often damaged self-esteem. This dynamic is an extension of the single-parent family's failure to resolve the co-parental relationship prior to remarriage.

Stepfamilies also need to establish clear boundaries within their household. Stepfamily subsystems which must be established are: the remarried couple; the divorced couple(s); the custodial parent-child; the noncustodial parent-child; the step-parent-step-child; the biological siblings (within and across households); and the step-siblings (within and across households). According to Katz & Stein (1983), three of the above are the "power" subsystems of the stepfamily which must be included for effective intervention: the remarried couple, the custodial parent-child and the divorced couple.

The establishment of roles is the second major stepfamily task. In contrast with the well established, socially prescribed family role relationships of husband/father, wife/mother, daughter/sister, and son/brother, the stepfamily roles of step-parent and step-sibling are guided by few norms. Critical issues are financial responsibility, child care responsibility, child compliance responsibility, parental authority, and emotional attachment (Visher & Visher, 1979). A key element of stepfamily roles is their ascribed versus biological nature. Stepfamily role relationships are "instant" and can be expected to remain secondary to biological relationships for many years, particularly when children are school-aged. Adolescents may never form close relationships with stepfamily members. The expectation of an "instantly" reciprocally, loving family is a myth which undermines the success of stepfamilies.

Role transitions are stressful for all families. In remarriage, role changes represent significant losses for children while representing important gains for adults. Children in single-parent families have often developed unique role capabilities and a particularly close relationship with their custodial parent. Remarriage alleviates the child's role responsibilities but also threatens their "special position" vis-a-vis the parent. Stepparents unexpectedly find themselves the target of wrath not appreciation for their parenting or housekeeping efforts.

BEST PRACTICES

Assessment

As indicated throughout the preceding section, children's school learning or behavior problems may emanate from their membership in or transition to a single-parent or stepparent family. It is recommended, therefore, in the course of a psycho-educational evaluation of single-parent or stepfamily children, that a family assessment interview be completed. The goals of the family assessment interview are to:

1. determine the reality of the family situation
2. evaluate the family's adjustment to that reality
3. formulate hypotheses regarding the possible connection between #1 and #2 with the child's school problem.

Table I outlines a recommended family assessment interview for use with single-parent and stepparent families. The interview is adapted from Katz & Stein (1983).

TABLE I: SINGLE-PARENT & STEPFAMILY INTERVIEW

A. *Presenting problem*

   1. Obtain a detailed description of the presenting problem, the extent, the duration, precipitating events, consistency across settings and across relationships.

   2. How is the family affected by the problem? Who is affected?

3. Does the family see a relationship between the child's school functioning and family operations?

Analysis: Symptomatic behavior by a child is often "functional." What family relationships are being heightened or maintained by the child's problem? What relationships are being stressed or discouraged? What parental perceptions and behaviors are becoming dominant? What parental behaviors are suppressed or excluded?

B. *Family composition and developmental history*

1. Complete diagram which identifies the family structure and developmental changes over time.

2. What are the satisfactions and dissatisfactions of significant relationships?

3. What has been the family's response to major developmental changes?

Analysis: How complex, how resolved, and how supportive or stressful is the family structure? Unresolved, stressful adult relationships are common sources of child distress. What are the major developmental issues facing the family currently? What family coping response can be predicted from previous developmental changes?

C. *Current family functioning*

Single-parent household

1. How long has (was) the single-parent family been in existence?

2. How did they become a single-parent family?

3. How do family members describe their experience as a single-parent family? What are satisfactions/dissatisfactions, rewards/stressors?

4. How are family roles accomplished (provider-economic, child care, housekeeping, child socialization, recreation, companionship, sexual)?

Custodial parent-child relationship

1. What is the relationship like? What do they do together? How do they typically get along? How is their relationship the same or different from the parent's relationship with other children in the family?

2. Has the relationship changed over the past few years as the family shifted from a nuclear to a single-parent or to a remarried family?

3. Does the parent view the parent-child relationship as the key relationship in their life? Does the child view the parent as the key person in their life? If not, which person or relationships are key for parent and child?

Cross-household relationsips

1. What are the custodial, visitation, and financial arrangements between households?

2. How often do the households communicate? Who talks to whom? What topics are discussed? What is not discussed?

3. How do family members across households get along? (Interviewer will need to inquire about specific dyadic relationships such as ex-spouses, stepmother-stepson, child-stepsibling, mother-stepmother, etc.)

Other parent-child relationships

1. What role does the co-parent, step-parent, unrelated substitute parent play? What role would they like to play? Do they feel encouraged or discouraged from enacting their desired role? By whom?

2. Do co-parents agree on rules and child rearing practices? How are disagreements settled?

3. How does the co-parent view the child and their problem?

4. How does the child view the co-parent?

Remarriage

1. How long has the stepfamily been in existence? What was the history of courtship? How are previous marriages or relationships by the couple characterized?

2. How do family members describe the stepfamily experience and functioning?

3. How does the couple describe their relationship? How do they perceive stepfamily life interfering with their relationship as a couple?

4. How do children get along in the family? across households? (check for rivalries, sexual attractions, coalitions against parents).

Analysis: Determine the clarity and appropriateness of boundaries within and between households. Determine the role allotment, role clarity, perceived role competence, and level of role strain experienced by family members. Identify unresolved emotional issues and cut-off relationships. Identify family coping strengths.

D. *External supports & stressors*

1. Explore the family's economic well-being. If inadequate, how are they coping?

2. Is parent's employment a source of stress or enrichment?

3. How extensive and supportive is the parent's support network? What type of social support network has the parent chosen (family of origin, extended, conjugal, insular)?

    Who is available for the parent in case of emergencies?
        for child care?
        for solace and talking through problems?
        for companionship, recreation, socializing?
        to meet sexual needs?
        to provide a sense of community?

4. How extensive and supportive is the child's support network?
    Who does the child identify as friend(s)?
    Does the child feel liked by peers?
    Who does the child go to if she/he has a problem?
    Does the child like school? Does his/her teacher like them?
    Does the child engage in extracurricular activities?

Analysis: Determine the adequacy of the support network. An inadequate external network indicates an intervention area which must be addressed regardless of other interventions to maintain gains.

It is recommended that the family assessment interview be completed with the *entire* family unit. While this represents a departure from typical school psychology practice, bringing the family together regarding the child's school problem provides invaluable data for the psychologist and may begin the intervention process.

Intervention

The school psychologist has numerous intervention choices in working with single-parent and stepparent families. The choice of interventions are determined by: the type of identified problem, the primary-source of the problem, the accessibility of the primary source to intervention, the goal of intervention, and the skill of the school psychologist. In addition it is expected that the school psychologist engages in both prevention and treatment in working with single-parent and stepfamilies. Following is a discussion of possible interventions for school psychologists across the three system levels of family, child, and school.

Family system intervention

The family is the optimal target of intervention when the family assessment interview indicates the family has not adequately transformed its structure to meet a changed family situation and this is undermining the child in accomplishing his/her developmental task of school performance. Family intervention techniques include: counseling, consultation, education, and mediation.

Family Counseling

The goal of family counseling is to change the established patterns of family interaction so they become supportive of the identified problem child's development. Family counseling is indicated (a) when children have developed chronic school behavior or learning problems which do not respond to school based interventions and (b) when the family acknowledges a possible relationship between the child's school problem and family situation and is "stuck" in resolving the problem.

There are many approaches to family counseling (Nichols, 1983; Gurman & Kniskern, 1982; Wolman & Stricker, 1983). For the school psychologist, family counseling approaches are recommended which permit the focus to remain on the parent-child relationship. Family counseling approaches which meet this criterion are: the behavioral approach (Patterson, 1975: 1983); the strategic approach (Haley, 1978; Madanes, 1981); the structural approach (Minuchin, 1974; 1981); the problem-solving approach (Epstein & Bishop, 1981).

One question often raised in family counseling with single-parent and step-families is who to include in the intervention. While there are no hard and fast rules, some guidelines are helpful.

1. When the boundaries between households are rigid or antagonistic, parents from both households should be involved. The counseling focus is on establishing a cooperative relationship between the co-parents.

2. When boundaries are too open between households or between co-parents, establish boundaries by intervening primarily with custodial household. (It is likely that the excluded person will sabotage the intervention at some point if not consulted; however, the inclusion of this person can be minimized).

3. When the child is the target of stress between two parents (a detouring triangle), involve the entire family. Focus the counseling on blocking the inappropriate anger toward the child and redirecting it to the locus of the tension. Look for opportunities to make a referral for marital therapy.

4. When the child is unmanageable, include the parent and child plus any substitute parents. The thrust of counseling is to build the authoritative capacity of the parent (see Patterson, 1982) and establish clear parent-child boundaries. An unmanageable parent-child interaction may be

supported by the lack of involvement of a second parent figure. Then the focus of counseling is to increase this parent's role.

5. Siblings or stepsiblings may "unite and conquer" parents. This is most feasible when the parent lacks authority and is treated from that perspective.

6. Stepsiblings may have serious rivalries which are upsetting the family system. If the step-siblings are adolescents, counseling may focus on that subsystem alone. With younger children, parents need to be involved as the mediators of disputes.

As a rule of thumb, in family counseling, always include one subsystem level above the manifestation of the problem.

Family counseling *should not* be attempted in the following conditions:

1. When the potential risks outweigh the benefits, for example, a remarriage is on the verge of separation-divorce.

2. When the family does not accept a connection between family and school problems, therefore, key family members refuse to participate.

3. When a family does not have and is not expected to have the capacity to restore adequate functioning.

4. When an individual family member's difficulties are independent of the family process.

5. When the child's problem can be effectively treated in the school context.

6. When the school psychologist is not adequately trained to conduct family counseling. This type of intervention should not be attempted without specific training in family counseling concepts and techniques.

Family Consultation

Family consultation refers to school-problem focused discussion with the family or parents. In contrast to the family counseling goal of changing family interaction patterns, the goal of family consultation is education. Family consultation would include: (a) increasing the family's understanding of "normal" and "abnormal" behavior in single-parent and stepparent families; (b) increasing the confidence of parents in their single-parent or stepparent role; (c) providing "expert" guidance to single-parents and stepparents; and (d) linking single-parent and stepfamilies with resources.

Family consultation is indicated (a) when families are functioning fairly well but lack information or experience with specific aspects of their current family developmental stage or (b) when it is a possible precursor to a marital or family counseling referral. Family consultation skills are expected to fall within the typical role and competence of the school psychologist and therefore require no discretionary use.

Family Mediation

Mediation assumes a conflict of interest between two parties. Requesting co-parents to meet in order to resolve issues "in the best interest of the child" is viewed as family mediation. Mediation differs from family counseling in that no effort is made to change the family system. Mediation is unlike consultation as there is no educational goal. In the mediator role, the school psychologist takes a neutral position toward the problem and the involved parties, although they may protect the child. Mediation ground rules include no discussion or expression of feelings regarding unresolved emotional issues between the parents. Thus the task in the mediation is to maintain authoritative control by keeping parents rational and task-oriented while blocking unacceptable emotional responses.

Although many family and family-school problems are appropriate for mediation, family mediation is especially useful for single-parent and stepparent families who are experiencing visitation difficul-

ties. Mediation is contraindicated when the conflict between parties is so high as to threaten violence or preclude rational discussion. A second consideration in the use of mediation techniques is an assessment of the motivation and ability of parents to comply with the "working agreement." Parents must have the capacity to separate their needs from those of the child. Finally, while mediation appears similar to techniques of problem-solving, the school psychologist is encouraged to gain competence in mediation techniques via workshops or readings (Woody, 1983).

Family Group Interventions

When the school psychologist encounters a growing number of single-parent or stepfamily problems, a group approach to intervention might be more cost effective. Family group interventions appropriate within the school context include family education groups and family support groups.

Support Groups

Support groups for families provide the opportunity for guided discussion and group problem-solving by members facing similar life situations. Support groups are neither focused on therapy or educational goals. The goal of a support group is self-help and mutual help. Support groups are expected to benefit both single-parent and step-parent families as each family type often feels their problems are unique and their families are out of control. Support groups are likely to be most useful for relatively functional families who are experiencing normal anxiety regarding a family transition. Support groups are also the obvious intervention approach for "insular" single-parent families; however, attendance is likely to require a buddy system approach.

Educational Groups

Education groups are time limited

groups for parents or families which focus on providing information regarding aspects of single-parent and stepparent family functioning. The advantage of this mode of intervention is its familiarity to the school psychologist and its acceptability within the public school system. Education groups are an adequate intervention mode for adaptive families. While all families are likely to benefit from education, severely dysfunctional families do not have the capacity to apply or sustain what is learned in an educational format to their situation (Patterson, 1983; Wahler, 1980). Group effectiveness is also limited if only one parent of a two parent system attends. Educational groups, therefore, are recommended only as a supplemental intervention for more severely distressed families.

Child system interventions

Intervention with the child system is recommended (a) to supplement ongoing interventions with parents or family; (b) to supplement the parental role when adults are unavailable or incapable of assisting the child's adaptation to family change; (c) to supplement the family's role in the child's socialization by expanding the child's social support network; and (d) when the child is an adolescent. Underlying child intervention guidelines is the assumption that children have less control over and less cognitive capacity to understand family stress factors than do parents. Child treatment, therefore, is expected to ameliorate but not to resolve school problems which originate in family dysfunction. Adolescents, on the other hand, have both the cognitive maturity and the developmental thrust of separation-individuation which enables them to benefit from individual or group counseling. Despite the limitations, child system interventions hold an important place in the treatment of single-parent and step-

families. In many situations, the school is the most stable and supportive environment available to the child. The school must often serve a temporary replacement function for poor or inaccessible parenting.

Individual or Group Child Therapy

Children who have experienced family disruptions benefit from either individual (Gardner, 1976) or group therapy (Cantor, 1977) by school psychologists. The focus of interventions with children are likely to center on the emotional resolution of the loss, irrational fears or beliefs regarding the disruption, and the development of skills to use school and peers as supports. Critical to the success of child-focused intervention is consideration of the developmental level of the child. Excellent, concise discussions of the developmental approach to treating children of divorce and remarriage are found in Robson (1982) and Wallerstein (1983). Children who have experienced loss of a parent through death require a different intervention focus. Clay (1981) provides an excellent compilation of resources on both death and divorce work with children.

Group interventions are expected to be particularly useful for adolescents (ages 10-18) who are already developmentally open to peer support and advice, but groups also help younger children "normalize" their feelings. In addition to a discussion format, bibliotherapy and films are likely to be helpful, particularly with younger children (see Clay, 1981).

Classroom Teacher Consultation

Parent surveys indicate that teachers hold negative expectations for the behavior and learning of children from divorced or single-parent families (Clay, 1981). Consulting with a problem child's classroom teacher helps the teacher adjust perceptions or expectations and subsequently change their behavior to converge with the idiosyncratic needs of the child as a result of a family change. Possible topics of teacher consultation include: accepting a nurturing role toward the child; clarifying who "owns" the problem (for example, a single parent who is too disorganized to monitor homework completion or getting to school on time) and redirecting blame to the appropriate source; providing greater structure in the classroom for the child (Wallerstein & Kelly, 1980); and recognizing bias in attitudes, speech, curriculum materials and homework assignments. Teacher consultation strategies are well explicated for school psychologists (Meyers, Parsons & Martin, 1979).

School system intervention

School system policies and attitudes have been established consistent with a social majority comprised of nuclear, intact families. As the traditional family structure alters, the school as an open system is increasingly pressured to respond. A discussion of possible school system level interventions to accomodate single-parent and stepfamily needs follows.

Clay (1981) completed a survey of 1,237 single parents in 47 states to get their appraisal of school programs and policies. Although Clay did not question stepfamilies, many of the problems pinpointed are applicable to the multi-household relationships characteristic of stepfamilies. Table II summarizes the identified school problem areas and recommendations for improvement.

School policies not only reflect but also impact on social change. School policies which encourage the continued involvement of custodial and noncustodial parents as well as stepparents in their children's school functioning communicate acceptance of a social reality. More importantly, they provide norms for noncustodial and stepparents regarding parental roles and responsibilities.

TABLE II: SCHOOL POLICIES & DISRUPTED FAMILIES

Area	Problem	Recommendations
Parent involvement in the school	1. Single, working parents have difficulty being involved with school	1. Schedule parent-teacher conferences in evenings/weekends
	2. School communication is typically negative	2. School personnel take the initiative in keeping parents informed especially of child's positive behavior or learning efforts
Non-custody parents	1. Seldom are provided information about child's school progress or school activities	1. Revise school forms to include information about noncustodial parent
		2. Establish & communicate guidelines to personnel re: communication with noncustodial parents policy.
		3. Send report cards & school activity notices to noncustodial parents

(Table II continued)

Area	Problem	Recommendations
Curriculum	1. Two-parent environment is seen as normal	1. Discuss concern with text review committee & publishers
		2. Use librarian to locate & order less biased materials
Before & after school care	1. Few desirable child options	1. Conduct needs assessment
		2. Explore possible program options
		3. Consider the educational benefits as well as child care benefits
Inservice training	1. School personnel lack information & hold biased perceptions	1. Conduct inservice training programs to increase knowledge, skills and awareness

SUMMARY

Single-parent and stepparent families have become increasingly representative of family life in the United States. These family forms place unique demands upon their child members; they also provide challenges to schools and to school psychologists.

Understanding stepfamily and single-parent family dynamics is the first step to effective practice. While both single-parent and stepparent families are highly variable, commonalities exist. Both family types face major issues of emotional loss and a transformation of roles and relationships. Both families experience one or several "normal" periods of chaos and reduced member effectiveness. Single-parent and stepfamilies differ, however, in the "manning" of their system. While single parents are stressed by too few members for family roles, stepfamilies are stressed by multiple, ambiguous roles. Single-parent and stepfamily systems present the school psychologist with common threads but unique designs.

The school psychologist has many practical choices available in working with single-parents and stepfamilies. A multi-level (child-family-school) and multi-goal (treatment-support-education-mediation) approach has been outlined and is recommended for school psychology practice.

Finally, schools as social institutions and school psychologists as advocates of children's mental health have a responsibility not only to be responsive to the needs of single-parents and stepparents, but also to serve as models for these challenging parental roles.

REFERENCES

America's children and their families: Key facts (1982). Children's Defense Fund. Library of Congress Catalog & Number: 82-072946.

Bass, B. A., Wyatt, G. E. & Powell, G. J. (1982). *The Afro-American family: Assessment, treatment, and research issues.* NY: Grune & Stratton.

Biller, H. B. (1974). *Paternal deprivation: Family, school, sexuality and society.* Lexington, MA: Heath.

Cantor, D. W. (1977). School-based groups for children of divorce. *Journal of Divorce, 1,* 183-187.

Carter, E. A. & McGoldrick, M. (1980). *The family life cycle.* NY: Gardner.

Clapp, P. (1981). Single parents and the public schools: How does the partnership work? National Committee for Citizens in Education.

Clapp, D. V. & Raab, R. S. (1978). Follow-up of unmarried adolescent mothers. *Social Work, 3,* 149-153.

Clay, P. L. (1981). Single parents and the public schools. National Committee for Citizens in Education.

Coletta, N. D. (1979). The impact of divorce: Father absence or poverty. *Journal of Divorce, 3,* 27-35.

Crohn, H., Sager, C. J., Brown, H., Rodstein, E. & Walker, L. (1982). A basis for understanding and treating the remarried family in J. Hansen & L. Messinger (Eds.) *Therapy with remarried families.* Rockville, MD: Aspen.

Dell, P. & Appelbaum, A. S. (1977). Trigenerational enmeshment: Unresolved ties of single-parents to family of origin. *American Journal of Orthopsychiatry, 47,* (1) 52-59.

Duberman, L. (1973). Step-kin relationships. *Journal of Marriage & Family, 35,* 283-292.

Durst, P. (1981). Post-divorce family relationships: A comparative study. Doctoral dissertation. The University of Texas at Austin.

Epstein, N. B. & Bishop, D. S. (1981). Problem-centered systems therapy of the family. In A. S. Gurman & D. P. Kniskern (Eds.) *Handbook of family therapy.* NY: Bruner-Mazel.

Gardner, R. A. (1977). *Psychotherapy with children of divorce.* NY: Jason Aronson.

Gurman, A. S. & Kniskern, D. P. (1981). *Handbook of family therapy.* NY: Bruner-Mazel.

Furstenberg, F., Jr. & Crawford, A. (1978). Family support: Helping teenage mothers cope. *Family Planning Prospective, 10,* (6), 322-333.

Glick, P. C. (1979). Children of divorced parents in perspective. *Journal of Social Issues, 35,* (4) 170-181.

Guidabaldi, J., Cleminshaw, H. K., Peery, J. D. & McLoughlin, C. S. (1983). The impact of parental divorce on children: Report of the nationwide NASP study. *School Psychology Review, 12,* (3), 300-323.

Haley, J. (1978). *Problem-solving therapy.* San Francisco, CA: Jossey-Bass.

Hetherington, E. M., Cox, M. & Cox, R. (1982). Effects of divorce on parents and children. In M. E. Lamb (Ed.) *Non-traditional families: Parenting and child development.* NJ: Lawrence Erlbaum.

Kantor, D. & Lehr, R. (1975). *Inside the family.* San Francisco, CA: Jossey-Bass.

Katz, L. & Stein, S. (1983). Treating stepfamilies. In B. Wolman & G. Stricker (Eds.) *Handbook of family and marital therapy.* NY: Plenum.

Kurdek, L. A. (1981). An integrated perspective on children's divorce adjustment. *American Psychologist, 36,* 856-866.

LaBarre, M. (1972). Emotional crises of school-age girls during pregnancy and early motherhood. *Journal of American Academy of Child Psychiatry, 11,* (2), 537-557.

Madanes, C. (1981). *Strategic family therapy.* San Francisco, CA: Jossey-Bass.

McLanahan, S. S., Wedemeyer, N. & Adelberg, T. (1981). Network structure, social support, and psychological well-being in the single parent family. *Journal of Marriage & the Family, 10,* 601-612.

Mendes, H. A. (1979). Single-parent families: A typology of life-styles. *Social Work,* (May), 193-200.

Mendes, H. A. (1976). Single fathers. *Family Coordinator,* (10), 439-444.

Meyers, J., Parsons, R. D. & Martin, R. (1979). *Mental health consultation in the schools.* San Francisco, CA: Jossey-Bass.

Minuchin, S. & Fishman, H. C. (1981). *Family therapy techniques.* Cambridge, MA: Harvard University.

Minuchin, S. (1974). *Families & family therapy.* Cambridge, MA: Harvard University.

Nichols, M. (1983). *Family therapy: Concepts & methods.* NY: Gardner.

Nye, F. I. & Berardo, F. M. (1973). *The family: Its structure & interaction.* NY: Macmillan.

Patterson, G. R. (1982). *Coercive family process,* Champaign, IL: Research Press.

Patterson, G. R. (1975). *Families,* Champaign, IL: Research Press.

Prosen, S. & Farmer, J. (1982). Understanding stepfamilies: Issues & Implications for Counseling. *The Personnel & Guidance Journal, 60,* (7), 393-397.

Richman, H. A. & Smith, H. D. (1983). Statement presented to House Select Committee on Children, Youth & Families, April.

Robson, B. (1982). A developmental approach to the treatment of children with divorcing parents. In J. Hansen & L. Messinger (Eds.) *Therapy with remarried families*. Rockville, MD: Aspen.

Rollins, B. C. & Calligan, R. (1978). The developing child and marital satisfaction in parents. In R. M. Lerner & G. B. Spanier (Eds.) *Child influences on marital and family interaction*. NY: Academic.

Rosen, R. H., Benson, T. & Stack, J. M. (1982). Help or hindrance: Parental impact on pregnant teenagers. *Family Relations, 31*, 271-280.

Rutter, M. & Garmezy, N. (1983). Developmental psychopathology. In P. H. Mussen (Ed.) *Handbook of Child Psychology*, Vol. IV. NY: Wiley.

Santrock, W., Warshak, R., Lindbergh, C. & Meadows, L. (1982). Children's and parents' observed social behavior in stepfather families. *Child Development, 53*, 472-480.

Shinn, M. (1978). Father absence and children's cognitive development. *Psychological Bulletin, 85*, (2), 295-324.

Smith, E. (1975). The role of the grandmother in adolescent pregnancy and parenting. *Journal of School Health, 45*, (5), 278-283.

Staples, R. & Mirande, A. (1980). Racial & cultural variations among American families: A decenniel review of the literature on minority families. *Journal of Marriage and the Family*, Nov., 887-903.

Visher, E. B. & Visher, J. S. (1979). *Stepfamilies: A guide to working with stepparents and stepchildren*. Secaucas, NJ: Citadel Press.

Wahler, R. G. (1980). The insular mother: Her problems in parent-child treatment. *Journal of Applied Behavior Analysis, 13*, 207-219.

Wallerstein, J. & Kelly, J. B. (1980). *Surviving the breakup*. NY: Basic Books.

Wallerstein, J. (1983). Children of divorce: Psychological tasks of the children. *American Journal of Orthopsychiatry, 53*, (2), 230-243.

Weiss, R. (1979a). *Going it alone*. NY: Basic.

Weiss, R. (1979b). Growing up a little faster: The experience of growing up in a single-parent household. *Journal of Social Issues, 35*, (4), 97-111.

Wolman, B. B. & Stricker, G. (1983). *Handbook of family and marital therapy*. NY: Plenum.

Woody, R. H. (1983). Arbitration of family disputes. In B. B. Wolman & G. Stricker (Eds.) *Handbook of family and marital therapy*. NY: Plenum.

Zill, N. & Peterson, J. L. (1982). Trends in the behavior and emotional well-being of U.S. children. Washington, DC: Child Trends, Inc.

ANNOTATED BIBLIOGRAPHY

Minuchin, S. (1974). *Families and family therapy*. Cambridge, MA: Harvard.
This is an easy-to-read, inexpensive introduction to family systems and to family counseling techniques. These structural family therapy strategies were derived from work with problem children in disadvantaged, multi-problem homes and are particularly useful to the "difficult" families encountered by the school psychologist.

Visher, E. B. & Visher, J. S. (1979). *Stepfamilies: A guide to working with stepparents and stepchildren*. NY: Bruner-Mazel.
This is the most comprehensive book currently available on stepfamilies. It discusses research, specific problems faced by stepfamily members, treatment implications, and provides additional resources for both the psychologist and the stepfamily. Available in paperback.

Wallerstein, J. & Kelly, J. B. (1980). *Surviving the breakup*. NY: Basic.
A comprehensive discussion is presented based upon clinical research of the impact of divorce on both children and parents. It addresses children's school-related changes and the impact of school on children's functioning. Available in paperback.

Weiss, R. (1979). *Going it alone: The family life and social situation of the single parent*. NY: Basic.
Sensitive and comprehensive coverage of single-parent family issues is discussed. The book is particularly useful for heightening awareness of school personnel to the problems and concerns of the single-parent. It is not a treatment-oriented book. Available in paperback.

BEST PRACTICES IN PLANNING INTERVENTIONS FOR ELEMENTARY STUDENTS

Jeffrey J. Cohen
Ardsley Union Free School District, New York

OVERVIEW

This chapter presents specific interventions that are used in elementary school settings to manage problem behaviors. The variety of techniques and their range of sophistication require the practitioner to weight numerous factors in choosing the most effective intervention. Some strategies are more appropriate in particular settings, with particular ages, for specific problems, or with particular teacher, student, and parent temperaments. Even the preferences of the school psychologist are considered, because each practitioner has an individual work style and perspective which impacts on treatment decisions.

At one time or another, many school psychologists become frustrated in their efforts to help parents and teachers manage student problems. One psychologist offers guidelines based on child development, while another refers the family for psychotherapy. However, specific approaches which focus directly on the presenting problem are less often available. When teachers and parents ask, "Can you help me *now?*", practitioners face a dilemma. They recognize that desired changes often occur slowly, but appreciate the need to see positive movement within a reasonable period of time. Some reach back into their training and experience for more active, timesaving methods, but without success. This need not occur, for there exists a voluminous albeit scattered literature describing a multitude of school-based strategies for all types of behavior problems. School psychologists are in an ideal position to bridge the gap between research and practice by introducing these techniques into the schools and adapting them to the demands of the situation. This broadens the options for direct service to students and strengthens the practitioner's role as a problem-solver.

Literature on school-based interventions developed in the mid to late 1960s focusing primarily on the classroom application of behavior modification techniques (Hall, Lund & Jackson, 1968; Madsen, Becker & Thomas, 1968). Behavioral strategies were popular for several reasons; (a) CONSISTENCY WITH TEACHER GOALS. They effected behavior change in more efficient, less time-consuming ways; (b) IMMEDIACY. They dealt with "here-and-now" problems of most concern to classroom teachers and did not probe historical issues; (c) SPECIFICITY. They pinpointed target behaviors clearly and provided operational clarity; (d) UNIVERSALITY. A variety of individuals could be taught to implement these techniques which freed the psychologist for other duties; (e) EFFECTIVENESS. Psychologists could demonstrate the close relationship between the strategy and subsequent behavior change; and (f) OPPORTUNITY. They extended the psychologist role beyond that of psycho-diagnostician.

The 1970s saw an acceleration of research linking internal cognitive processes to behavior change (Meichenbaum, 1977; Schinke, Gilchrist & Small, 1979; Wine, 1979). Meichenbaum, a major cognitive theorist, argued succinctly for the cognitive viewpoint when he stated that, "behavior therapy techniques as originally conceptualized and implemented, have over-emphasized the importance of environmental events . . . and, therefore, under-emphasized and often overlooked how a client perceives and evaluates those events . . . Environmental events, *per se*, although important, are not of *primary* importance, rather what the client says to himself about those events influences his behavior . . ." (1977, p. 108).

During the past 10 years, the work of researchers and practitioners has resulted in an explosion of behavioral and cognitive techniques. The range of problems tackled has also broadened to include acting-out behavior, poor academic performance, disorders ranging from enuresis to thumbsucking, distractibility, impulsivity, disturbed social interactions and many others (see School Psychology Review, XI, 1, Winter, 1982, Special Issue). Simultaneously, there has been renewed emphasis on the refinement of counseling and other psychodynamic- and humanistically-oriented treatment approaches. These diverse perspectives have converged on the schoolhouse and offered varied interventions for a wide range of problems. Within this naturalistic laboratory, the school psychologist is perhaps the professional best equipped to use this knowledge to greatest advantage.

BASIC CONSIDERATIONS

Table 1 presents the more common student problems. Classroom management difficulties remain the most frequently targeted group of behaviors. More articles are devoted to strategies for these disturbances than to any other classroom difficulty (see Walker, 1979). Teachers and parents point to acting-out students as the most disruptive of the teaching process, and consequently, as those from whom they most want relief. This explains the heavy concentration on behavioral strategies. The demand for techniques to reduce disruptiveness found a response

TABLE 1
Common School Behavior Problems

1. Classroom Management Problems
2. Poor Academic Performance
3. Anxiety, Poor Self-Esteem, Depression, Phobias
4. Substance Abuse
5. Sexual Behavior
6. Hyperactivity, Impulsivity, Distractability and Inattentiveness
7. Disturbed Relationships with Peers and/or Adults

in behavioral technology which offered relatively short-term behavior management. In addition, the more clearly observable behaviors associated with classroom disturbances lent themselves to behavioral intervention. For example, calling out, hitting, or leaving one's seat are definable actions which can be observed, counted, and targeted for change. The category of "Poor Academic Performance" shares this operational clarity. Measures of performance such as work rate, accuracy, amount and quality of homework completed, or test grades are easily identified (for example, Wilson & Williams, 1973). However, anxiety, poor self-esteem, depression, substance abuse, and sexual behavior are less easily defined in specific, identifiable, or public terms. They are often measured indirectly through questionnaires, self-reports, or observation, and are open to interpretation based on individual or subcultural value systems. Thus while behavioral strategies are available for these problems, there is increased emphasis on psychodynamic and humanistic approaches as well as on cognitive and related relaxation techniques (Digiuseppe & Kassinove, 1976; Meyers & Pitt, 1976).

Hyperactivity, impulsivity, distractibility, and inattentiveness use cognitive methods in addition to, and often in conjunction with behavioral interventions. Cognitive strategies are reasonable interventions considering the developmental irregularities and process breakdowns that occur in these disorders. The goal of treatment is typically the training and internalizing of cognitive controls. For example, self-instructional training (Kendall, 1977; Meichenbaum, 1977; Palkes, Stewart & Kahana, 1968) is designed to teach self-talk, an important regulatory process that guides behavior. Relaxation techniques are also used with distractible, impulsive students to train states which are incompatible with hyperkinetic behavior. If possible, medication is avoided. (Klein & Deffenbacher, 1977; McBrien, 1978).

Disturbed relationships with peers and adults are commonly seen as outgrowths of poorly-developed or inappropriate social skills. They lead to lowered self-esteem and avoidance of social contact. Interventions for resolving relationship problems combine behavioral, cognitive, and ego-building techniques to strengthen confidence and teach more effective styles of interaction (Camp, Blom, Herbert & van Doorninch, 1977; Slavin, 1977).

Two points are worth noting. First, certain problems are not manageable in the classroom. Complex issues such as chemical dependency, chronic depression, or vandalism are not easily resolved in the course of daily teaching. These and other behaviors require strategies at the individual, building, district, and community levels that use school psychologists, staff, and community members (see Steele, 1978). However, many problems are open to classroom approaches which the teacher, psychologist, parent, and student implement together. It is neither always advisable nor necessary to remove the stu-dent from class in order to provide treatment. Second, theoretical distinctions do not limit the creative use of techniques in new problem areas. It is not difficult to find cognitive approaches to self-esteem improvement (Lane & Miller, 1977) or counseling and behavioral methods combined into one strategy (Gumaer & Myrick, 1974). However, even the best approach finds limited success if it is implemented under inappropriate conditions.

BEST PRACTICES

The remainder of this chapter concentrates on 10 factors to consider when choosing interventions. They are not the only factors, but form a core of variables which highlight the importance of good planning. Specific practices will illustrate each factor. Table 2 summarizes these factors and the sample interventions.

STUDENT AGE — Intervention decisions must consider the student's age. For example, participation by students in a parent conference rests, to some extent, on age. Additionally, positive or negative contingencies selected for a behavior modification program must be age appropriate. Younger children often enjoy stickers or a smiling face on schoolwork, whereas teenagers prefer free time or lunch away from school. Numerous techniques have been developed specifically for particular ages while others were adapted to suit the needs of various age groups.

Schneider (1974), and Schneider and Robin (1976) describe the *Turtle Technique*, a method of helping young elementary students manage frustration, agression, and tantrums. The approach combines relaxation training, reward, and instruction in problem-solving. Children hear a story about Little Turtle who preferred to run and play with his friends

TABLE 2

Factors to Consider in Planning Interventions

Factor	Sample Intervention
1. Student Age	Turtle Technique Thematic Fantasy Play
2. Teacher Variables	Positive Grading Practices Teacher Behaviors to Improve Classroom Behavior and Performance
3. Parent Variables	Home-School Contingency
4. Student Variables	Contracting Self-Management
5. Number of Targets	Group Contingencies
6. Seriousness/Danger of the Problem	Instructed Repetition Timeout Overcorrection
7. Ethical/Moral Considerations	DRL-DRO Schedules
8. Availability of Time and Space	Psychosituational Classroom Intervention Anxiety and Relaxation
9. Administrative Support	Principal as Reinforcer Phone Calls for Absences
10. Setting	Systematic Praise and Ignoring Negative Reinforcement

rather than go to school. School was hard for Little Turtle and made him angry no matter how much he tried to stay calm. One day he met the wise, old turtle who told him how to pull in his arms, legs, and head to rest inside his shell whenever he got angry. He tried it in school and liked how it felt. He stayed in his shell until he felt better, and when he came out, his teacher was proud of him (see Schneider, and Schneider & Robin for story details). After hearing the story, the class practices the technique. When the teacher says the word "turtle," the children imitate Little Turtle by pulling their arms in close to their bodies and resting their chins on their chests. Imaginary frustrating experiences are presented, and stars are given for good performance. Then, relaxation techniques involving tensing and relaxing different muscles of the body are taught. Finally, relaxation is practiced in the turtle position and the children are encouraged to cue themselves with the word "turtle." Again, rewards are provided. Daily problem-solving sessions are held to practice alternatives to aggression and tantruming and are integrated into the turtle-relaxation position. Schneider reports that successful training involves 15 minutes daily for three weeks, gradually reducing to twice weekly.

Thematic Fantasy Play was described by Saltz, Dixon, and Johnson (1977). Preschoolers heard fairy tales and other stories, saw story pictures, and discussed the stories. Over several sessions, the children acted out the stories in pantomine while an adult narrated. Other children described and acted out everyday experiences or told fairy tales without acting them out. Fantasy play enhanced impulse control and increased the childrens' scores on measures of cognitive development. This technique is applicable to younger elementary children and capitalizes on the importance of "pretend play."

TEACHER VARIABLES — The choice of an intervention is influenced by teacher temperament in several ways, including their willingness to learn and use certain strategies, their skill and sensitivity implementing a given technique, and the degree of intrusion into classroom life allowed. Beginning with the least intrusive approach is a useful rule of thumb.

One such intervention is based on evidence that lower-achieving students are responsive to *positive grading practices* (Brown and Epstein, 1977). One group of teachers positively graded daily drill papers by marking correct answers with a "C", writing only the total number of correct at the top of the paper, and making positive comments on the paper about improved performance. Another group negatively graded papers by checking wrong answers, indicating the number wrong at the top, and making negative comments on lower grades. It was found that the lower scoring students on day 1 improved the most with positive grading in five treatment days.

When suggesting techniques to teachers, it is important to point out that no single strategy works magic. Consistent response patterns over time are necessary to create a classroom environment in which behavior is better managed and performance is enhanced. In this context, Table 3 condenses a variety of teacher behaviors which improved classroom behavior and performance. The variety underscores the point that combinations of techniques work best and that not all approaches are acceptable to all teachers. Knowing the teachers and their preferences increases the likelihood of a successful outcome.

Points 1 to 7 in Table 3 are abstracted from Jones and Miller (1974). Two effective teachers' responses that prevented high-intensity classroom misconduct were taught to two less effective teachers. The key element of the effective teachers' behaviors was quick yet mild reaction to disruptiveness before it escalated.

Points 8 to 10 were described by Simmons and Wasik (1976). They used sociometric data and peer influence in elementary settings to increase attentiveness to work. Seating was based on positive peer ratings. Students were asked to help the target student with classwork, and free time was given for completed work.

TABLE 3
Teacher Behaviors for Classroom Management

Behaviors	Citation
1. Brief Comments and Gestures 2. Close proximity and focused attention to the student 3. Quick yet mild responses 4. Disapproving expressions and vocal tones 5. Positive attention to a well-behaved student immediately following negative attention for misbehavior 6. Promoting and reinforcing the offender following positive attention to a good student 7. Timeouts	Jones & Miller, 1974
8. Seating students based on positive sociometric choice 9. Using peer influence — students help and encourage a target student 10. Group reward	Simmons & Wasik, 1976
11. Requiring a delay before responding to a question 12. Teaching about alternative responses to questions 13. Self-instructional training 14. Proximity to reflective models 15. Positive & Negative Feedback	Digate, Epstein, Cullinan, & Switzky, 1978
16. Providing independent learning activities 17. Allowing the student to question and receive answers 18. Individualized instruction 19. Positive feelings from teacher	Needels & Stallings, 1975
20. Openly monitor tests 21. Arrange conditions so cheating is risky 22. Provide reasonable chances for success 23. Think twice before punishing when student admits to *suspected* cheating	Winston, 1978
24. Systematic praise	Broden, Bruce, Mitchell Carter & Hall, 1970
25. Combining touch and verbal praise	Clements & Tracy, 1977

(Table 3 continued)

Behaviors	Citation
26. Soft Reprimands	O'Leary, Kaufman, Kass, & Drabman, 1970
27. I-messages	Peterson, et. al., 1979
28. Varying presentation rate to reduce off-task behavior	Carnine, 1976
29. Promoting and rewarding positive self-statements	Hauserman, Miller & Bond, 1976
30. Goal setting on tests	Gardner & Gardner, 1978
31. Verbal reinstatement of rule-breaking behavior	Karpowitz, 1977
32. Attributing skill and effort to improve self-esteem and achievement	Miller, Brickman & Bolen, 1975

Points 11 to 15 target impulsivity (Digate, Epstein, Cullinan & Switzky, 1978), and outline cognitive and behavioral techniques teachers integrate into their daily teaching.

Teaching behaviors in elementary classes with fewer absences are highlighted in points 16 to 19 (Needels & Stallings, 1975). When children worked in smaller groups, received more positive feedback from the teacher, and more actively participated in their learning, absenteeism was less common.

Points 20 to 23 suggest steps to control cheating. These techniques are derived, in part, from Winston (1978). One point stands out: if admissions of *suspected* cheating are punished, cheating does not stop but confessions do. Intermediate steps such as requiring the confessing student retake the test, but with a lower grade or completing some alternative project rather than simply fail are suggested.

Points 24 to 32 are summarized as follows: (24) The teacher is trained to systematically attend to and ignore attending and non-attending behavior respectively. Using this technique, one second grade boy positively affected the attending behavior of a boy next to him. Ignoring inappropriate behavior is not always feasible in a classroom situation, but requires consideration of both the teacher's skill and the behavior targeted (Broden, Bruce, Mitchell, Carter & Hall, 1970). (25) Touch (defined as friendly touching of both shoulders) adds power to verbal praise. Student age, student-teacher gender, and the degree of teacher comfort influence whether this suggestion is made (Clements & Tracy, 1977). (26) Techniques are suggested for behaviors the teacher can not ignore. For example, soft reprimands delivered near the child were more effective than loud comments and reduced attention for disruptiveness (O'Leary, Kaufman, Kass & Drabman, 1970). (27) I-messages are used instead of reprimands or disapproval. These are non-judgmental statements that describe the unacceptable behavior, the teacher's feeling, and the reason why the behavior was inappropriate. The teacher is instructed to say, "*(student's name)*, when you *(description of behavior)*, I feel *(emotion)* because *(reason)*". I-messages reduce disruptive behavior only as long as the teacher uses them (Peterson, et. al., 1979). (28) The teacher presents new tasks immediately following the student's response rather than waiting. Off-task behavior was reduced and task performance improved. When presentation rate is too slow, teaching is less productive (Carnine, 1976). (29) When elementary students behaved in a successful or positive way, they were prompted to say something good about themselves and then were rewarded with praise or a hug for their statements. Reinforcing positive self-statements increases measured self-esteem (Hauserman, Miller & Bond, 1976). (30) When students in a high school resource room set test goals with their teacher, test results improved (Gardner & Gardner, 1978). Goal setting with elementary school children is used less frequently. (31) Discipline is enhanced when the misbehavior is described to the student in some detail rather than stated vaguely (Karpowitz, 1977). However, behavioral reenactment of the episode adds no power. (32) When elementary school students are regularly informed that they are capable, good workers, their self-esteem and performance improve. This contrasts with telling students that they should be good. Attribution of skill and motivation is more effective in encouraging students than attempts to persuade them to do better (Miller, Brickman & Bolen, 1975).

Again, combinations of techniques integrated into the teacher's teaching style are far more successful in managing problem behavior than a "shotgun approach" in which one or another technique is attempted. The practitioner suggests strategies, but also encourages their use through training experiences. Helping teachers successfully use interventions enhances the practitioner's role as problem-solver.

PARENT VARIABLES — When parents play a role in the change process, the options for intervention are increased. One of the more flexible strategies capitalizing on parental involvement is the *home-school contingency*. In this technique, the contingency for school behavior and performance is delivered at home (Dougherty & Dougherty, 1977; Fairchild, 1976; Schumaker, Hovell & Sherman, 1977). There are several advantages to this procedure. First, the parent is involved with the child and the school in a new and productive way. This alone fosters change. Second, because a cooperative relationship between home and school is promoted, the school is portrayed as working in the child's interest. Another advantage is that the child is rewarded for school behavior, and may be less tense when communication between school and home occurs. Finally, the parent receives immediate feedback on the child's status in school.

In Karraker's study (1972) second graders brought home either a smiling or frowning face each day to represent math performance. The reward system was explained to parents by a letter, two one-hour conferences detailing principles of behavior and reinforcement, or one 15-minute conference which only discussed the report card procedure. Parents rewarded their child with a treat, special event, or something else of their choosing. For an unsatisfactory card, the parent did not punish the child. If no card came home, the parent asked about it, but said nothing more. Improvement in the children's math performance was significant and equal for all three parent instruction methods. This indicated that parents learn the approach without involved explanations of theory. This writer adapted the home-school procedure for a sixth grader who repeatedly talked out in class. On three randomly selected days each week, the teacher indicated the number of times the student was told to stop calling out. The procedure was outlined with the parents and a contingency selected. If he was told to stop talking out fewer than three times on the designated days, the student earned an extra half-hour of television that evening. When three or more reminders were given, he lost a half-hour of viewing. On each treatment day, parents were told the number of reminders given. After 16 weeks, talkouts were reduced from approximately five per 40-minute period, to approximately two per period.

Home school contingencies are successful for two reasons. For some teachers, reducing their responsibility for managing the procedure minimizes resistance. Parent-child communication about school is also improved by structuring the interaction positively.

STUDENT VARIABLES — Students are not always passive targets of change, but play an active role in managing their problems. In *contracting* (Homme, 1969), the student is an equal participant with the parent and practitioner and assumes responsibility for improvement. Contracting also provides an alternative to punishment because it rewards positive, rather than punishing negative behavior.

A contract is never a fixed document but is renegotiated as needed to modify the schedule, change an unsuccessful reward or make other alterations. It provides the opportunity to earn rewards for reaching achievable goals.

Brooks (1974) outlined the necessary components of a contract for a 15-year old truant whose mother unsuccessfully tried various threats and punishments. The contract included the student's name, a short statement of the problem, back-

ground information, the student's obligation in the contract, the reward schedule, agreement statements, and signatures of the student, the parents, and practitioner. (See Brooks for the complete contract.)

Gershman (1976) developed a contract for an eight-year old firesetter with academic, behavioral, and social problems in school. The contract structured the mother's rewards for appropriate school performance. A statement provided for contract changes through mutual agreement. The boy was assigned specific school tasks on "task cards" each day at home and was rewarded with points for their completion. He traded points for backup reinforcers. Improvement in performance was significant.

Self-management is another approach with active student participation (Jones, Nelson & Kaxdin, 1977; Workman & Hector, 1978). In the Humphrey, Karoly and Kirshenbaum study (1978), students as young as second graders rewarded and punished themselves for reading performance. Students received one cup with their name on it and another labeled "bank." In one condition, students corrected their work and rewarded themselves by transferring tokens from the "bank" to their cups. In the "response-cost" condition, students fined themselves for unsatisfactory work by returning chips to the "bank." Although both strategies improved work rate with no change in accuracy, self-reward was more effective. Working for reward is more motivating than working to avoid punishment. It is also more appealing to teachers who implement the approach in their classroom.

Self-recording, another self-management strategy, was shown to influence the behavior recorded (Broden, Hall & Mitts, 1971). A fifth grade student who displayed temper outbursts during a remedial reading class expressed the desire to improve his behavior. The author developed the following approach for the student. Each day the boy received a sheet of paper with a grid. Any time during class if he was attending to his work, he marked a "+" in the grid. If he had an outburst, he placed a "-" in a box. When he had no outbursts during class, the student checked a larger box marked "perfect day." No data was analyzed, yet after several weeks, the teacher reported that the student was no longer a disruptive influence in class.

When student self-assessment disagrees with an independent observer, or even when the student forgets to self-record, the effect operates. Self-management is useful when the teacher is reluctant to participate in the intervention, is pressed for time, or when the student is able to play the role of manager. In addition, evidence suggests that long-term changes are better sustained when students self-evaluate and reinforce their own behavior (see Jones et. al., 1977).

NUMBER OF TARGETS — Options for intervention depend on whether the target is one student, a group, a class, or an entire school. *Group contingencies* are flexible because the behavior of many students is managed simultaneously (see Litow & Pumroy, 1975 for further discussion). Sulzbacher and Houser (1968) described a group strategy to reduce the use of and reference to the familiar "finger." The teacher placed 10 consecutively numbered cards on a bracket in front of her desk. Each time the "finger" or reference to it occurred, she flipped a card and one minute of a 10-minute recess was lost by the entire class. The behaviors declined immediately. This strategy imposed the same contingency on all members of the class.

Ross and Levine (1972) implemented a group contingency to modify the behavior of one student. The teacher told the class that each time she saw the boy with his thumb in his mouth, she would put a check on the board. If there were less than 15 checks per day for two consecutive days, every child received candy. The rate of thumbsucking in this nine-year old immediately dropped to near zero.

Other group techniques use a contingency designed only for several students within a class (Swanson, 1979).

While group contingencies are powerful tools, there are potential drawbacks. First, group pressure, particularly in older populations, focuses on the student responsible for others' rewards. While peer influence is a positive force, this issue needs careful individual consideration. Some argue that an individual contingency is a better choice when the target is one student. Second, it is difficult to convince some teachers to reward or punish students not directly involved in the behavior.

On the positive side, the group contingency is useful with varied behaviors and populations (see Gresham, 1983), may earn a student positive attention from classmates, and is more practical and timesaving when the target population is a group.

A group contingency was used to creatively reduce stealing in a second grade class with an unknown "culprit" (Switzer, Deal & Bailey, 1977). Items such as nickels, gum, and pens were placed around the classroom. If no items were missing by mid-morning, students had 10 minutes of free time. Stealing was reduced in three classes while anti-stealing lectures had no such effect.

SERIOUSNESS OR DANGER POSED BY THE PROBLEM — While most students respond positively to obtain rewards, aversive interventions are chosen when behavior is highly maladaptive or the intervention is judged less aversive than the consequences of continued negative behavior. Lahey, McNeeds, and McNees (1973) used both *instructed repetition* (also called *massed practice* or *negative practice*) and *timeout* to control obscenities in a 10-year old. During four daily 15-minute sessions, the boy had to repeat his most frequently used obscenity rapidly and without stopping. While obscenities decreased by 50%, behavior problems increased. Neither the teacher nor the student liked the instructed repetition method. A timeout procedure was then introduced. After each obscene remark, the student was placed in a timeout room for at least five minutes, and then until he was quiet for one minute. Obscenities were markedly reduced with no negative side effects. Timeouts are effective when students are removed from something *positive;* removal itself is not sufficient. Furthermore, ethical, moral, and legal issues must be considered before timeouts are employed. Further discussion of timeouts can be found in Solnick, Rincover, and Peterson (1977).

Overcorrection (Azrin & Wesolowski, 1974) was first used with retarded populations, but is applicable to non-disabled students. Retarded adults who stole food from neighbors replaced the item and then added an identical item. While simple correction and timeouts were moderately successful, this method lowered stealing to a zero rate.

Aversive strategies are often combined with positive contingencies, but practitioners are still uneasy about problems of teachers' discomfort, emotional side effects, and parental consent. These concerns closely parallel the ethics and morality issue in strategy selection.

ETHICAL AND MORAL CONSIDERATIONS — Some teachers and psychologists object in principle to aversive interventions or to punishment of whole classes for the behavior of one or a few students. Some alternatives to punishment such as contracting have already been discussed. *DRL-DRO schedules* offer another opportunity to reward students rather than punish them.

Epstein, Repp, and Cullinan (1978)

demonstrated the use of *differential reinforcement of the low rates of responding* (DRL) which rewards for reduction in negative behavior, and the DRO schedule (differential reinforcement of other behavior) which rewards the absence of such behavior. A primary special education class used a token reinforcement system in which students earned tokens for appropriate performance and behavior. Tokens were traded for backup reinforcers (see McLaughlin, 1975, and Stattler & Swoope, 1970, for more on token systems). For the first 12 days, bonus tokens were earned for keeping obscenities below three per day. Then for five days, the cursing limit was reduced to two, then one per day for eight days, and finally none were allowed (DRO). The procedure dramatically reduced the number of obscenities.

DRL-DRO schedules have several advantages: When reasonable criteria are set, students reduce inappropriate behavior gradually and rate the procedure as fair. They are used with a variety of populations, as either individual or group contingencies and with a variety of behavioral problems. Most importantly, they reward a reduction of inappropriate behavior rather than punish its occurrence.

AVAILABILITY OF TIME AND SPACE — When school practitioners are faced with practical limitations of time and space, there are techniques that help. In *Psychosituational Classroom Intervention* or *PCI* (Bardon, Bennett, Bruchez & Sanderson, 1976), the practitioner works with problem students directly in the classroom. The practitioner focuses on issues as they arise from on-going classroom events. While a given student is the primary target, factors that trigger or maintain the problem behaviors also receive attention. Other students are brought into the process as they interact with the target student or affect his or her actions. Key elements are using natural occurrences as points of departure for intervention and focusing on ecological influence in misbehavior. The psychologist shows a student how to work on a task, intervenes in a fight, discusses past behavior with a few students, or deals with other important issues. Not all classrooms and teachers tolerate such intrusion, so careful planning and choice of teachers are crucial.

When time and space are available, options are limited only by the practitioner's creativity and judgment. This writer considers student anxiety a priority issue and has attempted to heighten sensitivity to the topic. He wrote several articles about anxiety in his regular middle school newspaper column. Articles covered such points as frequency of occurrence, triggering events, individual display, and methods of reduction. The topic was also addressed in a team teaching situation. Students were introduced to the concepts and techniques of relaxation with major emphasis on the student's personal power to manage anxiety without recourse to artificial substitutes such as drugs, alcohol, or cigarettes. One group of students requested further information, so a 10-week relaxation training experience was begun. Parent consent letters were sent home for signature. Activities included breathing exercises, practice in focused attention and body awareness, guided imagery, simple muscle relaxation, and other modified exercises to illustrate anxiety reduction. The introductory nature of the experience was stressed. Students did not become proficient users of relaxation techniques as a result of the "course." Questionnaires filled out after the 10 weeks indicated students enjoyed the experience. Guided imagery was the favorite exercise, while muscle relaxation was least popular. One student practiced at home. He reported fewer sleep problems although this was not verifiable. In sum, the goal of increasing awareness of

anxiety as a life issue was accomplished.

ADMINISTRATIVE SUPPORT — Relaxation training in schools is not possible without administrative support. Principals are the major tone-setters in the school, and are powerful reinforcing agents. In Copeland, Brown, and Hall's study (1974), the principal changed academic performance. Fifth grade students saw the principal for praise when they met math and reading performance criteria. Under these conditions, math and reading accuracy increased. In a related approach, the principal visited third-grade classrooms and asked students who met the "improved" criterion in math to stand and be praised. Over three weeks, math improvement was recorded.

The power of the principal is applied in other areas. In one technique (Sheats & Dunkleberger, 1979), the principal's secretary called students' homes after a predetermined number of abscences. She used a prepared script and increased the seriousness of the message as absences became more frequent. When compared to calls made by the principal, this approach was equally effective and reduced absenteeism by about one-third. It is helpful when the principal delegates authority with positive results. In this writer's school, a nurse's aide phones the home of each absent student. It is believed that this follow-up contributes to an average daily school attendance of 96%.

A third strategy requiring administrative support developed for unmotivated students and operates on the *Helper Therapy Principle* (Durlak, 1973). For many years, the idea that tutors benefit as much as students from the tutoring experience has been discussed. In this study, ninth-grade students were assigned to an elementary school teacher. They tutored students, marked tests, supervised on the playground, and performed other chores. They received both course credit and a grade. Questionnaires completed by student aides and teachers indicated improved self-esteem, work habits, and interpersonal relationships in these helpers. The effect on the elementary students was not assessed.

SETTING — Techniques are workable in some settings but not others. Zimmerman and Zimmerman (1962) described an 11 year old student in an inpatient residential treatment center class. He misspelled words deliberately, wrinkled clean sheets of paper, and laughed when these behaviors were noticed. For his intervention, the student spelled words on the blackboard and was ignored every time he misspelled them. When he spelled a word correctly, he was praised and the next word was given. With each new word, the number of incorrect spellings decreased. At the end of the intervention, he received an "A" and was praised, and joined in a pleasant activity with the teacher. In class, positive behavior was praised and inappropriate behaviors were ignored. Attention-getting behaviors disappeared in one month.

Another strategy used negative reinforcement to maintain a 12-year old in a day treatment program (Wasserman, 1977). The boy was destructive, made constant noises in class, refused to do classwork, and demanded to return home. His mother had placed him and refused to have him back. Positive contingencies had not been effective. For his intervention, he was told that efforts were being made to return him home, but that his behavior was intolerable. When his behavior did not meet clearly delineated daily criteria, one page of his residential return materials was completed. As he improved, standards for good behavior were raised. He was also counseled about his mother's rejection. Over two months, his behavior improved significantly.

These 10 guidelines should assist the practitioner in planning the most appropriate intervention. Some additional points are also relevant. (a) Strategies must be applied consistently for a specified length of time. It is not uncommon for parents and teachers to indicate that they "tried the technique yesterday" but it didn't work. Build a justifiable time frame into the method and stress the importance of following the plan. (b) Generalization of effects over settings or to different time periods is not automatic, but is planned. Maintaining positive behavior changes also requires planning. Refer to Walker (1979, chap. 7) for further information. (c) Parent knowledge and consent is a priority issue which has professional, practical, ethical, and legal implications. Parents have a right to know about and agree with attempts to alter their children's behaviors, attitudes, and feelings. Practically, chance for success improves when parents are involved in the change process. Finally, written consent is advisable, when aversive components are used or when non-traditional strategies are tried.

SUMMARY

School psychologists are involved with a wide variety of problem behaviors in the school setting. Working in such an action-oriented environment, they cannot choose which problems to tackle, but must be ready to manage any situation from social ostracism to truancy to a family death, to the day-to-day tensions of childhood and adolescence. While acknowledging that behavior and attitude changes need time to occur, the school psychologist recognizes the needs of teachers and parents for some timely relief. The literature suggests many approaches to school behavior problems, and practitioners strengthen their role in the educational process by bridging the gap between research and practice and bringing those strategies into the schools.

This requires a knowledge of the techniques available and skillful planning of their appropriate use. Ten factors: student age; teacher, parent, and student variables; the number of targets or students; the seriousness or danger posed by the problem; ethical and moral considerations, availability of time and space; administrative support; and setting, provide a framework for choosing the most workable interventions. Planning increases the chances of a successful outcome and enhances the psychologist's image as a problem-solver and valuable school professional.

REFERENCES

Azrin, N. H., & Wesolowski, M. D. (1974). Theft reversal: An over-correction procedure for eliminating stealing by retarded persons. *Journal of Applied Behavior Analysis, 7*, 577-581.

Bardon, J. I., Bennett, V. C., Bruchez, P. K., & Sanderson, R. A. (1976). Psychosituational classroom intervention: Rationale and description. *Journal of Psychology, 14*(2), 97-104.

Broden, M., Bruce, C., Mitchell, M. A., Carter, V., & Hall, R. V. (1970). Effects of teacher attention on attending behavior of two boys at adjacent desks. *Journal of Applied Behavior Analysis, 3*, 199-204.

Broden, M., Hall, R. V., & Mitts, B. (1971). The effect of self-recording on the classroom behavior of two eighth-grade students. *Journal of Applied Behavior Analysis, 4*, 191-199.

Brooks, B. D. (1974). Contingency contracts with truants. *Personnel and Guidance Journal, 52*(5), 316-320.

Brown, R. A., & Epstein, J. (1977). Interaction of achievement level and reinforcing properties of daily grading systems. *Education, 98*(2), 131-134.

Camp, B. W., Blom, G. E., Hebert, F., & van Doorninck, W. J. (1977). Think aloud: A program for developing self-control in young aggressive boys. *Journal of Abnormal Child Psychology, 5*, 157-169.

Carnine, D. W. (1976). Effects of two teacher presentation rates on off-task behavior, answering correctly, and participation. *Journal of Applied Behavior Analysis, 9*, 199-206.

Clements, J. E., & Tracy, D. B. (1977). Effects of touch and verbal reinforcement on the classroom behavior of emotionally disturbed boys. *Exceptional Children, 43*, 453-454.

Copeland, R. E., Brown, R. E., & Hall, R. V. (1974). The effects of principal-implemented techniques on the behavior of pupils. *Journal of applied behavior analysis, 7*, 77-86.

Digate, G., Epstein, M. H., Cullinan, D., & Switzky, H. N. (1978). Modification of impulsivity: Implications for improved efficiency in learning for exceptional children. *Journal of Special Education, 12*, 459-468.

Digiuseppe, R., & Kassinove, H. (1976). Effects of a rational-emotive school mental health program on children's emotional adjustment. *Journal of Community Psychology, 4*, 382-387.

Dougherty, E. H., & Dougherty, A. (1977). The daily report card: A simplified and flexible package for classroom behavior management. *Psychology in the Schools, 14*(2), 191-195.

Durlak, J. A. (1973). Ninth graders as student aides: Making use of the helper therapy principle. *Psychology in the Schools, 10*(3), 334-339.

Epstein, M. H., Repp, A. C., & Cullinan, D. (1978). Decreasing "obscene" language of behaviorally disordered children through the use of a DRL schedule. *Psychology in the Schools, 15*(3), 419-423.

Fairchild, T. N. (1976). Home-school token economies: Bridging the communication gap. *Psychology in the Schools, 13*(4), 463-467.

Gardner, D. C., & Gardner, P. L. (1978). Goal setting and learning in the high school resource room. *Adolescence, 13*, 489-493.

Gersham, L. (1976). Eliminating a fire-setting compulsion through contingency management. In J. D. Krumboltz & C. E. Thoresen (Eds.), *Counseling methods* (pp. 206-213). New York: Holt, Rinehart and Winston.

Gresham, F. M. (1983). Use of a home-based dependent group contingency system in controlling destructive behavior: A case study. *School Psychology Review, XII*(2), 195-199.

Gumaer, J., & Myrick, R. D. (1974). Behavioral group counseling with disruptive children. *The School Counselor, 21*(4), 313-317.

Hall, R. V., Lund, D., & Jackson, D. (1968). Effects of teacher attention on study behavior, *Journal of Applied Behavior Analysis, 1*, 1-12.

Hauserman, N., Miller, J. S., & Bond, F. T. (1976). A behavioral approach to changing self-concept in elementary school children. *The Psychological Record, 26*, 111-116.

Homme, L. E. (1969). *How to use contingency contracting in the classroom.* Champaign: Research Press Company.

Humphrey, L. L., Karoly, P., & Kirschenbaum, D. S. (1978). Self-management in the classroom: Self-imposed response cost versus self-reward. *Behavior Therapy, 9,* 592-601.

Jones, F. H., & Miller, W. H. (1974). The effective use of negative attention for reducing group disruption in special elementary school classrooms. *Psychological Record, 24,* 435-448.

Jones, R. T., Nelson, R. E., & Kazdin, A. E. (1977). The role of external variables in self-reinforcement. *Behavior Modification, 1*(2), 147-176.

Karpowitz, D. H. (1977). Reinstatement as a method to increase the effectiveness of discipline in the school or home. *Journal of School Psychology, 15,* 230-238.

Karraker, R. J. (1972). Increasing academic performance through home-managed contingency programs. *Journal of School Psychology, 10*(2), 173-179.

Kendall, P. C. (1977). On the efficacious use of verbal self-instructional procedures with children. *Cognitive Therapy and Research, 1,* 331-341.

Klein, S. A., & Deffenbacher, J. L. (1977). Relaxation and exercise for hyperactive impulsive children. *Perceptual and Motor Skills, 45,* 1159-1162.

Lahey, B. B., Mcnees, M. P., & Mcnees, M. C. (1973). Control of an obscene "verbal tic" through time-out in an elementary school classroom. *Journal of Applied Behavior analysis, 6,* 101-104.

Lane, J., & Muller, D. (1977). The effect of altering self-descriptive behavior on self-concept and classroom behavior. *Journal of Psychology, 97,* 115-125.

Litow, L., & Pumroy, D. K. (1975). A brief review of classroom group-oriented contingencies. *Journal of Applied Behavior Analysis, 8,* 341-347.

Madsen, C. H., Jr., Becker, W. C., & Thomas, D. R. (1968). Rules, praise, and ignoring: Elements of elementary classroom control. *Journal of Applied Behavior Analysis, 1,* 139-150.

McBrien, R. J. (1978). Using relaxation methods with first-grade boys. *Elementary School Guidance and Counseling, 12,* 145-152.

McLaughlin, T. F. (1975). The applicability of token reinforcement systems in public school systems. *Psychology in the Schools, XII*(1), 84-89.

Meichenbaum, D. (1977). *Cognitive-behavior modification: An integrative approach.* New York: Plenum Press.

Meyers, A. W., & Cohen, R. (Eds.). (1982). Cognitive-behavioral interventions for classroom and academic behaviors (Special issue). *School Psychology Review, XI*(1), Winter, 1982.

Meyers, J., & Pitt, N. W. (1976). A consultation approach to help a school cope with the bereavement process. *Professional Psychology,* 559-564.

Miller, R. L., Brickman, P., & Bolen, D. (1975). Attribution versus persuasion as a means for modifying behavior. *Journal of Personality and Social Psychology, 31*(3), 430-441.

Needels, M., & Stallings, J. (1975, March). *Classroom processes related to absence rate.* Paper presented at the annual meeting of the American Educational Research Association, Washington, DC.

O'Leary, K. D., Kaufman, K. F., Kass, R. E., & Drabman, R. S. (1970). The effects of loud and soft reprimands on the behavior of disruptive students. *Exceptional Children, 37,* 145-155.

Palkes, H., Stewart, M., & Kahana, B. (1968). Porteus maze performance of hyperactive boys after training in self-directed verbal commands. *Child Development, 39,* 817-826.

Peterson, R. F., Loveless, S. E., Knapp, T. J., Loveless, B. W., Basta, S. M., & Anderson, S. (1979). The effects of teacher use of I-messages on student disruptive and study behavior. *Psychological Record, 29,* 187-199.

Ross, J. A., & Levine, B. A. (1972). Control of thumbsucking in the classroom: Case study. *Perceptual and Motor Skills, 34,* 584-586.

Saltz, E., Dixon, D., & Johnson, J. (1977). Training disadvantaged preschoolers on various fantasy activities: Effects on cognitive functioning and impulse control. *Child Development, 48,* 367-380.

Sattler, H. E., & Swoope, K. S. (1970). Token systems: A procedural guide. *Psychology in the Schools, VIII*(4), 383-386.

Schinke, S. P., Gilchrist, L. D., & Small, R. W. (1979). Preventing unwanted adolescent pregnancy: A cognitive-behavioral approach. *American Journal of Orthopsychiatry, 49*(1), 81-88.

Schneider, M. R. (1974). Turtle technique in the classroom. *Teaching Exceptional Children, 7,* 22-24.

Schneider, M., & Robin, A. (1976). The turtle technique: A method for the self-control of impulsive behavior. In J. D. Krumboltz & C. E. Thoresen (Eds.), 2Counseling Methods (pp. 157-162). New York: Holt, Rinehart and Winston.

Schumaker, J. B., Hovell, M. F., & Sherman, J. A. (1977). An analysis of daily report cards and parent-managed privileges in the improvement of adolescents' classroom performance. *Journal of Applied Behavior Analysis, 10,* 449-464.

Sheats, D. W., & Dunkleberger, G. E. (1979). A determination of the principal's effect in school-initiated home contacts concerning attendance of elementary school students. *Journal of Educational Research, 72*(6), 310-312.

Simmons, J. T., & Wasik, B. H. (1976). Grouping strategies, peer influence, and free time as classroom management techniques with first- and third-grade children. *Journal of School Psychology, 14,* 322-332.

Slavin, R. E. (1977). How student learning teams can integrate the desegregated classroom. *Integrated Education, 15,* 56-58.

Solnick, J. V., Rincover, A., & Peterson, C. R. (1977). Some determinants of the reinforcing and punishing effects of timeout. *Journal of Applied Behavior Analysis, 10*(3), 415-424.

Steele, M. (1978). Enrolling community support. *Journal of Research and Development in Education, 11*(2), 84-93.

Sulzbacher, S. I., & Houser, J. E. (1968). A tactic to eliminate disruptive behaviors in the classroom: Group contingent consequences. *American Journal of Mental Deficiency, 1,* 182-187.

Swanson, L. (1979). Removal of positive reinforcement to alter learning disabled adolescents' preacademic problems. *Psychology in the Schools, 16*(2), 286-292.

Switzer, E. B., Deal, T. E., & Bailey, J. S. (1977). The reduction of stealing in second graders using a group contingency. *Journal of Applied Behavior Analysis, 10,* 267-272.

Walker, H. M. (1979). *The acting-out child: Coping with classroom disruption.* Boston: Allyn and Bacon, Inc.

Wasserman, T. H. (1977). Negative reinforcement to alter disruptive behavior of an adolescent in a day-treatment setting. *Journal of Behavior Therapy and Experimental Psychiatry, 8,* 315-317.

Wilson, S. H., & Williams, R. L. (1973). The effects of group contingencies on first graders' academic and social behaviors. *Journal of School Psychology, 11*(2), 110-117.

Wine, J. D. (1979). Test anxiety and evaluation threat: Children's behavior in the classroom. *Journal of Abnormal Child Psychology, 7,* 45-49.

Winston, A. S. (1978). Experimental analysis of admission of cheating: An exploratory study. *Psychological Record, 28,* 517-523.

Workman, E. A., & Hector, M. A. (1978). Behavioral self-control in classroom settings: A review of the literature. *Journal of School Psychology, 16*(3), 227-236.

Zimmerman, E. H., & Zimmerman, J. (1962). The alteration of behavior in a special classroom situation. *Journal of the Experimental Analysis of Behavior, 5,* 59-60.

ANNOTATED BIBLIOGRAPHY

Alpert, J. L., & Associates. (1982). *Psychological consultation in educational settings.* San Francisco: Jossey-Bass Publishers.
The author brings together case studies to present the theory and practice of consultation at each school level. The diversity of techniques in the consultation model are presented in "first-person" accounts.

Kronick, D. (1981). *Social development of learning disabled persons.* San Francisco: Jossey-Bass Publishers.
The book clarifies how cognitive disorders associated with learning disabilities affect the development of social skills. Issues in family relationships are also discussed. Techniques for enhancing the social development of learning disabled students are presented.

Meichenbaum, D. (1977). *Cognitive-behavior modification: An integrative approach.* New York: Plenum Press.
The author integrates cognitive and behavioral research to explain how cognitive processes underlie behavioral change and to develop interventions which may be applied to a variety of problem behaviors. Techniques such as self-instructional training and stress inoculation training are described.

Millman, H. L., Schaefer, C. E., & Cohen, J. J. (1980). *Therapies for school behavior problems: A handbook of practical interventions.* San Francisco: Jossey-Bass Publishers.
This book provides a multitude of research-based techniques for managing the spectrum of behavior problems that may occur in schools. Succinctly written digests encapsulate the important procedures for coping with each presenting problem, and the authors' commentaries help the reader apply the methods more productively.

Spivak, G., Platt, J. J., & Shure, M. B. (1976). *The problem-solving approach to adjustment: A guide to research and intervention.* San Francisco: Jossey-Bass Publishers.
Working from a cognitive model, and incorporating their own research and the work of others, the authors describe sets of interpersonal problem-solving skills which enhance social adjustment, and outline training programs to develop these problem-solving skills in children and adults.

BEST PRACTICES IN SCHOOL-BASED CONSULTATION: GUIDELINES FOR EFFECTIVE PRACTICE

Michael J. Curtis
University of Cincinnati

Joel Meyers
State University of New York at Albany

OVERVIEW

Two decades have passed since "consultation" was introduced as a major professional function for school psychologists. Those twenty years have witnessed notable progress in this area of service delivery.

School-based consultation originated in the 1960s based on dissatisfaction with the medical model which seemed to permeate traditional school psychology. Consultation emerged as part of what Hobbs (1964) called "mental health's third revolution" referring to the general revolt throughout professional psychology against failures of the "mental illness" orientation of the field. Although the "revolution" was not specific to school psychology, its effects were significant in the continued development of the specialty.

The 1970s brought a growing consensus among school psychologists that consultation should occupy a more dominant place in the delivery of services (Bardon & Bennett, 1974; Meacham & Peckham, 1978). Similar preferences of teachers, superintendents and other school personnel have been well established (see Gutkin & Curtis, 1982 for an extensive review of related studies), as have those of parents and students (Raffaniello, Curtis, Heintzelman, Shannon, Van Wagener, Vesper, Taylor, & Blennerhassett, 1980).

However, the merits of a consultative approach do not rest solely on the "preferences" of school psychologists and the consumers of their services. There is a substantial body of empirical support for the effectiveness of consultative methods.

Extensive reviews of the research literature which have been conducted by Medway (1979), Mannino and Shore (1975) and Fullan, Miles and Taylor (1980) regarding the efficacy of consultation support this conclusion.

Research also has examined the "preventive" value of consultative techniques with encouraging results. Consultation has been found to positively affect conditions and outcomes for children in a variety of ways such as: improved professional skills for teachers (Gutkin, 1980; Zins, 1981); teacher attitudes regarding the "seriousness" of children's problems (Gutkin, Singer & Brown, 1980); improved teacher information and understanding of children's problems (Curtis & Watson, 1980); generalization of consultation benefits to other children in the same classroom (Jason & Ferone, 1978; Meyers, 1975); reductions in referral rates (Ritter, 1978); improved long-term academic performance (Jackson, Cleveland & Merenda, 1975); and reduction of varying behavioral difficulties (Spivack, Platt, & Shure, 1976).

In view of the above information, it is only logical to assume that consultation would currently occupy a position of primary emphasis within the profession. Yet, despite twenty years of advocacy and mounting empirical support, there is a gap between the justified prominence of consultation and the reality that it continues to lack a place of priority in professional practice.

One reason for this inconsistency relates to the lack of a common understanding of consultation. This problem is caused by the overuse of the almost meaningless generic term "consultation." Consultation has been used to refer to practically every interaction between two professionals. However, as Curtis and Zins (1981) note, "consultation is beginning to achieve a level of sophistication whereby there is a fair degree of agreement and understanding regarding what is implied by the term when it is identified with a specific model" (p. xiv). Those with a background in consultation are very likely to understand what assumptions, objectives, and behaviors are associated with a particular model.

But the fact is, most school psychologists do *not* have a strong background in consultation. "The primary obstacle to the effective integration of consultation into school psychological services rests in the failure of training institutions to address this area" (Curtis, 1983, p. 9).

Surveys of school psychology training programs have found that a minority of the respondent institutions include an emphasis on consultation (Bardon & Wenger, 1974, 1976). In a recent survey (Meyers, Wurtz, & Flanagan, 1981), only 40% of the responding programs offered a course focused solely on training in consultation. There also is an absence of consultation offerings through continuing professional development programs which compounds the problem for practitioners who have never received formalized preparation in this area. There is a pressing need for systematic and intensive training which includes an integrated practice component.

BASIC CONSIDERATIONS

The three major models for school-based consultation are the behavioral, mental health and organizational. Comprehensive discussions of each model are presented by Bergan (1977), Caplan (1970) and Schmuck, Runkel, Arends and Arends (1977), respectively. Although the three approaches differ in terms of their theoretical bases, they reflect numerous areas of commonality. This chapter offers a model for consultation which integrates those elements that are common to the other models within a systems framework.

A Systems Model of Consultation

Throughout this chapter, consultation will be defined as: *a collaborative problem solving process in which two or more persons (consultant(s) and consultee(s)) engage in efforts to benefit one or more other persons (client(s)) for whom they bear some level of responsibility, within a context of reciprocal interactions.* This definition reflects nine major assumptions regarding effective consultation which are described below:

Assumption 1: Participants in Consultation.

Consultant and Consultee. For ease in clarification of roles, we tend to describe the participants in a consultative relationship in terms of distinct identities. The *consultant* is generally the person who provides assistance to the consultee (the caregiver) regarding a work-related concern. Typically, we think of the school psychologist as a consultant to a classroom teacher regarding a child for whom the teacher is responsible. However, other school personnel such as a principal or counselor also could be the consultee.

It is important to recognize that *a unique feature of the above definition is the potential for consultant and consultee to shift roles.* While the consultant (e.g., school psychologist) generally tries to help the consultee (e.g., teacher), there are times in the relationship when the teacher possesses the expertise needed to help the school psychologist. This is important because it emphasizes that *both* participants in the consultation relationship share power and influence in a process that truly is characterized as a reciprocal interaction.

Client. The client is the ultimate beneficiary of consultation. In a classroom situation, a student is typically the client. An entire class could be clients if consultation is focused on improving the professional performance of the teacher. Students would also be the clients in organizational consultation since the purpose would be to improve the educational environment for the benefit of students.

Assumption 2: Collaborative Relationship

One of the most fundamental principles underlying this definition is that a genuinely collaborative professional relationship among those engaged in the problem solving process is essential for success. Unlike the medical model which assumes that the expertise for solving any given problem rests primarily within the consultant, this model assumes that *both* the consultant and the consultee have knowledge and/or skills necessary for problem resolution. The success of this relationship is dependent on the following characteristics.

Coordinate Status. The relationship of those involved is non-hierarchical. The consultant does not operate from a position of authority, diagnosing the problem and then either carrying out the remediation directly or prescribing the program to be implemented by others. Rather, the consultant and consultee both contribute to the development of problem solving strategies.

Consultee Involvement in Consultation. It is essential that the consultee(s) is actively involved in the consultation process by helping to assess and diagnose the problem, as well as by contributing to the intervention plans. Through active involvement, the consultee develops a sense of "ownership" of the plan. In most cases, it is likely that the consultee will bear primary responsibility for implementation of the plan. Failure to establish ownership may result in the likelihood that the strategy will not be carried out as intended. Besides, it often is the consultee who has the best sense of what is possible within the context of the school and classroom. By contributing ideas, the consultee helps to ensure that appropriate recommendations are developed.

Consultee's Right to Accept or Reject Strategies. The consultee must feel free to accept or reject any of the consultant's ideas. The consultant does not have the authority to impose a plan on the consultees. Moreover, it would be counterproductive to do so. If forced to implement a plan, the consultee is likely to carry it out in a manner which will ensure its failure, if it is implemented at all. If the consultee does not believe in an idea, there is little likelihood that it will work (Curtis & Anderson, 1976a). If the consultant genuinely believes that the consultee is a coordinate member in the consultation process, ideas generated by the consultee deserve equal consideration with those of the consultant. Even in those cases where the consultant does not favor the suggestions of the consultee, the consultee's plan should be tried as long as it does not appear to have detrimental implications for the client. The primary goal is to find some way to help the client, rather than to "win" a struggle over whose plan will be used.

Consultation is Voluntary. Although

not always the case, consultation should be initiated by the consultee. When this occurs, it suggests that the consultee (a) recognizes that a problem exists, and (b) may be motivated to do something about it (Curtis & Anderson, 1976a). Unfortunately, there are many instances in schools where consultation is neither initiated by the consultee nor voluntary. Such situations are less likely to be effective than those in which the consultee is voluntarily involved.

Confidentiality. It is essential that information shared remain within the consultative relationship. The central issue here is one of trust. The likelihood of honest and open communication is diminished when the consultee believes that sensitive information may be available to others outside the relationship. Obviously, there is some information which of necessity must be shared with others (e.g., parents, administrators, or other specialists). However, under these circumstances, the consultant and the consultee should discuss ahead of time what information will be shared.

The "need to know" principle can be a helpful guide as to what information should be shared. In other words, only information that others need to know should be passed on. For example, both the principal and parents need to know about the behavioral program to be implemented for a given child. However, the teacher's feelings of inadequacy or anger regarding actions of the principal should not be a topic for outside discussion. This concept of confidentiality is intended to reflect upon the importance of an honest and open relationship. It does not relate to the legal status of confidential communication which is determined by the laws of each state.

Assumption 3: The Need for Confrontation

Confrontation is an important component of the consultation process since this technique can be necessary to push the consultee toward action. However, the term "confrontation" has a negative connotation to some people. Confrontation, as used here, is a professional process which is not destructive *and* which is devoid of hostility. In fact, confrontation must be implemented in a manner which avoids a win-lose struggle and which preserves the consultee's right to accept or reject the consultant's ideas.

Two distinct approaches to confrontation have been discussed in the literature and both can be useful. The first, *Indirect Confrontation*, was described first by Gerald Caplan (1970). He suggested that indirect techniques were advantageous because they do not break down defenses. An example of this approach is to discuss the consultee's problem (e.g., difficulty dealing with rebellious pupils) as if it were a problem of the client (e.g., "Be careful how you deal with Johnny because *he* has difficulty dealing with authority figures.") See Meyers, Parsons and Martin (1979) for a more detailed discussion of indirect confrontation.

While indirect approaches are sometimes the only way to help the consultee without stimulating resistance, this method can be so subtle that the message is not received by the consultee. Under these circumstances, it may be necessary to use the second major approach, *Direct Confrontation*. However, this must also be done in a way that minimizes consultee resistance. To do this, it must be based on a strong relationship between consultant and consultee. Direct confrontation is a purposeful process in which contradictions, conflicts within the consultee or other problems are clarified and discussed openly. Direct confrontation must be communicated in a tentative manner, leaving the consultee with the clear option to reject what is offered. For example, when trying to initiate a discussion of a new teacher's conflict about being the authority figure the consultant might say, "Let's spend a few minutes thinking about what you just said. Do you think it implies that one important issue may have to do with your own ambivalence about being an authority figure to the students?" By opening a direct discussion of such a problem it becomes more likely that the consultee will be able to plan alternative interventions. A more detailed discussion of the variety of conflicts that may be the focus of direct confrontation during consultation is presented in Meyers, Parsons and Martin (1979).

Assumption 4: Indirect Service

Consultation differs from direct service models such as counseling in that the consultant works primarily with another caregiver, rather than directly with the client. Typically, it is the caregiver (consultee) who works directly with the client. In other words, consultation is an indirect approach to service delivery which involves a triadic relationship. The consultant works with the consultee who, in turn, works directly with the client.

There can be situations in which a school psychologist would consult with a consultee *and* would engage in some form of direct service during the same period of time. One example occurs when a psychologist provides counseling services to a child and uses information obtained during counseling as a basis for consulting with the youngster's teacher. Such situations represent a combination of both direct and indirect services, with consultation being the indirect service.

Assumption 5: Responsibility for Client

Historically, consultation models have emphasized that it is the caregiver/consultee who is responsible for the client. While the consultee may retain *primary* responsibility, it is important to note that the school psychologist must also assume some level of responsibility for the client. Participation on multidisciplinary teams and demands for accountability in service delivery require that the consultant share in responsibility for outcome.

Assumption 6: Work-Related Focus

The focus of consultation is always on work-related concerns. This principle has two primary implications: (a) Consultation is differentiated from therapy based on this principle. While therapy focuses on personal concerns, the consultant is consistent in directing conversations towards work-related issues. When therapy is sought by the consultee, the consultant should make a referral to outside sources. This can be an important factor in defining the consultant's role clearly for the system. (b) The second implication is that while the consultant maintains a warm productive relationship with the consultee and uses procedures like empathy, the focus is not primarily on the consultee's feelings. Consultation is a problem solving process which involves two colleagues. Although attention would be paid to work-related feelings when they are relevant, the primary focus is on solving the problem at hand.

Assumption 7: Goals of Consultation

This consultation model, like every other, has two goals. The first is explicit within the definitions, i.e., to resolve the referral problem. The second is to improve the consultee's understanding of and ability to respond effectively to similar problems in the future.

Assumption 8: Systems Theory

A critical emphasis that is *not* reflected clearly in most other models is the basis in *systems theory* as illustrated by the inclusion of *reciprocal interaction* as one major concept. Operationally, this refers to the tendency for a change in any part of a system to affect other parts of the system. This concept moves away from the medical model view that the child "contains" problems and instead suggests that the child is part of a system. It is no longer sufficient to postulate that psychological disturbances are internal to the client. Attempts to resolve child-related problems in schools must be based on a sophisticated awareness of effects that the school and classroom environment have on the child, as well as of the child's effects on the environment.

The application of systems theory to consultation is valuable in two ways. First, it helps the consultant understand the consultative process itself as affected by numerous interactive variables (e.g., consultant characteristics, consultee characteristics, school climate, district philosophy) (Gallessich, 1973). Second, it offers a framework for examining child-related concerns and for developing strategies for addressing those concerns within the context of the child as *one* component in an environmental setting (system). Any problem reflects the interaction of numerous variables associated with the setting. An understanding of those variables is essential in developing meaningful interventions.

Assumption 9: Affective/Cognitive Components to Consultation

Consultation can be viewed as having two primary components (i.e., affective and cognitive).

Affective Component. This refers to those aspects of the consultative interaction which address the interpersonal relationship between the consultant and consultee. This component would relate to core elements such as coordinate status between consultant and consultee, involvement of the consultee in the process, the consultee's right to accept or reject consultant suggestions, the voluntary nature of consultation and the confidential nature of the interaction. It reflects *how the consultant views the consultee.*

Cognitive Component. This refers to those aspects of the interaction which reflect the consultant's theoretical base for problem solving. It reflects *how the consultant views the problem.* For example, the approach to the problem might indicate either a behavioral orientation (Bergan, 1977) or a mental health orientation (Caplan, 1970). The steps or stages for problem solving are included in the cognitive component and the same general pattern is consistent across different theoretical orientations. Whether the consultant uses behavioral, psychodynamic, or cognitive-behavioral theory, the steps to problem solving follow a sequence which includes problem clarification, strategy generation, planning for implementation, and planning for evaluation.

Consultant Skills In order to fulfill the requisites of both the affective and cognitive components, the consultant needs four areas of expertise. The first relates to the interpersonal process and reflects both knowledge and skills pertaining to effective communication and the establishment of positive relationships. Good reflective listening skills as well as the use of Rogers' core conditions (i.e., empathy, genuineness, and nonpossessive warmth) are needed for effective consultation and have been discussed by Gutkin and Curtis (1982) as the "technology of communication." It also is important to recognize that particular communication skills may have to be implemented in different ways depending on the socio-cultural context. For example, the way in which the consultant uses a skill like empathy may vary dramatically depending on whether the consultee is a teacher in a suburban upper middle class school district or an aide in a head start program located in an urban ghetto (see Raffaniello, 1981).

The second area of expertise relates to a strong foundation in the area of professional content specific to the consultant. In the case of the school psychologist, that would be a strong foundation in the understanding of human behavior. The view of human behavior adopted by the consultant will dictate the theoretical basis for problem analysis. Third, is expertise in problem solving accompanied by the ability to facilitate the problem solving process.

The fourth area of expertise is knowledge of systems theory. The systems model of consultation allows for the incorporation of other consultation models (e.g., behavioral, mental health, organizational) within a systems framework. The definition integrates those elements that are common to other models pertaining to relationship, goals, focus and being indirect in nature. It requires expertise in generic problem solving. Yet, it allows for differing theoretical orientations to human behavior. It establishes a context of reciprocal interaction within which problems are to be analyzed and resolved. This last element requires that consultants be skilled in systems analysis.

BEST PRACTICES IN
SCHOOL—BASED CONSULTATION

Consultation and Direct Services

Since the earliest offerings, there has been a tendency in the literature to present consultation as an indirect service delivery system which is independent, if not dichotomous from direct service delivery systems. You either do consultation or you do other things. The message almost becomes one of being a consultant, rather than a school psychologist (Curtis, 1983, p. 9).

Essentially what has occurred is a confusion between the *role* of the consultant and the *function* of consultation. In reality, relatively few school psychologists are able to secure roles as consultants, i.e., their sole function is consultation. On the other hand, many school psychologists have been successful in establishing consultation as an integral part of a comprehensive service delivery system (Curtis, 1983). "When direct service is applied appropriately, it invariably involves consultative aspects; thus to exclude direct service from consultation would be artificial" (Meyers et al., 1979, p. 89). In other words, consultation is most appropriately viewed as a set of skills that are complementary to and a part of direct services.

Entry into the System

Schools should not be viewed as isolated entities, but as systems which are influenced by the larger environment within which they exist, as well as by the various internal components of which they are composed. External factors such as legislation and community norms can affect the types of services expected. Internally, factors such as staff characteristics, morale and educational philosophy can influence receptivity to the use of mental health resources. For example, competition and anxiety among teachers may reduce their interest in collaborative efforts for improving classroom processes (Schmuck & Schmuck, 1979). It is essential that the practitioner maintain a systems perspective in understanding the numerous organizational variables that can influence consultation. Gallessich (1973) provides a helpful discussion of this topic.

Gaining Sanction. Implementation of consultation involves acceptance by relevant administrators, as well as by the caregivers themselves (Meyers et al., 1979). Entry is an important on-going process, and should not be conceptualized as a single event (Curtis & Zins, 1981). Acceptance should be secured at the highest level possible in order to gain support and reduce resistance. Many of the following issues should be clarified during negotiations (Zins & Curtis, 1984; Meyers et al., 1979).

1. *Clearly define the consultation role.* Topics such as the functional meaning of consultation, how it fits in and confidentiality should be discussed. Short- and long-term goals should be established.

2. *Involve all relevant administrators.* Avoid identification of consultation as one person's "pet project." Access to all levels of the organization is needed.

3. *Present the rationale for consultation.* What are the benefits to the system? Emphasize efficiency and effectiveness of service delivery, mental health promotion, early identification of problems and skills development in consultees.

4. *Provide accountability data.* Agree to provide both formative and summative evaluation data after a specified period of time. Zins (1981) describes an effective program using this technique.

5. *Establish formal and informal contractual agreements.* Once an understanding has been achieved, an agreement or "contract" should be established which specifies all areas of agreement (this does not necessarily refer to a formal written document).

6. *Make provisions for review/renego-*

tiation. Arrange for an evaluation of the effort after a specified period of time.

7. *Develop formal job descriptions.* Once agreed upon, the entire range of services to be provided should be clarified in writing.

8. Maintain open lines of communication. As with many other processes, fine tuning or even significant adjustments might be necessary as time goes by. Problems should be dealt with promptly.

After negotiating with the administration, acceptance must be secured from the teachers and other school personnel who might serve as consultees. One effective method for doing this is the use of an "entry presentation" at a faculty meeting (even when it is not initial entry, but the introduction of a new professional function). In essence, the approach to the presentation should reflect the assumptions and philosophy underlying the consultation model. It is essential that a "collegial" atmosphere be established. A "down-to-earth" explanation of consultation should be provided in very functional terms and all jargon avoided (Zins & Curtis, 1984). Issues should be covered such as what consultation is, appropriate concerns to be addressed, the consultant-consultee relationship, initiation, responsibility, confidentiality, and the benefits of consultation (Curtis & Anderson, 1976a; Gutkin & Curtis, 1982). It is important to recognize that this presentation will help to establish a climate conducive to implementing consultation. Nevertheless, a realistic understanding of what consultation *can* be will depend largely on the behavior of the consultant during the early stages of entry. Also, these same issues are brought up informally with individual teachers at the beginning stages of a particular consultation relationship.

Changing Role Expectations. "Role expectations essentially are determined by history, title and behavior" (Curtis &

Zins, in press). *History* refers to the expectations that have been established by the behaviors of those who previously have fulfilled the same role. *Title* infers that regardless of previous direct experiences, certain expectations are instilled by the title of the individual, e.g., "school psychologist." Most importantly, the *actual behaviors* of the individual school psychologist eventually will become the dominant influence in determining role expectations. It is common to find that a school psychologist's role is determined more by what others *expect* than it is by what they *desire*. Chandy (1973) has demonstrated that a brief in-service program can influence the frequency and manner in which consultants are used. It is essential that the school psychologist ensure that potential consumers and persons in influential positions have an accurate understanding of what the school psychologist *can* do before deciding what it is that they *will* do (Curtis & Zins, in press). The entry presentation described above is one way of contributing to that understanding. However, misconceptions regarding the consultant's role will continue to arise and must be dealt with on an individual basis through discussions as well as through the modeling of appropriate behavior by the school psychologist. Some psychologists have found it effective to repeat the entry presentation when role confusion persists. It is important to remember that change will be gradual, although some psychologists have achieved remarkable differences within the first year of concentrated effort.

Value Dilemmas. School psychologists frequently confront value dilemmas in their efforts to provide services to children and their families. Those same types of conflict will persist in efforts to provide consultation. The school psychologist can use skills in systems analysis to assess the various contextual elements that result in value dilemmas. The values of the organization are as significant as are those of the individual consultee. A prerequisite to considering the values of other components in the system, however, is that the consultant be fully aware of personal values. Undoubtedly, each of us must make personal decisions regarding those activities, goals and objectives that we are willing to support or even condone, and we are best able to make those decisions based on an awareness of the values of components of the system, as well as our own personal values.

Accountability — Assessing Impact. When an activity is new or represents a distinct change, it often is necessary to demonstrate the value of that activity to those in a decision-making position. In view of the widespread misuse of the term "consultation," the scarcity of appropriately conducted consultation in most settings, and the fact that it represents a significant change in the role expectations for the school psychologist, consultation requires program evaluation to demonstrate its efficacy. Such evaluations are conducted all too infrequently. Nevertheless, there is a variety of practical approaches to evaluation. Fairchild, Zins and Grimes (1983) have developed a multi-media program on accountability which includes a filmstrip, manual and book of accountability instruments. Also, Zins (1981) presents a case study which illustrates the use of data-based evaluation in the integration of consultation into school psychological services.

Downplay the Intended Change. It is important to recognize that consultation represents a dramatic shift in service delivery. Many people automatically resist change regardless of its potential positive effects. Therefore, it may be easier to gain acceptance for consultation by portraying it as an approach which is *similar to* rather than different from existing approaches. By minimizing the change involved, people may be more accepting at first. Then, as they become accustomed to the approach and see its benefits firsthand, they may be more receptive to expansion of the consultant role.

The Consultation Process

The consultation process can be conceptualized in stages which include: (a) entry, (b) problem clarification and (c) problem solution. Entry was discussed in the preceding section.

Problem Clarification

The purpose of this stage is to define the problem as specifically and as comprehensively as possible. It must be emphasized that the intent here is to understand the problem within an environmental context in terms of reciprocal interactions. How does each component of the environment interact to contribute to the problem? In order to move on to the stage of problem solution, we first must consider the influence of the teacher, other children, classroom structure, curriculum, school norms, parents, home environment and child (in the case of a child-related problem). It is essential that both the consultant and the consultee develop a thorough understanding of all aspects of the problem and the various factors contributing to it. Bergan and Tombari (1976) found problem identification to be the primary determinant of consultation outcomes. In other words, they found that when the consultant and teacher agreed that the problem had been identified correctly, "problem solution almost invariably resulted" (p. 12).

Early in the problem clarification process, the consultant attempts to determine the level of the system at which consultative intervention would be most effective. That is, the consultant must determine whether to provide consultation directed toward: (a) the child; (b) the teacher and the classroom; or (c) the school as an organization. Although child-related problems could be dealt with through consultation at the individual child level, a significant number of such problems are addressed most effectively by focusing on the teacher or the organization. In other words, there are some situations where factors associated with the teacher, the classroom, or the school organization contribute significantly to the problems of individual children. For example, at an organizational level, very low morale among the teaching staff is likely to contribute to an increase in the incidence of student behavior problems. Improving morale in these situations is often followed by a decrease in behavior problems.

Since it is desirable to function at a preventive level, the consultant should attempt to intervene at the level where it is possible to benefit the maximum number of children. If problems are caused in large part at the organizational level and consultative efforts are directed at the child level, the consultant essentially is using a bandaid approach and failing to address the *cause* of the problems. The same is true when problems are caused by the teacher. It is most efficient to focus consultation on the teacher rather than on individual students when the skills of the teacher are causing student problems.

The priority for intervention would be from highest to lowest in terms of preventive influence. Accordingly, the consultant would first choose to work at the organizational level, then the teacher level, and finally at the child level. Of course, in cases where organizational or teacher-centered factors were not of primary importance, the focus of consultation would be on the individual child.

Regardless of the level of intervention, problem clarification uses information collected through data generating strategies and/or interviewing techniques.

Data Generating Strategies. Consultation involves the use of information from a variety of sources other than consultative interactions. Among the data sources are assessment procedures, clinical interviews, observational systems, educational records, and medical records. Additional data sources which may be more pertinent to organizational consultation include surveys, questionnaires, personnel records, organizational correspondence, meeting minutes, and so forth.

Interviewing Techniques. Interviewing forms the basis for what most people see as consultation. It is that process of verbal interaction between the consultant and the consultee(s). First, it must be emphasized that all of the principles outlined earlier such as the characteristics of a collaborative relationship, work-related focus, dual goals, and systems emphasis form the foundation to the interactive process and serve as guidelines for the consultant's behavior.

Essentially, the consultant uses the skills of listening, asking questions and integrating information and ideas. Listening means interest in and attentiveness to what the consultee has to say. Questioning has been found to be the consultant behavior most highly correlated with overall effectiveness (Curtis & Anderson, 1976b). It tends to influence every other skill such as the abilities to establish a climate of trust, elicit information, and involve the consultee throughout the process.

The consultant should try to minimize the use of closed questions where the consultee can provide a "yes" or "no" response. Such questions, in essence, require the consultant to develop a mental checklist of possible information regarding the problem and to then request the consultee to indicate whether or not each possible piece of information is accurate. This method places most of the burden for information generation on the consultant who has to think of every conceivable possibility. It also limits the involvement of the consultee and thereby interferes with the collaborative relationship. In contrast, more open-ended questions require that the consultee provide a greater amount of information. Questions of this type tend to be more oriented toward stimulating the consultee to think about the problem under discussion. They also tend to facilitate the collaborative relationship by keeping the consultee actively involved in the process throughout. For example, instead of asking about a list of possible situations that might "set off" temper tantrums in a particular boy (Does he get upset when . . .?), the consultant might ask, "What kinds of things cause him to lose his temper?" Also, effective consultants tend to ask proportionately more questions and make fewer statements of fact or opinion. It is important to note however, that the process is collaborative and involves the active involvement of *all* participants. It would be inappropriate for the consultant to hold back ideas and become non-directive. What is important is that ideas are shared in a way that allows the consultee to accept or reject them.

A critical consulting skill is the ability to integrate information and ideas. Quite often, it is necessary to consider information regarding a client from a variety of sources (assessment and observational data, teacher perceptions). The amount of information is expanded even further in a systems model since the influence of several additional variables must be considered. It is essential that the consultant be able to integrate all of the information in a way that is meaningful to the problem at hand.

Two related skills that facilitate integration of material by both the consultant and consultee are clarification and summarization. Clarification is a technique in which the consultant presents his/her perception of what the consultee just said. This lets the consultee know that the consultant understands the consultee's experience and it helps the consultant ensure that he or she understands correctly what the consultee has just said. While clarification reflects one specific statement of the consultee, summarization is used to integrate a variety of information that has been presented by the consultee. The goal is to help develop a conceptual bond for diverse information that has been discussed. Neither clarification nor summarization is designed to bring premature closure to the discussion. Instead, the purpose is to facilitate continued exploration of the topic.

The problem presented initially by the consultee may not be the problem that eventually is dealt with. Information generated during problem clarification should confirm the "agenda" which is often more complicated than the initial referral, even when the referral remains a partial focus of consultation. It cannot be stated too strongly that the problem must be clarified *thoroughly* before the process moves to the problem solution stage. When this does not occur, consultation frequently fails. Furthermore, there are cases in which thorough problem clarification may be enough of an "intervention" to enable the consultee to resolve the problem without further assistance from the consultant (Curtis & Anderson, 1976a).

Problem Solution

Once the problem has been clarified thoroughly, the process moves to the problem solution stage. Since problem clarification will have been completed from a systems perspective, attempts at problem solution should reflect a similar approach.

As noted earlier, numerous articles have been published regarding the problem solving process and different steps have been suggested (Parnes, Noller & Biondi, 1977). Yet, as noted by D'Zurilla and Goldfried (1971), "there has been a remarkable degree of agreement among theorists and investigators working in different areas as to the general kinds of operations involved in *effective* problem solving . . ." (p. 111).

A representative list of the stages follows.

1. *Thoroughly clarify the problem.* Problem clarification, consistently identified as the first general stage has already been discussed.

2. *Specify objectives.* It is important that *specific* objectives be identified in an effort to reduce anxiety and to prevent the consultee from being immobilized regarding the problem. This step is particularly significant since global and vaguely defined problems inhibit problem resolution. The consultant should help the consultee identify objectives which are specific and realistic, and for which there is a reasonable probability of success.

3. *Explore resources available.* Although this might include information and materials available, as well as the assistance of other persons, professionals and parents, the consultee should not be overlooked as a resource. There may be a tendency to look too quickly for "outside" assistance.

4. *Evaluate and choose among alternatives.* Developing alternative strategies allows the consultee to compare and contrast the different approaches in deciding which one is most likely to prove effective in resolving the problem at hand. In reality, a systems approach might require

that several strategies be implemented in an effort to respond to the various environmental forces that contribute to the problem. Each strategy should be carefully examined. The consultant should strive to ensure that the strategy is selected based on its potential effectiveness. Other reasons should not be used (e.g., convenience, politics, etc.) unless the available options are equal in their potential efficacy. Since the consultee is the person who will carry out the plan, it is essential that the consultee is actively involved in this process. Therefore, the consultee should select the intervention strategy to be used.

5. *Clarify implementation procedures.* This step is particularly important. *Who* will carry out *what* action and by *when* must be clarified and agreed upon. A plan with tremendous potential will probably be of no value if it is not implemented as planned. Detail and responsibility are critical issues and they must be detailed if success is to be ensured.

6. *Implement the chosen strategy.* It is not safe to assume that the agreed upon plan will be implemented as planned. This does not necessarily infer that the consultee does not have the ability, or willfully chooses not to fulfill the agreement. There are many unanticipated legitimate obstacles that arise. These potential problems require systematic follow-up on the part of the consultant. In essence, this step reinforces the idea that consultation is an on-going process and not a one-time encounter.

7. *Evaluate the plan and recycle if necessary.* Planned evaluation of the intervention's effectiveness is essential. It is naive to think about problem solving in terms of finding *the* solution. There are few "guaranteed" solutions to problems involving human behavior, especially within a constantly changing environmental context. Therefore, it is essential that the consultant and consultee monitor

effectiveness once an intervention is implemented. Sometimes it will be necessary to revise the intervention. However, lack of success of the intervention also may occur because of a problem during the entry or problem clarification stages. For example, a problem with the entry stage can easily result in a consultee participating in consultation when all that was expected was that the consultant remove the problem with no involvement from the consultee. Similarly, an error in problem clarification could have resulted in interventions directed at an individual child, when what was really needed was a focus on the teacher or the entire school organization. Under these circumstances, the consultant would use the evaluation data as a basis for cycling back to an earlier stage of the consultation process.

SUMMARY

Consultation does not represent a panacea for the effective delivery of school psychological services. However, there is a substantial body of evidence indicating that consultation can contribute significantly to the ability of the school psychologist to meet the school-related needs of children and their families. However, one major problem which continues to hamper the field in this regard is inadequate emphasis on the specific skills necessary for successful consultation. This chapter has outlined some of the important skills that are needed. A more detailed discussion of consultation skills can be found in Parsons and Meyers (1984).

In order for school psychologists to be able to provide these needed services, adequate training must be made available. First, it is essential that school psychology training programs provide quality formalized training in consultation. Second, pre-service and in-service teachers should receive training in the skills necessary to work effectively as consultees (Meyers, 1982). To enable school psychologists to meaningfully respond to the needs and demands that they face in the schools, training programs will have to take these steps and school psychologists will have to be determined to integrate consultation into the school psychological services delivery system.

REFERENCES

Bardon, J. I., & Bennett, V. D. (1974). *School psychology.* Englewood Cliffs, NJ: Prentice-Hall.

Bardon, J. I., & Wenger, R. D. (1974). Institutions offering graduate training in school psychology: 1973-1974. *Journal of School Psychology, 12,* 70-83.

Bardon, J. I., & Wenger, R. D. (1976). School psychology training trends in the early 1970s. *Professional Psychology, 7,* 31-37.

Bergan, J. R. (1977). *Behavioral consultation.* Columbus, OH: Charles E. Merrill.

Bergan, J. R., & Tombari, M. L. (1976). Consultant skill and efficiency and the implementation and outcomes of consultation. *Journal of School Psychology, 14,* 3-14.

Caplan, G. (1970). *The theory and practice of mental health consultation.* New York: Basic Books.

Chandy, J. M. (1973). *The effects of an inservice orientation on teacher perception and use of the mental health consultant.* Unpublished doctoral dissertation, University of Texas at Austin.

Curtis, M. (1983). School psychology and consultation. *Communique', IX,* (7), 9.

Curtis, M. J., & Anderson, T. (1976a). *Consulting in educational settings: A collaborative approach* (slide/tape). Cincinnati: Faculty Resource Center, University of Cincinnati.

Curtis, M. J., & Anderson, T. (1976b). *The relationship of behavioral variables to consultant effectiveness.* Paper presented at the annual meeting of the National Association of School Psychologists, Kansas City.

Curtis, M. J., & Watson, K. (1980). Changes in consultee problem clarification skills following consultation. *Journal of School Psychology, 18,* 210-221.

Curtis, M. J., & Zins, J. E. (Eds.) (1981). *The theory and practice of school consultation.* Springfield, IL: Charles C Thomas.

Curtis, M. J., & Zins, J. E. (in press). The organization and structuring of psychological services within educational settings. In S. N. Elliott & J. C. Witt (Eds.), *The delivery of psychological services in schools: Concepts, processes, and issues.* Hillsdale, NJ: Lawrence Erlbaum.

D'Zurilla, T. J., & Goldfried, M. R. (1971). Problem solving and behavior modification. *Journal of Abnormal and Social Psychology, 78,* 107-126.

Fairchild, T. N., Zins, J. E., & Grimes, J. (1983). *Improving school psychology through accountability* (filmstrip). Washington, DC: National Association of School Psychologists.

Fullan, M., Miles, M. B., & Taylor, G. (1980). Organization development in schools: The state of the art. *Review of Educational Research, 50,* 121-183.

Gallessich, J. (1973). Training the school psychologist for consultation. *Journal of School Psychology, 11,* 57-65.

Gutkin, T. B. (1980). Teacher perceptions of consultation services provided by school psychologists. *Professional Psychology, 11,* 637-642.

Gutkin, T. B., & Curtis, M. J. (1982). School-based consultation: Theory and techniques. In C. R. Reynolds & T. B. Gutkin (Eds.), *The handbook of school psychology.* New York: John Wiley.

Gutkin, T. B., Singer, J. H., & Brown, R. (1980). Teacher reactions to school based consultation services: A multivariate analysis. *Journal of School Psychology, 18,* 126-134.

Hobbs, N. (1964). Mental health's third revolution. *American Journal of Orthopsychiatry, 34,* 822-833.

Jackson, R. M., Cleveland, J. C., & Merenda, P. F. (1975). The longitudinal effects of early identification and counseling of underachievers. *Journal of School Psychology, 13,* 119-128.

Jason, L. A., & Ferone, L. (1978). Behavioral versus process consultation interventions in school settings. *American Journal of Community Psychology, 6,* 531-543.

Mannino, F. V., & Shore, M. F. (1975). Effective change through consultation. In F. V. Mannino, B. W. MacLennan, & M. F. Shore (Eds.), *The practice of mental health consultation.* New York: Gardner Press.

Meacham, M. L., & Peckham, P. D. (1978). School psychologists at three-quarters century: Congruence between training, practice, preferred role and competence. *Journal of School Psychology, 16,* 195-206.

Medway, F. J. (1979). How effective is school consultation: A review of recent research. *Journal of School Psychology, 17*, 275-282.

Meyers, J. (1975). Consultee-centered consultation with a teacher as a technique in behavior management. *American Journal of Community Psychology, 3*, 111-121.

Meyers, J. (1982). *Consultation skills: How teachers can maximize help from specialists in schools.* Published by National Support Systems Project, University of Minnesota, M. R. Reynolds, Editor.

Meyers, J., Parsons, R. D., & Martin, R. (1979). *Mental health consultation in the schools.* San Francisco: Jossey-Bass.

Meyers, J., Wurtz, R., & Flanagan, D. (1981). A national survey investigating consultation training occurring in school psychology programs. *Psychology in the Schools, 18*, 297-302.

Parnes, S. J., Noller, R. B., & Biondi, A. M. (1977). *Guide to creative action.* New York: Scribners.

Parsons, R. D., & Meyers, J. (1984). *Developing consultation skills: A guide to training, development and assessment for human services professionals.* San Francisco: Jossey-Bass.

Raffaniello, E. M. (1981). Competent consultation: The collaborative approach. In M. J. Curtis & J. E. Zins (Eds.), *The theory and practice of school consultation.* Springfield, IL: Charles C Thomas.

Raffaniello, E. M., Curtis, M. J., Heintzelman, G., Shannon, P., Van Wagener, E., Taylor, C., Vesper, J., & Blennerhassett, L. (1980). *School psychologists' roles: Parent and student perceptions.* Paper presented at the meeting of the National Association of School Psychologists, Washington, DC.

Ritter, D. (1978). Effects of a school consultation program upon referral patterns of teachers. *Psychology in the Schools, 15*, 239-243.

Schmuck, R. A., Runkel, P. J., Arends, J. H., & Arends, R. I. (1977). *The second handbook of organization development in schools.* Palo Alto, CA: Mayfield Publishing.

Schmuck, R. A., & Schmuck, P. A. (1979). *Group processes in the classroom* (3rd ed.). Dubuque, Iowa: Wm. C. Brown.

Spivack, G., Platt, J. J., & Shure, M. B. (1976). *The problem-solving approach to adjustment.* San Francisco: Jossey-Bass.

Zins, J. E. (1981). Using data-based evaluation in developing school consultation services. In M. J. Curtis & J. E. Zins (Eds.), *The theory and practice of school consultation.* Springfield, IL: Charles C Thomas.

Zins, J. E., & Curtis, M. J. (1984). Building consultation into the educational service delivery system. In C. A. Maher, R. J. Illback, & J. E. Zins (Eds.), *Organizational psychology in the schools: A handbook for professionals.* Springfield, IL: Charles C Thomas.

ANNOTATED BIBLIOGRAPHY

Alpert, J. L. (1982). *Psychological consultation in educational settings.* San Francisco: Jossey-Bass.

Alpert and 16 co-authors present detailed case studies of successful consultative interventions. The cases involve various settings (elementary school, middle school, high school, college, entire school system, and community) and different approaches to consultation (behavioral, mental health, organizational). The detailed and candid reports offer insight into many practical issues in consultation.

Curtis, M. J., & Anderson, T. E. (1976). *Consulting in educational settings: A collaborative approach* (slide/tape). (1977). *Consulting in educational settings: Demonstrating collaborative techniques* (videotape). Cincinnati: Faculty Resource Center, University of Cincinnati.

The slide/tape program outlines the major concepts in the collaborative model of consultation. It is helpful both in training consultants and in preparing pre-service and in-service teachers for consultation. The videotape demonstrates effective consulting skills and can be used as part of a consultation training program.

Curtis, M. J., & Zins, J. E. (1981). *The theory and practice of school consultation.* Springfield, IL: Charles C Thomas.

Curtis and Zins organize reprinted and original articles by 41 authors in a logical sequence that reflects the development of consultation skills. The articles review the major consultation models, analyze research findings, and discuss issues and practical strategies relating to the provision of school consultation services.

Meyers, J. (1982). *Consultation skills: How teachers can maximize help from specialists in schools.* Published by the National Support Systems Project, University of Minnesota, M. R. Reynolds, Editor.

Meyers presents the basic issues in consultation that are important for teacher-consultees to understand. The module is appropriate for training both pre-service and in-service teachers in the skills necessary to be effective consultees. In addition to providing basic information, the module includes skill building exercises.

Meyers, J., Parsons, R. D., & Martin, R. (1979). *Mental health consultation in the schools.* San Francisco: Jossey-Bass.

The authors integrate the practice and research contributions of psychologists, social workers, psychiatrists, counselors, and educators with their own in providing a discussion of the special problems encountered by consultants, as well as strategies for avoiding or remedying such difficulties. Guidelines are also offered for implementing consultation in the schools.

BEST PRACTICES IN BEHAVIORAL OBSERVATION

Susan Epps
Iowa State University

OVERVIEW

To understand children and adolescents, it is important to observe them. They are observed each time they are administered a standardized test or interviewed. The data obtained from these sources are certainly useful. In general, however, the information derived is incomplete, perhaps even inaccurate. Gathering additional information about variables that affect students' behavior makes it possible to generate more effective interventions. Students must be observed in natural environments such as the classroom, lunchroom, or playground and not just in the artificial one-to-one testing situation where it is not possible to observe them influencing and being influenced by those around them. The purpose of this chapter is to assist psychologists in becoming acquainted with the use of observation strategies so that behavior can be *systematically* recorded and examined to provide objective information for making educational decisions. The chapter addresses observation as a problem-solving strategy with a focus on helping psychologists devise their own observation systems that are tailored to the needs of each case. With these observation skills, an extremely wide range of information is gathered. Although people sometimes think that behavioral assessment is used only to take data on inappropriate behaviors such as spit-ball throwing, pigtail pulling, or not completing assignments, it is also extremely useful for providing information on the extent to which appropriate behaviors occur. For example, just how often does Rachel share the chemistry set with other students who want to use it or compliment people when they do well on an assignment?

Behavioral observation serves at least six different purposes, each of which applies directly to the services provided by school psychologists. First, the correct use of behavioral observations provides objective, reliable, and valid data that strengthen the inferences made about those students who are assessed. For example, suppose a psychologist tests Charlie and notes that he frequently looked at other things in the testing room when he should have been trying to complete various tasks. The psychologist infers that Charlie is distractible. By observing him in the classroom, it is noted that Charlie looks up from his written work an average of three times per minute, a *rate* measure, for an average of 17 seconds per minute, a *duration* measure. These observations provide more data that strengthen the inference about Charlie's distractibility.

It is important to note that behavioral observation should not be used only to confirm the inferences made about students from the testing situation. These inferences could misrepresent the student since they are based upon a limited sample of behavior. Consider Charlie again. After he is tested and the inference is made that he is distractible, systematic observation in his classroom indicates that he looks up from his written work an average of 0.2 times per minute for an average of 2 seconds per minute. Hmmm, seems that Charlie really is not as distractible as was initially thought. Maybe he was just interested in those mobiles hanging from the ceiling in the room that was used for testing.

Second, behavioral observations provide a methodology to measure an infinite number of nonacademic behaviors. All those annoying behaviors the teacher reports can be measured. No test in the world provides objective data on all the behaviors that are of interest. In general, it is a good idea to take data on a student's desirable behaviors as well even when the primary interest lies in a certain inappropriate behavior.

Third, behavioral observation is used to measure academic behaviors. This application of behavioral-assessment techniques has largely been overlooked by school psychologists. Although standardized achievement tests provide normative data regarding a student's achievement level, they can also present an inaccurate picture if test reliability is low and content validity is suspect. For example, there is curriculum bias inherent in all standardized achievement tests; this bias means that the test items will match some school curricula more closely than others. The significance of this differential match is that students' test scores vary depending on which test is used. Jenkins and Pany (1978) provide a complete discussion of curriculum bias in achievement tests.

Behavioral-assessment techniques can be used to take data on academic behaviors thereby helping to circumvent this problem. For example, a psychologist can have students read from textbooks used in their classrooms and count the number of words they read correctly per minute. If it is the social-studies teacher who expresses concern about a student's performance, then the behavioral-assessment approach provides a flexible format. The psychologist has the student read from the social-studies book.

Use of behavioral assessment to examine academic behaviors is a very useful tool for school psychologists. It may help strengthen the inferences made about a student's academic achievement based on test performance. It also is handy when there are no tests to measure a certain content area. Systematic behavioral assessment may also *disconfirm* test results. Suppose Ross takes a test that has three addition problems on it, and he misses all three. Psychologist #1 might say, "Ross doesn't know how to add." Psychologist #2, however, says, "I need to give Ross more problems to check my hypothesis that he has difficulty with addition." So psychologist #2 uses a behavioral-assessment approach, gives Ross more addition problems, and determines a *frequency* measure. Psychologist #2 finds that of these 20 new addition problems, Ross got all correct. These behavioral data disconfirm the test data. It seems that Ross does not have a problem with addition; it just happened that the test contained those three that he did not know or he was just careless. For more information about using behavioral assessment to measure academic behaviors, typically referred to as formative evaluation, see Deno, Marston, and Mirkin (1982), Deno and Mirkin (1977), and Deno, Mirkin, and Chiang (1982).

Fourth, in addition to providing data on the student who has been referred, behavioral observation can be conducted to enable social-comparison data to be gathered within a classroom to determine how unusual a behavior is. For example, systematic observation indicates that Elizabeth gets up from her desk between 5 and 11 times in a 15-minute period. But before an intervention is planned that focuses on Elizabeth alone, it is necessary to take data on her peers as well. These social-comparison data help determine how unusual Elizabeth's out-of-seat behavior is. Systematic observation of three other students in her class who were randomly selected indicates median values of between 3 and 10 out-of-seat behaviors per 15-minute period. It seems that in this classroom, Elizabeth's behavior is not so atypical and that intervention directed toward a larger group of students or the teacher should be considered.

Fifth, behavior observations allow events and conditions that precede, accompany, and follow the behavior of interest to be analyzed. Students do not operate in a vacuum. They are influenced by people and materials around them. Much of the analysis of this reaction to environmental stimuli, such as teacher behavior, is missed when students are removed from their classrooms for assessment. A procedure for examining environmental factors and interpreting the observations made is discussed in the Methods section under narrative recording.

Sixth, behavioral observations help determine if the student has a repertoire (skills) or a motivational problem. If it is determined that the student does not have the skills to perform the behavior, he/she first must be taught those skills. If the student knows how to perform the behavior but does not do so, a motivational problem exists and reinforcement contingencies will need to be manipulated to correct the problem. Thus, behavioral observations are particularly useful in both skills and conditions analyses which in turn influence the type of intervention that is implemented. Psychometric testing alone provides limited information in this area.

For some referrals, systematic behavioral observations are sufficient. Other cases involve more extensive interviews and/or standardized testing. For these, behavioral observations are intended to serve as an adjunct to other procedures. They are used along with other assessment techniques to increase confidence in the inferences made about students and to clarify the nature of the problem. If observational data contradict data from other sources, hypotheses regarding the

problem need to be revised and/or more information gathered.

BASIC CONSIDERATIONS

Systematic behavioral observation has the potential to be a powerful assessment tool because it provides objective, reliable, and valid information. Like any other technique, however, observation systems can lead to inappropriate and even inaccurate conclusions if they are misused. Therefore, it is important to keep a number of basic considerations in mind when observations are completed.

When a referral is first made, psychologists often start off with situational analysis (see Unit 2 of Sulzer-Azaroff & Mayer, 1977). This analysis includes reviewing the student's records, observing in the classroom, and interviewing significant people in the student's environment. Frequently, the first step is to clarify the reason for referral. It is during this process that a psychologist begins to focus on target behaviors to observe systematically. Ultimately, these observational data are used to plan interventions. An essential yet often overlooked beginning step is to take a developmental perspective to evaluate the appropriateness of a particular behavior. For example, suppose that a kindergarten teacher expresses concern about Rebecca because she does not sit still for more than 10 minutes at a time. Psychologists who forget to do the situational analysis to clarify the nature of the concern and who do not take a developmental perspective might decide to target Rebecca's out-of-seat behavior. Such an analysis is quite inappropriate. Rebecca is a five year old; children of that age often have short attention spans and move around fairly frequently. Developmentally, her behavior is not really unusual. A move appropriate approach is working with the teacher to develop classroom activities that allow students to change tasks more often. Adopting the developmental perspective, then, helps keep psychologists on the right track because they are more likely to observe relevant behaviors and in turn, to generate more appropriate interventions.

Since behavioral assessment has the advantage of being used for such a wide range of verbal and nonverbal behaviors, it is important to be particularly careful when selecting target behaviors. Alessi and Kaye (1983) outline several variables that must be considered when determining which behaviors to observe. First, is the behavior important to the people involved? If the answer is yes, it still must be determined whether focusing on that behavior will help design meaningful interventions. Lahey, Vosk, and Habif (1981) discuss several behaviors such as attention deficits that are generally inappropriate to target. One of the main problems is that although interventions can be implemented that increase on-task behavior, they do not necessarily lead to improvements in academic performance. Targeting academic behavior, on the other hand, is more likely to lead to improvements both in academic and attending behaviors (cf. Broughton & Lahey, 1978; Hay, Hay, & Nelson, 1977; Holman & Baer, 1979).

A second factor to consider when selecting an appropriate target behavior is whether or not it is a prerequisite to other skills. Is it an enabling behavior that allows the student to perform other, more difficult behaviors? In the academic domain, school professionals generally do a good job of identifying prerequisite behaviors, such as learning to add before learning to multiply. They are less consistent, however, in identifying prerequisite behaviors for social skills. Although ultimately students need to be able to get along with people, first they must perform such prerequisite behaviors as maintain-

ing eye contact, initiating conversation, and responding when other people say something to them. It is these enabling behaviors that are usually best to target. It may be helpful to refer to Stephens (1978) to identify prerequisite behaviors to various social skills.

A third factor to consider when determining which behavior to observe systematically is whether it is comparable to peers' behavior in similar situations. When deciding whether or not a behavior is appropriate, it is necessary to examine the context in which it occurs and whether or not the behavior is of appropriate duration, frequency, and intensity. Since most third graders are expected to know how to read, Anna's reading behaviors should be targeted if her teacher expresses concern. (Note, it would also be appropriate to select reading behaviors for observation since they are enabling behaviors.)

In addition to considering which behaviors are appropriate to observe, it is important to pay careful attention to defining those behaviors. To ensure precision in the measurements, it is essential to operationalize the definition of the target behavior. The operational definition allows behaviors to be observed and measured accurately enough that two independent observers agree when these behaviors do and do not occur. If the behavior is not defined clearly enough to begin with, the observational data are inaccurate and faulty inferences and inappropriate educational decisions about those students will be made.

To provide operational definitions for each of those behaviors, the various behavioral dimensions of the response are specified. It is not always necessary to delineate all of them, although at least several are described. First, the *topography* of the response, its form or shape, is specified. For example, teachers may want a preschooler to tie shoes in a certain way or an adolescent to greet adults in a certain way. Specifying the topography of a behavior is particularly important for motor behaviors, but is also useful for verbal behaviors.

Second, the *intensity* dimension may be important. For example, when verbal behavior has been targeted, it could be specified that the student must say a given phrase loudly enough to be heard 3 feet away or softly enough not to be heard in another room. Handwriting and aggression are examples of other behaviors for which intensity is considered.

Third, it may be important to specify the *duration* of the behavior, namely, how long it lasts. How long does off-task behavior have to occur before it is counted?

Fourth, frequently the *accuracy* of a response must be defined, what constitutes a correct response. Suppose a psychologist is taking data on a mentally retarded student's dressing skills. Is credit given when shoes are put on independently regardless of whether or not they are on the correct feet?

And fifth, although infrequently, *latency* may be of interest. It refers to the time between presentation of a stimulus and occurrence of the behavior. Suppose a psychologist wants to take data on Joseph's following teacher directions. The first teacher direction observed asks for the reading group to start their silent-reading activity. Although it took him 4 minutes and 37 seconds to begin the activity, he did finally comply. Perhaps latency should be included when operationalizing direction-following behavior. If 1 minute were selected, Joseph's behavior is counted as not following directions.

An important step, then, in making systematic behavioral observations is to operationalize each target behavior by specifying the relevant behavioral dimensions. More information can be found in Chapter 4 of Alberto and Troutman (1982) and in Unit 4 of Sulzer-Azaroff and Mayer

(1977).

Once an appropriate target behavior has been selected and operationally defined, the next step is to decide how to measure it. The different methods of behavioral observation are discussed in the next session. After selecting an observation system, it is essential to ensure that it is technically adequate, an evaluation that also is done with standardized tests. Three criteria to consider when evaluating the soundness of our observation system are the extent to which it is objective, reliable, and valid (Sulzer-Azaroff & Mayer, 1977). Objectivity refers to measurement systems that are not biased by the observers' feelings or their interpretations of data. Operationalizing the definition of the target behavior by clearly specifying each of the relevant behavioral dimensions significantly increases objectivity. For example, Blair's impulsivity may be targeted for observation. The lack of objectivity is apparent since observers have idiosyncratic definitions of impulsive behavior. Specifying a more observable description such as responding to a question before 5 seconds have elapsed significantly increases objectivity. Sometimes observers think they have an objective definition for a behavior, but find that they really do not after observing for a few days. In this case, the definition of the behavior needs to be refined.

A second criterion to consider when evaluating the technical adequacy of an observation system is reliability, more appropriately called inter-observer agreement. Before actually beginning to take data, it is important to ensure that the measurement system is reliable. Two different observers should consistently agree on the behavior they observe; differences in the target behavior should not occur simply because people do not agree that the behavior occurred. Therefore, it is important to demonstrate high reliability, usually considered to be at least .90, of a measurement system by calculating coefficients of agreement. If the reliability coefficient drops below .80, there are problems and changes must be made before continuing to take data. Poor inter-observer agreement often means that the target behavior has not been defined precisely enough, or the observers may not have been trained sufficiently in using that particular observation system. Inter-observer agreement is calculated in different ways for different measurement systems (see Chapter 3 of Kazdin, 1982, or Units 5-6 of Sulzer-Azaroff & Mayer, 1977).

A third criterion to consider when evaluating the technical adequacy of an observation system is validity. An observation system is valid when it actually measures what it purports to measure. The validity of an observation system presupposes that it is both objective and reliable although these alone are insufficient to ensure that a measurement system is valid. There is usually not much of a problem when a domain is defined narrowly and specifically. For example, a psychologist could develop a valid measurement system of oral reading rate by having students read out loud from one of their books. Note, though, that there are likely to be differences in the validity of the measures depending upon whether students read a list of words in isolation or words from a passage. Most educational personnel consider the latter to be more valid. Similarly, a valid measure of sharing cound entail observing children as they play with their peers and counting how many times they give another child one of their toys.

The more broadly a domain is defined by using abstract terms, however, the more difficult it is to find a valid measurement system. Although a valid observation system for oral reading has been found, that does not mean that it is a valid system for the entire domain of reading including decoding skills, silent reading, comprehension, and reading for different purposes. Similarly, a valid observation system has been found for assessing sharing-toys behavior, but not for social skills in general. To increase the validity of assessments of these broader domains, multiple measures are necessary. Behavioral-observation techniques are still used, but it is necessary to sample additional behaviors in the domain. For example, to assess students' reading, behavioral-assessment techniques are used for oral reading by having the student read a passage out loud and for decoding by presenting the student with a list of nonsense words. Measures of permanent products such as workbook pages are also used to assess reading comprehension. To assess social skills, one could observe sharing, giving compliments, and appropriately receiving negative feedback, to name a few. Although the entire domain of reading or social skills cannot be assessed, the validity of the observation system is substantially increased by including measures of multiple behaviors. Each of these behaviors being observed, of course, needs to be operationally defined to maximize objectivity and reliability.

Another important consideration when conducting behavioral observations is deciding in which settings to observe. Whenever a referral is made, the first step is to clarify the reason for the referral and to decide on which behaviors to sample. Then different situations are selected for observation since a student's behavior is likely to vary as a function of different environmental stimuli. To examine the extent to which a particular problem occurs, it is important to observe the student in a variety of contexts. Alessi and Kaye (1983) outline a number of these. First, the behavior is observed both in structured and unstructured settings. An activity falls somewhere along this dimension depending on how specific the task instructions are and how closely the teacher monitors the activity. Most psychologists remember students they have observed whose behavior varied considerably depending on whether they were in structured or unstructured settings. Second, a student is observed in activities involving different numbers of students such as large-group, small-group, or one-to-one situations. Third, students are observed in their strongest as well as weakest subjects. And fourth, at a minimum, students are observed in at least two different settings. Since settings refer either to people or to places, a student could be observed with two different teachers and/or in two different classrooms. There is a setting change if Tessa is observed in Room 101 with Mr. Appleby and then observed in the same room with Ms. Grapple. There also is a setting change if Benjamin is observed in Room 203 with Mr. Rhett and in Room 301, again with Mr. Rhett. Students' behavior can vary in the presence of different adults and/or in different classrooms.

It is desirable to observe students in a variety of situations. When differences in a student's behavior are apparent in different settings, it is essential to analyze setting events to determine which variables are effecting differences in the behavior. The information gained from this analysis helps in designing an intervention. It may be more effective to modify some situational variable rather than to set up a formal intervention for the target student.

A particularly important yet often overlooked consideration is describing the setting and analyzing its features that can limit, direct, or facilitate behaviors. When data are taken and a student's behavior in one observation session is compared to behavior in another, differences may be evident that are a function of the way the data were taken and not of the student. The data are confounded and it is not known if changes in the student's behavior are real or a reflection of changes in the situation. Therefore, it is essential to ensure that the student's freedom and opportunity to respond are consistent across observations.

According to White and Liberty (1976), there are two questions to consider when comparing behavior counts. The first is whether or not a student was as free to respond in the first instance as in the second. Was there anything pacing, prompting, or inhibiting her in one situation but not in the other? For example, suppose Laurel's food stealing during lunch time is targeted and baseline data are taken. On the first day there are seven episodes of food stealing. This number is quite significant when a teacher has several other severely handicapped students in a lunch group. Therefore on the second day, the teacher put Laurel at an adjacent table and had the teacher associate monitor her. This modification inhibited Laurel's freedom to steal food; her food stealing on that day was two. Although it would appear that Laurel's food stealing was decreasing, a change in the environment was actually what accounted for the apparent improvement. Generally it is best to create situations in which the student is free from external constraints while responding. Only when the students are free to respond at their own pace can the effectiveness of program variables be assessed. If constraints do exist, as is often the case for highly disruptive behaviors, these need to be recognized, described, and kept as consistent as possible across baseline and treatment phases.

The second question to consider when comparing two behavior counts is whether or not the student has an equal opportunity to respond in both instances. For example, suppose that the target behavior was the number of independent steps Joshua completed in dressing himself. Training is in the third week and there has been considerable improvement in his zipping and buttoning skills. Then one day the weather is particularly warm, so Joshua puts on a T-shirt and a pair of elasticized shorts, thus eliminating the necessity to button his shirt or to zip his pants. By examining the data, it looks like there has been a dramatic drop in his dressing skills. This behavior change is explained entirely by an environmental variable, namely, a decrease in Joshua's opportunity to respond. In general, it is best to allow a student the same number of opportunities to respond in each session. For example, in individual treatment sessions to increase compliance, 20 requests are made at each session. For situations in which it is not possible to provide a constant number of opportunities, percentage rather than frequency of correct responses is used.

Using systematic observation systems, data can be taken on both academic and nonacademic behaviors of the referred student. Non-referred students who serve as comparisons also can be observed systematically. The social-comparison data help in interpreting the information gained about the referred student because they place the student within an environmental context. The psychologist not only learns about levels of the target student's behavior, but also about how atypical or uncommon it is within that classroom. Suppose a teacher expresses concern that Andrew rarely turns in his homework. Data are taken for a week to assess the frequency of the problem and indicate that he does not turn in his homework for three of the five days. However, it is not known whether Andrew's problem is unique to him unless social-comparison data are taken.

Alessi and Kaye (1983) outline several ways to select comparison students. First, the psychologist asks the teacher to suggest several average students in the same observation situation and then observes all of them, or randomly selects one of them. These should not be the best students, but rather the typical ones. There are two interpretations of the "same observation situation." It can refer to students who are average within the class as a whole, or it can refer to students who are average for a subgroup in the class such as one of the reading groups. A second way to gather social-comparison data is looking at the seating arrangement before going into the class and then selecting a student or students at random. Finally, the psychologist observes most, perhaps even all, of the students in the subgroup or entire class. When actually conducting the observation, data sometimes are taken on both the target student and comparison student at the same time if they sit close to each other. If they are far apart or if there is more than one comparison student, the psychologist alternates taking data on each. For example, the target student is observed during the first minute, comparison student number 1 in second minute, the target student in the third minute, comparison student number 2 in fourth minute, and so forth.

There can, of course, be limitations in the social-comparison data collected. It is particularly important to conduct several observations so that the extent to which there are reliable differences between the target and social-comparison students can be determined. The randomly selected student or students may really not be so typical. The best or worst student in the class inadvertently may have been selected. It is also important to note that even though the target student's behavior may be significantly different from the comparison students (see Deno & Mirkin, 1977, for a procedure to calculate discrepancy), the target student's behavior still may be within the acceptable range. The extent to which the behavior is considered acceptable depends on how developmentally appropriate it is as well as on the teacher's tolerance level. Keep in mind that if the target student's behavior is comparable to the comparison students' behavior, that does not necessarily indicate that the referred student has no behavioral difficulties. It is possible that the entire class does, too.

METHODS OF BEHAVIORAL OBSERVATION

Once a behavior has been targeted for observation and defined precisely in quantifiable terms, a procedure for measuring it must be selected. There are a variety of ways to measure behavior. The particular method chosen depends on a number of factors including whether the behavior is enduring or transitory, how much time is available to observe, and whether the psychologist or someone else, such as a teacher, takes the data. It is important to remember that there are relative advantages and disadvantages to each of the different observation systems. Consider these carefully and select the one that yields the most accurate estimate of the behavior. More detail on each of these can be found in Alberto and Troutman (1982), Alessi and Kaye (1983), and Sulzer-Azaroff and Mayer (1977).

Narrative Recording

A narrative recording is a continuous description of what occurs during an observation session. The observer writes down everything that occurs including behaviors of other people. The end product of this continuous recording looks something like a paragraph. The next step, then is to reorganize it into a sequence analysis which consists of three columns of information: (a) antecedent events and conditions that seem to precipitate the student's behavior, (b) the student's behavior, and (c) events that

follow as consequences of the acts. People sometimes refer to a sequence analysis as an "ABC" which stands for Antecedents, Behavior, and Consequences. A sequence analysis provides extremely useful information that not only helps to refine goals, but also to set up an intervention. Unit 2 of Sulzer-Azaroff and Mayer (1977) provides detailed information about a sequence analysis.

One final point is important to keep in mind before beginning narrative recordings or more systematic observations of a student: How representative is this observation of the student's typical behaviors? Was the student observed on a particularly good or bad day? The psychologist could ask the teacher if the behavior that occurred during the observation period was fairly typical of the student.

Measures of Permanent Product

If the behavior leaves some form of an enduring product, it is called a permanent product. The number of boxes packed, towels folded, worksheets completed, or toys broken all can be measured directly as soon as they occur or later. If the complexity of the tasks is kept constant, all that is necessary is counting the instances. Many behaviors are transitory, however, and cannot be measured after they occur; they must be measured as they are taking place.

Event Recording

Event recording is the number of times a behavior occurs in a given time interval such as 15 minutes, the lunch period, or the entire school day. Before event recording can be considered the appropriate measure, the target behavior must be discrete, that is, it must have a clearly definable beginning and end. Behavior such as finger eating or object throwing are discrete whereas on-task behavior often is not. A second requirement before event recording can be used is that each occurrence of the behavior has approximately the same duration. For example, if temper tantrums were the target behavior and event recording was to be used, observers would have to be sure that they recognize when a tantrum started and stopped and that each tantrum lasted about 2 minutes, 5 minutes, or whatever. If both of these criteria are not met, then event recording is an inappropriate measure. A third consideration before using event recording is that the behavior does not occur at too high a rate. If it occurs too rapidly, an accurate frequency count cannot be reliably determined.

Event recording can be done in many ways: with pencil and paper, with a reliable wrist counter similar to the one proposed by Lindsley (1968), with a hand counter, by marking on masking tape on the wrist, or by transferring tiny objects such as paper clips from one pocket to another. An observer who is only taking data and not having to instruct students will probably use pencil and paper. If the teacher is taking the data while continuing to teach, a convenient system needs to be worked out. Regardless of how the frequency data are taken, they are eventually recorded on a data sheet. Examples of these are found in Table 1.

Duration Recording

Duration refers to the amount of time in which a behavior occurs. Behavior must be discrete if duration recording is done. Stop watches are particularly suitable for measuring duration. They can be stopped and started without resetting to record total duration of a behavior for any given observation session.

Latency Recording

Latency refers to the elapsed time between a stimulus and when the person begins to respond. For example, the teacher presents an instructional prompt, "Start doing your math problems." After 14 seconds, the student begins to work the problems. Latency of responding is 14 seconds. Although latency is not one of the more common measures, it is very useful when determining how long it takes a student to respond to a request or to different types of prompts. An example of a data sheet for recording latency and duration is found in Table 2.

Interval Recording

For behaviors that are not clearly discrete, interval recording is appropriate. In such cases, event recording and duration recording are difficult. There are two types of interval recording. In the first, whole-interval recording, the behavior must occur continuously throughout the entire interval before it is scored. Behaviors that occur for very short periods of time, such as blinking or throwing an object, are not measured using whole intervals whereas behaviors occurring for longer periods, such as working on an activity, are. The observer determines the length of the interval; 10-second intervals are often used. If whole-interval recording was used and four out of the six intervals in a minute were scored, it is concluded that the student had engaged in that behavior for at least 40 seconds. Thus, whole-interval recording is used to estimate the duration of a behavior, and provides a measure of the minimal possible duration.

TABLE 1

Event Recording Data Sheets

1. *Single student, single behavior*

Student: _____ Observer: _____

Setting: _____

Operational Definition of Behavior(s): _____

Date	Obs'n Time Start Stop	Occurrences	Total Frequency

2. *Multiple students or behaviors*

Dates and Time of Observations

Students or Behaviors	3-5-84 10:00 - 10:15					
1						
2						
3						

TABLE 2

Latency and Duration Recording Data Sheet

Student: _____   Observer: _____

Setting: _____   Time Start and Stop: _____

Operational Definitions of:

Behavior initiation: _____

Behavior termination: _____

Date	Time		Latency	Time	Duration
	Presentation of Stimulus	Initiation of Response		Termination of Response	

In the second, partial-interval recording, the behavior only needs to occur for part of the interval to be scored. Whereas whole-interval recording underestimates the occurrence of the behavior, partial-interval overestimates it. The true level of the behavior lies somewhere between the two. Because each provides different estimates of the behavior, psychologists must be careful how they report the data. Thus, for example, they could say that Esther shared her tools in 40% of the intervals observed and not that she shared them 40% of the time. In addition, they briefly explain that this 40% is an under- or overestimate depending upon whether whole- or partial-interval recording was used.

Although interval recording is used to measure many behaviors, it is not appropriate for infrequent behaviors. Keep in mind, too, that although a psychologist as an outside observer can use this system with no difficulty, teachers cannot use it and continue to teach unless the observations are kept very brief. A prerecorded tape indicating the selected intervals is frequently used for interval recording. Examples of data sheets for interval recording are found in Table 3.

Momentary Time Sampling

In recording the occurrence of a behavior using a momentary time-sampling system, only behavior at the end of the interval is observed. One observes for 1 second or for 3 to 5 seconds at the end of each interval. Once the psychologist decides what amount of time to use, that same amount is consistently used to observe at the end of each interval.

Momentary time samples are used for behaviors that last a while. If the behaviors are too brief in duration, the observer misses them altogether. In this behavior-recording system, the interval is generally longer (e.g., 15 minutes) than it is for whole- and partial-interval recording (e.g., 10 seconds). It is a useful technique for teachers to take data while teaching. It is also useful for taking data on several students. At the end of the interval, the observer looks at each student in turn and records the presence or absence of the target behavior. Behaviors are grossly underestimated if long observation intervals are used.

As an example of a situation in which momentary time sampling is used, consider Charlotte who reads so much that she does not get her work done. Momentary time sampling at 10-minute intervals is used, and she is observed for 2 seconds at the end of each interval. At the end of 1

hour, six observations have been made. If reading was observed in two of them, the data would be interpreted as follows, "Charlotte was observed reading in 33% of the observations made." She was *not* observed reading 33% of the time because a continuous duration measure for the full hour was not made. Examples of data sheets for time sampling are found in Table 4.

SUMMARY

Behavioral observation is a powerful tool for gathering information, drawing inferences, and generating ideas about students. The focus of this chapter was on the *systematic* use of observation techniques to provide objective information for making educational decisions. Systematic behavioral observation provides a breadth of information and serves many different purposes. It provides valid data to strengthen inferences made about students who are assessed; it also yields information to disconfirm these inferences so that hypotheses about the problem must be revised and/or more information gathered. Behavioral assessment is used to measure both academic and nonacademic behaviors and to gather social-comparison data so that psychologists can determine how atypical a student's behavior is. Behavioral observations provide a methodology to analyze environmental events and conditions that influence these behaviors and to determine whether the student has a repertoire or a motivational problem. This information is important in order to develop the most appropriate intervention.

Like any other assessment technique, behavioral observations lead to inappropriate and even inaccurate conclusions if they are misused. Essential issues to consider are selecting appropriate behaviors to observe, precisely defining behaviors, choosing a measurement system, examining the technical adequacy of the observation system, determining settings in which to observe, and selecting appropriate social-comparison students.

There are a variety of ways to measure behavior including narrative recording, measures of permanent product, event, duration, latency, and interval recording, and momentary time sampling. It is important to consider the relative advantages and disadvantages of each and to select the observation system that yields the most accurate estimate of the behavior.

TABLE 3

Interval Recording Data Sheets

1. *Single student, single behavior*

Student: _____ Observer: _____

Date and Setting: _____ Time Start and Stop: _____

Operational Definition of Behavior: _____

_____

10-second Interval

Minutes	1	2	3	4	5	6
1						
2						
•						
•						
15						

2. *Multiple behaviors* (e.g., seeking teacher attention*, accepting criticism, making verbal exchange)

(Table 3 is continued on next page)

Minutes	T ATTN	ACC CRIT	V XCHG		T ATTN	ACC CRIT	V XCHG
1'-1				6'-1			
2				2			
3				3			
4				4			
5				5			
6				6			
2'-1				7'-1			
2				2			
3				3			
4				4			
5				5			
6				6			
3'-1				8'-1			
2				2			
3				3			
4				4			
5				5			
6				6			
4'-1				9'-1			
2				2			
3				3			
4				4			
5				5			
6				6			
5'-1				10'-1			
2				2			
3				3			
4				4			
5				5			
6				6			

* *Key:* + = appropriate, – = inappropriate
Target: observe during odd minutes   *Comparisons:* observe during even minutes

TABLE 4

Time Sampling Data Sheet

1. *10-minute intervals, 1-hour observations per day*

Date	10'	20'	30'	40'	50'	60'

2. *5-minute intervals, target student and social comparisons*

	5'	15'	25'	35'	45'	55'
Target						

	10'	20'	30'	40'	50'	60'
Peers						

REFERENCES

Alberto, P. A., & Troutman, A. C. (1982). *Applied behavior analysis for teachers: Influencing student performance.* Columbus, OH: Charles E. Merrill.

Alessi, G. J., & Kaye, J. H. (1983). *Behavior assessment for school psychologists.* Kent, OH: National Association of School Psychologists.

Broughton, S. F., & Lahey, B. B. (1978). Direct and collateral effects of positive reinforcement, response cost, and mixed contingencies for academic performance. *Journal of School Psychology, 16,* 126-136.

Deno, S. L., Marston, D., & Mirkin, P. (1982). Valid measurement procedures for continuous evaluation of written expression. *Exceptional Children, 48,* 368-371.

Deno, S. L., & Mirkin, P. K. (1977). *Data-based program modification: A manual.* Reston, VA: Council for Exceptional Children.

Deno, S. L., Mirkin, P. K., & Chiang, B. (1982). Identifying valid measures of reading. *Exceptional Children, 49,* 36-45.

Hay, W. M., Hay, L. R., & Nelson, R. O. (1977). Direct and collateral changes in on-task and academic behavior resulting from on-task versus academic contingencies. *Behavior Therapy, 8,* 431-441.

Holman, J., & Baer, D. M. (1979). Facilitating generalization of on-task behavior through self-monitoring of academic tasks. *Journal of Autism and Developmental Disorders, 9,* 429-446.

Jenkins, J. R., & Pany, D. (1978). Standardized achievement tests: How useful for special education? *Exceptional Children, 44,* 448-453.

Kazdin, A. E. (1982). *Single-case research designs: Methods for clinical and applied settings.* New York: Oxford University Press.

Lahey, B. B., Vosk, B. N., & Habif, V. L. (1981). Behavioral assessment of learning disabled children: A rationale and strategy. *Behavioral Assessment, 3,* 3-14.

Lindsley, O. R. (1968). A reliable wrist counter for recording behavior rates. *Journal of Applied Behavior Analysis, 1,* 77-78.

Stephens, T. M. (1978). *Social skills in the classroom.* Columbus, OH: Cedars Press.

Sulzer-Azaroff, B., & Mayer, G. R. (1977). *Applying behavior-analysis procedures with children and youth.* New York: Holt, Rinehart and Winston.

White, O. R., & Liberty, K. A. (1976). Behavior assessment and precise educational measurement. In N. G. Haring & R. L. Schiefelbusch (Eds.), *Teaching special children* (pp. 31-71). New York: McGraw-Hill.

ANNOTATED BIBLIOGRAPHY

Alberto, P. A., & Troutman, A. C. (1982). *Applied behavior analysis for teachers: Influencing student performance.* Columbus, OH: Charles E. Merrill.
Chapter 4 focuses on collecting and graphing data. It provides helpful suggestions for determining which observation system to use. It also includes excellent examples of data recording sheets.

Alessi, G. J., & Kaye, J. H. (1983). *Behavior assessment for school psychologists.* Kent, OH: National Association of School Psychologists.
This publication presents a comprehensive analysis of behavioral assessment and includes numerous examples of observation forms. A special feature is the accompanying videotape that illustrates several observation systems and provides supervised practice as the viewer takes data on target and social-comparison students.

Boehm, A. E., & Weinberg, R. A. (1977). *The classroom observer: A guide for developing observation skills.* New York: Teachers College.
This book provides a nice introduction to some important considerations when using behavioral observation systems. It includes a number of activities to complete and presents answers in the appendix. It also includes examples of data recording sheets.

Epps, S. (1983). *Designing, implementing, and monitoring behavioral interventions with the severely and profoundly handicapped.* Des Moines, IA: Department of Public Instruction. Although this manual focuses on interventions, Chapters 1 and 2 are devoted to observation systems which can be applied to any population. There are several practice exercises included along with answers in the appendix. It also contains information on training observers and graphing observational data.

Sulzer-Azaroff, B., & Mayer, G. R. (1977). *Applying behavior-analysis procedures with children and youth.* New York: Holt, Rinehart and Winston.
This comprehensive text provides detailed information primarily about behavioral interventions, but also about observation systems. It includes examples of data recording formats.

BEST PRACTICES IN THE ASSESSMENT OF
LIMITED ENGLISH PROFICIENT AND BILINGUAL CHILDREN

Giselle B. Esquivel
Fordham University

OVERVIEW

This chapter presents best practice alternatives in the assessment of limited English proficient (LEP) and bilingual children. This is a group of children who come from language minority backgrounds or whose families speak languages other than English. The assessment of language minority students is a complex process; one which is best conceptualized from an understanding of their unique needs, the assessment process itself, the legal and ethical issues involved, and professional implications for practice.

Needs of Language Minority Students

The number of children from linguistic minority backgrounds in our school systems is rapidly increasing. According to a recent national survey on education, elementary and secondary schools are struggling to absorb immigrant youngsters by the hundreds of thousands each year (Maeroff, 1983). Language minority students come from many diverse national backgrounds including Chinese, Hispanic, Russian, Haitian, Korean, and Indochinese. Some are children who migrated, alone or with their families, in pursuit of better opportunities or as political refugees. Others are first and second generation Americans who are, to varying degrees, still involved in the process of cultural adaptation. Also included in this group are Native Americans who speak a wide range of dialects and are moving from reservations into urban settings.

It is evident, from a historical perspective, that our society is becoming increasingly pluralistic. This is reflected not only by the number of linguistically and culturally different children in our schools, but also, more importantly, by the growing sensitivity to their needs.

Children from linguistic minority background have unique needs related to various sources of stress. Although these children come from diverse socio-economic backgrounds, a great majority belong to families who live in urban settings, work in unskilled positions, and earn low mean incomes, factors which render them more susceptible to the effects of poverty. Low levels of academic achievement and high drop-out rates have been reported for children in urban ghetto areas where a majority of these children reside (Pifer, 1979). In addition, epidemiological studies have suggested that children in urban areas are more subject to potentially stress-inducing events and, consequently, are more vulnerable to social-emotional problems (Canino, Earley, & Rogler).

Migration factors are another source of stress which affect a great number of language minority children. These include the severance of family ties, the loss of friends, difficulties in learning a new language or way of life, and intergenerational conflicts created when they become acculturated at a faster rate than their parents. Refugee children, in particular, may suffer from adjustment reactions as a result of having experienced war or political unrest in their native country (Brower, 1980). Sometimes these conflicts may form the basis for the development of greater flexibility and adaptive resources. However, these may also result in more enduring emotional problems in the absence of appropriate support systems.

Cultural and language factors often play a significant role in problems related to academic achievement. For example, the emphasis in some language minority cultures on mutual interdependence may clash with mainstream values of competitiveness required for school success. At times, pressures to achieve create conflicts in children who are coping with learning a new language. Although most immigrant children acquire conversational skills in English within one or two years, it takes them five years on the average to develop those aspects of language related to cognitive and academic functioning (Cummins, 1982). This problem is intensified for students who have had limited exposure to formal educational experiences and/or whose culture places minimal emphasis on verbal communication (McShane & Plas, 1984).

The problems of language minority children are exacerbated for those who suffer from handicapping conditions. In many instances the special needs of immigrant children have failed to be identified or appropriate interventions have not been provided for them in their native country. Families of children with limited resources have often been unable to afford supportive services. For example, some children with orthopedic handicaps obtain corrective devices or become involved in special gymnastics for the first time when coming to this country.

Although it is relatively easier to identify the problems of students with more obvious or severe handicaps, it is harder to assess the needs of those who exhibit difficulties which are intertwined with language and cultural factors. Diagnostic problems exist in the ability to distinguish between actual learning disorders and difficulties in language proficiency, or to differentiate cultural adjustment reactions from emotional problems. At the same time, the early identification and diagno-

sis of these problems, based on appropriate assessment procedures, is a critical issue.

Assessment of Linguistic Minorities

Historically, the assessment of language minority students may be characterized by the use of inappropriate procedures including the evaluation of children in their non-dominant language or with instruments standardized on a white middle class population. The resulting comparably lower performance of these children on tests was often attributed to genetic or hereditary factors (Garth, 1923). Minimal regard was given to environmental, cultural and language variables as possibly affecting performance. Consequently, this process resulted in inappropriate labeling and misplacement of many language minority students in special education classes (Mercer, 1973).

Since the 1960's, testing of linguistic minorities has been increasingly scrutinized. Factors that could account for observed differences have been identified, such as the relevance of cultural values and extent of acculturation, levels of English proficiency or degrees of bilingualism, the nature of testing conditions, language of the examiner, inadequacies of test instruments, and the failure to provide comparable education (Olmedo, 1981).

Growing research in the area of test bias with minorities has further demonstrated the potential bias in the use, or rather misuse, of tests with limited English proficient and bilingual students. These studies consistently indicate that administering verbal tests in English to such children yield meaningless or questionable scores if interpreted as tests of cognitive ability rather than as short-term predictors of achievement when English is the medium of instruction (Jensen, 1980). Similarly, issues in test translations and other alternative procedures have been identified (Oakland, 1977; Samuda, 1975).

Greater emphasis is now given to the multicultural aspects of assessment and to the influence of language, affective, and motivational variables (Anastasi, 1983). A recent trend is the study of culture-specific patterns in the performance of students from various ethnic and language groups on individually administered ability tests, when controlling for socio-economic status and level of functioning (Reynolds, 1983). Similar approaches have been applied in the area of personality assessment and in the clinical diagnosis of sub-cultural groups (Costantino, 1982b; Kasdan, 1976, 1983).

Legal and Ethical Issues

The re-definition of assessment and the increasing scrutiny of assessment practices has been partly related to greater involvement on the part of the judicial system in protecting the rights of children including those from language and ethnic minorities. Although there have been numerous court and legal decisions pertaining to the assessment of these children, three more prominent ones serve to highlight their significance.

The Diana versus The California State Board of Education class action suit in 1968 on behalf of linguistically different children who had been placed inappropriately in programs for the mildly retarded resulted in a consent decree which set broad guidelines for the assessment of these children. These guidelines set a precedent for the evaluation of children, taking into account their native language and socio-cultural background. This decision was followed by the 1974 Supreme Court ruling, in the case of Lau versus Nichols, that evaluations and educational instruction be provided in the native language of the child. Finally, the greatest impact was provided by Public Law 94-142, the Education of All Handicapped Act, which mandates that the evaluation of children be conducted in their dominant language and that appropriate individualized programs of instruction be provided.

Implications for School Psychologists

The appropriate assessment of an increasing number of language minority students poses a challenge for the school psychologist who is committed to meeting the needs of all children. Legal requirements often stipulate what needs to be done, yet fail to specify how the task should be accomplished. The process of assessing these children is beset with limitations posed by currently available instruments and the scarcity of research-based knowledge in this area. More importantly, there is a very limited number of both bilingual and monolingual school psychologists who are trained to work with LEP and bilingual/bicultural populations. These problems are not only confined to urban areas where there are large numbers of language minority students, but to rural areas as well. In these more isolated areas, difficulties in serving migrant handicapped students are intensified by few appropriate resources, materials, and qualified bilingual personnel (Helge, 1984).

BASIC CONSIDERATIONS

The development of alternative approaches for providing school psychologists with specialized competencies in the assessment of language minority students is an important and viable solution. Three major approaches through which these competencies may be developed are the training of bilingual school psychologists, the in-service training of monolingual school psychologists, and the training of interpreters.

Training of Bilingual
School Psychologists

Rosenfield (1982) describes the underlying thesis for her development of a university-based model training program as that of preparing bilingual school psychologists who are competent in the field of school psychology and who have additional competencies in working with LEP and bilingual students. These specialized competencies involve knowledge in the areas of linguistics, cross-cultural psychology, bilingual special education, and bilingual assessment (Figueroa, Sandoval, & Merino, 1982). Bilingual school psychologists can, in turn, share their expertise in these areas and sensitize others to the needs of language minority students.

In-Service Training

Another approach which has been used to meet the continuing education needs of practicing school psychologists in the area of bilingual assessment is the provision of in-service training. The primary goals of this model are to train monolingual school psychologists in non-biased assessment procedures, to carry out those tasks and services performed with greater sensitivity and awareness of the needs of the child with limited English proficiency, and to work with the resources within the school and community (Coulopoulos, 1982).

Training of Interpreters

The training of interpreters is another approach resulting from the problem of not having enough school psychologists who are competent in a variety of low incidence languages or regional dialects. It has been suggested that interpreters be trained in such aspects as how to establish rapport, how information gets lost in the interpretation process, how non-verbal communication supplements interpretation, and methods and techniques available to the interpreter. In addition, interpreters need to be aware of ethical practices such as maintaining confidentiality (Aliotti, 1981; Sandoval, 1981).

In summary, school psychologists may use different approaches for developing and applying those basic competencies which facilitate their assessment of language minority students. It is recognized that this may be a long-term process given the heterogeneity of language minority groups and the limited resources available. Therefore, it is important to consider more specific assessment alternatives.

BEST PRACTICES

Alternative procedures in evaluating LEP and bilingual students need to be perceived within the context of a broader view of assessment. This process involves a series of informal strategies, formal approaches, and preventive efforts.

Informal Approaches

Consultation
One of the first decisions that needs to be made in the assessment process is to identify the problem and nature of the referral and to determine if a student needs to be evaluated formally. This question is difficult to answer, especially for children who are recent immigrants and appear to exhibit learning or behavior problems which are not of an obvious or severe nature. Premature involvement with children in the testing process often results in aggravating the problem. Moreover, it may lead to inappropriate conclusions since it is difficult to determine what constitutes an actual disorder versus a transitional problem related to language, cultural and situational factors. At the same time, there is a need for the timely identification and remediation of problems.

Involvement in consultation with teachers working with the child serves as a means of problem clarification. Through a collaborative relationship between teachers and the school psychologist, the actual source and nature of the child's difficulties are identified. Some issues to ascertain are the child's past academic experience, the suitability of present instruction to the child's learning style, cultural factors which affect adjustment to the school situation, the appropriateness of services to develop English skills, and the relationship between language and academic achievement. Expectations in these areas are further clarified by the application of research findings. For example, children are often referred on the assumption that because they have acquired English conversational skills, their academic difficulties must be based on a learning problem. However, it takes students as many as five years to acquire the necessary cognitive skills in the second language for their performance to reflect a more accurate estimate of their true abilities (Cummins, 1980).

Parent Interview

Involving parents in the assessment process further facilitates the understanding of specific cultural values which affect the child's school adjustment. Some relevant issues to consider are the family's extent of acculturation, use of language at home, and attitudes towards school and academic achievement. Equally important is an understanding of parental attitudes towards exceptionalities, their perception of emotional problems, and their receptivity to the use of special education and mental health services (Acosta, Yamamoto, & Evans, 1982). For example, parents may hold cultural values which emphasize the use of family support systems in dealing with children's emotional problems rather than entrusting these to professionals in unfamiliar institutions. As a result, it is important for school psychologists to communicate with parents based on an understanding of these factors. Using interpreters or community members as "cultural consultants" who can explain cultural customs, values and beliefs held by the family is of value in this process (Acosta & Cristo, 1981). In addition, it is useful to have knowledge of differing family structures and roles, differing socialization patterns, and differing historically important themes in culturally diverse groups (Sandoval, 1981). Recent literature in the area of cross cultural counseling and ethnic family therapy serves as a source of information in this area (McGoldrick, Pearce, & Giordano, 1982).

Background Information

Disadvantaged language minority children often suffer from developmental, health and nutritional deficiencies which affect their learning. For example, otitis media (middle ear disease), the leading identifiable disease among American Indians and Eskimos, results in inadequate development of oral-linguistic processing skills (McShane & Plas, 1984). Stress factors play a role for those children whose families face economic difficulties or who are dealing with cultural adjustment problems. The extent of exposure to formal learning experiences, the pattern of mobility, age of arrival, and number of years in this country are variables which influence achievement and second language acquisition. Consideration of these important factors will provide significant diagnostic information.

Observations

Children from specific cultures express feelings or respond to stress in unique ways. Traditional values may emphasize the need for reserve or concealment of sadness behind a polite smile. Some may behave in ways which are appropriate within their own culture but not within the context of school. For example, some children avoid eye contact as a sign of deference when reprimanded. These behaviors are misinterpreted when observed from a mainstream culture perspective. Observations which are culture specific or evaluated in the light of the child's culture are more sensitive to these differences and form the basis for more valid interpretations.

Furthermore, observations need to be purposeful. School psychologists who are interested in understanding some unique aspect of a child's personality may want to focus specifically in observing how the child differs from peers within his or her own cultural group. On the other hand, observing a child's interaction with peers from other cultures may reflect a child's extent of acculturation, flexibility, and socially adaptive resources. Comparing a child's behavior in various settings provides additional information. Sometimes children who appear to be limited in school prove to be quite resourceful as they assume the role of interpreters or cultural mediators for parents in the community.

Some useful observational techniques include sociometric measures, naturalistic observations, behavioral procedures, classroom interaction scales, and anecdotal reports. These observations, however, are meaningful only when interpreted within the context of the child's unique cultural experience.

Child Interview

Communicating with children is one of the most significant ways to learn about them. Children are able to express feelings about their native country and reaction to loss of significant persons, reflecting their capacity for affective response. They recount stories and situations with others which reveal the nature of their interpersonal relationships. They relate possible conflicts with parental values or difficul-

ties in adjusting to the new culture which provide information about their coping and adaptive skills. In addition, verbal interaction may shed light on their reasoning ability, problem-solving style and language skills. The use of drawings and play activities are useful diagnostic tools for those children who are less verbal since these media of expression often reflect aspects of a child's individual and cultural experiences. Moreover, children are able to express conflicts through drawings, as evidenced by those of refugees from Cambodia (Boothby, 1983). Innovative personality assessment techniques and interventions which are culturally sensitive are being investigated for possible use (Constantino, 1982a).

Language Assessment

Language assessment procedures need to take into account the nature of language proficiency and the varying degrees of bilingualism which have been identified. Along the continuum are a group of children among the "new arrivals" who are native speakers but have no understanding of English. A second group of children are the "incipient bilinguals" who may have mastered surface aspects of English but have yet to acquire the deeper structures of this language (McCollum, 1981). Other degrees of bilingualism include the "dual bilingual," or children who have native like mastery of two languages; and the "pseudolingual," who have incomplete mastery of two languages (Dulay & Burt, 1980). This latter group of children, who show slow development in *both* languages, need to be observed carefully in terms of a possible language disorder or learning problem (Greenlee, 1981).

In assessing speech and language, particular attention needs to be given to the more dominant language since it is difficult to determine if errors are a function of language proficiency or actual disorders. Inappropriate labeling and involvement in a speech program may interfere with the child's normal interlanguage development (Anderson, 1981). Formal techniques include assessment of oral proficiency listening, speaking) and those more dependent on instruction or content (reading, writing). Informal techniques include naturalistic observations, analysis of written language samples, taped measures of interactions with peers and adults, and gathering such information as what television programs are watched or the language of books which are read for entertainment.

Academic Assessment

Academic skills are assessed through criterion-referenced measures and curriculum-based assessment strategies. These approaches, however, require some understanding of curriculum design and instructional methods (Reynolds, Gutkins, Elliott & Witt, 1984). Some informal diagnostic strategies include having the student provide written samples in both languages, solve tasks which require mathematical computation, and read from passages in both the native and English languages. These samples are task-analyzed in terms of required skills and nature of errors made. Having students verbalize their approach to a task also provides information about their problem-solving and reasoning abilities. Interventions are then developed based on knowledge of the student's strengths and weaknesses and unique learning style. A child's *own* rate of progress serves as the basis for determining the need for further assessment.

Formal Approaches

Non-Verbal Tests

The rationale for the use of non-verbal tests is that LEP and bilingual children usually do significantly better in tests of performance where the use of language is limited and the influence of culture reduced. Performance scales of standardized intelligence tests appear to have the greatest predictive validity for these students, and may provide a more accurate estimate of their actual abilities. For example, Block Design, a performance subtest on the WISC-R, has been found to have the most cross-cultural validity and to correlate significantly with classroom performance and mathematical ability. Raven Progressive Matrices is another instrument which has been successfully used with language and ethnic minority children and for which hypothetical national norms are available (Sigmon, 1983). This test is in the process of being restandardized. Other approaches include the use of non-verbal tests such as the SRA Pictorial Reasoning Test, without timing requirements; the Cattell Culture Fair Intelligence Test, and industrial tests as potential resources (Salny, 1983).

Verbal Tests

The use of standardized verbal scales is applicable primarily for language minority children who have been properly identified as English dominant. These children perform better on these tests than on those which have been developed or standardized in their native, yet non-dominant language. For example, it has been found that the disparity between verbal and non-verbal performance diminishes with increasing number of years in school. Nevertheless, findings need to be interpreted in light of the child's level of acculturation and sociocultural factors (Valencia, 1983).

Verbal tests also provide a picture of children's verbal processing skills and language proficiency when used qualitatively. Mercer (1983) has suggested that verbal portions of tests are good measures of a child's proficiency in cognitive academic aspects of English as their second language. In addition, comparing a child's performance on these verbal tests with their performance on equivalent versions standardized in their native country provides an estimate of level of acculturation.

Test Translations

Since the degree of bilingualism varies in children, they mix languages or alternate between two language systems in understanding and responding to questions. Their ability to express themselves in either language depends on the nature of the task or the context within which they learned the specific skill required. Consequently, the examiner may have to switch from one language to the other and to translate specific items or instructions.

Direct translations of tests, however, have inherent flaws in that they do not yield technically equivalent forms. Some words do not have exact counterparts, the level of difficulty may change as a result of the translation, there are many concepts which have no equivalents, and the test content remains culture bound (Olmedo, 1981). Nevertheless, the use of a profile analysis, combined with a qualitative interpretation of results, may have diagnostic significance. For example, the profile of limited English proficient students is characterized by lower scores on information, similarities and vocabulary and peaks in arithmetic and digit span. In addition, these children do significantly better in performance tasks. Language minority students who deviate from these patterns or do poorly in typical areas of strengths need to be assessed further for possible learning or perceptual difficulties (Cummins, 1982).

Standardized Translated Versions

The development of translated versions which are item analyzed and factor analyzed cross culturally is another approach which has been attempted as a means of correcting for difficulties inherent in direct test translations. For example, the Wechsler Intelligence Scale for Children-Revised has been adapted and standardized on various populations including children from Mexico, Spain and Hong Kong. These tests are applicable for students who reside in those countries or who have recently migrated to this country from them. However, they are inappropriate for language minority students whose cultural, academic and linguistic experiences are intermixed.

Local Norms

A more recent approach in response to the heterogeneity of language minority groups has been the development of local norms. For example, the WISC-R has been translated, item analyzed and re-standardized on a Hispanic population in Florida. The Mexican version of the WISC-R is also being adapted for use with children in California. Local norms are being developed for SEARCH as a screening instrument for younger children in New York City. Similar attempts to establish local norms are needed for a variety of other language minority groups. Although there are difficulties posed by within group differences and mobility factors, the development of local norms may prove to be a valuable alternative.

Supplemental Techniques

Additional supplemental approaches include De Avila's Cartoon Conservation Scale as a Piagetian measure; Torrance Tests of Creative Thinking, Figural Form; Feurstein's Dynamic Assessment of Learning Potential; and the Kaufman Assessment Battery for Children, based on information processing theory.

Other important approaches are the use of task analysis as part of a qualitative interpretation of subtests on traditional instruments (Kaufman, 1977); multipluralistic adaptive measures such as Mercer's SOMPA; and various techniques for testing limits (Sattler, 1982). In general, the most effective methods involve the use of multiple criteria and interdisciplinary team efforts

SUMMARY

There are no easy solutions to the problem of assessing LEP and bilingual students. Some alternatives have been presented which are helpful in this process. Ultimately, however, this issue needs to be addressed from a broader perspective. Involvement in prevention not only makes assessment more meaningful now, but it will eventually realize its purpose, which is to meet the needs of children. The following are some suggestions towards efforts at prevention:

1. Develop training programs which prepare school psychologists with additional competencies in working with language minority students and their families and which provide opportunities for the continued professional development of practicing school psychologists in this area.

2. Provide in-service training of school personnel, including teachers and administrators, to sensitize them to the needs of language minority students and to develop their expertise in providing appropriate services for them.

3. Involve language minority parents in the schools as a means of developing closer relationships between the family and the school system.

4. Work cooperatively with community agencies in developing supportive programs for children and their families. Use community resources to obtain information and volunteer-paraprofessionals and interpreters.

5. Develop affective education and counseling programs which are supportive of children dealing with acculturation stress, strengthen coping skills, and develop a healthy sense of bicultural (or multicultural) identity.

6. Develop interventions which are culturally appropriate, including cross-cultural counseling and culturally relevant instructional methods.

7. Develop regular education supportive programs which meet the literacy needs of immigrant students with limited educational experience.

8. Develop programs for culturally different students with gifted potential.

9. Develop mentorship and interest groups in professional organizations in the area of bilingual school psychology.

10. Increase the use of applied research in the area of bilingual school psychology.

REFERENCES

Acosta, F. X., & Cristo, M. H. (1981). Development of a bilingual interpreter program: An alternative model for Spanish-speaking services. *Professional Psychology*, 12(4), 474-482.

Acosta, F. X., Yamamoto, J., & Evans, L. A. (1982). *Effective psychotherapy for low-income and minority patients.* New York: Plenum Press.

Anastasi, A. (1983, November). *The nature of intelligence: A view from the 1980's.* Invited Address, Minority Assessment Conference, Tucson, Arizona, Arizona Conference on Applied Psychological Issues.

Aliotti, N. (1981, April). *Some strategies and training implications for the assessment of bilingual-bicultural children.* Paper presented at National Association of School Psychologists, Houston, TX.

Anderson, J. I. (1981). Considerations in phonological assessment. In J. G. Erickson & D. R. Omark (Eds.), *Communication assessment of the bilingual bicultural child.* (p. 96) Baltimore, MD: University Park Press.

Boothby, N. (1983). The horror, the hope. *Natural History*, 64-71.

Brower, I. C. (1980). Counseling Vietnamese. *Personnel and Guidance Journal*, 646-652.

Canino, I. A., Earley, B. F., & Rogler, L. H. (1980). *The Puerto Rican child in New York City: Stress and mental health.* (Monograph No. 4) NY: Hispanic Research Center, Fordham University.

Costantino, G. (1982a). Cuentos folkloricos: A new therapy modality. *Research Bulletin:* Hispanic Research Center, Fordham University 5(4), 7-10.

Costantino, G. (1982b). TEMAS: A new technique for personality assessment and psychotherapy for Hispanic children. *Research Bulletin*, Hispanic Research Center, Fordham Universty, 5(4), 3-6.

Coulopoulos, D. (1982). Inservice training of school psychologists in nondiscriminatory assessment of bilingual children. *Proceedings of a Conference on Psychoeducational Assessment of Pupils with Limited English Proficiency*. Albany, NY: Bureau of Bilingual Education.

Cummins, J. (1980). Psychological assessment of immigrant children: Logic or intuition? *Journal of Multilingual and Multicultural Development*, 97-111.

Cummins, J. (1982). Tests, achievement, and bilingual students. *Focus*, National Clearinghouse for Bilingual Education, 1-7.

Dulay, H., & Burt, M. (1980). The relative proficiency of limited English proficient students. *NABE Journal*, 4(3), pp. 1-23.

Feurstein, R. (1979). *The dynamic assessment of retarded performers*. Baltimore: University Park Press.

Figueroa, R. A., Sandoval, J., & Merino, B. (1982). *Preparing school psychologists to serve bilingual and limited English proficient children*. Davis: University of California, Dept. of Education.

Garth, T. R. (1923). A comparison of the intelligence of Mexican and mixed and full blood Indian children. *Psychological Review, 30*, 388-401.

Greenlee, M. (1981). Specifying the needs of a bilingual developmentally disabled population: Issues and case studies. *NABE Journal, 6*(1), 55-75.

Helge, D. (1984, January). The state of the art of rural special education. *Exceptional Children*. 294-305.

Jensen, A. R. (1980). *Bias in mental testing*, NY: MacMillan Publishing Co., 604-607.

Kasdan, M. B. (1976). Psychological test patterns among orthodox Jewish children. *Dissertation Abstracts International, 37* 3B 1438. (University Microfilms No. 76-21, 236)

Kasdan, M. B. (1983, November). *Psychological testing with subcultural groups: Some notions regarding test interpretation*. Paper presented at Minority Assessment Conference, Tucson, Arizona.

Kaufman, J. (1977, June). Can we learn by their mistakes: Assessment of multi-cultural children utilizing a task analysis approach. *Proceedings of a multi-cultural colloquium on non-biased pupil assessment*, Albany, NY.

Maeroff, G. I. (1983, August). Rising immigration tide strains nations schools. *The New York Times*, Sec. 12.

Marcos, L. R., & Alpert, M. (1976). Strategies and risks in psychotherapy with bilingual patients: The phenomenon of language independence. *American Journal of Psychiatry, 133*, 1275-1278.

McCollum, P. A. (1981). Concepts in bilingualism and their relationship to language assessment. In J. G. Erickson & D. R. Omark (Eds.), *Communication assessment of the bilingual bicultural child.* (pp. 25-41). Baltimore, MD: University Park Press.

McGoldrick, P., Pearce, J. K., & Giordano, J. (1982). *Ethnicity and family therapy*. NY: Guilford Press.

McShane, K. A., & Plas, J. M. (1984). The cognitive functioning of American Indian children: Moving from the WISC to the WISC-R. *School Psychology Review*, 13(1), 61-73.

Mercer, J. R. (1973). *Labeling the mentally retarded*. Berkeley: University of California Press.

Mercer, J. R. (1983, November). *The WISC-R: Implications for transnational assessment*. Invited Symposium, Minority Assessment Conference, Tucson, Arizona, Arizona Conferences on Applied Psychological Issues.

Oakland, T. (1977). *Psychological and educational assessment of minority children*. NY: Brunner/Mazel Publishers.

Olmedo, E. (1981). Testing linguistic minorities. *American Psychologist, 36*(10), 1078-1085.

Pifer, A. (1979). *Bilingual education and the Hispanic challenge*. Annual Report of the Carnegie Corporation of New York.

Reynolds, C. R. (1983, November). *Changing conceptualizations of race differences in intelligence*. Invited Address, Minority Assessment Conference, Tucson, Arizona.

Reynolds, C. R., Gutkin, T. B., Elliott, S. N., & Witt, J. C. (1984). *School psychology: Essentials of theory and practice*. NY: John Wiley & Sons.

Rosenfield, S. (1982, May). *Some problems and solutions concerning psychoeducational assessment of bilingual-limited English proficient-non-English dominant children.* Paper presented at the Invitational Conference, Psychoeducational Evaluation of Pupils with Limited English Proficiency, New York State Education Dept.

Salny, A. F. (1983). *Issues in the assessment of the bilingual child.* Paper presented at Symposium of New Jersey Association of School Psychologists, Somerset, NJ.

Samuda, R. J. (1975). *Psychological testing of American minorities: Issues and consequences.* NY: Dodd, Mead.

Sandoval, J. (1981, April). *Preparing school psychologists to serve bilingual and limited English proficient children.* Paper presented at Trainers of School Psychologists, Houston.

Sattler, J. M. (1982). *Assessment of children's intelligence and special abilities* (2nd ed.). Boston, MA: Allyn and Bacon.

Sigmon, S. B. (1983). Performance of American school children on Raven's Colored Progressive Matrices Scale. *Perceptual and Motor Skills,* 56, 484-486.

Valencia, R. R. (1983). Stability of the McCarthy Scales of Children's Abilities over a one-year period for Mexican-American children. *Psychology in the Schools,* 20, 29-34.

Seidner, S. S. (1981). Issues of language assessment: Foundations and research. *Proceedings of the First Annual Language Assessment Institute,* Illinois, National College of Education.
A series of articles useful in the assessment of language proficiency and the development of instructional interventions is presented.

Seidner, S. S. (1983). *Issues of language assessment:* Vol. II.
Language assessment and curriculum planning, Illinois, National College of Education.

ANNOTATED BIBLIOGRAPHY

Omark, D. R., & Erickson, J. G. (1983). *The bilingual exceptional child.* California: College Hill Press.
This book provides a thorough discussion of assessment and intervention issues related to bilingual exceptional children.

Powell, G. F. (1983). *The psychosocial development of minority group children.* New York: Brunner/Mazel Inc.
This book discusses the psychological development and emotional needs of children from various cultures.

RESOURCES

National Clearinghouse for Bilingual Education
1300 Wilson Boulevard, Suite B 2-11
Rosslyn, VA

National Indochinese Clearinghouse
Center for Applied Linguistics
3520 Prospect St., N.W.
Washington, DC 20007

Evaluation Dissemination and Assessment Center
3700 Ross Ave., Box 103
Dallas, TX 75204

Bilingual School Psychology Program
Resource Library, Room 1008, Fordham University
113 W. 60th St. & Columbus Ave.
New York, NY 10023

Dr. Lloyd H. Rogler, Director
Hispanic Research Center
Fordham University
Bronx, NY

Dr. Abbie F. Salny
Consultant International MENSA
143 River Drive
Elmwood Park, NJ 07407

BEST PRACTICES IN THE TRAINING OF SCHOOL PSYCHOLOGISTS: CONSIDERATIONS FOR TRAINERS, PROSPECTIVE ENTRY-LEVEL AND ADVANCED STUDENTS

Thomas K. Fagan
Memphis State University

OVERVIEW

This chapter is an overview of the relationships among professional training, accreditation, and credentialing organizations and discusses training practices in the United States. The information is useful to practicing school psychologists, persons seeking initial preparation in school psychology, and those with basic training who are considering advanced graduate work. The discussion helps the student and practitioner understand potential barriers encountered when one moves from one state to another and to recognize the general relationship between basic and advanced preparation. Avenues of exploration for persons seeking training with various specializations are provided. It is also intended to be useful to persons involved in establishing school psychology training programs and to trainers advising prospective students on program selections. This chapter should be an addition to the program's existing resources to assist student career explorations in school psychology (Fagan and Hohenshil, 1976).

Background

The earliest practitioners of school psychological services carried other titles and their formal training in school psychology was very limited. School psychological services were inaugurated in the early twentieth century in some major cities. The Chicago Bureau of Child Study, established in 1899, is usually considered the first public school program. Practitioners usually had preparation in psychology depart-ments which emphasized experimental studies. Their programs included few applied courses, except for limited study in clinical psychology, a method of individual examination and intervention emanating largely from the work of Lightner Witmer at the University of Pennsylvania. Much of the practice involved individual psychometric evaluation of children and adolescents suspected of being "mentally, physically or morally defective." At that time, few test instruments and theories were available.

The rapid growth of psychological science and public education in the first half of the twentieth century required the services of persons broadly trained in psychology and education with specific emphasis on the problems of education and school children. While the extent to which this orientation has become implemented in daily practice is debatable, the recognition has strongly influenced the training of school psychologists for decades. Early practitioners typically held bachelor's or master's degrees with considerably fewer holding the doctorate. Training emphasized the use of newly developed tests of intelligence, school achievement, motor skill, and so forth. The general purpose of psychological services in most settings was to assist school personnel in sorting children into more appropriate classroom placements including the relatively few but increasing number of special education programs. Owing to the diversity of problems and children in the schools, most practitioners operated as "generalists" who responded to a large variety of situations. Because of acute gaps in supply and demand, the service providers ranged from persons holding advanced graduate degrees in psychology to persons with teacher training and a "crash course" in intelligence testing.

Efforts to formalize programs of preparation and/or mechanisms for quality control of providers through credentialing procedures were not attempted for a considerable time. University graduate sequences appropriate for clinical psychology students planning to work in the schools were available in the 1920's. However, it now appears that the first programs of preparation actually labeled *school psychology* were in the undergraduate and graduate programs at New York University (See NYU School of Education Bulletin, 1929-30).

Little has been written about the development of training programs in school psychology during the period prior to 1950, though it was reported that at least 18 such programs existed at the time of the Thayer Conference in 1954. What little prior information is available suggests the leadership role was held by such institutions as New York University, Columbia University, Pennsylvania State University, Ohio State University, University of Michigan and the University of Illinois. Growth in the number of training programs has been dramatic in the past three decades. There are currently at least 200 institutions offering programs with at least 70 at the doctoral level.

Many persons contributed to the growth of programs: H. H. Goddard, J. E. W. Wallin, Francis Maxfield, Gertrude Hildreth, Percival Symonds, T. E. Newland, Boyd McCandless and countless more recent figures. Today several hundred trainers in over 200 institutions owe much to the planning and thinking of these persons. With the inauguration of the University of Illinois doctoral program in 1951 and the impetus of the Thayer Conference, the development of masters and doctoral programs became apparent. While the Illinois program established by T. E. Newland was not the first doctoral program in school psychology, it was probably among the first clearly organized and recognized programs. Early descriptions of the Illinois program reveal its sensitivity to both educational and psychological foundations, the need for broad-generalist preparation and other aspects still included in professional training standards.

Throughout this development of training programs, the issue of doctoral-nondoctoral preparation is observed. This issue has increased since the reorganization of the American Psychological Association (APA) in 1945. The greatest intensity has been observed since the APA Council of Representatives took a firm stand in 1977 on the doctoral-level requirement for the title "professional psychologist." The demand for doctoral level personnel is recognized in the growth of such programs in the past 20 years. Needless to say, the doctoral-nondoctoral issue is very complex and not the focus of this discussion. However, from a training perspective, it is worth noting that the percentage of school psychologists holding doctoral degrees has climbed from about 3% in 1970 to about 20% in 1980. This trend is judged to be persistent with gradual increases in the doctoral force relative to the nondoctoral force. Without significant changes in the areas of health services provision and credentialing, the doctoral degree will continue to be the choice only for those practitioners desiring to hold employment with the least professional and legal restrictions. For persons desiring full-time employment in school districts, the forecast is for continued nondoctoral demand in the vast majority of settings, private non-school practice with some practice restrictions specified in an increased number of states, and the continued availability of relatively large numbers of specialist level programs of training. Em-

ployment opportunities at both the doctoral and specialist levels are attractive,
particularly in rural and developing areas,
some urban districts, many non-school
settings, and private practice. They are
best for persons having specializations
and a higher degree of mobility.

BASIC CONSIDERATIONS

This section provides basic concepts
and information for prospective school
psychologists about the training, credentialing and practice of the profession. It is
organized around selected questions commonly posed to trainers by prospective
students and many practitioners.

1. *What is the typical training of the
school psychologist?*
Ramage (1979) provides a representative picture of the levels of degree common
to practitioners. The following table summarizes degrees held by respondents to
both her and an earlier survey:

PERCENT OF RESPONDENTS
HOLDING DEGREES

	Ramage (1979)[1]	Farling & Hoedt (1971)
Bachelors	1	1
Master's (1 yr)	22	28
Master's (2 yr)	39	63
Master's (3 yr) or Specialist	14	1
Doctorate	24	3

Despite sampling differences and
problems of return rates of less than 50%
in each study, it is safe to say that most
practicing school psychologists hold nondoctoral degrees. The two-year master's
and specialist levels are gaining in popularity and growth at the doctoral level is
also very pronounced.

The following summary table regarding number of students in training and
number of programs is adopted from
Brown and Minke (1984):

Students in Training	Number	Program Response Level
Total	7293	211
Master's	1466	80
Sixth Year	2526	174
Doctoral	2301	69

Again, the prominence of advanced graduate training is observed. As in the Brown
and Minke study, sixth year level refers to
programs meeting NASP accreditation
standards. The average sixth year program was reported to require 63 semester
hours. So defined, it is consistent with the
two-year, three-year and specialist levels
combined in the previously reported surveys. The terms "sixth year" and "specialist" degrees often represent similar levels
of graduate training. However, specialist
level typically involves a degree awarded
at the termination of work while the sixth
year level indicates at least one year beyond the master's but not necessarily a
separate degree. Since specialist degrees
are typically awarded for a *minimum* of
60 semester hours of graduate work, it is
not unusual to find such programs having
greater requirements and hurdles such as
terminal exams and research papers than
a sixth-year program entails. In the author's opinion, persons seeking training in
school psychology are wise to pursue
nothing less than a sixth-year program
of graduate preparation. The author's
forecast is that surveys in the 1990s
will most commonly reveal programs at
the specialist and doctoral levels,
fewer two-year master's programs and
practically no one-year programs. Additionally, practitioners will increasingly
hold specialist, sixth-year or doctoral
degrees with master's and bachelor's level

---

[1]The survey was conducted in 1976 and published in
1979.

personnel fading almost entirely within the next two decades.

Another way of responding to questions about typical training is to provide information about the content of degree programs. The *NASP Directory of School Psychology Programs* (Brown and Minke, 1984) provides a convenient source of information on the content areas required by each program. Each training institution is listed alphabetically within each state. The annual publication by the APA, *Graduate Programs in Psychology*, also provides information related to school psychology programs and is more specific than other sources in such areas as admission requirements, and retention rates. Since doctoral and nondoctoral graduate programs are increasingly complying with the standards advocated by the NASP and the APA (doctoral program standards only), the program content requirements of these associations' standards are also useful general references. More information about program content at various degree levels is discussed in a later section of this chapter.

2. *What resources are available to assist in the selection of a training program, level of preparation, and so forth?*

The few early works related to career selection in school psychology are largely outdated. Only in the past decade have materials specifically related to training been produced. In addition to the NASP and APA program standards and the survey documents mentioned above, certain other documents are helpful. The most specific source is Gerner and Genshaft (1981). It provides information related to such issues as degree, field experiences, credentialing requirements, program orientation, and interviewing questions. This document points out the often confusing relationship between a training program and the credentialing requirements of the state in which the program is located. This

is a major consideration at the non-doctoral level. Since most programs are organized to meet requirements of a particular state department of education (SDE) or other regulatory authority such as a psychology licensing board, the non-doctoral program even within institutions offering doctoral degrees often conforms closely to these requirements. With this in mind, *The Handbook of Certification/ Licensure Requirements For School Psychologists* (Brown, Horn and Lindstrom, 1977) is very useful in the decision-making process.

Students seeking guidance in the selection of entry-level training in school psychology should answer the following questions before exploring specific training institutions:

1.) Do you desire to work primarily in the public school setting?

2.) Do you desire to have a doctoral or nondoctoral degree completed in the near future (say five, ten years)?

3.) In what state, or at least region, do you intend to seek employment?

It is assumed that the person has already responded positively to related questions including: Do you desire to work with school-age children, many of whom have handicapping conditions? Or will you be comfortable employed in the public school environment? Generating specific responses to the above questions greatly narrows the range of selections. The previously mentioned *Directory of School Psychology Programs* and *Graduate Programs in Psychology* are then used to gather basic information on several institutions under consideration. Inquiries to these institutions provide sufficient program data to allow the student to make more specific decisions regarding the appropriateness of the program for the student's needs and interests. These resources are useful in decision-making for doctoral programs as well.

3. *Why are many school psychology programs operated from within a College of Education or other apparently non-psychology unit?*

Unlike most areas of education or psychology, school psychology has experienced a confusing history of credentialing, accreditation and locus of training. Throughout that history, training programs were located in psychology and non-psychology departments in both Colleges of Education and Colleges of Arts and Sciences. Anyone who scans through program data is surprised by the inconsistency of training locations. By departmental title there are at least a dozen different departments housing school psychology programs in the United States. The Brown and Lindstrom (1977) *Directory* which included Canadian programs, indicated summary data suggesting the following percentage distribution:

Academic Unit	Percent of all Programs (N=198)
Psychology	40
Education	42
Special Education	3
Counseling/Guidance	4
Interdepartmental	11

Special education, counseling and guidance, most interdepartmental programs and at least some of the psychology departments are in Colleges of Education; consequently, such colleges probably "house" more than half of the programs. These results are consistent with those of Goh (1977) which also indicated the presence of a program in a Graduate School of Professional Psychology. Thus diversity, perhaps even growing diversity is the norm not the exception in school psychology training. Without belaboring the analysis, the diversity is related to historical trends in the development of school psychology. These trends include selection of students from diverse educational and psychological backgrounds, conflicts between psychology and education departments, accreditation influences from differing agencies, and, until recent years, lack of clear professional identity. There is no indication that such departmental diversity will decrease.

From the standpoint of persons seeking school psychology training, the question then becomes whether or not academic location of the program makes any difference. The author knows of no study related directly to this question and there is no reason to judge the location of programs in one academic unit as consistently superior to another. Historically, distinguished programs have come from varying units. For example, the earliest programs at NYU were in the College of Education; the influence of the Teachers College, Columbia University is widely recognized, particularly through the period 1930-1970; the first APA accredited program was at the University of Texas, Department of Educational Psychology. Newland's program at the University of Illinois was interdepartmental, but administered from within Education. Even among APA accredited doctoral programs, the high frequency of programs located in education-related units is apparent in the published annual listing. Recognized programs in psychology units including the Universities of South Carolina, Rhode Island, and Florida State University are also found in these listings. Thus there is at least "soft" evidence for the recognition of strong programs in various units. Such recognition probably extends across doctoral and non-doctoral degree levels.

Employing school psychology faculty ratings of perceived importance of content areas, Goh (1977) provides results which strongly suggest that academic emphases do not differ significantly as a function of a program's departmental location. Though not a study of the various programs' quality levels, Goh's research provides one of the few comprehensive analyses of program content and is further discussed in the next section.

In 1984, the APA completed a pilot project on Program Designation which provides another avenue to evaluate the appropriateness of programs. It facilitates the assurance that a participating school psychology program is basically psychological, as defined by APA, in nature and meets certain criteria for administration and curriculum regardless of the institutional unit in which it is "housed." It is not an accreditation process, however, and does not assure the quality control that accreditation procedures seek.

It has been the author's impression that programs located within education units are often more flexible in admissions criteria and scheduling of classes. Thus I believe a student is more likely to be allowed to pursue graduate work on a part-time basis with a selection of daytime and evening courses in a non-psychology based program. Many psychology-based school psychology programs in the Southeast are actually "housed" in a College of Education where a "spread effect" has probably influenced greater flexibility than is the case in psychology units in Arts and Sciences. Rural programs are also different in these respects from urban programs. There are pragmatic concerns related to licensure or certification that encourage persons to seek one unit or another. In every instance there is no substitute for seeking direct answers to questions from the program director/administrator. With the rapid growth of training in the past ten years, even recently published directories cannot keep pace with the changes in policy and curricula. Among trainers it is well known that university publications such as Graduate Bulletins often lag one or two years on these matters. The program administrator is usually the most reliable source of in-

formation.

4. *What is the relationship among training, accreditation, and credentialing? Why are these relationships important?*

The levels of training programs and degrees conferred have direct and indirect relationships to the procedures and outcomes of both accreditation and credentialing. It is as important for the prospective practitioner to understand these relationships as it is to grasp other areas of professional preparation. The relationships dictate the type of title and practice one is eventually permitted. The complexity of these relationships is suggested by Figure 1. Practitioners and trainers understanding the intricate relationships between the organizations, committees, and programs represented in the chart should have little difficulty in recognizing the complex nature of accrediting and credentialing in school psychology. However they may feel powerless to change it. An introductory understanding of these relationships is obtained by reviewing the summary analysis in Figure 2. Imagine that Figure 2 is superimposed on Figure 1. What emerges are two major levels of quality control in the profession: (a) accreditation, the quality control over the preparation of persons desiring to function and call themselves school psychologists, and (b) credentialing, the quality control over the approving procedures for granting titles and functions to persons following professional preparation. A few guidelines will assist understanding the relationships of Figures 1 and 2.

1. Organizations, committees, and relationships in the top portion of the chart relate to accreditation; those at the bottom relate to credentialing.

2. Relationships in the top portion of the chart are typically conducted at the national level; those in the bottom portion at the state level.

3. Relationships in the left portion of

A Diagram Of Power And Authority For
Accreditation And
Credentialing In School Psychology

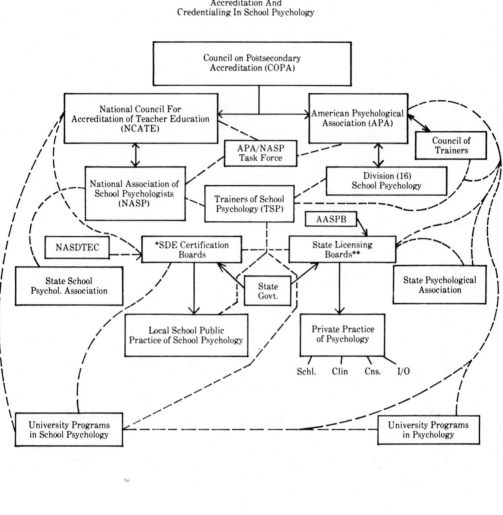

Important Terms

Accreditation	SDE Program Approval	Licensure
APA Approval	Certification	Credentialing

*SDE Certification Boards have power relationships to the NASDTEC
**State Licensing Boards have power relationships to the AASPB

FIGURE 1

Power-Authority Relationships Between
The Four Major Areas Of Control
In The Accreditation And Credentialling Process

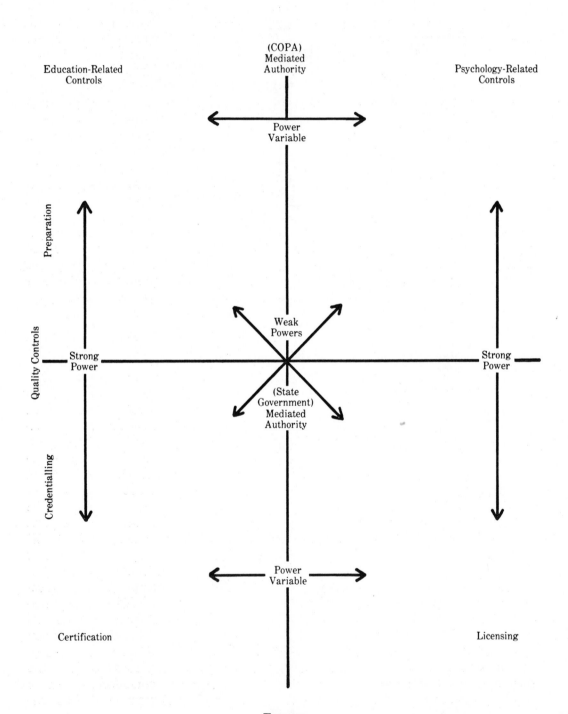

FIGURE 2

the chart relate to established structures and policies of education; those on the right relate to psychology.

4. Dotted lines are meant to indicate power or influence relationships; solid lines represent authority regardless of the extent of power that may co-exist.

5. It should be obvious that there is considerably greater power than authority relationships involved in quality control of these aspects of the profession. In fact, decisions to get involved in quality control are strictly voluntary for most training programs, agencies, committees, and individuals.

Even a cursory understanding of this must be conveyed to and comprehended by prospective trainees since it relates to decisions regarding program selection. Since most of the relationships in the education sector lead to certification while those in the psychology sector lead to non-school based private licensure, and since these credentialing mechanisms are authoritatively regulated at the state level, applicants should have some knowledge about the state(s) in which they would eventually like to practice. It is true that commonalities exist among state certification and state licensing authorities, but reciprocity of credentials and/or equivalence of credentialing requirements in school psychology is the exception, not the norm. Two examples demonstrate the importance of the decisions involved and the relationships in Figure 1.

1. Student "A" is interested only in employment as a school psychologist in his home state, has no interest in non-school setting practice and feels uncommitted at this time to pursuing a lengthy program of graduate preparation leading to a doctoral degree. "A", familiar with the non-doctoral nature of SDE certification in the home state and the fact that the SDE closely scrutinizes the programs of preparation, selects an institution which holds both NCATE accreditation at the specialist level

and SDE program approval, a state-level mechanism of quality control not unlike accreditation in some ways but available in only certain states. Upon completion of the program, "A" is automatically endorsed for certification by his institution and the SDE subsequently grants the certificate. "A" is now authorized to practice as a school psychologist in the public school systems of that state. Depending on the similarity of the home state's requirements to those of other states, "A" may or may not achieve similar certification elsewhere. Nor is "A" authorized, or perhaps even eligible, to apply for authorization for non-school practice as a school psychologist because licensing requirements in his state do not specify a non-doctoral credential. Should "A" move to another state with different certification requirements, no reciprocity with his SDE, and a doctoral-level only licensure requirement, "A" could be without any credential to continue practicing school psychology.

2. Student "B" is interested in maximizing flexibility in the marketplace and seeks preparation for school and non-school based practice. "B" also wishes to retain the title "school psychologist" in both sectors. "B" wants to practice in the same state as "A" but is interested in specializing in a particular area of school psychology. "B" selects an out-of-state institution that holds NCATE accreditation at the nondoctoral and doctoral levels, APA accreditation in school psychology at the doctoral level, and an advanced graduate concentration in the desired specialty. "B" notes also that the program requirements readily match those for certification of her home SDE. Upon completion of the doctoral degree which included a year internship, "B" returns to her home state and makes application for both certification via the SDE and licensure as a school psychologist via the State Board of Examiners in Psychology. After completing additional written and oral examination require-

ments, "B" is both certified and licensed to practice as a school psychologist in school and non-school settings, and privately. Should "B" choose to move to another state it is very likely that additional credentials for both public school and private practice could be obtained with only a minimum of additional examination or other requirements. Certification for "B" to practice in the schools would be practically guaranteed in every state.

The examples above are not meant to suggest any preference. They serve only to demonstrate the manner in which two different persons, defining their goals differently, achieve appropriate training. Many variations of these patterns could be employed to show the intricate relationships among training, accreditation and credentialing. For example, had the home state provided non-doctoral licensure for school psychologists to practice in the non-school sector or had all credentialing of school psychologists been under the control of the State Board of Examiners in Psychology, each person may have made substantially different choices for training. Thus, it is important for prospective entry-level and advanced students to consider the credentialing requirements of their chosen state(s) and the accreditation status of the training program.

Training Orientations and Specialties

Generalists versus Specialists

Throughout the history of school psychology most practitioners have performed a variety of functions while adapting to the range of problems presented them. The necessity for practitioners to have broad training to meet these conditions has long been recognized. Thus most training programs have espoused a generalist orientation which drew upon knowledge and skills from education, psychology, special education and related fields. The generalist model has prevailed in training despite the common reference to school

psychologists as "specialists" or members of "specialized services teams." This is true even for those practitioners holding Educational Specialist Degrees. The issue of whether practitioners should be trained as generalists or specialists has been discussed frequently although few published works on the subject exist.

With the rapid development of professional identity of the past two decades the issue gained attention in both training and practice. Recent publications have suggested the following:

1. There is evidence that students in rural or urban settings benefit from or are in need of specialized training experiences related to the socio-cultural characteristics peculiar to those settings.

2. There is evidence that specialized forms of training are more likely to occur in doctoral programs than in nondoctoral programs.

3. There is evidence of need for and growing interest in several areas of specialization, including consultation, early childhood, vocational school psychology, and neuropsychology.

Goh's (1977) survey bears directly on the second point and suggests considerable similarity of training emphases at the non-doctoral level with areas of specialization generally occurring at the doctoral level. Students seeking entry-level training can anticipate considerable commonality, though not uniformity, of training in the two-year Master's and Educational Specialist level programs. Considering the previous discussion, the commonality is greatest within a single state particularly if credentialing requirements are very specific to selected courses or course areas. Greater diversity at the doctoral level can be anticipated by beginning students or practitioners seeking additional degrees. This diversity is present both within and across states. Thus some states have doctoral programs that emphasize very different areas of specialization despite commonalities in the nondoctoral level across the same institutions and departments. Accreditation standards strengthen and support certain commonalities at the entry-level while encouraging either advanced generalist training or specialization at the doctoral level.

Of course, through experience, continuing education, and personal interests, many school psychologists specialize without obtaining a doctoral degree. For example, perhaps recognizing a need in their practice or district, they obtain additional information and skill in the assessment of low-incidence handicaps. These areas of expertise are common among practitioners, but differ from highly concentrated specializations obtainable either through graduate programs at the doctoral level or advanced graduate courses. Both nondoctoral and doctoral school psychologists have strong commitments to continuing education and recognize that there is no such thing as a terminal professional degree.

Some additional perspectives on the future are useful to the prospective student:

1. With continually increasing numbers of practitioners pursuing doctoral degrees, a work force of persons with specialized skills in the field of school psychology is developing.

2. There is a very definite trend in the direction of practitioners moving into non-school based practices in hospitals, clinics, professional groups, and into self-employment. With generalist level services common to most communities through school-based practitioners, non-school based school psychologists are forced to compete on the basis of specializations. It is also true that generalists in and out of the school setting seek the assistance of specialists. Thus exchange of referrals from one *school* psychologist to another *school* psychologist is becoming more common. In the past, such referrals were commonly

exchanged across groups such as school psychologists to clinical psychologists.

3. A strong employment market for nondoctoral generalists will persist. Employment opportunities for doctoral generalists and specialists both in and out of school settings should also persist, though at a lesser level.

4. Observing the developments in related professions, we can anticipate that school psychologists moving out of school settings will first seek employment in other agencies or self-employment and will eventually move into collective employment with other psychologists or health services providers. Such collectivity of services encourages specialization among those in the collective employment.

In the author's opinion, there will be continuing demand for both generalist and specialist school psychologists with certain characteristics of employment encouraging specializations. Prospective doctoral students should seriously consider their desire and need for either advanced generalist or specialization training. As in the case of previous questions posed for program selection, deciding upon specialization or non-specialization greatly simplifies the program choices. Choosing a particular area of specialization reduces the process even further.

The Content of Programs

Despite the growth and diversity of training levels and the complexity of relationships to accreditation and credentialing, the content of entry-level programs in school psychology has considerable similarity. Such stability reflects the influences of professional and political forces in our history and the realities of daily field practice. With recent program accreditation in school psychology, however, we observe the development of more comprehensive training than has previously existed at the entry level. Thus in the past ten years we have observed rapid growth in Master's and Specialist Degree and Doctoral programs that meet the NCATE/NASP and/or APA accreditation. Such interest was partially responsible for the joint accreditation project (1983-1984) between NCATE and APA. The continuation of that project is uncertain at this time. Program content is presented for entry-level and doctoral programs with the latter including example specializations.

Entry-Level Programs

Because entry-level (specialist) program guidelines developed by NASP have gained in acceptance, they provide one of the best means of determining expected program content. Such content is divided into broad areas as follows:

Psychological Foundations
1. Biological Bases of Behavior
2. Cultural Diversity
3. Child & Adolescent Development (Normal and Abnormal)
4. Human Exceptionalities
5. Human Learning
6. Social Bases of Behavior

Educational Foundations
1. Education of Exceptional Learners
2. Instruction & Remedial Techniques
3. Organization & Operation of Schools

Assessment

Interventions (Direct and Indirect)

Statistics & Research Design

Professional School Psychology
1. Legal and Ethical Issues
2. Professional Issues
3. Professional Standards

The guidelines also specify practica and internship experiences. Accredited programs are expected to have sixty semester hours or more credit embracing the academic and practica-internship experiences. As a general rule, students pursuing specialist level training on a full-time basis across consecutive years can expect a minimum of three years of study, including the internship. Greater specificity of these requirements may be obtained from the NASP documents. These guidelines are consistent with trainers' program emphases ratings in the Goh (1977) study. In that study, nine areas of emphasis were found to account for 73% of the total variance: (a) school-based consultation, (b) educational assessment and remediation, (c) behavior modification technology, (d) psychological evaluation, (e) psychotherapeutic procedures, (f) quantitative methods, (g) community involvement and consultation, (h) professional roles and issues, and (i) psychological foundations including child development and learning. These factors were present in both doctoral and nondoctoral programs with factors a, b, and c accounting for 49% of the variance at all levels!

Since areas of emphasis and accreditation guidelines are met through courses/experiences with varying titles, it is impossible to provide a listing of the common courses in all nondoctoral programs. However from surveys of course content and the NASP *Directory of Programs* (Brown & Lindstrom, 1977) it appears at least the following courses are present in most specialist level programs:

Advanced Statistics
Research Methods/Design
Child and Adolescent Development
Psychology of Learning
Intellectual Assessment
Personality Assessment
Educational Assessment
Educational Foundations (e.g., administration, curriculum)
Child Study Practicum
Seminar on School Psychology
Counseling/Psychotherapy
Consultation
Educational Remediation

Characteristics of Exceptional
Children
Behavior Management
Internship

The internship is full-time for one academic year or part-time over a much longer period. Guidelines for the internship and its supervision are available from NASP.

Doctoral Programs

Most doctoral programs in school psychology are offered in departments that also offer nondoctoral programs. In many instances, the doctoral track is more than an extension of previous levels although a career ladder approach is often available. Because of differences in some aspects of accreditation and the particular orientation of the doctoral program, such students pursue different courses and experiences than nondoctoral students even in the first few years of training. In other instances, the differences are minimal in the first two - three years and doctoral students are drawn from applicants who are already credentialed. It is important for prospective doctoral students to explore these differences since considerably more time may be required to complete doctoral work if a nondoctoral track is followed in the early years of graduate study. As a general rule, students pursuing doctoral degrees full-time across consecutive years can expect a minimum of four years of study which may or may not include the academic year of internship.

Goh (1977) reported factor results on combined doctoral-subdoctoral programs and analyzed emphases that trainers rated significant to the doctoral level. The only areas consistently cited were "school-based consultation" and "quantitative methods." These results support popularly held assumptions that advanced graduate training in school psychology differs most from previous training levels in providing specializations and additional research information/skills. A precise grasp of doctoral program content is not readily available from accreditation guidelines either NCATE/NASP or APA. The NCATE/NASP curriculum standards are by areas of competency, rather than courses and are the same for both doctoral and nondoctoral levels. They are meant to insure that practicing school psychologists emerging from either level of preparation have the same basic skills and competencies. The APA standards apply specifically to doctoral programs and are generic to professional psychology programs. Several areas of competency are specified in the APA Standards. Comparisons of the NCATE/NASP and APA Standards by the APA/NASP Joint Task Force have found them to be highly similar in curricular expectations. As a general rule, the doctoral student can expect to encounter additional statistics and research courses; a major research requirement, usually the dissertation; related requirements such as major area papers; additional written and oral examinations; and an internship experience. Some institutions accept previous internships completed at the entry-level. Advanced graduate coursework in psychology and education are also provided. Such coursework is a generalist concentration expanded from the entry-level, two or more small concentrations such as special education or behavioral interventions elected by the student, or a major specialization in one area such as vocational school psychology. Specializations are emphasized by several doctoral programs. Table 1 is a list of doctoral programs and associated areas of orientation. Most doctoral programs specify areas of specialization that students choose in consultation with an advisor. The presence of special orientations is not confined to the doctoral level. Some nondoctoral programs employ specialization. For example, Gallaudet College offers specializa-

Table I
Orientations of Doctoral Programs in School Psychology[1]

Areas of Specialization	University Identification Number
Applied Behavior Analysis	5, 23, 34, 65
Behavior Assessment/Intervention	11, 39, 53, 65
Behavioral Consultation	11, 47, 54
Behavioral Medicine	50
Child/Pediatric	66
Childhood Psychopathology	5
Clinical Psychology	1, 19, 48, 59, 60
Cognition/Instructional Psychology	12, 54
Computers in Education	47
Consultation	10, 12, 19, 23, 29, 31, 36, 53, 56
Counseling	10, 19, 35, 42, 47, 48, 57, 60, 64
Developmental Psychology	7, 12, 25, 26, 28, 41, 50
Discipline	23
Educational Psychology	35, 48
Experimental	35
Family Systems	7, 19, 21, 39, 57
Generalist Orientation with selected course emphases/concentrations	2, 3, 4, 6, 8, 9, 13, 14, 15, 16, 17, 18, 20, 22, 24, 27, 29, 30, 31, 32, 33, 37, 38, 39, 40, 43, 44, 45, 46, 49, 51, 52, 55, 58, 61, 62, 63
Gifted	25
Hispanic Handicapped	25
Learning Assessment	23
Measurement/Statistics	28, 34
Organizational Development	21, 37, 47, 53
Neuropsychology	25, 34, 42, 54, 57
Pediatric Psychology	35, 42
Preschool/Early Childhood	10, 25, 41
Program Evaluation	5, 25, 41
Psychoeducational Assessment	36, 39, 53, 56
Research/Field Experimental	11, 12, 25, 28, 41, 53, 56
Special Education	41, 42
Therapeutic Invervention	36, 56
University Teaching/Training	53, 54, 56
Vocational School Psychology	18, 39, 64

No.	Name	No.	Name
1.	Adelphi U.	9.	Indiana U.
2.	Arizona State U.	10.	Kent State U.
3.	Ball State U.	11.	Louisiana State U.
4.	Bryn Mawr College	12.	Loyola U. of Chicago
5.	Florida State U.	13.	Michigan State U.
6.	Fordham U.	14.	Mississippi State U.
7.	Georgia State U.	15.	New York U.
8.	Howard U.	16.	Northern Arizona U.

(Table 1 continued)

No.	Name	No.	Name
17.	Ohio State U.	43.	University of Nebraska at Lincoln
18.	Oklahoma State U.	44.	University of North Carolina
19.	Peabody College of Education Vanderbilt U.	45.	University of Northern Colorado
20.	Pennsylvania State U.	46.	University of Oklahoma
21.	Rutgers U.	47.	University of Oregon
22.	Syracuse U.	48.	University of the Pacific
23.	Temple U.	49.	University of Pittsburgh
24.	Tennessee State U.	50.	University of Rhode Island
25.	Texas A. & M. U.	51.	University of South Carolina
26.	Tulane U.	52.	University of South Dakota
27.	University of Alabama	53.	University of South Florida
28.	University of Arizona	54.	University of Southern Mississippi
29.	University of California, Berkeley	55.	University of Tennessee
30.	University of California, Santa Barbara	56.	University of Texas
		57.	University of Toledo
31.	University of Cincinnati	58.	University of Utah
32.	University of Colorado at Boulder	59.	University of Virginia
33.	University of Florida	60.	University of Washington
34.	University of Georgia	61.	University of Wisconsin at Madison
35.	University of Iowa	62.	University of Wisconsin at Milwaukee
36.	University of Kansas		
37.	University of Kentucky	63.	Utah State U.
38.	University of Maryland	64.	Virginia Polytechnic Inst. & State U.
39.	University of Massachusetts		
40.	University of Michigan	65.	Western Michigan U.
41.	University of Minnesota	66.	Yeshiva U.
42.	University of Missouri at Columbia		

tion with the hearing impaired.

In recent years professional degrees such as the Doctor of Psychology (Psy.D.) have emerged and made advanced training in non-traditional formats available to school psychologists. The Central Michigan University program, for example, stresses the interrelatedness of three areas of study: personal service, program development and evaluation, and administration-organization. The Psy.D. Program at Yeshiva University is tailored to the needs

---

[1]Responses are based on a survey of the 79 doctoral programs listed in the 1984 edition of the *Directory of School Psychology Programs*. In response to the survey mailed in March, 1984, 66 programs responded according to the survey request, 4 programs indicated they were not offering doctoral study specifically in school psychology, and 9 programs failed to respond. Responses are presented as reported with only minor attempts to combine areas, despite obvious similarities.

of already practicing school psychologists and offers part-time evening studies over a minimum of two years. Finally, some programs, such as New York University offers generalist orientation through all levels including the doctorate. As observed at the nondoctoral level, there is no substitute for the student obtaining first hand information from the program director.

A final note about specializations: Many program specializations are related to the faculty's expertise as much as to orientation of the administrative unit. Thus, specializations in particular programs often wax or wane as a function of faculty mobility and interests. For example, rural-urban specializations at the doctoral or nondoctoral levels are not always related to the geographic location of the program. Some students attend urban universities but obtain rural specialization as a function of selected courses, faculty expertise, and perhaps, most importantly, field experiences.

Non-Curricular Characteristics

There are many aspects of a program's overall quality that are not necessarily expressed in its curricular offerings. Gerner & Genshaft (1981) advise students to look for several factors when making program selections and even include some tips on interviewing. The APA and the NCATE/NASP Guidelines also specify many areas in addition to those for program content. Such aspects as the qualifications of the director and faculty, physical facilities, research interest, student production, admissions criteria, use of campus/community resources, and field supervision are very important. Since the accreditation of school psychology programs is based upon comprehensive review, the accrediting bodies' decisions provide an excellent source of information. The APA annually publishes a listing of accredited doctoral programs in the *American Psychologist*. NCATE publishes an *Annual*

List which includes its accredited programs in school psychology at the doctoral and nondoctoral levels. Listings of these programs may be obtained by writing to the following organizations:

> Accreditation Office
> American Psychological Assn.
> 1200 Seventeenth St., NW
> Washington, DC 20036
>
> NCATE
> 1919 Pennsylvania Ave.
> Suite 202
> Washington, DC 20006

Several states have a program approval process whereby the State Department of Education reviews school psychology programs either independently or concurrently with other reviews. For an indication of these states contact:

> National Association of State Consultants in School Psychology, c/o NASP, #10 Overland Dr., Stratford, CT 06497.

In other instances a program participates in regional accreditation activities. Names and addresses of the six regional accrediting bodies are available through the local or university library or from the listing in the June 16, 1980, *The Chronical of Higher Education* (*20*, No. 16, p. 8).

SUMMARY

Responses have been given to several commonly asked questions of prospective entry-level and advanced students in school psychology. The complex relationships of training, accreditation and credentialing were discussed in the context of program selection and the precautions needing to be taken. Example content of programs at both doctoral and nondoctoral levels as well as sources for additional information were presented. Accrediting agencies and program directors or staff are considered the most reliable sources of information about program content and organization. Opinions about future training directions and the employment situation for school psychologists are also presented. Upgrading of certification/licensure standards, gradual increases in the proportion of school psychologists holding doctoral degrees, increased specialization of practitioners, and a trend toward practice in non-school settings all suggest continued positive growth in school psychology and expanding employment opportunities in traditional and non-traditional settings.

REFERENCES/SUGGESTED READINGS

American Psychological Association. (1980). *Accreditation Criteria*, Washington, DC: APA.

American Psychological Association. (Published Annually) *Graduate Study in Psychology*. Washington, DC: APA.

Brown, D. T. & Lindstrom, J. P. (1977). *Directory of school psychology programs in the United States and Canada*. Washington, DC: NASP.

Brown, D. T. & Minke, K. M. (1984). *Directory of School Psychology Training Programs*. Washington, DC: NASP.

Brown, D. T., Horn, A. J. & Lindstrom, J. P. (1980). *The Handbook of certification/licensure requirements for school psychologists*. Washington, DC: NASP.

Fagan, T. K. & Hohenshil, T. (1976). The integration of career education into the training of school psychologists. *Psychology in the Schools, 13*, 334-340.

Farling, W. H. & Hoedt, K. C. (1971). *National Survey of school psychologists*. Washington, DC: NASP.

Gerner, M. & Genshaft, J. (1981). *Selecting a school psychology training program*. Washington, DC: NASP.

Goh, D. S. (1977). Graduate training in school psychology. *Journal of School Psychology, 15*, 207-218.

National Association of School Psychologists. *Standards for Training Programs in School Psychology* (revised edition includes Field Placement Standards). Washington, DC: NASP, in press.

National Council for the Accreditation of Teacher Education (NCATE). (1982). *Standards for the Accreditation of Teacher Education*. Washington, DC: NCATE.

Ramage, J. C. (1979). National Survey of school psychologists: Update. *School Psychology Review, 8*, 153-161.

BEST PRACTICES IN THE EVALUATION OF GIFTED CHILDREN

Ron Fischman
Montgomery County Intermediate Unit
Norristown, Pennsylvania

OVERVIEW

In the educational establishment, there is no diagnosis so fraught with political, emotional, economic, and educational issues as giftedness. This chapter relates these issues both to the characteristics of gifted students and to appropriate, varied techniques for their identification. Since there are individual differences in the gifted group, no one program meets all gifted children's needs. Therefore, *best practices* in identifying gifted students depend on both the types of gifted students and types of gifted programs.

Popular belief, literature, and lore have been unkind to those more intellectually capable than their peers. Perhaps a major cause of conflict with giftedness is its stereotype. On one hand, the "inferiority of superiority" (Sumption and Luecking, 1960) is stressed with comically pathetic intellects, pale and wan, who fall over their own feet. Such characters include the bespectacled child who writes poetry, wears a slide rule, and fears contact sports. Others are Mr. Peepers, Clark Kent, and assorted other four-eyed critters. On the darker side, are those gifted who frighten us by using their intellects to seduce, to control, and to destroy. Examples include Faust, Machiavelli, and Darth Vader.

A basic motive of research on giftedness in the late 19th and early 20th centuries was to challenge the stereotype of extreme giftedness as a precursor of insanity (Sumption and Luecking, 1960). Early findings of physical characteristics indicated that mentally gifted children were larger and healthier than average children (Hollingworth, 1972; Terman and Oden, 1947). Socially, the gifted child was a popular, outgoing, socially responsible leader who was less clique-ish than (his or her) average peers (Sumption, 1941; Terman and Oden, 1947; Lightfoot, 1957). More recently, Rimm and Davis (1977) and Duncan and Dreger (1978) independently found a constellation of personality traits of/for gifted and creative youngsters. Such children display greater verbal fluency, more sustained attention, quicker reaction time to questions, higher general energy levels, and more and varied play interests. Additional traits included greater self-confidence, independence, and risk-taking ability in competitive situations. While these findings were heavily biased by socioeconomic variables, they did cast serious doubt on earlier fears and stereotypes.

Although social characteristics distinguish the gifted child from (his/her) peers, they also stigmatize the child. Adults delight in the banter of gifted children who express themselves adroitly. Gifted children often display a canny sense for the interests of attentive adults. Yet, for a harried parent or teacher, a plethora of questions or arguments regardless of how sound or logical are much more grating than ingratiating. For average peers, the gifted's in-depth knowledge of a specific field or incomprehensible vocabulary is an irritation to which they respond physically or verbally. For the teacher or parent, the fluent, hard-hitting, verbal return to a question or comment is interpreted as flippancy.

Hollingworth (1942) described five major problems of very gifted children: (a) finding work challenging enough to maintain interest, (b) adjusting to less conceptually capable and less verbally proficient classmates, (c) choosing appropriately stimulating play, (d) conforming at various developmental levels to social situations, and (e) coping with one's social and familial origin and destiny. More recently, Ruth Strang (1956) reported that some gifted students struggle with feelings of inadequacy, inferiority, or dissatisfaction with relationships. For this reason alone, gifted programs are at times invaluable for bringing together children of similar concerns, vocabulary levels and senses of humor if not similar interests. With age-peers, gifted students must learn "to suffer fools gladly" (Hollingworth, 1942).

Gifted children often cope with inappropriate expectations and demands of adults and peers. Parents boast about their child's giftedness and rely upon that child for emotional support or social judgment. This demand gives the child much more power than he/she can handle and usually engenders stress in dealing with peers. Parents also demand unrealistically high expectations for success and consistency from their gifted children. Children exploit their gifted peers by egging them on to argue with teachers and cause intellectual mayhem in the classroom. In either exploitation, the question of peers and adults alike is, "How can a kid who was supposed to be so smart act so dumb?" This question accentuates the difference between intellectual ability and social and emotional development.

The old stereotype of frail and pale children engaged in abstruse issues still exists in the public. Among psychologists and educators, a newer although no less insidious stereotype has developed. It depicts the gifted child as so capable that he or she needs little educational help. Indeed, some professionals have stated that such children can get by on their own while others need the resources of the school much more. However, this very narrow view of the gifted child as merely an intellect completely ignores the much touted philosophy of educating the whole child.

Gifted children who are either socially immature or who are placed in untenable social situations are often highlighted as proof that they are not so smart after all. Moreover, if the gifted child does not fit the system, the system will find some far less desirable eligibility or placement.

The gifted most easily identified are those who fill the societal needs of a given time. Today, the ideal is the highly achieving, highly motivated student. In other times the model was the food gatherer, hunter, warrior, or philosopher. However, these gifted comprise only a small subgroup of the gifted population. Of great loss to us are gifted children who do not achieve academically because of emotional and social problems, cultural and language differences, or learning disabilities.

BASIC CONSIDERATIONS

Two major themes emerge in the literature on giftedness. The first is the need for multiple criteria in selecting gifted students while the second seeks a quicker and cheaper method of determining an I.Q. Both themes question the definition, nature of programming, and means for identifying giftedness.

Traditionally, definitions of giftedness stressed academic superiority. Therefore, it is not surprising that intelligence tests, the best predictors of academic success, were emphasized (Sumption and Luecking, 1960). Nevertheless, such definitions expected the gifted student to achieve in all areas and allowed for little inconsistency (Passow, 1975; Otey, 1981).

Recognizing the limitations of a narrowly defined, psychometrically based definition of giftedness, alternative multifaceted approaches were proposed. The definition in the 1972 report *Education of the Gifted and Talented*, by the Senate Subcommittee on Labor and Public Welfare represents most statements of multiple criteria in identifying giftedness.

Children capable of high performance include those with demonstrated achievement and/or potential ability in any of the following areas:

1. General intellectual ability
2. Specific academic aptitude
3. Creative or productive thinking
4. Leadership ability
5. Visual and performing arts ability
6. Psychomotor ability

Multi-faceted definitions of giftedness emphasized identification techniques that supplement basic scholastic achievement and aptitude assessment and the need for alternative assessment models. Gallagher (1975), Rubenzer (1979), and Otey (1981) stated that additional information such as teacher, parent or peer nomination and past achievement must be considered.

Dirks and Quarforth (1981) studied a depth versus breadth model of selecting gifted students. The former model chose students for superlative ability in one area while the latter selected students for lesser expertise in more areas. While results warrant further investigation, these different approaches selected different students who would benefit from different types of programs.

Delisle and Renzulli (1982) discuss a revolving door approach to gifted identification that stresses task commitment and product. This model assumes tht giftedness is topical, temporal, and behavioral. The model allows the inclusion of students for selected areas at selected times. For those with a greater breadth of interest, commitment or production, more inclusion is allowed. However, such a program is limited to the actual products of gifted students and may further entrench them in their own areas of interest. Thus, the lesson to be learned from viewing various models is that each model has its own

strengths, weaknesses, and application. Therefore, one model succeeds in a given situation but fails in another because of different needs, resources, and the types of gifted students served.

To develop an appropriate identification model for gifted in a specific situation, DeHaan and Havighurst (1965) proposed seven criteria.

1. The search for gifted is acceptable to all involved including *all* school personnel, parents and students.

2. The screening techniques must be appropriate for the situation and systematically applied.

3. Creative and personality factors are considered.

4. Non-cognitive factors such as social, physical, and emotional characteristics are also considered.

5. The evaluation process begins as early as possible in the child's scholastic career.

6. Screening for programming continues throughout the school year and through grade levels.

7. The identification process is flexible and includes culturally different, sensorally impaired, and handicapped youngsters.

The single most discussed issue in gifted identification is the intelligence quotient (IQ) (Gallagher, 1975). Grinter (1975) estimated that 95% of all children identified as gifted were classified by performance either on an intelligence or specific aptitude test. Yet, these instruments stress convergent thinking and have ceilings which are too low for some of the gifted population. IQ tests do not assess psychomotor skills or aesthetics, and there is a lack of interchangeability of IQ scores across tests due to differences in task demand, norming and statistics. On the Stanford-Binet Intelligence Scale (SB) especially, there is a lack of stability of IQ because different types of tasks are demanded at different age levels (Harrington, 1982). Since the SB appears easier for children younger than age 8, a majority of school psychologists prefer it to the age-appropriate Wechsler Scale for children below grade 2. (Sattler, 1974).

Another source of confusion is the norm differences between the revisions of the SB as well as between the Wechsler scales. The SB presents significant problems because the newer revision yields generally lower IQ scores (Fischman, et al., 1975; Sattler, 1974). Another issue is the precise effects of cultural and sex differences on test performance. For example, on the WISC-R, Karnes and Brown (1980) found that males perform significantly higher on Information, Similarities, Vocabulary, Comprehension, and Block Design while females do better on Coding. Also the degree to which the major IQ tests discriminate against certain ethnic or social groups is not understood.

Other techniques of assessing the IQ of gifted must be researched. There are few studies of the SOMPA and the McCarthy Scales. The recently introduced Kaufman Assessment Battery for Children whose underlying assumptions are so divergent from previous testing models must be carefully studied. Disturbingly, Alvino (1981) reports that psychometric techniques are often administered to groups for whom the instruments were not intended. Alvino also cautions against inappropriate generalizations or conclusions from limited test data.

A major drawback of the Stanford-Binet and the Wechsler Scale is the administration time, especially for high-achieving gifted children (Killian and Hughes, 1978). Yet, shorter IQ assessment techniques are usually preceeded with the caveat that such techniques are used only for screening and not for classification purposes (Dirks, et. al., 1981). When the behaviors sampled are reduced in number, test reliability is reduced and validity is questionable. Karnes and Brown (1979) found that

the Slosson Short Intelligence Test was not a good predictor of Stanford-Binet or Wechsler Scale IQs, especially at the extreme ends of the normal distribution. Rust and Lose (1980) found that the Slosson greatly overestimates the Stanford-Binet and Wechsler IQs. Hirst and Hirst (1980) used the Ammons Quick Test to predict Stanford-Binet and Wechsler IQs and found that the Ammons underestimated the cognitive abilities of gifted youngsters.

Since the purpose of short forms is screening, not classification, those who have been screened must be evaluated with longer, individual tests. To shorten this process, part of the longer test may be used as a screening tool. Karnes and Brown (1981) found that Similarities, Vocabulary, Block Design and Object Assembly are the most efficient predictors of the Wechsler Full Scale IQ. When the sum of Vocabulary and Block Design scaled scores is greater than 31, the error rate in predicting very superior functioning was approximately 3% (Elman, 1981). Using this technique, the screening and identification time is almost halved. Killian and Hughes (1978) report a correlation of .92 between the WISC-R Full Scale and the sum of Vocabulary and Block Design. Dirks and his associates (1981) question the use of Block Design now with the popularity of a very similar, commercial game, TRAC-4. These writers offer as an alternative set of pedictors the Similarities, Object Assembly, and Vocabulary subtests.

While most researchers agree that IQ is a good predictor of school success (Sattler, 1974), school success is not sufficient evididence of giftedness. Youngsters who function at or above the 98th percentile in achievement are not considered for gifted programming unless their IQs are commensurate with their achievement, a psychometric version of the tail wagging the puppy. This practice stresses the high-achieving, high-IQ students, and excludes the learning disabled, underachieving, and the culturally and linguistically different gifted. Schiff, Kaufman, and Kaufman (1981) found a distinct profile of WISC-R scores for gifted children with learning disabilities. These students' relative strengths lie in verbal comprehension and expressive skills, but they are relatively weak in sequencing and motor coordination tasks. They are more reactive to emotional situations and less organized than their non-learning disabled gifted peers and share behavioral tendencies with learning disabled students. Crompton (1982) cites peer influence, burnout, boredom, difficulty with family relations, and inappropriate curricula as causes of underachievement in the gifted. Of course, these are problems faced by most normal children, especially in adolescence. However, the youngster's giftedness may add to his emotional difficulties. Additional sources of underachievement are inappropriate identification of giftedness and poor instruction.

The Estes Attitude Scales are a good means to identify gifted students who underachieve in specific areas and/or general school-related tasks (Golicz, 1982). The Guidance Instrument For Talented Students (GIFTS) discriminated between achieving and underachieving gifted students at the secondary level (Perrone & Shen, 1982). On this instrument, underachieving gifted students earned lower scores on divergent thinking, goal orientation, task persistency, introspection, social awareness, and social effectiveness. Credence to this trend was added by Whitmore (1980).

A significant area of concern in the identification of gifted students is in the assessment of culturally different children. Torrence (1968) viewed the culturally different as a great, untapped reservoir of gifted. Gay (1978) describes Black gifted as keen observers with verbal proficiency and breadth of information, but

cautions that they may suffer from inferior schooling. Since most gifted programs focus on achievement and traditional IQ tests are derived from achievement-oriented tasks, Black gifted students are often overlooked. Chen and Goon (1978) found a higher percentage of gifted Asians compared to white populations. Gifted Asians had better peer relations and were more diligent than non-Asian gifted students. However, these children often came from homes of lower socio-economic status and had parents who did not speak English and had difficulty in communicating with school personnel.

In evaluating Black and Hispanic American children for gifted programs, language limitations and cultural differences are considered. Unfortunately, the psychometric adaptations suggested are not satisfactory. For example, La Escalla de Intelligencia Wechsler para Ninos (Wechsler, 1967) is a translation of the older Wechsler for Puerto Rican children. It asks for responses in inches and pounds, concepts foreign to most Central and South American children and even includes the "Cash or Collect upon Delivery" item in English. (Wechsler, 1967).

Gay's (1978) recommendation that the Structure of the Intellect Learning Abilities Test (SOI) (Meeker, 1975) be used for minority gifted children is also not satisfactory. Thompson and his associates (1978) found that subtests of the SOI such as arithmetic contain achievement tasks and several SOI scores that relate to performance on the Iowa Tests of Basic Skills. Performance on the SOI does, however, correspond to teachers' perceptions of students of various ethnic groups after an interaction lasting at least eight months (Cunningham et al., 1978). In conclusion, we have no acceptable psychometric means to identify giftedness in culturally different children.

In reaction to the difficulties of the psychometric strategies, alternatives were attempted or in some cases reintroduced. Alvino (1981) catalogued approximately 120 different techniques including various behavioral checklists, biographical inventories, and objective rating scales used in the U.S. to identify gifted children. Fears of subjectivity led to the exclusion of these techniques, but researchers have shown that behavioral rating systems have predictive value. Gear (1978) reviewed rating strategies and reported that early criticisms were "arbitrary" or "crude." After a training program, teacher accuracy in selecting gifted students by rating increases greatly even though teacher attitudes toward disadvantaged youngsters did not change significantly (Gear, 1978). Rust and Lose (1980) found that the Renzulli, Hartman and Calahan Scale was not a good predictor of WISC-R IQ. Passow (1975) reported that parent observations were usually realistic estimates of children's ability, especially when such information concerned specific aspects of the child's interactions within the home and neighborhood. Thus, teacher, parent and peer observation techniques are useful in identifying gifted youngsters who would be overlooked by traditional psychometric instruments.

BEST PRACTICES

Unfortunately the identification of gifted children has become synonymous with testing children or, even worse, in giving IQ tests to children. In the evaluating of gifted, the prejudices alight. There are so many children who *really* need help. We need a quicker way to *test* the gifted so that we have time for those children who really need us, that is, the children who are troubling their teachers, principals, and guidance counselors with disruptive, noncompliant, and oppositional behaviors. Unprejudiced practitioners who understand the characteris-

tics of gifted children must wonder how many of these disruptive students are gifted as well as naughty.

It should be quite apparent that before even attempting to lay test on child, the psychological practitioner in the school has several important questions to ask.

1. What is the nature of gifted programs in our school district?
2. Are programs at different educational levels articulated or disjoint?
3. What are the attitudes of teachers, administrators, special subject teachers, and parents toward gifted programming?
4. How do students feel about their gifted peers?
5. What are the community's political attitudes toward gifted programming?
6. Who should participate in the evaluation process?

Only after attempting to answer these questions realistically and honestly can strategies for the evaluation of gifted children be developed. Unfortunately, gifted programs are frequently ill-defined hodgepodges of enrichment activities which relate tangentially to classroom skills or any philosophical rationale. Many programs shift emphasis drastically from teacher to teacher or from level to level. When asked why she was teaching a unit on Spain to 4th grade gifted students, one teacher replied, "Because I was just there last summer."

Research has repeatedly demonstrated that teachers often have narrow, stereotypic prejudices of what gifted children are really like. Gifted children are at times regarded as receiving more than others rather than programming which is different and necessary. Upon returning to the regular classroom from a gifted, enrichment program, one young man enthusiastically raised his hand to share something, and the teacher responded, "You've already had your good time for today." Would this same response have been made to a child returning from speech therapy, a resource room for the emotionally disturbed, or an emergency marching band practice?

Real estate in both urban and suburban areas is often advertised in terms of local schools and program availability. Some upper middle class communities comprised of very achievement oriented, often gifted, managerial or professional parents who have a high need to achieve have a disproportionately high number of gifted children. These communities in particular may for political or financial reasons attempt to limit or underplay the nature of the gifted program. Unfortunately, many of the gifted children of such parents are overindulged due to parental guilt at working long hours or are overpressed to achieve. In either case, giftedness may manifest itself with the child's being emotionally disturbed or emotionally disturbing.

The diagnosis of mental giftedness should be a multidisciplinary team effort in accordance with Public Law 94-142 to include the students teacher, parents, unified arts teacher, the psychologist, a special educator and, when appropriate, the child as well. Using characteristics discussed previously, behavior checklists regarding attitudes, interests, and favorite activities are relatively easy to construct in a Likert response format. School districts enjoying greater supportive services in terms of statistical research specialists may wish to construct a decision matrix as suggested by Feldheusen and his associates (1981). Having all members of the team including the children and their peers complete the same or similar checklists provides valuable insight for the multidisciplinary team. The psychological practitioner must, however, be aware of his or her own prejudices regarding gifted children as well as prejudices and levels of understanding of other team members. Interestingly, members of such

teams in which this author has participated will often note that their own children are not in gifted programs. However, this author has never heard members of such teams make similar remarks about programs for mentally retarded or emotionally disturbed. At times, educating, guiding and counselling for team members may be as necessary as such activities for parents and children themselves.

To be complete, the evaluation process should include the following information:

1. A detailed reason for referral indicating reasons why the parents or classroom teacher or peers feel that the student to be evaluated needs special education.

2. A parental intake interview with developmental and medical history including the child's present medical conditions, reactions to stress, special interests as well as peer and authority relationships.

3. An educational history and present level of functioning including strengths and weaknesses, peer and authority figure relationships, special interests actively and persistently pursued and the specific nature of behavioral problems or infringement of school rules when applicable.

4. A review of club and extracurricular activities to determine excellence in areas other than academics.

5. A review of books borrowed in the school library which may reveal that an otherwise nondescript student could well be an Asimov authority, Dickens expert, or budding chess champion.

6. A psychological evaluation.

The Psychological Evaluation

The psychological evaluation for gifted children should be consistent with good psychological evaluation practices for any child referred. Presumably, the initial reason for referral is to determine an appropriate placement to meet the individual needs of the student for whom the general curriculum may not be in itself appropriate. The purpose of such an evaluation must be to gather information in a systematic manner to assist in a decision about placement, curricular modifications if appropriate, and special services within school and outside of school when necessary. The components of such an evaluation should include the following:

Background Information

Background information should be gathered carefully by a mental health professional to help that person understand the youngster's developmental history, medical history, and social and emotional development. Parental concerns, philosophy of rearing practices, and stress upon the family unit or individual members of the unit must be determined. Also differences in parents' rearing practices and the potential for the youngster's manipulating the parents should be sought. The psychologist or social worker gathering this information should attempt to determine the degree to which the parents may use a diagnosis of giftedness or the lack of such a diagnosis to foster unrealistic expectations.

Clinical Interview

Unfortunately, the interaction between psychologist and child is inappropriately summarized as "testing." As important as any score derived, perhaps much more important, is the informally gathered information that results from the clinical interview and from the psychologist's informal observations of the

youngster's responses to assessment kinds of tasks. For example, in the block counting task of the Stanford-Binet, one child may put each of six blocks in a designated space with thumb and forefinger in apposition, while another youngster may grasp two groups of three blocks. The level of vocabulary must also be considered. For example, one 6 year old youngster may respond to the question, "What is an orange?" with the statement, "Something round that's good to eat" while another youngster may respond with the statement, "A citrus fruit." While there are no scoring differences between the two responses, there are, certainly, qualitative differences of note.

In addition to the observations of language levels, the psychologist must assess the youngster's sense of humor, the degree to which he responds to subtleties, and of special note with some gifted children, the use of unusual verb tenses such as the future anterior tense. During the clinical interview, much information can also be sought about the youngster's motives, aspirations, fears, and concerns as well as his perception of himself with regard to authority figures and peers both at home and in school.

Psychometric Assessment

The intellectual assessment technique used to evaluate gifted youngsters should be one of the major, recognized techniques. While the Wechsler Intelligence Scale for Children-Revised Edition and the Stanford Binet (1972 Revision) both have objectionable qualities, they seem to be at the present time the two most widely used and most predictive of school success. Short forms are not particularly fruitful in predicting Full Scale IQ. If short forms or shorter intelligence tests are used, they should be used with extreme caution and only for screening purposes. Of interest in the near future will be studies indicating correlation between performance on various aspects of the Kaufman Assessment Battery for Children and achievement among various ethnic groups, age groups, and the two sex groups.

In addition to intellectual assessment, achievement should also be assessed. It is frequently taken for granted that gifted children will be high achievers. Oftentimes, this is not the case, especially with underachieving gifted and culturally different gifted. Even with high achieving gifted youngsters, it may well be that the youngster has specific problems in math and reading. Therefore, assessment techniques geared to the specific curriculum that the youngster is using in his school program would be valuable. An informal reading inventory based upon the reading series in the school program would provide very useful information along with a math assessment technique such as the Key Math Diagnostic Arithmetic Test.

The complete intellectual assessment usually includes a technique to consider eye/hand coordination and psychomotor performance. Assessment techniques such as the Beery-Buktenica Developmental Test of Visual/Motor Integration and the Bender-Gestalt are most frequently used and may well give some interesting information with regard to planning, organization, and general psychomotor skills. The interested reader should consider further research into the value of such information and its relative clinical importance as a technique which may be used at the beginning of an assessment to allay anxiety.

Emotional Assessment

In addition to the clinical interview which is quite valuable in gaining an insight into the youngster's perception of himself with regard to his parents, his siblings, and his peers both at home and in school, projective assessment techniques should be considered. The House-Tree-Person, the Sentence Completion technique, and various projective story techniques are valuable. With gifted youngsters, rich stories are provided in response to the stimulus pictures of the Children's Apperception Test, the Thematic Apperception Test, and other similar techniques such as the Scholastic Apperception technique. Youngsters' responses to the Rorschach tend to be very complete with many responses per card, and usually, gifted youngsters provide more whole responses at an earlier age than do their non-gifted peers. Occasionally, gifted youngsters may use the emotional assessment as a means of testing limits or of manipulating the psychologist. For example, several gifted youngsters evaluated by this author have attempted to speed up or slow down the telling of their stories to vary the writing rate of the examining psychologist. At times, a note of passive/aggressive glee was detected or projected by youngsters who questioned, "Am I going too fast for you." With regard to emotional assessment, it is not unusual to find that intellectually mature youngsters capable of dealing with a concept at a verbal, cognitive level, may be emotionally unable to accept that concept or deal with it appropriately. Thus, the examining psychologist must be very careful not to expect the gifted youngster to be equally mature in all areas of functioning.

A complete evaluation is necessary not only to determine whether or not a youngster may qualify for a program for gifted youngsters but to determine what kind of programming may be specifically appropriate for a given child. It may well be that a youngster would benefit from resources apart from the usual program for gifted children as provided by a school district. While some youngsters may require a program to give them more information, others may require programming to help them analyze and synthesize the kinds of information which they are capable of understanding on their own. Social skills such as taking appropriate intellectual risks, sharing, and developing receptivity to others' ideas of solutions to a given problem are indeed appropriate goals for gifted programming. In addition to information with regard to placement and program needs, it may well be that a gifted student requires professional help outside of the educational establishment in dealing with problems that he may have in terms of other children his own age in the neighborhood, in dealing with his perceptions of his parents' expectations of him or in dealing with guilt and concern about his or her being the only child among his siblings to have been designated as gifted. Parents may require supportive counselling to help them set appropriate expectations for their gifted children as well as to deal appropriately with their gifted and non-gifted children. Using their offspring to fulfill their own needs, parents can often make inappropriate demands upon their children which must be considered and restructured in an ongoing therapy situation.

SUMMARY

The diagnosis of gifted children is sometimes influenced by inappropriate stereotyping and the prejudiced notion that gifted children are always high-achieving and socially conforming. Such stereotyping often dictates a narrow psychometric approach in identifying gifted youngsters, a practice that would not be professionally tolerated in the diagnosis of socially and emotionally disturbed or learning disabled youngsters, or youngsters of any other exceptionality for that matter.

An equally disturbing stereotype is that educators understand how to educate gifted children. This notion can be refuted with the simplistic concept of, "a gifted program," a notion that denies the wide diversity of skills, abilities, and personality characteristics within the group that is designated as gifted. Indeed, research repeatedly demonstrates that unless well-trained specifically with issues concerning the gifted, most teachers rely upon popular stereotyping in identifying gifted youngsters.

After considering the inappropriate stereotypes, the least desirable practice in diagnosing gifted is to give them an IQ test. The psychological practitioner should determine the types of programming available, the problems that each individual may have, the strengths of each individual, and the general attitude of the school faculty and community toward gifted youngsters. Only then can the seasoned psychologist select or develop the means to assess intellectual, social, emotional, and academic assets of the student who may be gifted. In practice, the philosophy of identifying gifted students is no different from the philosophy of identifying any other exceptional child.

REFERENCES

Alvino, J., McDonnell, R. C., & Richert, S. (1981) National survey of identification practices in gifted and talented. *Exceptional Children, 48*, 124-132.

Chen, J. & Goon, S. W. (1976) Recognition of the gifted from among disadvantaged Asian children. *Gifted Child Quarterly, 20*, 157-165.

Crompton, M. F. (1982) The gifted underachiever in the middle school. *Roeper Review, 4*, 23-25.

Cunningham, C. H., Thompson, B., & Alston, B. (1978) Use of S.O.I. abilities for prediction. *Gifted Child Quarterly, 22*, 507-513.

DeHaan, R., & Havighurst, R. J. (1965) *Educating Gifted Children.* Chicago: University of Chicago Press.

Delisle, J. R., & Renzulli, J. J. (1982) The revolving door identification and programming model: Correlates of creative production. *Gifted Child Quarterly, 26,* 85-89.

Dirks, J. A., & Quarforth, J. (1981) Selecting children for the gifted classes: Choosing for depth. *Psychology in the Schools, 18,* 437-449.

Duncan, J. A., & Dreger, R. M. (1978) Behavioral analyses and identification of gifted children: Children's Behavioral Classification Project Instrument. *Journal of Genetic Psychology, 133,* 43-57.

Elman, L., Blext, S., & Sawicki, R. (1981) The development of cut off scores on a WISC-R in the multidimensional assessment of gifted children. *Psychology in the Schools, 18,* 426-428.

Feldhusen, J. F., Baska, L. K., & Womble, S. (1981) Using standard scores to synthesize data in identifying the gifted. *Journal for the Education of the Gifted, 4,* 177-186.

Feldhusen, J. F., & Kolloff, M. B. (1981) Me: A self concept scale for gifted students. *Perceptual and Motor Skills, 53,* 319-323.

Feldman, D. (1979) Toward a non elitist conception of giftedness. *Phi Delta Kappan, 60,* 660-663.

Fischman, R., Proger, B., & Duffey, J. B. (1976) The Stanford-Binet revisited: A comparison of the 1960 and 1972 revisions of the Stanford-Binet Intelligence Scale. *Journal of Special Education, 10,* 83-90.

Gallagher, J. J. (1975) *The Teaching of the Gifted Child.* Boston: Allyn and Bacon.

Gay, J. E. (1978) A proposed plan for identifying black gifted children. *Gifted Child Quarterly, 22,* 353-360.

Gear, G. H. (1976) Accuracy of teacher judgement in the identification of gifted children: A review of the literature. *Gifted Child Quarterly, 20,* 478-490.

Karnes, F. A., & Brown, E. (1980) Factor analysis of the WISC-R for the gifted. *Journal of Educational Psychology, 72,* 197-199 (a).

Karnes, F. A., & Brown, E. (1980) Sex differences in the WISC-R scores of gifted students. *Psychology in the Schools, 17,* 361-363 (b).

Karnes, F. A., & Brown, E. (1981) A short form of the WISC-R for gifted students. *Psychology in the Schools, 18,* 169-173.

Killian, J. B., & Hughes, L. C. (1978) Comparison of short forms of the Wechsler Intelligence Scales for Children — Revised in the screening of gifted children. *Gifted Child Quarterly, 22,* 111-115.

Landig, H. J., & Nauman, T. F. (1978) Aspects of intelligence in gifted preschoolers. *Gifted Child Quarterly, 22,* 85-89.

Lightfoot, G. F. (1951) *Personality Characteristics of Bright and Dull Children* (Contributions to Education, No. 969). New York: Bureau of Public, Teachers College, Columbia University.

Maddux, C. D., Schreiber, L. M., & Bass, J. E. (1982) Self-concept and social distance in gifted children. *Gifted Child Quarterly, 26,* 77-81.

Meeker, M., Mestyanne, L., & Meeker, R. (1975) *S.O.I. Learning Abilities Test: Examiner's Manual.* El Segundo, CA: S.O.I. Institute.

Gear, G. H. (1978) Effects of training on teachers' accuracy in the identification of gifted children. *Gifted Child Quarterly, 22,* 90-97.

Golicz, H. (1982) Use of the Estes Attitude Scales with the gifted underachiever. *Roeper Review, 4,* 22-23

Grenter, R. (1979) Identification Processes. Paper presented to Wisconsin Council for Gifted and Talented, February, 1975. In Rubenzer, R. Identification and evaluation procedures for gifted and talented programs. *Gifted Child Quarterly, 23,* 304-316.

Harrington, R. G. (1982) Caution: Standardized testing may be hazardous to the educational programs of intellectually gifted children. *Journal of Education, 103,* 112-117.

Hirsch, F. J., & Hirsch, S. J. (1980) Quick Test as a screening device for gifted students. *Psychology in the Schools, 17,* 37-39.

Hollingworth, L. S. (1926) *Gifted Children: Their Nature and Nurture.* New York: The MacMillan Company.

Hollingworth, L. S. (1942) *Children Above 180 IQ.* New York: World Book.

Karnes, F. A., & Brown, E. (1979) Comparison of the SIT with the WISC-R for gifted students. *Psychology in the Schools, 16,* 478-482.

Milgram, R. M. (1979) Perception of teacher behavior in gifted and nongifted children. *Journal of Educational Psychology, 71,* 125-128.

Milgram, R. M., & Milgram, N. A. (1976) Group vs. individual administration in the measurement of creative thinking in the gifted and nongifted. *Child Development, 47,* 563-565.

Otey, J. W. (1978) Identification of gifted students. *Psychology in the Schools, 15,* 16-21.

Passaw, A. H. (1975) The gifted and the disadvantaged. In Barbe, W. O., & Renzulli, J. (Eds.), *Psychology and Education of the Gifted.* New York: Halstead Press.

Passaw, A. H. (Ed.). (1979) *The Gifted and Talented: Their Education and Development.* The yearbook committee and associated editors, NSSE. Chicago: University of Chicago Press.

Perrone, P., & Chen, F. (1982) Toward the development of an identification instrument for the gifted. *Roeper Review, 5,* 45-48.

Pfeffer, J. S., Fischman, R., Proger, B. B., Weintraub, M., Schwartz, L. L., & Bernoff, R. (1982) *Final Technical Report: Project PATS: Potentially Academically Talented Students.* Norristown, PA: Montgomery County Intermediate Unit 23.

Rimm, S., & Davis, G. A. (1977) Characteristics of creatively gifted children. *Gifted Child Quarterly, 21,* 546-551.

Rimm, S., & Culbertson, F. (1980) Validation of gifted on instrument for the identification of creativity. *Journal of Creative Behavior, 14,* 272-273.

Rubenzer, R. (1979) Identification and evaluation procedures for gifted and talented programs. *Gifted Child Quarterly, 23,* 304-316.

Rust, J. O., & Lose, B. D. (1980) Screening for giftedness with the Slossen and the Scale for Rating Behavioral Characteristics of Superior Students. *Psychology in the Schools, 17,* 446-451.

Sattler, J. M. (1974) *Assessment of Children's Intelligence.* Philadelphia: W. B. Saunders, Co.

Schiff, M. M. (1981) Scatter analysis of WISC-R profiles for LD children with superior intelligence. Part I: Studies with new or unusual LD populations. *Journal of Learning Disabilities, 14,* 400-404.

Solly, D. C. (1977) Comparison of WISC and WISC-R scores of MR and gifted children. *Journal of School Psychology, 15,* 255-258.

Sternberg, R. J. (1982) Nonentrenchment in the assessment of intellectual giftedness. *Gifted Child Quarterly, 26,* 63-67.

Strang, R. (1965) The psychology of gifted children. In Barbe, W. (Ed.), *Psychology and Education of the Gifted.* New York: Appleton-Century-Crofts.

Sumption, M. H. (1941) *Three Hundred Gifted Children.* Yonkers, NY: World Book, Co.

Sumption, M. H., & Luecking, E. M. (1960) *Education of the Gifted.* New York: The Ronald Press.

Terman, L. M. & Oden, M. H. (1947) *The Genetic Studies of Genius. Vol. 4: The Gifted Child Grows Up.* Stanford, CA: Stanford University Press.

Thompson, B., Alston, H. L., Cunningham, C. H., & Wakefield, J. A. (1978) The relationship of a measure of structure of intellect abilities and academic achievement. *Educational and Psychological Measurement, 38,* 1207-1210.

Torrence, E. P. (1975) Assessing children, teachers and parents against the ideal child criterion. *Gifted Child Quarterly, 19,* 130-139.

Treffinger, D. J. (1980) Progress and peril of identifying creative talent among gifted and talented students. *Journal of Creative Behavior, 14,* 20-33.

Wechsler, D. (1967) *Escala de Intelligencia Wechsler para Ninos.* New York: The Psychological Corporation.

Wechsler, D. (1982) *Escala de Intelligencia Wechsler para Ninos — Revisada,* Research Edition. New York: The Psychological Corporation.

Wells, M. A., Peltier, S., & Glickauf, H. C. (1982) Analysis of sex role orientation of gifted male and female adolescents. *Roeper Review,* 46-48.

ANNOTATED BIBLIOGRAPHY

Gallagher, J. J. (1975) *The Teaching of the Gifted Child.* Boston: Allyn and Bacon.
Gallagher deals with basic educational problems of the gifted in a comprehensive, informative and interesting style. Reading this book only to understand the Palcuzzi Ploy is reason enough to consider this text as essential resource.

Renzulli, Joseph S. (1977) *The Enrichment Triad Model: A Guide for Developing Defensible Programs for Gifted and Talented.* Wethersfield, CT: Creative Learning Press
The key word of this short readable book is "defensible." The model is essentially behavioral. It is based on the idea of "gifted is as gifted keeps on performing."

Salvia, John and Ysseldyke, J. F. (1981) *Assessment in Special and Remedial Education,* Second Edition. Boston: Houghton-Mifflin Company.
This text provides a great review and resource reference for the practicing school psychologist. Of special interest are the authors' clear descriptions of test norms and norm-referenced statistics for making appropriate psychometric decisions.

Terman, L. M. and Merrill, M. A. *The Stanford-Binet Intelligence Scale,* 1972 Norms Edition.
Many practicing psychologists have not read the technical data of the instrument which they frequently use.

Wechsler, D. *Manual for the Wechsler Intelligence Scale for Children-Revised.* New York, NY, 1974: The Psychological Corporation.
There are, unfortunately, several misconstructions and misconceptions with regard to the Revised Form of the Wechsler. There have been changes in materials and questions between the WISC and the revised version of it. Of particular concern is the use of this instrument with youngsters younger than eight and older than fourteen years of age, and a review of the scaled score tables at various age levels is important to understand the relationships between raw score points and scaled scores, and therefore, Intelligence Quotients.

BEST PRACTICES IN ACADEMIC ASSESSMENT

Kathryn Clark Gerken
The University of Texas at Dallas

OVERVIEW

Psychologists have always been expected to assess children in order to identify the reasons for academic problems. Tindall (1979) reported that the first clients who appeared in 1896 at Lightner Witmer's psychological clinic were an adolescent with a reading problem and another adolescent with a spelling problem.

Whether one reads Gray's (1963) historical account of the development of school psychology or one of the more recent narratives (Tindall, 1979; Bardon, 1982), it is clear that school psychology is bound to the development of the testing movement and special education in the United States. During the latter part of the nineteenth century and the early part of the twentieth century, as psychology developed in America, so did testing, special education and mental health services. The early descriptions of school psychologists identified them as psychologists focusing on psychometric or clinical concerns. But it is also interesting to note that in a 1942 issue of the *Journal of Consulting Psychology*, broader types of functioning were described for the school psychologist than were present for many school psychologists in the 1970's.

BASIC CONSIDERATIONS

Ysseldyke and Mirkin (1982) state that the current efforts to use assessment data for the purpose of planning instructional interventions have their roots in the early research on individual differences. One can ignore the historical ties that appear to bind school psychology to special education and testing. However, the school psychologists of the 1980's cannot afford to disregard the present ethical and legal demands of the profession. The literature is replete with surveys conducted in the 1970's which indicate that neither psychologists nor other school personnel are pleased with the state of the art in psychological services. Nearly all the results of these studies indicate that school psychologists spend most of their time conducting psychoeducational studies. The data are inconsistent with regard to what psychologists, administrators, and teachers believe to be ideal roles for school psychologists. (See reviews: Ford & Migles, 1979; Gutkin, Singer & Brown, 1980; Hughes, 1981; Kahl & Fine, 1981; Landau & Gerken, 1979; Senf & Snider, 1980).

During the latter part of the 1970's, the consultative and facilitative role of the psychologist was emphasized because the consumer seemed to be asking for it and the psychologists desired change. In response to the public and professional hue and cry against testing, some psychologists simply "got out of the kitchen." Misuse of tests was rampant, but too many psychologists failed to assume responsibility for what was taking place. They simply wanted to assume a new role, preferably one in which they would not be scrutinized too closely. The fewer direct services they provided, the less responsibility they would have to assume for failures. Concern with appropriate assessment is not new, but has received more attention during the last decade. In 1966, Anastasi addressed the American Psychological Association about the responsibilities of psychologists in insuring the appropriate use of psychological tests. Her suggestions have been carried out by some but were never read or were ignored by many others. Responsible psychologists asked why the general public was opposed to testing and why the consumers of psychological services were specifically requesting a change in testing practices. It takes no more than a quick glance at traditional practices to understand why there was a desire for change. A common practice by school psychologists and other psychologists in the 1960's and 1970's (and still in existence throughout the United States) was to respond to any referral by administering a standard battery of tests under the assumption that the problem existed within the student.

The impetus for change was brought about by many factors. Yesseldyke (1979) reported the following as especially compelling:

1. Increased disillusionment on the part of classroom teachers with the kinds and quality of assessment.

2. Increased emphasis on the rights of children.

3. Mandated nondiscriminatory assessment.

4. Increased activity in mainstreaming handicapped children.

5. Increased movement toward individualization of instruction for increasing numbers of children.

6. Due process. (Ysseldyke, 1979, 106-107).

During the 1970's leverage, litigation and legislation mandated what ethical standards have always proposed — appropriate assessment. The courts no longer allow the schools and school personnel to plead ignorance as an excuse for negligence. The psychologist has a responsibility beyond testing. If he/she cannot perform assessment that complies with the standards set forth in law and the ethical standards of the profession, then arrangements should be made for someone else to do it.

Ysseldyke (1979) points out that one of the primary problems in the assessment of handicapped children has been the failure of assessors to differentiate strategies and tools relative to the kinds of decisions to be made. He suggests that evaluators need further or different training to insure that they (a) engage in and facilitate differential assessment, (b) view tests as samples of behavior and make appropriate selections based on what behaviors need to be sampled, (c) use technically adequate assessment devices, (d) make a valid assessment-intervention link, (e) use behavioral assessment, and (f) are skilled examiners.

Some psychologists have never had the training and expertise to perform adequate assessment; some have never understood that assessment goes beyond testing; some psychologists freely relinquished the role of assessor to those even less qualified to perform adequate assessment. Gresham (1983) summarizes the major problems with psychoeducational assessment as (a) obtaining insufficient assessment information, (b) using technically inadequate tests, and (c) using measures that yield inappropriate or educationally irrelevant information. He advocates using more than one method to assess the same student trait to obtain more valid and relevant information. What he says has been said before in different ways, but psychologists failed to apply this knowledge. Currently there are school psychologists, educational diagnosticians, counselors and other school personnel who assess children in the schools and make decisions regarding these children from inadequate and often inaccurate information. It is certainly time for school psychologists to ask what steps they can take to provide assessment leading to positive changes for students. It has been far too easy for school psychologists to blame inadequate assessment on the instruments themselves or on outside agents or agencies that govern school psychological services. School psychologists need to cease their search for the "ideal" test instrument that is technically adequate, comprehensive, precise, economical and useful. There are few if any instruments that fit that description, especially in the area of academic skills. The most important change in academic assessment is that concerned professionals are forced to restructure the assessment process.

A major goal of assessment is the acquisition of relevant information that contributes to the decision-making process. Assessment is a purposeful process that does not terminate after attaching labels. It leads to the clarification of the presenting problem and those factors which influence it, assists in making decisions concerning the types of intervention needed, and provides a means to evaluate the effects of intervention.

Ysseldyke and Mirkin (1982) point out that while there have been many critiques of assessment and decision-making practices, until recently there were limited data describing such practices. They report that Arter and Jenkins found the widespread practice of designing interventions based on modality preferences, even though little data to support such practice existed. Ysseldyke and Mirkin (1982) also reported that survey and computer-simulated investigations of assessment and decision-making practices reveal that (a) considerable assessment data are collected, (b) often there is no differentiation of data collection for different purposes, (c) measures of processes and abilities are used, (d) the majority of tests are technically inadequate, (e) the decision-making process is highly varied, (f) predictions of academic success are biased by referral data, and (g) assessment decisions are systematically biased as a function of students naturally occurring characteristics.

Academic Referrals

Although current referral figures are not available, it is unlikely that there will be a decrease of academic referrals during the next decade. P.L. 94-142 brought with it an increase in psychoeducational assessments. School personnel and parents sought services for students whom they never thought were eligible before. Declining scores on standardized tests, the "back to basics" movement, and minimum competency testing have resulted in increased psychoeducational studies to find out why many students appear unable to do satisfactory academic work. Often, it was hoped that, through testing, the psychologist would conclude that the reasons for low scores and failure were due to difficulties within the student rather than problems with the teachers, curriculum or school.

It is the responsibility of the person who conducts or directs academic assessment to insure that there is differentiated assessment based on (a) factors within the student such as overall ability and motivation, (b) factors in the student's instructional environment such as the curriculum and teaching methods and materials, (c) factors in the student's physical environment, and (d) factors in the student's interpersonal environment such as teacher-student interactions.

Preservice/Inservice Considerations

The psychologists who are able to meet the needs of the consumers of the 1980's (teachers, parents, and most of all, students) are those who have knowledge of basic measurement theory, learning theory, child/adolescent psychology, and the theories underlying basic skill development in reading, writing, spelling, and arithmetic. These psychologists also need to apply their knowledge in all of the above areas. For example, relative to their knowledge of measurement theory, they are able to analyze the strengths and weaknesses of the available assessment techniques and to match assessment techniques with the purpose for assessment.

If they wish to affect positive changes for students, the psychologists who participate in the academic assessment process must have different and/or additional skills beyond those now exhibited. They must recognize that performing worthwhile academic assessment may not be something everyone can or need do as long as there are enough skilled psychologists who can use their technical expertise and practical skills to assist classroom teachers in designing appropriate educational programs for children. Psychologists not only have a part to play, but also a responsibility to insure that academic assessment is done appropriately. Whether they provide indirect service to the student who has academic problems or direct service, the psychologists need the above knowledge and skills in order to provide the best possible services.

Figure 1

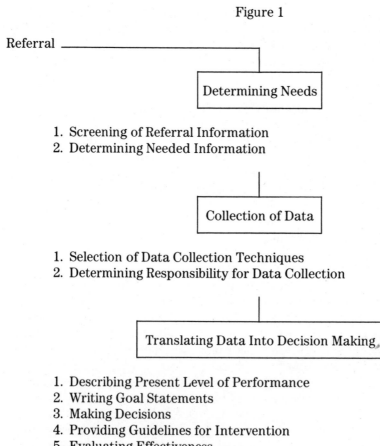

Referral

Determining Needs

1. Screening of Referral Information
2. Determining Needed Information

Collection of Data

1. Selection of Data Collection Techniques
2. Determining Responsibility for Data Collection

Translating Data Into Decision Making

1. Describing Present Level of Performance
2. Writing Goal Statements
3. Making Decisions
4. Providing Guidelines for Intervention
5. Evaluating Effectiveness

BEST PRACTICES

Effective psychological services depend upon an adequate needs assessment and a continuous assessment process. Psychologists must ask what decisions are being made, what information is needed to make those decisions, and where the information can be obtained. The rest of this chapter provides school psychologists with guidelines for determining strengths and weaknesses, establishing goals, and prescribing interventions for students with academic difficulties. Mash and Terdal (1974) state that it is the way assessment information is used that gives significance to this process. Academic assessment should not be performed unless it is useful in forming decisions of benefit to the child having academic difficulties.

The Assessment Process

Analysis of Referral

Figure 1 is an assessment model adapted from materials developed in 1978 at the Midwest Regional Resource Center (Holmes & Ford).

It is apparent that a thorough analysis of the referral or statement of the problem must take place before the collection or use of data. It is during this analysis that parents or guardians become involved in the assessment process. They also play an integral part in the collection and translation of data. The following questions are asked when determining needs:

1. Is there concern regarding academic skills?

2. Does the referral include descriptive samples of behavior?

3. What is known about school-related variables? (a) Does the student have sufficient general cognitive ability to perform the academic tasks? (b) What is the student's broad level of ability academically? What are specific strengths and weaknesses in academic areas? (c) Are there behavioral factors interfering with academic learning? (d) Are there factors within the school environment that affect the academic learning?

4. What is known about non-school related variables? (a) What is the student's general health? Are health factors including visual and hearing acuity within normal limits? (b) What is the student's rate of growth and motor development? Are these factors within normal limits? (c) Are there factors within the home environment that affect the academic learning?

5. What, if any, intervention efforts have been attempted?

Determination of Academic Expectations

If the referral analysis indicates some concern regarding academic skills, the school psychologist attempts to find out everything that is already known regarding the student's abilities before planning assessment. Are there examples of the student's written work, prior test results, other types of evaluations? What roles do others take in the student's academic learning? Decisions must be made about the additional data needed, how the data will be collected, and by whom.

In order to know what to assess, the psychologist must first understand the goals for this student in the academic areas. The psychologist finds out what textbooks are used in the school/classroom and obtains the scope and sequence charts, lists of objectives or whatever else is used in the school/classroom. The compilation of these charts and objectives may seem time consuming and inappropriate to the school psychologist. However, if the psychologist wishes to determine where a particular breakdown might be occurring, then he/she must understand what has already been introduced to the student, which skills are appropriate for the student's grade placement, the requirements of the academic tasks the student has failed, the instructional programs available to the student and the student's desire to perform the academic tasks.

The psychologist should make a notebook which contains the district/school/teacher goals in each academic area and the textbook scope and sequence charts for various academic areas. If the psychologist does not make a notebook, he/she needs easy access to the materials, which is not always possible. There are helpful books such as Aukermann's 1981 review of basal readers which contain evaluative information regarding text books.

Sources of Difficulties

The psychologist who is doing academic assessment must be familiar with the research literature regarding factors influencing academic skills because this information helps formulate the assessment questions that need to be answered. A review of the literature indicates that the difficulties students have in academic areas develop from many sources and there is a complex interaction of variables which influence academic attitudes and achievement. Gerken (1983) provides a review of the causes of errors in mathematics, spelling and writing. Reisman (1982) briefly reviews the factors influencing learning mathematics while Aaron and Poostay (1982) consider reading acquisition. The psychologist must remember that academic disabilities vary largely in the severity of the problem rather than in qualitatively distinct types of disabilities.

Determination of Appropriate Assessment Techniques

The most effective assessment process is the one in which the psychologist, classroom teacher and anyone else involved in the student's schooling work together to plan and conduct appropriate assessment. After analyzing the referral and determining expectations for the student, the assessment team reviews what is already known about the student's academic skills and formulates the questions to be answered. The exact roles for each team member depends on each individual's skills. Some divisions of role are very easy. It is necessary to gather more than one sample of behavior across settings. For example, the following data might be gathered for a student experiencing difficulty in mathematics.

1. A group survey test in math is administered by a teacher or psychologist.

2. Work samples are obtained from the classroom teacher and parents.

3. Observation of math skills are conducted by parents, teacher and psychologist.

4. An interview is conducted by both the classroom teacher and the psychologist.

5. A diagnostic test in math is selected by the psychologist, administered by the teacher, or selected and administered by both the psychologist and the teacher.

6. Informal analyses of survey tests, diagnostic tests, and work samples are completed by the classroom teacher and psychologist working together.

Value of Survey Tests.

The scarcity of technically adequate, useful academic assessment instruments necessitate the combination of formal and informal techniques both for testing and teaching. The psychologist will find it necessary to reconsider the use of group tests for screening rather than using inadequate individual tests. Reviews of various assessment instruments by Hammill and Bartel (1982), Salvia and Ysseldyke (1981), Taylor (1984), and Wallace and Larsen (1978) contain overlapping, even contradictory, but valuable information. Contrary to psychologists' popular belief in the inherent goodness of individual versus group tests, the reviews point out that group tests are often technically superior to the individual tests, have larger samples of behavior, and can be more directly linked to curriculum. Although Ysseldyke and Marston (1982) express some caution in using group reading tests, Salvia and Ysseldyke's (1981) review of five popular group-administered achievement batteries reveals that far more information can be obtained from a normative and/or criterion-referenced analysis of these instruments than from most of the individually administered multiple-skill or single-skill achievement tests.

The selection process goes beyond choosing a group versus individual, screening versus diagnostic, or norm versus criterion referenced instrument. The quest is for instruments that are technically adequate, provide large enough samples of behavior, and are linked to the curriculum. A technically-adequate test that results in scores and no other information is not useful for planning intervention. The achievement test whose content does not reflect the curriculum in the school or classroom also has limited value. Leinhardt and Seewald (1981) point out that whenever a set of test scores are used to evaluate the impact of instructional programs, the extent of overlap between the tests and what is taught is critical. This knowledge is also vital when evaluating individual's strengths and weaknesses. Leinhardt and Seewald (1981) discuss two basic approaches for dealing with overlap. The first approach is a systematic analysis of curricula and tests to select the best-fitting test; the second approach is to directly measure the extent of overlap through teacher responses and criterion measures. The psychologist is not expected to undertake such an analysis but must be aware of the work that has been done.

There is nothing wrong with beginning assessment with a survey test or measure of overall academic performance as long as assessment does not stop there. The psychologist should ask to see the results of any recently administered, technically adequate survey test and should discuss the results with the teacher and student. If the record booklet and answers are available, an analysis of the errors is made. If the student has not had a recent survey test, then the psychologist should select a technically adequate one that provides the most information concerning the acquisition of the specific academic skills and concepts. It is important to note student's behaviors and discuss responses with him/her after testing is completed. The examiner must ask the student how he/she determined the answers, etc.

Both normative information and descriptive information are obtained from the survey test. These results help pose specific questions regarding the student's academic knowledge and skills. Many of the technically-adequate group achievement tests are both norm and criterion-referenced and have specific objectives linking assessment with curriculum. It is interesting to note how infrequently school psychologists and other school personnel use the data from group tests to effect changes for students.

Value of Diagnostic Tests

Although there are a myriad of diagnostic tests to assess academic areas, few of them provide sufficient information about individual strengths and weaknesses. If a technically adequate survey test has already been used to identify broad areas of difficulty, there is no need to waste time administering an inadequate diagnostic test. Some of the standardized diagnostic tests could be used as informal tests to identify specific problem areas.

Hambleton (1982) states that the ten-year battle for supremacy in the testing world is nearly over. There is no winner. Both criterion and norm-referenced tests have important roles to play in providing data for decision-making. There are significant differences in the instruments, but they have much in common. Many criterion-referenced tests are available and range considerably in content, grade levels, and technical quality. Hambleton (1982) reports that there is substantial room for improvement in the preparation of commercially available criterion-referenced tests. He offers suggestions for selecting criterion-referenced tests in terms of preliminary, practical, content, and technical considerations. He presents 38 questions which cover the content and technical considerations. He makes it clear it is essential to prepare a clear statement of the intended uses of the test information before a criterion-referenced test is selected.

Numerous books and articles have been written about the development of teacher-made tests or informal inventories. Guidelines differ but also share commonalities that are beneficial in developing a test. Such tests/inventories also vary and can take the form of a very thorough inventory to a checklist for a specific instructional technique. An example of a thorough mathematics inventory is the Sequential Assessment of Mathematics Inventory (SAMI) by Reisman (1978) which is available commercially from Merrill Publishing. Hambleton (1982) describes the steps for building a criterion-referenced test and Gerken (1983) summarizes various guidelines for developing informal evaluations of mathematics, spelling, and writing. Suggestions for developing an informal reading inventory are available from several sources (Elliott & Piersel, 1982; Hammill & Bartel, 1982; Wallace & Larsen, 1978).

However, criterion referenced instruments have their shortcomings. There are usually no standardization data or information regarding the technical adequacy of the instruments. The content may be dated or too limited, the interpretation of these inventories can be highly subjective, and the most critical component for scoring them may be the expertise of the examiner. Although the most helpful instruments are those developed from the students' own textbooks, unless the examiner/ test developer has knowledge about the specific academic area as well as knowledge of test construction, there must be cautious interpretation of the results.

Observation

Observation by both the classroom teacher and the psychologist is a very beneficial technique in analyzing a student's skills in reading, writing, spelling or mathematics. It can be used formally or informally, but it should be part of every step of the assessment process. Observation may be used for environmental assessment. Such assessment is done through checklists, videotapes, direct observation, detailed environmental analyses, etc. It is used to add information to the quantitative and qualitative aspects of other assessment, confirm findings from informal and formal assessment, or assess specific skills, behaviors, and interactions which have not been studied previously. It is used to reduce the redundancy in formal testing. There are numerous types of observation techniques, but the four basic methods are anecdotal records, checklists, behavioral rating scales, and systematic observation.

Observation can be as simple as looking at a sample of a child's work or as complex as a rigorous naturalistic observation system which requires that normative peer data be obtained as well as data regarding the target child. Within each of the techniques of observation, there will be a great deal of variability depending on what is to be observed and who is doing the observation. One might decide to combine several observation techniques or simply use one to gather information, keeping in mind the strengths and weaknesses of each technique.

Interview

Bartel (1978) and Schoen (1979) suggest that the oral interview can be used to provide additional information regarding a student's error strategies or check out hypotheses derived from assessment and daily work. McAloon (1979) stresses the importance of using questions to diagnose and remediate. He indicates that the teacher or diagnostician must ask questions that have the greatest potential for posing misconceptions. Bartel's (1978) list of procedures for the interview was adapted from the work of others as well as her own experiences.

1. Select one problem area at a time.

2. Begin with the easiest problems first.

3. Tape or keep a written record of the interview.

4. Have the child simultaneously solve the problem in written form and explain what he or she is doing.

5. Allow the child to solve the problem without hints that something is being done incorrectly.

6. Avoid hurrying the pupil (Bartell, 1978, pp. 118-119).

Schoen (1979) believes that the oral interview can yield at least partial answers to these questions:

1. Why does a particular skill, concept, or problem seem difficult for some students?

2. How are students interpreting the symbols they see and explanations they hear?

3. How does the class, or specific students in it, view mathematics?

4. How does a particular change in instructional approach change the students' perceptions and strategies?

5. What individual traits does each student possess that may help explain his or her learning problems? (Schoen, 1979, p. 37)

It is apparent that the amount of time needed for an oral interview seriously limits its usefulness. Therefore it should be used only when additional information is needed to pinpoint the problem area.

Informal Analysis Techniques

In order to complete a diagnostic evaluation one must know how a student learns. What errors does he/she make? What is the rationale for the errors, and what needs to be learned in order to remediate the situation? An accurate diagnosis reveals the cause of errors and suggests ways to eliminate them. Errors can be evidenced in the student's daily work, on tests, etc.

How does a psychologist analyze errors? It simply requires examination of errors to determine if any consistent pattern exists. The basic steps in error-pattern analysis are to: (a) find and mark the errors; (b) fill in the correct response; (c) describe the errors; (d) state a tentative conclusion; (e) confirm the conclusion by observing the student's performance in other situations where the same skills are required, and (f) make a diagnostic hypothesis.

Error pattern analysis is a major part of the process for mathematics, spelling and written expression. It can be conducted quickly if there has been direct observation of the student completing the academic tasks, but is more difficult if only the questions and answers are available. Ashlock (1982) and Reisman (1978) are excellent resources for studying error patterns and their analysis in mathematics.

Miscue analysis is a term used by Kenneth Goodman and associates to describe oral reading errors. The deviations in oral reading are called "miscues". This suggests that errors are not random, but in fact are cued by the thought and language of the reader. A miscue analysis of any reading selection is possible. However, a Reading Miscue Inventory (RMI) has been developed (Goodman & Burke, 1972). The authors suggest that the inventory be used as the basic evaluation tool in the reading curriculum. The five steps for using the RMI are:

1. *Taping oral reading* — The student reads an unfamiliar selection onto audio tape. The teacher marks the reader's miscues on a worksheet. The student is asked to retell the story in his/her own words.

2. *Marking miscues* — The teacher replays the tape and confirms/evaluates the worksheet information and calculates a Retelling Score.

3. *Using RMI Questions and Coding Sheet* — The Comprehension Pattern and the Grammatical Relationships Pattern are determined.

4. *Preparing the RMI Reader Profile* — The pattern of student's strengths and weaknesses is portrayed in graph form.

5. *Planning the Reading Program* — Each miscue is analyzed with regard to its graphic, syntactic, and semantic similarity to the test. The patterns of strengths and weaknesses provide the basis for the reading program.

Miscue analysis is viewed as a beginning for measuring comprehension. Other systems can be investigated. (Johnston, 1983).

Task Analysis

The breaking down of a task or objective into all of its component parts is called task analysis. It assists in identifying all the subtasks which the learner must be able to perform to accomplish a larger task. Many criterion-referenced and/or informal tests use a form of task analysis to structure their items in order of difficulty. Commercial and computer-based programs to analyze pre-academic and academic skills have now been developed. Several books have been written which teach the skills of task analysis.

The following are very simple guidelines for conducting a task analysis. It is used as both an assessment and intervention tool. Task analysis requires the isolat-ing, describing, and sequencing of the subtasks which will enable the student to perform an instructional objective (Bateman, 1971). The psychologist begins with the problematic instructional objective, breaks it into subtasks, constructs a checklist with a test item for each subtask, administers the checklist, and teaches the student the subtasks not known (Holmes & Ford, 1978, p. 54). One concentrates on the objective that is being assessed or taught and considers only those behaviors which can be seen, heard, measured or counted.

Reisman's (1977) outline for a task analysis is:

1. Identify those concepts or skills that are necessary prerequisites to the end goal.

2. Word those prerequisites in behavioral terms.

3. Use them as teaching and testing guides for the instructional program.

4. Be sensitive to any changes that must be made in sequence of presentation, or to any gaps in the learning hierarchy that might become apparent as a request of evaluation feedback (Reisman, 1977, p. 50).

She suggests that either a descending or an ascending task analysis can be performed. Either start with the end goal and work down to the simplest behavior or start with the simplest behavior and work up step by step.

Summary

When choosing informal assessment or analysis techniques, it is important to remember that each technique can be useful in obtaining information about students. However, each is just one part of the assessment process and is not valid alone. One of the major weaknesses of informal techniques is lack of specificity in pinpointing behavior to be observed, writing behavioral objectives, or performing a task analysis. Intra and interrater reliability and/or test retest reliability data must be gathered for these techniques.

The Intervention Process

How does the assessment process lead to decision making? In spite of all that has been written there remain two major purposes for assessment: (a) the determination of eligibility for special education services and (b) the development of an individualized instructional program. In order to translate data into decision making the multi-disciplinary assessment team must do the following: (a) record data for each area of investigation; (b) determine present level of performance by describing the student's strengths and weaknesses; (c) summarize what the student can do; (d) establish priorities; and (e) write goal statements. The above activities cannot be separated from the decision-making process. If priorities and goals have not been established then the type of intervention needed for a particular student cannot be determined. At this point the team needs to determine the student's eligibility and need for special education services. It is necessary to review the criteria for special services and compare the statement of the student's level of performance with that criteria. Even if the student is eligible for services, it must be determined whether this is the optimal way to achieve the goals set forth. The proper collection of appropriate information is very important to making decisions and developing an effective intervention program for each student regardless of eligibility for special education services.

Although much has been written touting the use of assessment data to plan intervention and it appears there are many diagnostic-prescriptive teaching models to choose from, Ysseldyke and Mirkins' (1982) analysis of the available literature indicates this is not true. They believe there are basically two major diagnostic prescriptive teaching models with the abilities-analysis approach on one end of the continuum and the skills-analysis approach on the other. Variations of both models are interspersed along the continuum. Efforts to demonstrate support for the abilities-analysis approach through descriptive research, gain-score research, or aptitude-treatment interaction have not been successful. Relative to the research on skill training, Ysseldyke and Mirkin (1982) report that there have been many single-subject studies in which direct and continuous measurement procedures were successful. However, there have been very few studies in which the effects of the systematic application of direct and continuous assessment were contrasted with other approaches. Ysseldyke and Mirkin (1982) believe that the results of the existing studies provide empirical support for direct and continuous measurement of performance. They also recognize the need for additional research to isolate the components of an effective formative evaluation system.

Direct assessment is now recommended as the alternative to psychometric testing (Dickinson, 1980), just as criterion-referenced testing was touted in the 1970's as the alternative to norm-referenced testing. But Ysseldyke and Mirkin (1982) point out the need to look at dimensions other than directness of measurement. They cite a model of measurement by Van Etten and Van Etten that considers directness and frequency of measurement: Type I — indirect and non-continuous assessment; Type II — indirect and continuous assessment; Type III — direct and non-continuous assessment; and Type IV — direct and continuous assessment. It is believed that the more direct and continuous the data collection system becomes, the more precise the teaching-learning process will be.

It is clear from Ysseldyke and Mirkin's (1982) and this author's reviews of the intervention-methods literature regarding academic skills that research does not support one program of remediation or instruction. It takes the cooperative efforts of all members of the assessment team to develop an individualized intervention program. The evaluation of the effectiveness of the intervention is a continuous ongoing process.

SUMMARY

During the latter part of the nineteenth century and throughout the twentieth century, psychologists have been expected to assess students with academic problems. Far too often that assessment has ended with diagnosis and labeling. There have been few data indicating that the assessment led to successful interventions for the students. An abundance of articles have appeared in the professional and popular literature that indicate little satisfaction with the state of the art in assessment.

The concerns are varied, but relative to academic assessment they focus on the need to know exactly what academic skills a student does or does not have in order to remediate or at least alleviate some of the student's deficits. It is clear that psychologists who are going to conduct or direct academic assessment need additional and/ or different training. The role of psychometrician is viewed with disfavor by psychologists, but few psychologists have performed that role well. The psychologist must be able to transfer into practice the knowledge acquired in measurement, learning, and development as well as those theories underlying the basic academic skills of reading, writing, spelling and arithmetic. These are not the only skills needed, but would add much to the assessment process.

The assessment process that contributes to positive changes for students takes the combined efforts of all the people involved in the student's academic experiences.

REFERENCES

Aaron, I. E. & Poostay, E. J. (1982). Strategies for reading disorders. In C. R. Reynolds & T. B. Gutkin (Eds.). *The handbook of school psychology.* (pp. 410-435). New York: John Wiley & Sons.

Anastasi, A. (1967). Psychology, psychologists, and psychological testing. *American Psychologist.* 22(4), 297-306.

Ashlock, R. B. (1982). *Error patterns in computation* (3rd edition). Columbus, Ohio: Charles E. Merrill.

Aukermann, R. C. (1981). *The basal reader approach to reading.* New York: John Wiley & Sons.

Bardon, J. (1982). The psychology of school psychology. In C. R. Reynolds & T. B. Gutkin (Eds.) *The handbook of school psychology* (pp. 3-14). New York: John Wiley & Sons.

Bartel, N. W. (1978). Problems in mathematics achievement. In D. D. Hammill & N. R. Bartel, *Teaching children with learning and behavior problems* (2nd edition). Boston: Allyn and Bacon.

Bateman, B. D. (1971). *Essentials of teaching.* San Rafael, California: Dimensions.

Dickenson, D. J. (1980). The direct assessment: An alternative to psychometric testing. *Journal of Learning Disabilities.* 13 (9), 8-12.

Elliott, S. N. & Piersel, W. C. (1982). Direct assessment of reading skills: An approach which links assessment to intervention. *School Psychology Review.* 11(3), 267-280.

Ford, J. D. & Migles, M. (1979). The role of the school psychologist: teachers' preferences as a function of personal and professional characteristics. *Journal of School Psychology.* 17(4), 372-378.

Gerken, K. C. (1983). *Guidelines for the school psychologist: The diagnostic process in mathematics, spelling, and written expression.* Des Moines, Iowa: Iowa Dept. of Public Instruction.

Gray, S. W. (1963). *The psychologist in the schools.* New York: Holt, Rinehart & Winston.

Goodman, Y. M. & Burke, C. L. (1972). *Reading miscue inventory manual.* New York: Macmillan.

Gresham, F. M. (1983). Multitrait-multimethod approach to multifactored assessment: Theoretical rationale and practical application. *School Psychology Review*, 12(1), 26-34.

Gutkin, T. B. & Singer, J. H., Brown, R. (1980). Teachers reactions to schoolbased consultation services: A multivariate analyses. *Journal of School Psychology*. 18(2), 126-134.

Hambleton, R. K. (1982). Advances in criterion-referenced testing technology. In C. R. Reynolds & T. B. Gutkin (Eds.) *The handbook of school psychology*. (pp. 351-379). New York: John Wiley & Sons.

Hammill, D. D. & Bartel, N. R. (1982). *Teaching children with learning and behavior problems* (3rd edition). Boston: Allyn and Bacon.

Holmes, R. L. & Ford, K. K. (1978). *The appraisal process in special education*. Des Moines, Iowa: Midwest Regional Resource Center.

Hughes, J. N. (1981). Consistency of administrators' and psychologists' actual and ideal perceptions of school psychology activities. In J. L. Carroll (Ed.) *Contemporary School Psychology* (2nd edition). Branden, Vermont: Clinical Psychology.

Johnston, P. H. (1983). *Reading comprehension assessment: A cognitive basis*. Newark, Delaware: International Reading Association.

Kahl, L. J. & Fine, M. J. (1981). Teachers' perceptions of the school psychologist as a function of teaching experience, amount of contact, and socioeconomic status of the school. In J. L. Carroll (Ed.) *Contemporary School Psychology* (2nd edition). Branden, Vermont: Clinical Psychology.

Landau, S. E. & Gerken, K. C. (1979). Requiem for the testing role. *School Psychology Digest*. 8(2), 202-206.

Leinhardt, G. & Seewald, M. A. (1981). Overlap, what's tested, what's taught? *Journal of Educational Measurement*. 18(2), 85-96.

Mash, E. J. & Terdal, L. G. (1974). Behavior therapy assessment: Diagnosis, design, and evaluation. *Psychology Reports*. 35, 587-601.

McAloon, A. (1979). Using questions to diagnose and remediate. *Arithmetic Teacher*. 27, 44-48.

Reisman, F. K. (1978). *A guide to the diagnostic teaching of arithmetic* (2nd edition). Columbus, Ohio: Charles E. Merrill.

Reisman, F. K. (1977). *Diagnostic teaching of elementary school mathematics*. Chicago: Rand McNally.

Reisman, F. K. (1982). Strategies for mathematics disorders. In C. R. Reynolds & T. B. Gutkin (Eds.) *The handbook of school psychology* (pp. 436-452). New York: John Wiley & Sons.

Salvia, J. & Ysseldyke, J. E. (1981). *Assessment on special and remedial education* (2nd edition). Boston: Houghton Mifflin.

Schoen, H. L. (1979). Using the individual interview to assess mathematics learning. *Arithmetic Teacher*. 27, 34-37.

Senf, L. B. & Snider, B. (1980). Elementary school principals assess services of school psychologists nationwide. *Journal of School Psychology*. 18(3), 276-282.

Taylor, R. L. (1984). *Assessment of exceptional students*. Englewood Cliffs, New Jersey: Prentice-Hall.

Tindall, R. H. (1979). School psychology: The development of a profession. In G. D. Phye & D. J. Reschly (Eds.) *School psychology perspectives and issues* (pp. 3-24). New York: Academic Press.

Wallace, G. & Larsen, S. C. (1978). *Educational assessment of learning problems: Testing for teaching*. Boston: Allyn and Bacon.

Ysseldyke, J. E. (1979). Issues in psychoeducational assessment. In G. D. Phye & D. J. Reschly (Eds.) *School psychology perspectives and issues* (pp. 87-121). New York: Academic Press.

Ysseldyke, J. E. & Marston, D. (1982). A critical analysis of standardized reading tests. *School Psychology Review*. 11(3), 257-266.

Ysseldyke, J. E. & Mirkin, D. The use of assessment information to plan instructional interventions: A review of the research. In C. R. Reynolds & T. B. Gutkin (Eds.) *The handbook of school psychology* (pp. 395-409). New York: John Wiley and Sons.

ANNOTATED BIBLIOGRAPHY

Gerken, K. C. (1983). *Guidelines for the school psychologist: The diagnostic process in mathematics, spelling, and written expression*. Des Moines, Iowa. Iowa Department of Public Instruction.
This manuscript briefly reviews the factors which influence learning in the above academic areas, presents guidelines for assessment, and provides an overview of instructional practices in these areas. The appendices contain examples of skill hierarchies and informal assessment techniques.

Hammill, D. D. & Bartel, N. R. (1982). *Teaching children with learning and behavior problems* (3rd edition). Boston: Allyn and Bacon.
The critique of assessment instruments is not as thorough in this text as in others. However, the features that make this book a valuable resource are the overview provided for each academic skill area and the review of teaching techniques/materials.

Reynolds, C. R. & Gutkin, T. B. (Eds.) (1982). *The handbook of school psychology.* New York: John Wiley & Sons.
Chapter 13 contains Hambleton's comprehensive review of criterion-referenced testing. Ysseldyke and Mirkin (Chapter 15) succinctly state the need to utilize only those assessment-intervention approaches that have empirical support. Aaron and Poostay's coverage of reading disorders (Chapter 16) and Reisman's introduction to math disorders (Chapter 17) are somewhat limited in scope, but valuable.

Salvia, J. & Ysseldyke, J. E. (1981). *Assessment in special and remedial education* (2nd ed.). Boston: Houghton Mifflin.
This book is a valuable text for introducing psychoeducational assessment as well as a valuable resource for information concerning assessment instruments. It does differ from most other introductory assessment texts in two major ways: its thorough coverage of basic measurement concepts and its critical evaluation of the technical adequacy of assessment instruments.

Taylor, R. L. (1984). *Assessment of exceptional students.* Englewood Cliffs, New Jersey: Prentice-Hall.
The format of this book is similar to other introductory assessment texts. However, its unique features make it worth reading and having as a resource. A review of relevant research is provided for each standardized test that is presented. Formal and informal procedures for diverse populations are reviewed.

BEST PRACTICES IN ASSISTING IN PROMOTION AND RETENTION DECISIONS

Robert B. Germain   Michele Merlo
University of Rhode Island

OVERVIEW

This chapter provides the school psychologist with background for, and a model of, best practices in assisting in promotion and retention decisions. The information required to make these decisions is multi-faceted and psychologically complex, so it is likely that the school psychologist might have a unique perspective to offer in the decision-making process.

Background

Retention, or nonpromotion, is the practice of requiring a child to repeat a particular grade. The term is also applicable when a child of appropriate chronological age does not begin kindergarten or first grade in the designated school year.

The practice of retention began in the 19th century, shortly after the introduction of graded-schools. The question arose concerning how best to handle pupils who were not prepared for the next grade (Seldon, 1982; Rose et al, 1983). In the 1930's, educators became concerned with the possible negative impact that retention might have on the social and emotional functioning of children (Rose, et. al., 1983). While this concern has resulted in a decline in the percentage of children being retained since the beginning of the century (Walker, 1973; Safer, Heaton, & Allen, 1977), nonpromotion is still widely used. Reports indicate that as recently as 1971 over one million school children were retained (Bocks, 1977).

BASIC CONSIDERATIONS

Despite almost three-quarters of a century of research on this topic, a review of the literature does not result in a secure position about the effectiveness of retention. Therefore, a school psychologist must be aware of the diversity of the ideas and research in this area to provide assistance in individual cases and policy-making. This section presents a systematic overview of these ideas and this research which impacts on the specific options for best practices.

Promotion

Ideas

The primary argument in favor of promotion is that "more of the same" will not be effective; the experience that did not produce success the first time should not be expected to produce success when tried again.

Research

There are numerous research studies which show that promoted children do better, academically and/or socially, than retained children (e.g. Anfinson, 1941; Sandin, 1944; Goodlad, 1954; Morrison & Perry, 1956; Coffield & Bloomers, 1956; Kamii & Weikart, 1963; Chansky, 1964; Dobbs & Neville, 1967; Abidin et al, 1971; Godfrey, 1972; and White & Howard, 1973). Using predominantly elementary pupils, and to a lesser extent junior high school students, these studies examined a variety of factors such as reading and math achievement, school adjustment, emotional adjustment, popularity, and self concept.

Research Critique

The primary weakness in these studies is the comparability of the promoted and retained groups. Only three studies cited by Jackson (1975), the latest of which was published in 1941, employed a design in which students considered for retention were randomly assigned to either the promotion or retention "condition." Some studies did match students based on race, sex, SES, age, and IQ. However, without random assignment of children to conditions, the variables that led some children to be retained and others to be promoted may bias the results in favor of the promotion group. It is likely that the promoted groups were "better" prior to promotion on some relevant dimensions.

The second problem with this group of studies is that the vast majority of analyses which favor the promoted over the retained group report mean differences which do not reach statistical significance. Jackson (1975) reports that only one of 18 analyses in support of promotion actually reached statistical significance.

Summary

While a large number of studies show that promoted children do better both academically and socially than retained children, there is a general lack of statistical significance and a consistent design problem which would unfairly bias the results in favor of the promotion groups. However, the supporters of promotion would argue that the burden of proof should be on those who favor retention since it is this latter group who is proposing the need for a non-normative educational practice.

Retention

Ideas

Arguments in favor of retention consider both academic and social-emotional functioning. First, it is argued that students who have not mastered the work of one grade level are not ready to undertake the academic work of the next grade level. They will be better able to make significant academic growth during the year they are retained. Second, it is argued that this mastery of skills provided by retention will increase self-esteem. Third, for some children, an extra year allows them to mature socially.

Research

Many research studies show that retained children make significant academic and/or social-emotional gains during the retained year (Lobdell, 1954; Coffield & Bloomers, 1956; Stringer, 1960; Chase, 1968; Scott & Ames, 1970; Finlayson, 1977; and Elligett & Tocco, 1983). These studies have measured the developmental maturity, reading and math achievement, grade point average, and self concept of elementary and junior high school students.

Research Critique

The primary weakness in these studies is that retention was not systematically compared to any other treatment condition. It cannot be concluded that the gains made by children were due to retention and would have been any less substantial if the children had been promoted.

Summary

While numerous studies show that retained children make academic and social-emotional gains during the retained year, a general design problem precludes attributing the gains to the retention process.

However, some supporters of retention would argue that all the studies mentioned thus far document two things: (a) retention is not beneficial for everyone for whom it is used; and (b) it is still potentially beneficial for some individuals. The next section analyzes the situations in which retention might be an effective alternative.

Circumstances
for Retention

The studies described above all tried to determine whether promotion or retention has a consistent advantage over the other. It is not surprising that these results are mixed. Rather than attempting to answer the "either-or" question, a more appropriate question is, "Is retention more effective for certain populations than for others, and, if so, under what circumstances is retention the best alternative?"

Child Factors

Ideas

In both an early study (Saunders, 1941) and a recent one (Gruszka, 1983), elementary school principals mentioned low academic skills and general social and social-emotional im-maturity as the two most common reasons to recommend retention. Principals in Gruszka's study described children who are most likely harmed by retention as those with below average IQ, children in need of other services such as special education, students in later grades, or youngsters who were large physically.

There are several theoretical ideas which help put these ideas and the subsequent research into perspective. A fundamental issue about which behaviorists, learning theorists, and supporters of competency-based and mastery education would agree is that certain skills and tasks are prerequisite to others. To the extent that certain specific tasks and skills have not been learned, progress will not be made on more advanced tasks. This would include tasks in both the cognitive and social-emotional domains. In this view, those children who show specific skill or task-related deficits which are fundamental to the learning experiences in the next grade should be retained.

There are also maturationists (Ames,

Gillespie, & Streff, 1972; Ames, Gillespie, Haines, & Ilg, 1979) who believe that physiological immaturity affects cognitive and/or social-emotional behavior. For those immature students, the mere allowance of more time to mature warrants the use of retention.

Cognitive-developmentalists such as Piaget or Feuerstein would claim that there are some children for whom the next grade's experiences would be inappropriate because they have not developed the cognitive structures or operations to successfully deal with those experiences. This could be due to biological maturity and/or the quality or quantity of previous learning experiences.

Research

Sandoval and Hughes (1981) compared successful to unsuccessful retained children. They found that for retained first-grade children, those who learned the most in the year prior to retention also learned the most during the retained year, and those who were initially highest in social development and self-esteem made the most gains in these areas. As noted by the authors, their design did not allow for flawless comparisons with a group of promoted students. The latter group was superior to the successful retained group in math, but not in reading. Since it is likely that retention decisions were made more frequently on the basis of reading than math skills, promotion may not be more effective in those skill areas in which the student has deficits. This supports the theoretical arguments above.

Sandoval and Hughes also identified a group of children who made little if any gains during the retention year. These were children whose scores on most measures of achievement and adjustment were at the lower extreme of the distribution. Similarly, Stringer (1960) found that of the group of children who did not benefit from retention, some were emotionally disturbed and many had lagged behind their peers in achievement by two or more grade levels. These studies support the contention that retention should not be used in place of special education.

Gredler (1980a, 1980b) would agree that in instances where a child has learning or emotional difficulties, retention will not solve the problem. His concern is that students with special needs will be overlooked by maturationists who assume that the child's problems will go away merely with time.

Stringer reported that unsuccessful retained students were those who were retained in higher grades (seventh and eighth). Reinherz and Griffin (1980) also found this age effect, noting that a much larger percentage of second and third graders, as contrasted with first graders, made unsatisfactory progress.

Finally, Sandoval and Hughes (1981) report that certain child factors were not predictive of success. These include the child's physical size and visual-motor development.

Summary

The students who are most likely to benefit from retention are those who do not have the academic and/or social skills to benefit from promotion, who have good learning and/or social-emotional potential, and whose deficits are due to a lack of adequate learning experiences.

Family Variables

Some investigators believe that parent involvement and family support can be important in the initial retention decision as well as in the ultimate success of the nonpromotion (Stringer, 1960; Lieberman, 1980). The data do not support this contention, though only short-term studies have been done. For example, Sandoval and Hughes found that family variables were not significant in discriminating

successful from unsuccessful retained students.

Systems Factors

There are a number of diverse systems factors which can potentially affect a promotion/retention decision. These will be reviewed in the following sections.

Teacher and Classroom Factors

Sandoval and Hughes (1981) found that the degree of confidence a teacher had in the retention decision was a significant predictor for each of the three groups of successfuly retained children —the academically, emotionally, and socially successful. There are at least two possible inferences: (a) there was a self-fulfilling prophecy effect; or (b) teachers are well informed by their experience with a student about whether or not retention would be appropriate.

Another finding from this study is that the philosophy of the teacher was not significantly related to success. However, children who had the same teacher both years and those attending open classrooms which provided individualized instruction achieved greater affective gains than their counterparts.

Policies

There does appear to be general agreement that an appropriate promotion/retention policy is better than no policy. Yet it is relatively uncommon for a policy to exist. In one study, 81% of the teachers surveyed reported that their school had no written policy regarding retention (Miller, Frazier, & Richey, 1980). In another study (Abidin et al, 1971), there was no documented reason provided for 24% of the retained students.

There is evidence that in the absence of a formal policy, children may be retained on the basis of irrelevant or inappropriate variables such as disruptive (rather than immature) behavior (Caplan, 1973; Minde, et al, 1971); race and socio-economic status (Flynn, 1971; and Walker, 1973); or gender (Sister Josephina, 1962; Chansky, 1964; Sabatino and Hayden, 1970), with males outnumbering females by at least two to one.

Another policy weakness is that the process of making retention decisions is typically not as systematic as is the process for special education decisions. For example, Gruszka found that 49% of the principals reported that parental consent was never required and an additional 11% reported that it was required only for kindergarten.

Alternative Services

Whether or not retention is the best decision for a child depends in part on the other options available within a school system. Following are some alternatives to simple promotion and retention.

1. Special education services. This may include anything from placement in a self-contained or resource room to consulting teacher help for those students who meet the federal, state, and local guidelines on the basis of the intellectual, academic, physical, and behavioral/emotional status.

2. Transition classrooms. This can be a class where two grades are completed in three years (e.g. kindergarten, first, and second grades), or, following a similar model, where one grade is completed in two years.

3. Open, non-graded, and/or individualized instruction classrooms. This represents a maximally flexible curricular arrangement in which students are provided with instruction geared to their current academic level.

Related Policies

There are two related policy issues which bear upon the potential appropriate uses of retention. The first involves policies of graduation standards. In the

past 10 years, an increasing number of states have made earning a high school diploma contingent on the achievement of a certain level of basic skills. Local or state-wide policies which relate to graduation requirements may impact on retention and promotion decisions in secondary schools. The research fairly consistently supports the conclusion that it is better to retain children earlier rather than later in their school career. These factors would need to be considered in formulating a system-wide policy.

The second policy issue concerns students whose intellectual functioning is above the criteria for mental retardation, but whose academic skills are significantly below grade level. Many of these students are currently classified as learning disabled (LD). There is no question that there is a group of students for whom the regular classroom's typical curriculum and methods are inappropriate and who do not qualify for special education services under any other handicapping condition criteria. However, the possibility exists that the overwhelmingly large number of LD students represents significant misclassifications. Rather than being retained, students without the academic skills necessary to be successful in the subsequent grade are often socially promoted. In later grades their academic achievement is severely discrepant with their potential, and they are classified as LD. Yet, it is the consistent inadequacy of their learning experiences (i.e. consistently being presented with material "over their heads"), and not a learning disability which may account for this discrepancy.

Both of these policy issues, graduation requirements and LD misclassification, give evidence of a large number of students who are not handicapped yet who are not being adequately served by regular education. It is unlikely that retention is appropriate for more than a small percentage of these students. For most of them, inappropriate instruction that did not work the first time will not work after one or two more tries. Rather, our system's failures must be ameliorated through greater support for teachers and related staff to allow them to develop and implement appropriate instructional systems.

Economic Issues

The longer a student stays in school, the more it costs the school district and the taxpayers. Coffield and Bloomers (1956) state that, "A failed pupil represents added operational costs which cannot be justified" (p. 236) given the available research evidence. Thompson (1979) also cites the high cost of retention policies to schools. Therefore, in light of the economic considerations, any decision to retain a child must be defended more strenuously as being clearly in the child's best interests.

Related Decisions

Once it has been decided that a child should be retained, an important related decision is whether to place the child with the same teacher during the retained year. Gruszka reports that almost three quarters of the principals surveyed reported that they would be in favor of placing a student with a different teacher. Presumably this is because the teaching-learning interaction had not been successful, and there may be teacher or child frustration and negative feelings (Lieberman, 1980). Reasons to keep the same teacher would involve the teacher's knowledge about the child, continuity in programming, and rapport. Sandoval and Hughes (1981) found significantly greater gains were made by the students who were taught by the same teacher both years.

BEST PRACTICES

Models Previously Developed

Recently, Lieberman (1980) and Light (1981) have independently developed multi-factor decision models as guides for educators involved in making retention decisions for individual children. Lieberman's model consists of 27 components under three general categories: child, family, and school. The factors are not given standardized weights. School personnel review these variables and make their decisions based on "rational problem solving."

Light's model, which consists of 19 variables, involves a more quantitative approach, offering cutoff scores to be used as guidelines by school personnel when making retention decisions about particular students. Sandoval (1980) reports that the score has limited reliability, and, in a study of concurrent validity, the measure failed to accurately identify to-be-retained children. Nevertheless, these models are appealing in their scope and comprehensiveness, and serve to identify variables which must be systematically considered by decision-makers who are well-informed by the existing research.

CURRENT BEST PRACTICES

Policies and Procedures

1. A formal retention policy is important to prevent inconsistent, haphazard, or discriminatory retention practices. This policy should include the specific information upon which the decision is to be based, the standards and circumstances which will be applied to the information, and the procedures to be followed in decision-making. These are discussed below.

2. The development of the policy should be coordinated with other district policies relating to academic standards, such as those relating to graduation requirements. This consideration is intended to prevent,

for example, social promotion through the elementary grades, and retention for long-standing academic deficits in junior or senior high school.

3. The decision-making process should be treated with the same seriousness accorded special education decisions. That is, parental permission and involvement should be obtained, a multi-disciplinary team should be responsible for guiding the assessment and for making the decisions, and finally, goals, objectives, and evaluation procedures should be specified.

Other Systems-Related Best Practices

1. Because the benefits of retention are, at best, limited to a very small segment of the population, it is important that school systems continually develop the range of alternative services available to students. Ideally, there would be no need for retention, as consistently individualized instruction and evaluation procedures would meet each child's needs. Services such as effective and multi-faceted special education classes, transition classrooms, and increased individualization within classrooms can be provided for many students who otherwise would have been retained.

2. When retention is used, it should not be assumed that the same instructional procedures which failed to work for the child the first time will work the second time. Rather, alternative instructional procedures may be warranted, and this may require a school system to provide greater supportive services for regular classroom teachers.

3. Because the benefits of retention are at best ambiguous, and at worst costly to both the student and the school district, the effectiveness of retention decisions should be evaluated.

4. Retention will result in increased variation in age, interests, and physical and social maturity within classrooms. To prevent resistance to retention on this

basis, efforts to emphasize the value of heterogeneity would be helpful.

Best Practices: When Should a Particular Child Be Retained?

The ideas and research reviewed on promotion and retention result in only one firm conclusion:

1. Do not use retention when a child is handicapped and therefore in need of other special services.

Other than this one conclusion, there are several defendable positions about whom to retain. The first is mutually exclusive of the others:

2. Retain no one. Jackson's (1975) statement is still applicable:

> "There is no reliable body of evidence to indicate that grade retention is more beneficial than grade promotion for students with serious academic or adjustment difficulties . . . Thus, those educators who retain pupils in a grade do so without valid research evidence to indicate that such treatment will provide greater benefits to students with academic difficulties than will promotion to the next grade" (p. 627).

The following perspectives are not mutually exclusive, and must be thought of as tentative considerations.

3. For a child with academic or readiness deficits, where these deficits derive from a history of inadequate learning experiences in the home, it does not seem appropriate to delay entrance into school. One more year of inadequate learning experiences will not provide the child with the needed skills. The child needs learning experiences geared to his or her present level of skills.

4. For a child with academic deficits which derive from a lack of instruction in school (e.g. from excessive absences or frequent moves), retention with typical classroom instruction might be most appropriate.

5. For a child who has developed academic deficits in spite of receiving the typical classroom instruction, one alternative is to retain the child and modify the content and/or process of instruction. This alternative requires flexibility on the part of classroom teachers, who in turn may require additional supportive services.

6. For a child with behavioral and/or social deficits, where these deficits derive from a lack of social and peer interaction (i.e. a child who has been isolated from agemates), it does not seem appropriate to delay entrance into school. One more year of isolation will not provide the child with the needed skills.

7. For a child with behavioral and/or social deficits, where these deficits seem to be a part of a general immaturity (e.g. people experience the child as being "babyish;" developmental milestones were typically reached at a later age than average), many people would support delayed entrance into school or retention. However, the research has not supported this opinion.

8. Retain in the earlier, rather than in the later grades as much as possible.

9. In cases where a child is retained, he or she may be placed with the same teacher again if the child and teacher have had a positive experience with each other and the teacher is willing and able to individualize instruction for the child.

SUMMARY

The practice of retention has been studied for almost three quarters of a century. Most studies which purport to show either advantage of promotion or benefits of retention have severe design flaws. Few address the most appropriate concern of determining the population and circumstances that make retention the most effective alternative.

While the benefits of retention have not been substantially documented, a re-view of literature and research suggests that some students are likely to benefit from retention. They are ones who have average potential for intellectual or social-emotional development. They may have academic or behavioral deficits related to inadequate learning experiences which make it unlikely that they will succeed in the subsequent grade. Yet, their deficits are not of such severity that they would qualify for special education services.

It is clear that there are numerous students who do not achieve at grade level and who are not rightfully eligible for special education. While retention can help a small percentage of these students, many of them are unlikely to benefit from another year of the same content and methods of instruction. Alternative instructional procedures could be developed, but these require the provision of considerably more support for the regular classroom teachers.

While there is continued ambiguity over precisely who should be retained, there is little doubt that it is beneficial to establish a written policy on retention and to follow a systematic procedure in decision-making.

REFERENCES

Abidin, R., Golladay, W., & Howerton, A. (1971). Elementary school retention: An unjustifiable, discriminatory and noxious educational policy. *Journal of School Psychology, 9,* 410-417.

Ames, L. B., Gillespie, C., & Streff, J. W. (1972). *Stop School Failure.* New York: Harper & Row.

Ames, L. B., Gillespie, C., Haines, J., & Ilg, F. L. (1979). *The Gesell Institute's child from one to six.* New York: Harper & Row.

Anfinson, R. (1941). School progress and pupil adjustment. *Elementary School Journal, 41,* 507-514.

Bocks, W. (1977). Non-promotion: "A year to grow?" *Educational Leadership, 34,* 379-383.

Caplan, P. (1973). The role of classroom conduct in the promotion and retention of elementary school children. *Journal of Experimental Education, 32,* 225-237.

Chansky, N. (1964). Progress of promoted and repeating first grade 1 failures. *Journal of Experimental Education, 32,* 225-237.

Chase, J. (1968). A study of the impact of grade retention on primary school children. *Journal of Psychology, 70,* 169-177.

Coffield, W. & Bloomers, P. (1956). Effects of nonpromotion on educational achievement in the elementary school. *Journal of Educational Psychology, 47,* 235-250.

Dobbs, V. & Neville, D. (1967). The effects of nonpromotion on the achievement of groups matched from retained first graders and promoted second graders. *Journal of Educational Research, 60,* 472-475.

Elligett, J. K. & Tocco, T. S. (1983, June). The promotion/retention controversy in Pinellas County, Florida. *Phi Delta Kappan,* 733-735.

Feuerstein, R. (1979). *The dynamic assessment of retarded performers.* Baltimore: University Park Press.

Feuerstein, R. (1980). *Instrumental enrichment: an intervention program for cognitive modifiability.* Baltimore: University Park Press.

Finlayson, H. (1977). Nonpromotion and self-concept development. *Phi Delta Kappa, 59,* 205-206.

Flynn, T. M. (1971). Implicit criteria used to determine promotion for normal and retarded students. *Psychology in the Schools, 8,* 204-208.

Godfrey, E. (1972). The tragedy of failure. *Education Digest, 37,* 34-35.

Goodlad, J. (1954). Some effects of promotion and nonpromotion upon the social and personal adjustment of children. *Journal of Experimental Education, 22,* 301-328.

Gredler, G. (1980a). The birthdate effect: Fact or artifact? *Journal of Learning Disabilities, 13,* 9-12.

Gredler, G. (1980b). Cumulative retention rate as an index of academic progress: A third look. *Journal of Learning Disabilities, 13,* 15-18.

Gruszka, M. (1983). *A survey of nonpromotion policy and practice in Rhode Island Elementary Schools.* Unpublished manuscript.

Jackson, G. (1975). The research evidence on the effects of grade retention. Review of *Educational Research, 45,* 613-635.

Josephina, S. (1962). Promotion, a perennial problem. *Education, 82,* 373-376.

Kamii, C. & Weikart, D. (1963). Marks, achievement, and intelligence of seventh graders who were retained (nonpromoted) once in elementary school. *Journal of Educational Research, 56,* 452-459.

Lieberman, L. (1980). A decision-making model for in-grade retention (nonpromotion). *Journal of Learning Disabilities, 13,* 268-272.

Light, H. W. (1981). *Light's Retention Scale.* San Rafael, California: Academic Therapy Publications.

Lobdell, L. G. (1954). Results of a nonpromotion policy in one school district. *Elementary School Journal, 54,* 333-337.

Miller, M., Frazier, C., & Richey, D. (1980). Student nonpromotion and teacher attitude. *Contemporary Education, 51,* 155-157.

Minde, K., Lewin, D., Weiss, G., Lavigueur, H., Douglas, V., & Sykes, E. (1971, Nov.). The hyperactive child in elementary school: A five-year controlled follow-up. *Exceptional Children,* 215-221.

Morrison, I. E. & Perry, I. F. (1956). Acceptance of overage children by their classmates. *Elementary School Journal, 56,* 217-220.

Reinherz, H. Z. & Griffin, C. L. (1970). The second time around: A study of achievement and progress of boys who repeated one of the first three grades in school. *School Counselor, 17,* 213-218.

Rose, J. S., Medway, F. J., Cantrell, V. L., & Marus, S. H. (1983). A fresh look at the retention-promotion controversy. *Journal of School Psychology, 21,* 201-211.

Sabatino, D. A. & Hayden, D. L. (1970). Psychoeducational study of selected behavioral variables with children failing the elementary grades. *Journal of Experimental Education, 38,* 40-57.

Safer, D., Heaton, R., & Allen, R. (1977). Socioeconomic factors influencing the rate of nonpromotion in elementary schools. *Peabody Journal of Education, 54,* 275-281.

Sandin, A. A. (1944). Social and emotional adjustments of regularly promoted and nonpromoted pupils. *Child Development Monographs,* No. 32. New York: Bureau of Publications, Teachers College, Columbia University.

Sandoval, J. (1980). Reliability and concurrent validity of Light's Retention Scale. *Psychology in the Schools, 17,* 442-445.

Sandoval, J. & Hughes, G. P. (1981). *Success in non-promoted first grade children.* Final report. Davis California: California University, (ERIC Document Reproduction Service No. ED 212 371).

Saunders, C. M. (1941). *Promotion or failure for the elementary school pupil?* New York: Teachers College, Columbia University.

Scott, B. A. & Ames, L. B. (1969). Improved academic, personal, and social adjustment in selected primary-school repeaters. *Elementary School Journal, 69,* 431-439.

Selden, S. (1982). Promotion policy. In H. E. Mitzel, J. H. Best & W. Rabinowitz (Eds.), *Encyclopedia of Educational Research* (Vol. 3). New York: The Free Press.

Stringer, L. A. (1960). Report on a retention program. *Elementary School Journal, 60,* 370-375.

Thompson, M. (1979). Because schools are burying social promotion, kids must perform to pass. *American School Board Journal, 166,* 30-32.

Walker, W. E. (1973). The slow-progress student in graded and nongraded programs. *Peabody Journal of Education, 50,* 191-210.

White, D. & Howard, J. (1973). Failure to be promoted and self-concept among elementary school children. *Elementary School Guidance and Counseling, 7,* 182-187.

ANNOTATED BIBLIOGRAPHY

Jackson, G. (1975). The research evidence on the effects of grade retention. *Review of Educational Research, 45,* 613-635.
Jackson provides a substantial review of the promotion and retention controversy dating to 1973. He reviews data, studies, arguments, and critiques from each side, including in his summary a good deal of detail. This is an excellent overview of the thinking and research up to that time.

Sandoval, J. & Hughes, G. P. (1981). *Success in non-promoted first grade children.* Final report. Davis California: California University (ERIC Document Reproduction Service No. ED 212 371.
Describe a systematic study of 78 retained children, and recognize the strengths and limitations of their design. Their results are substantial and well-presented, and the article would serve as a good starting point for the design of further studies.

Light, H. W. (1981). *Light's Retention Scale.* San Rafael, California: Academic Therapy Publications.
Discusses Light's Retention Scale. While the scale itself may not be empirically validated, the manual includes a description of a variety of factors one may wish to consider when making a retention/promotion decision. Research findings related to these factors are reviewed as is the research on social promotion, retention, and retention as a discriminatory practice.

Rose, J. S., Medway, F. J., Cantrell, V. L., & Marus, S. H. (1983). A fresh look at the retention-promotion controversy. *Journal of School Psychology, 21,* 201-211.
Discusses several important issues, presenting a historical perspective followed by a summary of the current trends in policies and retention rates. A brief review of the research literature and some of the relevant philosophical issues serve as a springboard for a discussion on the retention/promotion decision-making process.

Elligett, J. K. & Tocco, T. S. (1983, June). The promotion/retention controversy in Pinellas County, Florida. *Phi Delta Kappan,* 733-735.
Presents a description of a district-wide promotion and retention policy instituted in 1977, and empirical results of data collected through 1982.

BEST PRACTICES IN SOCIAL SKILLS TRAINING

Frank M. Gresham
Louisiana State University

OVERVIEW

Social skills are important in school settings for a variety of reasons. Children and youth who are deficient in social skills and/or who are poorly accepted by peers have a high incidence of school maladjustment, school suspensions, expulsions, dropping out, delinquency, childhood psychopathology, and adult mental health difficulties (see Gresham, 1981a, 1981b for reviews).

Social skill deficiencies have also been related to the social outcomes of mainstreaming. Mainstreamed handicapped children are often poorly accepted or socially rejected by nonhandicapped peers. The social interactions between mainstreamed handicapped children and their nonhandicapped peers occur at low rates and/or are more negative in nature (Gresham 1982a, 1983a).

Social skills have been related to other measures of classroom functioning such as academic achievement, attending behavior, question-asking, and teacher acceptance (Cartledge & Milburn, 1978). Several social skills differentiate mainstreamed handicapped children from their nonhandicapped peers. Stumme, Gresham, and Scott (1982) found that the skills of independent work, expressing feelings, positive attitude toward self, appropriate movement around the school environment, and attending behavior best discriminated mainstreamed emotionally disabled from nonhandicapped students.

The foregoing paragraphs strongly suggest that social skills are extremely important for children and youth to learn and use in school settings. School psychologists assist children to develop these skills by assessing and remediating their social skill deficiencies.

BASIC CONSIDERATIONS

Social Competence

Social competence and social skills represent two distinct constructs. McFall (1982) states that *social skills* are the specific behaviors that an individual exhibits in order to perform competently on a task. In contrast, *social competence* is an evaluative term based upon judgments that a person has performed a task adequately. These judgments are based upon opinions of significant others such as parents or teachers, comparisons to explicit criteria including number of social tasks performed correctly in relation to some criterion, or reference to some normative sample.

The issue of social competence can be recast in terms of social validity: the determination of the clinical, applied, and/or social importance of exhibiting certain behaviors in particular situations (Kazdin, 1977; Van Houten, 1979; Wolf, 1978). That is, behavior is considered socially competent if it predicts important social outcomes for individuals (Gresham, 1983b). The concept of social validity is more thoroughly discussed in the next section.

Reschly and Gresham (1981) conceptualized social competence as being comprised of two components: (a) *adaptive behavior* and (b) *social skills*. Adaptive behavior for children and youth includes independent functioning skills, physical development, language development, and academic competencies (see Reschly this volume). Social skills include *interpersonal behaviors* such as accepting authority, conversation skills, cooperative behaviors, *self-related behaviors* including expressing feelings, ethical behavior, positive attitude toward self, and *task-related behaviors* such as attending behavior, completing tasks, following directions. Details regarding these social skills are found in recent publications (see Gresham, 1981b, 1983a; Stumme et al., 1982; Stumme, Gresham & Scott, 1983; Stephens, 1978).

Definitions of Social Skill

At least three general definitions can be distilled from the accumulated literature on children's social skills. One definition is termed the *peer acceptance definition* in that researchers primarily use indices of peer acceptance to define social skill. Thus, children and youth who are accepted by their peers are said to be socially skilled. The major drawback of a peer acceptance definition of social skill is that it cannot identify what specific behaviors lead to peer acceptance or popularity. Consequently, social behaviors to target for remediation are not identified for the poorly accepted child. This is analogous to knowing that a child scored at the 2nd percentile in academic achievement. Such data do not provide useful nor specific information for intervention purposes.

Another frequently used definition is termed a *behavioral definition*. This approach defines social skills as those situationally specific responses that maximize the probability of producing and/or maintaining reinforcement and minimize the probability of punishment or extinction. Naturalistic observations are typically used to behaviorally assess social skills. This definition has the advantage over the peer acceptance definition in that antecedents and consequences of particular

social behaviors are identified, specified, and operationalized for assessment and intervention purposes. In spite of this, the behavioral definition does not ensure that these social behaviors are in fact *socially skilled, socially significant,* or *socially important.* Merely increasing the frequency of certain behaviors that researchers define *a priori* as social skills does not impact upon goals or outcomes valued by society at large (Gresham, 1983a).

A final and perhaps a better-conceived definition of social skills is termed a *social validity definition.* According to this definition, social skills are those behaviors which, within a given situation, predict important social outcomes for children. These important social outcomes are: (a) peer acceptance or popularity; (b) significant others' judgments of social skill; and/or (c) other social behaviors known to consistently correlate with (a) and (b) above. This definition has the advantage of not only specifying behaviors and situations in which a child is deficient, but also defines these behaviors as "socially skilled" based upon their relationships to socially important outcomes such as peer acceptance and teacher acceptance.

Conceptualization of Social Skill Problems

Social skill problems are classified into four types depending upon whether or not the child knows how to perform the skill and the presence or absence of emotional arousal responses such as anxiety or anger. The four types are as follows: (a) *skill deficits,* (b) *performance deficits,* (c) *self-control skill deficits,* and (d) *self-control performance deficits.* Although this conceptualization is primarily speculative, there is empirical support for the majority of social skills problems described below (Camp, Blom, Herbert & van Doorninck, 1977; Gottman, 1977; Gresham, 1981a, 1981b; Meichenbaum, 1977; Van Hasselt et al., 1979).

Skill Deficits

Children with *social skill deficits* either do not have the necessary skills in their repertoire to interact appropriately with peers or they do not know a critical step in the performance of a given social skill. These skill deficits are similar to what Bandura (1969, 1977a) refers to as acquisition or learning deficits.

Skill deficits can be clarified by using school examples. A child who does not know the "+" operation sign has a skill deficit in that he/she does not know what behavior to exhibit when seeing the addition sign. Likewise, a child may not know how to join an ongoing activity or game in which other children are involved. The child may not know what to say, how to say it, and/or what to do in this type of situation. Remediation of this type of skills deficit focuses upon teaching the child via modeling, coaching, or behavior rehearsal how to join ongoing play activities.

A similar example can be used to elucidate a skills deficits in which a child does not know a critical component of a given skill. A child may know the "+" operation sign, but may not know what to do when confronted with a problem such as $32 + 19 = $ _____ Although the child knows what to do when seeing the "+" sign, he/she has left out the regrouping component of addition when responding to the problem $32 + 19 = 41$.

An example of a social skills problem in which a child leaves out a critical component is giving a compliment. The child is able to formulate a reason for giving a compliment knows how to phrase a compliment, and discriminates the most appropriate time for giving a compliment. However, the child does not know how to compliment others in a clear and sincere voice. Given this assessment, an intervention would focus upon teaching the child how to compliment clearly and sincerely. Most *social skill deficits* are remediated through modeling, coaching, and/or behavior rehearsal (Gresham, 1981b, 1982b, 1983c; Gresham & Lemanek, 1983). Figure 1 presents a classification of childrens' social skills problems.

Figure 1.

CLASSIFICATION OF SOCIAL SKILL PROBLEMS

	Acquisition Deficit	Performance Deficit
Emotional Arousal Response Absent	Social Skill Deficit	Social Performance Deficit
Emotional Arousal Response Present	Self-Control Skill Deficit	Self-Control Performance Deficit

Performance Deficits

A *social performance deficit* describes children who have the skills in their repertoires, but do not perform them at acceptable levels. Performance deficits are thought of as a deficiency in the number of times a social behavior is emitted and are related to a lack of motivation or an absence of opportunity to perform the behavior. It is important to realize that fear, anxiety, or other emotional arousal responses do *not* enter into a social performance deficit. The presence of emotional arousal responses that prevent the acquisition or performance of social behaviors are termed *self-control skill* and *self-control performance deficits*, respectively.

The key in determining whether a social skills problem is a performance deficit is whether or not the child performs the behavior. Thus, if the child does not perform a behavior in a classroom situation, but performs the behavior in a role playing situation; it is a *social performance* deficit. Also, if the child performed the behavior in the past, it is probably a performance rather than a skill deficit. Given that difficulties either in stimulus control or reinforcement contingencies are functionally related to social performance deficits, training strategies focus upon antecedent and consequent control techniques. These strategies include peer initiations (Strain, Shores, & Timm, 1977), sociodramatic activities (Strain, 1975), contingent social reinforcement (Allen, Hart, Buell, Harris, & Wolf, 1964), token reinforcement programs (Iwata & Bailey, 1974), and group contingencies (Gamble & Strain, 1979).

Self-Control Skill Deficits

This type of social skill problem describes a child who has not learned a particular social skill because some type of emotional arousal response has prevented the *acquisition* of the skill. One emotional arousal response that interferes with learning is *anxiety*. Anxiety has been shown to prevent the acquisition of appropriate coping responses, particularly concerning fears and phobias (see Bandura, 1969, 1977a, 1977b for comprehensive reviews). Hence, children do not learn how to interact with peers because anxiety or fear prevents approach behavior. In turn, avoidance of or escape from social situations reduces anxiety thereby reinforcing isolation behaviors.

Another emotional arousal response that prevents the acquisition of social skills is impulsivity, the tendency toward short response latencies in social situations. Children who exhibit impulsive behavior fail to learn appropriate interaction strategies because their behavior often results in rejection by peers who avoid the impulsive child. As a result, the target child is not exposed to models of appropriate behavior or is placed on an extinction schedule for his/her social responses.

This behavioral formulation suggests that the target child emits aversive social behaviors as a result of an impulsive response style. This results in rejection by peers, parents, and teachers. Consequently, the behaviors of significant others in the child's environment that lead to avoidance of the target child are reinforced. In turn, the target child's behavior is either punished by verbal or physical reprimands, or extinguished by ignoring. The outcome of this sequence of events is that the child does not learn the skills for appropriate interaction.

Several studies in the literature have described the skill-deficient child (Bryan, 1978; Camp et al., 1977; Meichenbaum & Goodman, 1971; O'Leary & Dubey, 1979; Zahavi & Asher, 1978). Determination of a self-control skill deficit rests upon two criteria: (a) the presence of an *emotional arousal response*, and (b) the child either *not knowing* or *never having performed* the skill in question. Teaching strategies typically take the form of anxiety-reducing techniques such as desensitization or flooding, coupled with modeling/coaching and *self-control strategies* including self-talk, self-monitoring, self-reinforcement (see Kendall & Braswell, 1982; Kendall & Wilcox, 1979; Meichenbaum, 1977; Urbain & Kendall, 1980 for reviews).

Self-Control Performance Deficits

Children with self-control performance deficits have the specific social skill in their repertoires, but do not perform the skill because of an emotional arousal response and problems in antecedent and/or consequent control. That is, the person knows how to perform the skill, but does so infrequently or inconsistently. The key difference between self-control skill and performance deficits is whether or not the child has the social skill in the repertoire. In the former case, the skill has never been learned, in the latter case, the skill has been learned but is not exhibited consistently. Two criteria are used to determine a self-control performance deficit: (a) the presence of an emotional arousal response and (b) the inconsistent performance of the skill in question. Interventions with this type of problem typically focus upon self-control strategies to teach the child how to inhibit inappropriate behavior, stimulus control training designed to teach discrimination of potentially conflictful situations, and/or reinforcement contingencies for appropriate social behaviors (Blackwood, 1970; Bolstad & Johnson, 1972; Bornstein & Quevillon, 1976; Drabman, 1973).

BEST PRACTICES

A number of procedures have been identified as effective social skills training strategies. The myriad of strategies are classified under four major headings: (a) *manipulation of antecedents*, (b) *manipulation of consequences*, (c) *modeling*, and (d) *cognitive-behavioral techniques*.

Manipulation of antecedents focuses upon identifying and changing those environmental events that precede or set the occasion for appropriate social interaction. Having a child's peers initiate positive social interactions, changing a child's seat to promote interaction, and playing games are examples of this type of social skills training strategy.

Manipulation of consequences represents a class of procedures which manipulate events consequent to a child's behavior. These procedures are predicated on the assumption that poor social skills result from the lack of reinforcement for appropriate behavior. Examples of these procedures include contingent social reinforcement, token systems, group contingencies, and home-based contingency systems (Gresham, 1981b).

Modeling procedures use either live or symbolic modeling displays to teach social skills. In modeling, the entire behavioral sequence of a given social skill is demonstrated either in person (live modeling) or in film/videotape format (symbolic modeling). The most effective modeling procedures use reinforced modeling displays, coping rather than mastery models, and models who are similar in age and sex to observers (Gresham, 181b).

Cognitive-behavioral techniques involve coaching, self-control strategies such as self-instruction, self-monitoring, or self-reinforcement, and covert modeling/behavior rehearsal to teach social behavior. While effective with some children, there is currently little research to support the efficacy of these strategies with cognitively impaired children such as the mildly retarded.

Structured Learning: An Overview

The *structured learning* approach to social skills training (SST) is based upon a *directive teaching* model (Stephens, 1978). *Directive teaching* is skill training oriented within a diagnostic-prescriptive model of teaching that consists of four steps. *First,* behaviors are defined and stated in observable terms that specify both the movements which make up the behavior and the conditions under which behavior occur. *Second,* behaviors are assessed using the procedures described in Brockman's chapter in this book on social skills assessment. *Third,* teaching strategies are prescribed to fit the student's needs as determined by the assessment. *Fourth,* the effects of the teaching procedure on the performance of social skills are empirically validated. This define-assess-teach-evaluate (DATE) model is applied continuously to each deficient social behavior the student exhibits.

Directive teaching is predicated on the research literature that suggests the best way to teach both academic and social skills is through direct instruction. If a child cannot read, teach reading skills. If a child cannot carry on a conversation, teach conversational skills. Much instructional time and effort have been unnecessarily wasted by trying to remediate processing deficits in the academic arena or personality traits or predispositions in the social skills arena. The key point to remember is that the most *effective means of teaching social behavior is by teaching it directly.* The vast literature supporting social learning theory (Bandura, 1969, 1977a) indicates that most social behavior is learned either through *tuition* or *modeling.* As such, school psychologists use those procedures that have the strongest base of research support to teach social skills.

Components of Structured Learning

Structured learning as presented here consists of five basic steps: (a) *establishing the need;* (b) *identifying skill components;* (c) *modeling;* (d) *rehearsing behavior,* and (e) *generalization training.* Each of these components is discussed in the following paragraphs.

Establishing the need. The first step in SST is to establish the need for the child to perform the social skill in question. This makes the skill relevant for the child, specifies why it is important, what benefits are derived from learning the skill, and what disadvantages might accrue from not knowing or not performing the behavior.

The need to perform particular social skills is established by reading stories about same-aged children, discussing the advantages of the skill in a group, or using films, filmstrips, or other audio-visual equipment. For example, discussion of the advantages of performing the skill could relate to specific problem situations children are experiencing. Remember that the purpose of this first step is to *make the skill and its probable outcomes salient for the child.* Chances are the child has not really thought about the performance of the skill and its consequences.

Children are also taught to discriminate between short-term and long-term consequences for performing particular social skills. Examples of short-term consequences include receiving recognition in the group, avoiding homework assignments, and so forth. Long term consequences include popularity, respect from teachers and peers, and the like. Before teaching each skill, identify several short-term and long-term consequences.

Identifying skill components. This step immediately follows the discussion regarding the need to perform the skill. Elicit from the group the specific behaviors in proper sequence that make up the skill. In other words, *task analyze* the social skill to be taught. The specificity and number of subtasks identified are, in part, dictated by the age and degree of sophistication of the group. When there are too many steps in the analysis, they are often placed out of sequence or even forgotten.

A recurrent question in task analyses of social skills is: *How large do I make the subtasks?* First, much of the social skills research has used relatively *molecular behaviors* such as eye contact when speaking, number of on-topic questions, number of assertive responses, and physical proximity to other people during interaction. Other research has focused upon relatively *molar behaviors* such as sharing with others and cooperation.

Neither *molecular* nor the *molar* levels of analyses are the most appropriate for task analyzing social skills. The rule for task analysis is *analyze* at *the level of what people do.* That is, people do not just have good conversational skills (molar interpretation), they *perform* the following: (a) identify a topic for conversation; (b) greet another person; (c) make eye contact; (d) make introductory small talk; (e) decide if the other person is listening, and (f) move to the topic of conversation identified at Step (a). Each of these steps is directly taught in its proper sequence and mistakes in the performance or sequencing of these steps are corrected. A molar approach does not provide specific feedback on why the performance was unsatisfactory. By the same token, a molecular conceptualization is not likely to be very meaningful to children (e.g., "You only looked at the person 46% of the time while you were speaking"; "You had only two on-topic questions in a five-minute conversation").

It is strongly recommended that children participate in the analysis of the components (subtasks) of a social skill. For example, for the skill of friendship, a film or story is presented that depicts children successfully making friends. It is followed by a discussion to identify specific responses that helped the characters to make friends. As the component behaviors are generated, they are listed and sequenced on a chalkboard or chart.

Step 1 — Say, "Hi, how are you? My name is _____. "What's yours?"

Step 2 — Ask something like, "Where are you from?" or "What are you doing?"

Step 3 — Invite him or her to do something, "I want to play checkers. Would you like to play with me?"

In identifying component behaviors, trainers use the child's own words as much as possible and take into consideration developmental levels and cultural differences. Handicapped children probably require more prompts in identifying specific behaviors and in correctly sequencing responses. Moreover, handicapped children require relatively more repetitions of the response identification and sequencing phases to facilitate overlearning of the responses. They probably also need *verbal prompts* since many of these children especially the mildly retarded do not spontaneously use the strategies that were taught.

Modeling. Modeling is one of the most effective and efficient ways of teaching social behavior. It is used to inhibit or disinhibit behavior and has been employed to teach a variety of social behaviors. Modeling is efficient in the sense that component behaviors of a particular social skill are not taught using a time-consuming shaping process. Since shaping involves reinforcement of successive approximations to the desired terminal response, it is a relatively lengthy, drawn-out procedure. Modeling, on the other hand, presents the entire behavior at once and also teaches how the specific behaviors in a sequence can be integrated into a composite behavior, the social skill.

The psychological processes that are required to learn and perform a skill through modeling are: (a) *attention*, (b) *retention*, (c) *motor reproduction*, and (d) *motivation*. A person has to *attend* to the modeled behavior, *retain* the behavior in memory, have the motor skills necessary to reproduce it, and have some incentive or motivation to perform the modeled behavior. The first two processes, attention and retention, are necessary for *learning* or *skill acquisition*. Modeling remediates both skill and performance deficits, although it is used primarily to teach new social behavior or to demonstrate proper response integration and sequencing. Modeling is also used to remediate *self-control* deficits. It has been demonstrated that exposure to proper models reduces certain emotional arousal responses (Bandura, 1977a).

Modeling takes a variety of formats including videotape or film modeling, verbal modeling via books and stories, and live modeling. For most purposes, live modeling is the most practical and flexible teaching procedure.

Modeling displays are presented in a clear and detailed manner, call attention to the component behaviors, and use several different models if necessary. Members of the group monitor whether or not each of the steps was followed and properly sequenced. Each step is verbally identified when modeling the skill to make each component behavior more salient.

The modeling procedure works like this when teaching social behavior. After having established the need for performing the skill and having identified the skill components, the facilitator chooses another child with whom to role play the skill. The steps are verbalized aloud while modeling the skill (e.g., "First, I say hello", "Then, I ask the other person's name." "Finally, I ask them if they want to play."). The skill is modeled several times with different partners depending upon the complexity of the skill and the sophistication of the group.

After the modeling display, a discussion follows and provides answers to the following questions.

1. What behaviors occurred?
2. Did the model complete all of the responses the group listed on the board?
3. Were the responses properly sequenced?
4. Was the model effective in performing the skill? Why?
5. How do you think the model felt after performing the skill? Why?
6. What other responses might the model have used in this situation?

This discussion helps children think about consequences of social skills, assists them in retaining the steps necessary to perform the social skill, and teaches them to discriminate effective from ineffective performances.

It is not necessary for the facilitator to always be the model for particular social skills. One may want to form an SST group using *peer confederates* who have a high level of social skills. These children are trained before the group starts and effectively provide the modeling displays. When working with groups of handicapped children, the use of nonhandicapped peer confederates is a major step in the successful *social integration* of handicapped children into the mainstream of the school environment.

Rehearsing Behavior. The purpose of this step is to have students practice or exercise the skill with each other and receive feedback from the leader and peers regarding the quality of skill performance. Observed behavior are not necessarily learned unless some mechanism is put into operation whereby the observed behavior is retained and subsequently reproduced. Modeled behaviors are practiced by the child before they are produced in real-life situations. *Behavioral rehearsal* represents a form of structured role playing that enables the student to act out and practice the new behaviors.

The behavior rehearsal phase uses the

same behaviors that were modeled except that in this step, two students in the group practice the skill. This step is initiated by asking for two volunteers to rehearse the skill. It serves as an additional modeling display for the group.

Response feedback is a critical component of the behavior rehearsal phase since feedback about performance is necessary for the child to make corrections to improve skills. Feedback takes a variety of forms including corrective instructions or praise, tangible reinforcers for correct performance, and/or self-evaluation whereby the child evaluates his/her own performance.

Behavior rehearsal sequences are followed by a discussion for the purposes of indicating better ways of performing the skill, suggesting alternative responses, and social reinforcement. Coaching is a direct instructional technique that primarily uses *verbal instruction* and *feedback* in teaching social behavior. Both the modeling and behavior rehearsal phases contain a large coaching component. This combination of modeling, behavior rehearsal, and coaching often leads to better skill performance than any single procedure.

Generalization training. Social skills are relatively useless unless they are performed in "real-life" settings and situations. For social skills to have any functional or adaptive value, they must be generalized from instructional settings into other settings, to other persons, and over time.

Stokes and Baer (1977) suggest the following strategies for programming generalization.

1. Look for a response that enters a "natural" community; in particular teach children to cue their potential natural communities to reinforce their desirable behaviors.

2. Train more exemplars and diversify them.

3. Loosen experimental control over stimuli and responses involved in training; in particular, train different examples concurrently, and vary instructions, discriminative stimuli, social reinforcers, and backup reinforcers.

4. Use stimuli that are likely to be found in generalization settings; in particular, use peers and tutors.

5. Reinforce accurate self-reports of desirable behavior; apply self-recording and self-reinforcement techniques whenever possible.

SUMMARY

Social skills are not only important for school-age children and youth, but also represent an area in which school psychologists can expand and modify their roles. Social skills are related to academic achievement, teacher and peer acceptance, cognitive development, and classroom behaviors such as work completion, attention to task or asking questions. Social skills are related to the social outcomes of mainstreaming and the differentiation of handicapped from nonhandicapped children.

A conceptualization of social skills deficits was presented based upon the presence or absence of the social behavior in the child's repertoire (skill versus performance) and the presence or absence of emotional arousal responses (self-control). Relationships between specific social skills deficits and remedial social skills training strategies were discussed.

A structured learning approach to social skills training based upon a *directive teaching model* was presented as the most efficient and effective teaching procedure. Components of this procedure were definition, assessment, teaching, and evaluation of social skills training. Specific social skills training strategies included modeling, coaching, behavior rehearsal, response feedback, and generalization training for conceptualizing social difficulties from an intervention/training standpoint.

REFERENCES

Allen, K. E., Hart, B. M., Buell, J. S., Harris, F. R., & Wolf, M. M. (1964). Effects of social reinforcement on isolate behavior of a nursery school child. *Child Development, 35*, 511-518.

Bandura, A. (1969). *Principles of behavior modification*. New York: Holt, Rinehart, & Winston.

Bandura, A. (1977a). *Social learning theory*. Englewood Cliffs, NJ: Prentice-Hall.

Bandura, A. (1977b). Self-efficacy: Toward a unifying theory of behavior change. *Psychological Review, 84*, 191-215.

Blackwood, R. O. (1970). The operant conditioning of verbal mediated self-control in the classroom. *Journal of School Psychology, 8*, 251-258.

Bolstad, O. D., & Johnson, S. M. (1977). The relationship between teacher's assessment of students and students' actual behavior in the classroom. *Child Development, 48*, 570-578.

Bryan, T. S. (1978). Social relationships and verbal interactions of learning disabled children. *Journal of Learning Disabilities, 11*, 107-115.

Camp, B. W., Blom, G. E., Herbert, F., & Van Doorninck, W. J. (1977). "Think Aloud": A program for developing self-control in young aggressive boys. *Journal of Abnormal Child Psychology, 5*, 157-169.

Cartledge, G., & Milburn, J. (1978). The case for teaching social skills in the classroom: A review. *Review of Educational Research, 48*, 133-156.

Drabman, R. S. (1973). Child-versus-teacher-administered programs in a psychiatric hospital school. *Journal of Abnormal Child Psychology, 1*, 68-87.

Gamble, R., & Strain, R. S. (1979). The effects of dependent and interdependent group contingencies on socially appropriate responses in classes for emotionally handicapped children. *Psychology in the Schools, 16*, 253-260.

Gottman, J. M. (1977). The effects of a modeling film on social isolation in preschool children: A methodological investigation. *Journal of Abnormal Child Psychology, 5*, 69-78.

Gresham, F. M. (1981a). Assessment of children's social skills. *Journal of School Psychology, 19*, 120-133.

Gresham, F. M. (1981b). Social skills training with handicapped children: A review. *Review of Educational Research, 51*, 139-176.

Gresham, F. M. (1982a). Misguided mainstreaming: The case for social skills training with handicapped children. *Exceptional Children, 48*, 422-433.

Gresham, F. M. (1982b). Social skills instruction for exceptional children. *Theory Into Practice, 20*, 129-133.

Gresham, F. M. (1983a). Social validity in the assessment of children's social skills: Establishing standards for social competency. *Journal of Psychoeducational Assessment, 1*, 297-307.

Gresham, F. M. (1983b). Social skills assessment as a component of mainstreaming placement decisions. *Exceptional Children, 49*, 331-336.

Gresham, F. M., & Lemanek, K. L. (1983). Social skills: A review of cognitive-behavioral training procedures with children. *Journal of Applied Developmental Psychology, 4*, 439-461.

Iwata, B. A., & Bailey, J. S. (1974). Reward versus cost token systems: An analysis of the effects on students and teacher. *Journal of Applied Behavior Analysis, 7*, 567-576.

Kazdin, A. E. (1977). Assessing the clinical or applied importance of behavior change through social validation. *Behavior Modification, 1*, 427-451.

Kendall, P. C., & Braswell, L. (1982). Assessment for cognitive behavioral interventions in the schools. *School Psychology Review, 11*, 21-31.

Kendall, P. C., & Wilcox, L. E. (1979). Self-control in children: Development of a rating scale. *Journal of Consulting and Clinical Psychology, 47*, 1020-1029.

Leland, H. W. (1978). Theoretical considerations of adaptive behavior. In A. Coulter & H. Morrow (Eds.), *Adaptive behavior: Concepts and measurements*. New York: Grune & Stratton.

MacMillan, D. (1982). *Mental retardation in school and society* (2nd ed.). New York: Little Brown.

McFall, R. M. (1982). A review and reformulation of the concept of social skills. *Behavioral Assessment, 4*, 1-33.

Meichenbaum, D. (1977). *Cognitive behavior modification*. New York: Plenum Press.

Meichenbaum, D., & Goodman, J. (1971). Training impulsive children to talk to themselves: A means of developing self-control. *Journal of Abnormal Psychology, 77*, 115-126.

O'Leary, S. G., & Dubey, D. R. (1979). Applications of self-control procedures by children: A review. *Journal of Applied Behavior Analysis, 12*, 449-465.

Reschly, D. J., & Gresham, F. M. (1981). *Use of social competence measures to facilitate parent and teacher involvement and nonbiased assessment.* Unpublished manuscript. Iowa State University.

Robinson, N., & Robinson, H. (1976). *The mentally retarded child.* New York: McGraw Hill.

Stephens, T. M. (1978). *Social skills in the classroom.* Columbus, Ohio: Cedars Press.

Stokes, T., & Baer, D. (1977). An implicit technology of generalization. *Journal of Applied Behavior Analysis, 10,* 349-368.

Strain, P. S. (1975). Increasing social play of severely retarded preschoolers with sociodramatic activities. *Mental Retardation, 13,* 7-9.

Strain, P. S., Shores, R. E., & Timm, M. A. (1977). Effects of peer social initiations on the behavior of withdrawn preschool children. *Journal of Applied Behavior Analysis, 10,* 289-298.

Stumme, V. S., Gresham, F. M., & Scott, N. A. (1982). Validity of *Social Behavior Assessment* in discriminating emotionally disabled from nonhandicapped students. *Journal of Behavioral Assessment, 4,* 327-342.

Stumme, V. S., Gresham, F. M., & Scott, N. A. (1983). Dimensions of children's classroom social behavior. *Journal of Behavioral Assessment, 5,* 161-177.

Urbain, E. S., & Kendall, P. C. (1980). Review of social-cognitive problem-solving interventions with children. *Psychological Bulletin, 88,* 109-143.

Van Hasselt, V. B., Hersen, M., Whitehill, M. B., & Bellack, A. S. (1979). Social skill assessment and training for children: An evaluative review. *Behavior Research and Therapy, 17,* 413-437.

Van Houten, R. (1979). Social validation: The evolution of standards of competency for target behaviors. *Journal of Applied Behavior Analysis, 12,* 581-591.

Wolf, M. M. (1978). Social validity: The case for subjective measurement or how applied behavior analysis is finding its heart. *Journal of Applied Behavior Analysis, 11,* 203-214.

Zahavi, S. L., & Asher, S. R. (1978). The effect of verbal instruction on preschool children's aggressive behavior. *Journal of School Psychology, 16,* 146-153.

ANNOTATED BIBLIOGRAPHY

Cartledge, G., & Milburn, J. F. (1980). *Teaching social skills to children: Innovative Approaches.* New York: Pergamon Press.

This brief book presents an excellent overview of the conceptualization, assessment, teaching, and generalization of social skills with child and adolescent populations. Chapters focus upon social isolation, early childhood, severely handicapped, and behaviorally disordered groups. Twenty-six pages in the appendix are devoted to a listing of resources for teaching social skills.

Goldstein, A. P., Sprafkin, R. P., Gershaw, N. J., & Klein, P. (1980). *Skillstreaming the adolescent: A structured learning approach to teaching prosocial skills.* Champaign, Illinois: Research Press.

This brief book presents a curriculum for teaching social skills to adolescents focusing upon adolescents. *Structured Learning* consisting of modeling, role-playing, feedback, and transfer training is suggested to teach 50 social skills crucial for adolescent social development. The book also contains a teacher rating scale for the 50 social skills as well as examples of homework assignment forms to promote generalization.

Gresham, F. M. (1981). Social skills training with handicapped children: A review. *Review of Educational Research, 51,* 139-176.

Behavioral techniques derived from social learning theory to training social skills are reviewed. Studies using both handicapped and nonhandicapped populations are included. The literature is divided into four broad areas for review purposes: (a) manipulation of antecedents, (b) manipulation of consequences, (c) modeling, and (d) cognitive-behavioral techniques. It is concluded that social skills training is a potentially useful approach to successful mainstreaming of handicapped children.

Stephens, T. M. (1978). *Social skills in the classroom.* Columbus, Ohio: Cedars Press.

This is the most comprehensive social skills curriculum available as it contains specific procedures for teaching 136 social skills. These social skills are grouped under four broad categories: (a) Environmental Behaviors; (b) Interpersonal Behaviors; (c) Self-Related Behaviors; and (d) Task-Related Behaviors. The curriculum is appropriate for children ranging from kindergarten through 8th grade. Numerous resources and references for teaching social behavior are in the Stephens' social skills curriculum.

Walker, H. M., McConnell, S., Holmes, D., Todis, B., Walker, J., & Golden, N. (1983). *The Walker Social Skills Curriculum: The Accepts Program.* Austin, Texas: Pro-Ed.
This curriculum is designed to teach critically important teacher-child and peer-to-peer social-behavioral competencies essential for a successful adjustment to the behavioral demands of mainstream settings. It is designed for mildly and moderately handicapped children in primary and intermediate grades. A placement test, a nine-step instructional procedure, scripts for teaching social skills, and activities are contained in the program

BEST PRACTICES IN FACILITATING ORGANIZATIONAL CHANGE IN THE SCHOOLS

Robert G. Harrington
University of Kansas

OVERVIEW

It is easy to think of Citibank of New York, AT&T, and General Motors as organizational systems. These are all powerful corporations with many different divisions, employing large numbers of people and requiring a coordination of all personnel and services. Although it may not be quite so obvious, schools are organizational systems, too, just like these big businesses. Organizational systems are composed of individuals working together to reach common goals. Unlike these three profit-making corporations, however, the primary goal of school systems is to educate children. All professional staff working in a school system, not just the classroom teacher, share this responsibility.

Because schools represent unique organizational systems the kinds of organizational dysfunctions encountered by them may be unlike those of any big business. For example, educators may spend a great deal of time and exert much effort in trying to reach some undefined educational goals dictated by society at large. When these educators fail to reach these nebulous and constantly changing goals they may feel blamed and frustrated. In fact, the real problem may rest not with individual teachers but with the organizational plan itself. It may be that the goals as stated are unattainable, conflict with each other, or possibly cannot be measured accurately with present instrumentation. Another organizational problem to which school organizational systems may be prone involves miscommunication. Opportunities for collaboration among teaching staff may be few if individual teachers seek commentary and reactions mostly from the supervising principal and that principal communicates with individual staff members and not the group. The result can be poor interpersonal relations, stress, and eventually teacher burnout. To simply establish better person-to-person communication between any two teachers will not solve this problem. A systematic attempt to increase communication among all staff members in the system is required. Finally, organizational problems may arise in the process of adopting new system-wide educational programs designed to serve large groups of children. A case in point involves one school system which adopted an assertive discipline model for managing students. It was soon observed that children's attitudes toward school turned extremely negative, parents complained and teachers became exasperated. It would have proven futile to deal with this situation on a child-by-child basis. Alternatively, a more expeditious and rational approach would be to review the school's classroom management model and redesign it as appropriate.

What should be clear by now is that each one of these case examples has one point in common. Each requires the school consultants to break out of the case consultation mindset from time to time and rethink referrals from the broader organizational "systems" perspective. Without the "system" perspective such problems will inevitably be localized in the classroom setting when in fact, changes at the broader level of the organizational "system" may be required. The strategies involved in diagnosis and intervention for change at the organizational level are considerably different from those typically employed by most school psychologists working with an individual teacher, child or parent. Consequently, the purpose of this chapter is fivefold:

1. to describe in detail how schools fit the characteristics of organizational systems.

2. to explain the qualifications and role of the school-based OD consultant.

3. to apply the principles of planned change to the public school system.

4. to illustrate the functions of the school psychologist as an organization renewal consultant with a case illustration.

5. to provide an annotated bibliography of related references for further reading.

BASIC CONSIDERATIONS

When schools are described as organizational "systems" it means that they are composed of many different groups of professionals. For example, schools employ curriculum specialists, regular classroom teachers, special education personnel, administrators, and special education support personnel like school psychologists. Each of these groups has a distinct and specialized service to offer. Despite these distinctions, an organization, such as a school, can function efficiently only when all these groups of individuals are working together in a coordinated manner. If this is not the case, then their individual efforts, however well-intentioned, may be at odds with their other colleagues.

Systems are not static entities. They are dynamic (see figure 1) (Gordon, 1983). A system is fueled by some rather basic resources called *inputs*. The inputs for schools include tax dollars to support the educational process; school buildings, books, computers, and libraries to facilitate learning; and teachers to conduct the educational experience. All of these basic inputs contribute to the teaching and learning process. Without the benefit of any one of these inputs effective teaching and learning may not occur. This combined effort is called *transformation*. After all this effort, most systems will produce some *output* or product. Some of the products school patrons have come to expect include high achievement test scores, high literacy rates, good citizens, and entrance for their children into colleges. School systems may be evaluated on how well they achieve these goals.

A number of assumptions and values positions underlie a systems approach to organizational development (French & Bell, 1978; Huse, 1980). The school consultant interested in effecting change at the organizational level should be aware of these. It is assumed that because system components are interdependent, organizational change may be complex by its nature. Systems change also implies a dynamic and open organization capable of adaptation and improvement in response to feedback from the external environment. When one subsystem changes in response to a felt need, related changes will ripple throughout interconnected subsystems. Consequently, organizational renewal may result in some power shifting from the administrative level to the staff in a school system. For these reasons, individual goals and school organizational goals may need to be revised. Systems consultation also assumes the consultant is capable of simultaneously and accurately perceiving the organizational gestalt with its many interrelated subsystems. To explore an organizational development strategy suggests a conscious decision to enlarge the data base used by organization members in decision making. Another major assumption of any organizational renewal efforts is that most individuals have drives toward personal growth if provided a stimulating environment. OD places great trust in organization mem-

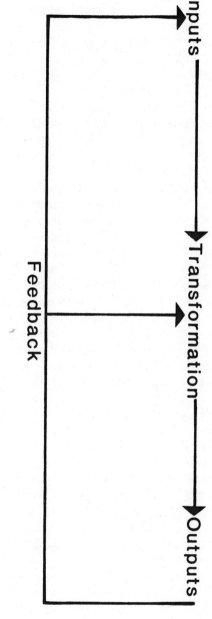

Figure 1. The Basic Systems Model

bers by presuming that they can and are willing to contribute to organizational goals if given the opportunity. A final assumption of most organizational change efforts is that it is not sufficient to change only individuals within a system. Any improvements in the human subsystem of the organization need to be maintained through appropriate changes in the supporting appraisal, compensation, training, staffing, task and communications subsystems. When these values and assumptions are not made explicit hidden agendas between the OD consultant and his/her client(s) can grow and trust may diminish.

The Qualifictions and Functions of the School-Based OD Consultant Qualifications of Systems Change Agents

The activities involved in organizational development in the schools require a blend of professional skills and personal qualities. Professional qualifications include: (a) diagnostic ability; (b) basic knowledge of behavioral science techniques; (c) knowledge of the theories and methods within the consultant's own discipline; (d) goal-setting ability; and (e) problem-solving ability (Miles & Schmuck, 1976). Furthermore, in order to be effective the competent OD consultant must also possess a range of personal qualities. The change agent should be cognizant of personal needs, motivations, and skills in relation to the requirements of the job. The ability to evaluate the situations within the system objectively is critical. Imagination and flexibility may be needed to create the optimal intervention plan to match a unique problem. Honesty, consistency and trust are at the core of the consultation relationship. Finally, the consultant's self-image should be built on a foundation of stability and security. This is because even the best school consultant

can expect to receive occasional feedback which could make a less self-confident individual feel vulnerable and defensive (French, Bell, & Zawicki, 1978).

Change agents may arise internally within an organization or may be hired externally. It has been suggested that schools would be well-advised to hire or assign internal facilitators; however, the typical pattern has been to employ external facilitator-consultants (Gordon, 1983). Both types have certain advantages and disadvantages. On the one hand, internal agents compared to external agents may possess more complete knowledge of the organization and represent a known, readily-available reference person. On the other hand, such individuals may be too close to the problem, hold biased views and create additional resistance if viewed as part of the problem. The advantages of the external agent include more objective views of the organization and more experience in dealing with diverse problems. Potential disadvantages include less knowledge of the organization, an unknown track record and longer start-up time.

School psychologists seem to be especially well-suited to serve in a consultative capacity on issues of organizational renewal for several reasons. By their job descriptions, school psychologists are mainly involved in facilitation of behavior change. The traditional model has been one of individual intervention rather than systems intervention. On the other hand, however, it is not uncommon for school psychologists to comment that many of their cases involve similar themes or problem situations. Such pervasive problems should be cues that there may be a larger problem at the level of the organizational system. A systems analysis rather than an individualized intervention could be not only more efficient but also could serve to prevent similar future problems. Also, because school psychologists already serve school districts in a consultative capacity, they may enjoy some of the advantages of both internal and external change agents. That is, by working regularly with both teachers and administrators they may enter with a broader knowledge of the complete organizational system. Also, because they are not directly involved in the administration or delivery of instruction, they may have more objective views of the teacher-administration relationship. For these reasons, school psychologists would seem to fit the profile of school organizational consultants and would be well-advised to consider conceptualizing selected cases within this framework (Neale, Bailey & Ross, 1981).

Some individuals, of course, are especially well-suited to function as change agents because their regular job descriptions include organizational change agent duties, because they are temporarily assigned change agent responsibilities, or because they have special skills and expertise.

Role and Function of the Consultant-Facilitator

A school psychologist interested in stimulating and planning for organization renewal will be carrying out various roles and functions in the process. Four roles stand out as paramount (see figure 2) (Lippitt, 1969).

As a *planning leader*, the OD consultant will organize individuals and groups to begin the coordination and communication prerequisite to a systems intervention. As an *information and communications link*, the school psychologist will serve to collect organizational information from a systems perspective, clarify the information found, synthesize and integrate the information into a sequence of events, test the reality base of information and communication, provide expert

information when needed, and serve as a communication link between members of the organization. As a *learning* specialist, the school psychologist would apply learning theory and effective educational methods to teach people how to improve the organizational system. As a consultant to *management*, the school psychologist would serve to clarify for the school administration the benefits to be derived from a systems approach to problem-solving and serve to facilitate communication and information flow between administration and staff. It is extremely important to begin the OD consultation from a base of support founded not only with staff but also with school administration. The change agent should be careful to present him/herself as a reference on how to help an organization to learn rather than as an expert on the actual management problems which the organization is trying to solve. Once the school psychologist's role and function in the organizational development process has been clarified, he/she is ready to initiate the first steps involved in planned organizational change.

BEST PRACTICES

Change is inevitable in any organization. In fact, continuous flux is normal. Many of these changes are unplanned if not random. On the other hand, strategic change involves consciously planned changes which either will permit the organization to avoid an imminent threat or take advantage of an impending opportunity (Tichy, 1983). To avoid management by crisis, managers must be able to control organizational stress as it is encountered and develop effective ways of continuously carrying out diagnosis and planned change. As a liaison between administration and staff, the school psychologist can be of great assistance in this regard.

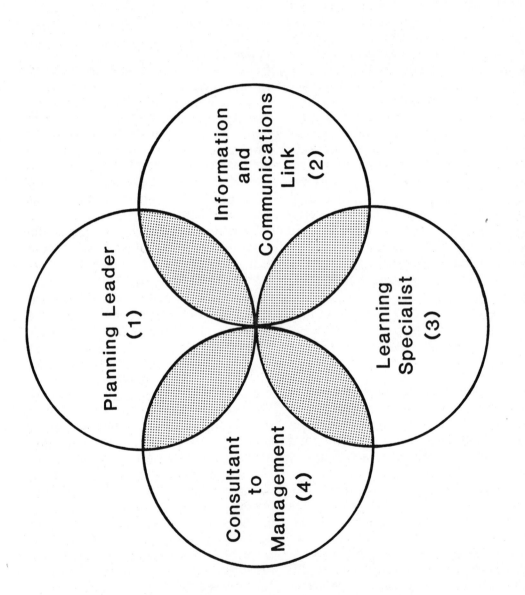

Figure 2. Key Roles of the Organizational Consultant

Planned change is conceptualized as consisting of a dynamic seven-step process: scouting, entry, diagnosis, planning, action, evaluation, and termination (see figure 3) (Cunningham, 1982; French, 1978; Short, 1973). The famous social psychologist Kurt Lewin (1951) has conceptualized the process of planned change as one of "unfreezing" and "refreezing" the system so that change might take place in the interim. During the four "unfreezing" stages systems members stop, collaboratively review the functioning of their organization and cosider alternative actions. In essence, the "unfreezing" sets the stage for change to occur. The "change" phase involves actively moving toward change. During the last two "refreezing" stages the system is refrozen in so far as equilibrium and stabilization should be restored within the system. For the purpose of illustration, the seven steps of the planned change process will be explained in the context of a typical school system consultation a school psychologist might encounter (see figure 3). The planned change model to be described is suitable for internal as well as external consultants.

Phase 1: Scouting. During this phase the change agent is exploring the need for help within the school system. The change agent needs to assess the system's readiness for change while the school system judges the change agent's abilities and interests in producing change. By the end of the scouting phase, there should be a mutual agreement between the OD consultant and the school system whether to proceed or not and an entry point should be selected.

Take, for example, the case of a school district trying to implement a state department of education's new guidelines for the identification of learning disabled children. Conflict and frustration among teachers, support staff, school administration and parents had been noted. Since the organizational problem persisted for over six months, planned change using an organizational consultant was considered. The school psychologist OD consultant began by "scouting" the problem in collaboration with the Director of Special Education. Both parties agreed there was an organizational problem, were committed to improving the situation and after some discussion, felt like they could work together cooperatively to facilitate a resolution.

Phase 2: Entry. To begin the OD process, the change agent defines for the client system how the following stages of the planned change process will be carried out. Included in this informal agreement are expectations about goals, roles and methods of those involved in the change effort. If the administration seems threatened and defensive, a power struggle could arise between the OD consultant and administration and the planned change effort will be unsuccessful. In the case example, the Director of Special Education was somewhat defensive because he felt blamed for the problem situation. After some clarification that the goals and techniques to be used could be effective and that he would not be blamed for the problem situation, he agreed to cooperate and assist in any way he could.

Phase 3: Diagnosis. The purpose of the diagnostic phase is to define the problem, specify goals and evaluate what resources are available to deal with the problem. The OD consultant's main activity is to identify the subsystem in which the problem is perceived to be located and the interrelationships between that subsystem and other parts of the school system. The change agent must also assess individuals' commitment to change within that subsystem. One of the most efficient methods of systems diagnosis is to refer to an elaborated systems model complete with subsystems such as the one depicted in figure 4.

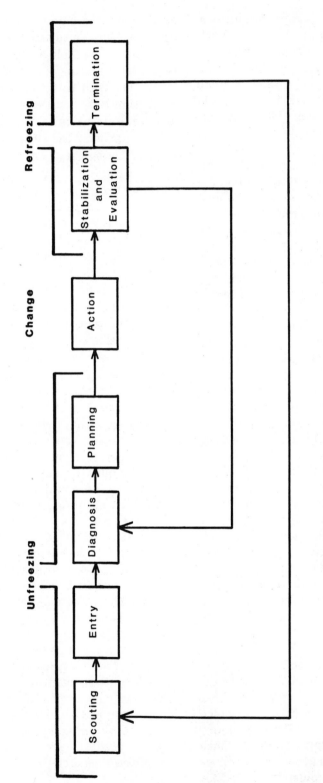

Figure 3. Planned Change and Lewin's Topology of Change

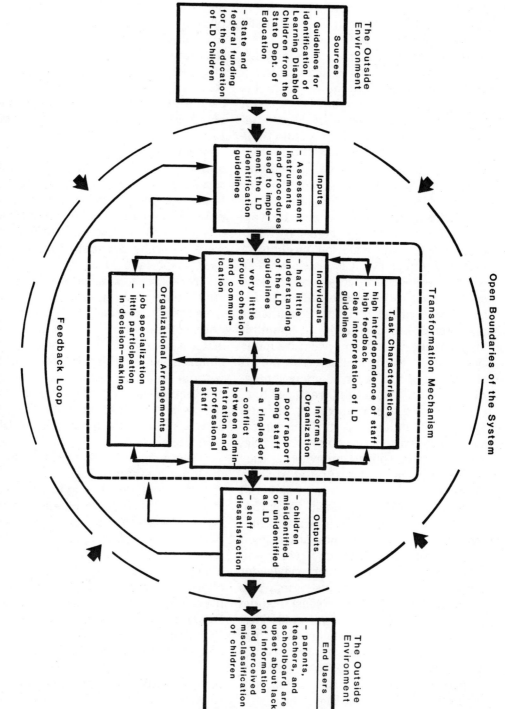

Figure 4. Diagram of a System in Interaction with its Environment

This model makes it clear that the LD guidelines originated from the State Department of Education and as such the State Department represented the primary *source* of the misunderstood LD guidelines. The school psychologist had a great deal of *input* into the system in this case since the LD guidelines required a severe discrepancy between intellectual ability and achievement for a child to be placed in a LD resource room. The director of special education exerted a great influence in interpreting the LD guidelines for the staff. The interpretation of these LD guidelines had specific effects on the various organizational subsystems. By referring to the transformation mechanism depicted in figure 4, it is possible to see what these specific effects were. The *task characteristics* of interpreting the LD guidelines required high interdependence among staff, good feedback and communications, and a clear and accurate interpretation of the guidelines. The fact is that the staff had received many contradictory memos from the Director of Special Education interpreting the guidelines. Many of the individuals in the organization disagreed regarding how the guidelines should be applied and whether they always had to be interpreted strictly. Consequently, the group cohesion and communications broke down. Poor rapport developed within the informal organizational subsystem. Some staff aligned with the special education director and others banded together under a ringleader teacher against the administration. This situation led to conflict, dissension and a poor attitude toward the LD guidelines. Factors which further deteriorated the situation included the *organizational arrangement* of the staff. There was very little overlap or integration of job contents among the staff. The school psychologist provided the test results. The other staff saw the test results as the primary criterion for inclusion in the LD

program and felt eliminated from the decision-making process as a multidisciplinary team. It should be understood that all of these organizational subsystems interacted to transform or affect the original task of identifying LD children. In this case, as the sybsystems impinged on each other, the problem became exacerbated. Initial misunderstandings among *individuals* led to further alienation and less collaborative decision-making. The *outputs* of this system became self-evident to a State Department compliance review team out on a routine site visit. They noted that a number of children were misidentified or left unidentified, staff were generally dissatisfied and the *end users*, especially parents, were upset for several reasons. Some believed that their children would be automatically released from the LD program if their children did not meet the severe discrepency formula criteria. Parents of other newly-referred children believed their children would fail without some LD assistance. Many parents perceived the staff and administration as incompetent because of their lack of agreement on the interpretation of the guidelines.

The most common methods used to diagnose a systems breakdown such as this one include questionnaires, interviews, personal observations and comparisons between the organization's present performance with its previous performance data. Of course, the change agent's ability to "sense" the overall organizational climate represents another important diagnostic approach (Herriott & Gross, 1979). Selection of specific diagnostic techniques should be tailored to fit the situation (Schmuck, 1977).

After interviewing individual staff, administrators and parents and upon reviewing educational files of children referred for possible LD placement, the school-based OD consultant working on this case was able to pinpoint the origins of the system's dysfunction. The symptoms of organizational dysfunction could be all linked to poor communication within and outside the organizational system. The LD guidelines from the state department of education were not explicit and required too much interpretation. The Director of Special Education had never held a planning committee meeting with his staff to develop a district policy. Staff and parents received misinformation about the rationale for the guidelines. They thought the state department's major motivation was to save funds by identifying fewer children as LD. With this kind of diagnostic information gathered, the school-based OD consultant was ready to move to the planning phase.

Phase 4: Planning. Alternative intervention plans are formulated based on the data already gathered during the diagnostic phase. Goals are specified and action steps are outlined. One action plan may be selected over another if the latter is vulnerable to staff resistance. Likewise, the source of power to be used to bring about the change and the appropriate subsystem to which the intervention will be directed must be considered. All planning should be conducted cooperatively not only with the administration, but also with representatives from the rest of the staff. This move is intended to ensure mutual commitment to and satisfaction with the plan among all members of the organization.

The plan developed for the LD guidelines case problem involved three major goals agreed upon by staff and administration. These included the following:

Goal Number 1: The requirements of the LD guidelines will be understood by all staff and administration. To accomplish this goal a state department of education representative was requested to present an in-service to all administrators and staff to clarify discrepancies and answer questions on implementation of

the LD guidelines.

Goal Number 2: Communication between staff, parents and administration will be improved. A staff representative was appointed to serve as a liaison with the director of special education and other school administration. The staff representative, along with interested parents, met regularly with the administration to discuss problems, especially regarding the LD guidelines. The staff liaison and director of special education agreed to work cooperatively with parents to resolve future problems.

Goal Number 3: Efforts will be made to increase rapport among staff. After conferring with state department officials, it was clarified that the discrepancy formula was not the only placement criteria. In fact, the decision was to be based on a multidisciplinary team decision using a variety of other criteria in conjunction with the discrepancy formula. This new understanding opened the door for enriched cooperation among staff. The OD consultant also presented an in-service on LD preassessment requirements and how team members could contribute collaboratively in the process. This model set a friendlier tone for future staffings.

Phase 5: Action. The finalized intervention plans constructed during phase four are implemented during the action phase. Successful implementation depends on the accuracy of the work done during the previous few phases. If failure occurs it is often the result of improper diagnosis, failure to involve a key person or group in a power position, or failure to anticipate the consequences of the proposed action. Because subsystems are interdependent, a change in one subsystem is bound to inadvertently influence other subsystems. Such interactions must be taken into consideration. In the case study under discussion, intervention plans were implemented smoothly and without repercussions.

Phase 6: Stabilization and Evaluation. Once the change has stabilized the results of change need to be evaluated for effectiveness. If not, the OD consultant may need to return to the planning stage for future action planning. The extent of the evaluation required depends on the scope or significance of the project. Best practice would dictate that ongoing evaluation should proceed throughout the OD consultancy and not just at the conclusion.

Phase 7: Termination. It is important to predetermine criteria for success. If the intervention is successful the school psychologist may terminate active involvement or may continue to monitor progress on an intermittent basis. In the LD guidelines case, staff relations improved markedly, and increased support for the LD guidelines was reported as communication increased.

Optimizing Success

Simply working through the seven stages of planned change in a lockstep manner may not be sufficient to ensure the school psychologist success in organizational consultation. According to theory and research successful organizational development has explicit distinguishing characteristics (Bowers & Franklin, 1977; Schmuck, Arends & Arends, 1974; Neale, Bailey & Ross, 1981). Conversely, unsuccessful efforts tend to feature mistakes or inattention relative to some of these dimensions. Specifically the following represent important conditions and phases for optimal success and a provocative list of guidelines for practice from the consultant's point of view:

- Link knowledge to action, resources to users.
- Continually restate the goals of the consultation.
- Be prepared to undertake proce-

dures for increasing organizational readiness.
- Make it clear that successful OD requires sustained effort over many months.
- Assess progress at each stage to ascertain how much of earlier stages need to be recycled.
- Be sure the macro-design includes micro-designs for recycling the process of trust-building, goal-setting, and diagnostic information gathering.
- Establish collaborative relationships with key authorities.
- Engage all participants in introductory discussions.
- Clarify interpersonal relationships between consultants and clients.
- Tell clients that a formal diagnosis will precede training.
- Insist on collecting data on present conditions.
- Use formal and informal methods of data collection.
- Use diagnosis for feedback to clients and for further planning.
- Don't let personal biases get in the way.
- Adapt the themes of training, data feedback, confrontation, and process consultation to the local situation.
- Build the macro-design to encompass the mode of intervention, the focus of attention, and diagnosed problems.
- Phase the work to meet short- and long-term intervention goals. Include time to renegotiate the plan.

SUMMARY

Schools have always been organizational systems but recognition as such has come only recently. The smooth functioning of any school system is affected by a complex interaction of inputs, a transformation mechanism, and outputs. Consequently, when schools fail it often may not be the fault of any one individual. As opposed to intervention on a case by case basis school psychologists might reconceptualize cases with similar referral problems in a systems framework. As systems consultants, school psychologists could serve as planning leaders, as communication and information links, as learning specialists and as consultants to school management. The basic model from which most planned change strategies have been derived include the following components: scouting, entry, diagnosis, planning, action, evaluation, and termination. A case example has been provided to illustrate best practices in this planned change process. Ultimately, success in facilitating organizational development requires the application of many of the skills school psychologists already possess and a willingness to reframe the school organization itself as the client when appropriate.

REFERENCES

Bowers, David G., & Franklin, Jerome L. *Survey-guided development I: Data Based organizational change.* La Jolla, California: University Associates, 1977.

Cunningham, William G. *Systematic planning for educational change.* Palo Alto, California: Mayfield Publishing Company, 1982.

French, W. L. A checklist for organizing and implementing an OD effect. In W. L. French, C. H. Bell, Jr., & R. A. Zawacki (Eds.), *Organization development: Theory, practice and research.* Dallas, TX: Business Publications, 1978.

French, Wendell, L., & Bell, Cecil H., *Organization Development: Behavioral science interventions for organization improvement* (2nd ed.). Englewood Cliffs, NJ: Prentice-Hall, 1978.

French, W. L., Bell, C. H., Jr., & Zawacki, P. S. (Eds.), *Organization development:* Theory, *practice and research.* Dallas: Business Publications, 1978.

Gordon, Judith R. *A diagnostic approach to organizational behavior.* Boston: Allyn and Bacon, Inc., 1983.

Herriott, Robert E., & Gross, Neal. *The dynamics of planned educational change.* Berkeley, California: McCutchan Publishing Corporation, 1979.

Huse, E. H. *Organization development and change* (2nd ed.), St. Paul, MN: West, 1980.

Lewin, Kurt. *Field theory in social science.* New York: Harper & Bros., 1951.

Lippitt, Gordon L. *Organizational renewal.* New York: Appleton-Century-Crofts, 1969.

Miles, M. B., & Schmuck, R. A. The nature of organization development. In R. A. Schmuck & M. B. Miles (Eds.), *Organizational development in schools.* La Jolla, California: University Associates, 1976.

Neale, Daniel C., Bailey, William J., & Ross, Billy E. *Strategies for school improvement: Cooperative planning and organization development.* Boston: Allyn and Bacon, Inc., 1981.

Schmuck, Richard, Arends, Jane, & Arends, Richard. *Tailoring consultation in Organization development for particular schools.* Eugene, Oregon: Center for Educational Policy and Management, 1974.

Schmuck, Richard A., Runkel, Philip J., Arends, Jane H., & Arends, Richard I. *The second handbook of organizational development in schools.* Palo Alto, California: Mayfield Publishing Company, 1977.

Short, L. E. Planned organizational change. *MSU Business Topics*, 1973, pp. 53-61.

Tichy, Noel M. *Managing strategic change: Technical, political and cultural dynamics.* New York: John Wiley & Sons, Inc., 1983.

ANNOTATED BIBLIOGRAPHY

Conoley, Jane, & Conoley, Collie W. *School consultation:* A guide to practice and training. Elmsford, NY: Pergamon Press, 1982, 244 pp.
Good consultation skills are basic to all organizational improvement attempts in the schools. This book represents a brief, practical training guide on the skills, techniques and stages of consultation. A variety of representative consultation models are described. The prospective organizational consultant should find this book helpful in highlighting the skills necessary to be a successful OD consultant.

Cunningham, William G. *Systematic planning for educational change.* Palo Alto, California: Mayfield Publishing Company, 1982.

Instead of always reacting to school-based problems, this book explains why a more preventative approach to avoiding such problems may be worthwhile. Continuous systematic planning is the key to this approach. The benefits of advance planning are explained and strategies for developing and implementing system-wide plans are introduced. To be most effective school consultants need to be aware of issues in planning for educational futures rather than the present alone. The perspective presented in this book adds a new dimension to the role of the school psychologist serving as an OD consultant in the schools.

Gordon, Judith R. *A diagnostic approach to organizational behavior.* Boston: Allyn and Bacon, Inc., 1983, 434 pp.

This book presents readings and case studies focusing on the diagnosis of organizational systems. Chapters deal with strategies for describing, understanding, explaining, and predicting behavior in organizations. A basic understanding of organizational dynamics and an overview of how organizations might be improved are emphasized.

Neale, Daniel C., Bailey, William J., & Ross, Billy E. *Strategies for school improvement:* Cooperative planning and organizational development. Boston: Allyn and Bacon, Inc., 1981.

In times of diminishing resources school improvement through planned change may be more necessary than ever. The philosophy of this book is that all staff need to cooperate to effect this change. On this note, this text proceeds to describe a model of organizational development based on the partnership of staff and administration. An especially relevant chapter is devoted to a discussion of change agent roles and tactics.

Tichy, Noel M. *Managing strategic change.* New York: John Wiley & Sons, 1983, 702 pp.

Change within organizations is inevitable. The purpose of this book is to assist organizational consultants in managing major reorientation in an organization based upon the three organizational "basics": technical aspects of work, power and value.

BEST PRACTICES IN CONDUCTING RE-EVALUATIONS

Timothy S. Hartshorne
Wichita State University

E. Brent Hoyt
Silver Lake, Kansas

OVERVIEW

School psychologists are very familiar with re-evaluations. For many school psychologists, particularly those trained since the advent of PL 94-142, their very first assessment as practicum student was re-evaluation. Many more undoubtedly expect to complete their careers with a re-evaluation. Then why, with a practice this familiar, is there need for a best practice chapter? Perhaps because familiarity has led to contempt. This occurs when re-evaluations are relegated to a time-consuming, seemingly insignificant routine. Because they are seen as making so little difference, re-evaluations become appropriate tasks for beginning psychologists or are farmed out on a contract basis.

The above is clearly a negative point of view, but one that fits far too often. This chapter considers the validity of the perception that re-evaluations are excessively time consuming and that their impact on the lives of children is insignificant.

There is very little research data on re-evaluations, most likely because it has generally been viewed as a repeat of the original assessment procedures. There have been, however, at least three surveys of common practice in re-evaluations.

Martin (1979) examined the initial and retest results for 145 students in a southeastern urban school system. He found evidence that the psychologist's recommendation significantly impacted on placement decisions, but that this was more true for initial than for re-evaluation placement decisions.

Elliott, Piersel and Galvin (1983) surveyed 40 psychologists in four states concerning current practice in re-evaluations. They found that, while re-evaluations constitute a considerable proportion of the evaluations performed by psychologists during the year, take anywhere from three to five hours to complete, and were perceived by the psychologists as important checks on the appropriateness of diagnosis and placement, their significance in terms of changes in the educational placement or program was very small.

Similar findings come from a survey of 112 Kansas psychologists conducted by the Kansas Association of School Psychologists (1984). The respondents indicated that, in general, re-evaluations tend to be a repeat of the original test battery, and that in very few cases do they result in a change of placement or program.

This survey data tends to support the negative viewpoint: re-evaluations do not result in major changes in children's programs, and since a majority of psychologists are re-administering the original battery of tests, they are undoubtedly time-consuming and repititious. To spend such a large amount of time on an activity with such little impact is likely to lead to frustration. Is this necessary? Are psychologists required, for example, to re-administer the original battery of tests? In fact, are tests always a necessary part of re-evaluation?

Rules and regulations regarding re-evaluations vary from state to state with the only constant being the federal rules and regulations (USDHEW, 1977). Section 12a.534 states:

Each State and local educational agency shall insure: (a) That each handicapped child's individualized education program is reviewed in accordance with 121a.340-121a.349 of Subpart C, and (b) That an evaluation of the child, based on procedures which meet the requirements under 121a.532, is conducted every three years or more frequently if conditions warrant or if the child's parent or teacher requests an evaluation.

Part (b) really pertains to the school psychologist's involvement with re-evaluation. It specifies the three year requirement while noting that this is the maximum time allowed. It then makes reference to Section 121a.532 Evaluation Procedures, noting that a re-evaluation must be based on techniques which meet these requirements.

Because clarity is so important in considering what is truly required in a re-evaluation, each of the six points under Section 121a.532 will be reviewed:

(a) Tests and other evaluation materials:

    (1) Are provided and administered in the child's native language or other mode of communication, unless it is clearly not feasible to do so;

    (2) Have been validated for the specific purpose for which they are used; and

    (3) Are administered by trained personnel in conformance with the instructions provided by their producer.

This point essentially insists on a valid assessment process.

(b) Tests and other evaluation materials include those tailored to assess specific areas of educational need and not merely those which are designed to provide a single general intelligence quotient.

In other words, an IQ does not an assessment make.

(c) Tests are selected and administered so as best to ensure that when a test is administered to a child with impaired sensory, manual, or speaking skills, the test results accurately reflect the child's aptitude or achievement level or whatever other factors the test purports of measure, rather than reflecting the child's impaired sensory, manual, or speaking skills (except where those skills are the factors which the test purports to measure).

This is an interesting point because it suggests that one ought not only evaluate the child's handicap, but also the child's abilities. Note that none of the above points insist that a *test* be given, but rather designate characteristics that any procedure used must have.

(d) No single procedure is used as the sole criterion for determining an appropriate educational program for a child.

Note that this point says "procedure" rather than "test."

(e) The evaluation is made by a multidisciplinary team or group of persons including at least one teacher or other specialist with knowledge in the area of suspected disability.

Thus re-evaluation must use the multidisciplinary team.

(f) The child is assessed in all areas related to the suspected disability, including, where appropriate, health, vision, hearing, social and emotional status, general intelligence, academic performance, communicative status, and motor abilities.

Thus, the child's assessment must be appropriate.

Nothing in those rules and regulations requires the administration of a test as part of the initial evaluation, or by extension, a re-evaluation. Of course, when one attempts to identify a handicapping condition according to the definitions in the rules and regulations (Section 121a.5), tests are going to be necessary. But in the case of re-evaluation, identification has already been made and this evaluation serves other purposes.

To support this position, it is necessary to provide some definitions for the terms *test, evaluation,* and *assessment.* As Cronbach (1970) notes, there is no completely satisfactory definition of the word *test.* He nevertheless offers the following: "A test is a systematic procedure for observing a person's behavior and describing it with the aid of a numerical scale or a category-system" (p. 26).

Compare the above with the definition of *assessment* given by Ysseldyke (1979). "Assessment should be viewed broadly as the process of collecting data for the purpose of making decisions for or about students" (p. 87). Note how different this is from the definition of a test given by Cronbach. There is no mention of a scale, and it is only as systematic as the process which is used. Ysseldyke goes on to say, "Assessment is not synonymous with testing; testing is simply one part of assessment. Assessment includes several means of data collection . . ." (p. 87).

Return now to the rules and regulations pertaining to evaluation criteria and re-examine part (f) which requires that the child be *"assessed* in all areas related to the suspected disability." By using Ysseldyke's definition of assessment, it is now implied that tests may or may not be a part of the process. But the term which is used most frequently in the rules and regulations, and is harder to define satisfactorily, is evaluation.

Ross-Reynolds (1983), while advocating something broader, notes, that in daily practice the term "re-evaluation" is often construed to mean testing. Is that what the rules and regulations refer to? If so, why do they use the phrase in (b) "Tests and other evaluation material?" Is it possible that they intended the term evalua-

tion to mean what Ysseldyke means by "pupil evaluation?" He states (1979): "Considerable data are collected in educational environments for the purpose of helping professionals evaluate the extent to which individual children are making progress in their educational programs" (p. 88). This certainly sounds consistent with the purpose behind these rules and regulations.

Evaluation, then, could be described as the process of examining the kinds of progress a child is making in an educational program. Such an evaluation requires that an assessment, with or without tests or testing, takes place to make accurate and effective decisions. Re-evaluation, then, is re-examining the kind of progress a child has made in a program recommended no more than three years previously. There is nothing in the federal rules and regulations requiring that a test be given as a part of this process.

Two points require emphasis. First, to say that the federal rules and regulations do not insist on the administration of a test for re-evaluation does not mean it is always appropriate to omit tests. It simply gives the multidisciplinary team considerable latitude in the procedures to adopt. Second, individual state rules and regulations *may* be more restrictive. Psychologists are urged to read their own state rules and regulations very carefully before arriving at any conclusion.

This overview has considered the definitions of the major terms used by the federal rules and regulations: test, assessment and evaluation. From this, the conclusion was drawn that it is possible to perform a re-evaluation without administering a test. However, from the review of re-evaluation surveys, it appears that, in practice, re-evaluations tend to be heavily test-based and duplicate the battery administered three years previously. It also appears that, in a vast majority of cases, re-evaluations serve no more than a regulatory function. This leads to the basic consideration of this chapter: what is the purpose of re-evaluations, can they serve more than a perfunctory function, and what might be considered best practices in carrying them out?

BASIC CONSIDERATIONS

If the evaluator takes the term "re-evaluation" seriously, then the most basic consideration is evaluation of what? There are three primary possibilities. First, one might evaluate the qualifications of the child for a special education program. This is a matter of examining the entrance requirements for a program and comparing the child against those criteria. In this instance, re-evaluation is re-checking the match between child and admission standards.

Second, one might evaluate the effectiveness of a particular educational program or plan. A means for doing so might be judging the plan's effectiveness in meeting the program goals. A re-evaluation in this case examines the extent to which the program has met those goals over a period of time and results in a judgment concerning its likelihood to meet these or additional goals in the future.

Third, evaluation might focus on the current needs of a particular child. In the educational context, this means an assessment of the child's ability to learn effectively under particular educational conditions. This data would then be used to descibe the ideal learning environment for the child. This ideal is then compared with the current environment to evaluate the child's present needs. A re-evaluation in this context is compared with a previous evaluation to find any changes in the child's educational needs.

All three possibilities are evaluation because, in each case, a judgment is made. Does the child have the qualities required

for a particular program, is a program effective in meeting its goals, and is there a match between the child's educational needs and current program? An appropriate assessment, conducted by the multidisciplinary team ought to address itself to all three considerations.

Ross-Reynolds (1983) proposed a model for re-evaluations which is highly cosistent with the above discussion. She suggested that re-evaluations be both summative and formative. The former addresses both process (program implementation) and product (program outcomes), while the latter addresses recomendations for program modifications. She noted that administering standardized tests was not always appropriate, described the validity issues of the evaluation model and suggested that psychologists consider criterion-based measures.

Support for this model came from a survey of Iowa psychologists by Lohry (1980). These psychologists believed that an intelligence test was not required for re-evaluation. The primary goal of re-evaluation was seen as measurement of academic progress (program outcomes or program effectiveness) by 56% of the sample. Another 44% saw confirmation of placement (formative evaluation or matching the child's needs with the current program as the primary goal). Thus these psychologists recognized the summative and formative evaluation implications of re-evaluations.

Re-evaluations, then, ought to be real evaluations; an evaluation of the effectiveness of a major intervention in the life of a child. Such an evaluation calls upon assessment techniques somewhat different from the usual armament of the school psychologist and includes some unfamiliar concepts and procedures. It is less likely to become routinized or repetitive, and may have a more genuine impact on the life of the child.

BEST PRACTICES

Re-evaluation considers three primary areas: the continuing match between child and program admission standards, the effectiveness of the program in meeting previously identified needs, and the nature of current needs. This concept is put in the context of the entire child assessment process.

A training module developed by the School Psychology Network (Tucker, 1981) considers assessment to be a series of sequential stages from pre-referral to educational intervention. What effectively moves the process from one stage to another is the presence of unanswered educational and diagnostic questions. The goal of the psychological evaluation is to gather data relevant to these diagnostic concerns. The answers are considered to be hypotheses which are, at least partially, confirmed or disconfirmed by the outcome of the educational intervention. This makes the three year re-evaluation essentially confirming or disconfirming the original hypotheses. Thus, every re-evaluation begins with an examination of the diagnostic questions and the tentative answers.

There are at least two methods for examining these questions and answers. One administers the previous assessment battery to see if the same conclusions result. Currently, this is the usual procedure. It is evident that it is a waste of time because it puts the cart before the horse. This process answers questions that may not be relevant today.

The second alternative begins with a re-evaluation of the original diagnostic questions to see if they continue to be of concern. This is done by an interview of each team member and/or in a meeting of the multidisciplinary team. If these questions do continue to reflect the major areas of concern, the next consideration is examination of the answers previously obtained. If the program developed is a good match for the child, shows evidence of being effective, and continues to reflect the child's needs, then there is good evidence to support the previous hypotheses. If, on the other hand, either a different set of questions emerges or the previous answers have not held up well over time, there is need for a new assessment to develop an alternative program. This process is charted in Figure 1.

FIGURE 1

Flow Chart of Re-Evaluation Procedures

re-examine diagnostic questions
    ↓
are questions still of concern? — no → develop new questions
    |
    yes   ↓
    ↓
have previous answers held up? — no → assessment conducted
    | ↓
    yes   answers hypothesized
    ↓   ↓
    end   ←   program developed

A key point in this process is the consideration of the durability of previous conclusions because this is the heart of the re-evaluation. These answers led to the current placement and educational program for the child. Team members who worked with the child over the intervening period have varying degrees of evidence and confidence in the past decisions. If everyone is satisfied that the program has met and continues to meet the child's needs, then that concludes the re-evaluation. If, on the other hand, one or more team members provide data such as anecdotes, child records, observations, suggesting a mismatch between child and program, then a formal assessment is conducted.

A re-evaluation, then, always begins with a consideration of the diagnostic questions from the previous evaluation and the team members' assessment of the adequacy of the conclusions after three years hingsight. Questions of the child's continued eligibility, the program's effectiveness, and the current needs must be addressed. These might be answered to the team's satisfaction without any testing because a plethora of data has built up over a three-year period. If such data does not satisfy the team, then and only then, is additional information collected through an assessment which may or may not include testing.

The team is most likely influenced by several factors in its deliberations. One consideration is certainly the confidence expressed in the original diagnostic conclusions. For example, if a child had been diagnosed as mentally retarded with an IQ of 60 and commensurate adaptive behavior, there is more confidence in the eligibility as compared to a child with an IQ of 69 and considerable scatter in the adaptive behavior profile.

Another consideration is confidence in the program. There are certainly differences in quality between special education classrooms and teachers, and differential weight is given to reports of student progress in weak versus strong programs.

The number of years a child has been in a program is also a factor. A child coming up for a first re-evaluation is considered differently from one who has been in the program for nine years with steady progress and no evidence to support a modification.

The age of the student is also important. A child of 16 or 17 is likely to show less change in standardized test scores than a child of six or seven, and the former's proximity in finishing school makes a change in placement less desirable.

Finally, the consistency of previous evaluations is an important consideration. If all previous data agree with the diagnostic conclusions that were drawn over the years, there is less need for further confirmation.

The key to re-evaluation is the multidisciplinary team's initial review of the diagnostic questions and determination of additional assessment needs. They do this at an initial meeting or one member conducts structured interviews with each team member prior to the initial meeting. This has the distinct advantage of insuring that each team member comes to the meeting after consideration of the case and that appropriate data relative to team concerns have already been compiled. The second author has developed a format for these interviews which is available upon request. They basically cover perceptions concerning the accuracy of available test data, performance of the child, changes that have been observed, and areas of concern.

Re-evaluations were intended to insure that special education placement does not become a dead-end for the child. But they can be much more. They are an important means of accountability and provide a feedback loop to the diagnostic and educational decision-making process. Careful attention to this goal helps assure that children's needs continue to be met, and that re-evaluations do not become routine, mechanistic, and boring procedures.

SUMMARY

Survey data on re-evaluation suggests that this procedure is perceived as a re-administration of previous assessment instruments which has limited impact on the educational programs of most children. It has been suggested that this is a very narrow perspective. An appropriate re-evaluation serves two extremely important purposes. First, it provides important feedback to the members of multidisciplinary teams about the conclusions and decisions they made about a child three years previously. Second, it helps insure that educational programs continue to be responsive to the changing needs of the child.

Additionally, it has been suggested that an appropriate re-evaluation considers three areas: first, whether a child continues to meet the admission requirements for a particular program, second, whether the program has had success in meeting previously identified needs, and third, whether the child's needs have changed and warrant a new program. Each team member presents evidence concerning these issues, and only when new questions arise is additional assessment data collected. Deliberation generally includes such factors as confidence in the previous diagnosis, confidence in the program, length of time in the program, age of the child, and the consistency of previous evaluations.

It is claimed that re-evaluations are excessively time consuming and have little real impact on the lives of most children. Regarding the first issue, the current practice of re-administering the original test battery is considered a waste of time because it addresses the previous answers rather than the questions concerning the child's current problems. Since questions are likely to change over three years, answers to old questions are unlikely to be very useful. By following the above recommended procedures for best practice, some re-evaluations are more time consuming than a simple re-administration of the previous battery because some specialized assessment is required to answer the new questions, or re-answer the old ones. But this makes these cases more interesting and challenging which compensates for loss of time. In a majority of cases, re-evaluations take a lot less time. If the original evaluation was a good one and the program developed appropriately, data collected during the three-year period will point to the continuation of the placement. Needed modifications are fairly apparent without requiring much additional assessment. This procedure is not advocated because it is less time consuming, but because it has a better chance of having a positive impact on the life of the child.

REFERENCES

Cronbach, L. J. (1970). *Essentials of psychological testing* (3rd Ed.). New York: Harper & Row.

Elliott, S. N., Piersel, W. C., & Galvin, G. A. (1983). Psychological re-evaluations: A survey of practices and perceptions of school psychologists. *Journal of School Psychology, 21,* 99-105.

Kansas Association of School Psychologists (1984). (Survey of Kansas School Psychologists). Unpublished raw data.

Lohry, D. A. (1980). The actual and ideal roles of the school psychologist in three-year reevaluations of learning disabled students in Iowa as perceived by the school psychologist. *Dissertation Abstracts Interventional, 41,* 2018A.

Martin, F. (1979). Is it necessary to retest children in special education classes? *Journal of Learning Disabilities, 12,* 388-392.

Ross-Reynolds, J. (1983). Three year reevaluations: An alternative to the reevaluation-means-retest model. In Iowa Department of Public Instruction, *Communicating psychological information in writing* (pp. 75-89). (Available from Jeff Grimes, Department of Public Instruction, Grimes State Office Building, Des Moines, Iowa 50319.)

Tucker, J. (1981). *Sequential stages of the appraisal process: A training module*. Minneapolis: National School Psychology Inservice Training Network.

USDHEW (1977). Education of handicapped children: Implementation of Part B of the Education of the Handicapped Act. *Federal Register, 42* (163), 42474-42518.

Ysseldyke, J. E. (1979). Issues in psychoeducational assessment. In G. D., Phye & D. J. Reschly (Eds.), *School psychology: Perspectives and issues* (pp. 87-121). New York: Academic Press.

ANNOTATED BIBLIOGRAPHY

Helton, G. B., Workman, E. A., & Matuszek, P. A. (1982). *Psychoeducational assessment: Integrating concepts and techniques*. New York: Grune & Stratton.
This excellent text provides a review of law, litigation, ethics, assessment instruments, all in the general context of a branching assessment system, and a perspective of the child as client. Only a page is devoted to re-evaluations, but the book is recommended for its intelligent approach to the process of psychoeducational assessment.

Martin, R. (1979). *Educating Handicapped children: The legal mandate*. Champaign, IL: Research Press.
Written by a lawyer, this review of law and litigation in the education of handicapped children is thorough, informative, and amazingly enjoyable reading. It is extremely helpful in understanding the intent and extent of legal influences on the assessment process, and the questions yet to be tested.

Ross-Reynolds, J. (1983). Three year reevaluations: an alternative to the reevaluation-means-retest model. In Iowa Department of Public Instruction, *Communicating psychological information in writing* (pp. 75-89). (Available from Jeff Grimes, Department of Public Instruction, Grimes State Office Building, Des Moines, Iowa 50319).
This article provides a Why, What, How and How will you know perspective for re-evaluations. A program evaluation model is brought to bear on the process of pupil evaluation. Summative and formative evaluation procedures and concepts are utilized in this re-consideration of the process. An illustrative case report is included.

Ysseldyke, J. E. (1979). Issues in psychoeducational assessment. In G. D. Phye & D. J. Reschly (Eds.), *School psychology: perspectives and issues* (pp. 87-121). New York: Academic Press.
While this chapter does not address itself to reevaluations, it is recommended for its discussion of the nature of assessment and evaluation as processes, its consideration of the nature of various assessment models, and its call for well considered change in assessment strategies and activities.

BEST PRACTICES IN VOCATIONAL ASSESSMENT FOR HANDICAPPED STUDENTS

Thomas H. Hohenshil
Virginia Tech

Edward M. Levinson
Indiana University of Pennsylvania

Kathy Buckland Heer
Virginia Tech

OVERVIEW

The vocational aspects of school psychology practice have become increasingly important during the 1970's and 1980's. As a result of several significant pieces of federal and state legislation, more handicapped youth are enrolled in school and they are staying longer. Rather than dropping out, or being "dropped out" prior to junior and senior high school, handicapped students are entering these secondary education settings in record numbers. Developing and implementing the appropriate kinds of educational and support services for them is troubling schools across the nation (Heller, 1981; Hohenshil, 1982).

National concern for the handicapped and their career development is growing as these students leave the protected educational environment and enter the competitive employment market. Research indicates that the gap between school and work is frequently much wider for handicapped than nonhandicapped individuals (Harrington, 1982). They, more than any other group, need assistance in bridging this gap. To leave the career development of handicapped students to chance, as has been the case all too often in the past, frequently commits them to disproportionately high rates of unemployment and underemployment (Batsche, 1982). Vocational eduction is presently assuming a much greater role in career training for students with special learning needs. This results in larger numbers of these students moving from special education programs in elementary schools to various types of vocational education programs at the secondary level to gain employment skills. (Miller & Schloss, 1982).

Although it is clear that a number of support services are necessary to assist handicapped students in career development, this chapter is specifically devoted to the topic of vocational assessment and the roles that school psychologists play in this important process. This is not to downgrade the other services that school psychologists provide to handicapped students, parents, and other educational personnel. However, assessment has been a traditional function of school psychological services and the vocational aspects of psychological assessment are essential for the proper educational placement of handicapped adolescents. Even though the contents of this ·chapter are directed toward the vocational assessment of handicapped youth, most of the models and procedures described are also useful with persons without handicapping conditions.

It is the view of an increasing number of psychologists that there should be a vocational component in every junior high and senior high psychological evaluation. In addition, *comprehensive* psychological evaluation deals with the vocational aspects of personality and educational development. Determining the appropriate vocational placement for handicapped adolescents is just as critical to school success as determining the appropriate special education placement at the elementary level. Each vocational program requires a specific set of vocational aptitudes, interests, academic skills, physical abilities, and personality. For a psychological evaluation to be helpful, all of these factors are considered. This requires a shift in emphasis from primarily academic considerations to those necessary to assist in the career planning process.

BASIC CONSIDERATIONS

School psychological services, like other educational services, should support the primary emphases of the different levels of the educational system. This is such a critical point that these emphases are briefly reviewed:

Elementary School — The basic emphasis of the elementary school has traditionally been the acquisition of the basic skills of reading, writing, arithmetic, and social and citizenship skills.

Junior High School — A primary emphasis of the junior high school has traditionally been exploration of various curricular and career options to assist students in the decision-making process as they enter high school.

High School — The major emphasis of the high school has traditionally been preparation for entry level employment or preparation for the next level of the education system. This occurs through vocational education programs, college preparatory programs, or some combination of the two.

Unfortunately, many special educators and school psychologists have performed as if the junior high and high school emphases did not exist for handicapped youth. Traditionally, the goals of most secondary special education programs were similar to those provided in elementary schools. Many special educators believed that if handicapped students did not learn to read, write, and do arithmetic in elementary schools, then they should get another six years of the same curriculum. It is becoming increasingly clear that more attention must be devoted to exploration and career preparation at the junior and senior high levels.

If they are asked what they want for their handicapped children after 12-14 years of schooling, parents respond that they want them to be independent, self supporting, self directing individuals. It is virtually impossible for this to happen in our society unless a person is *occupationally* independent. An emphasis upon "academic" skills alone does not achieve this goal. Occupational independence for many handicapped students will not happen unless considerable attention is focused on the acquisition of occupational skills in our junior and senior high schools.

The Career Planning Process

The basic purpose of vocational assessment is to provide information and assistance in the career planning process. The basic model is the same whether students make the career decisions themselves or whether they are made for them by placement committees. As noted in Figure I, the career planning process is broken down into the following seven basic steps.

One of the most important components of this model is Step 1 — determining the decision to be made with a particular student. If a student is eight years of age, regardless of the handicapping condition, no decision is made about what the student will do for the rest of his or her life. At this level, more career and self awareness activities are probably the most appropriate. If the student is 14-21 years of age, career exploration and career prepartion activities are most appropriate. Obviously, the specific decision regarding career development depends upon such factors as age, level of mental ability, social and emotional maturity, occupational experience, and the handicapping condition.

Vocational assessment information is particularly useful in Step 2 of the model — collection of appropriate information. Vocational assessment procedures and instruments generally focus upon the internal information aspects of Step 2 by helping individuals and placement committees learn more about student interests, aptitudes, values, small and large motor co-

Figure 1

CAREER PLANNING MODEL

Step 1 — *Determine Decision to be Made*
  — Depends upon student's level of educational and psychological development

Step 2 — *Collect Appropriate Information*
  — Internal Information
              Interests
              Aptitudes
              Values
              Aspirations
              Achievement
              Personality
              Small/large motor coordination

  — External Information
              Types of occupations available
              Personal requirements for entry
              Educational requirements
              Economic & social consequences
              Relation of curriculum to various career options
              Application process for entrance

Step 3 — *Generate Alternative Career Options*

Step 4 — *Select Primary Alternative & Specify Secondary Alternatives*

Step 5 — *Reality Testing in Sheltered Environment*
              School courses
              Co-op programs
              Simulated work experience
              Observation

Step 6 — *Evaluate Results of Reality Testing*

Step 7 — *Continue to Pursue Primary Alternative*

      or

      Return to Step 4 to consider secondary career alternatives

ordination, achievement, and personality — all important aspects of the career planning process. In fact, the quality of information developed through Step 2 clearly determines the quality of career options in Step 3. Vocational assessment information also provides valuable data to evaluate the results of reality testing included in Step 6 of the model. Certainly the more individuals know about themselves, the better the career decisions they make. Cutting down on the error factor in career decisions results in a reduction of frustration and occupational and curriculum changes. If students, handicapped or otherwise, are knowledgeable about themselves and various career options, research indicates they make more realistic choices. The same is true for the decisions and recommendations for future education and training made by placement committees (Anderson, 1982; Levinson, 1984).

Uses of Vocational Assessment

As noted in Figure 2, the three basic uses for vocational assessment data are viewed on a continuum.

Many handicapped students have literally no occupational goals while others have unrealistic notions. For these students and their placement committees, the primary purpose of vocational assessment is to *generate* alternative courses of action and potential career alternatives. A second use of vocational assessment information deals with the *selection* of occupational and training alternatives. Some students have multiple career goals, have explored three or four occupational alternatives and need help in choosing among them. A third use is *confirmation*. Students as well as placement committees request vocational assessment to confirm a decision they tentatively made. This type of model is also viewed as a continuum of stages through which everyone goes. Students, handicapped or not, need to generate occupational alternatives, and to confirm that the alternative selected is appropriate.

Figure 2

USES OF VOCATIONAL ASSESSMENT

Generation of Alternatives	Selection from Alternatives	Confirmation

/ _____ / _____ /

BEST PRACTICES

There are a variety of vocational assessment techniques which psychologists use to facilitate the career planning process for handicapped students. These techniques are presented in Figure 3.

Work experience is one of the best vocational assessment techniques. There is no better way to determine whether students like to do something (interest), whether they are good at it (aptitude), and whether they want to pursue an occupation through specific job training. Unfortunately, most research indicates that handicapped students, as a group,

Figure 3

VOCATIONAL ASSESSMENT TECHNIQUES

Work Experience

Simulated Work Experience

Work Sampling

Performance Tests

Behavioral Observation

Interviewing

Paper and Pencil Tests

have little actual part or full-time work experience. Thus, in many situations, work experience is not a realistic assessment tool.

Simulated work experience is another excellent vocational evaluation technique. Here students are placed in an environment which simulates actual working conditions in an occupation or group of occupations. Many of the career exploration programs at the junior high and early senior high levels are simulated work experiences. Vocational education programs are really simulated work experiences (exploration), especially for those students who have not had an opportunity to participate in career exploration experiences.

A third technique is *work sampling*. Work sampling is a process whereby certain job functions from a single occupation or group of related occupations are performed by the student while under the observation of a trained examiner. There are a variety of commercial and locally-constructed work sampling programs which are currently in use. Performance tests such as the performance section of the General Aptitude Test Battery, the Crawford Small Parts Assembly Test, and even the performance sections of the revised Wechsler scales provide important information for the career planning process. Indeed, much data derived from a traditional psychological evaluation are vocationally relevant.

Behavioral observation and *interviewing* are two useful vocational assessment techniques. We recommend that psychologists include a vocationally oriented interview as part of every psychological evaluation. Talk with students about their work experiences, their occupational likes and dislikes, course preferences, leisure activities, and career and lifestyle aspirations. This is an excellent technique to determine a student's position in the career planning process described in Figure 1, as well as to formulate vocational assessment goals. These vocational assessment goals are dramatically different for students who have little idea of what they might do than they are for those who have significant work experience in occupations they would like to pursue in the future. The same is true with respect to self knowledge about vocational aptitudes, interests, values, and so forth. The behavioral observations of parents and teachers are also excellent sources of information. For example, it is important to ascertain if the student interview data parallel the observations of teachers and parents. If not, then this certainly has relevance for determining additional vocational evaluation, counseling, and exploration techniques.

Group psychometrics (paper and pencil) techniques are what most people think about first when vocational assessment is mentioned. One of the most obvious short-comings of this technique is that the reading level of many tests is too high for exceptional students. In these instances, it is necessary to use some of the non-reading interest inventories which are available. For students who are orthopedically handicapped, paper and pencil instruments generally do not provide enough useful information about vocational aptitudes and physical limitations which are of vocational relevance. Here, work sampling procedures and performance tests are more useful. Certainly the specific vocational evaluation techniques selected by the psychologist depend upon the presenting handicapping condition (Hohenshil, 1982).

Assessment Continuum

Another way to conceptualize a framework for vocational assessment is to use an experiential continuum as depicted in Figure 4.

Work experience and simulated work

Figure 4

EXPERIENTIAL CONTINUUM

Work Experience Simulated Wk. Experience	Work Sampling Performance Tests	Behavioral Observation Interview	Paper & Pencil

/_____/_____/_____/

experience are closely related to actual occupational performance and have the highest degree of face validity. Many experts in vocational rehabilitation suggest that work experience, simulated work experience, and work sampling procedures also have the highest predictive validity. However, empirical research data to support the reliability and validity of work sampling procedures is not as convincing as one would hope.

One could construct another continuum of time and expense for the above techniques. Here, work experience, simulated work experience, and work sampling procedures are much more expensive in terms of time, personnel, and the initial cost of the work sampling equipment. It takes several days or longer to cycle a student through all of the work samples included in some of the commercial work sampling batteries. Generally, the most expensive and time consuming procedures are reserved for those students with the greatest disabilities. In many of these instances, the client is observed performing a wide variety of job functions before an accurate job training recommendation is made.

Proposed Assessment Battery

Following is a proposed vocational evaluation battery for use with handicapped secondary students. Readers wish-

Figure 5

PROPOSED APPRAISAL BATTERY

Mental Ability

Achievement

Small/Large Motor Coordination

Personality — Social Maturity

Vocational Interest

Vocational Aptitude

Vocational Adaptive Behavior

Career Maturity

ing to deal with each component of the battery in depth should consult the annotated bibliography.

As with any psychological evaluation, the specific components of a battery depend upon the presenting handicapping condition as well as the basic purpose of the referral. Mental ability and achievement in the basic academic skills are extremely important data in the career planning process because they are probably the most accurate predictors of success in any vocational or academic program. We would be the last to suggest that psychologists dump their Wechsler scales on the road as they enter the high school parking lot. Subscale information from the Wechsler scales is extremely important in an occupational perspective.

Small and large motor coordination are also vitally important factors in vocational assessment and career planning because coordination is a high priority in most trade and industrial occupations, such as plumbing or construction. Measures of motor coordination are necessary to predict the probability of success in most vocational areas. In addition to traditional techniques in motor and perceptual assessment, work sampling and various types of performance tests are included as part of vocational assessment batteries.

Personality and social maturity are necessary for job success in most occupations to some degree. In fact, research indicates that most people lose their jobs because they cannot get along with their coworkers and supervisors, not because they lack specific occupational skills. For example, in sales social skills are critically important, while they are less important in most trade and industrial occupations such as plumber, electrician, construction worker, or machinist. Thus, personality and social maturity assessment are necessary components of a comprehensive vocationally-oriented battery.

Interest and aptitude assessments are efforts to determine vocational likes and dislikes, as well as what abilities can be developed with further training. In some instances, interests and aptitudes are assessed through traditional paper and pencil psychometric techniques. The deciding factor is whether or not a particular handicapping condition interferes with the proper use of these instruments. Low reading level, various sensory deficits, and orthopedic handicaps may require such "non traditional" methods as work sampling and various types of behavioral observation or nonreading interest inventories. Most work sampling techniques

include items to assess vocational interests as well as vocational aptitudes. This is not to say that school psychologists should be proficient in the administration of time consuming work sampling procedures, but they should know enough about them to recommend certain procedures and to integrate the results into appropriate placement plans for handicapped students.

Career maturity is similar to the concept of mental maturity. Career maturity instruments are designed to assess students' levels of self knowledge, career information, and career decision making skills in relation to others of their age group. In general, most career maturity inventories lack norms on students with various types of handicapping conditions. Therefore, they must be interpreted with caution.

A number of vocationally oriented adaptive behavior measures are coming on the market. Previously, most adaptive behavior measures were developed for either young children or adults. Few were available for use with secondary school youth. This situation is slowly being rectified and a number of these measures are listed in the annotated bibliography.

A vocationally oriented interview is used to determine the goals of vocational assessment and training. Not all students require the entire battery. Many components of the battery are the same as those school psychologists already use to assess academic skills, personality and social functioning. What is different is that the traditional procedures are interpreted with emphasis upon their implications for career planning and placement (Hohenshil, 1982).

Levels of Vocational Assessment

The experienced clinician selects and chooses particular techniques for a specific student or group of students. The composition of the test battery depends upon the disability and decision to be made. Most vocational evaluation programs are developed to comprise a two or three level evaluation scheme as follows:

Level 1 evaluation. A level 1 vocational assessment includes such traditional information as mental ability, academic achievement, adaptive behavior, social skills, and physical dexterity information, as well as data obtained through vocationally oriented interviews with the students and their parents/guardians. Information from teachers is also critical and includes data about work habits and attitudes, interests, aptitudes, and achievement levels. Information from the cumulative records such as group test data, grades, and medical background is also useful. A Level 1 vocational assessment is recommended for *all* special education students.

Level 2 evaluation. A Level 2 vocational assessment includes the information in Level 1 plus formal assessment of vocational interests and vocational aptitudes. Selected work samples and a short term exploratory vocation experience may also be components of a Level 2 evaluation. The minimum information required in Level 2 vocational assessment consists of two types of data: a vocational interest inventory and a vocational aptitude test. Selected work samples and a short term exploratory experience are optional. A Level 2 vocational assessment is usually recommended for *all* special education students.

Level 3 evaluation. Level 3 assessments are usually reserved for the more severely disabled. They normally occur in a centrally located evaluation center due to the nature of the equipment required. Level 3 includes the types of data included in Levels 1 and 2 as well as administration of comprehensive work samples and exploratory vocational course experiences. All medical data (vision, auditory, and physical) is carefully reviewed and referral for additional medical evaluation may be required.

Examples of Vocational Assessment Programs

Texas. Texas has developed a three level vocational evaluation scheme similar to that outlined above. Figure 6 presents the Texas model of vocational assessment.

The Texas guidelines describe two types of vocational assessment, Basic Vocational Assessment and Comprehensive Vocational Assessment. The Basic Vocational Assessment is referred to as Levels 1 and 2 assessment, and is recommended for all special education students. Level 3 is reserved for those who are more seriously disabled. If a placement committee is able to determine an appropriate vocational option based on assessment Levels 1 and 2, Level 3 assessment is not necessary. Special education teachers, school counselors, rehabilitation counselors, school psychologists, parents, medical personnel, social workers, vocational educators, specially trained work/vocational evaluators and other appropriate persons are involved at all three levels.

Virginia. Virginia has developed a series of vocational assessment regional centers. The Southside Special Education Consortium (SSEC) located in Amelia, Virginia, an example of such a regional program, provides special education and related services to seven primarily rural public school divisions. Recognizing the comprehensive nature of vocational assessment, SSEC uses a two phase, multidisciplinary team approach in the vocational assessment of handicapped students in school divisions served by the consortium. Phase 1 assessment is conducted at the time of a student's special education re-evaluation in either the 6th, 7th, or 8th grades and is completed within the student's home school division. In

Figure 6

THE NATURE OF ASSESSMENT

VOCATIONAL ASSESSMENT WILL . . .

ASSESS . . .	USING . . .	TO RECOMMEND . . .
Vocational interests	Interest tests Tour of vocational programs Work samples Job tryouts	
Dexterity, coordination, and physical skills	Dexterity tests Physical ability tests Work samples Medical records	Specific vocational training areas
Prevocational and functional life skills	School records Checklist of skills filled out by teacher/ parent Observation during testing Work samples Job/classroom tryouts	Vocational program placement level (resource, disadvantaged, or regular vocational classroom) Job placement Teaching techniques and curriculum modifications
Vocational learning style	Work samples Job/classroom tryouts	Training in prevocational and life skills
Basic education skills	Diagnostician's report Teacher check-lists Work samples	Training in work adjustment skills (work behaviors, attitudes, habits) Additional community support services
Vocational aptitude and ability	Dexterity tests Pencil and paper aptitude tests Diagnostician's report Checklist of list skills Work samples Job/Classroom tryouts	

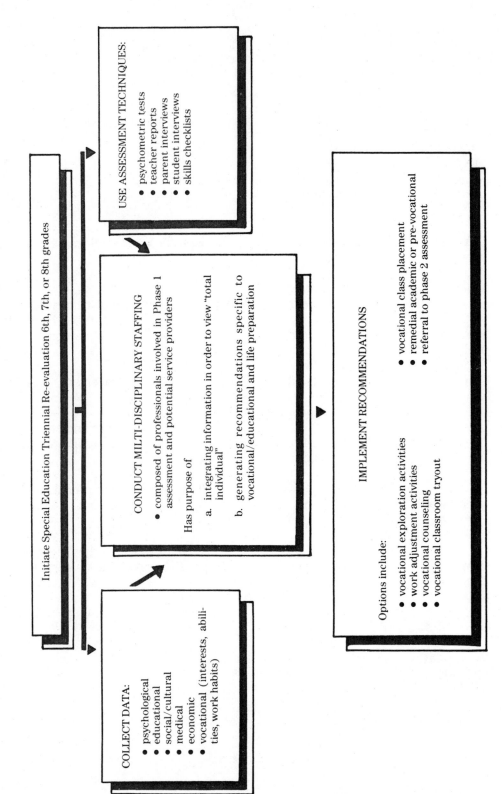

Figure 7 PROPOSED PHASE 1 VOCATIONAL ASSESSMENT   (to be completed in student's home school division and interfaced with special education triennial re-evaluation)

Initiate Special Education Triennial Re-evaluation 6th, 7th, or 8th grades

USE ASSESSMENT TECHNIQUES:
- psychometric tests
- teacher reports
- parent interviews
- student interviews
- skills checklists

CONDUCT MULTI-DISCIPLINARY STAFFING
- composed of professionals involved in Phase 1 assessment and potential service providers

Has purpose of

a. integrating information in order to view "total individual"

b. generating recommendations specific to vocational/educational and life preparation

COLLECT DATA:
- psychological
- educational
- social/cultural
- medical
- economic
- vocational (interests, abilities, work habits)

IMPLEMENT RECOMMENDATIONS

Options include:
- vocational exploration activities
- work adjustment activities
- vocational counseling
- vocational classroom tryout

- vocational class placement
- remedial academic or pre-vocational
- referral to phase 2 assessment

Figure 8 PROPOSED PHASE 2 VOCATIONAL ASSESSMENT

(to be done at comprehensive vocational assessment center, and interfaced with special education triennial re-evaluation, if possible)

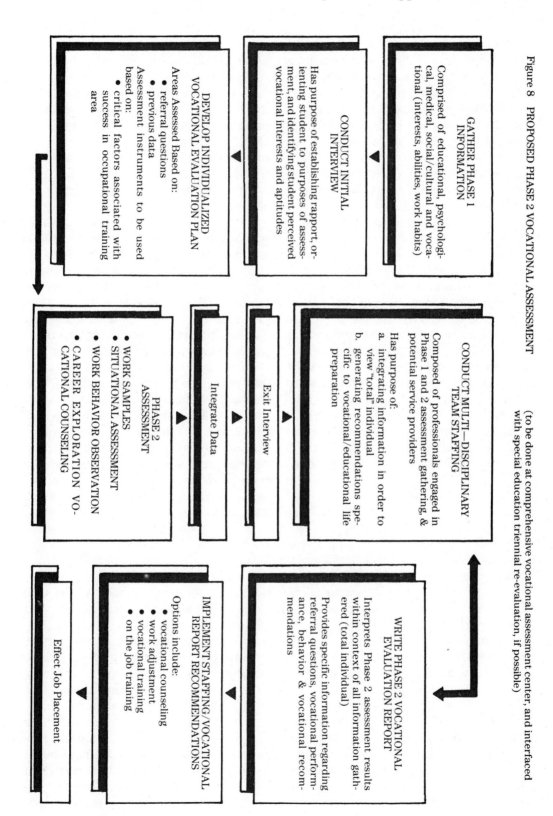

GATHER PHASE 1 INFORMATION

Comprised of educational, psychological, medical, social/cultural and vocational (interests, abilities, work habits)

CONDUCT INITIAL INTERVIEW

Has purpose of establishing rapport, orienting student to purposes of assessment, and identifying student perceived vocational interests and aptitudes

DEVELOP INDIVIDUALIZED VOCATIONAL EVALUATION PLAN

Areas Assessed Based on:
• referral questions
• previous data

Assessment instruments to be used based on:
• critical factors associated with success in occupational training area

CONDUCT MULTI—DISCIPLINARY TEAM STAFFING

Composed of professionals engaged in Phase 1 and 2 assessment gathering, & potential service providers

Has purpose of:
a. integrating information in order to view "total" individual
b. generating recommendations specific to vocational/educational life preparation

Exit Interview

Integrate Data

PHASE 2 ASSESSMENT

• WORK SAMPLES
• SITUATIONAL ASSESSMENT
• WORK BEHAVIOR OBSERVATION
• CAREER EXPLORATION VO-CATIONAL COUNSELING

WRITE PHASE 2 VOCATIONAL EVALUATION REPORT

Interprets Phase 2 assessment results within context of all information gathered (total individual)

Provides specific information regarding referral questions, vocational performance, behavior & vocational recommendations

IMPLEMENT STAFFING/VOCATIONAL REPORT RECOMMENDATIONS

Options include:
• vocational counseling
• work adjustment
• vocational training
• on the job training

Effect Job Placement

addition to the information typically gathered as part of the special education re-evaluation process, vocational aptitudes, job attitudes, and general educational development are obtained. Following information gathering, a multi-disciplinary staffing consistent with the special education process is conducted in which all information is shared, and recommendations are made relative to educational, vocational, and life preparation. Figure 7 details the Phase 1 assessment process.

A Phase 2 assessment is initiated during the 8th, 9th, or 10th grade, but only upon referral of the more seriously handicapped student. It is conducted at a regional vocational assessment center. Phase 2 is generally reserved for those students who require a more comprehensive evaluation. The Phase 2 assessment is about a four and a half day process. It includes such assessment techniques as work sampling, situational assessment, and simulated work experiences. Where possible, it is also interfaced with the student's triennial re-evaluation. Figure 8 describes the Phase 2 evaluation process.

Who does what?

Vocational assessment is a multi-disciplinary process in almost all of the currently functioning programs. Those involved include vocational and special education personnel, school psychologists, school counselors, rehabilitation counselors, medical personnel, parents, vocational/work evaluation specialists, and students. Who does what in this process depends upon the characteristics of the school system; qualifications that a staff possesses; and the availability of services from various social agencies. School psychologists provide a wide variety of services, the nature and breadth of which depend upon their training, experience, interest, and employer expectations. In some school divisions, school psycholo-

gists are routinely conducting Level 1 and Level 2 evaluations and participate as staff members for Level 3 assessments. School psychologists may also either head the development of vocational assessment programs or serve as important members of the planning committee. Work sampling procedures are typically conducted by specially trained vocational/work evaluators, although a few psychologists are also employed in this capacity.

Regardless of the specific roles that school psychologists play in the vocational assessment process, most traditionally trained psychologists need additional knowledge and skills in vocational education and vocational assessment areas to function effectively. This is occurring through inservice education of practicing psychologists and some training programs include vocational aspects as a regular part of their programs. Regardless of how a school psychologist acquires the necessary knowledge and skills, a minimal level of training includes: (a) knowledge of vocational education programs and the student aptitudes necessary for success in each program, and (b) knowledge and skills in vocational assessment procedures and techniques.

SUMMARY

A critical need exists for the vocational development of students. This need is especially prevalent among handicapped adolescents. With school psychologists' training, experience, and unique expertise, they are the appropriate professionals to facilitate this development. School systems, alone or in combination, are devoting more attention to the vocational development of exceptional youth because more handicapped students are entering secondary schools. This chapter familiarized school psychologists with the basic tenets of vocational assessment which provide useful information for the career decision-making process. Obviously, school based vocational assessment programs are developed with local needs and resources in mind. Consequently, diversity among school divisions and states is expected in both the development and operation of vocational assessment programs. Likewise, diversity exists among the roles school psychologists play in such programs. In school divisions where no such programs exist, school psychologists may assume a leadership role in the development and implementation of such programs. In schools where programs already exist, the psychologists' roles range from providing a complete vocational assessment to discussing the vocational implications of the data gathered from traditionally used psychological assessment instruments.

Regardless of their roles in the vocational assessment and planning process, most school psychologists need to upgrade their skills in the vocational aspects of the practice of school psychology. It is our hope that this chapter serves as an important tool in the acquisition of the necessary knowledge and skills to function more effectively in vocational/secondary settings.

REFERENCES

Anderson W. T. (1982). Assessment roles for vocational school psychologists. *The Journal for Vocational Special Needs Education*, 4(3), 14-17.

Batsche, C. J. (1982). *Handbook for vocational school psychology*, Des Moines, Iowa: Iowa Department of Public Instruction.

Harrington, T. F. (1982). *Handbook of career planning for special needs students*. Rockville, Maryland: Aspen Systems Corporation.

Heller, H. W. (1981). Secondary education for handicapped students: In search of a solution. *Exceptional Children, 47*, 582-583.

Hohenshil, T. H. (1982). School psychology + vocational counseling = Vocational school psychology. *The Personnel and Guidance Journal, 61*(1), 11-13.

Hohenshil, T. H. (1982). Secondary school psychological services: Vocational assessment procedures for handicapped students. In T. H. Hohenshil, W. T. Anderson, & J. F. Salwan (Eds.), *Secondary school psychological services: Focus on vocational assessment procedures for handicapped students*. Blacksburg, VA: Virginia Tech in cooperation with the Virginia Department of Education, the NASP National Committee on Vocational/Secondary School Psychology, and the Virginia Association of School Psychologists. (*ERIC Reproduction Number*, ED 229704), pp. 1-7.

Levinson, E. M. (1984). Vocational/career assessment in school psychological evaluations: Rationale, definition, and purpose. *Psychology in the Schools, 21*, 112-117.

Miller, S. R. & Schloss, P. J. (1982). *Career-vocational education for handicapped youth*. Rockville, Maryland: Aspen Systems Corporation.

ANNOTATED BIBLIOGRAPHY

Handbook for vocational school psychology (1982). Des Moines, Iowa: Iowa State Department of Public Instruction.
This five chapter handbook provides a broad overview of the vocational aspects of the practice of school psychology. Chapters three and four provide an indepth treatment of vocational assessment procedures and the roles that school psychologists should play in this process.

Journal for Vocational Special Needs Education (Spring, 1981), 3(1).
This special issue is devoted to the topic of vocational evaluation for special needs students. It contains seven articles on a number of vocational assessment topics, including work sampling, vocational evaluation of secondary educable mentally retarded students, and the individualized vocational plan. The journal is the official publication of the National Association of Vocational Education Special Needs Personnel, a division of the 50,000 member American Vocational Association.

Journal for Vocational Special Needs Education (Spring, 1982), 4(3).
This special issue is devoted to the topic of the vocational aspects of the practice of school psychology. The nine articles in the special issue are devoted to such topics as the current status of vocational school psychology, assessment roles in vocational programs, vocational school psychology in corrections and rehabilitation settings, and future prospects for school psychologists practicing in various vocational and secondary settings.

Vocational assessment of students with special needs
(1982), Austin Texas: Texas Education Agency
(State Department of Education).
This 120 page manual describes the vocational
assessment process for handicapped junior
and senior high school students. The manual
provides a well balanced outline for the process of developing and operating a comprehensive vocational assessment system, student
characteristics, suggested instruments, and
suggestions for vocational IEP activities.

*Secondary school psychological services: Focus on
vocational assessment procedures for handicapped students* (1982). Blacksburg, VA: Virginia Tech in cooperation with the NASP National Committee on Vocational/Secondary
School Psychology, the Virginia Department of
Education, and the Virginia Association of
School Psychologists, (*ERIC Reproduction
Number*, ED 229704).
This document comprises the proceedings of
the National Conference on Secondary School
Psychological Services: Focus on Vocational
Assessment Procedures for Handicapped Students. It contains 16 chapters on various
aspects of vocational assessment for handicapped junior and senior high students. Chapter topics include the vocational assessment
of the mentally retarded, learning disabled,
emotionally handicapped, orthopedically
handicapped, and students with various sensory disabilities.

BEST PRACTICES IN NEUROPSYCHOLOGICAL ASSESSMENT

George W. Hynd
University of Georgia
Medical College of Georgia

Jeff Snow
University of Southern Mississippi

OVERVIEW

For over two decades now, it has been recognized that a significant number of children with adequate ability do not learn as well as their peers. From the beginning it was assumed that the learning disorders had a neurological basis. Although the definition of learning disabilities published in the *Federal Register* in 1976 did not specifically state the neurological etiology of learning disabilities, it was implied by the listing of " . . . such conditions as perceptual handicaps, brain injury, minimal brain dysfunction, dyslexia and developmental aphasia" (p. 56977).

This definition was widely acclaimed as a good beginning, but its limitations were recognized by many. For this reason the National Joint Committee for Learning Disabilities (NJCLD) which included representatives from six professional educational organizations was formed. Its task was to produce a more precise and conceptually meaningful definition of learning disabilities. The efforts of this organization resulted in the following definition:

> *Learning Disabilities* is a generic term that refers to a heterogeneous group of disorders manifested by significant difficulties in the acquisition and use of listening, speaking, reading, writing, reasoning, or mathematical abilities. These disorders are intrinsic to the individual and *presumed to be due to central nervous system dysfunction.* Even though a learning disability may occur concomitantly with other handicapping conditions (e.g., sensory impairment, mental retardation, social and emotional disturbance) or environmental influences (e.g., cultu-

ral differences, insufficient/inappropriate instruction, psychogenic factors), it is not the direct result of those conditions or influences. (Emphasis added, Hammill, Leigh, McNutt, & Larson, 1981, p. 336)

If one assumes that the estimated incidence rate is conservatively 3% of the population of the United States, then there are an estimated 6,600,000 persons with some form of learning disability. This is indeed a significant figure. It has been estimated that the number of children with a severe reading disability alone probably exceeds the total number of children suffering from cerebral palsy, epilepsy, and severe mental retardation (Duane, 1979).

Only limited evidence exists that documents neuroanatomical abnormalities in the brains of severely learning disabled children (see Rosen & Galaburda, 1984). If central nervous system dysfunction cannot be documented, then it is inappropriate to diagnose learning disability by the wording of the NJCLD definition (Hynd & Snow, 1984). From this perspective, one must defend one's diagnosis and document in some fashion the neuropsychological etiology of the learning disability. For this reason school psychologists should be familiar with the basics of neuropsychological assessment, the advantages and disadvantages of various approaches, and professional issues related to appropriate training.

The reality of diagnosis of learning disabilities in the schools, however, often rests solely on a documented discrepancy between measured achievement and potential. Thus, determining the presence or absence of central nervous system dysfunction is irrelevant to differential diagnosis for placement purposes. Even if this is indeed the case, the results of a neuropsychological assessment are valuable for two reasons. First, the neuropsychological examination helps differentiate learning disorders that are not due to neurological dysfunction. Thus, cases in which emotional disturbance manifests as a learning disability are more accurately discerned. Many children with emotional disturbance do not evidence the soft neurological signs associated with many learning disabilities. A second instance where a neuropsychological examination is helpful is in determining whether or not the learning disability is due to neuropsychological dysfunction. If the learning problem is not associated with neuropsychological dysfunction, then direct intervention in the area of deficit is most appropriate. If the neuropsychological evaluation reveals correlated dysfunction, then the intervention is more productive if it is initially focused on the learning of compensatory educational strategies (Hynd & Snow, 1984).

Consequently, the neuropsychological evaluation documents central nervous system dysfunction for differential diagnosis and in cases where the initial diagnosis has been made using other diagnostic criteria, contributes to the choice of intervention.

Professional Preparation

Many school psychologists receive some, if limited, preparation in the area of neuropsychological screening and assessment through their professional training (Hynd, Quackenbush, & Obrzut, 1980). Generally, however, this training is limited to one course in the biological foundations of behavior and some exposure to neurological screening devices in clinical assessment courses. To date, only a few programs offer any formalized study in child neuropsychology for the school psychologist. Continuing education experiences are the primary mode of receiving advanced preparation in neuropsychological screening and assessment. The school psychologist wishing to pursue expertise in this area of specialization should receive more formalized training experiences. Proposed guidelines have been outlined elsewhere (Hynd, 1981). It is obvious that it is the responsibility of the school psychologist to pursue appropriate professional experiences that allow him or her to offer qualified services.

BASIC CONSIDERATIONS

Prior to discussing the various approaches to neuropsychological assessment of school-age children, two points need to be briefly addressed. First, how the results of the neuropsychological assessment are integrated with those of the traditional psychoeducational battery is discussed. Second, instances when school psychologists refer a child to a neurologist or other physician are considered.

Interfacing Neuropsychological and Psychoeducational Results

The results of the neuropsychological examination are integrated into the format and conceptual framework of the traditional psychoeducational battery. For instance, if one administers the Luria-Nebraska Neuropsychological Battery-Children's Revision, many of the subtests relate directly to abilities and modalities assessed by other instruments in the psychoeducational battery. In the report, the school psychologist includes the results of the Intelligence Scale on the Luria-Nebraska in the section reporting the usual WISC-R results. Results of the Luria-Nebraska Motor, Rhythm, Visual, and Tactile Scales are integrated into the section on perceptual-motor functioning. In other words, the results are not discussed separately as they relate to "brain" function but are integrated into the report format as they relate to the "processes" important to learning. In this fashion the results are complementary to rather than separate from the typical report generated by the school psychologist.

Making a Referral to a Neurologist

The neuropsychological screening or assessment that a school psychologist conducts is used to make a determination as to whether or not evidence exists as to the neuropsychological basis of some learning disorder. Using the data derived from such assessment, the school psychologist enhances the probability that the referral to a neurologist is appropriate.

There are three situations in which a neurological examination is warranted (Oppe, 1979). First, a child who is suspected of suffering some neurological disease obviously sees a neurologist. Some neurological diseases most notably the muscular dystrophies are first manifested as learning or behavioral problems. A gradual decline in intelligence and achievement over a period of time and a positive family history are excellent indicators that a referral is necessary.

A second situation when a referral is indicated is when there are no obvious neurological difficulties or positive family history, but the behavior itself warrants medical evaluation. Extremes in hyperactive behavior or suspected petit mal (absence) seizures are examples.

Finally, the neurological exam is useful as a screening device in identifying neurologically-based disorders of learning (e.g., learning disabilities). As Oppe (1979) points out, though, the neurologic examination is less valuable in this third situation since it is likely to elicit the "soft" signs more typically associated with disorders of higher cortical processes. It is here, of course, where the neuropsychological evaluation in the hands of an appropriately trained school psychologist provides meaningful information regarding the diagnosis and treatment of learning disabilities.

BEST PRACTICES

Neuropsychological assessment of school-age children is a complex procedure involving the integration of knowledge from a number of different areas. In order to complete a neuropsychological evaluation with a child, the school psychologist needs a working knowledge in areas pertinent to neuropsychology including functional neuroanatomy, cerebral vascular systems, and so forth, as well as an understanding of testing and developmental psychology. The importance of prerequisite knowledge of basic neuropsychology is obvious to the completion of valid neuropsychological assessments; however, the relevance of the other two areas are less apparent and therefore merit further discussion.

Considerations

The use of standardized tests has been a major influence within the discipline of neuropsychological assessment. An understanding of the basic principles of psychometrics such as reliability, content and discriminate validity is important for any school psychologist using standardized tests. In relation to neuropsychological assessment it is particularly important that the psychologist be aware of data pertinent to the construct validity of the measures used. Two of the more commonly used neuropsychological batteries have been the focus of criticism in terms of adequate construct validity (Hynd & Snow, 1984). The concerns have centered around such issues as the influences of IQ level on the test results or the number of discrete constructs which are measured by the test battery (Seidenberg, Giordani, Berent, & Boll, 1983; Snow & Hynd, 1984; Snow, Hynd, & Hartlage, 1984). Generally, the school psychologist who uses standardized batteries in a neuropsychological assessment needs assurance that the tests measure discrete constructs relevant to the evaluation. Only then can the evaluation contribute useful information beyond that which is provided by a more traditional psychoeducational assessment.

In addition to knowledge about psychometrics, the school psychologist who uses neuropsychological assessment procedures should understand basic neuropsychological development. This is particularly important in terms of the types of tasks which are selected for the evaluation. For instance, Golden (1981) argued that the prefrontal lobe areas do not become active until adolescence. Therefore, he concluded that tasks which assess these cortical areas are not included when evaluating a child. On the other hand, Luria, (1973) stated that the prefrontal lobes mature at about ages four to seven years. These conflicting theoretical viewpoints indicate the importance of developmental considerations in clinical neuropsychology. The school psychologist considers the age of the child being evaluated and determines what tasks are most appropriate. Consequently, a fundamental understanding of the theoretical and empirical literature pertinent to neuropsychological development becomes increasingly important.

The factors discussed above are just some of the many elements which are considered by the school psychologist. It is important that the complexity of the assessment be understood and that the person completing the evaluation has the appropriate training and prerequisite knowledge. Based on this information, the following section provides a brief review of the concept of functional systems as well as examines some basic approaches used in neuropsychological assessment.

Functional Systems

The functional system is a key concept in neuropsychology. One of the most influential theorists who put forth this concept was Luria (1973; 1980). He moved away from strict localizationism of neurological functioning. Luria (1980) felt that a function was a complex network involving different areas of the nervous system. More specifically, Luria (1973; 1980) indicated that a functional system was a group or chain of interconnected nervous system acts. Therefore, most behaviors involve the coordinated activity of a number of different cortical areas. Further, it is important to remember that each of these cortical areas contributes a unique qualitative aspect to the functional system (Luria, 1973). This is particularly relevant to the clinical approach of neuropsychological assessment and testing.

Clinical Approach

The clinical approach of neuropsychological assessment is best exemplified by Luria's system of evaluation (1980). According to Luria (1980), brain lesions lead to qualitative changes in behavior. This concept emphasizes the importance of the functional system since each component in the chain of behavior contributes a particular qualitative aspect to the behavior resulting from that functional system. Therefore, lesions in different components of a functional system lead to different qualitative deficiencies in the performance of the behavior. It is the observation and analysis of these qualitative deficiencies which play a central role in the clinical approach.

According to Luria (1980), a neuropsychological assessment is goal oriented with the central objective being the explanation of a syndrome resulting in functional impairment. To obtain this objective, Luria (1980) proposed a three stage assessment model.

The first stage involves an interview and administration of preliminary tests. The interview provides the psychologist with some indication of the person's social-emotional status and also the person's physiological/psychological complaints. Next, a battery of preliminary tests are administered. These tests include visual, auditory, kinesthetic, motor, and sensorimotor tasks as well as more complex measures involving the integration of functions such as reading. These preliminary tests screen for deficiencies and provide the neuropsychologist with clues as to which processes are affected.

At the second state of assessment, the neuropsychologist uses follow-up measures based on the results of the preliminary examination. These more specific tasks allow the psychologist to analyze the functional systems' qualitative deficiencies to determine their component links and common position within the central nervous system; this localizes the lesion. According to Luria (1980), focusing on a syndrome analysis or commonality among a group of impaired behaviors provides a more reliable means of localizing the brain dysfunction.

The third and final state is arriving at an overall conclusion. This identifies and describes the defect, indicates if possible the pathological factors contributing to the defect, and clarifies how various mental functions indicate the deficit (Luria, 1980).

It should be noted that the clinical approach relies primarily on observation and qualitative analysis of the errors made by the person and not on specific test profiles. A somewhat different approach is the standardized test battery. The most common batteries for use with school-age children are the Halstead-Reitan tests (Reitan-Indiana Neuropsychological Test Battery for Children) and the Luria-Nebraska Neuropsychological Battery-Children's Revision.

Halstead-Reitan Batteries

The Halstead Neuropsychological Test Battery for Children designed for children 9-14 years of age and the Reitan-Indiana Neuropsychological Test Batery for Children designed for children 5-8 years of age are comprehensive tests which involve a number of different types of measures (for a discussion of the subtests, see Selz, 1981): However, research results with the batteries have been somewhat variable among different populations of school age children.

The Halstead-Reitan Batteries have been shown to effectively differentiate brain-damaged children from normal controls (Reitan & Davison, 1974). These studies have consistently shown that brain-damaged children score significantly lower than normal controls on the different tests (Selz, 1981). However, while this type of validation data is important in a clinical interpretation and use of test results such as discriminating brain-damaged from non-brain damaged children, the school psychologist who uses the batteries for educational diagnosis and intervention needs other sources of information. In this regard, several studies have been completed which provide data on learning disabled (LD) children.

In general, the test batteries do appear to be effective in differentiating between LD, brain damaged, and normal children (Selz, 1981). However, some possible conceptual problems limit the utility of these data (Hynd & Snow, 1984). The first problem relates to the development of the batteries. Reitan merely took measures with high discriminant validity and simplified them for use with children. Aspects of developmental neuropsychology were not taken into account. A second confounding variable is the influence of IQ variation on test results and differences. A recent study found a significant influence of IQ on 6 of the 14 tests (Seidenberg, et al., 1983). Therefore, the school psychologist must carefully assess the results obtained from a more conventional psychoeducational evaluation and determine what additional information is provided by the Halstead-Reitan batteries with LD children.

Luria-Nebraska Neuropsychological Battery-Children's Revision

The Luria-Nebraska Neuropsychological Battery-Children's Revision (LNNB-CR) is a relatively new instrument designed to provide a comprehensive assessment of neuropsychological functioning of children 8 to 12 years of age. Development of the battery centered around revision of the adult version of the test, the Luria-Nebraska Neuropsychological Battery (LNNB) (Golden, Hammeke, & Purisch, 1978). The development of this test involved administration of the LNNB to a group of children with above average achievement. Inappropriate items and instructions needing modification for children were identified. Three revisions of the battery were tested with groups of normal children until a fourth and finalized form was completed. This version was then standardized on a sample of 125 children.

The battery consists of 11 scales and has a total of 149 items. The scales of the LNNB-CR are Motor Function, Rhythm, Tactile, Visual Functions, Receptive Speech, Expressive Speech, Writing, Reading, Arithmetical Skill, Memory, and Intellectual Processes. Each item of the battery is scored on a 3-point scale (0, 1, 2). Item scores are summed within each scale and this total is then converted to T-scores with a mean of 50 and a standard deviation of 10.

As with the Halstead-Reitan batteries, research results with the LNNB-CR are variable. The battery appears effective in discriminating between brain-damaged and normal children. However, the utility of the test battery with LD children is inconclusive. The primary concerns focus on the construct validity of the LNNB-CR with LD children and the influence of IQ and academic achievement on test results (Snow & Hynd, 1984; Snow, Hynd & Hartlage, 1984). It is important that the school psychologist be aware of these possible limitations.

SUMMARY

The conclusions and recommendations that result from a neuropsychological assessment should be educationally relevant. In order to provide a more comprehensive and useful evaluation, it is recommended that the schol psychologist integrate both qualitative error analysis and standardized test scores. These data, when combined with results obtained from more traditional psychoeducational batteries, are valuable in evaluation and remediation.

In summary, a multitude of factors have contributed to a growing awareness as to the neurological conceptualization of learning disability in children. Responding to this awareness, school psychologists have begun using neuropsychological screening and assessment with children suspected of having a learning disability. Appropriate training experiences, knowledge as to when to refer the child to a neurologist, and familiarity with different conceptual approaches to clinical neuropsychological assessment are central factors in providing appropriate services.

REFERENCES

Duane, D. D. (1979). Toward a definition of dyslexia: A summary of views. *Bulletin of the Orton Society, 29,* 56-64.

Federal Register (1976). *Education of handicapped children and incentive grants program.* U.S. Department of Health, Education, and Welfare, *41*, 56977.

Golden, C. J. (1981). The Luria-Nebraska Children's Battery: Theory and initial formulation. In G. W. Hynd & J. E. Obrzut (Eds.), *Neuropsychological assessment and the school-age child: Issues and procedures.* New York: Grune & Stratton, Inc.

Golden, C. J., Hammeke, T. A. & Purisch, A. D. (1978). Diagnostic validity of a standardized neuropsychological battery derived from Luria's neuropsychological tests. *Journal of Consulting and Clinical Psychology, 46,* 1258-1265.

Hammill, D. D., Leigh, J. E., McNutt, G., & Larsen, S. C. (1981). A new definition of learning disabilities. *Learning Disability Quarterly, 4,* 336-342.

Hynd, G. W. (1981). Training the school psychologist in neuropsychology: Perspectives, issues and models (379-404). In G. W. Hynd & J. E. Obrzut (Eds.), *Neuropsychological assessment and the school-age child: Issues and procedures.* New York: Grune & Stratton, Inc.

Hynd, G. W. & Snow, J. H. (1984). Assessment of neurological and neuropsychological factors associated with severe learning disabilities. In P. J. Lazarus & S. S. Strichart (Eds.), *Psychoeducational evaluation of children with low incidence handicaps.* New York: Grune & Stratton, Inc.

Hynd, G. W., Quackenbush, R., & Obrzut, J. E. (1980). Training school psychologists in neuropsychological assessment: Current practices and trends. *Journal of School Psychology, 18,* 148-153.

Luria, A. R. (1980). *Higher cortical functions.* New York: Basic Books.

Luria, A. R. (1973). *The working brain.* New York Basic Books.

Oppe, T. E. (1979). The neurological examination (1-17). In F. C. Rose (Ed.), *Pediatric neurology.* Oxford: Blackwell Scientific Publications.

Reitan, R. M. & Davison, L. A. (Eds.) (1974). *Clinical neuropsychology: Current status and applications.* Washington, DC: V. H. Winston & Sons.

Rosen, G. D. & Galaburda, A. M. (1984). Development of language: A question of asymmetry and deviation. In J. Mehler & R. Fox (Eds.), *Neonate cognition: Beyond the blooming buzzing confusion.* Hillsdale, NJ: Lawrence Erlbaum Associates, Inc.

Seidenberg, M., Giordani, B., Berent, S., & Boll, T. J. (1983). IQ level and performance on the Halstead-Reitan Neuropsychological Test Battery for older children. *Journal of Consulting and Clinical Psychology, 51,* 406-413.

Selz, M. (1981). Halstead-Reitan neuropsychological test batteries for children (195-235). In G. W. Hynd & J. E. Obrzut (Eds.), *Neuropsychological assessment and the school-age child: Issues and procedures.* New York: Grune & Stratton, Inc.

Snow, J. H. & Hynd, G. W. (1984). Determining neuropsychological 'strengths' and 'weaknesses' on the Luria-Nebraska: Good practice or wishful thinking. *Journal of Consulting and Clinical Psychology, 52,* 695-696.

Snow, J. H., Hynd, G. W. & Hartlage, L. (1984). Differences between mildly and more severely learning disabled children on the Luria-Nebraska Neuropsychological Battery-Children's Revision. *Journal of Psychoeducational Assessment, 2,* 23-28.

ANNOTATED BIBLIOGRAPHY

Hynd, G. W., & Obrzut, J. E. (Eds.) (1981). *Neuropsychological assessment and the school-age child: Issues and procedures.* New York: Grune & Stratton, Inc.
This book provides an overview of various approaches to neuropsychological assessment with school-age children. The twelve chapters are divided into four sections: (1) Neuropsychological Perspectives on Education, (2) Issues in Neuropsychology, (3) Diagnostic and Clinical Procedures, and (4) Neuropsychology in the Schools. Case studies are provided in the assessment chapters.

Lezak, M. D. (1983). *Neuropsychological assessment* (2nd ed.). New York: Oxford University Press.
Lezak provides an updated overview of the many different tests and techniques used in clinical neuropsychological practice. The book devotes most of its focus to adult assessment. The standardized neuropsychological batteries are not given much attention.

Luria, A. R. (1980). *Higher cortical functions in man* (2nd ed.). New York: Basic Books.
This revised and expanded second edition is a truly significant contribution to the neuropsychology literature in that Luria's theories regarding brain-behavior relations are fully explored. It is an excellent resource.

Rose, F. C. (Ed.) (1979). *Pediatric neurology*. Oxford:
    Blackwell Scientific Publications.
    An edited volume with 39 chapters, this book
    serves as an excellent resource for a quick
    overview of a number of common disorders
    found in school-age children. The chapters on
    cerebral palsy, neuromuscular disease, hydro-
    cephalus, the epilepsies, and head injuries are
    particularly worthwhile.

BEST PRACTICES IN PROCEDURAL SAFEGUARDS

Michael L. Kabler

OVERVIEW

During the late 1960's and early 1970's numerous lawsuits were filed in behalf of children who had been misidentified as handicapped and inappropriately placed in special education programs. Litigation also occured in this time period which addressed the concerns of parents who wanted access to their children's records while simultaneously protecting privacy (Weintraub, Abeson, Ballard & LaVor, 1976).

As a result of this waive of litigation, the U.S. Congress adopted the Education for All Handicapped Children Act of 1975 (Public Law 94-142) and the Family Educational Rights and Privacy Act (FERPA) (U.S. Congress, 1975, 1974). These laws have had very extensive influence on many educational and psychological practices since their enactment. School districts and state education agencies throughout the country responded to these laws by developing administrative procedures which are designed to implement the requirements set forth in the federal legislation and concomitant state legislation. Wide variation has been noted in the manner with which school district personnel including school psychologists responded to these requirements (Budoff, 1978; Pryzwansky & Bersoff, 1978). In some schools the psychologists welcomed these laws and regulations. They now had a legal basis for advocating fuller involvement of parents in the education of their children. In other settings there has been an opposite response ranging from outright refusal to involve parents to the establishment of procedures which comply with the law but discourage parent involvement and access to information.

Since 1976 a significant reduction in the frequency of the latter response has been observed.

BASIC CONSIDERATIONS

The purpose of this paper is to address selected issues and professional practices relevant to school psychology in the implementation of procedural safeguards extended to children and their parents. Procedural safeguards refer to those specific procedures which are designed to ensure that due process of law is afforded individuals as guaranteed by the U.S. Constitution. It includes those activities which the school district carries out in providing appropriate notices to parents regarding proposed actions, obtaining informed consent of parents, involving parents in decision making and providing an impartial review mechanism in the event an unresolvable disagreement between the school district and the child's parents develops. Presently, PL 94-142 and FERPA regulations are the most important federal requirements addressing procedural safeguards in the schools.

PL 94-142 Regulations were initially assigned to Title 45 of the Code of Federal Regulations and designated Part 121a. With the creation of the Department of Education the regulations were transferred to Title 34 (Education) of the Code of Federal Regulations (CFR) and redesignated 34 CFR Part 300; however, the individual section numbers were not changed. In the redesignated regulations some minor revisions were made to accommodate the new Department of Education. Subpart E of PL 94-142 Regulations deals with the procedural safeguards set forth in the Act (U.S. Dept. HEW, 1977). This section includes specific procedures addressing due process procedures for parents and children, protection in evaluation procedures, least restrictive environment, and confidentiality of information. The focus of this chapter is placed on selected areas which are most directly related to the role and function of the school psychologist. Since appropriate evaluation procedures are addressed in other chapters, attention is given to that area only as it relates to the issues of notice and consent. In addition to the issues of providing prior notice and obtaining consent, the areas of protecting the confidentiality of information and due process hearings are addressed.

Whereas PL 94-142 relates only to handicapped or suspected handicapped children, the Family Rights and Privacy Act (FERPA), commonly referred to as the Buckley Amendments (Section 438) to PL 93-380, is applicable to all children and their parents. FERPA and its regulations provide for parent access to their children's records and ensures that confidentiality of educational records is maintained. School psychologists are confronted daily with situations where their actions are governed by the aforementioned legislation and regulations.

School psychologists should be familiar with selected sections of federal regulations developed for implementing the requirements of PL 94-142 and PL 93-380, Section 438. Copies of the complete regulations can be obtained by contacting your U.S. or congressional district representative. The FERPA regulations and the most relevant sections of the 94-142 Regulations are also reproduced in the *Handbook of School Psychology* (Reynolds and Gutkin, 1982). In addition to these Federal requirements each of the fifty states has laws which are applicable. State requirements reflect those at the federal level but may contain additional specifics.

Copies of state regulations are available from school districts and state departments of education. A review of federal and state rules is important in order to have first-hand knowledge of what is legally required rather than relying exclusively on the interpretations of administrators, colleagues and other secondary sources.

While the regulations cited above provide the legal basis for best practices, the codes of ethics and standards for the practice of school psychology of the National Association of School Psychologists (NASP) and the American Psychological Association (APA) are equally important in providing a professionally ethical basis for practices. School psychologists should be familiar with these standards. Copies of the respective standards are available from NASP and APA. The NASP Code of Ethics and Standards are reproduced in Appendices I and II. Sections are cited in Table 1 in relationship to areas addressed in the section on "best practices."

School psychologists are likely to be familiar with local policies and procedures developed to assist the school district comply with federal and state requirements. School psychologists should reexamine these policies and procedures in light of what is presented in the following paragraphs and the sections of ethical standards cited in Table 1.

As noted by Budoff (1978), school personnel who have developed these policies think legalistically. Schools review federal and state requirements and develop their own procedures for implementation. Many administrators, school psychologists, teachers and other educational personnel perceive the procedural safeguards as biased against them (Budoff, 1978). This attitude is one of the major reasons that so many local policies are developed with too much emphasis on what is minimally required by the regula-

Table 1

Relevant Sections of APA and NASP
Standards for Professional Ethics

APA Principle	NASP Principle	Content Area
Principle 5 Confidentiality	I. Professional Competency (Subpart c)	Confidentiality of Records
	III. Professional Relationships With the School (Subparts b. & c.)	
Principle 8 Assessment Techniques	IV. Professional Relationships With the School (Subpart d.)	
	V. Professional Relationships With the Parent (Subpart d.)	
Principle 5 Confidentiality	III. Professional Relationships With the Student	Prior Notice and Consent
Principle 6 Welfare of the Consumer	V. Professional Relationships With the Parent	
Not applicable directly	Not applicable directly	Due Process Hearings

tions. While minimum requirements or the "letter of the law" need to be met, local procedures should also be designed to address the "spirit of the law."

The spirit of the procedural safeguard requirements is to increase parent involvement in the educational decision-making process and to provide an appropriate public education for all handicapped children. Perhaps there is enough latitude in local policies that actual practices in which school psychologists engage can shift substantially without the necessity of a change in the written documents or codes or regulations.

BEST PRACTICES

School psychologists' concerns about procedural safeguards predates the enactment of the federal legislation (McDermott, 1972; Fisher, 1968; Trachtman, 1963, 1972). With the federal legislation in place, however, there is a much broader need and interest on the part of school psychologists in this area.

The federal legislation has settled some issues for the school psychologist such as the parent consent issue for the handicapped and access to copies of the school psychologist's report, but raises many more. This section addresses some of these issues and offers solutions which are consistent with the spirit as well as the letter of federal law and regulations and the standards for professional conduct.

This section is organized into three major components:
1. prior notice and parental consent;
2. confidentiality of records; and
3. due process hearings.

Prior Notice and Parental Consent

The intent or "spirit" of the requirements for prior notice to parents and obtaining consent before an evaluation is to increase parent awareness and involvement in educational decision-making for their children. Bersoff noted that it is critically important for school psychologists to "pay as much attention to the process as to the substance of assessment" (1982, p. 1058). He further observed that the involvement of parents concerning an impending psycho-educational evaluation is the most crucial requirement. Bersoff's rationale for this view is based on the need to conduct an unbiased assessment.

Relevant Federal Regulations

The sections of PL 94-142 and FERPA Regulations which deal with prior notice and consent are presented in Table 2. These regulations require prior notice in many more instances than those for which consent is required. Parental consent is required in only three instances: prior to an initial preplacement evaluation, before releasing information to outside agencies and before the initial placement of a handicapped child into special education. Prior notice is required, however, in a number of other instances. Table 2 lists those instances where prior notice is required.

Relevant Professional Standards

Pertinent sections of the professional standards for ethical conduct are presented below:

NASP Principle:
V. Professional Relationships with parents.
Parental involvement is a significant influence on efforts to improve a student's capacity for coping with demands. Failure to obtain parental support may compound pressures acting on the student and increase adjustment and learning difficulties. Conferences . . . a. The school psychologist

Table 2

Summary of PL 94-142 and FERPA Requirements
for Prior Notice & Consent

When Notice Is Required for District Action	When Consent Is Required for District Action	Relevant Regulations
Referral for preplacement evaluation		34 C.F.R. Section 300.504(1)
Refusal to conduct an evaluation requested by parents		34 C.F.R. Section 300.504 (a) (2)
Referral for reevaluation		34 C.F.R. Section 300.504 (a) (1)
Conducting the pre-placement evaluation	Conducting the pre-placement evaluation	34 C.F.R. Sections 300.504 (a) (1) & (b) (1)
Conducting a reeavaluation		34 C.F.R. Section 300.504 (a) (1)
Development of an initial IEP		34 C.F.R. Section 300.504 (a) (1) 300.345 (a) (1)
Refusal to develop an Initial IEP		34 C.F.R. Section 300.504 (b) (1)
Initial placement in Special Education	Initial placement in Special Education	34 C.F.R. Section 300.504 (a) (1) & (b) (1)
Review of IEP		34 C.F.R. Section 300.504 (a) (1)
Refusal to review IEP		34 C.F.R. Section 300.504 (a) (2)
Modify the IEP or the student's special education program		34 C.F.R. Section 300.504 (a) (1)
Refusal to revise an IEP or change placement		34 C.F.R. Section 300.504 (a) (2)
	Release of information to outside agencies (many exceptions are noted in the Regulation)	34 C.F.R. Section 99.30, 31 (a) (2-10) & 34 (a) (1) (i) (ii) 34 C.F.R. Section 300.571 (a) (1) & (b)
Release of information to another school or school system in which the student seeks to enroll (two exceptions are noted in the Regulation)		34 C.F.R. Section 99.31 (a) (2) & 34 (a) (i) (ii)
Maintenance of records is no longer necessary to provide an education		34 C.F.R. Section 300.573 (a)
Refusal to amend records at parental request		34 C.F.R. Section 99.21 (c) & 300.567 (c)
Request for an impartial hearing to override parent's decision		34 C.F.R. Section 300.504 (a) (1) & 506 (c) (2)

recognizes the importance of parental support and seeks to obtain this by assuring that there is parent contact prior to seeing the student. The . . ."

APA Principles:
Principle 6. states in part: Psychologists fully inform consumers as to the purpose and nature of an evaluative, treatment, educational or training procedure, . . ."

The above sections of the NASP and APA standards of professional conduct are applicable to all children and their parents not just the handicapped or those suspected of being handicapped. There is no conflict between professional standards and the legal requirements. The principal difference is the implicit and explicit statement in the professional standards that it is the school psychologist who is providing the notice and communicating with the student and parent. Although there is nothing in the regulations requiring that the student be provided with information, the NASP and APA standards do.

Suggested Practices for Notice Activities
Prior notice and parent involvement is viewed as an ongoing process which is the responsibility of all school personnel. If prior notice and parent involvement are everyone's responsibility and the school staff operates with an attitude of openness and desire to keep parents informed, there is very little likelihood that the parents will become distrustful of school officials and become adversaries. The best procedural safeguards are those which strengthen the parent-school partnership leading to collaborative efforts to benefit the child.
Practices are established in the school district so that parents are never surprised that their child is being considered for a referral to the school psychologist.

This is accomplished by putting procedural safeguards in place which require classroom and building staff to communicate regularly with parents about their children's progress in school. This means more than the usual six or nine week grade reports. It requires that opportunities be created for communication between the child's teacher and the child's parent. The better the communication is with the parent before the school personnel perceive a problem with the child's progress in school, the more likely the parents are to be receptive to the suggestion that there is a problem. Some excellent suggestions for teachers in conducting parent-teacher conferences are offered by Stephens and Wolf (1980).

While school psychologists are not directly responsible for the operation of any school program, it is incumbent upon professionals to use their influence in the system to establish practices which will enhance the education of all. In most school districts, communication prior to referral is limited to one conference and is usually accomplished by the teacher and/or building principal at the time consent for the evaluation is sought (Kabler, Carlton & Sherwood, 1981). This approach complies with the mandate of 94-142 Regulations; however, it falls considerably short of what could be considered a "best practice." This traditional approach of relying on the principal or teacher to recognize a problem, attempt to solve it, discuss it with the child's parents and refer to the school psychologist for a psycho-educational evaluation must be abandoned. Approaches where the school psychologist is involved early as a consultant to the teacher and child's parent regarding their concerns about the child represents preferred practices in implementing procedural safeguards. It is also consistent with research findings showing that an effective way of addressing some children's problems is to treat them in their regular classroom before referral for an evaluation (Ysseldyke, Thurlow, Graden, Wesson, Deno, & Algozzine, 1982).

Using a consultative approach is not new to school psychologists. This role is viewed as a part of procedural safeguards established to keep parents fully informed about the district's plans to initiate any changes in educational placement or to propose an evaluation.

At the onset of involvement, the school psychologist explains his or her role to the parent as a consultant to help the teacher and/or the parent solve the child's problem. Maximally, this entails an explanation of: (a) any data collection including interviews with the teacher or the parent, and review of records; (b) methods of intervention that are likely to be developed; (c) pros and cons of using the intervention methods; and (d) the intention to keep them informed of any changes recommended for their child and obtain parental approval before implementation. Minimally, school psychologists meet with parents and discuss their consultant role and seek the parents' approval.

If consultation does not result in a solution to the child's problem and a comprehensive evaluation is needed, the school psychologist meets with the parents to explain the evaluation procedure and their rights under PL 94-142. Again this is a departure from the approach which entails mailing the parents a notice or having the teacher or principal notify the parents of their rights. This approach is recommended because it ensures that the evaluation procedures are explained fully and specifically. Because the school psychologist has been working on the child's case with the teacher and parent, the psychologist is better able to select appropriate instruments. These tests are then discussed with the child's parent to ensure that they are fully informed about the evaluation.

Information about the evaluation which is mandated requires only a minimal characterization of each procedure or test (Bersoff, 1982). However, ethical standards and best practice require a fuller explanation. It is suggested that when the evaluation procedures are discussed with the parents that the following be included: (a) reason for the referral including a description of any reports, tests or records used to make the decision to refer; (b) general description of the areas of functioning to be assessed and methods to be used; (c) specific instruments to be used, brief description of each with examples of the type of content and discussion of the strengths and weaknesses of each; (d) description of the potential outcomes of the evaluation and use of the information; and (e) explanation regarding what the psychologist report will include and with whom the results of the evaluation will be shared.

An additional suggested practice is having the parent and child explain what they perceive as the purpose of the evaluation and its potential outcomes. Bersoff (1982) refers to this process as mutual disclosure. It is a necessary component of prior notice activities which builds trusting and honest relationships (Pryzwansky & Bersoff, 1978).

In addition to presenting the above information verbally, there must also be provisions for it to be given to the parent in writing. Additional specifics are required by the PL 94-142 Regulations in Section 300.505. The reader is referred to *Due Process in Special Education* (Shrybman, 1982), for a detailed discussion of the specific requirements.

Suggested Practices for Obtaining Consent

Parental consent is required by the PL 94-142 Regulations in two instances: the pre-placement evaluation and the initial placement in special education. It is recommended, however, that consent be obtained orally for each proposed action which effects the evaluation and/ or educational placement of the child.

Broadening the situation for which consent is obtained furthers the involvement of parents and is consistent with the view that "parents are at least equally capable as the school staff in deciding what is best for their children" (Bersoff, p. 309, 1973). It also strengthens cooperation between parent and school and decreases the likelihood of any major conflicts which could result in a request for an impartial hearing.

School psychologists should be directly involved in obtaining oral and written consent when the proposed action involves an evaluation or treatment procedure which they will be implementing. When obtaining consent, the school psychologist must be especially careful to be sure that it is voluntary. (For a discussion of the legal requirements and conditions of consent, refer to Bersoff, 1982.) Consent cannot be contingent upon any conditions explicit or implied. Care must be taken to ensure that parent consent is not due to the recommendation of the professional. Rather, the potential benefits to the child should be the reason for the decision.

One method used to help guarantee voluntary written consent is to review all the necessary prior notice and the nature of the consent with the parent. Provide a consent form and a self-addressed, stamped envelope and instruct the parents to make their decision at home and return the form to the school.

Another approach is to provide the parents with all of the information at the time of the conference but not ask for consent. Inform them that a consent form will be mailed for completion and return.

A third method construed as a best practice is to obtain consent at the time of the conference but have it go into effect at some future date. This gives the parents an opportunity to change their minds during which time the district has no authority to proceed.

All of these approaches address obtaining written parent consent. In the case of oral consent, the school psychologist uses a procedure for a "cooling off period." No action would be taken until consent is verified at a later date.

By obtaining verbal or written consent for actions which are not covered in PL 94-142 requirements and by using procedures which help to ensure consent is voluntary, school psychologists communicate that parental involvement as important. These approaches help build a trusting, open relationship which serves to the benefit of children.

Confidentiality of Records

In the late 1960s and early 70s school records including school psychologists' reports were not accessible to parents or students. School records were shared with other agencies on a regular basis, however, without notifying parents or students of majority age. School psychologists routinely refused to share psychological reports with parents on the grounds that they contained information which needed interpretation. These practices, among others, prompted the Associate Director of the New York Civil Liberties Union to write: "There are only two public institutions in the United States which steadfastly deny that the Bill of Rights applies to them. One is the military and the other is the public schools." (Glasser, 1969, p. 190).

FERPA and its regulations were enacted and promulgated for the express purpose of ensuring that the rights of children, adult students, and their parents are protected. It is unfortunate that federal legislation was the principal impetus to bring about this change, particularly in relation to the practice of school psychology. However, it is almost certain that parent access to psychological reports would still be denied on a widespread basis without the federal mandates. This seems likely because of the position taken by professionals during the litigious years. It was thought that parent and student access would render school psychological reports inconsequential formalities of no help to anyone (Trachtman, 1972).

School Psychologists' Written Reports

Vestiges of the past still haunt the profession. This is evidenced in such practices as having the school psychologists' reports maintained in a locked file in the principal's inner office or worse, only filed in a central location with access controlled by the school psychologist. This occurs while all other educational records are in cumulative files in the outer offices of a school building. Another practice is that of stamping *only* the school psychologist's report as *CONFIDENTIAL.*

These practices suggest that the school psychologists' report is more confidential than other educational records. Under the law a student's Individual Educational Plan (IEP), multidisciplinary team report, group test scores, school psychologist's report and all other records are treated equally. It is the author's view that the school psychologist's report should be maintained in the same controlled file as the other records. It should not be stamped *confidential* unless other records are in accordance with a policy for determining which records are so designated. By treating the school psychologist's report no differently than other educational records, there will be further movement away from psychological secrecy and the adversarial relationship which this fosters between psychologists and our student and parent consumers.

To encourage full disclosure, the school psychologist should adopt the practice of providing a copy of his/her written report to the parents. Such an approach helps ensure that the school psychologist only reports factual information which is pertinent to the referring problem, that the data supports inferences and conclusions, that the recommendations are supported by the data, and that children's and their families' privacy is not unduly invaded.

A "best practice" which goes beyond providing a copy of the report would entail a conference with the parents to discuss the written report (Bersoff, 1973; 1978). Using this approach the school psychologist meets with the child and parents, critiques the report and provides the parents and child the opportunity to present a dissenting view in writing. Bersoff (1978) also states that the psychologist then obtains permission to disseminate the report to school personnel. This last step is impractical in most school systems since one of the purposes of the evaluation was sharing information with school personnel. It is feasible, however, for such an approach to work. It should not be dismissed as unthinkable. While obtaining such consent before the evaluation is not required by federal regulations, standards of professional conduct do (APA, 1981). Although NASP (1976) ethical standards do not require it, the requirement for obtaining parental support would be clearly met if consent were obtained.

Test Protocols

Unlike the school psychologist's report, test protocols are maintained in a separate file from the other educational records. The purpose of this is not to prevent access to the test protocols by the child's parents; but to protect the security of tests.

Although FERPA contains a provision which excludes records from parental access when maintained in the sole possession of the preparer, it is unlikely that protocols meet the criteria for classification as a "sole possession" record. To qualify for exemption under this provision the record must be: (a) a private note created solely by the individual possessing it; (b) a personal memory aid; or (c) maintained in sole possession of the preparer and not revealed to any other person (including the student) except for the possessor's temporary substitute (U.S. Dept. of HEW, 1976). Bock (1982) has noted that in relation to these requirements, test protocols fail on all three counts. First, they are created by the student and the psychologist. Second, protocols are not used as memory aids; rather they represent a record of the child's responses. Third, the information is almost always shared with someone else, either the parent, or the student or other educational personnel. Other persuasive arguments have also been put forth which clearly indicate that test protocols are accessible to parents (Bersoff, 1982).

It is consistent with Principle 8 of the APA Ethical Principles of Psychologists, and Principles III and V of the NASP Principles for Professional Ethics (APA, 1981; NASP, 1976), for school psychologists to adopt practices which provide parents access to test protocols. Of course best practices in this area will ensure that the security of tests is not compromised.

While school psychologists are encouraged to establish practices whereby parents are given access to test protocols, implementing procedures where protocols are routinely reviewed in detail with parents is not considered a best practice. However it is recommended that the school psychologist meet with the parents of all children evaluated to share information.

Such a post evaluation conference is helpful in demonstrating to the parent that the school psychologist remains open to input and wants to share the findings in a full and complete manner. This approach also prevents parental concern over the psychologist's findings. If the parents feel that the psychologist has nothing to hide, they will have little reason to request access to protocols.

By discussing results with the parent, the psychologist learns where the parents disagree with findings. Bersoff (1973; 1978) advocates holding such a conference with the parent and student immediately after an evaluation for the purpose of checking the validity of the examiner's impressions and interpretations made by the psychologist.

Whether it occurs with the child and parent or parent only and whether it occurs immediately after testing or sometime later, best practices dictate that it does occur. In addition to the benefits previously cited, this approach also helps ensure that the evaluation and subsequent interpretation is done in an unbiased manner.

In some districts school psychologists do not meet with parents following the evaluation. Such practices, while legal, are more likely to raise the anxiety of parents, thereby creating an adversarial relationship. School psychologists should not encourage practices which remove them from the opportunity to have a personal conference with the child's parents following an evaluation in which they have been a major evaluator.

Even though school districts implement practices which build trusting relationships, there are still circumstances which arise that prompt parents to request access to their children's test protocols. When responding to such a request, care must be taken not to project an image of having something to hide.

Most often when parents ask for copies of test protocols they are really communicating some other message. Parents are often interested in knowing how the scores on their child were derived. If they are in disagreement with the school psychologist's findings they may be saying; "I don't trust you. Show me how you did it."

Regardless of the real message, the first response is to set up a conference to review the records, including test protocols. At the conference the psychologist may want to provide parents with a copy of the front page of the test protocol. However, parents should not be given a copy of the inside pages of the protocol nor should they be permitted to copy any of the items or use a tape recorder. This procedure of copying the first page only is consistent with the policy of at least one major test publisher, The Psychological Corporation. (Kray, 1983).

During the conference the test protocol is reviewed by discussing each subtest, what it purports to measure and its relationship to the child's score on the test. The primary purpose of this conference is to be helpful to the parents in understanding their child's performance. If the parents indicate that they are certain that the recorded responses are in error because they have observed the child give correct responses at home, the school psychologist should accept the information, note it and indicate that in the testing situation the recorded response reflects the response which was given.

Most of these conferences result in both parties satisfaction. However, in those instances where dissatisfaction is expressed with the test results, it is advisable to suggest that an independent psychological evaluation be obtained. Since the school district must provide for an independent evaluation at no cost to the parents, offering such an evaluation at this time is appropriate. This further demonstrates that the best interest of the child is primary. The school psychologist indicates that information from the independent evaluation will be considered before any decision regarding the child's educational services are made.

Due Process Hearings

When procedural safeguards have been implemented which reflect the best practices and philosophy discussed in the preceding sections, the likelihood of an impartial due process hearing is minimal. However, if a hearing were requested and the practices discussed earlier have been implemented, the tone of the hearing and the related contacts between parties will be much more matter of fact. Because the hearing will have been requested by one of the parties on the basis of a difference in the interpretation of facts and not because one party distrusted the other nor because of repeated negative, unpleasant and unresponsive contacts (Budoff, 1978).

When an impartial hearing is requested, school psychologists should encourage all parties to seek a resolution of their differences acceptable to all involved because nobody really wins at a hearing. When the decision favors the district, the parents are expected to comply. When the decision favors the parents, district personnel are expected to comply. District personnel usually want cooperation, not resented compliance. Parents want an ally not an enemy (Michaelis, 1980). School psychologists should offer their services as a facilitator to assist the school personnel and parents to explore their differences and search for a solution. If the parties are unwilling to participate in a conference to resolve their conflict with one particular school psychologist serving as a facilitator, another district psychologist may be appropriate.

Although there are many other professionals who can serve effectively as a facilitator, it seems that a school psychologist is the most likely professional to have training in interpersonal communication and conflict resolution. In some states due process regulations set forth provisions which encourage, but do not require, that efforts be made to resolve the differences without a hearing (Ohio Department of Education, 1981). These provisions encourage resolution with the least formality possible. Such an approach is consistent with Budoff's (1978) view that parents and school officials should avoid an adversarial relationship, if at all possible.

When resolution of differences is not possible even with the help of an outside impartial mediator and a due process hearing proceeds, school psychologists may be active participants as witnesses in the proceedings. This is very likely to occur when the issue involves the diagnosis of a handicapping condition or the initial placement of a child into special education. Since most school psychologists are employed by school districts, most are witnesses for the school district. Once the conflict has progressed to the stage where a hearing has been requested, the school psychologist should consult with the district administration before making any direct contacts with the parents. Efforts, of course, can continue to be made to find a resolution, but this should only be done with the district administration having knowledge of and participating in such efforts. Otherwise, such efforts will be unsuccessful.

Due process hearings which occur under PL 94-142 have become very much like courtroom trials (Shrybman, 1982). The parents and school district are usually represented by attorneys and the hearing officer is often an attorney. Evidence is presented by both sides; witnesses present testimony and are cross-examined. The hearing officer listens to the testimony, examines all of the documentation presented, and writes a decision.

Participation in a due process hearing is an unlikely occurrence for most school psychologists. However, all school psychologists should carry out their daily activities as though they expected to be called as a witness on every case. In this manner school psychologists monitor their own assessment practices, oral and written communications, counseling activities and consultation services much more effectively and are less likely to violate PL 94-142.

When involved in a due process hearing the school psychologist should adhere to the following guidelines which have been adapted from Shrybman (1982 pp. 391-402).

• Polish your skills; review current textbooks and other professional literature relevant to the handicapping condition and any other areas in which you are giving testimony; brush up on the technical information of the test manuals for the instruments used with the student; confer with other school psychologists.

• Prepare notes and review them with your legal counsel and supervisor; point out any problems you see with the case.

• Don't memorize a script; be spontaneous on the witness stand.

• Answer the questions directly and succinctly; avoid the use of jargon; don't volunteer information which is not requested.

• Project an image of sincerity and concern; avoid humor.

• Be honest; don't try to match your testimony to that of another witness; try to be an impartial witness who is reporting the facts.

• Listen carefully to the question; if a question is unclear don't answer it; ask to have the question repeated or rephrased.

The guidelines stated above address only a few major areas with which the school psychologist should be concerned in preparing for a due process hearing. The reader is referred to Shrybman's book *Due Process in Special Education* (1982) for additional specifics.

SUMMARY

Procedural safeguards mandated by PL 94-142 and FERPA to protect the rights of students and their parents have been identified and reviewed. Discussion was focused on safeguards which addressed prior notice and consent, confidentiality of records and due process hearings.

Throughout the chapter an emphasis has been placed on the discussion of practices for implementing the requirements which encourage cooperation between school personnel and parents. Communication between school personnel and parents in the early contacts regarding the child's difficulties in school are seen as vitally important in establishing a strong and effective working relationship.

The school psychologist has a major role in the implementation of procedural safeguards in the areas of providing prior notice and obtaining consent for evaluation services. Such a role is certainly consistent with the APA and NASP Codes of ethical conduct.

Requirements which protect the confidentiality of information call for the implementation of practices which ensure parental access to all educational records and for obtaining parent consent before release of such records. School psychologists are encouraged to share any and all information with parents. Practices such as providing copies of the school psychologist's report to the parents help ensure that information is not withheld. Access to test protocols is provided under controlled conditions which ensure that parents are fully informed about the test instrument and their child's performance while protecting the security of the test.

The principal role for the school psychologist in relation to the due process hearing requirements is to help ensure that there is never any reason for a hearing to actually take place. If a hearing is requested and efforts to reconcile the conflict fail, the school psychologist must prepare to be an effective impartial witness who is committed to providing factual information and expert opinion.

Implementation of the best practices discussed here strengthen the relationship and cooperation among parents, school administrators and school psychologists. Special education procedural safeguards truly are a maze (Anderson, Chitwood, & Hayden, 1983) which must be negotiated; school psychologists should assume a principal role in helping others particularly parents to negotiate it effectively to best serve all children.

REFERENCES

American Psychological Association. (1982). *Ethical Principles of Psychologists.* In C. R. Reynolds & T. B. Gutkin (Eds.), *The handbook of school psychology.* New York: Wiley & Sons.

Anderson, W., Chitwood, S. & Hayden, D. (1983). *Negotiating the Special Education Maze.* Englewood Cliffs, New Jersey: Prentice-Hall, Inc.

Bersoff, D. (1982). The legal regulation of school psychology. In C. R. Reynolds, and T. B. Gutkin (Eds.), *The Handbook of School Psychology,* New York: John Wiley and Sons.

Bersoff, D. N. (1978). Procedural safeguards. In *Developing criteria for the evaluation of due process procedural safeguards provisions.* Wash., DC: U.S. Dept. of HEW.

Bersoff, D. (1975). Professional ethics and legal responsibilities: On the horns of a dilemma. *Journal of School Psychology, 13,* 359-376.

Bersoff, D. (1973). "The Ethical Practice of School Psychology, A Rebutal and Suggested Model." *Professional Psychology, 4,* 305-312.

Bock, F. (1982). Ethical concerns and issues in school psychology. *The Ohio School Psychologist, 27,* 14-15.

Budoff, M. (1978). Implementing due process safeguards from the user's viewpoint. In *Developing criteria for the evaluation of due process procedural safeguards provisions.* Washington, DC: U.S. Dept. of HEW.

Glasser, I. (1969). Schools for scandal — the Bill of Rights and public education. *Phi Delta Kappan, 41,* 190-194.

Kray, K. (September 21, 1983). Personal communication.

McDermott, P. A. (1972). Law, Liability, and the School Psychologist: Systems of Law, Privileged Communications, and Access to Records. *Journal of School Psychology, 10,* 299-305.

Michaelis, T. (1980). *Home and School Partnerships in Exceptional Education,* Rockville, Maryland: Aspen Systems Corp.

National Association of School Psychologists. (1982). Principles for Professional Ethics. In C. R. Reynolds & T. B. Gutkin (Eds.), *The handbook of school psychology.* New York: Wiley & Sons.

Ohio Department of Education. (1981). *Rules for the education of handicapped children.* Columbus, Ohio: Author.

Pryzwansky, W. and Bersoff, D. (1978). "Parental Concern for Psychological Evaluations, Legal, Ethical, and Practical Considerations." *Journal of School Psychology, 16,* 274-281.

Shrybman, James. (1982). *Due Process in Special Education.* Rockville, Aspen Publications.

Stephens, T. M., and Wolf, J. (1980). Effective Skills in Parent-Teacher Conferencing. Columbus, OH: NCEMMH, The Ohio State University.

Trachtman, G. M. (1972). Pupils, parents, privacy, and the school psychologist. *American Psychologist, 27,* 37-45.

U.S. Department of Health, Education and Welfare (HEW). (1976). Privacy rights of parents and students. *Federal Register, 41,* N. 118.

U.S. Department of Health, Education & Welfare (HEW). (1977). Education of handicapped children. *Federal Register, 42,* 42474-42518.

Weintraub, F. J., Abeson, A., Ballard, J., LaVor, M. L. (Eds.). (1976). *Public policy and education of exceptional children.* Reston, VA: The Council for Exceptional Children.

Ysseldyke, J., Thurlow, M., Graden, J., Wesson, C., Deno, S. & Algozzine, B. (1982). *Generalizations from five years of research on assessment and decision-making.* Minneapolis, Minnesota: Institute for Research on Learning Disabilities, University of Minnesota. (Research Report No. 100).

ANNOTATED BIBLIOGRAPHY

Anderson, W., Chitwood, S. & Hayden, D. (1982). *Negotiating the Special Education Maze.* Englewood Cliffs, New Jersey: Prentice-Hall, Inc.
This book is written principally for parents. It provides excellent practical suggestions to parents for increasing involvement in the educational decision-making process. School psychologists will find these suggestions of great value in helping implement best practices in procedural safeguards.

Bersoff, D. N. (1982). The legal regulation of school psychology. In C. R. Reynolds & T. B. Gutkin (Eds.), *The Handbook of School Psychology.* New York: John Wiley & Sons.
Bersoff's chapter provides review of the historical background and current legal regulation of school psychology. His discussion covers constitutional principles as the basis for the legal intervention in school psychology and the impact of the courts and law on three major roles: (1) testing, (2) intervention and therapy and (3) research.

Michaelis, T. (1980). *Home and School Partnerships in Exceptional Education.* Rockville, Maryland: Aspen Systems Corp.
Dr. Michaelis presents major communication and organizational pitfalls which will confront school personnel in their efforts to implement the requirements of PL 94-142. The target audience for the book is school personnel. School psychologists will find the examples of procedures and forms helpful in increasing parent-school collaboration.

Shrybman, James A. (1982). *Due Process in Special Education.* Rockville, Maryland: Aspen Systems.
PL 94-142 and PL 93-112 Section 504 requirements are thoroughly covered in this book. It is well organized into seven parts with 29 chapters. The regulations are presented with an interpretation and suggestions for implementation. This reference provides broad coverage of special education laws.

BEST PRACTICES IN DEALING WITH DISCIPLINE REFERRALS

Howard M. Knoff
State University of New York at Albany

OVERVIEW

While school psychologists spend much of their time with special education procedures and responsibilities, their attention to *non*-special education discipline referrals has become increasingly important. Discipline has long been recognized as a major problem in American schools (Gallup, 1983). Further, it received additional publicity in the report of the National Commission on Excellence in Education and from national political and educational leaders. The successful resolution of school discipline problems is a complex task involving many more professionals than the school psychologist. These problems require analyses of the school organization and the specific dynamics of the problem itself. Individuals potentially involved with the case and its resolution are identified. Ideally, a referral problem encourages the school district to move toward more preventative school and community programming. While this is beyond the scope of the typical school psychologist and this chapter, the school psychologist is a significant participant at the direct service level and provides feedback which facilitates organizational and preventative change.

The present discussion is geared to the practicing school psychologist who receives discipline referrals requiring direct service and programming. The school psychologist can use this chapter to: (a) distinguish between students with different types of acting-out patterns; (b) identify the skills and knowledge they need to address discipline referrals comprehensively; (c) integrate consultation processes into the referral and problem-solving process; and (d) review a problem-solving process involving problem identification, problem analysis, intervention, and evaluation.

Acting-Out Students and Discipline Referrals

A discipline referral generally includes some type of acting-out behavior which disrupts the classroom's educational process. Acting-out behavior takes different styles, forms, and intensities. However, not all acting-out behaviors are considered within the discipline domain.

Quay and Peterson (1979) recently revised and improved the Revised Behavior Problem Checklist, a factor analytically-derived behavior rating scale which analyzes children's and adolescents' deviant behavior. The Revised Behavior Problem Checklist (RBPC) is used to distinguish among different clusters of behaviors so that discipline problems are more clearly defined. The RBPC consists of four major scales: Conduct Disorder, Socialized Aggression, Attention Problems-Immaturity, Anxiety-Withdrawal and two minor scales: Psychotic Behavior, Motor Excess. Based on the items which comprise these scales (Quay, 1983), they are conceptually grouped into three types of "acting-out" or atypical behavior patterns:

1. Discipline Problems: Conduct Disorders and Socialized Aggression Scales;

2. Emotional Disturbances: Psychotic Behavior and Anxiety-Withdrawal Scales; and

3. Maturational Delays: Attention Problems-Immaturity and Motor Excess Scales, and the Anxiety-Withdrawal Scale. (The latter is included because it overlaps considerably with the Attention Problems-

Immaturity Scale.)

Discipline problem students are characterized as exhibiting conduct disorders (disruptive, annoying, impertinent behaviors; frequently engaging in fighting, external blaming, and denial behaviors) and socialized aggression (always in trouble; associates with a "rougher," "delinquent" crowd; stays out late at night; has poor control or supervision from parents). Discipline problem students are *not* emotionally disturbed, maturationally delayed, or organically involved. Nevertheless, these other student problems require intervention and psychological attention. Discipline problem students present behaviors which range from mildly to significantly disruptive. Regardless of the level of disruptiveness, these behaviors are goal-oriented, adaptive to the student's self-perceived needs, predictable, and alterable.

To summarize, the RBPC is used to define discipline problems and to contrast them with other types of atypical behavior patterns. The RBPC and other behavior rating scales analyze and characterize a referred student's behavior pattern. Indeed, the correct classification of a referral as a discipline, emotional disturbance, or maturation delay problem dictates the direction of the school psychologist's entire problem-solving and consultation process.

BASIC CONSIDERATIONS

There are no identified sets of skills, knowledge, or training experiences which perfectly predict one's success in resolving discipline referrals. Success is often a relative experience which is influenced by (a) those individuals directly involved with a discipline referral (the referred student, referral source, school psychologist); (b) those groups who participate in the intervention program (the child study or intervention team, parents and nuclear family, peers); and (c) those organizational fac-

tors and characteristics which guide and structure the interventions (school policy, resources, and flexibility; out-of-school mental health and support agencies). While school psychologists function within these interdependent factors, they work most effectively with sound backgrounds in (a) personality theory; (b) consultation theory; and (c) multidisciplinary/group processing. A great deal of professional and interpersonal persistence is also important.

Most school psychologists take at least one comprehensive personality theory course in their graduate training. Unfortunately, many school psychologists (over-) emphasize one psychological orientation or perspective such that they analyze their discipline referrals exclusively within that perspective. This practice results in the rejection of explanations and interventions which might better address a particular discipline situation or behavior. Wolfgang and Glickman (1980) categorized psychological orientations and personality theorists relevant to discipline problems into a continuum with three anchoring points:

1. *Intrapsychic orientations* emphasize a referred student's potential to recognize and reflect upon his or her negative behavior and to "grow" toward change and appropriate behavior when supported by a warm consistent environment (Theorists: Carl Rogers, Thomas Gordon [TET], Eric Berne and Thomas Harris [TA], Louis Raths and Sidney Simon [Values Clarification]).

2. *Interactionalist orientations* emphasize the effects of both individual personality and environmental factors on negative behavior, suggest that disciplined students need structure, direction, and support toward behavioral change and that these students must take responsibility for that change (Theorists: Alfred Adler and Rudolf Dreikurs [Social Discipline], Fritz Redl [Dynamic/Therapeutic

Milieu Approach], William Glasser [Reality Therapy]).

3. *Extrapsychic orientations* emphasize the need for interventions which structure a student's behavioral change by altering social learning conditions, reinforcement schedules and contingencies, and cognitive strategies and determinants (Theorists: Albert Bandura [Social Learning], Arnold Goldstein [Structured Learning Therapy], B. F. Skinner, Garth Blackham, and Adolph Silberman [Reinforcement Models], Donald Meichenbaum [Cognitive Behavior Modification], James Dobson [the Punishment Model]).

School psychologists must consider all three orientations and their respective theorists with all discipline referrals. They understand the orientations' theoretical backgrounds, their practical implications, and their abilities to suggest effective, realistic interventions. In this way, discipline problems are addressed more comprehensively and with greater breadth and depth.

Consultation is a collaborative process which guides the interpersonal and helping relationship between the school psychologist and a referral source including teachers or parents. Often, the development of this relationship is the most critical event which influences the successful or unsuccessful resolution of a discipline referral. Just as school psychologists consider the potential of each psychological orientation with a discipline referral, they also maintain their openness toward using any of the seven primary consultation models. These models are the Process, Organizational Development, Behavioral, Mental Health, Advocacy, Psychoeducational, and Strategic consultation models. Depending on the discipline problem and its related issues, the school psychologist uses one or any combination of consultation models for maximum effectiveness (see Knoff, 1984). Examples of when to use the individual models follow:

Process Consultation is used when a child study team disagrees on the best intervention plan and this disagreement is related to a lack of leadership, inappropriate decision-making processes, and the poor relationships among team members. Process consultation addresses these individual, task, and maintenance characteristics by building the team's cohesiveness and task clarity. This ultimately facilitates a more effective consideration of the task at hand, the discipline referral.

Behavioral Consultation is used when a referred student's behavior is discreetly defined and analyzed, when environmental conditions are causally affecting or supporting the behavior, and when behavioral techniques or therapies are clearly the intervention of choice.

Mental Health Consultation is used when a teacher, aside from mis-managing the referred student's behavior, is unable to relate interpersonally with the student due to lack of knowledge, experience, confidence, or objectivity. The consultant here works with the teacher to resolve these issues so that the intervention process is maximized.

Advocacy Consultation is used when a teacher or child study team misrepresents a discipline problem as emotional disturbance and improperly recommends an inappropriate special education placement. The consultant here attempts to educate the team members in psychology and special education law and ultimately writes a dissenting opinion while advocating with the parents to appeal any team decisions.

Strategic Consultations are used when a student's misbehavior is a manifestation of a home problem including a parental separation or divorce that is not addressed fully by a school's educational and mental health staffs. The school psychologist here strongly encourages private counseling and then becomes a liaison between the private practitioner and the child study team. In this way, important information is shared between the school and private psychologists so that consistent intervention styles and strategies are used.

To summarize, consultation processes and skills significantly influence the referral and resolution of discipline problems. Good consultation skills encourage the teacher's referral of an appropriate problem; it also enhances the teacher's willingness to keep the student in the regular class while trying a series of interventions. More specific reviews of consultation are found in Conoley (1981) and Curtis and Meyers (this issue).

While multidisciplinary/group processing skills overlap with process consultation skills, there are subtle yet important differences. Multidisciplinary skills are used proactively by school psychologists to understand the characteristics and dynamics which facilitate positive relationships among the diverse professions represented in school systems. Process consultation skills, however, are more often used reactively as the consultant enters a poorly-functioning team or group, assesses its processing difficulties, and begins a group intervention. Given a discipline problem, the school psychologist is often a member of a formal or informal group which minimally includes the referring teacher, school principal, parents, and guidance counselor or social worker. Because the team must work efficiently together to resolve the referred problem, the school psychologist benefits from a sound understanding of multidisciplinary/group processing skills. While beyond the scope of this discussion, the reader is referred to the *School Psychology Review*'s recent theme issue (Maher & Pfeiffer, 1983) on "Multidisciplinary Teams in the Schools."

Finally, school psychologists who deal closely with discipline problems need persistence. There are no guarantees that an intervention program will succeed; ours is not yet a perfect science. At best, school psychologists work within a probability model. That is, their interventions are chosen for their greatest probability for success given an analysis of the discipline referral, consideration of the three psychological orientations and related personality theorists, and identification of the appropriate consultation models. If the intervention is unsuccessful, they re-evaluate these procedures and their problem-solving strategy and try again. Interventions may be unsuccessful, but the school psychologist and child study team really never "fail." There is no blame associated with unsuccessful interventions; there are just too many intervening variables which negatively influence what may be an appropriate intervention.

Again, school psychologists need persistence. Despite a realization that they are doing their best, sometimes discipline referrals involve a number of intervention attempts, frustration, and time. For the teacher and child study team, recognition that intervention is housed within a probability model decreases frustration and burn-out especially when success is not immediate. For the school psychologist, this perspective decreases expectations that school psychologists have "all of the answers all of the time."

BEST PRACTICES

The discussion so far has alluded to the importance of a problem-solving strategy when dealing with discipline referrals. This strategy, which is not specific to discipline problems, involves problem identification, problem analysis, intervention, and evaluation procedures. It represents a logical, organized approach to any problem and has been used for personality assessment (Knoff, 1983), consultation (Bergan, 1977; Meyers, Parsons, & Martin, 1979), and individual therapy (Goldfield &

Davison, 1976). This problem-solving strategy is outlined below in the context of discipline referrals and the best practices currently in the field. The discussion is guided by one major assumption: there is no single "best practice" in any of the problem-solving steps. School psychologists must use their background skills to individualize the problem-solving process with each referral.

Problem Identification

During problem identification, the school psychologist evaluates the discipline referral to determine whether the targeted behaviors are actually present and truly disruptive. Sometimes, consultation with the referring teacher reveals that the target problem is only one facet of a larger problem that includes, yet extends beyond, the referred student. Thus the problem-solving process, geared to direct student-centered intervention, is used only when the discipline problem directly involves the referred student. That is, the student is not a scapegoat for a more pervasive classroom or organizational problem.

Problem identification involves two components: a normative comparison and a developmental comparison. The normative comparison analyzes the referred student's misbehavior in the environment, for example, in the classroom, school building, or district where it occurs. Three behavioral characteristics which can be objectively observed and quantified are used to make the comparisons: the frequency, duration, and intensity of the target behaviors (Sulzer-Azaroff & Meyer, 1977). More specifically, the school psychologist observes the referred student and randomly-selected peers in the same class at the same time to compare the specified target behaviors differentially. If the referred student's target behavior significantly differs from that of his or her peers

on one or more of these characteristics, the student is identified correctly as a discipline problem (Tombari, 1980). However, if the behavior is typical of the peer group, for example, talking without raising one's hand, the class is best identified for a group intervention.

The developmental perspective analyzes misbehavior in the context of expected child and adolescent development and maturation. A specific behavior pattern or style is not considered misbehavior if typical of a child's chronological age. For example, the presence of short attention spans in kindergarten students is developmentally expected; it is not an appropriate discipline referral for the school psychologist. Some behaviors are developmentally appropriate but still disruptive in the classroom. For these referrals, the school psychologist explains why the behavior is not considered misbehavior and then proceeds to recommend developmental or maturational interventions. Rather than focusing on behavior change, these interventions emphasize developmental growth.

The developmental comparison is also used to distinguish between misbehavior and emotionally disturbed behavior. While these distinctions are determined by one's theoretical orientation, the Revised Behavior Problem Checklist again helps to discriminate among these behavior patterns. As with developmentally-delayed behaviors, emotionally disturbed behaviors often require educational settings, staff, and interventions which differ from those addressing misbehavior.

The school psychologist using the developmental comparison applies developmental theory and research to practical classroom interventions. This requires a continuing review of the major developmental textbooks and periodicals and the ability to communicate this knowledge to teachers and administrators. Using the developmental normative comparisons, the school psychologist discriminates discipline referrals from maturational delays and emotional disturbance while educating teachers on differing perspectives and intervention requirements.

Problem Analysis

Problem analysis encompasses (a) a definition or description of an individual's misbehavior, the misbehavior situation, and the misbehavior environment; (b) an understanding of the misbehavior such that variables which cause, support, or maintain it are identified successfully; and (c) an informed direction toward a group of potential interventions with a high probability of success. This process is best accomplished by using as many as four different analytical procedures separately or in concert: the ecological/systems, group process/social psychological, developmental/psychoeducational, and theoretical/psychological analyses.

The *ecological/systems analysis* integrates the ecological perspective (Bronfenbrenner, 1979; Garbarino, 1982) and the family systems perspective (Haley, 1978; Minuchin, 1974) together. The former perspective believes that misbehavior is related to the interactions among the referred student; classroom and school characteristics such as teachers, peers, curricula; family and community characteristics including siblings, religious affiliations, out-of-school peer groups; and societal values and ideologies. The latter perspective believes that an individual's behavior is shaped by and reflects existing family and group norms and behaviors. The integrated analysis assesses misbehavior with the *entire* "ecological system" (student, school, family, community). This "ecosystem", *not* the referred student alone, "owns" the problem and is targeted for intervention. This analysis identifies ecosystem strengths and weaknesses, interactions which explain misbehavior, and

previous successful and unsuccessful interventions. Much of this is accomplished through the systematic analysis of student, school, family, and community interaction patterns and attitudes. These interactions are outlined in one or more "eco-maps" (Newbrough, Walker, & Abril, 1978; Wahler, House, & Stambaugh, 1976).

The *group process/social psychological* analysis investigates the impact of interpersonal dynamics and group development on classroom norms and individual student misbehavior. This analysis includes a diagnostic assessment of students and staff using questionnaires and surveys, diagnostic observations of the classroom or school building, and individual and group interviews or discussions as related to the misbehavior and where it occurs (Flanders, 1970; Schmuck, 1982). Ultimately, the misbehavior is analyzed within the context of classroom (group) development across eight variables: teacher and student expectations and goals; school, class, and interpersonal norms; cohesion-building interactions; leadership roles; decision-making processes; conflict management procedures; communication styles; and attraction between individuals and groups (Schein, 1969; Schmuck & Schmuck, 1982). Often, this analysis also identifies negative teacher and classroom practices or interactions which decrease teacher effectiveness and positive classroom climate.

The *developmental/psychoeducational analysis* investigates the potential impacts of atypical physiological, perceptual, learning and cognitive, socialization, and other developmental/psychoeducational areas on the referred student's age-expected versus actual referred behavior. Here the school psychologist uses norm- and criterion-referenced assessments, standardized and non-standardized tests, and formal and informal tools and approaches. Use of adaptive behavior scales; behavior rating scales; social skills analyses; parent, teacher, and student interviews; and other assessment approaches are also appropriate (see the relevant chapters in this *Manual*).

The *theoretical/psychological analysis* uses the various psychological theories and orientations to understand and contrast typical behavior and misbehavior. These orientations have been discussed above (Wolfgang & Glickman, 1980). The reader is referred to the various theorists for their individual analysis and interpretation procedures.

There is no standardized way to use the four problem analysis perspectives and procedures. The developmental/psychoeducational analysis is the foundation to the assessment. It decides if the referred behavior *is* misbehavior and then determines where the student is functioning in the various developmental areas. The ecological/systems analysis then provides an extensive diagnostic picture of the misbehaving student and the significant interacting systems and issues within the ecosystem. If appropriate, the classroom system is then analyzed using group process/social psychological procedures. Finally, the referred student's behavior is assessed within one of the theoretical/psychological perspectives in preparation for intervention.

Intervention

The school psychologist, pressured by teachers, administrators, or child study teams, too often begins intervention prematurely. An intervention's success is determined primarily by good problem identification and sound problem analysis. In fact, these two procedures create a logical foundation for intervention. There are three broad intervention areas available: empirical/teacher strategies, individual/self-management strategies, and theoretical/psychological strategies. Any intervention plan, given the complexity of the

referred behavior and its analysis, is likely to use a number of strategies from any or all of these areas.

Empirical/teacher strategies have been empirically tested. They prevent and respond to potential or existing misbehavior (Hipple, 1978; Jones & Jones, 1981). These "good-teacher" strategies have broad theoretical support, and suggest ways to encourage positive teacher-student relationships. Examples might include intervening with the precursors of misbehavior before it actually occurs, using physical proximity with a frustrated or misbehaving student, reprimanding with a normal or quiet-pitched voice, and intervening in a non-punitive matter-of-fact manner.

Student/self-management strategies are techniques which initially are taught by a teacher or school psychologist to the child but eventually are managed by the referred student to prevent or interrupt misbehavior. These strategies are more behaviorally-oriented and include cognitive behavioral techniques (Meichenbaum, 1977), relaxation techniques, problem-solving strategies (Goldfried & Davison, 1976), and systematic modeling approaches (Bandura, 1977).

Theoretical/psychological strategies follow directly from the specific theorists in the theoretical/psychological analysis component. Paralleling the three major orientations of Intrapsychic, Interactionalist, and Extrapsychic are Non-Interventionist, Interactionalist, and Interventionist strategies, respectively (Wolfgang & Glickman, 1980). Below, the major intervention strategies from each theorist along the discipline continuum are listed. The reader is encouraged to investigate these theorists and strategies further.

Non-Interventionists

Gordon (TET, 1974) discusses critical and active listening, reflection of feeling and statement, and "no lose" interventions.

Berne and Harris (TA, 1969) discuss understanding the referred student's and teacher's internal states (Parent, Child, or Adult), encouraging communications from Adult to Adult states, teaching the student to analyze and recognize his/her internal state, and modeling Adult reactions to stressful situations.

Raths and Simon (Value Clarification, 1966) discuss active listening, probing and understanding the student's value system, and modeling alternative behaviors to specific situations using classroom exercises.

Interactionalists

Dreikurs (Social Discipline, 1982) discusses intervening in the motivation behind the student's misbehavior (attention-getting, power and control, revenge, helplessness or inadequacy) using the classroom to model democratic functioning, logical and natural consequences, and using encouragement instead of reinforcement.

Redl (Dynamic/Therapeutic Milieu Approach, 1975) discusses techniques supporting self-control, techniques involving task assistance, techniques of reality and value appraisals, techniques using the pleasure-pain principle, and life-space interviewing.

Glasser (Reality Therapy, 1969) discusses confrontation, student contracting, "classroom meetings," and systematic time-out procedures.

Interventionists

Goldstein (Structured Learning Therapy, 1980) discusses integrating roleplaying, modeling, behavioral objectives and reinforcements, and behavioral homework assignments.

Blackham and Silberman, Skinner (Reinforcement Models, 1975) discuss contingency contracting; primary and secondary reinforcers; shaping and chaining behavior; reinforcement schedules; positive, aversive, and punishing reinforcements; and "time-out" (see also Sulzer-Azaroff & Mayer, 1977, for an excellent review).

Dobson (Punishment Model, 1970) discusses reinforcement strategies until physical intervention and isolation are necessary.

Evaluation

Evaluation assesses the problem-solving process in general and the implemented interventions specifically. This usually involves an evaluation of changes in the student's misbehavior as well as the child study team's satisfaction with the consultation and change process. The assessment incorporates both formative and summative evaluation. The former occurs during the interventions to determine intermediate levels of success and areas where the intervention needs adaptation to provide greater success. The latter occurs when the intervention programs are completed or discontinued as a final evaluation of their utility and success. Finally, the evaluation investigates both intended and unintended effects (Payne, 1982).

Evaluation often includes both subjective and objective data and is program- or intervention-oriented. Additional information on the evaluation process is found elsewhere (Conti & Bardon, 1974; Knoff, 1982; Maher, this issue; Stufflebeam, et al., 1971).

SUMMARY

Discipline problems are referred in increasing numbers to school psychologists. Initially, school psychologists must distinguish emotionally-disturbed behavior from behavior due to maturational delays. Misbehavior is distinguished and defined through behavior rating scales, most notably Quay and Peterson's (1979) Revised Behavior Problem Checklist. Here, discipline problems include those characterized as Conduct Disorders and Socialized Aggression.

To competently address discipline referrals, school psychologists need a sound theoretical and applied background in personality theory, consultation theory, and multidisciplinary/group processing. Discipline problems and their resulting interventions are conceptualized within a probability model where interventions are chosen for their high, but not perfect, probability of success.

Discipline problems are best analyzed within a problem-solving process which includes problem identification, problem analysis, intervention, and evaluation. There is no standardized or actuarial approach to discipline referrals. However, a systematic approach considering the perspectives and approaches discussed above increases school psychologists' success and confidence in their expertise.

REFERENCES

Bandura, A. (1977). *Social learning theory.* Englewood Cliffs, New Jersey: Prentice-Hall.

Bergan, J. R. (1977). *Behavioral consultation.* Columbus, Ohio: Charles E. Merrill.

Blackman, G. J., & Silverman, A. (1975). *Modification of child and adolescent behavior,* (2nd edition). Belmont, California: Wadsworth Publishers.

Bronfenbrenner, U. (1979). *The ecology of human development.* Cambridge, Massachusetts: Harvard University Press.

Conoley, J. C. (Ed.) (1981). *Consultation in schools: Theory, research, procedures.* New York: Academic Press.

Conti, A., & Bardon, J. I. (1974). A proposal for evaluating the effectiveness of psychologists in the schools. *Psychology in the Schools, 11,* 32-39.

Dobson, J. (1970). *Dare to discipline.* Wheaton, Illinois: Tyndale House Publishers.

Dreikurs, R. (1982). *Maintaining sanity in the classroom.* New York: Harper and Row.

Flanders, N. A. (1970). *Analyzing teacher behavior.* Reading, Massachusetts: Addison-Wesley.

Gallup, G. H. (1983). The fifteenth annual Gallup poll of the public's attitudes toward the public schools. *Phi Delta Kappan, 65,* 33-47.

Garbarino, J. (1982). *Children and families in the social environment.* New York: Aldine Publishers.

Glasser, W. (1969). *Schools without failure.* New York: Peter H. Wyden Publishers.

Goldfried, M. R., & Davison, G. C. (1976). *Clinical behavior therapy.* New York: Holt, Rinehart, and Winston.

Goldstein, A. P., Sprafkin, R. P., Gershaw, N. J., & Klein, P. (1980). *Skillstreaming the adolescent.* Champaign, Illinois: Research Press.

Gordon, T. (1974). *T.E.T.: Teacher effectiveness training.* New York: Peter H. Wyden Publishers.

Haley, J. (1978). Beginning and experienced family therapists. In A. Ferer, M. Mendelsohn, & A. Napier (Eds.), *The book of family therapy.* Boston: Houghton Mifflin.

Harris, T. A. (1969). *I'm O.K. — You're O.K.: A practical guide to transactional analysis.* New York: Harper and Row.

Hipple, M. L. (1978). Classroom discipline problems? Fifteen humane solutions. *Childhood Education, 54,* 183-187.

Jones, V. E., & Jones, L. S. (1981). *Responsible classroom discipline.* Boston: Allyn and Bacon.

Knoff, H. M. (1984). The practice of multimodal consultation: An integrating approach for consultation service delivery. *Psychology in the Schools, 21,* 83-91.

Knoff, H. M. (1983). Personality assessment in the schools: Issues and procedures for school psychologists. *School Psychology Review, 12,* 391-398.

Knoff, H. M. (1982). The independent psychodiagnostic clinic: Maintaining accountability through program evaluation. *Psychology in the Schools, 19,* 346-353.

Maher, C. A., & Pfeiffer, S. I. (1983). Multidisciplinary teams in the schools: Perspectives, practices, possibilities. *School Psychology Review, 12* (Theme issue).

Meichenbaum, D. H. (1977). *Cognitive-behavior modification: An integrative approach.* New York: Plenum.

Meyers, J., Parsons, R. D., & Martin, R. (1979). *Mental health consultation in schools.* San Francisco: Jossey-Bass.

Minuchin, S. (1974). *Families and family therapy.* Cambridge, Massachusetts: Harvard University Press.

Newbrough, J. R., Walker, L. S., & Abril, S. (March, 1978). *Workshop on ecological assessment.* Paper presented at the meeting of the National Association of School Psychologists, New York City.

Payne, D. A. (1982). Portrait of the school psychologist as program evaluator. In C. R. Reynolds & T. B. Gutkin (Eds.), *The handbook of school psychology.* New York: Wiley and Sons.

Quay, H. C. (1983). A dimensional approach to behavior disorder: The Revised Problem Behavior Checklist. *School Psychology Review, 12,* 244-249.

Quay, H. C., & Peterson, D. R. (1979). *Manual for the Behavior Problem Checklist.* Privately printed.

Raths, L. E., Harmin, M., & Simon, S. B. (1966). *Values and teaching: Working with values in the classroom.* Columbus, Ohio: Merrill Publishing.

Redl, F. (1975). Disruptive behavior in the classroom. *School Review, 83,* 569-594.

Schein, E. H. (1969). *Process consultation: Its role in organization development.* Reading, Massachusetts: Addison-Wesley.

Schmuck, R. A. (1982). Organization development in the schools. In C. R. Reynolds & T. B. Gutkin (Eds.), *The handbook of school psychology.* New York: Wiley.

Schmuck, R. A., & Schmuck, P. A. (1982). *Group processes in the classroom,* (4th ed.). Dubuque, Iowa: William C. Brown.

Stufflebeam, D., Foley, W., Gephart, W., Guba, E., Hammond, R., Merriman, H., & Provus, M. (1971). *Educational evaluation and decision making.* Itasca, Illinois: F. E. Peacock.

Sulzer-Azaroff, B., & Mayer, G. R. (1977). *Applying behavior-analysis procedures with children and youth.* New York: Holt, Rinehart, and Winston.

Tombari, M. L. (1980). *Assessing the emotionally disturbed.* In T. Oakland (Ed.), *Nonbiased assessment modules.* Austin, Texas: The University of Texas Press.

Wahler, R. G., House, A. E., & Stambaugh, E. E. (1976). *Ecological assessment of child problem behavior.* New York: Pergamon Press.

Wolfgang, C. H., & Glickman, C. D. (1980). *Solving discipline problems: Strategies for classroom teachers.* Boston: Allyn and Bacon.

ANNOTATED BIBLIOGRAPHY

Wolfgang, C. H., & Glickman, C. D. (1980). *Solving discipline problems: Strategies for classroom teachers.* Boston: Allyn & Bacon. (176 pgs.)
A practical, clearly written book which provides a conceptual model of discipline and integrates a number of important theorists and their strategies into it. It includes reviews of Gordon (TET), Berne and Harris (TA), Values Clarification, Dreikurs (Social Discipline), Glasser (Reality Therapy), and Behavior Modification. "Mainstreaming" techniques, and how to translate the theories into practical intervention programs are also discussed.

Millman, H. L., Schaefer, C. E., & Cohen, J. J. (1980). *Therapies for school behavior problems.* San Francisco: Jossey-Bass. (530 pgs.)
An excellent volume which reviews the recent literature across a number of common referral problem concerns. Annotated bibliographies are presented which encapsulate the most important studies. Included in the review are classroom management problems, immature behaviors, insecure behaviors, habit disorders, disturbed peer relationships, and disturbed relationships with teachers.

Sulzer-Azaroff, B., & Mayer, G. R. (1977). *Applying behavior-analysis procedures with children and youth.* New York: Holt, Rinehart, and Winston. (525 pgs.)
A comprehensive volume which discusses the major behavior analysis and behavior modification techniques in the field, reviews the literature in each area, and provides practical applications to school settings. The discussion includes observation of target behaviors; stimulus control; methods to reduce, extend, and maintain behavior; and ways to decide what approach to use given specific background characteristics.

Dreikurs, R., Grunwald, B. B., & Pepper, F. C. (1982). *Maintaining sanity in the classroom: Classroom management techniques.* (2nd ed.). New York: Harper & Row. (353 pgs.)
An excellent summary of the theory and techniques of Dreikurs and his social discipline perspective. Dreikurs advocates the democratic classroom and blends a child-oriented view of education with the realities and responsibilities which children need. It discusses ways to work with discipline referrals, logical consequences and their utility, and ways to cope with special academic and behavioral problems.

Quay, H. C., & Peterson, D. R. (1983). *Protocol and Interim Manual for the Revised Behavior Problem Checklist.* Coral Gables, Florida: Box 248074, University of Miami, 33124.
Is one of the best and most researched behavior rating scales available to analyze behavior disorders in the schools. A psychometrically sound instrument, the RBPC consists of 89 behavioral descriptors which are rated 0 - Not a Problem, 1 - A Mild Problem, and 2 - A Severe Problem. Factor analyses of these descriptors have identified four major scales (Conduct Disorder, Socialized Aggression, Attention Problems-Immaturity, Anxiety-Withdrawal) and two minor scales (Psychotic Behavior and Motor Excess).

BEST PRACTICES IN PARENT TRAINING

Jack J. Kramer
University of Nebraska — Lincoln

OVERVIEW

This chapter is designed to provide school psychologists with an overview of best practices in parent training. The emphasis is on the empirical literature, and the presentation is encyclopedic in nature. Individuals desiring a training manual or an exhaustive review of the literature need to look elsewhere. The chapter will be most helpful to those who seek specific information about various practices in parent training and others who use this material as a first resource before proceeding to a more extensive examination of the literature.

Recently there has been a prolifertion of programs and literature in the area of parent training. The literature has been characterized as "a mixture of tradition, opinion, misconception, politics and last, but hopefully not least, valid information" (Sherrets, Authier, & Tramontana, 1980, p. 34). It is obvious that a great deal more is known than was the case only a decade ago. There remains, however, some confusion about effective practice and the conditions which promote positive change in parents and children.

Definitions

Attempts to improve parents' ability to positively impact on children are classified into one of three general areas: parent education, parent therapy, and parent training. This manner of classification is not new (e.g., Abidin & Carter, 1980; Fine, 1980); however, it remains a useful means of categorizing approaches.

Parent education refers to lecture/discussion models designed to disseminate information, heighten awareness, and change attitudes. According to Abidin and Carter (1980) this model was predominant to 1965. It is easy to see why this approach has continued appeal with school psychologists. Faced with a multitude of demands for one's time, a desire to reach many people, and difficulty getting or keeping parents together, school psychologists have often turned to short-term lecture/discussion "workshops." In other instances, school psychologists are asked to make presentations in classes for future parents. The major problem with this approach is the consistent failure to document either behavioral or attitudinal change (Auerbach, 1968; Brim, 1959).

These brief presentations may also result in a variety of other problems. For example, in many instances it is difficult to evaluate the extent to which participants have mastered the principles and techniques which were discussed. An evaluation of this type has seldom been included in the parent education model. Thus we may fail to discover that some parents are inappropriately using techniques such as operant conditioning which have profound effects upon behavior. This does not mean that parent education programs have no place in the school psychologist's arsenal. However, it suggests that practitioners should be aware of the fact that disseminating information does not necessarily lead to behavioral or attitudinal change. They should be careful not to suggest to parents that they go home and implement briefly discussed management strategies.

Knowledge of behavior change principles can be effectively taught on a verbal level in a very short period of time. Flana-

[263]

gan, Adams, and Forehand (1979) demonstrated that following 40 minutes of instruction in the use of "timeout," parents participating in either written or lecture types of instruction scored as high on a written test as did those taught through either a role playing or modeling formats. However, on a test that measured the ability to use timeout in response to videotaped analogue scenes, high to low scoring groups were ordered as follows: role playing, modeling, lecture, written. This suggests, as has a previous analysis (O'dell, 1974), that while the "what" of behavioral technology can be taught through lectures and discussions, the "how" requires more direct intervention.

Parent therapy typically refers to efforts to work with parents with more serious problems such as pervasive, long-term family conflicts. Whereas people often come to parent education with a desire to learn more about parenting, their children, teaching, and learning; parents come to therapy because of problems which interfere with family relationships. Parent therapy is much more likely to be individualized and of unspecified duration (Patterson, Chamberlain, & Reid, 1982). Most school psychologists are not involved in parent therapy, and the reader is referred to other sources (e.g., Farrington & West, 1980) for a more thorough discussion of the research in this area.

Finally, parent training refers to programs designed to equip participants with *skills* which are expected to produce changes in parental attitude and behavior as well as concomitant changes in the behavior and adjustment of children. They range from very general programs aimed at improving the ability "to parent" to very specific, discrete efforts designed with a particular purpose in mind. Examples of the latter type include attempts to teach specific behavior change techniques like timeout or reinforcement, procedures related to certain behavioral problems such as aggression or communication deficits, or skills to be used by particular adult populations such as parents of retarded or abused children.

Though training programs are emphasized in this chapter, references are made to parent education and therapy. It should be noted that attempts to alter behavioral patterns of parents in ways that positively impact on children do not occur in a vacuum. The importance of a functional, ecological orientation to the study of human behavior cannot be over-emphasized (Bernstein, 1982). The value of this approach for school psychologists has been detailed elsewhere (Reynolds, Gutkin, Elliott, & Witt, 1984). The practitioner who remains attentive to the myriad of factors which influence children, parents, and families will undoubtedly have the most to provide to parents in search of assistance.

History

References to parent education in the U.S. can be traced to the early 19th century (Crooke & Glover, 1977). Although the concept of parent training is not new, Western society has assumed that parenting skills are as innately and biologically determined as the ability to become a parent. It has also been assumed that the mother possesses these skills and that whatever deficits she has will surely be remedied through her own childhood experiences or on-the-job training. The problem with these assumptions is the lack of scientific basis for them (Silcock, 1979). Parenting skills are no more inherent than driving a car or playing chess. Nor are they strictly the domain of the mother.

At the turn of the century, when extended families were the rule rather than the exception, a variety of family members trained prospective parents in the art of child rearing. With training taking place in the home, the "supervisors" were available on a full-time basis to provide training, feedback, and reinforcement. Now nuclear families are the norm with many consisting of no more than one or two adults. There are no live-in trainers for today's parents. Planned, systematic prepartion for parenthood in our society has been a non-event. The need to involve parents as full partners in advocacy, programming, teaching, and participation in child management decisions is obvious.

BASIC CONSIDERATIONS

The organization of the material which is included in this section has, to a large extent, been borrowed from Fine (1980). He conceptualized the first three areas listed below as "ethical considerations." Each individual (trainer and consumer) should be informed of these issues before entering into parent training. It is also obvious that it will ultimately be the responsibility of the trainer to see that this information is presented, or at a minimum available, to participants.

Qualifications of the Parent Trainer

There are no generally recognized standards for parent trainers. Groups have been led by ministers, teachers, nurses and lay persons as well as mental health professionals. It appears that with a minimum of supervised experience (3-10 sessions totaling 10-20 hours), paraprofessionals, graduate students, and masters level therapists can be trained to successfully implement a wide variety of parent education and training programs. Some commercially available programs provide explicit steps to follow for those desiring to become certified as a leader. *Parent Effectiveness Training* is one

example (Gordon, 1970) and these approaches should not be faulted for their attempts. One cannot help but wonder, however, if the ultimate criterion should not be outcome data. That is, has the trainer/program been demonstrated to be effective? In rare instances this can be accomplished through research such as that conducted by Rex Forehand and associates at the University of Georgia and Gerald Patterson and associates at the Oregon Social Learning Center. However, this level of validation is beyond most school psychologists.

Trainers should provide participants with information about their educational background, as well as their experience in parent training and in working with children. Practitioners can permit individuals to talk to former participants who present a balanced point of view regarding the benefits and limitations of training. A list of previous participants who agree to be contacted should be available upon request.

Henry (1980) asserts that most school psychologists have the prerequisite skills to be effective parent trainers. He is correct in maintaining, however, that, if feasible, practitioners are wise to serve an apprenticeship before attempting to solo as a parent trainer.

Claims, Promises, Permission and Protection

According to Fine (1980) "most parent education programs hope to achieve at least some of the following goals: (a) offer parents greater self-awareness; (b) help parents to use effective discipline methods; (c) increase parent-child communication; (d) encourage families to have more fun together; and (e) give parents useful information on child development" (p. 17). While these are desirable goals, can parents be promised that participation will lead to any or all of these outcomes? The research evidence, as well as my own experience, suggests that an unequivocal "no" is the only possible answer. Trainers must be very clear about what they can and cannot promise or accomplish.

It is, of course, appropriate and necessary to detail the types of activities, the length/number of sessions, the size of the group, the manner in which members are selected for participation (Abidin & Carter, 1980; Dangel & Polster, 1984) and the goals of training. School psychologists must differentiate among their activities, their goals, their expectations and the claims provided by the publishers of the training manuals and materials that are used. Although most training programs and self-help manuals are published prior to validation studies, some make questionable claims of effectiveness.

Although it may not be necessary in all cases, some practitioners have asked parents to sign a consent form prior to participation in training activities (see Cooper & Edge, 1978, for an example of a form). The form is dated, signed by the parents and the group leader, and explains, in varying degrees of detail, the activities to be completed and the responsibilities and rights of the parties involved. If the training activities are part of a research project, then consent is mandatory and the research guidelines of the American Psychological Association and the National Association of School Psychologists are applicable.

Acceptance/Rejection of Values

Although it is generally acknowledged that children should not be physically or verbally abused, it is much more difficult to make judgments about right and wrong when confronted with the many decisions that parents face everyday. Parents have

been known to balk at using the bedroom for time-out because of concern that the child might develop an aversion to the bedroom or going to sleep at night. If parents cannot be convinced that this is an atypical response, then a trainer should look for a more acceptable alternative. In other instances, some parents may want to work on developing interpersonal communication skills with their children, while others may be driven by the thought of using their new found behavior management skills to teach their children to eat vegetables. While it is conceivable that a trainer might find one of these goals more desirable than the other, it is important to be careful not to use one's status as group leader, as a school psychologist, to impose values on others. Although school psychologists will never be able to completely avoid this problem, it is an important concern to be aware of, for we must be careful not to unfairly influence others to be what we think they should be. Parents have different values, are incapable of being perfect, and have the right to disagree or abandon training.

Consumer Satisfaction

In a recent review of the literature McMahon and Forehand (1983) concluded that the majority of studies that assessed consumer satisfaction fell under the heading of parent training. Most concentrated on consumer satisfaction with treatment outcome (Tavormina, 1975) and/or with the therapist (Baum & Forehand, 1981). There are fewer examples in which the satisfaction of parents with treatment procedures (Kazdin, French, & Sherich, 1981) and teaching format (O'dell et al., 1982) were assessed. The Therapy Attitude Inventory (Eyberg & Johnson, 1974) and the Treatment Evaluation Inventory (Kazdin, 1980) are two of the most widely used tools for measuring satisfaction. Very little attention has been directed towards the relative satisfaction level of children with treatment. In general, however, consumers rated behaviorally oriented training groups higher than other approaches (McMahon & Forehand, 1983).

BEST PRACTICES

The following sections review practices which are most likely to increase the probability of success of parent training efforts.

Training Parents: Programs and Materials

The growth of the parent training industry during the last decade has been immense. The school psychologist faces a difficult task choosing materials to use in the training process. A useful reference is Abidin (1980) who provides short reviews of 29 programs. An examination of three of the most popular approaches is provided below. The most used programs have been classified (Henry, 1980) as predominately behavioral (e.g., *Living with Children*, Patterson & Guillon, 1976), Adlerian (e.g., *Systematic Training for Effective Parenting*, Dinkmeyer & McKay, 1976), or interpersonal communication (e.g., *Parent Effectiveness Training*, Gordon, 1975). While there is more research to support the behavioral approaches, it should not be assumed that because a program espouses a behavioral point of view that it has been researched and validated. The fact is most programs have not been not studied before being marketed (McMahon & Forehand, 1980; Stevens & Pfost, 1982).

Parent training programs are typically thought of as comprehensive programs designed to improve general par-

enting skills. There are, however, a number of programs available which teach very specific skills such as time-out (Nay, 1975), toilet training (Azrin & Foxx, 1974), and shopping with children (Greene, Clark, & Risley, 1977). When used in conjunction with minimal therapist contact, these programs has been demonstrated to be effective (McMahon & Forehand, 1980).

The literature has not confirmed the same likelihood of success for all the broad-based programs referred to earlier (Dinkmeyer & Mckay, 1976; Gordon, 1970; Patterson & Guillon, 1976). Only the Patterson and Guillon program has been found to consistently produce positive changes in parent attitude and behavior *as well as* desirable change in children's behavior (Christenson, Johnson, Phillips & Glasgow, 1978). Widespread use of the STEP and PET programs have occurred in the absence of demonstrated effectiveness (Doherty & Ryder, 1980; Henry, 1980; Rinn & Markle, 1971, Tavormina, 1980). Proponents of these often cite evidence of changes in parent attitude and emotions (e.g., Gordon, 1980) and suggest that behavioral change will follow. There is also a good deal of reliance on testimonials from previous program participants. It is nice to know that some parents feel better about their parenting skills following participation in STEP and PET and are willing to be quoted as supporting the particular benefits of a program. As suggested earlier, however, the proof is in the outcome data. To date, there is little well designed research which indicate that these programs are effective in producing behavioral changes in parents or children.

What does this suggest for the practicing school psychologist? It indicates the "cash validity" (Salvia & Ysseldyke, 1976) is not sufficient reason for choosing a particular training program. Care must be taken to match a trainer's goals with appropriate materials. Programs such as those described in this section may prove to be useful in providing structure for the new parent trainer. Analysis of the literature suggests, however, that a thorough knowledge of learning principles combined with skill in teaching parents how to apply those principles contributes more to effective outcome than the use of any particular packaged program.

Training Special Groups of Parents

Parents of aggressive/conduct disordered/non-compliant child. The child so described has developed an effective behavioral repertoire for coercing reinforcers through some combination of disobedience, fighting, stealing, lying, crying, and temper tantrums. These behaviors exist at a much higher rate than is normal.

Gerald Patterson and associates at the Oregon Social Learning Center have spent years investigating these behavior problems and have developed highly structured programs designed to help parents in the treatment of these problems. Specific descriptions of this program are provided in Horne and Patterson (1980). The literature is replete with examples of similar programs which have proven successful (e.g., Forehand & McMahon, 1984). Common elements of such training programs include: multiple sessions (5-8 minimum); homework assignments; didactic as well as experiential instruction; concentration on discrete, identifiable behavioral problems; and emphasis on teaching parents the skills necessary for building new behaviors as well as eliminating problem behaviors. It is interesting to note that even these programs report a 25-33% failure rate (Horne & Patterson, 1980).

Abusive and neglectful parents. As used here abusive parents are those who mistreat, neglect, emotionally deprive, or sexually molest their children. This group has been described as socially isolated, having low self-esteem, having unrealistic expectations of their children, and relying on punitive child management techniques (Steele, 1975). Clearly work with this group falls under the heading of "parent therapy" as defined earlier. There is an extensive literature indicating that this group, which is much more heterogeneous than the label abusive parent implies, can be helped through a variety of methods including casework, individual therapy, group therapy, marriage and family interventions, direct child intervention, and parent training (Martin, 1980). Recent studies have demonstrated that instruction in child management and self-control skills reduce the risk of abuse in these homes (Denicola & Sandler, 1980; Wolfe & Sandler, 1981).

Parents of handicapped children. The emotional and behavioral demands that handicapped children place upon parents has been extensively documented. The educational and training needs of these parents often begin at birth. In some cases, however, school psychologists are the first to tell parents that their children are experiencing educational handicaps.

Evidence suggests that early involvement with other parents of handicapped children in programs designed to increase knowledge regarding both their child's disability and educational options serve to ameliorate the negative impact that a handicapped child has on the family (Canino & Reeve, 1980). There is research which suggests that behaviorally oriented training workshops are effective in teaching the parents of mentally retarded children (Rose, 1974), hyperactive children (Dubey, O'Leary, & Kaufman, 1983), and behaviorally disordered children (Evans & James, 1982) how to manage behavior more effectively. Similar evidence is found documenting the effectiveness of behavioral programs in teaching language and communication skills to handicapped youngsters.

The programs described above for special populations of parents is far from exhaustive. Training for parents of preschool children, rural children, learning disabled children, children of divorced parents, foster children, and disturbed adolescents have been undertaken with varying degrees of success. The areas that have been described in more detail are used as examples of effective interventions. It is apparent that the school psychologist who thoroughly understands his/her population, who explicitly defines his/her objectives, and who implements experimentally validated training approaches is most likely to achieve success.

Bibliotherapy

As was indicated earlier, there are numerous parent training manuals available for almost every purpose imaginable. Recent reviews of this literature focused on self-help manuals with a behavioral orientation (Bernal & North, 1978; McMahon & Forehand, 1980; O'Farrell & Keuthen, 1983). When taken in conjunction with more general reviews of bibliotherapy approaches (e.g., Stevens & Pfost, 1982), the following conclusions are drawn: (a) most manuals have not been validated prior to publication; (b) self-administered, written instructions seldom lead to behavioral change; (c) self-help manuals are effective when used in conjunction with minimal therapist contact; and (d) there is great variability in the level of readability of parent training manuals.

It is recommended that school psychologists use self-help parent training manuals in the same manner as was earlier suggested for parent education programs. They increase the knowledge base, and teach basic principles but when used in the absence of professional contact, they seldom lead to behavioral change in parents or in children.

Maintenance and Generalization of Training

The available research indicates that a functional relationship exists between the contingencies imposed by parents and child behavior. Parents can learn to implement contingencies in a fashion that promotes learning in their children. O'Dell (1974) has suggested that there are three criteria for demonstrating that parent training is effective in producing and maintaining change in parental behavior: parents learn the necessary skills, changes are implemented, and skills are maintained and generalized to new areas. Although there are contradictory findings (Dubey, O'Leary, & Kaufman, 1983) it appears that simply teaching important child development and child management concepts are not enough to insure that the criteria cited above are met. As in other areas, exposure to the principles of behavior change, modeling, practice, immediate and extensive feedback, and contact with a skilled professional are functionally related to the learning of parenting skills. Less is known, however, about the conditions which promote maintenance and generalization.

Previous analysis has suggested that parent trainers need to be concerned with four types of generalization: temporal, setting, behavioral, and sibling (Forehand & Atkeson, 1977). In the past, many researchers were more concerned with assessing whether parent training worked as opposed to whether the effects generalized. Others ignored or inappropriately assessed generalization (Forehand & Atkeson, 1977). Although few definitive statements can be made, it appears that: if parents learn to appropriately use behavioral change strategies they are likely to generalize the use of the techniques to siblings (Lavigueur, Peterson, Sheese, & Peterson, 1973), involvement in a long-term (5-10 weeks) parenting program may be necessary for obtaining behavioral generalization (Wells, Forehand, & Griest, 1980), teaching knowledge of social learning principles enhances temporal and setting generality (McMahon, Forehand, & Griest, 1981), and use of a self-control package with parents increases the likelihood of temporal generality (Wells, Griest, & Forehand, 1980). A decade ago O'dell (1974) concluded that there was little known about the conditions that could be reliably expected to produce generalization of the effects of parent training. The problem remains.

SUMMARY

It should be apparent that there is an extensive literature and much controversy in the area of parent training. It is an area of great diversity, with variability in theoretical approaches, in practice, and in populations served. An attempt has been made to highlight procedures for dealing with that diversity. More specifically, definitions were included, basic considerations were outlined, best practices were suggested, and resources for more detailed examination were provided.

To conclude, a brief examination of the work of Bernstein (1982) is provided. In this analysis of the factors to be considered by individuals desiring to train behavior change agents, four questions are asked of trainers: "(a) What problems must behavior change agents be able to solve? (b) What skills are most likely to lead to solutions to those problems? (c) What techniques should be used to teach those skills? (d) What procedures are most likely to assure generalization of those skills" (p. 1)?

Bernstein suggests that while we must be concerned with studying and changing the behavior of individuals, we will be best served by approaches which allow us to integrate findings in a way which contribute to our understanding of the many interdependent systems which impact upon human behavior. The challenge remains for school psychologists to use this information in an efficient manner.

REFERENCES

Abidin, R. R. (Ed.) (1980). *Parent education and intervention handbook.* Springfield, IL: Charles C. Thomas.

Abidin, R. R., & Carter, B. D. (1980). Workshops and parent groups. In R. R. Abidin (Ed.), *Parent education and intervention handbook* (pp. 107-129). Springfield, IL: Charles C. Thomas.

Auerbach, A. B. (1968). *Parents learn through discussion.* New York: Wiley.

Azrin, N. H., & Foxx, R. M. (1974). *Toilet training in less than a day.* New York: Simon & Schuster.

Baum, C. G., & Forehand, R. (1981). Long-term follow-up assessment of parent training by use of multiple outcome mesaures. *Behavior Therapy, 12,* 643-652.

Becker, W. C. (1971). *Parents are teachers.* Champaign, IL: Research Press.

Bernel, M., & North, J. (1978). A survey of parent training manuals. *Journal of Applied Behavior Analysis, 11,* 533-544.

Bernstein, G. S. (1983). Training behavior change agents: A conceptual analysis. *Behavior Therapy, 13,* 1-23.

Brim, O. G. (1959). *Education for childrearing.* New York: Free Press.

Christenson, A., Johnson, S. M., Phillips, S., & Glasgow, R. E. (1978). Cost effectiveness in behavioral family therapy. Unpublished manuscript.

Cooper, J. O., & Edge, D. (1978). *Parenting: Strategies and educational methods.* Columbus, OH: Charles E. Merrill.

Croake, J. W., & Glover, K. E. (1977). A history and evaluation of parent education. *The Family Coordinator*, 151-158.

Dangel, R. F., & Polster, R. A. (1984). *Parent training.* New York, NY: Guilford Publications.

Denicola, J., & Sandler, J. (1980). Training abusive parents in child management and self-control skills. *Behavior Therapy, 11*, 263-270.

Dinkmeyer, D., & McKay, G. (1977). *Systematic training for effective parenting.* Circle Pines, MN: American Guidance Service, Inc.

Doherty, W. J., & Ruder, R. G. (1980). Parent effectiveness training: Criticisms and comments. *Journal of Marital and Family Therapy, 11*, 409-419.

Dubey, D. R., O'Leary, S. G., & Kaufman, K. F. (1983). Training parents of hyperactive children in child management: A comparative outcome study. *Journal of Abnormal Child Psychology, 11*, 229-246.

Eyberg, S. M., & Johnson, S. M. (1974). Multiple assessment of behavior modification with families. Effects of contingency contracting and order of treated problems. *Journal of Consulting and Clinical Psychology, 42*, 594-606.

Farrington, D. P., & West, D. J. (1980). The Cambridge study in delinquent development. In S. A. Mednick & A. E. Baert (Eds.), *Prospective longitudinal research: An empirical basis for primary prevention.* Oxford: Oxford University Press.

Fine, M. J. (Ed.) (1980). *Handbook on parent education.* New York: Academic Press.

Fine, M. J. (1980). The parent education movement. In M. J. Fine (Ed.), *Handbook on parent education* (pp. 3-26). New York: Academic Press.

Flanagan, S., Adams, H. E., & Forehand, R. (1979). A comparison of four instructional techniques for teaching parents to use time-out. *Behavior Therapy, 10*, 94-102.

Forehand, R., & Atkeson, B. M. (1977). Generalization of treatment effects with parents as therapists: A review of assessment and implementation procedures. *Behavior Therapy, 8*, 575-593.

Forehand, R., & McMahon, R. J. (1984). *Helping the non-compliant child.* New York, NY: Guilford Publications.

Gordon, T. (1970). *Parent effectiveness training.* New York: McKay.

Greene, B. F., Clark, H. B., & Risley, T. *Shopping with children.* San Rafael, Calif.: Academic Therapy.

Henry, S. A. (1983). Current dimensions of parent training. *School Psychology Review, 10*, 4-14.

Horne, A. M., & Patterson, G. R. (1980). Working with parents of aggressive children. In R. R. Abidin (Ed.), *Parent education and intervention handbook* (pp. 159-184). Springfield, IL: Charles C. Thomas.

Kazdin, A. E. (1980). Acceptability of alternate treatment for deviant child behavior. *Journal of Applied Behavior Analysis, 13*, 259-273.

Kazdin, A. E., French, N. H., & Sherick, R. B. (1981). Acceptability of alternative treatments for children: Evaluations by inpatient children, parents, and staff. *Journal of Consulting and Clinical Psychology, 49*, 900-907.

Lavigueur, H., Peterson, R. F., Sheese, J. G., & Peterson, I. W. (1973). Behavioral treatment in the home: Effects on an untreated sibling and long-term follow-up. *Behavior Therapy, 4*, 431-441.

McMahon, R. J., & Forehand, R. (1980). Self-help behavior therapies in parent training. In B. B. Lahey and A. E. Kazdin (Eds.), *Advanced in Clinical Child Psychology: Vol. 3* (pp. 149-176).

McMahon, R. J., & Forehand, R. (1983). Consumer satisfaction in behavioral treatment of children: Types, issues, and recommendations. *Behavior Therapy, 14*, 209-225.

McMahon, R. J., Forehand, R., Griest, D. L. (1981). Effects of knowledge of social learning principles on enhancing treatment outcome and generalization in a parent training program. *Journal of Consulting and Clinical Psychology, 49*, 526-532.

Martin, H. P. (1980). Working with parents of abused and neglected children. In R. R. Abidin (Ed.), *Parent education and intervention handbook* (pp. 252-271). Springfield, IL: Charles C. Thomas.

Nay, W. R. (1975). A systematic comparison of instructional techniques for parents. *Behavior Therapy, 6*, 14-21.

O'dell, S. (1974). Training parents in behavior modification: A review. *Psychological Bulletin, 7,* 418-433.

O'dell, S. L., O'Quin, J., Alford, B. A., O'Briant, A. L., Bradlyn, A. S., & Giebenhain, J. E. (1982). Predicting the acquisition of parenting skills via four training methods. *Behavior Therapy, 13,* 194-208.

O'Farrell, T. J., & Keuthen, N. J. (1983). Readability of behavior therapy self-help manuals. *Behavior Therapy, 14,* 449-454.

Patterson, G. (1977). *Families: Applications of social learning to family life.* Champaign, IL: Research Press.

Patterson, G. P., Chamberlain, P., & Reid, J. B. (1982). A comparative evaluation of a parent training program. *Behavior Therapy, 13,* 638-650.

Patterson, G., & Guillon, M. (1976). *Living with children: New methods for parents and teachers.* Champaign, IL: Research Press.

Reynolds, C. R., Gutkin, T. B., Elliott, S. N., & Witt, J. C. (1984). *School psychology: Essentials of theory and practice.* New York: Wiley & Sons.

Rinn, R. C., & Markle, A. (1971). Parent effectiveness training: A review. *Psychological Reports, 41,* 95-109.

Rose, S. D. (1974). Training parents in groups as behavior modifiers of their mentally retarded children. *Behavior Therapy and Experimental Psychiatry, 5,* 135-140.

Salvia, J., & Ysseldyke, J. E. (1981). *Assessment in remedial and special education.* Boston: Houghton Mifflin.

Sherrets, S. D., Authier, K. J., & Tramontana, M. G. (1980). Rationale, history, and funding sources. *Journal of Clinical Child Psychology.*

Silcock, A. (1979). Parenting in the early years: Current perspectives. *Australian Psychologist, 14,* 289-300.

Steele, B. (1975). Working with abusive parents from a psychiatric point of view (D.H.E.W. Publication No. (OHD) 75-70). Washington, DC: U.S. Government Printing Office.

Stevens, M. J., & Pfost, K. S. (1982). Bibliotherapy: Medicine for the soul? *Psychology, 79,* 21-25.

Tavormina, J. B. (1975). Relative effectiveness of behavioral and reflective group counseling with parents of mentally retarded children. *Journal of Consulting and Clinical Psychology, 43,* 22-31.

Tavormina, J. B. (1980). Evaluation and comparative studies of parent education. In R. R. Abidin (Ed.), *Parent education and intervention handbook* (pp. 130-155). Springfield, IL: Charles C. Thomas.

Wells, K. C., Forehand, R., & Griest, D. L. (1980). Generality of treatment effects from treated to untreated behaviors resulting from a parent training program. *Journal of Clinical Child Psychology, 13,* 217-219.

Wells, K. C., Griest, D. L., & Forehand, R. (1980). The use of a self-control package to enhance temporal generality of a parent training program. *Behavioral Research and Therapy, 18,* 347-353.

Wolfe, D. A., & Sandler, J. (1981). Training abusive parents in effective child management. *Behavior Modification, 5,* 320-335.

ANNOTATED BIBLIOGRAPHY

Abidin, R. R. (Ed.). (1980). *Parent education and intervention handbook.* Springfield, IL: Charles C. Thomas.
This handbook provides a comprehensive overview of a number of issues which are directly related to parent training. It is divided into three sections: general issues, working with special populations, and reviews of parent education materials. It is not a training manual and serves to provide wide ranging, thought provoking analyses.

Bernstein, G. S. (1983). Training behavior change agents: A conceptual analysis. *Behavior Therapy, 13,* 1-23.
Although this review does not directly address the issue of training parents, it is an excellent analysis of the questions which trainers must answer if they are to be successful in equipping parents with the skills which will allow them to change behavior. Particular attention is paid to the importance of an ecological orientation.

Cooper, J. O., & Edge, D. (1978). *Parenting: Strategies and educational methods.* Columbus, OH: Charles E. Merrill.
An excellent source for individuals wanting to learn about effective interventions for a variety of specific child behavioral problems. The bulk of the text is devoted to specific interventions and case studies are provided. Useful material for trainers is included in a series of appendices (e.g., parent consent form, training assignments, reinforcement menu, etc.).

Forehand, R., & Atkeson, B. M. (1977). Generality of treatment effects with parents as therapists: A review of assessment and implementation procedures. *Behavior Therapy, 8*, 575-593.
A thorough review of procedures that have been utilized to assess and implement generalization of the effects of parent training. Useful for the practitioner wanting to learn about reliable and accurate methods of training generalizable skills and for assessing the extent to which they have been successful.

McMahon, R. J., & Forehand, R. (1980). Self-help behavior therapies in parent training. In B. B. Lahey and A. E. Kazdin (Eds.), *Advanced in Clinical Child Psychology: Vol. 3* (pp. 149-176). New York: Plenum Press.
A review of bibliotherapy approaches to parent training is provided. Self-administered, self-help approaches appear to offer a great deal in terms of cost-effectiveness. This review highlights the potential benefits as well as the shortcomings of this approach. Suggestions for practitioners and future research are enumerated.

BEST PRACTICES IN EVALUATING EDUCATIONAL PROGRAMS

Charles A. Maher
Rutgers University

Louis J. Kruger
Rutgers University

OVERVIEW

In most school systems, school psychologists are involved in various educational programs & services. These include individualized education programs (IEPs), resource rooms, special and regular classroom instruction, pupil counseling, parent education, staff development training, and psychoeducational assessment procedures.

Most educational programs in school systems are evaluated by school professionals including psychologists. These program evaluation efforts, though, are typically not formal large scale undertakings. Usually the efforts are not even thought of as program evaluation by those involved. The process of gathering information about an educational program to further develop or improve it is what all school professionals do. When school psychologists ask questions like: "Is there a need for parent counseling?," "Are our psychoeducational assessment procedures occurring as planned?," and "Are IEP goals being attained?;" when they gather information to answer these questions; and when they make program decisions using the information, educational program evaluation is occurring.

In this chapter, educational program evaluation is viewed as a process of gathering information and making judgments so that programs are continually developed and improved (Maher & Bennett, 1984). Professionals involved in evaluating the range of educational programs that exist in school systems recommend this practical way of viewing program evaluation.

BASIC CONSIDERATIONS

A fundamental consideration to evaluating any educational program is having a clear understanding of what constitutes the *program*. Such an understanding is important and practical because those involved must know just what is the focus of evaluation. Maher and Bennett (1984) define a program as an organized configuration of resources, designed to assist an individual, group, or an organization attain clearly stated purposes. goals, or functions. In this sense, resources are the "critical mass" of the program, the means by which it is implemented: Human resources are the program's staff, administration, and consultants. Technological resources include materials, methods, procedures and approaches. Informational resources encompass policies, goals, and data bases. Financial resources are monies used for program operations. Finally, physical resources refer to such things as the facilities in which the program occurs.

Employing this definition of an educational program, many kinds of programs can be identified. Educational programs in a school system can be organized into five areas (Maher & Bennett, 1984).

1. *Assessment programs* are designed to gather information about pupils and programs for decision-making. Examples are: preplacement evaluation, IEP annual review, and district-wide standardized achievement testing.

2. *Instructional programs* are designed to enhance pupils' functioning in areas of academic achievement and functional living. Examples include: reading, mathematics, and language arts programs

3. *Related service programs* are designed to benefit pupils in communication, movement, and socialization. Examples are: speech and language therapy, physical therapy, or social skills training.

4. *Personnel development programs* are designed to enhance capabilities of staff, parents, and aides to more effectively educate children. In-service education, parental involvement, committees, and paraprofessional training are examples.

5. *Administrative programs* are designed to assure that other educational programs occur effectively and efficiently. Examples are: pupil case management procedures, program-oriented budgeting, and policy development approaches.

A second consideration involved in evaluating educational programs is knowing how the program is designed. In this regard, a *program's design* is reflected in material that describes the program. Documentation such as a written description of the individual, group, or organization standing to benefit from the program, the program's purpose and goals, the methods and activities to be employed during the program, and the roles and responsibilities of staff carrying it out provide information about the program's design. Without clearly written information about how a program is designed, appropriate judgments cannot be made about the extent to which an implemented program has deviated course and what particular program has resulted in goal attainment. Just what constitutes the program is unknown.

Another consideration is the organization within which the educational program is embedded. An educational program is part of a larger school organization that includes various factors affecting how programs are designed and implemented. An understanding of school organization, particularly the "readiness" of a school sytem for educational program

evaluation, helps in deciding what programs are appropriate candidates for various kinds of evaluation activities (Cronbach, 1982).

Finally, a fourth important consideration involves relying on standards when designing and carrying out evaluations. Four such program evaluation standards exist (Joint Commission, 1981). First, any approach to evaluating educational programs must possess *utility*. The evaluation must provide information useful for program development and improvement. Second, an evaluation to be undertaken must be considered in terms of *feasibility* in that the endeavor is sensitive to political, fiscal, and other practical realities of the organization. *Propriety*, a third standard, refers to ethical and legal responsibility to protect individuals and groups such as teachers, pupils and parents, who are asked to serve as data sources of the evaluation. *Accuracy*, the fourth standard, assures that evaluation occurs in technically defensible ways in terms of the instruments, tests, and procedures employed.

BEST PRACTICES

Best practices in evaluating educational programs are derived from the above considerations and occur as three sequential, interrelated evaluation tasks. These tasks are: (a) assessing organizational context; (b) developing and implementing an evaluation; and (c) analyzing and communicating evaluation information. These tasks occur for any kind of educational program to be evaluated including an assessment, instruction, related service, personnel development, or administrative program.

Assessing Organizational Context

Organizational factors either hinder or encourage attempts at evaluating an educational program. To assure that evaluation activities are successful, the first best practices task is minimizing organizational factors that inhibit an evaluation from being carried out as well as maximizing factors that facilitate an evaluation occuring as planned.

In assessing the organizational context of a school system for program evaluation, various readiness factors are considered to (a) determine if problems exist; (b) identify areas of organizational strength; and (c) design ways of intervening to minimize problems that have been detected. First, the *availability* of funds and evaluation personnel that can be allocated in sufficient amounts to an evaluation is important to consider. Determining availability of funds and evaluation personnel is particularly important in situations where the evaluation endeavor occurs across more than one school site or over an extended period of time such as an entire school year. Second, the *values* of school staff involved in the evaluation need to be understood. If key staff members do not perceive educational program evaluation as compatible with the school's prevailing philosophy and norms, the chances of evaluation being successfully carried out are minimal. Third, it is important to know what the *idea* of program evaluation means to school administrators and staff prior to planning an evaluation. If, for example, the majority of staff view program evaluation as large scale, highly controlled experimental research, then the notion of evaluation as a means to assist in continued development and improvement needs to be presented and discussed with these members. Fourth, if the school or school district in which evaluation is to occur is not administratively stable such as when a special services director who is supportive of program evaluation is about to leave the district for other employment, the *circumstances* for going ahead with

an evaluation may not be appropriate. In contrast, a fifth factor, *timing*, has to do with recent events or developments in the system that suggest the "Time is Right" for an educational program evaluation. For example, timing for evaluation activities might be appropriate if the state recently provided additional funding for such activities.

Three other organizational readiness factors round out the list that are considered before proceeding with designing and implementing an evaluation. *Obligation* refers to the extent to which district staff perceive a need for program evaluation and are willing to participate in it. If staff do not feel obligated about program evaluation, another factor, *resistance* to program evaluation participation, results. A final, but most important factor, one closely related to obligation and resistance, is *yield* or "pay-off." For example, administrators may see evaluation as being a positive event in that meaningful information for educational decision-making results from an evaluation. On the other hand, instructional staff might consider program evaluation as yielding negative consequences such as increased paperwork.

Two options which can be employed to assess organizational readiness in relation to the above eight factors are (a) interviewing school staff with respect to the factors or (b) administering a questionnaire such as the "Organizational Readiness for Program Evaluation Questionnaire" (Kiresuk & Lund, 1979). Information indicating lack of organizational readiness for program evaluation in any area then is used as a basis for developing an organizational intervention intended to increase readiness. For example, assessment of the organizational readiness factors indicates insufficient funds to support the evaluation effort. In this instance, a grant writing intervention is initiated to secure necessary funding from a state discretionary account to support program evaluation efforts. Similarly, interventions are planned and implemented for other factors considered impediments to organizational readiness. (A discussion of assessing readiness and how to intervene can be found in Maher, 1984, and Maher & Bennett, 1984.)

Designing and Implementing an Evaluation

Designing a plan for evaluating any educational program begins by focusing attention on key questions. Six such questions are considered appropriate to address in an evaluation. All questions, however, may not be necessary for a particular program.

Question 1: Is the program of interest capable of being evaluated? An affirmative response to this question is a necessary prerequisite to program implementation evaluation and outcome evaluation (Wholey, 1981). Two methods can be used to collect data about the extent to which a program is evaluated. First, materials that describe major aspects of the program's design — its purpose, goals, objectives, activities, staff — can be reviewed, such as a program grant document or procedure manual. A second method is interviewing staff who are engaged in operating or supervising the program about the major design aspects. Once such information has been gathered, the program's design is evaluated in terms of clarity and comprehensiveness. Clarity refers to the extent to which goals and objectives of the program are understandable, observable, and measurable, especially to staff who implement the program. Comprehensiveness refers to how inclusive the design is. For example, all individualized education programs should address state and federally mandated requirements, whereas a social skills training program focuses on important skill needs of the pupils. If the design of a program is found

lacking in clarity or comprehensiveness, the deficiencies are rectified prior to evaluating program implementation or outcome. Without rectifying these deficiencies, other kinds of evaluation questions are meaningless since the nature of program is not known.

Question 2: To what extent was the program implemented as planned? Evaluation information gathered in response to this question is useful in documenting compliance with legal requirements and ethical standards for programs. It also helps in deciding what activities or parts of a program need to be altered.

Various methods are used to evaluate program implementation. These methods focus on four implementation questions: (a) Who received the program?; (b) Who provided the program service?; (c) What activities and methods were employed in implementing the program?; and (d) What difficulties arose during implementation? One procedure for evaluating program implementation is to observe and record the activities of the program as they are being implemented by the program staff. However, due to the time consuming and obtrusive nature of this procedure, it is better suited to gathering information about materials and facilities. Survey approaches such as questionnaires and interviews are also used to evaluate the extent to which a program has occurred as planned. For example, questionnaires and interviews can provide information about staff perceptions of program operation and possible reasons for departures from the program's design. Another method that is used to evaluate program implementation is reviewing permanent products, such as lesson plans, to determine amount of teaching time spent in various instructional areas. The main disadvantage of the permanent product review method is that it involves making an inference from a product to a staff member's performance. For example, if a teacher's lesson plan lists certain instructional activities, it might be inferred that the activities actually occurred when they did not. Alternatively, implementation data can be recorded on a log at specified time intervals. This approach, likewise, shares a disadvantage with the survey method as being a retrospective account of program implementation. Since all methods of evaluating program implementation possess specific advantages and disadvantages, a multi-method evaluation approach is recommended (Patton, 1978).

Question 3: To what extent have program goals been attained? An appropriate response to this question requires that program goals are described, and objectives are stated as observable and measurable activities or products. For example, if the goal of a pupil group counseling program is to improve school attendance, a program objective that reflects the goal might be that pupil attendance would increase on the average of 50 percent following program completion as determined by official school records. Without clearly stated goals and objectives, a goal-based evaluation cannot be conducted in an appropriate manner (Joint Commission, 1981; Maher & Bennett, 1984).

For instructional programs, either criterion-reference or norm-reference frames are used to assess goal attainment. A test based on a criterion-reference frame informs decision-makers about an individual's or group's mastery relative to a sequence of skills reflected in program goals and objectives. A test using a normative frame of reference, however, provides information about an individual or group relative to a comparison or norm group. Normative reference frames are derived from the range of performance within which most members of the norm group scored. Thus, average goal attainment from the norm of a test occurs when

a score falls between the 16th and 84th percentiles (2 standard deviation units from the mean). Two major caveats, however, pertain to the use of norm-referenced tests. First, the test employed should be one that measures skills that are taught in the program and are stated in program goals and objectives. Second, the test's norm group should have characteristics relevant to the group or individual being assessed.

Criterion and norm-referenced tests are among the five methods which are used to gather goal attainment information. Naturalistic observations, interviews, questionnaires, and permanent product review approaches also are used (Maher & Bennett, 1984; Tuckman, 1982). A number of recording schedules have been developed for naturalistic observation. Behavioral recording schedules, however, differ from one another with respect to the type of information generated and in their advantages and disadvantages (Bergan, 1977).

Goal attainment scaling (Kiresuk & Lund, 1978) is a procedure that is used in school systems to summarize goal-related data derived from one or more of the above five methods. In goal attainment scaling, a goal is operationalized in terms of five possible outcomes, or "goal indicators", arranged on a goal attainment schedule from "most unfavorable" to "best anticipated." Goal attainment scaling allows relative judgments to be made about goal attainment and generates a summary goal attainment score. The goal attainment scale lends itself to both individualized program and group program evaluation, particularly for special education programs. (See Maher, 1983, for a detailed discussion of this approach.)

At least three pitfalls are recognized with respect to evaluating educational program goal attainment. One of these is the use of content or behaviors that do not accurately reflect the objectives being measured. Another common pitfall is the use of a too limited sample of behavior or performance for assessing each objective. This decreases the reliability of the measurement. A third is attributing a particular level of goal attainment to the program without suitable conditions necessary for evaluating cause-effect relations (Cronbach, 1982).

Question 4: What are the reactions of consumers to the program? Consumers include individuals participating in the program and groups indirectly impacted by the program, such as a private foundation that provides funding. Consumer reactions are useful in evaluating the "social validity" of the program (Kazdin, 1977). Furthermore, consumer reaction data can indicate unintentional effects and suggest ways the program can be improved. Two commonly assessed consumer reaction variables are satisfaction ratings of staff and parents, and individuals' perceptions of the extent to which program goals were attained.

Surveys are the typically employed method of obtaining consumer reaction data. Questionnaires are particularly efficient when a large group of individuals are surveyed. Also, individual or group interviews can be useful to clarify concerns about a program and to follow-up on particular responses obtained from a questionnaire. Although consumer reaction evaluations can be used as a means of evaluating any type of educational program, their most widespread use is with individualized programs and staff development programs (Maher & Bennett, 1984).

Question 5: Was the program responsible for the observed outcomes? This is a question concerning cause-effect relationships. For any educational program that has realized its goals, factors other than the program could be responsible for goal attainment outcomes. A cause-effect evaluation question, therefore, asks whether non-program factors are the cause of the outcomes. Problems exist in determining cause-effect relationships of most educational programs in school systems. In these settings, legal and ethical considerations often prevent use of the type of outcome evaluation approaches, particularly experimental designs, that have been recommended in attributing outcomes to an education program (Cronbach, 1982).

Nevertheless, in attempting to gather information relative to a cause-effect evaluation, evaluation approaches other than experimental ones can be used. Some of these approaches are more useful than others in determining whether or not the program produced the outcomes. For example, one evaluation approach that often is employed involves assessment at two points in time. Pupil performance related to program, goals and objectives are examined prior to the implementation of the program and after the program or some phase of the program. This approach provides a baseline of data to which the post program data are compared. Although this approach rules out some possible non-program causative factors, it still does not allow confident judgments to be made regarding cause-effect relationships. For example, although all children have received the same reading program, it could be said that the children would have learned as much without the program just because they have grown older.

In the time series approach, frequent assessments are made of pupil progress relative to goals and objectives at various points prior to, during, and after the program. The time series approach is particularly useful for gathering information on goals and objectives that reflect rates and amounts of skill development. This approach provides valuable information about appropriateness of goals, degree of goal attainment, and maintenance of goal attainment. Moreover, it helps rule out more non-program factors than the approach where data on pupil progress are only collected prior to and following the program. The time series approach thereby increases confidence in cause-effect judgments. Further information on the time series approach is found in Kazdin (1976), Kratochwill (1978), and Maher and Bennett (1984).

Another approach to determining cause-effect relations involves comparing educational performance of one group of pupils with a group that did not receive the program. If the pupils receiving the program have a greater degree of goal attainment than those who did not receive the program, it is possible that the program was responsible for the intended effects. A major difficulty in implementing this outcome evaluation approach is obtaining groups of pupils who are similar with respect to initial levels of goal attainment and other relevant characteristics. (See Cook & Campbell, 1979 for more detailed discussion of this approach.)

Question 6: What possible effects, other than goal attainment, might result from the program? This is an important but often overlooked question. Most programs targeted to pupils or staff result in effects other than the intended ones. Such unintended effects are judged either negative or positive in their impact on a group that received the program.

Maher and Bennett (1984) recommend a means of evaluating a program's related effects with respect to classroom instructional programs, as well as related service programs, such as pupil counseling. They outline four sequential, interrelated activities that occur in evaluating related effects: (a) assessing the learning environment and behavior of students in the classroom before program implementation; (b) determining the extent of program implementation; (c) assessing learning environment and behavior in the classroom following implementation; and (d) determining whether any changes in pupils and teachers not specified in goals and objectives can be attributed to the program.

Developing an evaluation plan. Once evaluation questions have been selected, an evaluation plan is developed. For each question, the methods, procedures, and instruments needed to gather information about each question are specified. Evaluation roles and responsibilities are determined which denote what various individuals are to do. An example includes deciding what teachers collect data and which professional analyzes them. It is pivotal that consensus be obtained from program managers and staff regarding evaluation roles and responsibilities, and that timelines for carrying through on evaluation activities are specified before the plan is implemented.

Implementing the plan. In implementing an educational program evaluation, a team approach is recommended. A team approach has several advantages. It reduces resistance to evaluation by including key managers and staff as team members. Inclusion of individuals possessing multiple perspectives on the educational program helps clarify questions and issues relative to the evaluation (Patton, 1978). The team approach also allows for division of evaluation responsibilities among members thereby decreasing amount of time any one individual spends on evaluation activities. Furthermore, assigning overlapping tasks to team members potentially increases reliability of the data gathered. Often, there are benefits to including as team members those who are directly involved in the operations of the program being evaluated. Those who have direct involvement with the program, for example, might be highly invested in assessing outcomes and have ready access to the data needed for the evaluation effort.

Prior to and during an evaluation, organizational sanctions and supports are actively sought. Maher's (1984) investigations of the implementation of innovative programs and procedures suggest that it is critical to obtain organizational sanctions and supports. An example is obtaining formal approval from a school principal before proceeding with evaluation activities. Failure to secure necessary organizational sanctions and supports may reduce the likelihood of implementing an evaluation as planned.

Analyzing and Communicating Evaluation Information

The third task in evaluating educational programs involves analyzing and communicating evaluation information. If program evaluation is to serve program development and improvement purposes, then data gathered by means of evaluation activities must be analyzed and communicated to program managers and staff in understandable ways.

Analyzing data from program evaluation activities. Descriptive and inferential statistical approaches are employed to analyze data derived from program evaluation activities. A descriptive statistical approach involves tabulation and summarization of data that have been collected about the program. Descriptive statistics frequently includes: (a) measures of central tendency such as the mean or median; (b) measures of variability such as the range of scores; and (c) depiction of data in frequency distributions such as graphs and tables. The types of descriptive statistical procedures employed depends on a number of factors including the evaluation question being asked, the specific evaluation approach used, and the individual or group to whom the data are being communicated. Graphs or tables, for example, can be appropriate descriptive procedures for presenting data to parents and school administrators.

A wide variety of inferential statistical procedures are useful in making judgments whether or not the results of a program occurred by chance. The procedures selected are determined by such factors as the number of pupils in the program group, the type of evaluation questions asked, and the evaluation approach used. Most importantly, though, consultation and technical assistance can be sought from a statistician or professional evaluator when considering whether it is appropriate to employ inferential statistics in analyzing program evaluation data. More detailed discussion of data analysis procedures as they pertain to evaluation of individualized and group programs is found in Kazdin (1976), Kratochwill (1978), and Cook and Campbell (1979).

Communicating evaluation information. In communicating evaluation information, decisions are made about the mode in which the information is communicated. Evaluation information is communicated in either written or oral modes. The mode used depends on a number of factors including who is provided the information, the purpose of the communication, and type of information. A written report implies formal documentation of evaluation results. It is used as a tool for program improvement as well as for documenting the program's worth or merit to groups such as a board of education or external funding agency. Several strategies exist for presenting a written report: (a) tailoring the degree to which the report includes technical terms to the individual group receiving the report; (b) providing the audience with a draft of the report that can be revised; and (c) providing the opportunity for additional meetings with the recipient to discuss ways in which the information can be used. The content of the report encompasses the purposes of the evaluation, evaluation methods, implementation and outcome results, and recommendations for program planning, development, and improvement. Tables, graphs, and other illustrations can be included in the report to enhance written material and emphasize important points.

Oral communication is most often used to report evaluation information within the context of ongoing professional contacts or meetings. It is more suitable for use with administrators and coordinators who do not have time to read written reports. Maher and Bennett (1984) recommend that content of an oral evaluation report include: (a) an emphasis on program goals achieved; (b) identification of program goals not achieved; (c) acknowledgement of the efforts of the evaluation team members; (d) causes for the program's outcomes when appropriate and defensible; and (e) implications of the information for program planning.

SUMMARY

Educational program evaluation is considered a process of gathering information, and making judgments about a program for purposes of program development and improvement. In terms of evaluating educational programs, considerations basic to evaluation were discussed in this chapter, including (a) understanding the definition of a program; (b) recognizing the various kinds of programs that can be evaluated; (c) being knowledgeable about the nature and scope of the design of a program to be evaluated; (d) understanding the organizational context within which the program is embedded; and (e) adhering to program evaluation standards when designing and implementing an evaluation. Best practice in evaluating educational

programs was then considered as encompassing tasks of assessing organization context, developing and implementing an evaluation, and analyzing and communicating evaluation information. The task of assessing organizational readiness was described as gathering information and making judgments about organizational factors that inhibit evaluation endeavors so that interventions to alleviate these factors occur. Developing and implementing an evaluation was discussed by focusing on key evaluation questions. These questions were concerned with the clarity and comprehensiveness of the design of a program as a basis for evaluation, the extent to which the program was implemented as planned, and the nature and degree of program outcomes. Various methods, procedures, and instruments were considered as means to gather relevant evaluation information. Analyzing and communicating evaluation information were discussed as being necessary to making program results meaningful to administrators, staff, and other individuals and groups.

REFERENCES

Bergan, J. R. (1977). *Behavioral consultation.* Columbus, OH: Charles E. Merrill.

Cook, T. C., & Campbell, D. T. (1979). *Quasi-experimentation: Design and analysis issues for field settings.* New York: Rand-McNally.

Cronbach, L. J. (1982). *Designing evaluations of educational and social programs.* San Francisco, CA: Jossey-Bass.

Joint Commission on Standards for Educational Evaluation. (1981). *Standards for evaluation of educational programs, projects, and materials.* New York: McGraw-Hill.

Kazdin, A. E. (1976). Statistical analysis for single case experimental designs. In M. Hersen & D. Barlow (Eds.), *Single case experimental designs: Strategies for behavior change.* New York: Pergamon Press.

Kazdin, A. E. (1977). Assessing the clinical or applied significance of behavior change through social validation. *Behavior Modification, 1,* 427-452.

Kiresuk, T., & Lund, S. B. (1978). Goal attainment scaling. In C. C. Attkission, W. A. Hargreaves, M. J. Horowitz, & J. E. Sorensen (Eds.), *Evaluation of human service programs.* New York: Academic Press.

Kratochwill, T. R. (Ed.). (1978). *Single subject research: Strategies for evaluating change.* New York: Academic Press.

Maher, C. A. (1983). Goal attainment scaling: A method for evaluating special education services. *Exceptional Children, 51.*

Maher, C. A. (1984). An approach to implementing programs in organizational settings. *Journal of Organizational Behavior Management,* in press.

Maher, C. A., & Bennett, R. E. (1984). *Planning and evaluating special education services.* Englewood Cliffs, NJ: Prentice-Hall.

Patton, M. Q. (1978). *Utilization-focused evaluation.* Beverly Hills, CA: Sage.

Tuckman, B. (1981). *Evaluating instructional programs.* Boston, MA: Allyn and Bacon.

Wholey, J. C. (1981). *Evaluation: Promise and performance.* Washington, DC: Urban Institute.

ANNOTATED BIBLIOGRAPHY

Attkisson, C., Hargreaves, W. A., Horowitz, M. J., & Sorensen, J. (Eds.). (1978). *Evaluation of human service programs.* New York: Academic Press.
This book includes a range of chapters dealing with program evaluation within the realities of operating human service systems. Chapters are devoted to issues such as organizational factors that influence evaluation and decision-making, evaluating indirect services in schools, use of management information systems to support program evaluation activities, and cost-effectiveness evaluation.

Cook, T. C., & Campbell, D. T. (1979). *Quasi-experimentation: Design and analysis issues for field settings.* New York: Rand-McNally.
This book goes into detail about various approaches that help make judgments about program effectiveness, and approaches that are employed in school settings particularly for evaluating large scale educational programs. Various evaluation approaches are discussed in terms of their usefulness in ruling out factors other than the educational program that were responsible for program outcomes.

Cronbach, L. J. (1982). *Designing evaluations of education and social programs.* San Francisco: Jossey-Bass.
Specific guidelines are offered on ways of planning and conducting evaluations that accurately reveal how educational and social programs are serving their clienteles. Advantages and disadvantages of the many evaluation techniques available including a notion of what is gained and lost in employing each of them are pointed out.

Joint Committee on Standards for Educational Evaluation, (1981). *Standards for Evaluation of Educational Programs, Projects, and Materials.* New York: McGraw-Hill.
This book, developed by a committee of distinguished professionals in psychology, education, and measurement, identifies and elucidates 30 separate standards. These standards correspond to four main concerns about any evaluation — its utility, feasibility, propriety, and accuracy. Each standard is explained and clarified through commentary which includes overview of intent, guidelines for applications, creativity, and illustration of the standards' application.

Kratochwill, T. R. (Ed.). (1978). *Single subject research: Strategies for evaluating change.* New York: Academic Press.
An edited textbook that provides a range of material on the applications of single subject (n = 1) evaluation strategies to make judgments about whether changes observed in a program client were due to the program. Numerous illustrations as well as practical guidelines for using the approach with pupils in educational programs are provided.

Maher, C. A., & Bennett, R. E. (1984). *Planning and evaluating education services.* Englewood Cliffs, NJ: Prentice-Hall.
This resource book presents a comprehensive overview of planning and evaluating a wide range of service delivery programs for exceptional children and youth. The approach encompasses all special education programs including assessment, instruction, related services, staff development, and administration. The practical methods and procedures described encourage a systematic, explicit, data-based approach to decision-making for each program area. This book shows school personnel how to improve programs so that they are targeted to the specific needs of their school district. It includes numerous tables, graphs, charts, and checklists to illustrate concepts and suggested procedures.

BEST PRACTICES IN WORKING WITH SEVERELY AND PROFOUNDLY HANDICAPPED CHILDREN

Christopher Matey
Miami University

OVERVIEW

Valletutti (1984) points out that the group of children referred to as severely and profoundly handicapped includes more than just severely and profoundly retarded children. Severe and profound handicaps include children with multiple handicaps, any one of which occurring singly would not constitute a severely disabling condition. For example when deafness or blindness constitute a single disability, the effects are more easily managed in educational settings. More significant obstacles to learning are met when deafness and blindness occur together. Similarly the disability referred to as autism involves multiple handicapping conditions, including communication problems, social relating deficits and cognitive disabilities. The combination of these handicaps results in significant learning problems requiring educational procedures unique to the severely and profoundly handicapped (SPH) groups.

Additional factors in defining the SPH group include the educational considerations of curriculum and SPH learner characteristics. The curriculum for SPH children deviates significantly from traditional instruction. Rather than presenting a watered-down version of the educational program for nondisabled children, educational programs for SPH children provide instruction in areas previously considered the exclusive domain of parents, occupational therapists and physical therapists (Valletutti, 1984). Objectives frequently addressed include toilet training, dressing, and appropriate use of utensils in eating. The training of these objectives must take into consideration two important characteristics of SPH children: (a) they have great difficulty generalizing skills learned in one setting to another; (b) they learn primarily through direct teaching rather than by observation and imitation. These learner characteristics and the aforementioned curriculur considerations shape the discussion of assessment and educational programming issues which are the focus of this chapter.

Given the preceding definition of children with severely and profoundly handicapping conditions, it is possible to anticipate the problems in working with them by the traditionally trained school psychologist. Most practitioners lack a background in dealing with children who are sensorily impaired, who have severe communication handicaps, who are severely physically disabled, and who are severely or profoundly mentally retarded. Emphasis in training has been on the high incidence handicaps such as children with learning disabilities and mild mental retardation. In addition, school psychology training programs do not deal extensively, if at all, with issues involved in assessment and programming for children functioning at preschool developmental levels. Two additional areas of deficient training are experience in interacting with SPH children and in developing teaching strategies for addressing special learning problems in educational settings.

The intent of this chapter is to provide the practicing school psychologist with the necessary background and resources so that when it is necessary to assist in the educational planning for a child with a severe or profound handicap, guidelines for professional practice are available.

The traditionally trained school psychologist is likely to produce an evaluation that attempts to describe the SPH child in terms of IQ and/or mental age. This approach fails because traditional tests such as the WISC-R, Stanford-Binet, Wide Range Achievement Test, and Bender are usually far beyond the abilities of this population. Often the child is described as being "untestable" and a recommendation is made for placement in a special education program. There is little discussion of instructional objectives or teaching strategies. Consideration of the traditional approach described above results in the following areas of training and knowledge being considered prerequisites to involvement with children with SPH conditions:

1. A familiarity with normal developmental skill sequences from birth to age five;

2. The ability to use criterion and norm-referenced instruments appropriate for interviewing caretakers and observing the child;

3. The ability to assess children's functional skills and to generate instructional objectives and educational strategies;

4. A knowledge of evaluation procedures and instruments which address the sensory and/or response limitations of the SPH group;

5. An opportunity to observe in classrooms for SPH children in which appropriate teaching strategies are employed.

We now proceed to address the first four areas. In regard to the fifth, refer to both the general guidelines for informal assessment presented later and to the section on classroom programming to structure observations.

Best practices in both the areas of assessment and programming are addressed. These two sets of activities are integrally related and it is difficult to address one area without raising questions about the other. For the purpose of exposition, however, these two areas are discussed under separate headings, acknowledging that overlap in content occurs.

Assessment Models

Bagnato and Neisworth (1981) emphasize the importance of linking assessment to classroom instruction. The term "linkage" in this case simply refers to a direct connection between assessment and instruction. A concern for establishing such linkages pervades our discussion of assessment activities.

Development versus Functional Models

Two basic approaches to assessment that incorporate a concern for developing linkages are the developmental approach as exemplified by Bagnato & Neisworth (1981) and Haring and Bricker (1976) and the functional approach as exemplified by Lou Brown and his colleagues (Brown, Falvey, Vincent, Johnson, Ferrara-Parish, & Gruenewald, 1980; Brown, Branston-McClean, Bumgart, Vincent, Falvey & Schroder, 1979). Both of these approaches are appropriate for use with SPH children although each has strengths and weaknesses that are pointed out in the discussion that follows.

The developmental approach is based on the assumption that the normal sequence of development observed in nondisabled children provides the guidelines for assessment and instructional planning for disabled children. Proponents of this view employ developmentally based assessment tools and curricula such as the Learning Accomplishment Profile-Diagnostic Edition (Lemay, Griffin & Sanford, 1978) and the Learning Accomplishment Profile Curriculum (Sanford, 1978) produced by the Chapel Hill Outreach Training Project. This approach involves looking at the child's level of functioning in each of a number of domains such as cognition, language development, fine and gross motor skills, social-emotional development, and self-care skills. The evaluator simply assesses the skills that the child possesses in each domain sequence and chooses skills that follow the child's highest skill level as instructional objectives to be taught in the classroom. By linking assessment to programming using the developmental model, educators have a basis for ongoing assessment and program planning.

Brown's objections to the developmental approach are most easily demonstrated in its use with older children. As children reach adolescence the need to develop functional, age appropriate skills becomes acute. Use of the developmental approach results in a teacher instructing a nineteen-year old in a task such as placing a shape in a box, a task far more appropriate for a four-year old. All too often educational programs for SPH individuals persist in instructing students in skills that are ultimately of little value to them. Brown et al. are concerned about the ultimate use of skills which are taught to SPH children and base their model on this criterion of ultimate functioning.

The criterion of ultimate functioning means that children are taught only those skills which enable them to function more effectively in the environment. Those skills that are taught are functional because they assist the child in adapting to the environment. These functional skills are based not only on the current environments but also on subsequent environments (such as potential work sites, the community transportation system and public areas such as parks) where the child would be expected to function. Functional skills are selected in five domains (a) domestic, (b) vocational, (c) recreation/leisure, (d) general community functioning, and (e) interaction with nonhandicapped persons. By directing assessment and programming activities using the criterion of ultimate functioning as a guide, it is argued that more appropriate educational programs are developed for children (Brown et al., 1980; Switzky, Rotatori, Miller, & Freagon, 1979).

Assessment of functional skills are preceded by a determination of the critical activities in current and subsequent environments in which the child is expected to participate. Once this is done, assessment begins by analyzing the skills necessary to successfully complete a certain activity; this process involves doing a student repertoire inventory (Brown et al., 1980) which has several steps. Step one involves completing an inventory of the sequence of behaviors for a designated activity as done by a nondisabled person. In step two the evaluator assesses the disabled person's ability to perform this activity. Step three involves an analysis of the discrepancies between the behaviors required of the nondisabled person and the abilities of the disabled person. Based on these discrepancies adaptations are considered that enable the disabled person to successfully complete the skill sequence. A list of possible adaptations and examples are found in Brown et al. (1979). The assessment is linked to educational programming by developing approaches to teach the child to use these adaptations in the actual environments in which the activity is completed.

The major shortcoming of the functional approach to assessment is that it does not emphasize remediating deficiencies reflected in the discrepancies between what the nondisabled and disabled person do. It is assumed that attempts were previously made to remediate the deficiency which justify using an alternative adaptation to circumvent the person's disability. The advantage of the functional approach is that training focuses on age-appropriate skills by making adaptations for the person's disability.

Both the developmental and functional approach to assessment are reasonable alternatives for organizing assessment activities. It has been argued (Gill & Dihoff, 1982) that with children who are younger and/or closer to the normal range of intellectual functioning, the developmental approach is more appropriate. With persons who are older and/or farther from normal intellectual functioning, the functional approach is more appropriate. Other attempts to integrate the best of both approaches are found in Guess, Horner, Utley, Holvoet, Maxon, Tucker, and Warren (1978) and Holvoet, Guess, Mulligan, and Brown (1980).

BEST PRACTICES

In conducting an assessment of a child with a severely or profoundly handicapping condition, it is important to recognize that that the psychologist finds direct test approaches less useful than with learning disabled and mildly retarded children. With SPH children, data obtained from interviews with caretakers, such as, parents or guardians and from observations in settings familiar to the child are essential. Emphasizing this point, Mulliken & Buckley (1983) state that interviews and observational data are the only valid sources of information about more severely disabled children who are difficult to assess with standardized assessment tools. Each of the three data gathering processes — interview, observation, and direct testing are discussed along with examples of assessment guides

and instruments that assist in completing each process.

Interviewing

Parents, others with primary responsibility for care, and teachers possess a wealth of knowledge about the child that is essential to program planning. Especially in the areas of self-care skills, such as, dressing, eating, and toileting, and in the area of social-emotional adjustment, significant others provide data relevant to a comprehensive evaluation that is difficult to obtain from observation and testing alone. A review of some issues related to using parents as sources of assessment data follows. It is assumed that a thorough assessment involves a complete history and review of records.

The accuracy of parental reports of children's skills is often questioned by practitioners. A study by Hayes & Oates (1978) revealed that parental evaluations of children's abilities often differ from professionals' views, but that professional findings are not always more accurate than the parents'. In addition, assessment errors are more likely to occur if the evaluation is done solely in a clinic setting. Gradel, Thompson, and Sheehan, (1982) made a similar comparison and found that when differences between parent and professional evaluations differed, it was usually in the direction of parental overestimation. This tendency simply reflects the parents' larger data base rather than signaling parental pathology; it also suggests that professionals underestimate children's functioning.

If discrepancies are found between parental reports and professional judgments of children's abilities, an attempt is made to resolve them. In many cases the discrepancies are attributable to differences in setting and approaches to management. There are, however, cases where the parent distorts information, thus reflecting either a defensive reaction to a threatening situation or, in rare cases, a pathological condition. In most cases, discrepancies are resolved in a satisfactory manner.

In addition to obtaining more reliable and valid information about the child, involving parents results in their feeling more a part of the assessment team. This is likely to promote feelings of mutual trust and to increase the probability that parents accept team recommendations.

An additional benefit of parental involvement is that the examiner is better able to make decisions regarding (a) the appropriate setting for the formal testing session, (b) the types of direct test measures that are most revealing of the child's abilities, and (c) the kinds of procedures, such as, reinforcers or degree of structure that make for an optimal performance on the part of the child.

One final benefit of parent participation is that better assessment of parental adjustment to the child's disabilities is made. There is a considerable body of literature regarding the parental adjustment process including Buscaglia (1984) and Darling (1979). Perhaps empathic involvement of the parents in the assessment process facilitates more accepting feelings as a result of attaining a better understanding of their child's abilities. Guidelines for conducting an interview are found in Mulliken & Buckley (1983).

There are a number of assessment instruments that are completed through an interview with a person familiar with the child. A number of these instruments are reviewed below. This list is intended to be representative of available measures rather than an exhaustive list of all available instruments. In addition, it is recognized that these instruments are intended to assist in structuring the interview. The examiner goes beyond the content of the instrument to deal with other issues.

Title: **Cain-Levine Social Competency Scale** (Cain, Levine, & Elzey, 1977)
Areas Assessed: Communiction skills, social skills, initiative, self-help.
Standardization: 716 Mentally Retarded Individuals, age 5-10 to 13-8, IQs 25-59.
Technical Data: test-retest reliability = .98; yields percentile ranks and a profile of abilities.
Comments: Guidelines for administration are excellent. Developmentally sequenced objectives are widely spaced. Use of this instrument to provide linkage with curricula requires considerable task analysis. The items represent functional skills.

Title: **Callier-Azusa Scale for Deaf-Blind** (Stillman, 1974)
Areas Assessed: Cognition/communication/language, socialization, daily living skills, motor development, perceptual abilities.
Standardization: None.
Technical Data: Rough age-equivalent scores are possible to obtain for each area assessed. A profile may be plotted.
Comments: This is a very useful tool that is easily translated into instructional objectives. Its applicability extends beyond just the deaf-blind population. It is also useful with profoundly handicapped individuals whose skills do not exceed a 12-month developmental level.

Title: **Camelot Behavioral Checklist** (Foster, 1974)
Areas Assessed: Communication, social, self-help, home duties, motor skills, vocational behavior, economic behavior, responsibility, independent travel, numerical ability.
Standardization: 624 mentally retarded subjects (ages and IQs are not reported).
Technical Data: Test-retest reliability = .93. Yields percentile ranks, a profile of abilities and an overall score.
Comments: This scale is appropriate for use with students who are becoming more

involved in the community. It is weak in skills at the lower developmental levels. There are training programs referenced to each of the items on the checklist. This facilitates linking assessment data to curriculum.

Title: **Developmental Profile II** (Alpern, Boll & Shearer, 1980)
Areas Assessed: Communication, social, self-help, physical, academic.
Standardization: 3008 normal children, ages birth through 9 years representative of national percentages in terms of social class and race, but drawing 98% of the subjects from Indianapolis and Seattle, thus lacking an adequate nationally based sample.
Technical Data: Interrater reliability = .99. Correlates with Vineland Social Maturity Scale. Yields age scores for each area and for total score.
Comments: This is a good screening measure but is of very limited use for developing linkages with curricula. Items do not represent sequentially functional abilities.

Title: **Oliver: Parent Administered Communication Inventory** (MacDonald, 1978)
Areas Assessed: Background information, play, attention, imitation, receptive language, early expressive language.
Standardization & Technical Data: None.
Comments: This instrument is completed by the parent at home over the course of a week to ten days while observing the child. While it does not yield scores, it does provide information highly relevant to educational planning. It has the advantage of involving the parent in developing a greater sensitivity to the child's communication skill development. It should be used only with children who are nonverbal or who are just beginning to speak.

Title: **TARC** (Sailor & Mix, 1975)
Areas Assessed: Communication, social, self-help, motor.

Standardization: 283 severely handicapped, 3 to 16-years old.
Technical Data: Interrater reliability = .85. Test-retest r = .80. Yields standard scores.
Comments: This is appropriate for lower functioning children and is helpful in deciding on educational objectives addressed in the classroom.

Title: **WISCONSIN Behavior Rating Scale** (Song & Jones, 1980)
Areas Assessed: Gross and fine motor, expressive and receptive language, play, socialization, domestic, eating, toileting, dressing, and grooming.
Standardization: 325 severely and profoundly handicapped, 184 nondisabled children.
Technical Data: Interrater r = .86-.99. Correlation with Vineland = .97. Yields percentile ranks and age scores for each area and for total score.
Comments: WBRS permits comparison to both SPH and nondisabled children although the samples are small. There are special items for deaf-blind children. Generally, the items reflect skills ordinarily mastered by children during the first 3 years.

As a result of the interview, a considerable amount of information about the child is acquired. This data base permits transition to the observation phase of the assessment.

Observation

Valletutti (1984) states that because there is a dearth of formal tests and procedures available for use with SPH children, informal diagnostic assessment is more essential than with other groups. This is true not only because of the technical barriers imposed upon the assessment by the SPH child's disabilities, but also because of most examiners' lack of experience with this group. A review of some of these and other issues involved in observational assessment preceeds an analysis of some of the assessment instruments that are used with SPH children.

Because of the low-incidence occurrence of SPH children, there are few opportunities for the average school psychologist to develop assessment skills in this area.[1] As a result of deficient background, most psychologists feel ill-at-ease with a child who is nonambulatory, not toilet trained, and who drools on the examiner and/or the assessment materials. Wright (1983) describes this uncomfortable feeling as reflecting a "requirement of mourning" for the child's disability. It is expected that this type of reaction renders the psychologist less capable of engaging in a formal assessment using a standardized measure. An informal, observational approach gives an opportunity to ease into the assessment without being imposed upon by the requirement of a formal, direct-test measure.

Another perspective for viewing the informal observational assessment takes into account SPH children's limitations in terms of attention and concentration. Standardized tests ordinarily require strict adherence to administration procedures and limit the modifications examiners make. The observational assessment session permits the examiner to experiment with modifying tasks as well as factors that have an effect on attention and motivation. Using rewards, varying the amount of structure, and employing a test-train-retest approach enables the examiner not only to more accurately assess the child's skills but also to provide the teacher with additional information

about how to teach the child in the classroom. This approach has been discussed by Gil and Dihoff (1982) in regard to cognitive assessment but applies equally well to other areas.

In addition to the examiner and child variables discussed above, the setting in which the evaluation occurs is another important consideration. This is important due to SPH children's more limited range of social experiences which results in a more limited ability to adapt to new surroundings. Thus they perform less well due to the strangeness of the setting (MacBeth, 1971). In addition, it is probably more important to discover how SPH children have learned to adapt to familiar surroundings than how well they can adapt to new settings. In order to accommodate these considerations, it is good practice to observe the child in a familiar setting. This could be either the home or school.

Observation affords the opportunity for the parent to observe the examiner's interactions with the child. In some cases the parent assists by interpreting the child's behaviors including speech, gestures, or facial expressions. In all cases, such parental overview greatly demystifies the procedure and facilitates acceptance and a better understanding of the assessment.

Some general guidelines for observation are presented below (Matey, 1975) followed by a representative list of additional instruments and some attempts at providing more specific guidelines for observation.

1. Fine and gross motor skills are observed by having the child play with toys and other materials. If the child is seen in the home, parents are asked to bring out

[1]It has been suggested (Forcade, 1983) that regionalization of psychological services provide for an opportunity for specialization in SPH assessment. This permits a psychologist to develop expertise in this area. It is the opinion of the author, however, that all school psychologists should acquire skills in this area of assessment.

favorite toys. If in a familiar setting, materials with which the child is comfortable are chosen. For example, it is important to determine how a child grasps and places objects. This is assessed using puzzles, peg boards, shape balls, form boards, paper and pencil, and the like. If the child needs assistance in performing motor tasks, the degree of assistance is noted.

2. Social relating skills are best evaluated in the informal assessment. The psychologist observes whether the child establishes eye contact, looks up for feedback as to correctness of a response, ignores others, and so on. The evaluator determines how well the child responds to direction from an adult by giving simple commands and observing the respones. Odd mannerisms and unusual preoccupations such as arm flapping, finger flicking, or string twirling and the conditions under which they occur are noted. The evaluator assesses readiness for a more formal school program by trying to simulate such an experience. This is done by structuring a situation in which the child is sitting down at a table and various tasks are presented with accompanying demands. Various reinforcers are also attempted and their effectiveness determined.

3. Self-care is assessed to the extent that the examiner has time and opportunities occur. Parent reports are checked in the areas of relative dependence in toileting, eating, dressing, and such. Measurement devices which focus on parent interview for obtaining information in this area were discussed earlier.

4. Communication skills are often impaired in SPH children. Record a sample of each child's expressive communication skills and observe how well the child responds to others' attempts to communicate. This begins on a basic level with a determination of whether or not the child turns when someone calls his name or whether he points toward something he wants. Often communication is prompted by creating a need such as taking a desired object from the child. Normally, however, if given an unstructured play situation in a familiar environment, even children with communiction handicaps express themselves to the extent that they are able. At this point only record what was observed.

5. Cognitive and academic skills are assessed informally by presenting various tasks in a play-like manner. The child's facility with preacademic skills such as puzzles, and color and shape discrimination, overlaps with other areas, including motor assessment; it also includes skills more readily classified as cognitively based. The evaluator presents picture books, counting tasks, simple reading exercises, and the like to determine the child's relative readiness for academic instruction.

A listing of structured instruments for collecting assessment data via observation follows:

Balthazar Scales of Adaptive Behavior (Balthazar, 1971). These scales assess abilities in the areas of eating, dressing and toileting. There is standardization data based on 451 5 to 57 year old ambulatory retarded persons. Percentile ranks are available for each area and reliabilities in the .90s have been obtained. Validity studies with the AAMD Adaptive Behavior Scales showed concurrence with each subscale. The authors of the previously discussed Wisconsin Behavior Rating Scale indicate compatibility with the Balthazar Scales.

Brigance Inventory of Early Development (Brigance, 1978). Areas assessed include preambulatory skills (very relevant to SPH children), gross and fine motor, self-help, prespeech, speech and language, readiness, reading, and math. This is a criterion-referenced instrument and is specifically designed for linkage with classroom programming. Psychologists will find the fine and gross motor assessment portions valuable in rounding out a multifactored evaluation. Age bench marks corresponding to the average ages at which normal children acquire certain skills are provided and assist in determining relative strengths and weaknesses in a child's abilities.

Development Sequence Performance Inventory (Dubose, Dmitriev, & Oelwein, 1980). Areas assessed include fine and gross motor, cognition, communication, and social/self-help. Items are grouped in terms of five age groups: 0-18 months, 18 months-3 years, 3 years-4 years, kindergarten, and 6 to 9 years. This instrument was designed to be used to link directly with classroom programming objectives.

Learning Accomplishment Profile: Diag. Ed. (Lemay, Griffin & Sanford, 1978). This instrument focuses on assessment in five areas: fine and gross motor, cognition, language and self-help. It was standardized on thirty-seven nondisabled children and items are arranged in age levels. Reliability of .98 is reported. The LAP-D requires ninety minutes for administration. It is designed to be used with the Learning Accomplishment Profile curriculum. The LAP-D is attractively packaged and involves materials that are more likely to hold the attention of SPH children.

Portage Project Checklist (Shearer, 1975). This informal observational checklist has a corresponding card file system for each item describing activities designed to teach the specific skill. While originally designed for use by parents in home programming, these materials are excellent resources for the psychologist and novice teacher.

Psychoeducational Profile (Schopler &

Reichler, 1976). Areas assessed are imitation, perception, fine motor, gross motor, eye-hand integration, cognitive performance and verbal skills. While originally designed for use with autistic children in mind, this tool is useful for many SPH children. An accompanying volume provides suggestions for programming.

There are a number of additional procedures useful in conducting an observational assessment. While often less structured than the instruments reviewed above, they nevertheless provide clinically valuable sources of data upon which educational programming decisions are solidly based.

Informal Assessment of Autistic Children (Bodenheimer, 1982). Areas assessed include behavior, socialization, communication and pre-academics. This article describes a developmentally based series of tasks which form the basis for clinical observations of the learning characteristics of autistic children functioning at the two to seven-year levels.

Developmental Activities Screening Inventory (Dubose & Langley, 1977). This instrument assesses skills in fine-motor coordination, cause-effect relationships, means-end relationships, association, number concepts, size discrimination, and sensation. A total age-level reference score is obtained. More importantly, the DASI's unique value lies in its inclusion of objective administration procedures. Use of these procedures enables the examiner to learn about the child's processing strengths and weaknesses. In addition, instructional suggestions are offered for each task.

Environmental Prelanguage Battery (Horstmeier & MacDonald, 1978a). This guide examines prerequisite language skills including functional play and motor imitation, early receptive language, verbal expression, and beginning social conversation. Approximate age bench marks are provided for each subarea. The unique feature of this instrument is that it involves a test-train-retest format which provides insights into children's learning processes particularly relevant to language training in prerequisite skills. There is an accompanying volume, *Reading, Set, Go: Talk To Me* (Horstmeier & MacDonald, 1978b) which describes activities useful for teaching each objective on the assessment protocol.

Informal Cognitive Assessment (Gill & Dihoff, 1982). The authors advocate using both standardized and nonstandardized procedures for assessing cognitive functioning. These informal procedures are based on a Piagetian model of cognitive development and address the content of the preoperational period. The areas assessed include play, drawing, haptic perception, sorting tasks, and number equivalence and seriation. The authors emphasize that the value of their approach lies not so much in determining whether or not the child solves the tasks; rather, it is important to note the processes by which the child goes about attempting task solution.

Symbolic Play Scale Checklist (Westby, 1980). The checklist is designed to analyze a child's play as it relates to stages of developmental play and linguistic development. This checklist is easy to use and valuable for integrating data about abilities across areas.

Ordinal Scales of Psychological Development (Uzgiris & Hunt, 1975). In combination with Dunst's manual (Dunst, 1980), the Ordinal Scales provide an informal assessment of cognitive skills in the sensorimotor stage.

Following completion of the interview and informal assessment, the examiner has a wealth of information regarding the SPH child's abilities. Additional data is available from standardized, direct-test measures although in the evaluation of SPH children, the findings from these instruments do not have the same significance as they do with learning disabled and mildly retarded children.

Direct-Test Assessment

It is widely recognized that the more traditional approach to psychoeducational assessment of SPH children is of limited value (Dollar & Brooks, 1982; Gill & Dihoff, 1982; Mulliken & Buckley, 1983). Limitations include a lack of measures designed for and standardized on SPH children, the existence of few measures useful with persons functioning below the two year level, and the problems inherent in attempting to adhere to standardized instructions with a population that approaches tasks in a generally nonstandard manner. It is in the light of these limitations that best practices in evaluation of SPH individuals focus on procedures described in the interview and observation sections of this chapter.

The foregoing is not intended to totally disparage the use of standardized tests. It is necessary to use these tests especially in the area of cognitive skills. This important area of assessment is the exclusive domain of the psychologist and, if approached judiciously, reveals data useful in the educational planning for SPH children. In this section the focus is on assessment of cognitive skills.

Gill and Dihoff provide a rationale for assessment of the intellectual skills of SPH children. They reason that the more that is known about a person's cognitive skills, the better the match between those cognitive skills and the tasks on which the person is trained in other areas. For example, if a person has not yet attained object permanence, tasks requiring the ability to recognize that an object is present even though out of sight would be inappropriate.

One necessary procedure in the assessment of SPH children is to administer a test of cognitive ability. This requirement follows from the need to classify individuals for administrative purposes. Unfortunately the examiner is limited by the constraints inherent in the available instruments. The tests of cognitive ability used by school psychologists are usually not within the realm of ability of most SPH children. This applies to all three Wechsler Scales and the Stanford-Binet Intelligence Scale. Despite these limitations, there are guidelines for best practices which the psychologist follows.

There are few instruments available which tap intellectual skills below the age of two. The Bayley Infant Scales (Bayley, 1969) and the Cattell Infant Intelligence Scale (Cattell, 1940) include items that are within the range of ability of most SPH children. The drawback is that both of these instruments suffer from a lack of norms for individuals older than 30 months. The Bayley, however, has the advantage of being administered in a flexible manner, thus enabling the examiner to make observations about adaptations that are relevant to classroom programming. It is recommended that when a test of intellectual ability which is appropriate in terms of the person's age and sensory and/or response limitations is not available, the psychologist administer the Bayley Scales and derive an "age equivalent score" (p. 33, Bayley, 1969). This age equivalent score is *not* translated into an IQ score but merely serves as a reference point for planning. Beyond simply reporting the age equivalent score, it is possible to regroup Bayley items using the Kent Scoring Adaptation (Reuter, Stancin &

Craig, 1981) to permit an analysis of strengths and weaknesses in intellectual skills. This procedure is analagous to the Binetgram described by Sattler (1981). By taking this approach, no one is "untestable" as is often the case if a WISC-R or Stanford-Binet is used. If the Bayley administration is accompanied by an informal assessment of cognitive skills (see the Piagetian approach of Gill & Dihoff described earlier) a comprehensive assessment of each SPH child's cognitive skills is achieved.

In support of the procedure described above, there is evidence that with the SPH population objective measures of intellectual ability such as the Bayley are predictive of both later test performance and educationally related outcomes (Baker, 1979; Dubose, 1976; DeMyer, Barton, Alpern, Kimberlin, Allen, Yang, & Steele, 1974). The results of these studies apply to children labeled multiply handicapped, autistic, and psychotic.

While many SPH children are assessed using the guidelines discussed above, there are some individuals who are evaluated using standardized measures appropriate to the child's age and abilities. The most common approach is to use a response-fair test that circumvents the child's disability. Examples of these are the Hiskey-Nebraska Test of Learning Aptitude (Hiskey, 1966) and the Leiter International Performance Scale (Leiter, 1948) for individuals who are nonverbal or who have a hearing impairment. It is recognized that with *all* nonverbal children, an assessment that addresses nonverbal intellectual ability is necessary. This is important because there are many children who have severe receptive and expressive communication impairments in the absence of a hearing-impairment, but who have normal or near-normal cognitive ability. Other response-fair tests include those that require only a pointing response or which are administered if the person indicates yes and/or no in some way such as a finger tap or eye blink. These tests include the Pictorial Test of Intelligence (French, 1964), the Columbia Mental Maturity Scale (Burgemeister, Blum, & Lorge, 1972), and the Peabody Picture Vocabulary Test-Revised (Dunn & Dunn, 1981).

There are occasions when adaptations in test materials or directions for administration are modified. In all cases of such modifications, they must be reported in detail and any interpretation of standardized scores resulting from modified administration is made in a tentative manner. A discussion of these kinds of modifications is found in Murray (1980) and Mulliken & Buckley (1983).

The procedures described above are primarily intended to enable the examiner to provide data necessary for classification. It is recognized, however, that standardized testing is supplemented by observational data.

Integrating Assessment Data

Following completion of the three processes of data collection, the examiner must integrate the assessment data using either developmental domains found on many of the developmentally based assessment tools or the curricular areas recommended by Brown et al. A concise description of the child's abilities in each domain/area provides (a) a baseline for judging progress at a later date, and (b) a basis for selecting educational goals and/or strategies for making adaptations to enable the child to engage in chronologically age-appropriate activities. It is particularly important to include information about learning processes that assists teachers in individualizing their approach to the child. The outcome of this integration of data is a comprehensive evaluation that is judged to have an acceptable level of reliability and validity.

Issues in Classroom Programming

Planning an individualized educational program for a SPH child requires skills that overlap but go beyond the skills necessary for planning educational interventions with more mildly disabled children. As with the less handicapped, practitioners must be thoroughly schooled in the techniques and principles of operant conditioning such as behavior shaping techniques, reinforcement schedules, baseline data collection procedures, and task analysis. There is a set of procedures, however, that are unique to the SPH population reviewed briefly below. A more extensive discussion for those practitioners new to the area is found in Richard Foxx's two recent books, *Decreasing Behaviors of Severely Retarded and Autistic Persons* (Foxx, 1982a) and *Increasing Behaviors of Severely Retarded and Autistic Persons* (Foxx, 1982b).

The teaching techniques unique to the SPH group follow directly from two important characteristics of SPH children mentioned earlier, that is, their problems generalizing and their difficulties learning by imitating. The difficulties encountered in generalizing benefit from use of a "zero degree inference strategy" (Brown, Neitupski, and Hamre-Nietupski, 1976). This teaching strategy requires the teacher to reassess a skill taught to a child every time it is applied to a new situation. Before generalization is said to have occurred it must be shown that the child demonstrates the behavior in response to three different persons, in three different settings, using three different sets of materials, and in response to three different language cues. Using these criteria as a guide it is important to consider varying the setting and other stimuli in planning teaching strategies.

Another set of teaching techniques follows from SPH children's difficulties in learning by imitation or observation. Many programs begin by teaching imitation skills as is often the case in language training programs for autistic children (Koegel, Rincover, and Egel, 1982). Many times skills are taught using physical guidance which involves the instructor in actually moving the child through the skill. Physical guidance is used to teach imitative skills, dressing skills, or eating skills. When physical guidance is used there must always be an attempt to fade, or gradually remove, the physical guidance. Fading occurs in teaching a child to eat with a fork when the teacher moves his/her hands down the arm from the hands over a large number of learning trials until his/her hands are merely touching the child's elbows. Later the teacher needs only physically prompt the child by touching the child's elbow in order to get the child to use the fork. Prompts may also be verbal. These kinds of techniques help to circumvent the difficulties SPH children have in learning by imitation.

One additional set of behaviors that are found almost exclusively in the SPH group include (a) self-stimulatory behaviors such as rocking, finger flipping, and hand flapping; (b) self-injurious behaviors such as head slapping, picking or scratching at sores, or head banging; (c) scavenging such as picking up and hoarding trash or specific objects such as cigarette butts; and (d) destructiveness. These and other maladaptive behaviors require procedures such as restitution which involves returning the environment or situation to its previous state; overcorrection which involves restitution followed by continued practice of appropriate behaviors; differential positive reinforcement of (a) behaviors incompatible with the undesirable behavior and (b) other behaviors. All of the above procedures involve a much greater degree of intrusion into the child's personal space. This intrusiveness follows from the SPH child's relative inability to imitate behaviors of others at a distance. These and other techniques are but a few of many special procedures that are effectively used with SPH children. Interested readers are referred to Foxx's books for a more comprehensive introduction.

SUMMARY

Working with severely and profoundly handicapped children requires an orientation that is different in emphasis from that used in working with mildly handicapped children. Rather than depending on formal, standardized testing, there is a greater dependence on data obtained from interviewing others familiar with the child and observation in settings familiar to the child. In addition psychologists choose between a functional and developmental approach or elect to integrate the two models. Both approaches are used to establish linkages with classroom curriculum, an essential step in making assessment information relevant to educational programming. The process of developing teaching strategies must take into consideration SPH children's difficulties in imitation and generalization. A thorough grounding in operant condition techniques and teaching procedures used primarily with SPH persons is necessary. The ability to effectively assess SPH children's needs and to assist in developing educational programming goals only come from working "hands-on" with these unique individuals. With the framework provided in this chapter, the practitioner is guided in beginning to become actively involved with SPH children.

REFERENCES

Alpern, G. D., Boll, T. J., & Shearer, M. S. (1980). *Developmental Profile II.* Aspen, Colorado: Psychological Development Publications.

Bagnato, S. J. & Neisworth, J. T. (1981). *Linking Developmental Assessment and Curricula.* Rockville, Maryand: Aspen Systems Corp.

Baker, A. (1979). Cognitive functioning of psychotic children: A reappraisal. *Exceptional Children, 45,* 344-348.

Balthazar, E. (1971). *BALTHAZAR Scales of Adaptive Behavior.* Champaign, Illinois: Research Press.

Bayley, N. (1969). *Manual for the Bayley Scales of Infant Development.* New York, New York: Psychological Corp.

Bodenheimer, C. (1982). Informal diagnostic assessment of autistic children. In Peter Knoblock (Ed.), *Teaching and Mainstreaming Autistic Children.* Denver, CO: Love Publishing, 1982.

Brigance, A. H. (1978). *Brigance Diagnostic Inventory of Early Development,* Worcester, MA: Curriculum Associates.

Brown, L., Branston-McClean, M. B., Bumgart, D., Vincent, L., Falvey, M. & Schroeder, J. (1979). Using the characteristics of current and subsequent least restrictive environments in the development of curricular content for severely handicapped students. *AAESPH Review, 4,* 407-424.

Brown, L., Falvey, M., Vincent, N., Johnson, F., Ferrara-Parrish, P. & Gruenewald, L. (1980). Strategies for generating comprehensive, longitudinal, and chronological-age-appropriate individualized education programs for adolescent and young adult severely handicapped students. *Journal of Special Education, 4,* 199-216.

Brown, L., Nietupski, J., & Hamre-Nietupski, S. (1976). The criterion of ultimate functioning and public school services for severely handicapped students. In M. A. Thomas (Ed.), *Hey, Don't Forget About Me: New Directions for Serving the Severely Handicapped.* Boston, MA: The Council for Exceptional Children.

Burgemeister, B. B., Blum, L. H., & Lorge, I. (1972). *Columbia Mental Maturity Scale* (3rd Ed.). New York: Harcourt, Brace & Jovanovich.

Buscaglia, L. (1983). *The Disabled and Their Parents* (revised ed.) Thorofare, NJ: Charles B. Slack, 1983.

Cain, L. F., Levine, S., Elzey, F. F. (1977). *Cain-Levine Social Competence Scale.* Palo Alto, CA: Consulting Psychologists Press.

Cattell, P. (1940). *Cattell Infant Intelligence Scale.* New York: Psychological Corp.

Darling, R. B. (1979). *Families Against Society: A Study of Reactions to Children with Birth Defects.* Beverly Hills, CA: Sage Publications, Inc.

Demeyer, M. K., Barton, S., Alpern, G. D., Kimberlin, C., Allen, J., Yang, E., & Steele, R. (1974). The measured intelligence of autistic children. *Autism and Childhood Schizophrenia, 4*(1), 42-60.

Dollar, S. J. & Brooks, C. (1982). Assessment of severely and profoundly handicapped individuals. In J. T. Neisworth (Ed.), *Assessment in Special Education,* Rockville, MD: Aspen Systems Corp.

Dubose, R. F. (1976). Predictive value of infant intelligence scales with multiply handicapped children. *American Journal of Mental Deficiency, 81,* 388-390.

Dubose, R. F., Dmitriev, V., Oelwein, P. (1980). *Developmental Sequence Performance Inventory.* Seattle, WA: Model Preschool Center for Handicapped Children, University of Washington.

Dubose, R. F., Langley, M. B. (1977). *The Developmental Activities Screening Inventory.* New York, New York: Teaching Resources.

Dunn, L. M., & Dunn, L. M. (1981). *Peabody Picture Vocabulary Test-Revised.* Circle Pines, MN: American Guidance Service.

Dunst, C. (1980). *A Clinical and Educational Manual for Use with the Uzgiris and Hunt Scales of Infant Psychological Development.* Baltimore: University Park Press.

Forcade, M. C. (1983). Procedures in the evaluation of children with low incidence handicapping conditions. In D. W. Barnett, *Nondiscriminatory Multifactored Assessment: A Sourcebook.* New York: Human Sciences Press.

Foster, R. (1974). *Camelot Behavioral Checklist.* Lawrence, Kansas: Camelot Behavioral Systems.

Foxx, R. (1982a). *Decreasing Behaviors of Severely Retarded and Autistic Persons.* Champaign, IL: Research Press.

Foxx, R. (1982b). *Increasing Behaviors of Severely Retarded and Autistic Persons.* Champaign, IL: Research Press.

French, J. L. (1964). *Pictorial Test of Intelligence.* Boston: Houghton-Mifflin.

Gill, G., & Dihoff, R. Nonverbal assessment of cognitive behavior. In B. Campbell and V. Baldwin (Eds.), *Severely Handicapped/Hearing-Impaired Students.* Baltimore: Brookes.

Grudel, K., Thompson, M. S. & Sheehan, R. (1982). Parental and professional agreement in early childhood assessment. In J. T. Neisworth (Ed.), *Assessment in Special Education,* Rockville, MD: Aspen Systems Corp.

Guess, D., Horner, R. D., Utley, B., Holvoet, J., Maxon, D., Tucker, D. & Warren, S. (1978). A functional curriculum sequencing model for teaching the severely handicapped. *AAESPH Review, 3*, 200-215.

Haring, N. & Bricker, W. (1976). Overview of comprehensive services for the severely/profoundly handicapped. In N. Haring & L. Brown (Eds.), *Teaching the severely handicapped.* Vol. I, New York: Grune & Stratton.

Hayes, S. C. & Oates, R. K. (1978). Parental and professional assessment of developmental handicaps in children. *Australian Journal of Mental Retardation, 5*(4), 135-137.

Hiskey, M. (1966). *Hiskey-Nebraska Test of Learning Aptitude.* Lincoln, NE: Union College Press.

Holvoet, J., Guess, D., Mulligan, M., Brown, F. (1980). The individualized curriculum sequencing model: A teaching strategy for severely handicapped students. *Journal of the Association for the Severely Handicapped, 5*, 337-351.

Horstmeier, D. S., & MacDonald, J. D. (1978a). *Environmental PreLanguage Battery.* Columbus, OH: Charles E. Merrill.

Horstmeier, D. S. & MacDonald, J. D. (1978b). *Ready, Set, Go: Talk To Me:* Columbus, OH: Charles E. Merrill.

MacDonald, J. D. (1978). *Oliver: Parent Administered Communication Inventory,* Columbus, OH: Charles E. Merrill.

Koegel, R. L., Rincover, A., & Egel, A. L. (1982). *Educating and Understanding Autistic Children.* San Diego, CA: College-Hill Press.

Leiter, R. G. (1948). *Leiter International Performance Scale.* Chicago, IL: Stoelting Company.

Lemay, D. W., Griffin, P. M., & Sanford, A. R. (1978). *Learning Accomplishment Profile: Diagnostic Edition* (Rev. Ed.). Winston-Salem, NC: Kaplan School Supply.

MacBeth, N. J. (1971). Early detection of apparently retarded child: Psychological and behavioral aspects. *Australian Journal of Mental Retardation, 1*(7), 224-228.

Matey, C. (1975). *Guidelines for Assessment of Low Incidence Handicapped and Multi-Impaired Children.* Dayton, OH: Miami-Valley Regional Center for Handicapped Children.

Mulliken, R., & Buckley, J. J. (1983). *Assessment of Multihandicapped and Developmentally Disabled Children.* Rockville, MD: Aspen Systems Corp.

Murray, J. (1980). *Developing Assessment Programs for the MultiHandicapped Child.* Springfield, IL: Charles C Thomas.

Reuter, B., Stancin, C., & Craig, M. (1981). *Kent Scoring Adaptation of the Bayley Scales of Infant Development.* Kent, OH: First Chance Project.

Sailor, W. & Mix, B. J. (1975). *The TARC Assessment System.* Lawrence, Kansas: H & H Enterprises, Inc.

Sanford, A. (1978). *Learning Accomplishment Profile.* Winston-Salem, NC: Kaplan School Supply.

Sattler, J. (1982). *Assessment of Children's Intelligence and Special Abilities,* 2nd Ed. Boston: Allyn and Bacon, Inc.

Schopler, E. & Reichler, R. (1976). *Psychoeducational Profile.* Chapel Hill, NC: Child Development Products.

Shearer, D. (1975). *The Portage Guide to Early Education: The Portage Project.* Portage, WI: Cooperative Educational Service Agency 12.

Song, A. & Jones, S. E. (1980). *Wisconsin Behavior Rating Scale.* madison, WI: Center for Developmentally Disabled,.

Stillman, R. D. (1974). *Collier-Azusa Scale: Assessment of Deaf-Blind Children.* Reston, VA: Council for Exceptional Children.

Switzky, H., Rotatori, A. F., Miller, T., & Freagon, S. (1979). The developmental model and its implications for assessment and instruction for the severely and profoundly handicapped. *Mental Retardation, 17*, 167-170.

Uzgiris, I. C., & Hunt, J. McV. (1975). *Assessment in Infancy: Ordinal Scales of Psychological Development.* Urban, IL: University of Illinois Press.

Valletutti, P. J. Introduction and overview. In P. J. Valletutti and B. M. Sims-Tucker, (1984). *Severely and Profoundly Handicapped Students: Their Nature and Needs.* Baltimore: Brookes.

Westby, C. E. (1980). Assessment of cognitive and language abilities through play. *Language, Speech and Hearing Services in Schools, 11*, 154-168.

Wright, B. (1983). *Physical Disability: A Psychsocial Approach,* 2nd Ed., Philadelphia, PA: Harper & Row.

ANNOTATED BIBLIOGRAPHY

Bagnato, S. J., & Neisworth, J. T. *Linking Developmental Assessment and Curricula.* Rockville, Maryland: Aspen Systems Corp., 1981. Bagnato and Neisworth advocate use of a multisource, multimeasure, multidomain approach to assessment. In a comprehensive review of developmental assessment tools that are consistent with such an approach, the authors indicate how assessment data can be related to, or linked with, curricula that are commonly used with preschool aged children. Bagnato and Neisworth provide a comprehensive discussion of the developmental approach to assessment and its relevance to educational planning.

Brown, L., Falvey, M., Vincent, N., Johnson, F., Ferrara-Parish, P., & Gruenewald, L. Strategies for generating comprehensive, longitudinal and chronological-age-appropriate individualized education programs for adolescent and young adult severely handicapped students. *Journal of Special Education*, 1980, 4, 199-216.

This article articulates the position of those advocating the functional approach to assessment in terms of both rationale and general assessment procedures. Examples are provided along with guidelines for involving parents.

Foxx, R. *Decreasing Behaviors of Severely Retarded and Autistic Persons*. Champaign, IL: Research Press, 1982.

Foxx, R. *Increasing Behaviors of Severely Retarded and Autistic Persons*. Champaign, IL: Research Press, 1982.

These companion volumes provide an easily understood explanation of the application of behavior management techniques with se-

verely and profoundly handicapped persons. Numerous examples accompany discussions of procedures along with exercises which the reader can use to test for understanding.

Mulliken, R. & Buckley, J. J. *Assessment of Multihandicapped Disabled Children*. Rockville, Maryland: Aspen Systems Corp., 1983.

This comprehensive text begins with separate chapters dealing with legal issues, the impact of the social environment on the disabled child, the roles of professionals, and the referral process. Seven chapters follow, each deals with the special problems associated with a separate domain: nonverbal behavior, cognitive skills, psychomotor skills, self-care and adaptive behavior, emotional disorders, communication skills, and educational achievement. Recommendations for communicating results and for planning interventions precede case studies illustrating the application of the approach.

Valletutti, P. J. & Sims-Tucker, B. M. *Severely and Profoundly Handicapped Students: Their Nature and Needs*. Baltimore, Maryland: Brooks, 1984.

This edited volume provides a thorough overview of the educational problems associated with five groups of children with severe and profound handicaps in the following areas: mental retardation, physical disabilities, emotional disturbance, language disorders, and sensory impairments (deaf-blind). Not only are the characteristics of each group provided, but each chapter also includes a discussion of recommended treatment approaches.

BEST PRACTICES IN COMPUTER APPLICATIONS

C. Sue McCullough
Lane Education Service District
Eugene, Oregon

OVERVIEW

In school psychology, computers are used primarily to assist the practitioner in completing daily tasks more efficiently and accurately. The focus of this chapter will be on uses of the microcomputer in the applied setting of the public schools. A brief glosssary appears at the end of the chapter.

Today, school psychologists use computers for test administration, test scoring, and test analysis. Psychological reports are prepared on computer word processors. Further, computer data management programs are employed to manage test, observation and interview data in ways that allow school psychologists better use of the information collected.

Computer utilization can be a double-edged sword for school psychologists. While computers offer welcome assistance with clerical tasks, psychologists may constrict their role by how they choose to use the computer. Thus, only computer applications that expand the role of the psychologist should be considered as best practices in computer applications. For example, therepautic interventions are possible with videodisk-computer interactive systems. Interactive interview programs collect intake data allowing psychologists to follow up with in-depth clinical interviews. Computer networks offer the possibility of improved communication and sharing of diagnostic and remedial information among school psychologists. Computer games, simulations and programming provide innovative intervention strategies to increase time on task and attention to details or to teach problem-solving and logical reasoning skills. Finally, best practice dictates that the school psychologist use some means to evaluate computer programs and their uses before purchase or implementation in daily practice.

BASIC CONSIDERATIONS

Computers, a relatively recent phenomena, emerged in the late 1970's. Schools and individuals are purchasing them in increasing numbers. Thus, there is pressure at all levels to become "computer literate."

There is considerable debate on the meaning of "computer literate." For the purposes of this chapter, "computer literate" is defined as possessing basic knowledge about (a) what computers can and cannot do, (b) how to load and run programs, and (c) what applications are possible in school psychology. The first two parts of the literacy definition are supplied in any introductory course on computers with hands-on experiences. The third part of the definition is the focus of this chapter.

Computer terminology, like psychological terminology, can be an impediment to understanding basic concepts. If words like "hardware," "software," "template," "modem," or "telecommunication networks" are foreign to the reader's vocabulary, it is suggested that the glossary at the end of the chapter be reviewed before proceeding further. Knowing basic definitions of terms should assist in understanding the descriptions of computer applications to school psychology.

Best practices in computer applications in school psychology demand high standards for professional use of computers. The professional and technical quality of any software must be of the highest level. Normative standards, statistical validity, and a solid research base must be maintained regardless of the media used to present or score the evaluation procedures. Test security must be preserved. Records stored or manipulated on the computer must be kept confidential and uses other than for required record keeping must be carefully monitored to prevent abuse and assure confidentiality and anonymity. Software that purports to interpret data must be reviewed by a panel of experts to determine it's accuracy, research justification, and applicability. School psychologists have to guard against abuse of the technology that could occur through exploitation of the hardware or software, or through using computers to preserve practices that have no rational basis other than continuation of the status quo.

Commercial software which lends itself to adaptation to the school psychologist's needs is preferred. Single function software tends to be too limiting and inflexible in areas like report writing or data management. However, other applications such as test scoring may demand single function software. However, even there, some flexibility is desired, as in scoring the test even though only selected subtests were given. Biases for adaptability, professional and technical quality, and ethical standards form the basis of the remarks that follow.

BEST PRACTICES

There are numerous ways in which computers can aid school psychologists. As an example, assume that a child has been referred for having a short attention span, poor coordination, and impulsive behavior. The child is experiencing significant difficulty with reading and math tasks, and there is some question as to the child's overall ability to perform at an average level in the school setting. Several interventions have been tried within the regular classroom, but the child continues to experience significant learning problems.

How could a computer help the school psychologist serve this child?

Assessment and Observation

First, more specific information is needed to answer the referral questions. The child is observed directly within the classroom setting. He is asked to play some computer games in which attention to task, co-ordination, and reaction time are recorded. Tasks similar to those on the computer may be tried manually for comparison. Informal or criterion-referenced reading and math tasks are presented on the computer. The computer records and statistically analyzes the child's responses while the psychologist observes the child's behavior during testing. Based on the child's performance, the computer generates randomly selected reading and math problems that are then printed for the child to try with paper and pencil. Data from the paper and pencil tasks can be entered into the computer for response analysis.

The school psychologist adds the response analyses to the clinical interview and observation data collected while working with the child. Norm-referenced tests are administered to determine overall potential, and to compare the child to the appropriate norm-referenced group. These tests are scored to obtain raw scores on subtests, then the raw scores are entered into the computer to obtain standard scores and statistical analyses. While the child was being evaluated, the parents and significant others completed an intake interview at the computer. Together with the direct observations and clinical interviews, this information provides important data for diagnostic and remedial purposes.

Report Writing

After computer analyses of the norm-referenced data are studied and compared with other information, a psychological report is prepared using a computer word processor. Depending on whether the psychologist is dictating the report for someone else to process, or typing the report directly on the word processor, the time to complete the report may be cut by 75%.

There are several report writing methods that use word processing programs. Typing on a word processing program is similar to typing on a blank piece of paper. However, the editing capabilities and computer memory make it easier to add, delete or modify the text without having to retype the entire report. Saving the report on a disk makes it possible to recall the document later and make changes or customize the report in a variety of ways. It is possible to use the word processor to create reports "from scratch" or from other text files. Examples of some of these time-saving methods follow. Note the variations in the amount of standardization or customizing that is possible with the different methods.

1. Form Text. Reports are created from routinely used blocks of text. This method is similar to filling-in-the-blanks on a form. The text is repetive, consistent, and standard for all readers and no attempt is made to individualize the information. The form text is supplemented by the addition of information related to the case.

2. Report Generators. Report generator programs produce a Form Text type of report from data entered into the computer either directly from taking tests on the computer or from raw data entered by a clerk. Typically, little or no information regarding behavioral, observational or clinical variables is considered. The report is primarily based on test data.

3. Customized Insert Standardized Text. Some word processing programs allow building a set of customized commands which can be user defined. Special markers within a standardized text format allow insertion of customized information unique to that report. For example, suppose the customized command, CC01, is defined as the "child's first name." Any time there is a reference to the student by first name, the word processing program inserts the information specified in the customized command into the specially marked place in the standard text format. It is possible to create any customized command desired or to define innumerable questions. For instance, CC05 = Primary concern expressed is ... or CC08 = Teacher reported social function is (avg./ above avg./ below avg.). Parts of the report will be repetitive, consistent and standard across all reports with unique information inserted as needed.

4. Starter Text Files. Starter text files refer to incomplete paragraphs related to a specific topic that have been stored on a computer disk and are readily retrieved for inclusion in a report. Starter text paragraphs provide a framework of frequently used blocks of text written by professionals in their own style. A data base of text files is built over time by incorporating the most frequently used phrases or topics. Commercially prepared starter text files are also available. Content of the starter text files is dependent upon the purpose of the report and the communication and organizational style of the writer. Some possible topics around which starter paragraphs can be built include identifying information, referral concerns, background information, achievement or educational recommendations.

Data Management

In addition to preparing the psychological report on the computer, the data on a child is entered into a computer data base for record keeping purposes. An IEP program that is part of the data manager is used to generate individual goals and objectives for the child. New data is entered into the computer to monitor progress in meeting these goals and objectives. The computer provides the school psychologist with daily or weekly reminders of the status of children on behavioral programs or those needing annual or three-year re-evaluations.

If the school psychologist decides to proceed with a behavioral intervention in the classroom setting, data recorders are available to assist in the data collection. Data management programs can be set up which allow effectiveness-of-intervention data to be produced. Data may be graphed at any point, reminders generated to check on specific children, and current status of any child retrieved.

The psychologist may prepare comparative graphs of the child's performance using the data entered into the program. These graphs visually show discrepancies or progress in the child's performance.

Quarterly and annual reports needed by the administration are generated from data already entered into the data manager. Some examples of the variety of ways data can be sorted include: by handicapping condition, by school, by age, by sex, by teacher, or by psychologist. Thus, all the children evaluated at a particular school by a particular psychologist are listed in alphabetical order along with any other information desired. The same data can be sorted by handicapping condition with the schools listed alphabetically and the children within the school with that handicapping condition counted. The computer produces reports formatted as needed for other statistical information.

From time to time, the school psychologist uses the computer spreadsheet to make budget projections or modifications, do statistical comparisons, or complete other tasks that require numerical manipulation.

A computer career information system is available to give guidance on career choices to secondary students. Occasionally the school psychologist checks in on a statewide or national telecommunication network to obtain information on workshops of interest, recent changes in federal legislation, and employment information, or to seek assistance in solving a special employment problem for a multiply-handicapped child.

Computer Assisted Instruction

The school psychologist is also developing knowledge of educational software, tutorials, simulations, and drill and practice programs that may be used to teach or remediate basic concepts. The psychologist evaluates the software from the perspective of the learning environment it creates and the special needs of the children who use it. A program that demands fifth-grade reading skills or uses a screen filled with closely spaced text is not appropriate for the reading disabled referral. Extraneous distractors such as noises, music, or dancing elves is inappropriate for a distractible child.

Another consideration is the research concerning the effectiveness of computer-assisted instruction over traditional teaching. In the absence of such information, the psychologist must determine the appropriateness of any intervention or remediation strategy with reference to the needs of the child and the resources of the classroom.

Specialized uses of the computer exist for low incidence handicapped children.

For instance, there are computers that read a book to a blind child, computer language boards that allow a mute child to speak, and adapted computers that enable physically disabled children to communicate, if only with a blink of their eyes. The school psychologist can obtain information about these specialized adaptations from telecommunication networks which include large data bases such as ERIC. There are also special education journals devoted to the topic.

Interventions

For the school psychologist who conducts therapeutic interventions, one promising procedure uses a videotape-computer combination. The pupil is videotaped in a particular setting, then views the tape with the psychologist and the computer. The computer stops the tape at various places and asks the child questions designed to increase the child's awareness of the relationship between his/her personal behavior and the behavior of others in the environment. If the videotape is viewed by the child alone, the computer presents a multiple-choice format to elicit responses. This same procedure has been used in counseling to help clients analyze their communication with each other.

Best practices using the computer with a child have involved using the computer as a tool to ascertain behavioral information directly, to provide accurate assessment data, to compute statistical analyses, to produce psychological reports more effectively, to graph results for pictorial presentation, to prepare an individualized educational plan, to generate quarterly or annual reports from data already stored in the data base, to give reminders, to assist in therapeutic or remedial interventions, to gather and share information via telecommunication networks, to advise on career choices via career information systems, and to manipulate numerical data for budgetary or research purposes.

Best practices with computers have preserved the non-replicable expertise of the school psychologist in analyzing, both data-based and clinically subjective information; in synthesizing the data into appropriate recommendations for interventions; and in operationalizing those recommendations. The computer can record the response but not facial, posture and hand gestures or voice inflection. The computer can produce analyses of the data, but again without the subjective observations and syntheses of data that enable meaningful decision making. Most importantly, the computer cannot replace the smiles and hugs from a child and the feelings of satisfaction when a professional job has been well done.

Evaluation

Best practices dictate that school psychologists evaluate the computer tools they propose to use. Numerous published guidelines exist to assist in this process. Computer applications are so new that the "state of the art" is reflective of the lack of standards and guidelines for software development. Therefore, caution is necessary before adopting or adapting commercial software into daily practice. Software exists that could do more harm than good to the children we serve. For instance, test analyses that have no foundation in research, recommendations that focus only on test scores excluding environmental, behavioral and personality variables, could lead to serious misdiagnosis or ineffective interventions. It is imperative that high standards be set for software used by school psychologists to encourage the development of high quality programs.

When evaluating programs, allow a few weeks time to become familiar with them. Evaluate such factors as documentation, ease of use, reliability, interpretive validity, professional utility, and technical quality. It often takes a few trials before a new user becomes comfortable with a program. In fairness to the program evaluation, some adjustment time should be allowed. Best practices would suggest that any program be used for a 30 day review period. The program should be treated very carefully during that time to avoid damage and is never copied. Vendors who will not allow a 30 day review period should not receive school psychologists' business. If a program is returned as unsatisfactory, include the evaluations to inform the producer of the reasons for the return.

Templates may be sold along with the programs. Templates are files that have been created to run on a particular piece of software. For instance, data managers and spreadsheets may have templates available to assist in organizing data on special education populations. The templates save the development time needed to establish such files so data can be immediately entered. Word processing programs may have templates available that contain typical psychological report statements. The content of these templates should be evaluated as judiciously as the original program itself.

Best Practices as a Tool

Best practices in computer applications in school psychology primarily focus on using the computer as a tool to assist in performing daily tasks more efficiently, more accurately and more effectively. When a computer is first used by the school psychologist, an adjustment time is necessary in order to become proficient in its use. Further, unless templates are purchased that have been developed by other school psychologists for specific professional uses, there needs to be allowance for development time as files are set up and evaluated. A decision will need to be made regarding which, if any, "old" files need to be entered into the data base. It is a good idea to enter some "old" files to test the newly-developed file for omissions or formatting problems, to perform a variety of "sorts" on the data and to practice transfer of the data to other programs, such as spreadsheets for numerical manipulation, word processors for inclusion in reports or graphing programs to produce pie, bar or line graphs. This "period of adjustment" is very important to the successful utilization of computers in the school psychologist's daily practice.

Using the computer as a tool is the best practice. The computer assists with test administration, test scoring and analysis, data management, manipulation and display, psychological and statistical report-writing and production, and research. For tasks that are repetitive in nature or demand storage and manipulation of large amounts of data, the computer can assist in creating a higher level of professional competence. Through telecommunication networks, communication with other professionals is facilitated. Promising practices or legislative changes can be known long before they appear in print.

Best practices also must include using the computer in innovative ways for therapeutic and remedial applications. Unique intervention strategies might include (a) using a spreadsheet program such as Visicalc to set up a classroom "bank" where good behavior would earn "deposits" and poor behavior would earn "withdrawals;" (b) using a video recorder to record a child's or group's behavior and then combining it with a computer to allow individual analysis of problem behaviors; or (c) using a computer program that compels cooperation among participants to achieve a goal, such as a stock market game or an activity called "lemonade." Computers offer limitless possibilities for unique applications if we unleash our imaginations.

Best Practices as a Tutor

Computers may also be used as a tutor. School psychologists should have an understanding of the variety of educational programs available on computers, as well as the knowledge to evaluate these programs. Before recommending use of these programs to teach or remediate learning problems, the evaluation should include examination of content, technical presentation and response demands of the program. This information needs to be evaluated in relation to the child's psychological, physical and emotional needs. Tutorials, simulations, or drill and practice programs that present information in a manner incomprehensible to the child do no better job of teaching than a teacher doing the same thing. School psychologists need to resist the temptation of thinking that a computer can teach better. If working on a computer does not solve a child's learning problems any better than other strategies, it is most likely not the fault of computer but rather indicates a need to reevaluate the validity of the diagnosis and remediation recommendations. Computers have great motivational influence with children when they are first employed. However, this advantage is lost with poor utilization such as turning the micro into an electronic workbook.

Computers offer great hope for individualization of education. Micros are infinitely patient and repeat things over and over. They provide immediate feedback. They offer a variety of response modes including spatial, sequential, audi-tory, or verbal orientations. Thus, with careful choice of programs, a variety of special needs can be met. Best practice demands that school psychologists be aware of these distinctions before making recommendations for incorporating educational software into a remediation program.

Best Practices as a Tutee

When children teach the computer rather than the computer teaching the child, a new and potentially powerful learning environment is created. This function of the computer as a tutee is represented primarily by programming tasks. The child has control of this environment within the limits of the programming language. LOGO, a programming language developed especially for children, gives immediate feedback on the child's mastery of this environment in the form of the graphics produced by the child. The implications of this function of computers for best practice in school psychology include:

1. Understanding the cognitive and emotional effects of learning to program the computer. For instance, what age is optimum to begin programming instruction? Are young children capable of learning the problem-solving and reasoning skills required?

2. Recommending the tutee function in appropriate cases where achieving control over some part of the environment and achieving success in the academic setting is an important need for the child.

3. Recommending learning to program in BASIC, LOGO, or some other language from a knowledge of the kinds of problem-solving skills provided by each language. The logic of each language is different.

4. Examining whether programming skills generate into other realms of learning. For instance, do the problem-solving strategies transfer to the social setting?

SUMMARY

One final caution is offered about the best practices applications of computers in the school psychology profession. Seymour Papert, developer of LOGO, warns of the dangers of the QWERTY phenomena, that is, preserving practices that have no rational basis beyond continuation of the status quo. The QWERTY arrangement of the keys on the typewriter keyboard dates back to a time when keys stuck — this problem no longer exists with the use of electronic impulses. Though more efficient and faster arrangement of keys exist, the QWERTY keyboard reigns. Using the computer as a tool can enhance the professional practice of school psychology. Misusing it can freeze us in our tracks. Do we want to do what we do now better, or even expand and enhance our role in the schools? Computers can help us do both, but only if we are cognizant of the dangers of defending a dead horse. For instance, computer-adapted testing looms on the horizon. Computer-generated criterion-referenced tests developed from a large data base of questions and answers in the basic skills are becoming available now. Will norm-referenced testing be necessary with such information that can be updated as often as desired? Will teachers have the skills to analyze this mass of information? Will school psychologists adapt to the change? What will we add to the process?

Computers are impacting on the schools, children, teachers, administrators and school psychologists. Computers hold the potential to make positive changes in the best practices of school psychologists. It is up to us as professionals to enter this information age enlightened and able to make judgements about how we will use computers. If we do not accept this responsibility, someone else will do it for us, and we may not like the outcome.

GLOSSARY

COMPUTER — A device that can input, store, manipulate and output data. It can automatically follow a program (a detailed step-by-step set of instructions).

DATA — Facts, recorded measurements and other information. In the computer field, the word data usually refers to information to be processed by a computer.

DATA BASE — A collection of data. Often this term refers to a computerized collection of information about people, and occurs in a discussion of privacy and security.

DATA MANAGEMENT OR PROCESSING — The processing of (raw) data to produce information and reports and/or to solve problems.

DISK — A storage device consisting of a flat circular rotating surface coated with magnetic iron oxide. It is usually used as secondary storage and looks like a phonograph record. Access time to a disk is about 25 to 100 milliseconds.

FILE — A collection of related records treated as a unit. For example, detailed information about one student might constitute a record, and all records for one school might constitute a file.

HARDWARE — The physical machinery of a computer system. It includes the central processing unit (CPU), primary storage, secondary storage, input devices and output devices.

MEMORY — A computer's storage device(s). Most computers have a primary memory with very fast access which is relatively small, and secondary storage which can contain a large number of characters of information, but has slower access time.

MODEM — A modulator-demodulator device that transmits electrical impulses over telephone lines allowing transmission of data from one computer to another.

PERIPHERAL EQUIPMENT — A computer system consists of a main central processing unit (CPU) and peripheral equipment. Peripherals include secondary storage, card reader, line printer and other input/output devices.

PROGRAM — A detailed step-by-step set of directions telling a computer how to perform a procedure. It may be written in a wide variety of computer languages.

SECONDARY STORAGE — The relatively slow access part of a computer's memory system. It may consist of magnetic disks, magnetic tape devices, bubble memory, and/or charge-coupled devices.

SOFTWARE — Computer programs.

SPREADSHEET — A program designed to manipulate numerical data, such as budget forecasts, statistical analysis or accounting records.

TELECOMMUNICATION NETWORKS — Utilizing telephone lines and modems, provides a large variety of information services to subscribers, including electronic mail, special interest bulletin boards, up-to-the-minute information on stocks, research, government announcements, etc.

TEMPLATE — Blank forms or files that have been created to run on a particular piece of software, ready to begin accepting data entry. For example, there are home budget management templates for spreadsheets or IEP templates for data management software.

TERMINAL OR MONITOR — An input or output device, a display mechanism.

TIMESHARING — A method of computer usage, or type of computer system where many people use the computer at the same time. The computer system shares its resources among its users through different terminals.

WORD PROCESSING — The use of computers to help automate a typewriter. Materials are typed and stored in a computer memory where they can be changed. Final copy is then typed out very quickly by the computer.

ANNOTATED BIBLIOGRAPHY

Computer and Technological Applications in School Psychology (CTASP) Newsletter, National Association of School Psychologists, Alex Thomas, Editor, 4107 Barclay, Port Clinton, Ohio.
Published quarterly; free to NASP members, $10 annually for non-members. CTASP Newsletter contains articles of interest to computer-using school psychologists, software reviews, and information exchanges.

International Council for Computers in Education, *Computing Teacher* Journal, University of Oregon, Eugene, Oregon, 97402.
Publishes 9 times annually, the *Computing Teacher* emphasizes the instructional use of computers, including teaching about computers, using computers, teacher education and the impact of computers on curriculum. Special Education Special Interest Group publishes newsletter.

International Council for Computers in Education, (ICCE) booklets: Metzger, Merrianne, Ouellette, David, and Thormann, Joan, *Learning Disabled Students and Computers: A Teacher's Guidebook*, 1983.
Excellent discussion of concerns and adaptations of computers for learning disabled students.

Microsift, Northwest Regional Laboratory, *Evaluator's Guide for Microcomputer-Based Instructional Packages*, 1982.
Excellent guidelines for evaluating instructional software.

Harper and Stewart, *Run: Computer Education*, Brooks Cole Publishers, Monterey, CA, 1983.
This is an edited collection of articles on a variety of topics relevant to computers in education. While some of the articles are dated because of the many changes in the computer field, many of them are classics that deserve repetition. The quality of the articles varies greatly.

Montana Department of Education, *Computers in the Schools*, Helena, Montana, 1983.
An excellent guide to incorporating microcomputers into the schools with many practical suggestions, evaluation forms, questions to answer, guidelines, etc.

Papert, Seymour. *Mindstorms, Children, Computers and Powerful Ideas*. Basic Books, Inc., Harper, 1980.
A book with revolutionary ideas for educating children using microcomputers. Papert presents a philosophy for computer applications, something missing in most applications articles. His ideas have implications for school psychologists in raising questions about assessing children's learning through products or through observing the learning process with computer applications.

Schwartz, Marc D. *Using Computers in Clinical Practice, Psychotherapy and Mental Health Applications*, The Haworth Press, 1984.
A collection of articles on a variety of applications in psychological practice including computerized assessment, intake interviews, diagnosis, data management, and therapy adjunct, such as social skill development or sexual dysfunction training.

BEST PRACTICES IN INTERVIEWING

James P. Murphy
Rider College

OVERVIEW

The psychologist arrives in the school building and sees Ms. Burke who talks excitedly about one of her students. The psychologist listens carefully for a few minutes, clarifies the concern, communicates support, and makes an appointment to discuss the situation further. Next, the psychologist attends a regularly scheduled meeting with the building principal and guidance counselor which involves consulting, planning, and listening to their concerns. Following this, a psychological evaluation is conducted with a child which includes a structured interview schedule. In the afternoon a parent conference is held to discuss assessment results and intervention strategies for a student who was recently evaluated. Subsequent to this conference, the psychologist attends a child study team meeting at which concerns about several students are shared by various professionals. The psychologist clarifies, probes, provides support and asks questions which help define problems and areas of responsibility. Following a brief counseling session with a student, the psychologist makes several phone calls to outside agencies to acquire information about clients and hurries to meet with a parent who has requested a conference to discuss concerns about her daughter.

Although the description of a fairly typical day for many school psychologists may be slightly exaggerated, practicing school psychologists do indeed become involved in each of the above activities, all of which require different types of interviewing skills.

The effective practice of school psychology in the 1980's involves a great deal of interviewing. In earlier times, the major thrust of service delivery has been testing large numbers of students and arranging special education placements. Today psychologists have an expanded role which requires effective communication skills in several different settings. The psychometrist administered the tests, and if any interviewing was done, it was usually conducted by the school principal. With the enormous demand for psychological services in the 1960's, school psychology students usually received minimal training and supervised experience in the process of interviewing. As the profession of school psychology evolved, it became more and more important for psychologists to conduct interviews as part of the assessment/intervention process and in the dissemination of information to various persons involved in a child's life. Recently, graduate programs have included the acquisition and enhancement of interviewing skills among the competencies necessary for the provision of school psychological services.

Interviewing in various forms and with various purposes has become so much a part of the daily routine of most school psychologists that little attention is paid to what takes place during the interview process. As a result, there is a tendency to become less rigorous in preparation for and sensitivity to issues which arise during this type of communication. The purpose of this chapter is a review of the basic structure of interviewing as it is applied in various settings as well as consideration of general principles of effective interviewing. Strategies specific to different types of interviews are presented as are interviewer behaviors which facilitate desirable outcomes. Procedures and conditions which reduce the effectiveness of the interview are also discussed. The overall goal of the chapter is to provide easily accessible information for practitioners to review and use in their daily activities. "Best practices" in interviewing involve the integration of knowledge of effective communication with the genuine personal style of the interviewer, and include the selection of appropriate techniques for each situation encountered.

BASIC CONSIDERATIONS

Various definitions of an interview have appeared in the social sciences literature. Bingham and Moore (1941) describe an interview as a serious conversation which is directed to a specific purpose other than satisfaction in the conversation. Kahn and Cannell (1961) state that an interview is an interactional process and both the interviewer and the respondent contribute to the communication of results. According to Fenlason, Ferguson, and Abrahamson (1962), an interview is viewed as a verbal and nonverbal interaction with more than one person working toward a common goal. In general, an interview has been conceptualized as being different from a conversation in that it usually involves more interaction surrounding a rather narrow topic in the respondent's experience. It is viewed as being goal oriented with specific roles and responsibilities incumbent upon the interviewer and the respondent. Since it is different from a conversation, specific means of attaining various goals have been developed. Richardson, Dohrenwend, and Klein (1965) delineate two broad categories of interviewing: standardized or structured and nonstandardized. Both are used in the practice of school psychology. The standardized interview is used when the same information is collected from more than one respondent. This can be

accomplished by using a schedule in which the sequencing and wording of the questions are held constant from respondent to respondent. Examples of this include the *Stanford Binet Intelligence Scale* (1972) and the *Wechsler Intelligence Scale for Children-Revised* (1974). A standardized interview can be conducted using a nonschedule approach in which the interviewer is well prepared in terms of what information needs to be obtained, but has the flexibility to vary the wording and sequence of the questions as conditions dictate. The *Vineland Social Maturity Scale* (Doll, 1965), the *Preschool Attainment Record* (Doll, 1966), and the *ABIC* (1978) are examples of nonschedule standardized interviews. A third type of interview, the nonstandardized interview does not specify in advance all items of information desired. It is most useful in situations where the psychologist is not aware of all relevant forces impinging upon the respondent. In practice, these three types of interviewing are often combined and employed at various times during comprehensive parent or teacher interviews.

School psychologists interview parents, teachers, children and adolescents, persons from agencies outside the school who work with their clients, and administrators. Interviewing has become a necessary and desirable procedure for several purposes. A prime reason for conducting interviews is to obtain relevant and accurate information from the respondent. Examples include taking developmental histories from parents, obtaining educational histories of students from parents and school administrators, and interviewing agency personnel regarding treatment histories. A second valuable purpose for interviewing is clarification of concerns of consultees and clients. Interviewing with parents and teachers who have referred a student are partially geared toward obtaining an operational definition of their conception of the problem. A third purpose of interviewing is to assist the psychologist in the collection of data as part of the diagnostic process. The necessity of sharing information with clients and consultees represents still another purpose for interviews. The above represent somewhat artificial distinctions and quite often interviews serve more than one purpose. For example, diagnostic information concerning the respondent's feelings is obtained during the taking of histories. Also, when providing information to clients, the problem identification is usually refined and clarified as the information is shared by the psychologist. However, the primary purpose of the interview dictates which constellation of interviewer behaviors are most appropriate.

BEST PRACTICES

A discussion of the most effective practices in interviewing would be superficial in nature and not particularly helpful to the practitioner if its scope were limited to a list of "do's" and "don'ts."

Just as a comprehensive psychoeducational evaluation involves more than the administration of tests, a successful interview involves more than the collection of information through questioning. Psychologists must integrate their knowledge of personality, motivation, mental health, and learning with an understanding of the interview process. Best practices, thus, involve an application of the knowledge, attitudes, abilities, and specific skills which result in increasing the probability of desirable outcomes from various types of interviews.

In the following section, conditions which lead to effective interviews are reviewed along with interviewer attitudes and abilities which have been found to lead to desirable respondent participation. Finally, specific interviewing skills which can be applied depending upon the goals of a particular interview are discussed.

Criteria for an Effective Interview

Richardson, Dohrenwend, and Klein (1965) suggest several criteria which must be met for an effective interview to take place. One criterion is the presence of a satisfactory level of participation by the respondent. According to Kahn and Cannell (1961), respondents communicate if they believe that it results in a change or action that is desirable to them. Respondents are motivated to participate when they receive gratification from the interaction and the relationship.

A second criterion for an effective interview is the validity of the obtained response. This is evaluated through external validity checks, the evaluation of the internal consistency of the responses, and the assessment of the style and manner of the responses. The communication of certain attitudes through appropriate interviewer behaviors greatly increases the validity of the responses.

Other criteria necessary for effective interviewing include the collection of relevant data which are both task specific and sufficiently clear to minimize interpretation. Finally, the full range of subject matter should be covered.

Inhibiting factors. Gorden (1969), Garrett (1942), and Kahn and Cannell (1961) discuss factors which inhibit effective interviewing. Low respondent motivation, difficulties with memory, and the psychological inability to produce information all tend to reduce the validity of the interview. Inadequate responses due to lack of understanding of the questions, insufficient rapport, or a belief on the part of the respondent that the question goes beyond the limits of the interview may also inhibit communication. If the respondents perceive that they are being questioned in a patronizing or condescending fashion, the response level is not appropriate and one of the main conditions of an effective interview is lost. Other inhibitors of communication include competing demands for the respondent's time and a tendency for certain clients to give socially desirable responses.

· *Facilitating factors.* The following section describes factors which facilitate the interviewing process. The interview is usually initiated by the interviewer, but even when it is client initiated, it is the task of the interviewer to communicate a general expectation of cooperation. This is accomplished both verbally by asking for cooperation and nonverbally by communicating that cooperation is expected through nonverbal cues. The use of praise and sympathetic understanding increases the level of respondent participation. The strong verbal and nonverbal expression of interest in the respondent along with an honest and upfront as opposed to a clever and manipulative interviewing approach also facilitates valid responses.

The interview strategy developed prior to the actual interview, if planned properly, greatly facilitates effective communication. Strategy includes the choice of a time, place and structure for the interview on the basis of the probable effect upon the client's comfort level. Interviewers must decide how to present themselves in such a manner as to maintain authenticity while maximizing the respondent's willingness to participate.

Interviewing techniques include specific forms of verbal and nonverbal behavior used during the interview. The timing of questions, the maintenance of a nonjudgmental attitude, and the avoidance of shock, surprise or disgust increase the validity of the interview. The avoidance of impertinence or taking the role of a teacher or advisor also facilitate meaningful communication and afford respondents the opportunity to qualify their responses. The use of language appropriate to the cultural and intellectual level of the respondent and the ability to confine the information to a few pertinent ideas in-

crease the comfort level of the respondent.

Interviewer Attitudes Which Lead to Effective Interviews

In analyzing attitudes and skills in preparing to interview, it is important to be cognizant that constructive, lasting results ordinarily come from satisfying and successful experiences. The interviewer must be able to create, as Kahn and Cannell (1961) state, "The psychological climate in which free communication thrives" (p. 79). The school psychologist must possess an attitude of acceptance, have positive regard for the respondent, and be nonjudgmental concerning the material presented by the respondent (Garrett, 1942; Fenlason, Ferguson, & Abrahamson, 1962).

Empathy, the ability to see the world through the eyes of the respondent while maintaining professional objectivity, is particularly important in interviewing. In addition to these attitudes, the degree of interviewer empathy depends upon several additional factors as described by Gorden (1969). The degree to which the interviewer's knowledge of the respondent is complete and accurate affects the interviewer's ability to be empathetic. In addition, the extent to which interviewers have experienced the same situation or the degree to which they are able to imaginatively construct such a situation from various elements of several similar situations also affects the ability to empathize.

Skills and Abilities Which Facilitate Effective Interviews

The above attitudes are necessary to successfully perform the tasks required of the interviewer in a successful interview. The skills and abilities described below are very important in communicating the desirable attitudes. The successful interviewer must be able to withstand stress, possess extensive knowledge of the subject matter, and be capable of flexibility in the formulation of questions.

Interviewers must have self-awareness in terms of how they are perceived as a listener. Essential interviewing skills include effective listening and observation. According to Gorden (1969), interviewers must accurately receive verbal and nonverbal communication. Receiving information, hearing and observing accurately, and remembering what is said are fundamental to the interviewing process. While this may seem to be relatively easy, interviewers should be careful that their level of fatigue and anxiety do not interfere with the accurate reception of information. In addition, the expectations of the interviewer should not distort the accurate reception of the information. The interviewer should be able to detect and correct misunderstandings of questions by the respondent as well as recognize resistance. The interviewer should also be able to discern mixed messages and other incongruities between the verbal and nonverbal communication. There is a high level of concentration, active participation, comprehension, and objectivity in the effective use of listening skills by the interviewer, according to Fenlason et al. (1962). The use of reflective and active listening as well as perception checking enable the interviewers to communicate both their interest and the accuracy of their listening.

In addition to listening and observing, effective interviewers are able to critically evaluate information. They are constantly aware of the quality and quantity of the responses as well as the degree of respondent cooperation. Visual and auditory nonverbal communication is analyzed and compared with verbal content. It is incumbent upon the interviewer to distinguish among the irrelevant, potentially irrelevant, and the clearly relevant information presented by the respondent. In addition, the interviewer must be aware of factors which might inhibit the respondent and result in an inappropriate level of respondent participation. Interviewers interpret the material for themselves but do not pass the interpretation along to the client. It is also important to remember that dealing with the emotional needs of clients take priority over the collection of facts especially when it is obvious that their ability to process information is impaired because of their emotional needs.

A third set of skills and abilities enable the interviewers to regulate their nonverbal behavior. These include the appropriate use of questioning, probing, and other modes of verbal and nonverbal expression. These are discussed in the following sections.

Interviewer self-awareness. In order to meet the criteria for an effective interview described in the previous section, interviewers must remember to maintain a level of self-awareness prior to the session. Using principles of communication described by Rogers (1958) and Gordon (1970), interviewers may initially conduct a self-assessment to increase their awareness of how they are viewed by the client. The self-assessment includes an awareness of the immediately visible characteristics, professional characteristics such as degrees, previous experience, and personal characteristics. Although the interviewer remains genuine throughout, certain characteristics may or may not be shown to the respondent until the relationship has been established. The interviewer must also select the appropriate type of interview based on the characteristics of the respondent. In addition, the interviewer should have extensive knowledge of the subject matter and a clear understanding of the purpose of the interview (Richardson et al., 1965).

Skills in interview management. It is desirable for the interviewer to accurately communicate questions to the respondent while maintaining sufficient rapport to maintain the respondent's ability to answer the questions. To do this, according to Richardson et al. (1965) and Garrett (1942), the interviewers prepare the physical setting so that they are able to provide undivided attention and record the information accurately and in a non-threatening manner. In addition, it is essential that the interviewers make determinations about what is relevant and use probes to maximize the clarity, validity and completeness of the responses. Kahn and Cannell (1961) suggest that an important task of the interviewers is to control the session to bring about a small stream of communication consisting almost entirely of items relevant to the purpose of the interview. Thus, interviewers must maximize the forces to increase communication and direct and control the interview toward specific objectives.

Questioning techniques. After deciding upon the general strategy of the interview and tending to the tasks dealing with self-awareness, interviewers must pose questions in a fashion that facilitates the goals of the interview. There are many questioning techniques from which to choose. Questions can be open-ended or closed, leading, encouraging, or confronting. Gorden (1969) describes two types of questioning: the funnel sequence and the inverted funnel sequence. In interviews designed to obtain a detailed description of a situation, the funnel sequence is most appropriate. In this sequence, the questioning flows from general, open-ended questions to specific, closed questions (see Figure 1). The advantages of this technique are that the respondents follow their own line of thinking and add information as it comes to them. In addition, interviewers avoid imposing their frame of reference on the client. When the respondent is not motivated to speak spontaneously, the inverted funnel sequence is

more appropriate. In this technique concrete examples are initially elicited, with generalization of information occurring later in the interview (see Figure 2).

Figure 1.
Illustration of a funnel sequence

1. Please tell me your concerns about your child.

2. Which of these concerns do you believe to be the most important?

3. Tell me more about this concern.

Figure 2.
Illustration of inverted funnel sequence

1. Tell me about the specific incidents that led you to refer this child.

2. What do you think these incidents reflect in the child's current functioning?

3. How would you describe the child's overall functioning?

The use of questions as followups to earlier questions is desirable and proceeds in different ways. The antecedents of a question lie in the *immediately preceding question* or in any *earlier question* posed by the interviewer. This technique is designed to increase interviewer control of the session and the questions are intended to elicit additional information. A drawback of this method is that the interview often proceeds in a fragmented, disjointed fashion.

Two other areas from which antecedents of questions are derived include the *immediately preceding response* and the *earlier response*. These are called response antecedents and are extremely valuable techniques in interviews. These questions enhance the feeling of active participation on the part of the respondent. Such methods as the use of feelings, reflections, summary statements, and confronting questions are designed to have the respondent clarify earlier responses. The use of respondent antecedents are also often an effective way of moving from one line of questioning to another.

Leading questions are avoided because they produce distorted responses from parents, teachers, and especially from children.

Probes and topic control. The key in probing during interviews is in using the right probe at the right time. Gorden (1969) and Kahn and Cannell (1961) discuss several important aspects of probing. The use of probes is tied into the amount of topic control sought by the interviewer. For example, the least directive probe is the silent probe followed by the use of an encouraging phrase or nonverbal cue. A controlled, nondirective probe used to stimulate more communication from the respondent reflects slightly more topic control. A probe requesting immediate elaboration such as "tell me more" adds additional control while with the immediate clarification probe the interviewer tells the respondent exactly what type of information is sought. Probing is useful when a partial response has been obtained, when an inaccurate response has been given, when either no response or an irrelevant response has been elicited, or when the respondent has verbalized a problem in responding.

Issues Specific to
Various Types of Interviews

The following section deals with different types of interviews commonly conducted by school psychologists. While all of the factors mentioned previously apply, each situation described below has slightly different demand characteristics.

Initial interviews — psychologist initiated. This type of interview requires first and foremost, the establishment of a positive working relationship. A clear, concise statement which communicates the rationale for the interview, coupled with verbal and nonverbal cues indicating interest and a desire to provide service, are crucial elements in this type of interview. The time and place are, as much as possible, at the respondent's convenience and the relevant information is collected with efficiency and tact. Finally, the psychologist must determine the perception of the problem by the interviewee. In this type of interview, the use of appropriate questioning and probing skills, in addition to the initial presentation of the interviewer as a caring person, are the major skills and abilities necessary for success.

Initial interview — parent/teacher initiated. A slightly different emphasis is desirable when someone requests an interview with the psychologist. In this type of interview, it is most desirable and appropriate to use empathic listening skills. The use of listening skills allows the client to state and elaborate his or her concerns in a nonjudgmental atmosphere of acceptance and interest.

The extensive use of listening skills in client-initiated interviews better enables the interviewer to determine both the content of the client concerns and any underlying or hidden agenda. Listening empathically also allows clients to determine their comfort level in terms of self-disclosure. Appropriate use of clarifying questions, summary statements, and perception checking are also emphasized. Finally, a realistic determination by the psychologist as to the degree he/she is able to be of service occurs. The psychologist then communicates this to the client to ensure mutually agreeable expectations.

Post-assessment interviews. Interviews with parents and teachers following the psychoeducational evaluation of a student are often difficult and complex. These interviews involve the presentation of information to persons who probably do not possess a great deal of training in psychology and, furthermore, who have an emotional investment in the student. This is particularly true when the parent is the respondent. It is not uncommon for a parent to enter this type of interview with anxiety and discomfort over not only what is said to them about their child, but also over the potential reactions of the spouse and other family members. Parents often find themselves in the position of trying to understand cognitively the content of the information while attempting to deal with their emotional reaction to what is being said to them.

A prime consideration in this type of interview, and one that is often overlooked by psychologists, is the need to determine how much information can be processed by the client in one session with a minimum amount of distortion. Practitioners have been encouraged to inform the client in great detail of the factors which underlie specific recommendations about their children. In addition, education is currently in a period of full disclosure of, student data to parents. This trend, while helping to correct some past abuses, has often resulted in too much irrelevant information being exchanged during post-assessment interviews. This may leave parents overwhelmed, confused, and not necessarily better informed.

In order to deal effectively with this problem, psychologists should plan these interviews with great care. It is extremely important to convey information in concise, clear, understandable fashion at a level of complexity which is appropriate to the client. In addition to the sharing of information, it is equally important for psychologists to maximize their understanding of how the client is perceiving the content and also of how they are reacting emotionally to what they are hearing. Appropriate use of observation skills, perception checking, and reflective listening better insure effective communication and result in less distortion of information by the client.

SUMMARY

School psychologists are currently engaging in interviewing as part of their day-to-day provision of psychological services. Interviewing has become a vital tool for the definition of problems, collection of important data, dissemination of information, and motivation of clients and colleagues. The communication of empathy, acceptance and caring are crucial elements in the effective use of interviewing. Valid information can be obtained provided that the interviewer establishes sufficient rapport, uses appropriate forms of questions and probes, and avoids a patronizing or condescending tone.

Interviews should not be conducted in a perfunctory manner lest the psychologist lose credibility as a person who is interested in helping the client. Preparation for interviews include a self-assessment on the part of the interviewer in which biases, objectives, manner of presentation, and skills and techniques are reviewed. During the interview, the psychologist must maintain concentration and listen attentively to the client's content and feelings messages and avoid overloading the client with too much information or using confusing or anxiety raising language.

REFERENCES

Bingham, W. & Moore, V. (1941). *How to interview.* New York: Harper & Row.

Doll, E. (1966). *Preschool Attainment Record (PAR).* Circle Pines, MN: American Guidance Service.

Doll, E. (1965). *Vineland Social Maturity Scale.* Circle Pines, MN: American Guidance Service.

Fenlason, A., Ferguson, G., & Abrahamson, A. (1962). *Essentials in interviewing.* New York: Harper & Row.

Garrett, A. (1942). *Interviewing: Its principles and methods.* New York: Family Service Association of America.

Gorden, R. L. (1969). *Interviewing: Strategy, techniques and tactics.* Hollywood, IL: Dorsey Press.

Gordon, T. (1970). *Parent effectiveness training.* New York: Wyden Press.

Kahn, R. & Cannell, C. (1961). *The dynamics of interviewing.* New York: John Wiley & Sons.

Mercer, J. & Lewis, J. (1978). *Adaptive Behavior in Children (ABIC).* System of multicultural pluralistic assessment (SOMA). New York: The Psychological Corporation.

Richardson, S., Dohrenwend, B., & Klein, D. (1965). *Interviewing: Its forms and functions.* New York: Basic Books.

Rogers, C. (1958). The characteristics of a helping relationship. *Personnel & Guidance Journal, 37,* 6-16.

Terman, L. & Merrill, M. (1972). *Stanford-Binet Intelligence Scale.* Boston: Houghton Mifflin.

Wechsler, D. (1974). *Manual for the Wechsler Intelligence Scale for Children-Revised.* New York: Psychological Corporation.

ANNOTATED BIBLIOGRAPHY

Fenlason, Ann, Ferguson, Grace, and Abrahamson, Arthur. (1962). *Essentials in interviewing.* New York: Harper & Row.
Written in a clear style with many examples and entire interviews, this work would serve as a good review of the principles and practices of effective interviewing. Particularly useful are the sections which demonstrate how one's basic knowledge of human behavior can be applied in the interview process.

Garrett, Annette (1942). *Interviewing: Its principles and methods.* New York: Family Service Association of America.
With economy of words, the author presents basic mental health principles along with a review of the need for empathy and self-awareness. In addition to the principles of Rogerian therapy, very practical considerations as well as specific examples of effective practices are described. Rereading this work, especially during the times when one is quite busy, may serve to put the school psychologist's role back in perspective.

Gorden, Raymond L. (1969). *Interviewing: Strategy, techniques, and tactics.* Hollywood, IL: Dorsey Press.
This work deals primarily with the technical aspects of interviewing. Strategies to increase reliability and validity are discussed. Tactics, techniques, and specific interviewer skills are emphasized. This reference would serve as a good comparison to one which deals with the philosophical aspects of interviewing.

Kahn, Robert, and Cannell, Charles (1961). *The dynamics of interviewing.* New York: John Wiley and Sons.
The theories, principles and techniques presented in this work were heavily influenced by Rogerian theory and Lewin's field theory. The communication process in general is discussed, along with the psychological bases for interviewing. A section of the book is devoted to transcripts of interviews with comments from the authors.

Richardson, Stephen, Dohrenwend, Barbara, and Klein, David (1965). *Interviewing: Its forms and functions.* New York: Basic Books.
This book deals primarily with the actual interview process. Consideration is given to the question and answer process, factors which increase the participation of the client, and the content of questions. It could be most helpful to practitioners who want to critique their interviews in terms of their technical soundness.

BEST PRACTICES IN WORKING WITH FAMILIES OF HANDICAPPED CHILDREN

Joseph N. Murray
Kent State University

OVERVIEW

Historically, school psychologists were perceived by themselves and others as psychometrically oriented diagnosticians, who were directed more toward assessing and remediating individuals while minimizing the importance of external factors impinging upon those individuals' lives. Within the last decade, school psychologists assumed more responsibility for the welfare of handicapped children. Public law 94-142, the Education For All Handicapped Children Act, and consequent state legislation caused school psychologists to work with a broader spectrum of handicapped children. With greatly increased public awareness resulting from this legislation, parents became sensitive to children's rights and aware of the available services and programs. Indeed, more services and programs came into being because of federal funding. Concurrent with this series of events, there was a movement away from normative, individualized testing. It was felt that testing was restrictive and described children as statistical entities rather than human beings. Today it is recognized that school psychologists look at more than the child when assessing and programming. They must be mindful of the child's immediate environment, his family, and the more distant environment, the community, if they are to be effective change agents for the child and family.

The purpose of this chapter is to focus on the family, and to provide suggestions which will help school psychologists who work with families of handicapped children. The theme suggests that, as professionals, we all too often focus on the observable, behavioral aspects of a disability while ignoring or minimizing the residual or secondary effects of a handicapped child on a family. As Hayden (1974) writes, "all the members of my family are disabled. But most people recognize only the disability of my deaf sister." School psychologists need to assess and program with respect to the entire family, not just the handicapped child within the family.

BASIC CONSIDERATIONS

School psychologists working with families having handicapped children should be sensitized to numerous factors which are either less existent or nonexistent in families not having handicapped children. Awareness of the following concepts and their implications are of critical importance when moving through the diagnostic-remedial continuum.

Cultural values and the handicapped. Persons handicapped by physical, mental or behavioral differences often fail to meet society's standards. Conformity in America is valued, deviance abhorred; perfection is prized, defect rejected; independence is valued and equated with maturity; competition is held in high esteem. Self-perception of handicapped children and their parents' perceptions of themselves and their children are often distorted by the child's inability to measure up to cultural standards. School psychologists work with children and families who often hold negative perceptions of themselves or others.

Psychological aspects of parents having handicapped children. While we cannot assume that the presence of a handicapped youngster within a family creates a consistent psychosocial profile, it appears that some commonalities exist among these families. Friedrich and Friedrich (1981) reported that these families experience more stress and less marital satisfaction, show less psychological well being and more need for support, and are slightly less religious than families without a handicapped child. An awareness of these psychosocial factors causes professionals to approach handicapped children and their families from a different perspective.

Intra-family dynamics. An important consideration in working with families is to determine as much as possible about how the family members react to the handicapped child and how their relationships to one another are affected. An awareness of mothers', fathers' and siblings' feelings and reactions plus those of other family members often have a direct bearing on the types of strategies which are successful. Consequently, assessment strategies should include ways to gain this information.

Intensity. Fueled by possible guilt, sorrow, anger and often frustration, parents of a handicapped child demonstrate much greater emotional intensity than parents of the nonhandicapped. The emotional manifestations run from apathy to various types of behavioral reactions. Consideration, sensitivity, and allowance for emotionality are important. Rationality and maturity are key words for psychologists working with such families.

BEST PRACTICES

Best practices in working with handicapped children and their parents insure that sufficient information from the child, family and community is available to effectively improve the lives of all concerned. The focus of the rest of the chapter is on ideas which facilitate the acquisition of information to help the psychologist understand handicapped children and their families.

Components of Effective Family Intervention

School psychologists develop assessment models which insure that two major things occur: (a) The model is comprehensive enough to gain individual information about the child while integrating this information with assessment data from the family; (b) Additionally, the diagnostic information leads to appropriate prescriptive programming and is eductionally as well as life-related.

A good assessment model has numerous components, each of which is not necessarily used in every assessment situation. While each of the assessment factors is gathered, the school psychologist interprets data as they relate to both the child and the family as it pertains to education and life itself. To facilitate this, psychologists break assessment and remediation into domains such as self help, personal-social, cognitive, academic, motor, and language. The following assessment components typify best practices by a school psychologist working with handicapped children and their families.

Screening. A screening checklist is used to give the psychologist an overall view of the child and his family and to provide further direction to the assessment process. A good screening checklist includes the following sections with numerous items under each (Murray, 1980): Visual, Auditory, Speech, Language, Listening, Behavioral Factors, Psycho-Motor, and Social-Emotional.

Parent interview. The importance of this assessment component is often minimized. A good parent interview gathers information about the child's problem as perceived by the parents. Ideally both parents are interviewed. The interviewer concludes the interview with information about the medical/developmental history of the child, an awareness of the child's daily and weekly schedules, and the child's strengths and weaknesses across all domains.

Medical assessment. Handicapped children often have multiple medical problems which are related to learning or behavior problems. The medical problem may not be related to the primary handicapping condition and, as such, may be overlooked. As an example, a physician may discover a severe respiratory infection in a moderately retarded child which, if corrected, will solve numerous problems. Unfortunately, many school systems do not employ medical consultants. Consequently, the medical component of the assessment model is often weak. In the absence of physicians, nurses serve as medical consultants.

Testing. Both normative and non-normative testing are used with handicapped children. Normative testing often gives perspective to the relative deficiency of the child's performance, and also allows psychologists to note gains or regressions over time. Unfortunately, with certain handicapping conditions such as some cerebral palsy cases, normative testing isn't effective. Children are penalized in testing by their impairment and the results are not valid. Non-normative or criterion-reference tests allow the psychologist to assess how children adapt to their everyday environment. Non-normative testing often involves family members and resulting data are used to design individual prescriptive plans for the handicapped child. For example, multiple domain scales are responded to by parents, ceilings in each domain are determined, and specific deficits at the ceiling and beyond are established as behav-

ioral goals. Ideally, parents and school personnel work cooperatively to insure that these goals are met.

Screening, parent interview, cumulative data, observation, medical assessment and testing all represent vehicles for obtaining information. School psychologists, however, also need sensitivity to the feelings of family members and how these feelings cause them to behave differently. The next section of this chapter is devoted to discussing how the presence of a handicapped child affects mothers, fathers, and siblings. An awareness of these concepts is an important component of effective assessment and programming.

The Family:
Mother, Father and Siblings

The reader is advised that the following concepts and tendencies are not applicable to all parents. However, there are commonalities of behavior among mothers, fathers, and siblings and the psychologist needs to be sensitive to them.

Mother

Mothers have similarities in their reaction to a handicapped child including feelings of loss and intense longings for the desired child. Failure to produce the desired child gives rise to feelings of guilt and inadequacy. One mother described her reactions by saying that she sometimes thought of herself not as a person with her own feelings and hopes, but as a robot — "the caretaker." She had become separated from her real self. It took time after the birth of her handicapped child to get back to herself. "I now realize —with some sadness and I'll admit a sense of loss — what could have been and hasn't been — that I've been pulled away from my real self" (Murphy, 1981). This mother goes on to say that she still has twinges of guilt when she acts as the 'creator' of her own behavior to the exclusion of attending to the needs of her handicapped child. Whether these feelings of guilt and inadequacy are socially induced or are in some way related to bonding does not matter as one attempts to understand and work with mothers of handicapped youngsters.

In addition to feelings of guilt and inadequacy, the probability of greatly exaggerated intensity across all emotions exists in these mothers. This heightened intensity is not necessarily a negative characteristic and is often channelled in a positive direction. School psychologists must be aware of the emotional intensity of mothers of handicapped youngsters.

Handicapped children's needs are more numerous than those of their peers. In addition to usual child care activities, the mother's responsibilities also include physical therapy, transportation to distant schools and special home teaching. Eventually, the mother becomes physically and emotionally exhausted. Do not consider giving this mother several suggestions for her to work with her handicapped child at home. That could represent the proverbial last straw.

Those mothers who do not make a satisfactory adjustment often avert their feelings of grief by establishing a guilty, depressed attachment to the child. They fail to adequately relate to other members of the family because they feel that they must give their lives to the care of the damaged child. It is also possible that they identify themselves with their own defective child, adding to their own sense of deficiency and failure. (Featherstone, 1980).

Not all mothers, however, fail to adjust to having a handicapped child and it is indeed unfair to suggest that the previous descriptions are universally applicable. Many mothers adapt successfully by doing one of two things: They have another baby or they join other parents of exceptional children in political or organizational activities. Few mothers undertake both simultaneously. Apparently, these behaviors are arrived at over time and after much pain. After a sufficient period of time, the adjustment process ideally moves the mother to a point where she spends time and effort caring for her personal needs. Once she gives herself permission to care for herself, she can take active steps to identify what she needs and likes to do. As she begins to do more things, coping becomes easier and she finds much more about which to be hopeful (Berry, 1981).

Fathers

A father of a handicapped child responding in a group discussion said, "I suffer for myself in terms of what I expected — what I hoped for in a son. But that's the suffering that goes with a loss like this. I suffer because he's got to, but also because I myself have had a loss. Yet, what have we lost? Only something I imagined" (Murphy, 1981). The phrase "only something I imagined" represents the extension of one's self or, from another perspective, the male ego. In time, many fathers adjust to the realization that they will not be able to be their child's magical teacher — the one whose irresistable and enlightening touch the child awaits and who causes the beauty of the child to flower. A common behavior among many fathers of handicapped youngsters is removing themselves from the scene. This removal, it can be speculated, is often directly related to the hurt which the father experiences as he realizes the improbability of his child serving adequately as an extension of his ego. In addition to some fathers bowing out of their handicapped children's lives, there is a very practical reason for playing less of a role in their children's lives.

Traditionally, in our society the man works outside the home. The job typically carries with it immediate daily responsibilities which change the father's focus away from the child for large periods of time. Said simply, it allows fathers to escape from the child's problems, albeit a temporary escape. Mothers, by contrast, often stay at home with their handicapped child. In essence, our social system which traditionally emphasizes the man as the major breadwinner in a family has created a coping mechanism for fathers by providing them with a respite. Absence from the home causes a number of father-related characteristics to emerge. The father has far less knowledge of the handicapping condition than the mother who quite naturally becomes 'expert' on cerebral palsy, epilepsy or whatever condition exists. Over time, realization of this lack of knowledge further contributes to his absence simply because he is somewhat of a stranger to it. The term 'denial,' frequently used in describing the behavior of fathers having handicapped youngsters, is perhaps tied into the fact that fathers necessarily spend much time away from home. Fathers do not develop a frame of reference which allows them to compare their child to nonhandicapped children. Mothers, by contrast, consistently have the opportunity to see their handicapped son or daughter in relation to 'normal' children and are constantly reminded of developmental differences. Because of this lack of time with the child, fathers can and often do avoid reality on two bases: They deny the extent of the actual handicap, and they do not reach the level of emotional intensity, particularly profound sorrow, that mothers do. In essence, the wider scope of the father's life is directly responsible for modifying his perceptions and feelings toward his handicapped child.

Fathers of handicapped children, more so than mothers, receive gratification and recognition from their jobs. In our society mothers are responsible for successful child rearing and as a conse-

quence, particularly with mothers having handicapped children, the place for them is seen to be at home. This denies mother the possibilities for enhancement of self esteem from job-related activities. Adding to this interference with improving self image is mother's constant failure to see her child measure up to either society's standards or her own, thus providing a constant threat to her self-image. Men, oriented more to career, at best have the opportunity for improving their self esteems on the job and under the worst circumstances are often able to remove themselves from the home for a socially encouraged and acceptable reason — to work.

Siblings

Are there specific behaviors and feelings among the siblings of handicapped children? After talking to several hundred mothers and fathers, one researcher concluded that brothers and sisters of the cerebral palsied, retarded, deaf, and blind accept their handicapped sibling and present few significant continuing problems to their parents (Barsch, 1968). Several other investigators asked parents about the adjustment of the normal siblings and also offer evidence that children with a handicapped brother or sister manage as well as those in ordinary families.

Variables such as religion, relative age, sex, income, family size, degree of retardation, type of physical handicap and parental attitudes all contribute to the sibling's adjustment. This suggests that too much complexity and individualization exists within families to permit any conclusions about siblings of handicapped children. Research studies on this topic, because of their normative nature, cause one to formulate conclusions which are not applicable in individual circumstances. There are, in fact, certain commonalities among siblings of handicapped which are best discovered through less formal methods. The remainder of this section on siblings relates the views of parents and siblings as they reflect on and respond to the questions, "Are there specific behaviors and feelings which exist among the siblings of handicapped children?"

Recently, in a graduate-level class in non-normative assessment, the topic being addressed was related to family dynamics in a special-child family. A student in that class made the point that she had a very difficult adjustment lasting many years as she grew up with a deaf sister. This student, nearly 30 years of age, married, and long since separated from the sister and parents on a daily basis, related her adjustment difficulties. She resented the attention given to her sister, harbored anger towards both the sister and parents, and finally was guilty about the resentment and the anger. It was fairly obvious that even after several years, this sister of a handicapped child still felt intense emotions.

Disability, with its built-in liabilities, carries with it many advantages. Special attention, recognition, and privileges are often unwittingly given by parents to their handicapped children, perhaps to modify their own guilt or sorrow. This special treatment may result in negative feelings and reactions by normal siblings.

Experienced school psychologists have more than likely heard parents refer to the above-average ability of their special child's brother or sister. The message in these references is something like, "We do have the ability to produce an offspring with ability." Handicapped children, because of less ability and because of the special feelings of the parents, *are* often treated differently. Parents having ego and identity needs often overemphasize the capabilities of 'normal' siblings. These two points regarding the advantages stemming from being handicapped and the increased expectation placed on normal siblings almost certainly cause very real behavior changes in the siblings of a special child. To conclude, however, that there exists a commonality of emotional responses among the siblings of handicapped children would be to ignore individuality. Emotions of siblings do not fit tidy categories. Loneliness, anger, guilt, embarrassment, identification, and confusion merge and battle with one another.

Family communication is often interfered with by the presence of a handicapped child and siblings are expected to be involved in this problem. In some family situations, discussion of topics related to a specific handicap or even general disabilities are inhibited, increasing confusion, misunderstanding, and intensifying feelings of all involved. Often the very opportunity to talk is lessened by the time needed to care for the handicapped child. Siblings desiring to share the day's happenings have that opportunity consistently taken away from them only to find a fatigued, less receptive parent listening to those accomplishments at a later time. Embarrassment on the part of siblings cause them to act and talk differently around their special brother or sister. Embarrassment, in fact, creates distance between children, thus having a direct effect on communication.

It should be mentioned that strength of character, responsibility, understanding, empathy, acceptance and a host of positive characteristics result from having a special brother or sister. School psychologists, however, should be mindful of possible negative consequences to holistically assess and help families. One may have excellent assessment and remedial skills when working with specific handicapping conditions, but failure to deal with the *family dynamics* will seriously impair one's overall effectiveness.

School Psychologists and Parents

School psychologists working with parents of special children often deal with great emotional intensity. The manifestation of emotions can run from apathy to various types of behavioral reactions at the opposite end of the continuum. Psychologists must be sensitized to these emotions, many of which may distort parents' perception and modify their behavior causing psychologists to approach the task somewhat differently than if they were working with parents of nonhandicapped children.

Psychologists who have worked with special children and their parents are aware of the anger which is often directed toward professionals. This anger has given parents' groups a dubious reputation among professionals. Psychologists, social workers, and educators who are invited to speak to parent groups often find themselves harassed by a barrage of angry questions. While the intensity and the emotions harbored by parents are in part responsible for anger directed at professionals, there are also numerous other factors. Knowing what parents want from professionals, and often do *not* get, should help professionals better understand anger held by many parents.

Information

Looking to professionals for information carries with it numerous residual ideas and problems. Parents associate absolute knowledge and solutions with authority figures (professionals). When the reality hits parents that the professional does not have any or all of the answers, there is disappointment, disillusionment, anger, and frustration. Not getting the 'desired' information, incidentally, creates a frequently observed type of parental behavior called "shopping around." Consider a mother who had taken her child to nine different places in five years.

She obtained a different diagnosis each time — 'retarded,' the first one said; 'aphasic,' the second one said; then she got 'autistic,' 'hard of hearing,' and 'minimally brain damaged.' For parents wanting definitive information, this type of experience is frustrating and anger-producing. Further complicating the interaction process between parent and professional is the frustrated reaction of the psychologist when forced to acknowledge that desperately sought answers are unavailable. Psychologists' frustrations might well distort their perception of parents, thus introducing another complication to the interaction process.

At times psychologists have substantial information but do not share it with the parents. Psychologists may not want to deal with the pain of the parents' reaction. There may be a tendency on the part of the psychologist to spare parents pain. Parents, for the most part, want the truth and psychologists withholding information or evading questions may implicitly criticize parents' good sense. When psychologists discuss a child's problems candidly with the family, they convey respect for their intelligence and judgment.

Parents' inability to get information may result from improper training of professionals in low-incidence disabilities. Unfortunately, people have an amazing facility in generalizing and assuming that an authority figure is knowledgeable in all areas. Recent legislation has put demands on school psychologists to be knowledgeable of developmental disabilities and disorders of young children. School psychologists have not had good training in these areas, and universities failing to adapt their curricula to meet the new role needs of school psychologists are not filling this void. Until changes are made, many school psychologists will find themselves lacking information sought by parents. How frustrating it is for parent and professional alike to be impotent.

Support

The second helpful quality of professionals desired by parents is a multidimensional characteristic, support. Listening may well head the list. Listening conveys respect and time. Parents desperately need to be heard and may well benefit most from a nondirective approach by the psychologist.

Understanding on the part of the professional provides support to parents. Complete understanding of the parents' thoughts and feelings is not possible for the professional. The professional who unthinkingly says, "I understand" may indeed create a sense of falseness and reduce credibility. Perhaps the best one can do is try to understand and respond realistically. Support groups, be they specifically related to a handicapping condition or generally directed toward parents of handicapped children, provide for the "understanding" sought by parents. Credibility is assured and each parent knows that the other understands.

Parents beset by unrelenting problems develop a lack of confidence in themselves. This is brought about because of the accentuated emotions, the lack of a frame of reference, and the need to 'survive' day to day. Emotions temporarily distort judgment. Several negative occurrences resulting from poor judgment lessen the confidence of a parent. The handicapping condition is often unique, disallowing the parent an opportunity to make decisions based on a well-established knowledge base. Often the sheer mechanics of caring for a handicapped child create chronic fatigue, depression and a sense of hopelessness. At a point in time, parents either refrain from making decisions on their own as their confidence level wanes or they require approval or advice from others. Professionals need to steer parents away from this dependency level with reassurance and move them in a direction which stresses independence and confidence. Helping in this way allows professionals to indeed be meaningful support persons.

Encouragement

One of the biggest mistakes made in working with special parents is giving 'false' encouragement. There is a natural tendency to want to say something to console others. Parents, however, quickly learn to view platitudes at best as an act of kindness and at worst as a serious credibility weakness, especially when delivered by professionals. Parents don't want to hear, "Everything is going to be alright," when their common sense tells them it won't be.

Encouraging parents to provide some time for themselves is one of the most therapeutic things professionals can do. Parents of special children often withdraw from the world and consequently need to be encouraged to continue contacts outside the immediate family to maintain a necessary broader perspective.

One of the truisms that exists among many handicapped people and among their parents is that they do not want sympathy, praise or pity. Properly related encouragement stresses realistic thoughts of how parents might improve a situation. Parents want reassurance, but back away from praise given on an emotional basis.

Care

To care is to go beyond oneself into the life of another, and to realize that the meaning one has to fulfill in life is beyond oneself; it is never merely oneself. Albert Schweitzer's message to a group of aspiring physicians suggested that only those who had sought and found how to serve would really attain happiness in their careers. In addition to developing a sound technical knowledge base, successful professionals have either learned or been endowed with this caring characteristic. What is important is an understanding of the components of this quality. Frankness on the part of the professional to the parent, respect for the child, and legitimately listening and responding to the parents' ideas and concerns are all major characteristics of caring. Nevertheless, frankness is a difficult attribute to learn and to use. It takes courage and confidence on the part of the professional and psychological insight into others. The true professional finds a way, however, to honestly share the most unpalatable information with parents.

Showing respect to the child through listening and by making realistic conversation gives a message to the parents. "My child is an individual, a person." Parents desire normalcy in their child and a professional relating in an unaffected way toward the child brings that goal closer. Personalizing of the handicapped child, while not a highly technical skill, is an essential part of showing care to both child and parent. Legitimate responding and listening is probably interfered with most by the pressure of time. School psychologists, reacting to time presses, often do not offer an opportunity for parents to work through their concerns. In an ideal setting, psychologists agree or disagree with parents, thus demonstrating meaningful listening. They do not expect passive acquiescence from parents and do not assume the omnipotent role of an arbiter rather than advisor. Caring is all of these things which, when synthesized, suggest the need for authenticity.

Helping in Decision Making

Helping is a key word, not directing or telling parents what to do, but helping them to decide. Again, school psychologists may have the technical information, but of prime importance is their ability to prepare parents for decision making — to properly address certain necessary requisites which facilitate decision making. What are the characteristics of persons which permit effective decision making? What do psychologists need to be aware of in readying parents for decision making? The following criteria are offered.

• Parents should be able to verbalize and accept their feelings. In tandem with this concept, of course, is the need for a person to whom they can relate meaningfully.

• Often, but not always, a mutual support group is helpful. This support group can provide information for decision making as well as allow for emotional support and confidence building.

• Parents having decision-making capability have remembered to satisfy their own needs and have developed interests beyond the world of their handicapped child. They have not allowed that child to dominate their lives.

• Parents have developed a belief in something to live for. This belief may be a religious faith, is often represented by giving and sharing to other parents, and it may be something quite unrelated to the handicapping situation. Whatever that something is, it often represents a removal of the parent from the immobility created by being caught up in the constraining life which can be imposed by a handicapped child.

• Accepting that life is not fair and that one's sense of justice will be constantly outraged will help persons to attain objectivity and reduce sorrow and self pity, thus permitting more capable decision making.

SUMMARY

The major themes of this chapter stressed the need for school psychologists to be more than technical experts in childhood disorders and emphasized certain characteristics of behavior which tend to occur in families having handicapped youngsters. The words *tend to occur* are an important qualifier, for they carry with them an implicit message that not all families having special children manifest these behaviors. In fact, many families having handicapped children are healthier and stronger than so-called nonhandicapped families. By focusing on the family dynamics aspect of handicapping conditions, it is hoped that the reader will be more sensitized to the subtleties which may exist within families having handicapped children and which need to be constantly addressed along the diagnostic-remedial continuum.

REFERENCES

Barsch, R. H. (1968). *The parent of the handicapped child: Study of child-rearing practices.* Springfield, IL: Charles Thomas.

Berry, J. (1981). Art of coping and hoping. *Exceptional Parent, 35* (11).

Featherstone, H. (1980). *A difference in the family life.* New York: Basic Books.

McDavis, R. J. (1982). Counseling needs of handicapped students and their parents. *School Counselor, 29,* 232-38.

Murphy, A. (1981). *Special children, special parents.* Englewood Cliffs, NJ: Prentice-Hall.

Murray, J. (1980). *Developing assessment programs for the multihandicapped child.* Springfield, IL: Charles Towson.

ANNOTATED BIBLIOGRAPHY

Featherstone, H. (1980). *A difference in the family life.* New York: Basic Books.
   The author of this book is an Assistant Professor of Education at Wellesley College and the mother of a handicapped child. The book discusses how the lives of family members are affected by the presence of a handicapped child. How they cope, the fear, the anger, guilt, personal inadequacy and loneliness which are experienced is expressed. The book is well researched and represents more than one person's feelings and opinion.

Murphy, A. (1981). *Special children, special parents.* Englewood Cliffs, NJ: Prentice-Hall.
   This book discusses over 200 critical incidents with parents, relatives, and others who come into contact with handicapped children. Coverage includes a series of not commonly discussed, yet important, issues in the lives of special families, including doubting, believing, hoping, daring, enjoying, feeling, loving, and single-parenting.

BEST PRACTICES IN WORKING WITH COMMUNITY AGENCIES

Jeanne M. Plas   Blanche Williams
George Peabody College of Vanderbilt University

OVERVIEW

What is the thing to do if a boy much smaller than yourself begins to fight with you? Perhaps you become involved with his social worker, his physician or his probation officer.

In recent years the complexity of our world, individual lives, and systems has demanded that school psychologists broaden their range of responsibilities. They find that students who formerly were exclusively involved with family, neighborhood and other carefully chosen social groups are now dealing with many different and sometimes unwanted relationships and social demands. Today's students are gaining more experience with the world than did their predecessors. This situation widens the array of potential involvements for the school psychologist.

As these social trends develop, school professionals are forced to face squarely the extent to which their singular effect on a child's life has been limited. No longer can the psychologist, for example, hope that educational testing, report-writing, and classroom placement will necessarily solve a child's academic or behavioral problem. A reasonable response demands that one's professional view is broadened to include numerous areas for potential assessment and intervention and that doors are opened for the participation of many other adults in the process. The psychologist is often called upon, explicitly or otherwise, to focus on many aspects of a child's life rather than simply on the identified problem. It is sometimes necessary to understand influences as remote as the welfare system and the pediatrician's office.

Working with community agencies and other professionals increases the school psychologist's effectiveness dramatically. The needs of children are many; especially the needs of special children. As a result, professional services not provided by the schools must sometimes be brought to bear on behalf of a child. Often, the school psychologist is the only professional who has access to the whole of the child's life. Often, it is the school psychologist who identifies the needs and is in a position to direct the child and family to the services which can respond to those needs. Thus, the school psychologist who sees his or her role as encompassing frequent contacts with professionals outside the school is in the best position to serve the needs of the whole child.

After expanding the view of the school psychologist's role it is possible to begin to see children as participants in many interactions involving physicians, attorneys, judges, welfare agents, clinical psychologists and a host of other professionals and administrators. Consequently, the issues broaden as do the numbers of people and settings with which to be concerned. Potential channels for new kinds of effort and influence appear which challenge the traditional role of the school psychologist.

School psychology began with well-defined limits. The school psychologist functioned within the school system by responding to referrals from teachers, testing children and making recommendations for placement and services. As psychologists sought greater effectiveness in dealing with teacher referrals, they soon began to redefine their roles. Out of this has grown the more recent trend toward consultation with teachers. Consultation models incorporate a desire to draw on the strengths of the child, the teacher, and the educational setting in order to reframe the goals of the psychologist's involvement. The principle of least disruption to the child's life enables psychologists to help teachers learn to deal effectively with "problem children."

Such a principle, by taking the focus off problems and placing it onto human and environmental strengths, dramatically alters the definition of consumer of school psychological services. Traditionally, one helped a needy individual by carrying full responsibility for problem solving. In contrast, consultation models focus on the consumer as an active participant in the change process. The elimination of the directive, magician-psychologist expands the possibilities of a school psychologist's effectiveness because responsibility is viewed as a shared enterprise, thus compounding the energy available for problem solving.

The school psychologist's role has widened further with the introduction of ecological approaches which allow all settings in which the child is a participant to be considered as potentially significant areas for assessment and intervention. Psychologists have learned the value of interviewing and observing families and peer groups and of reframing problems so that significant others were drawn into the intervention process.

Although the growth of the consultation and ecological models allows today's school psychologists the freedom and the responsibility to step further away from the traditional testing role, the current literature does not reflect the particular importance of the school psychologist as a liaison agent between the school and other agencies with which children are involved. Whether designated as liaison by parents, school officials or other pro-

fessionals, it is often the school psychologist who provides the best link among the school, the family and various agencies because of his or her association with the institution in which the child spends several hours a day and because of his or her training and experience in human relations, professional jargon, and educational matters (cf. Plas, 1981). In cases where direct service to a child or teacher is neither needed nor desired, the psychologist may decide to intervene within the liaison role. The situations in which one finds oneself in a position to work with representatives of community agencies are numerous. Each is identified in a different way, at a different point in the assessment process, and with its own impacts upon the child, the family, the school, and other agencies. Consider these examples and the school psychologist's possible involvement: Jimmy's isolation from school peers increases as his parents engage in a custody battle; the psychologist finds that Ritalin has been prescribed for Robert apparently without regard for his history of non-troublesome classroom behavior; the results of Pam's recent car wreck are affecting her ability to carry out former school activities; having been suspended from school for violent behavior, Linda is arrested the next day for shoplifting; John's community mental health caseworker has called for a behavior modification plan to be implemented in the classroom.

The role of the psychologist changes as the need for dealing with other professionals becomes apparent. One enters new systems, focuses on new concerns, and deals with different values, vocabularies, and status positions. Outside of the familiar school system, there are new challenges in assessment and communication. Perhaps the first important practical issue involves facing power structures which initially appear less clear than those within one's own system.

BASIC CONSIDERATIONS

The Significance of Power and Influence

The first item of business when working with an agency is to assess the influential relationships within it, between the professionals with whom one is dealing, and among significant representatives of other relevant systems including oneself. Little positive movement is made without regard for the structures and perceptions of power among the individuals and groups involved. The psychologist derives recommendations for the most useful type of communication and the most promising liaison role from his or her own assessment of power issues within each new setting or relationship.

"Power" is taken here to mean direct and indirect control over needed resources. Indirect power refers to non-coercive impact, or "influence" (cf. Plas, Hoover-Dempsey, and Wallston, in press); direct power, of course, is more easily identifiable. It is important to note that power is not considered here to be a negative factor within human relations, but an element that exists in all of them. Direct power that is exerted in cruel ways to serve an individual's selfish needs is certainly negative and undesirable; however, the vast majority of direct and indirect power transactions which occur on a daily basis are supportive of community and individual functioning. The grocer, for example, exerts direct, benign power when he or she does not give you your bag of groceries until you have paid for them. In a similar way, a physician uses direct power when he or she decides what medical information is released at a school psychologist's request. Your brother-in-law exerts indirect power (i.e., influence) when he suggests to your spouse that a nursing home should be considered for an aging and ill parent. Similarly, indirect power is in play when a social worker's disapproving look indicates that a foster parent's housekeeping standards are not adequate.

In every case, power regulates the flow of needed resources. These resources may be material such as food, grades on a report card, or money. Important resources also can be less tangible such as information, approval, or love.

All systems, including schools, health agencies, juvenile courts and the like, contain a complex set of power relationships. Power is sometimes associated with a person's role or status (for example, agency directors who have power as a result of the responsibilities associated with the position) or with a person's personal characteristics, such as the highly intelligent member of a pupil personnel services team who is respected as a result of his or her abilities.

It is important to become aware of the patterns of power in any organization or other unit with which the school psychologist comes into contact. For example, it is important to know who actually controls the flow of information from a pediatrician's office. Is it the physician? Or is it the head nurse or administrative assistant? Within the juvenile justice system, does the judge make the real decisions about placement or does the judge routinely accept the advice of the court social workers or probation officers? In each case, the psychologist's efficiency and effectiveness is influenced by his or her understanding of such issues.

Often, power relations are reciprocal; that is, there is mutuality of power. In other cases, one party seems to possess more power than the other. It is important to note such reciprocal influences within the organizations that the school psychologist contacts. Moreover, it is especially important to develop a sense of the power reciprocity between oneself and various agencies and individual community members affecting the life of the child. Wherever possible, mutuality of influence is sought since equality best serves the individual interests of children.

The most effective use of social power occurs after one understands the dynamics involved. The presence of direct and indirect power is assessed most quickly by noting the behavior of others. To the extent that persons attend, heed, and comply, power of some sort has been exerted. The level of cooperation which parents, for example, give to various professionals such as physician, social worker, and mental health counselor often indicates the level of power that parents perceive in these professionals. Assessment of one's own beliefs about personal effectiveness is also necessary as is assessment of the self-efficacy beliefs of others. Because low self-efficacy beliefs often result in more coercive and selfish means of asserting power, it is especially important to assess on this dimension. Again, behavior provides the important clues.

Consideration of Personal Styles

Prescriptions for performing good liaison work and for dealing with power, however, are ony as good as their goodness of fit with one's personal style. In addition to the limitations and resources of the school and the community agency to one's own status and that of others involved, and the expertise of oneself and others, one has personal characteristics that are always potential strengths on which to draw. Personal theoretical and philosophical orientations encourage certain liaison styles and render others less comfortable. Training and experience account for the presence of some skills and the absence of others. Personality characteristics are also important. Some effective psychologists, for example, are low-key and generally unobtrusive while others are good joke tellers and freely express their feelings.

These and other personal considerations must not be denied when entering a relationship with a community agency. Personal style always interacts with the model of practice that is selected; but sometimes the interaction does not facilitate effective functioning. For example, a naturally low-key, reticent person is not optimally effective as a confrontive, "hot-seat" group therapist; and without adequate training and consistent self-monitoring, an outgoing and talkative person is not a good listener.

While the school psychologist's functioning is enhanced by a knowledge of his or her personal style of relating, such knowledge is especially crucial for effective work with personnel located outside of the school. Often, involvement with these people is relatively brief and infrequent. In this case, personal styles are more obvious and of greater importance than they may be over the course of long-term professional relationships.

BEST PRACTICES

There are many modes of relating with professionals from other systems and a variety of functional roles develops in given situations. Any number of them are productive choices for the performance of liaison activities. Three are described below as examples of "best practices" but should be approached in light of the following caveat: Most efficient and most effective service is provided when a role is purposefully adopted with regard to the needs of the identified client, the needs of the school which one represents, a preliminary assessment of (or best guess about) the community agency to be entered — including its power structure and patterns of influential relationships — and an assessment of one's personal style. Further, efficiency and effectiveness is increased to the extent that one clarifies the functional characteristics of that role for oneself and for any others with whom a social contract is to be made explicit.

Although each of these practices is recommended for consideration by school psychologists dealing with community agencies, none is expected to provide a "magic answer" in any given situation. Therefore, the descriptions that follow include examples of the problems that are inherent to each one. The truly "best practice" is to undertake a role thoughtfully, to anticipate possible stumbling blocks, and to approach one's task with an attitude of flexibility.

The Advocacy Role

The psychologist who adopts a child advocacy role is placing absolute primacy on the child's welfare. Too often, school psychologists intuitively favor an advocacy approach but are not consciously aware of the implications of their choice and the values that they thereby assert. A child advocate believes that children possess rights independent of those afforded by the parents and views children as largely incapable of assuring the attainment and maintenance of these rights (Berlin, 1975). When a survey of the child's relationships substantiates such a belief in a given case, adoption of an advocacy role is crucial.

The advocacy role demands expert assessment and use of inter- and intra-agency power relationships. This particular approach also requires great sensitivity to one's own personal style. Nothing impedes progress more disastrously than a child advocate who terrorizes other professionals in the name of a single, "holy" value — the immediate rights and needs of the child.

An effective advocate is one who uses power and self-knowledge to link the strengths found within and among all agencies involved. Gentle reminders that the child is the most useful focus of attention often works wonders. Respect for the positions of professionals who operate within models other than the advocacy position is, of course, always essential.

The functioning of a child advocate is most problematic and least effective when community agencies and schools are experiencing difficulties in territoriality and the flow of hierarchial authority. In such cases, child welfare often takes a back seat to "turf wars" and line-of-authority problems. The child's needs wait while the adult professionals iron out difficulties over rights and responsibilities concerning the child. This turf problem is most acute for the advocate because even the first sign of trouble brings about great frustration. In the advocacy role, the school psychologist must guard against a self-righteous indignation that easily causes one's attention and energy to shift to "petty" problems rather than the child's very real needs.

The Process Facilitator Role

This approach has been discussed under a variety of labels (e.g., Davis & Sandoval, 1982; Feldman, 1979; Halpern, 1983; Plas, 1981; Tyler, Pargament & Gratz, 1983). With a specific set of strategies and values, the process facilitator approaches others concerned with the child as a whole or with various aspects of the child's functioning. School psychologists in this role are concerned primarily with communication patterns and routinely initiate numerous notes and phone calls to keep information flowing and communication channels open. In this role, the psychologist values the sharing of power and decision-making among all responsible parties. Often, meetings are held that involve personnel from several agencies as well as parents, grandparents and, whenever possible, the child.

The major difficulty with implementation of the process facilitator role probably resides in other professionals' lack of familiarity with it. The collaborative approach that it requires may initially surprise agency and school personnel who often expect the school psychologist to "solve" problems and to act as "expert." The psychologist as facilitator, however, rejects the expert role, preferring to demonstrate that the power for change resides within the natural environment of the child.

As process facilitators, school psychologists must continually clarify for themselves the goals and motives of everyone concerned since funtioning is affected adversely by the traditional expectations of other professionals with whom the school psychologist works. Making the social contract explicit at the very beginning of involvement usually avoids many of these difficulties later. Even after the contract has been set, it is wise to anticipate the inevitable role misinterpretations which follow. The public is accustomed to psychologists attempting to "cure" and to "fix;" it more rarely identifies the psychologist as an enabler or as a liaison professional.

The Consultee Role

As consultee, the school psychologist is in the position of receiving consultation services on behalf of an identified client or clients (cf. Baizerman & Hall, 1977; Caplan, 1963). Unlike the roles previously mentioned, this one makes the school psychologist the direct beneficiary of service, the aim of which is to empower the psychologist to affect the child's life in a particular positive way.

In the role of consultee, the school psychologist acts as an agent of the school, making him or herself available to welfare workers, probation officers or physicians to effect any school-related changes specified in an outside agency's plan for the child. This role is probably the most traditional one in which school psychologists have interacted with non-school professionals. It has proven effective for the psychologist who is skilled at information acquisition and interpretation and who has the support of a variety of school-based arenas for action. If principals, teachers, students and staff trust the psychologist, then an outside consultant has an excellent chance of working effectively for the client through the school psychologist as consultee.

On the other hand, the school psychologist functions as consultee on his or her own initiative when information outside the scope of his or her professional expertise is necessary. The difficulty in this position comes about in scheduling a consultation session if the other professional must account financially for each hour of his or her time. Ideally, one's school system is convinced to pay for such a session if the administrators believe that the psychologist uses the hour to open lines of communication with an important individual or agency whose services are of benefit within the school's long range plans. Otherwise, and perhaps more fruitfully, the psychologist negotiates a trade of professional expertise. When face-to-face consultation is not arranged with the expert, a few well-designed questions allow the psychologist a brief but helpful telephone contact leading directly to an intervention strategy or to other information resources.

A Case Illustration

The school counselor has referred Joe for testing because of his failing grades in math, social studies and science. It is the spring of Joe's eighth-grade year, and the counselor is concerned that failure of these courses will prevent his entering high school next fall. She believes that repeating the eighth grade would be particularly disruptive to his social development, since he is alredy two years behind his peers and strikes her as immature and dependent.

Joe's school records reveal that he moved into the school district during his third-grade year, that he began kindergarten at age 6 and that he repeated the third grade. His latest group achievement test scores fall consistently in the low-average range. His teachers report that Joe is never disruptive but that he fails to turn in many homework assignments and has passed very few tests this year. His B's, C's and D's from previous semesters have dropped to C's, D's and F's.

Joe himself reports that he completes most of his homework assignments and has "flunked a couple of tests but mostly made A's." He appears confused when confronted with the possibility of failing the eighth grade and talks eagerly about going to high school. He reports having many friends at school but will name none; his "best friend" is a 9-year-old neighbor.

Joe's mother, Mrs. Craft, is also confused about her son's failing grades and explains that she thought he was doing well on homework and tests. Her recent concerns have been his apparent inability to learn to do simple tasks at home, his sexual acting out, and his "depression." She remarks also that he was born with "hairline brain damage," was in special education classes from pre-school through half of third grade, and is currently being treated by the psychiatrist at the local community mental health center. She signs a permission form for release of records from the mental health center.

According to the psychiatrist's notes,

Joe is currently being "maintained on Haldol" and is seen once every two months for a check-up. No problems with the medication are noted.

How would three different school psychologists approach Joe's case?

The advocate. Assessment indicated that Mrs. Craft, a single parent, was able to mobilize few resources to handle Joe's problems and preferred to "turn him over to the professionals." Further Joe's case had been "staffed" with the psychiatrist at the mental health center because "it sounded like that boy needed some kind of medication." Therefore, school psychologist Janet McMillan decided that only the forcefulness of an advocacy position would succeed in obtaining better services for Joe, resulting in more productive and appropriate performance of home and school tasks. She immediately gathered information on the uses and side effects of Haldol, an antipsychotic medication, and telephoned the psychiatrist. Within a logical, assertive framework she presented the case that Joe's original problems did not seem to warrant an antipsychotic treatment and that his current problems might be due in part to the medication. She asked that the prescription of this medication be reconsidered and that the psychiatrist refer Joe's case for further staff evaluation with the prospect of family, group, or individual therapy in mind.

In consideration of her concern about some of the psychiatrist's defensive responses and the issues of power that are thereby problematic, Janet then telephoned the mental health center's clinical director and described her position as that of a school psychologist whose concerns for a mutual client had led her to become involved with the staff psychiatrist. She went on to describe the problems in which she was intervening as advocate and requested that Joe's case be re-staffed so that his needs might be reconsidered. She received from the clinical director a promise that Joe's case would undergo re-staffing procedures within two weeks and that she would be notified as to the outcome.

Pleased with her progress so far, Janet is awaiting a telephone call from the mental health center and plans to continue her cooperative advocacy position until Joe begins to receive more appropriate help from the agency.

The process facilitator. School psychologist Susan Campbell's major concerns in this case are the coordination of services among professionals and the information needs of all of them. Defining herself as liaison agent, she met with Joe's mother and made a list of all the agencies with which Joe had had significant contact. She also asked formally about family relationships and found that an older son, greatly admired by Joe, is out of state in a training program, that Joe's father, remarried and living 60 miles away, maintains irregular contact with his sons, and that Mrs. Craft's boyfriend had recently "taken Joe under his wing." With her, Susan decided to request records pertaining to Joe's birth, his early care by a neurologist, and his years in special education prior to the family's move into this school district.

She then telephoned the psychiatrist, explained Joe's current school and family problems, and asked whether the medication or any other factors he has noticed might play a role. The ten-minute discussion, in which Susan gathered some helpful information, ended with the psychiatrist's thanks and expression of his wish that Mrs. Craft would become similarly involved. Susan telephoned Mrs. Craft to report on the physician's cooperation and elicited a promise from her to accompany Joe on his next visit to the mental health center. She also arranged a time for an after-school conference that would be convenient for both Mrs. Craft and Joe.

Susan next spoke informally with Joe's math, social studies, and science teachers about monitoring his classroom behavior for a period of two weeks and invited them to the conference at which they could share and discuss their data. She prepared a memorandum containing all "new" information and a report of the teacher-monitoring plans, sent it to the school counselor, and invited her also to attend the after-school conference.

By the date of the conference, Susan had received one set of records through the mail and was able to summarize the information it provided, including WISC scores and a report of Joe's progress in elementary school classes for "delayed" children. She called Mrs. Craft, reported that she had received that set of records, and reminded her of the meeting.

The conference was dominated by the three teachers' reports, but Susan kept much of the focus directed toward Joe himself and asked for his responses throughout. She helped Joe, the teachers and Mrs. Craft work out an acceptable format for reporting to each other on assignments due, completion of assignments, and grades received.

Following Joe's next appointment with the psychiatrist, at which Mrs. Craft was present, Susan telephoned him to discuss his perception of Joe's problems and progress and to inform him of the teachers' reports of classroom behavior. The physician expressed concern about Mrs. Craft's interaction with her son and explained that he had referred them to the agency's clinical staff for family therapy. Susan asked to be kept informed by representatives of the mental health center and suggested that a meeting of Joe, Mrs. Craft, the psychiatrist, the family therapist, Joe's brother, and herself be planned during the brother's next vacation from school.

Susan continues to keep the lines of communication open among the various significant actors in Joe's life. The psychiatrist is currently considering a change in Joe's medication, an idea that was prompted by Susan's reports of teachers' observations of his behavior.

The consultee. As Joe's school psychologist, James Duke was surprised at Mrs. Craft's report of her son's previous placement in special education classes and the diagnosis of brain damage given to him at birth. With Mrs. Craft's help, he requested hospital and school records. When they arrived, he studied them carefully but was left with several questions concerning the kind of organic impairment and the extent of developmental delay that Joe had experienced.

James arranged a telephone interview with one of Joe's early childhood physicians who clarified many of the details. James felt that Joe should have been followed by a neurologist after the family's move during Joe's third-grade year but was unsure about suggesting to Mrs. Craft that she consult a neurologist at this point.

James found that a neurologist was affiliated with the local hospital for handicapped children. He decided to speak with the hospital's chief psychologist about the possibility of receiving short-term consultation services from members of the hospital staff and negotiated a contract through her (and with the approval of his school administrators), whereby he received "medical consultation as needed" in exchange for his expertise in assessment of educational needs.

James is now planning his first meeting with the neurologist from whom he hopes to gain a greater understanding of issues surrounding brain damage: its assessment, prognoses for adolescents like Joe, associated syndromes, family adjustment patterns, achievement expectations,

and effects of medication. Through such a consultee role, he hopes to broaden his own knowledge so that he can appropriately advise Joe, Mrs. Craft, and Joe's teachers.

SUMMARY

The effectiveness of the school psychologist is often facilitated by professional interaction with community agencies. Such involvement may be initiated out of obvious necessity, but often it provides a helpful alternative outside the traditional range of the school psychologist's activities. By considering the roles of advocate, process facilitator and consultee and matching them thoughtfully with the needs of all involved and with one's own personal style, the school psychologist can broaden his or her impact in the school system. Consciously attempting these and other roles with professionals from community agencies is encouraged because of the flexibility that is added to one's helping skills. As always, the school psychologist's goal is effective assessment and intervention for the benefit of school children; productive contact with outside agencies increases the effectiveness with which school psychologists proceed toward their goals.

REFERENCES

Baizerman, M., and Hall, W. T. (1977). Consultation as a political process. *Community Mental Health Journal, 13*, 142-147.

Berlin, I. N. (Ed.) (1975). *Advocacy for Child Mental Health.* New York: Brunner/Mazel.

Caplan, G. (1963). Types of mental health consultation. *Journal of American Orthopsychiatry, 33*, 470-481.

Cherniss, C. (1977). Creating new consultation programs in community mental health centers: Analysis of a case study. *Community Mental Health Journal, 13*, 133-141.

Davis, J. M. and Sandoval, J. (1982). Applied ethics for school-based consultants. *Professional Psychology, 13*, 543-551.

Feldman, R. E. (1979). Collaborative consultation: A process for joint professional-consumer development of primary prevention programs. *Journal of Community Psychology, 7,* 118-128.

Halpern, R. (1983). Direction Service: Linking handicapped individuals and their families with needed services. *Journal of Community Psychology, 11,* 187-198.

Kipnis, D. (1976). *The Powerholders.* Chicago: University of Chicago Press.

Perkins, D. V., and Thompson, J. R. (1974). An assessment of physicians' attitudes toward community mental health. *Community Mental Health Journal, 10,* 282-291.

Plas, J. M. (1981). The psychologist in the school community: A liaison role. *School Psychology Review, 10,* 543-551.

Plas, J. M., Hoover-Dempsey, K. V., & Wallston, B. S. (in press). A conceptualization of professional women's interpersonal fields: Social support, reference groups, and people-to-be-reckoned-with. In I. G. Sarason & B. R. Sarason (Eds.), *Social Support: Theory, Research, and Application.* The Hague: Martinus Nijhof.

Tyler, F. B., Pargament, K. I., and Gatz, M. (1983). The resource collaborator role: A model for interactions involving psychologists. *American Psychologist, 38,* 388-398.

Winett, R. A., Calkins, D., Douglas, C., and Prus, J. (1975). The role of resource linker in the public schools. *Journal of Community Psychology, 3,* 85-87.

ANNOTATED BIBLIOGRAPHY

Davis, J. M., and Sandoval, J. (1982). Applied ethics for school-based consultants. *Professional Psychology, 13,* 543-551.
Straightforward advice based on both ethical and practical considerations is compiled here for the school-based consultant. Although the article refers specifically to within-system consultation, its approach can easily be made applicable to professional interactions involving more than one system. A collaborative consultation model is urged, with self-awareness, flexibility, and adherance to basic ethical principles cited as the means for its successful application.

Halpern, R. (1983). Direction Service: Linking handicapped individuals and their families with needed services. *Journal of Community Psychology, 11,* 187-198.
This article describes a program designed to assist handicapped individuals and their families in locating, acquiring and effectively using community services. It demonstrates an exemplary approach by which consumers are helped to identify their own needs and strengths, become primary agents in satisfying their needs, and make contributions in their areas of strength, while environmental capacity for support of both consumers and service providers is increased. The author's identification of "paradoxes and challenges" will be particularly helpful in guiding liaison agents as they structure their own roles along similar, though not necessarily identical, lines.

Kipnis, D. (1976). The use of power. In Kipnis, D., *The Powerholders* (pp. 39-58). Chicago: University of Chicago Press.
Having defined power as the satisfaction of a need by inducing appropriate behavior in others, Kipnis devotes this chapter to an examination of various means by which such influence is exercised. He emphasizes ecological concerns, including the resources available in different institutional settings and the demands and limitations inherent in different role relationships. Making heavy use of published empirical studies on resistance, compliance, and the exertion of power, the author presents a two-part model of the rational process by which means of influence are chosen. This chapter is recommended as a guide to diagnosing the power strategies of others and understanding one's own motivations, resources and use of power.

Plas, J. M. (1981). The psychologist in the school community: A liaison role. *School Psychology Review, 10,* 72-81.
This article addresses the difficulties in moving toward a consultation/liaison role by offering a theoretical perspective for the contemporary school psychologist and a practical guide through a seven-step liaison process. A review of Nicholas Hobbs' Project Re-Ed, the classic example of a total liaison approach to service delivery, follows.

Tyler, F. B., Pargament, K. I., and Gatz, M. (1983). The resource collaborator role: A model for interactions involving psychologists. *American Psychologist, 38,* 388-398.
The authors focus on the multidirectionality of influence when the psychologist collaborates with other competent resource people. They encourage the professional to view such collaboration as a growth process for everyone involved, assuming that each participant's contribution will be both useful and limited. They make recommendations for resolving difficulties in relationships of shared power and describe collaborative functions within both hierarchical and horizontal frameworks. Empirical research is highlighted.

BEST PRACTICES IN ORGANIZING PROFESSIONAL SUPPORT GROUPS

Jack H. Presbury and Harriet C. Cobb
James Madison University

OVERVIEW

What is a Professional Support Group?

In his best selling book *Megatrends,* John Naisbitt (1982) predicts the course of our society through the next era of its development. Among his salient themes was the prediction that as our culture becomes more technologically efficient, we must carefully attend to our human needs and maintain our social contacts. In his words, "high-tech" requires "high-touch." Naisbitt believed that the encroachment of electronics, politics, and computers into our personal lives dramatized our desire to institutionalize new ways of being together. He stated that the human potential movement came about in reaction to technological growth and that we are all becoming more concerned with our relationships, our personal growth and our spirituality. These are examples of "high-touch" attempting to keep pace with high-tech.

Naisbitt also pointed out that the hierarchial or pyramidal structure of our organizations including our schools has failed to meet human needs. There is a growing recognition that professional isolation and burnout together with the failure of people to actualize their full potential in their work constitute a waste of human resources. If people are to creatively and enthusiastically perform their duties and make real contributions to the organizational mission, then it will be accomplished through new patterns of interaction. Naisbitt suggests that the structure which provides "high-touch" possibilities and releases human potential is networking:

"Simply stated, networks are people talking to each other, sharing ideas, information, and resources. The point is often made that networking is a verb, not a noun. The important point is not the network, the finished product, but the process of getting there — the communication that creates linkages between people . . ." (p. 192)

Professional peer support groups are networks of people within an organizational hierarchy who perceive themselves as having common needs and goals and who work together to solve problems, affirm each other, and improve their skills. Usually, these are groups of people who occupy the same role within the organization. In a school system, these may be groups of supervisors, principals, teachers, or pupil personnel workers who understand the nature of each others' concerns and who are interested in professional growth.

Current Practices in Schools and Other Settings

A review of the literature on networking and support groups reveals that while there is a great deal of activity in this area, there is very little generalized information on organizing and maintaining such groups. Most support groups and organizations have emerged at a grass roots level in response to a specific need. It has long been the custom in graduate schools for students, for example, to form study groups to divide and share responsibilities for learning. Ethnic minorities, women's groups, and neighborhood groups have developed networks and support systems because of common needs and interests (Welch, 1980). For a long time, businesses have employed leadership groups, "think tanks," teams, "buddy systems," or mentoring relationships to maximize the productivity of their employees. The one feature all these groups have in common is that they are horizontal; that is, they are comprised of members who are roughly at the same level in the heirarchy, rather than vertical or pyramidal in their organization. In general, support groups are composed of peers.

The structure and organization of most school systems work against the ad hoc formation of peer support groups. Teachers spend most of their day in a classroom with non-peers; principals, often assigned one to a school, are cut off from contact with their peers; school psychologists travel from one school to another and in rural settings may be the only such employee; counselors have impossible case loads and special education teachers sometimes teach in areas isolated from the rest of their colleagues. Only recently have many schools considered the problem of professional isolation (Winslow, 1977), burnout (Morocco, (1981), and the special needs of beginning teachers (Tisher, 1979). The usual way in which school professionals come together is through faculty-staff meetings in which the needs and demands of the system are articulated or through inservice education whose current status is generally considered to be "deplorable" (Hutson, 1979). If professional support groups are organized, in most school settings this is done consciously and deliberately by someone willing to take the initiative.

Thinking it Through-Then Going Ahead

The next two sections of this chapter are devoted to ways of planning and implementing strategies for a successful program. In the section entitled *How to View It*, a reference model is offered: the Professional Development Qube (P.D.Q.) with ideas drawn from the literature on group dynamics and professional stage development. The P.D.Q. serves as a systematic method for planning and analysis. In the section entitled *How to Do It*, best practices from many sources are brought together. Though this discussion generally refers to school systems as settings, it is also intended to be relevant for applications beyond the school.

BASIC CONSIDERATIONS

Technique without a theory is incomplete. An understanding of the needs and objectives of the client population provides a theoretical basis for success as well as a sound rationale for administration. In addition, an assessment of personal skills and ability to provide the needed service is necessary. A folk-poet from Tennessee once said that in order to know where you're going, you've got to know where you're at.

Viewing Yourself as Qualified

A major problem with the initiation of a professional support group within a school system is that no one knows whose job it is. Organizing such a group is a task unfamiliar to many school psychologists. The first thing to recognize is that, in the areas of human relations, consultation, and group behavior, school psychologists are as qualified as counselors and other psychological support personnel (Dyer and Vriend, 1980) and more qualified than most people in the school organization. People trained in staff development such as principals and other supervisory personnel may be less able to conduct a professional support group because of their lines of authority and evaluative roles (Moracco and McFadden, 1982). The school psychologist's flexibility of schedule, frequency of contact with people at all levels of the educational hierarchy, and the perception on the part of the teachers and others that the school psychologist possesses expertise in human emotions and behavior makes the psychologist qualified to initiate professional support groups.

Viewing What Professionals Need

Professionals whether teachers, school psychologists, or principals, share the same human needs. One useful definition of what people need comes from Shutz (1967). He states that we all have needs for affection, inclusion, and control. A successful professional support group meets the needs of its members. In a professional setting, the need of affection is often manifested as the need to be liked or cared about, to be considered "ok" regardless of minor idiosyncracies, and to maintain self-esteem in the workplace. The need for inclusion consists of feeling part of the group, knowing one's place in terms of the hierarchy, and being a valuable contributor to the group. This is the social sense of belonging. The need for control in the group is having the power to decide how much access other people have to one's private life and how much influence one has over the process of the group. It also refers to how competent people feel articulating their professional role. In the case of the classroom teacher, for example, the need for control exists in one's ability to manage classroom behavior and convey the lesson content. To be seen as a professional able to control the many demands of a role is also to experience oneself as belonging (inclusion)

and maintaining self-esteem (affection). Each of us needs affection, inclusion, and control in different combinations depending, in part, on the situation.

Viewing Where Professionals Are

Many authors suggest that teachers and other professionals develop through predictable stages (Fuller and Brown, 1975; Cruickshank and Callahan, 1983; Watts, 1980). Stage One of professional development has been characterized as the survival stage in which the emphasis is on control and adequacy (Dunleavy, et al., 1983). Stage One professionals bring a freshness and enthusiasm from their recent training and their new ideas can be a source of inspiration to professionals at other stages of development. On the other hand, because of their dramatized needs for control and belonging, these beginners may adopt inefficient habits and become constrictive in their styles. Stage One teachers adopt their teaching style within the first six months and, if unduly threatened, may value discipline as the primary goal and instruction as secondary. Stage One professionals need support in the areas of control, inclusion, and affection, in that order. What they need most is a concrete solution to an immediate problem.

Stage Two professionals are characterized by their increasing comfort in the area of control. This is the stage of adequacy. They have developed strategies which make their lives easier and have skills which are appropriate to the demands of their role. They may become bored with their duties and desire to be stretched by new challenges or they become complacent and tend to burnout or, as Truch (1980) suggested, to "rustout." They require new ideas and feedback to keep them going.

Stage Three professionals are at the

level of mastery. This is the possible equivalent to Erikson's stage of generativity (1968) in which the master teacher, for example, can become a mentor to beginning teachers by sharing wisdom and an accumulated set of strategies. The paradox of this stage is that the professional who has achieved mastery often experiences control needs because the system has no format for exploiting the resource of the Stage Three professional. If this is the case, the master professional feels a sense of isolation in which belonging needs again arise. The master teacher whose skills are not prized or used feels like the "old war horse" — not in control, not quite belonging, not cared about.

Viewing the Group Process

Professional support groups are an alternative to the classical continuing education or inservice methods of staff development used by most school systems. While such groups do not replace other methods, they have the unique quality of meeting affection and inclusion needs as well as bringing information to group members. Because professionals develop through stages in their careers, their need patterns are different at various times. In addition to the "high-touch" quality of professional development groups, the opportunity exists to tailor such groups to the particular needs of the members. According to Watts (1980), most existing inservice planning is like administering a non-specific antibiotic to the whole population without knowing what the germ is or who is suffering from the disease.

Using the concept of human needs (affection, inclusion, control) and the notion of professional stage development (survival, adequacy, and mastery), the school psychologist who organizes professional support groups begins to analyze the processes or activities needed in each group. A group of master teachers at Stage Three, for example, profits only minimally from an experience designed to explore new theories of classroom management. They might be dispersed, however, among groups of Stage One teachers to share what they already know in this area.

If the professional support group does not match the needs and experience of its members, it cannot succeed. This is axiomatic for any group. These group processes have been divided into a three category continuum: Theory, Technique, and Support. A group only involved with theory stays philosophical and at the level of ideas. One involved with technique concerns itself only with the practice and application of certain skills. A group involved with support spends time affirming and giving feedback to members. Theory groups have no need to get anything done. Their value is in the gaining of new perspectives and they are characterized by conceptual distance from the mundane. Technique groups have little tolerance for delay. Their criterion for success is what works. Support group members need to feel good about each other and to clarify relationships. Obviously, these categories are not exclusive of each other. These processes happen in all groups at different times.

The PDQ Professional Development Qube

For the school psychologist who is visual and profits from conceptual models, the authors have developed the Professional Development Qube (PDQ) as a quick reference for understanding groups and planning for objectives. Figure 1 shows the three "How to View It" axes already discussed: (a) needs, (b) stages, and (c) processes.

Taking these axes into consideration

FIGURE 1
PROFESSIONAL DEVELOPMENT QUBE
(P.D.Q.)

**A QUICK REFERENCE FOR
ANALYZING AND DESIGNING PROFESSIONAL SUPPORT GROUPS**

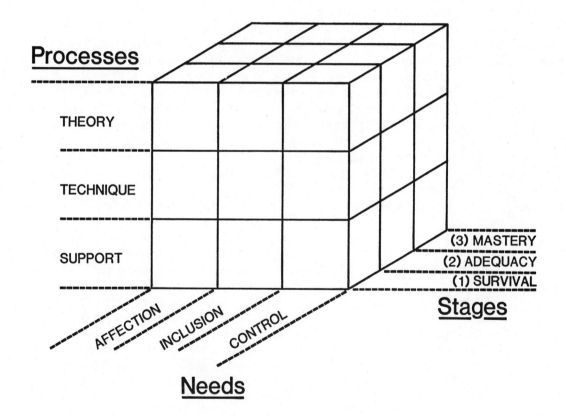

Presbury and Cobb © 1983

when designing professional support groups, one sees what is needed and analyzes problems when groups are not working. Specific issues, concerns, and topics are determined by the group members but the psychologist influences the design of the group to maximize success. Returning to the example of the beginning teacher with classroom management concerns, the process of theory and the need for affection are "on the back burner." The most urgent need is control and the most useful process is technique. Of course, all the other needs and processes are present in the requirements of the Stage 1 teacher, but the most efficient communication is, "Try this, it might work." Why it works is somewhat irrelevant.

Before organizing a professional support group, it is helpful to use a quick reference in planning. The school psychologist uses the axes of the PDQ to ask, "What do these people need most: affection, inclusion, control?" "At what stage of development are they: survival, adequacy, or mastery?" "Therefore, what process emphasis is most effective: support, technique, theory?"

BEST PRACTICES

Getting Started

A few guidelines are necessary before beginning to help an organization adopt a peer support system. Perhaps most important to remember is that to enlist the full emotional investment of the people involved, planning of the program and the setting of all agenda(s) must involve the potential participants (Douglas, 1977). This is initiated as an informal needs assessment in which people brainstorm topics and issues for group discussion. It must be remembered that until an atmosphere of trust is developed in these groups only superficial concerns are con-

sidered. No one is willing to expose feelings of inadequacy or problems which make them appear foolish.

The purposes of professional support groups are explained to those in authority who endorse the program so that attempts to organize them are not thwarted. The ideal situation has the administration agree that school time is used or some other compensation such as inservice credits is given. If everyone agrees that professional support groups are a good idea, but they are made a moral issue such as "true professionals would do this on their own time," not much can be expected to happen. An effective commitment by administration lends legitimacy to the enterprise (Sell, 1982). Schools must at least be open to the idea that inservice includes participation and not just information gathering; that learning takes place in a style appropriate to the individual learner; and that learning is facilitated by interactions which generate a sense of trust and collegiality (LaPlant, 1979).

It is sometimes easy to lose sight of the individual needs and stages of development of the group participants. The PDQ is a reminder that some groups are very eager to exchange ideas for classroom management, teaching, or dealing with parents. Others at different stages and with different needs may wish to form study groups and deal at the conceptual level. Still others desire a more spontaneous and low structure meeting. Nothing can kill a group faster than the facilitator who believes all groups should be nitty-gritty, true-confession style encounters!

Predictable Group Development

Groups, regardless of purpose, move through somewhat predictable phases. Without this understanding, group members become discouraged and think the group is not working. In general, the first phase is the Orientation Stage (Stanford, 1977) in which people mill around and negotiate their purpose together. They feel awkward and seek a structure. The Norm Establishment phase occurs when the rules are set up. It is usually at this stage that people feel they are off and running. Often, however, the next stage is Conflict. Here someone states discomfort with the course of the process such as too theoretical or too personal-supportive and wishes to renegotiate. After this follows the Productivity phase. Eventually there comes a Termination phase when the group has either done its work to the satisfaction of the members or they seek to continue and, therefore, begin the cycle again. If the group explicitly understands these predictable phases, they can manage their own process and not be discouraged or mystified by it.

Group Size and Format

The ideal size of a professional support group is three to five members according to Harvey (1982), although groups up to twelve have been successful. Membership in the group should be voluntary, although a commitment should be made by each member to be present at each meeting for a specified length of time. A grading period or a semester are convenient markers. At the end of this period, commitments are renewed. A regular time for beginning and terminating the meeting is established and adhered to. A specific agenda for group activity is agreed upon, though this is constantly renegotiated. A group which desires a theory process might agree to research articles on the topic and report to each other in the next meeting. The group seeking answers to specific problems (technique) might agree to have someone express a

concern and the others offer opinions or advice. The group seeking something more on the order of comraderie and fellowship (support) might agree to wait and see what comes up in each meeting rather than have homework assignments.

A group which stays at the level of theory becomes emotionally dried up since the need being met is more control than affection. On the other hand, a group which becomes extremely personal leaves some members feeling overexposed or unsafe. This type of group strives for affection at the expense of control. In general, groups balance themselves, but the psychologist conducting the group should consider the following guidelines: (a) Make the rules of the group intervention explicit. (b) Agree that what is said in the group is confidential. (c) Adhere strictly to the time limit. (d) Try to move from impersonal-abstract issues to personal issues. (e) Do not gossip about people not present in the group. (f) Keep a balance between intellectual and emotional issues. A group which includes the human needs of affection, inclusion, and control, and strikes a balance among the processes of theory, technique, and support stands a very good chance of being productive and satisfying to its members.

Kirschenbaum and Glaser (1978) offer several helpful guidelines in their book *Developing Support Groups: A Manual for Facilitators and Participants*. It is recommended for the school psychologist who decides to develop such a group. As with any group, there is some risk of problems involving group dynamics. For example, one person may attempt to dominate the group by taking too much of the group's attention. While ideally, each member monitors his or her own level of participation, some intervention on the part of the leader in the form of a tactful comment may be necessary. Other individual styles may hinder group progress such as the "Imposer" who must be right at all times or the "Blocker" for whom no idea seems acceptable. The group leader must be prepared to redirect the group to avoid having the others become disillusioned. It is not unusual for groups to increase the inevitable socializing component to the detriment of the other functions. If the group begins to develop this pattern, it is appropriate for the leader to bring the issue before the group in an effort to find a solution.

The issue of whether groups are composed of people from all stages of professional development or homogeneous, with people with the same level of professional concerns, is moot. In addition, whether groups are leaderless, have rotating or nominal leadership is an open issue in the literature. The authors favor nominal leadership so that someone is responsible for the process. These leaders then become the consultees of the school psychologist who organized the program. As in all consulting relationships, the goal is that the members take over and sustain their own groups and that the program organizer succeeds in helping the participants toward revitalization and independence.

An Example of the Organization of Teacher Support Groups

In the beginning of the school year, one of the authors was invited by a high school faculty to be the guest speaker at an inservice. The topic was *Classroom Management* and three case histories were sent to the speaker prior to the meeting. The plan was that the speaker solve the behavior problems in the case histories which would be followed by a discussion entitled, "Yes, but I already tried . . ." where the teachers said what they had actually done.

While this appeared to be a game or trap called "lynch the psychologist" it also was an opportunity to introduce the idea of professional support groups in which

the teachers shared their techniques for classroom management. In the meeting, rather than offer the expected solutions, the suggestion was made that the focus of the meeting be: "How do you go about finding support in the school system when you need answers to such concerns." A discussion followed, the idea of support groups was introduced, and five teachers volunteered to start a support group with the assistance of the psychologist.

For six months the group met after school for one hour every two weeks. At each session one person presented an issue on which he or she needed help. Someone else in the group volunteered to be the helper. These two people then interacted for 15 minutes without interruption from the group. At the end of that time, the group discussed how helpful the interventions of the helper had been as well as offered their perspective on the issue presented. Usually, each problem took the entire hour. The stress of the meetings was as much on how to become a better helper as it was to solve the presenting problem.

At the end of the six-month period the faculty went on retreat and invited the psychologist to conduct another inservice, this time on *Teacher Support Groups*. The faculty was divided into groups with the original group members serving as the leader of one of the five groups. In a day long workshop they practiced being better helpers. At the end of the day, the faculty voted to devote every other faculty meeting to teacher support groups. Support from the administration was already arranged. The previously trained faculty members became the ongoing group leaders and nearly all the faculty opted to be involved. The psychologist did not actively participate after that time. After a year the groups remained intact and the administration and faculty reported them to be satisfactory.

An analysis reveals crucial elements in this successful program organization. (a) A willing and cooperative administration existed, (b) A small prototype program was undertaken which fed trained people back into their collegial system, (c) Confidentiality and a definite structure within the groups were maintained, (d) Stage Three professionals were used to contribute their resources, (e) Finally, the need for peer contact and support existed, which can be accepted as a given in all school systems.

A Peer Support Group for School Psychologists

One of the authors was involved as a member of a peer support group comprised of rural school psychologists, each working as the only psychologist in his/her respective district. Once a month the four met on a Friday afternoon to discuss cases, exchange ideas, and offer mutual support. Although the group focused initially on the theory and techniques processes, it evolved into primarily a support group that offered feedback regarding personal strengths and weaknesses. Members left the group sessions feeling refreshed and ready to face the challenge of working in isolated settings.

The success of this year long group was due to several factors. A commitment was made to maintain it as a priority in spite of hectic schedules. Support from supervisors was given for the time away from usual routines. A point was made of keeping them informed of new approaches learned that could be implemented in the school systems. As with the previously described teacher support group, definite structure was designed.

SUMMARY

A professional support group offers its members many benefits including stimulating ideas, practical help, and support. While professionals are at different stages in their career from development; from survival, to adequacy, to mastery, a peer support group helps meet varying needs for inclusion, control, and affection. The Professional Development Qube (PDQ) provides a quick reference for designing and analyzing a professional support group that is appropriate for its members.

The school psychologist is in a unique position to be a catalyst in the development of a peer support group program in a school system. Acting as a facilitator for a group and/or a trainer of potential peer leaders, the school psychologist uses his or her skills in human relations, consultation, and group dynamics. Additionally, the school psychologist clearly benefits from participation as a member in a peer support group comprised of other psychologists, counselors, or pupil personnel workers. The goals of increasing both professional and personal growth are met within the framework of a peer support group. If Naisbitt is correct in his prediction that the future threatens an even more depersonalized world, then the school psychologist performs the important humanistic function of helping people maintain their "high-touch" contacts in a high-tech world.

REFERENCES

Cruickshank, D. R. and Callahan, R. (1983). "The other side of the desk: Stages and problems of teacher development," *The Elementary School Journal*, Vol. 83, No. 3, pp. 251-258.

Douglas, A. P. (1977). "Change processes at the elementary, secondary, and post-secondary levels of education," in Nash, N. and Culbertson, J. (Eds.), *Linking processes in educational improvement*, Columbus, Ohio: University Council for Educational Administration, pp. 44-45.

Dunleavy, T.; Ferguson, J.; Pastel, J.; Pleasants, F.; Washenberger, D. (1983). *Review of the literature and teacher survey for the Virginia Beginning Teacher Assistance Program*, Roanoke, Virginia: Roanoke City Schools, unpublished paper.

Dyer, W. W. and Vriend, J. (1980). *Group counseling for personal mastery: Everything you need to know to lead any group in any setting*, New York: Sovereign Books.

Erikson, E. H. (1968). *Identity: Youth and crisis*, New York: W. W. Norton and Company.

Fuller, F. F. and Brown, O. H. (1975). "Becoming a teacher," in Ryan, K. (Ed.), *Teacher education*, The seventy-fourth yearbook of the National Society for the Study of Education, Part 2, Chicago: University of Chicago Press.

Harvey, K. D. (1982). *Help! Forming a teacher support group*, Denver, CO, unpublished paper.

Hutson, H. (1979). *Inservice best practices: The learnings of general education*, Bloomington, IN: National Inservice Network.

Kirschenbaum, H. and Glaser, B. (1978). *Developing support groups: A manual for facilitators and participants*, LaJolla, CA: University Associates.

LaPlant, J. (1979). *Principlals inservice program*, Dayton, OH: Institute for Development of Educational Activities.

Morocco, J. C. (1981). *Burnout in counselors and organizations*, Ann Arbor, MI: ERIC Clearinghouse on Counseling and personal services.

Morocco, J. C. and McFadden, H. (1982). "The counselor's role in reducing teacher stress," *The Personnel and Guidance Journal*, pp. 549-552.

Naisbitt, J. (1982). *Megatrends: Ten new directions transforming our lives*. New York: Warner Books.

Roseland, R. W. and Hacker, L. (1982). "Self-help groups and professional involvement," *Social Work*, pp. 341-346.

Schutz, W. (1958). *FIRO: A three dimensional theory of interpersonal behavior*, New York: Holt, Rinehart and Winston.

Schutz, W. (1967). *Joy: Expanding human awareness*, New York: Grove Press.

Sell, D. (1982). *A model for faculty development in the community college*, unpublished paper.

Stanford, Gene (1977). *Developing effective classroom groups*, New York: Hart Publishing Company.

Tisher, R. P. (1979). *Teacher induction: An aspect of the education and professional development of teachers*, paper presented for the National Invitational Conference "Exploring issues in teacher education: Questions for future research," Austin, TX.

Truch, S. (1980). *Teacher burnout and what to do about it*, Norato, CA: Academic Therapy Publications.

Watts, H. (1980). *Starting out, moving on, running ahead or how teacher's centers can attend to stages in teacher's development*, Occasional Paper No. 8, San Francisco: Far West Lab for Educational Research and Development.

Welch, M. S. (1980). *Networking: The great way for women to get ahead*, New York: Harcourt, Brace, and Jovanovich.

Winslow, M. B. (1977). *Administrators: Two local efforts to combat administrative isolation*, paper presented to the Annual Meeting of the American Education Research Association, New York.

ANNOTATED BIBLIOGRAPHY

Kirschenbaum, H. and Glaser, B. *Developing support groups: A manual for facilitators and participants*, LaJolla, California: University Associates, 1978.
This is an excellent guide for establishing and implementing support groups. Kirschenbaum and Glaser provide numerous practical suggestions including how to invite potential members, how to conduct the first meeting, and how to avoid group process "pitfalls." The manual is helpful for both group leaders as well as participants.

Corey, G., Corey, M., Callahan, P., and Russell, J. *Group techniques*. Monterey, California: Brooks/Cole Publishing Company, 1982.
Corey et al provide a complete overview of the issues and skills involved in group work. Specific techniques such as setting goals, preparing members to get the most from the group, and dealing with resistance or conflict are described in detail. The stages of group process are elaborated with suggestions for effective leadership outlined. This book is especially useful for those who have not had extensive experience in leading adult groups.

BEST PRACTICES: ADAPTIVE BEHAVIOR

Daniel J. Reschly
Iowa State University

Adaptive Behavior has been emphasized in numerous authoritative accounts of psychoeducational assessment practices. Assessment of adaptive behavior is a mandatory, indispensible component of mental retardation classification and programming. There is little argument on that point. Adaptive behavior is also viewed as an important component of the multifactored evaluation that is required in the classification/placement and re-evaluations of all handicapped students. Best practices in school psychology, whether viewed from the perspective of legal mandates or considerations of what is good for students, reflect ample consideration of adaptive behavior.

The diverse meanings and many uses of adaptive behavior data are discussed in this chapter. Theory and research are cited where necessary to establish the basis for best practices. There is careful scrutiny of concepts of adaptive behavior, seen here as the single most important consideration in developing best practices. Conception of adaptive behavior is more easily resolved than it first appears; much of what has been written in recent years ignored earlier theory, research, and common practices thereby, probably unintentionally, obscuring much useful information. The origin of current concerns about adaptive behavior is discussed along with how these "recent" formulations are parallel to and sometimes identical with earlier conceptions. The review of this information provides a broader and sounder basis for the fundamental principles and best practices.

OVERVIEW

The construct that is now called adaptive behavior is not new. The most widely cited definition of adaptive behavior is, "... the effectiveness or degree with which the individual meets the standards of personal independence and social responsibility ..." (Grossman, 1973, p. 11; 1977, p. 11; 1983, p. 1). The *same phrases* were used by Doll at least as early as 1953 where social competence was defined as "... the functional ability of the human organism for exercising *personal independence* and *social responsibility*." (Doll (1953), p. 10, emphasis added). Still earlier, Doll's (1941) influential definition of mental deficiency established six criteria, the most important of which was, "social incompetence due to mental subnormality." Adaptive behavior and the two dimensional concept of mental retardation (intelligence and adaptive behavior), both thought by some to be quite recent, are at least 40 years old!

There is much more theory, research, and professional practice to use in developing best practices for the 1980s than some accounts suggest. The claims that the construct of adaptive behavior was "discovered" about 1960, and measures of adaptive behavior were not developed and then only in rudimentary form until the 1970s are simply inaccurate! *Social competence* as used by Doll and other mental retardation scholars throughout most of this century and *adaptive behavior* refer to the same construct. And the old theory, research, and professional practices in social competence are relevant to contemporary discussions of adaptive behavior, a point emphasized in an excellent, comprehensive review by Leland, Shellhaus, Nihira, and Foster (1967).

[351]

Adaptive behavior is tangentially related to several current research trends or professional issues. Much of this information is indirectly related to best practices in use of adaptive behavior data, and is therefore mentioned briefly. Further information on the relationship between adaptive behavior and placement bias litigation, one of the most controversial issues today, is available in Reschly (1981, a, b, 1982), Mercer (1973, 1979) and Bersoff (1982). The apparent decline in the number of students classified as mildly retarded in school settings is also related, at least in part, to adaptive behavior (Macmillan & Borthwick, 1980; Polloway & Smith, 1983). Rather large changes in numbers of students classified as handicapped were produced by very narrow, rigid concepts of adaptive behavior. As noted earlier, the question of what the construct of adaptive behavior means is crucial to all other considerations in this chapter.

BASIC CONSIDERATIONS

Conception of Adaptive Behavior

There are many definitions of adaptive behavior. For example, Heber (1959) discussed adaptive behavior in terms of meeting the ". . . natural and social demands of the environment." That isn't very specific. Since 1973, the key phrases in the American Association on Mental Deficiency (AAMD) definition have been personal independence and social responsibility (Grossman, 1973, 1977, 1983). Other definitions cited by Coulter and Morrow (1978) emphasize concepts like the dual influence of social role and social setting; developmental level and environmental demands; task demands and cultural norms; and so on. Definitions of adaptive behavior provide only a vague, elusive sense of what that construct means.

Developmental. There are several common features in adaptive behavior concepts. Perhaps the most salient is that all definitions of adaptive behavior suggest developmental criteria, meaning that expectations vary with the age of the individual. One of the clearest statements of developmental criteria is provided in the AAMD mental retardation classification system. Different criteria are provided for three broad age categories: preschool, school-age, and adult. During the preschool period the primary criteria are sensory motor skills development; communication skills including speech and language; self-help skills such as dressing, eating, and toileting; and socialization including interacting appropriately with others. During the school age years, denoted as childhood and early adolescence by AAMD, the most important criteria are use of basic academic skills in practical situations; use of reasoning and judgment in coping effectively with the environment; and the acquisition of social skills such as participation in group activities and establishing and maintaining satisfactory interpersonal relationships. In late adolescence and adulthood the principal criteria are independent functioning in the community and vocational responsibilities including economic self-support. These criteria, paraphrased and quoted from p. 25 of Grossman (1983), are conceptualized as a hierarchy. All of the criteria from earlier ages are included in the criteria for later ages. Thus, adolescents are expected to master self-help skills, a criterion from the pre-school period. Parents of adolescents who want rooms cleaned and personal articles picked up understand that mastery of adaptive behavior criteria from previous ages is uncertain and inconsistent. This is an example of a general problem in typical performance measures.

Environmental/Cultural Conditions. Another common and salient feature of adaptive behavior conceptions is emphasis on expectations for performance which in turn are understood to vary among environments and cultures. Opportunities to demonstrate specific capabilities as well as demands to perform certain roles vary considerably. Crossing a street properly with a traffic light is a reasonable and important skill for a child or a young adolescent residing in a city. That skill is classified within the general criterion of using reasoning and judgment to cope efficiently with the environment. But environments vary. If the nearest stoplight is 12 miles away and a busy street even farther, as was the case where I spent my childhood, this particular skill is not evoked, demanded, or necessitated by the environment. These kinds of variations are widely recognized and accepted. Other possible variations such as the importance of school achievement in the conception of adaptive behavior are not as universally accepted.

General Domains of Adaptive Behavior. In addition to age appropriateness and cultural context, there is implicit consensus regarding several dimensions or domains of adaptive behavior. Nearly every adaptive behavior measure has items on basic self-help skills such as looking after personal needs, avoiding obvious dangers, and moving about the environment independently; on understanding and using money; and on getting along with others. For adults, there is nearly universal agreement that adequate functioning in two general areas constitutes appropriate adaptive behavior: independent functioning in the community and economic self-support. An adult who functions adequately in these two very general areas meets minimal criteria for adaptive behavior competencies and cannot be regarded as mentally retarded regardless of how low the IQ is! It should be noted that independent functioning as conceptualized for adults includes very

broad sets of behaviors: looking after oneself, meeting minimum requirements expected of all citizens, and refraining from behaviors that excessively or unacceptably endanger or offend other persons are among the general classes of behavior involved.

Differences Among Conceptions of Adaptive Behavior

Although there are several areas of agreement among concepts of adaptive behavior, areas of disagreement are apparent, and must be addressed in carrying out best practices. These areas of debate are primarily restricted to the school age years. The degree to which cognitive/academic competencies are included is the basic area of disagreement. This disagreement has vast implications for the criteria used to assess adaptive behavior, for the setting(s) examined, for the very influential decision on who judges or reports on adaptive behavior competencies, and for how an adaptive behavior examination is carried out. For example, Mercer's (1979) concept of adaptive behavior eliminates consideration of underlying intellectual skills. This seems unwise for several reasons.

School psychologists must seek resolutions to these areas of disagreement, both in terms of general policies and as applied to specific cases. These disagreements are the reason that conception of adaptive behavior is the single most important issue in determining and implementing best practices in this area.

Developmental Task Theory. Before analyzing these areas of disagreement, a brief digression to developmental task theory might help clarify some issues. Developmental task theory suggests key challenges for each age period. Resolution of these challenges usually occurs through a combination of repeated environmental interactions with personal growth and development. Both learning and maturation are involved in interdependent and inseparable ways. Cultural context usually determines the specific *content* of the developmental challenge. Furthermore, each stage depends on mastery of prerequisite skills from previous stages, and in turn, each stage involves acquisition of skills that are prerequisites to the successful resolution of challenges at later stages.

The general nature of the developmental challenge at the school age period is acquisition of competencies required for participation in adult roles. This is apparently a nearly universal expectation existing across a wide variety of societies and economic systems. As noted earlier, the content of the developmental challenge, that is, the specific domains of behavior, is determined by each society. In modern technological societies, acquisition of various cognitive skills, basic literacy and communication skills, concepts of time and number, and so on is strongly emphasized. These cognitive skills are to a large degree acquired in schools, and there are rather strong expectations that children and youth meet these developmental challenges through adequate performance in a school setting. Moreover, there is virtual uniform emphasis on adequate achievement in academic settings among nearly *all* sociocultural groups in the United States (Bickel & Bond, 1981).

Adaptive Behavior: School Setting. If basic cognitive operations and literacy skills are emphasized by all sociocultural groups, if these skills are taught to a large degree in school settings, and if these skills are very important to adequate adaptive behavior in adulthood (Edgerton, 1967, 1984), then the school setting and academic achievement must be viewed as integral, essential components of adaptive behavior during childhood

and adolescence. This fundamental question, whether or not the school setting and academic achievement are properly included in a conception of adaptive behavior for children and youth, is resolved further by consideration of two additional sources of information. First, the AAMD concept of adaptive behavior has always included emphasis on learning, cognitive skills, and school performance. This was especially true of the 1959 and 1961 AAMD concepts (Heber, 1959, 1961). More recent versions (Grossman, 1973, 1977, 1983) adopted a broader perspective that still preserves emphasis on academic performance: "Difficulties in learning are usually manifested in the academic situation, but in evaluation of adaptive behavior, attention should focus not only on the basic academic skills and their use, but also on skills essential in coping with the environment, including concepts of time and money, self-directed behavior, social responsiveness, and interactive skills." (Grossman, 1983, p. 26). If the AAMD is acknowledged as authoritative on mental retardation and adaptive behavior criteria, then inclusion of the school setting and academic skills as *part* of the concept of adaptive behavior is indisputable.

Pertinent to the question of academics and adaptive behavior is consideration of the underlying intellectual skills for various adaptive behaviors. Everyone acknowledges the importance of handling money in this society. It is impossible to perform this skill competently without mastery of the concept of number, arithmetic operations, and the values of coins and paper money. There are many other universally endorsed adaptive behaviors that require mastery of intellectual skills. Intelligence and adaptive behavior certainly are not the same, but they are related. This relationship was recognized in the social competence literature (Leland, et. al., 1967) and will quite likely be rediscovered in the foreseeable future.

Adaptive Behavior in Non-School Settings. Acquisition of complex skills and competent performance of various rules outside of school is also expected of school-age children and youth. A conception of adaptive behavior focusing only on the school setting as was the common, but incorrect interpretation of the Heber (1959) AAMD scheme is excessively narrow and inadequate. Research and theory development arising out of the concern for the six-hour retarded child and minority overrepresentation in self-contained special education classes (Mercer, 1973, 1979; PCMR, 1970) have emphasized social roles and social settings outside of school.

There is a great deal of non-academic learning and developmental change over the school age years. Most children are expected to acquire and demonstrate a variety of competencies that have little to do, at least directly, with the school setting and academic skills. A wide range of self-help skills and social skills are typically acquired during these years. These skills are also emphasized in developmental task theory, and are prerequisite to adequate adaptive behavior during adulthood. Social skills and peer relationships, universally emphasized in adaptive behavior concepts, are discussed by Frank Gresham and Patricia Brockman in other chapters in this volume.

Summary of Adaptive Behavior Conceptions

For school-age children two broad settings are considered in conception of adaptive behavior. Decisions about adaptive behavior that do not consider both school and nonschool settings are based on inadequate information. Furthermore, the overlap among the domains of intelligence, adaptive behavior, and social skills (see Gresham, this volume) must be recognized (see Figure 1). Certain intellectual skills are prerequisite to independ-

ence and specific social skills are fundamental to social responsibility. The associations among these areas in our conceptual scheme including the moderate level correlations among good measures of the three domains are necessary to accurately describe human adaptation. This conception provides the basis for assessment procedures and decision-making strategies that in turn constitute the basis for best practices.

Purposes for Adaptive Behavior Assessment

Clarification of purpose is an essential step in the assessment process (Coulter & Morrow, 1978; Salvia & Ysseldyke, 1981). Adaptive behavior is typically assessed for the purpose of making either classification/placement or program planning/intervention decisions. Depending on which of these is the major goal, different procedures and instruments for assessing adaptive behavior are applied.

The classification/placement purpose involves decisions about current level of performance, degree of discrepancy from grade or age expectancies, degree and type of need, and eligibility for special programming. The questions are addressed from the perspective of a comparison of the individual student's performance to some group, usually a representative sample of other students. These comparisons are called *norm referenced*.

Assessment instruments and other data collection procedures for classification/placement decisions should meet certain requirements. The items should be *representative* of some domain of behavior. The sample of items or observations should be sufficient to infer the individual's level of competence in the area. The inferences about degree of discrepancy from expectations should be based on comparisons to a representative sample,

FIGURE 1

The Continuum of Social Competencies

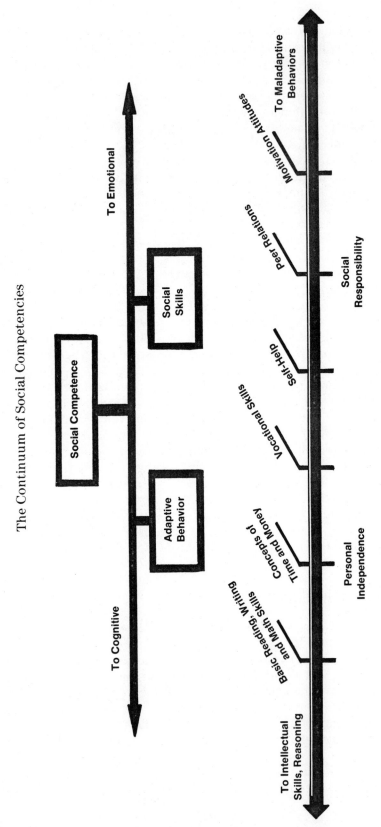

that is, good norms. The scores used in these comparisons should have relatively equal units throughout the scale, and so on. The scores should be highly reliable if decisions are made about individuals. If the scores for a particular instrument are not highly reliable (e.g., .9 or above) then multiple sources of information using different instruments or data collection procedures should be developed and considered in making decisions. Finally, if inferences are made about underlying traits such as intelligence or psychological processes, the instrument must have good predictive validity relative to appropriate criterion behaviors in educational settings.

Program planning/intervention decisions require somewhat different types of assessment information and different types of instruments. Rather than general degree of need or overall strengths and weaknesses, information is needed on very specific skills or competencies. Data collection from this perspective, called criterion referenced, is designed to pinpoint what the child can and cannot do in some important domain of behavior. The items on such instruments should provide *thorough* coverage of the important skills or competencies *rather* than a representative sampling. The items or observations should be related to important objectives and, ideally, to clearly specified interventions.

Most current adaptive behavior instruments or observation procedures do *not* meet the necessary criteria for both purposes. In nearly all cases, a particular instrument or observation procedure has desirable characteristics for norm referenced, classification/placement decisions *OR* criterion referenced, program planning/intervention purposes. Of course, many instruments do not meet the criteria for either.

Target Population

In addition to conception and purpose, another basic consideration is the target population whose adaptive behavior is assessed. A general distinction is made here between mildly handicapped, borderline, and normal groups on one hand and the more severely handicapped on the other. Adaptive behavior assessment for the school-age severely handicapped usually focuses on more rudimentary adaptive behavior skills. A fundamental self-help skill like dressing may appear as a single or a small number of items on a classification/placement device or procedure. If the purpose is primarily program planning/intervention, the same self-help skill might be subdivided into many more specific skills which are components of the overall behavior. In the former case, the decision to be made is level of mental retardation: moderate, severe, or profound, as well as determination of the *general* pattern of adaptive behavior skills. In the case of program planning/intervention, the purpose is to pinpoint specific skills and subskills that are mastered or not mastered. The decision to be made is to determine where to begin the intervention, for example, picking up a piece of clothing, putting the arm into a sleeve, or buttoning a shirt. Program planning/intervention generally involves far more items or observational units because instructional information needs to be more precise.

Adaptive behavior assessment for school-aged mildly handicapped to normal groups requires a greater range of items as well as items reflecting more complex behaviors. Here again, though, the distinction between types of decision is very important. An important domain for these groups might be what is called Economic/Vocational on one recently published scale, or Earner/Consumer on another, both of which include the skill of handling money. Making correct change might be an item on a general classification/placement procedure. The same skill, handling money, might be subdivided into many components such as adding, subtracting, value of coins, and so forth on a procedure used for program planning/ intervention.

Adaptive behavior instruments and procedures vary considerably depending on target populations. Methods intended for the severely handicapped usually involve simpler, more rudimentary skills whereas those designed for mildly handicapped to normal groups usually involve more complex skills. Obviously, age group, preschool versus childhood or adolescent, is another factor on which adaptive behavior procedures vary. Variations in target population are reflected in the norms for the instrument, a very important consideration in classification/ placement decisions. A very basic consideration is to examine different adaptive behavior assessment procedures to determine which or what combination best matches the purpose for assessment and the target population.

Assessment of Adaptive Behavior

The assessment of adaptive behavior is guided by considerations regarding concept, purpose and target population. These considerations provide a basis for careful scrutiny and wise use of existing procedures. Adaptive behavior measures are not as technically adequate nor as well developed as measures of cognitive functions. Recently published authoritative psychoeducational assessment texts (Salvia & Ysseldyke, 1981; Sattler, 1982) describe the limitations of currently available adaptive behavior instruments. The typical recommendation in these sources as well as in the 1983 revision of the AAMD Manual is to consider several indices of competence rather than a single score and to use multiple instruments or procedures and several sources of information. All recent authoritative commen-

taries urge caution in the selection and interpretation of adaptive behavior information. All have suggested the importance of clinical judgment and a broad variety of information in determination of adaptive behavior status.

Clinical judgment doesn't mean guessing, intuition, or entirely subjective decision making. Clinical judgment is exercised properly as a means to evaluate numerous kinds of data from various sources. Adaptive behavior is a broad, complex construct. Evaluation of adaptive behavior must be correspondingly broad using diverse kinds and sources of data. A single global score or the results from a single instrument are never sufficient to reach conclusions about adaptive behavior. Two extreme views to avoid are to completely ignore adaptive behavior instruments because of their technical limitations and to apply every known adaptive behavior scale under the guise of being thorough. Clarification of the kind of information, sources and instruments/ procedures is provided in Table 1.

In Table 1, the adaptive behavior assessment for children and adolescents is organized around two major settings, in school and out of school. Several indices of adaptive behavior are suggested. Much of this information, particularly that pertaining to classroom performance, is already (or should be) gathered routinely as part of a multifactored assessment. The assessment of adaptive behavior outside of school should involve multiple sources of information including interviews with the student and the parent.

Adaptive Behavior Instruments. Formal, standardized adaptive behavior instruments are used in practically all situations involving preplacement or re-evaluations of handicapped students. A list of these instruments is provided at the end of this chapter. The instruments vary markedly along the dimensions of concept, purpose, and target population.

TABLE 1

Conception of Adaptive Behavior for School Age Children

ADAPTIVE BEHAVIOR: SCHOOL BASED

Rationale:
1) Mastery of literacy skills is a key developmental task for persons between the ages of 5 and 17.

2) The expectation for and emphasis on educational competencies is common to most if not all major sociocultural groups.

Assessment:
1) Collection and consideration of a broad variety of information including teacher interview, review of cumulative records, examination of samples of classroom work, classroom observation, results of group standardized achievement tests, results of individual achievement tests, diagnostic achievement tests, and other informal achievement measures.

ADAPTIVE BEHAVIOR: OUTSIDE OF SCHOOL

Rationale:
1) Mastery of a variety of non-academic competencies also is expected, and a key developmental task between the ages of 5 and 17.

2) The expectations for and opportunities to develop non-academic competencies may vary among sociocultural groups.

Assessment:
1) Collection of information on social role performance outside of school in areas such as: peer relations, family relationships, degree of independence, responsibilities assumed, economic/vocational activities, etc.

2) Method of collecting data may include formal measures, interviews with parents, interview with student, etc.

None is sufficient alone; all must be supplemented by other formal or informal methods of gathering information.

Adaptive Behavior Instruments: Characteristics and Problems. Standardized adaptive behavior instruments with a few exceptions involve *third party respondents.* Third party respondent means that the adaptive behavior examination seeks information from a person who knows the child or client. Questions like "Can Bob dress himself?" (Yes or No) or "How often does Alice fix food for herself using the stove?" (Sometimes, often, or never) are answered by someone who knows the child. The indirect nature of many adaptive behavior procedures creates a number of problems such as respondent lack of information and respondent bias. Interpretation of adaptive behavior information from third party respondents must take into account the biases the respondent might have and how well informed the respondent is concerning the client's competencies. Most respondents have some limitations in these areas. Teachers know little about what the student does in the home; parents may be well informed about activities in the home, but know little about school performance or peer relations. Either perspective is too narrow. Both are important for school-age students.

Another important characteristic is that most adaptive behavior instruments are typical performance measures (Cronbach, 1984). Typical performance measures assess what a person *usually* does, rather than their best possible performance under standardized conditions. These measures are inherently less reliable because of the influence of situational factors (Ted may make his bed sometimes, but not others; or Carol may have good social skills with peers, but not with adults) and various response sets. Response sets may be intentional, as in respondent bias, or unintentional. An example of an unintentional response set is acquiescence in which a respondent agrees with or adopts a middle ground on most items. This response set is probably quite common on items using an always, sometimes, or never format. A respondent who is not thoroughly familiar with the client and who is attempting to be helpful may say "sometimes" to many items as part of an acquiescence response set. This acquiescence could inflate the score markedly, but still not be recognizable as a response set, bias, or faking (which of course it isn't). The only solutions to the response set problem are to seek multiple sources of information and to observe the behavior in a natural setting where appropriate and possible.

The *norms* for adaptive behavior scales, if they exist at all, are often based on non-randomly selected samples from a single state or a specific geographic region. Until very recently, there were no adaptive behavior scales with norms based on a stratified representative sample of the United States population. The norms should be related to the target population for the instrument. For instruments intended for use in making classification/placement decisions with the mildly handicapped to normal populations, norms based on stratified representative samples are more important. The stratified representative sample requirement is not as stringent for instruments used with the more severely handicapped.

The validity evidence for many adaptive behavior instruments is weak at best. However, these instruments should have validity evidence to support the kinds of interpretations suggested in the examiner's manual. Content validity is an important first step, but insufficient. Other evidence, particularly criterion-related validity, is especially important for instruments intended for making classification/placement decisions with the mildly handicapped. Correlations of approximately zero with other conventional measures cannot be offered as evidence that something important and, implicitly, valid is being measured.

There has been a good deal of debate over the appropriate validity criteria for certain adaptive behavior instruments (Goodman, 1979; Mercer, 1979). Criterion-related validity evidence from large scale studies of these measures will soon be published (Reschly, Graham-Clay, & Gresham, 1984; Taylor, 1983). The general findings from these studies is that out-of-school adaptive behavior as judged by parents is not closely related to other appropriate criteria. For instance, the author found very low correlations among peer relations as judged by parents and peer relations as measured by a sociometric measure. Obviously, validity can't be assumed. It is always wise to keep in mind Salvia and Ysseldyke's (1981) caveats regarding case validity. Popular tests are not necessarily good and there is no substitute for well conceived and carefully gathered observation, rating scale, and interview data to corroborate or disconfirm results from standardized measures.

Another characteristic on which adaptive behavior instruments and procedures differ is educational relevance. Direct measures of classroom learning such as classroom observation, samples of daily work, and classwork examinations obviously have considerable relevance to adaptive behavior in the school setting. In contrast, parental perceptions of social role performance outside of school, particularly their best guesses concerning what the child does outside of the home, are not closely related to most educational decision making. The student's competencies and activities outside of school should certainly be considered, particularly as they relate to preparation for the adult adaptive behaviors of independent functioning and self-support. But parental perception of out-of-school performance is not sufficient. Other indices must be considered including, at a minimum, what is called in the AAMD scheme, "application of basic academic skills in daily life activities, application of appropriate reasoning and judgment in mastery of the environment, and social skills (participation in group activities and interpersonal relationships" (Grossman, 1983, p. 25). The educational relevance topic brings the discussion to the final basic consideration: decision making using adaptive behavior data.

Decision Making Using Adaptive Behavior Data

In the previous discussion of purposes of adaptive behavior assessment, the importance of first clarifying the deci-

sion to be made and then matching the assessment procedure to the decision was emphasized. If this very basic, but essential, step is ignored or accomplished haphazardly, the assessment of adaptive behavior will founder (regardless of other factors, like the technical adequacy of instruments) *because the wrong information is gathered!* In addition to choice of assessment method to match purpose, recall or review the other basic considerations, all of which are crucial to the decision-making process. The remainder of this section is devoted to discussion of adaptive behavior scores and scales, classification criteria involving adaptive behavior, placement decisions, and adaptive behavior interventions.

Scores and Scales. There has been a lot said about the imprecision of any single adaptive behavior index. Imprecision of single indices is not unique to this area, but is perhaps a more prominent problem due to the general difficulty of adaptive behavior measurement. In addition to *those* problems, adaptive behavior scales are *not* sufficiently precise to justify the use of single, global scores or exact cut-off scores (see Grossman, 1983, p. 42-46). Scores and scales should be used, as well as comparisons to various standards, as the basic information from which a clinical judgment of adaptive behavior is made. But a specific numerical cut-off score is *not* recommended, here or in other sources (Grossman, 1983; Salvia & Ysseldyke, 1981; Sattler, 1982).

Classification Criteria. Classification criteria that include adaptive behavior directly as does mental retardation generally reflect the concerns about the imprecision of these instruments. The AAMD (Grossman, 1983) warns against the use of specific cut-off scores or single global scores because the adaptive behavior component of the AAMD classification criteria is less precise than the intellectual component. The intellectual component is described as *"significantly subaverage* general intellectual functioning" which is further defined as"IQ of approximately 70 and below on an individually administered general intelligence test." In contrast the adaptive behavior component, "deficits in adaptive behavior," has no modifying adjectives like significantly subaverage; there are no numerical criteria or amount of discrepancy stated or implied; and no general kind of assessment instrument or procedure is suggested. Clearly, a different decision-making process is intended in the AAMD system depending on whether the intellectual functioning or the adaptive behavior dimension is involved. The former involves an approximate cut-off score and a specific kind of measurement instrument. The latter, adaptive behavior, does not.

The AAMD definition of mental retardation is included in the PL94-142 Rules and Regulations (Federal Register, 1977). However, specific classification criteria are not stated in these rules and regulations for mental retardation or for other handicapping conditions. Adaptive behavior is also mentioned in the section "Protection in Evaluation Procedures Provisions," which specifies areas to consider in placement procedures with all handicapped students (Federal Register, 1977). Again, definition and classification criteria are not provided.

State Department of Education (SDE) definitions and classification criteria, which we are usually obligated to apply in classification/placement decisions, vary considerably (Patrick & Reschly, 1982). Most SDEs *do* include adaptive behavior in the definition of mental retardation and many mandate that adaptive behavior be assessed. However, most do *not* specify domains of adaptive behavior assessed, settings considered, measurement procedures, classification criteria such as score cut-offs or ranges, or how adaptive behavior is combined with other

information (such as intelligence) in making decisions. In the absence of SDE specifications on these variables, the role of school psychologists in determining adaptive behavior status is both crucial and challenging. Decisions about these variables are fundamental to the best practices.

Placement Decisions. Adaptive behavior is central to the extremely controversial issues of "six hour" retarded children and overrepresentation of minority students in special education programs for the mildly retarded. Much litigation over this issue has occurred and is continuing, including the landmark Larry P. case which has now been decided in a Federal District Court and the Ninth Circuit Court of Appeals (Larry P. 1979, 1984).

A fundamental issue often ignored by the courts is appropriate classification/placement decisions with minority students. A major dilemma exists with students who have very low general intellectual functioning, very low in-school adaptive behavior, but out-of-school adaptive behavior which is viewed as normal by their parents. These are almost by definition six-hour retarded children. Disproportionate numbers of these students are members of minority groups.

Reschly's decision-making strategy (1982) for the child just described is reproduced as Figure 2. This scheme requires part-time special education placement in what are called resource programs if out-of-school adaptive behavior is within broadly conceived normal limits. The part-time placement addresses the very serious educational problems that exist due to very low intellectual functioning and very low adaptive behavior in school. To *not* classify such students or to *declassify* already placed students with the adaptive pattern described above is *not* a solution to the problem. Such students should be maintained in part-time or resource

FIGURE 2

A Tentative Scheme for Use of Adaptive Behavior Information
in Classification and Selection of Program Option

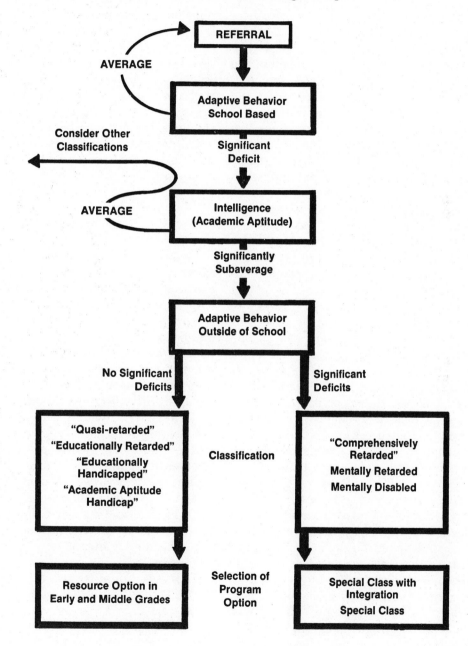

placements unless in-school adaptive behavior improves markedly or the part-time placement is clearly insufficient.

The placement decision strategy suggested in Figure 2 makes heavy use of adaptive behavior information. Depending on SDE Rules and Regulations, it provides one solution to the dilemma of the six-hour retarded child. Although classification as handicapped is required, the emphasis is on keeping the youngster in the regular classroom as much as possible — usually half or more of the school day. This solution provides help to students who have serious educational difficulties and significant limitations in general intellectual functioning and school adaptive behavior. However, the assistance is focused on academic goals, the major problem, with the degree of separation from regular education and the attendant stigma minimized.

The application of this strategy to placement decisions must be guided by SDE requirements and local district policies. As noted earlier, decision-making procedures with adaptive behavior are frequently *not* described by the SDE or in local policies. Unless contraindicted by state and local requirements, this strategy is recommended as a means to resolve the dilemma of classification/placement with so called "six hour" retarded students.

Program Planning and Interventions. Adaptive behavior data are important to good educational programming with all students and, perhaps, even more so with the handicapped. The functional (applied practical) academic skills are crucial to attainment of the major indices of adult success for the mildly handicapped: independent functioning and self-support. Careful description of current success in acquiring and applying these skills to practical, everyday situations is a major component of evaluations at all checkpoints: preplacement, annual reviews, and three-year reevaluations. These specific skills and other essential domains of adaptive behavior are the principal focus of educational programming.

Social skills and interpersonal relationships are at the other end of the adaptive behavior continuum (recall Figure 1). As Gresham notes in another chapter in this volume, most mildly handicapped students have social skills deficits. Social skills and adaptive behavior objectives are part of the IEP, and psychologists should assume major roles in fostering social competencies. These roles should involve counseling, consultation, and group intervention.

BEST PRACTICES

Adaptive behavior assessment is essential to classification/placement and program planning/intervention decisions with handicapped students. The multifactored assessment provided for all handicapped students at preplacement and reevaluation should reflect consideration of adaptive behavior information. This information influences decisions including IEP objectives. Adaptive behavior is the central theme in decisions about the mentally retarded. The preplacement and reevaluations, the IEP, psychological interventions, and annual reviews involving mentally retarded students should reflect careful consideration of adaptive behavior information. The following best practices in assessment and use of adaptive behavior are suggested:

1. *Basic Considerations: Concept, Target Population, and Purpose are Specified.*

The essential first step is to clarify the purpose for assessment, the target population, and the concept of adaptive behavior. To ensure this, it is very desirable to explicitly state the decision to be made and include that statement in the psychological report. This statement includes the decision(s), the target population, and the concept of adaptive behavior being applied. Target population has to do with the age of the student and the general level of behavior; that is, severely retarded versus mildly handicapped to borderline or normal. Concept refers to the major domains of adaptive behavior considered and the settings that are important with the specific case.

2. *Adaptive Behavior Assessment Must Be Matched To the Conception, Purpose, and Target Population*

It is better to gather relevant information with unstandardized instruments than to gather irrelevant information with standardized instruments. As noted and emphasized previously, there are a variety of indices of adaptive behavior. The indices that most closely match the purposes and target population are emphasized.

Where feasible and appropriate, formal adaptive behavior measures are used. When formal adaptive behavior measures are not feasible or are inappropriate due to the nature of the target population, the decision to be made, and so forth, other sources of data are gathered and considered. The other sources include structured and unstructured interviews with the students, parents, or other adults, problem behavior checklists, rating scales, observations, and the like.

3. *Adaptive Behavior Is Considered In All Multifactored Evaluations And, Where Appropriate, Included Explicitly in Classification/Placement and Program Planning/Intervention Decisions.*

This consideration should be apparent in comments made in reports. Deficits in adaptive behavior have a clear influence on decisions.

4. *Adaptive Behavior Is The Central*

Theme In Decisions About Mentally Retarded Students

Adaptive behavior is very important in classification/placement decisions and indispensable to educational programming with all levels of mental retardation.

5. *The Limitations in Adaptive Behavior Assessment Are Considered in Interpretations and Decision Making.*

These limitations establish the necessity of considering several indices of adaptive behavior; the use of informed clinical judgment; the avoidance of single, global scores; and the application of flexible decision rules rather than arbitrary cut off scores.

SUMMARY

Adaptive behavior is a relatively new name for an old and venerable construct. This construct is the intricate capability of human beings to acquire personal independence and social responsibility. Beyond this general statement, exact meaning and precise definition of adaptive behavior are elusive, a not uncommon circumstance with psychological constructs.

There is consensus on certain characteristics of adaptive behavior. It is viewed as developmental, as culturally relative, and general domains of behavior are subsumed in the adaptive behavior construct. The AAMD descriptions of different indices of adaptive behavior at different ages is perhaps the best single source of information on adaptive behavior skills (Grossman, 1983). The salient criteria for preschool ages are self-help skills, psychomotor development, and language. Learning in academic settings, application of skills in mastery of the environment, and social skills are the predominant adaptive behavior criteria for children and youth. Independent func-

TABLE 2

Some Recently Published Adaptive Behavior Measures[1]

Normative Adaptive Behavior Checklist and *Comprehensive Test of Adaptive Behavior* by Gary Adams, published in 1984 by Charles E. Merrill, 1300 Alum Creek Drive, Columbus, OH 43216.

Scales of Independent Behavior by Robert H. Bruininks, Richard W. Woodcock, Richard F. Weatherman, and Bradley K. Hill, published in 1984 by DLM Teaching Resources, One DLM Park, Allen, TX 75002.

Vineland Social Maturity Scale Revision, by Sara S. Sparrow, David A. Balla, and Domenic V. Cicchetti, published in 1984 by American Guidance Service, Publishers' Building, Circle Pines, MN 55014.

Childrens' Adaptive Behavior Scale Revised by Richard H. Kicklighter and Bert O. Richmond, published in 1983 by Humanics Inc., P.O. Box 7447, Atlanta, GA 30309.

AAMD Adaptive Behavior Scale School Edition, revised and standardized in 1981 by Nadine Lambert and Myra Windmiller, distributed by Publishers Test Service, 2500 Garden Road, Monterey, CA 93940.

Adaptive Behavior Inventory for Children by Jane Mercer and June Lewis, published in 1978 by the Psychological Corporation, 7500 Old Oak Blvd., Cleveland, OH 44130.

---

[1]No endorsement of the measures listed nor, for that matter, disapproval of measures not listed, is intended or implied. These measures are used most appropriately in conjunction with other sources and indices of adaptive behavior.

tioning and self-support are the primary criteria for adults.

Effective adaptive behavior assessment with informal devices or standardized inventories varies according to concept of adaptive behavior, target population, and purpose for assessment. The major issues in adaptive behavior conception have to do with whether prerequisite intellectual skills are included and whether both the school and non-school settings are included for children and youth.

Adaptive behavior is an important component of a multifactored assessment with all students and indispensible in the area of mental retardation. Adaptive behavior assessment procedures are not sufficiently well developed to allow decisions based on single instruments. Most are not sufficiently comprehensive or technically adequate. Use of global scores or precise cut-off points in decision making is also *not* appropriate. Information from a variety of adaptive behavior indices are used in decision making. The adaptive behavior information, because it deals directly with skills prerequisite to assumption of normal adult roles, is a crucial area for assessment and interventions with handicapped students.

REFERENCES

Bickel, W. E., Bond, L., & Carter, A. (1981). Educational priorities among urban black populations. *Journal of Negro Education, 50*, 3-8.

Bersoff, D. (1982). Larry P. and PASE: Judicial report cards of the validity of individual intelligence tests. In T. Kratochwill (ed.) *Advances in school psychology, Volume II*, Hillsdale, NJ: Lawrence Erlbaum Associates.

Coulter, W. A. & Morrow, H. W. (1978). *Adaptive behavior: Concepts and Measurements.* New York: Grune & Stratton.

Cronbach, L. J. (1984). *Essentials of psychological testing 4th Ed.* New York: Harper & Row.

Doll, E. A. (1941). The essentials of an inclusive concept of mental deficiency. *American Journal of Mental Deficiency, 46*, 214-219.

Doll, E. A. (1953). *Measurement of social competence.* Circle Pines, MN: American Guidance Service.

Edgerton, R. (1967). The cloak of competence: Stigma in the lives of the mentally retarded. Berkeley, CA: University of California Press.

Edgerton, R. B., Bollinger, M., & Heir, B. (1984). The cloak of competence: After two decades. *American Journal of Mental Deficiency, 88*, 345-351.

Federal Register (1977). Regulations implementing Education for All Handicapped Children Act of 1975 (Public Law 94-142). Author, August 23, p. 42474-42518.

Goodman, J. (1979). Is tissue the issue? A critique of SOMPA's models and tests. *School Psychology Digest, 8*, 47-62.

Greenspan, S. (1979). Social intelligence in the retarded. In N. R. Ellis (Ed.) *Handbook of mental deficiency, psychological theory and research, 2nd ed.* Hillsdale, NJ: Lawrence Erlbaum.

Grossman, H. J. (Ed.) (1973). *Manual on terminology and classification in mental retardation.* Washington, DC: American Association on Mental Deficiency.

Grossman, H. J. (Ed.) (1977). *Manual on terminology and classification in mental retardation.* Washington, DC: American Association on Mental Deficiency.

Grossman, H. J. (Ed.) (1983). *Classification in mental retardation.* Washington, DC: American Association on Mental Deficiency.

Heber, R. (1959). A manual on terminology and classification in mental retardation. *American Journal on Mental Deficiency Monograph Supplement 64(2).*

Heber, R. (1961). Modifications of the "Manual on terminology and classification in mental retardation." *American Journal of Mental Deficiency, 65(4)* 499-500.

Larry P. v. Riles 495 F. Supp. 926 (N. D. Cal 1979) (decision on merits).

Larry P. v. Riles United States Court of Appeals, Ninth Circuit, No. 80-427. Jan. 23, 1984.

Leland, H., Shellhaase, M., Nihira, K., & Foster, R. (1967). Adaptive behavior: A new dimension in the classification of the mentally retarded. *Mental Retardation Abstracts, 4*, 359-387.

MacMillan, D. L. & Borthwick, S. (1980). The new mentally retarded population: Can they be mainstreamed? *Mental Retardation, 18*, 155-158.

Mercer, J. (1973). *Labeling the mentally retarded.* Berkeley, CA: University of California Press.

Mercer, J. (1979). *System of Multicultural Pluralistic Assessment Technical Manual.* New York: Psychological Corporation.

Patrick, J. & Reschly, D. (1982). Relationship of state educational criteria and demographic variables to school-system prevalence of mental retardation. *American Journal of Mental Deficiency, 86*, 351-360.

PCMR (1970). *The six hour retarded child.* Washington, DC: President's Committee on Mental Retardation, United States Government Printing Office.

Polloway, E. A. & Smith, J. D. (1983). Changes in mild mental retardation: Population, programs, and perspectives. *Exceptional Children, 50*, 149-159.

Reschly, D. (1981a). Psychological testing in educational classification and placement. *American Psychologist, 36*, 1094-1102.

Reschly, D. (1981b). Evaluation of the effects of SOMPA measures on classification of students as mildly retarded. *American Journal of Mental Deficiency, 86*, 16-20.

Reschly, D. (1982). Assessing mild mental retardation: The influence of adaptive behavior, sociocultural status and prospects for nonbiased assessment. In C. Reynolds & T. Gutkin (Eds.) *The handbook of school psychology.* New York: Wiley Interscience.

Reschly, D. J., Graham-Clay, S. L. & Gresham, F. M. (1984). *Multifactored Nonbiased Assessment: Convergent and Discriminant Validity on Social and Cognitive Measures with Black and White Regular and Special Education Students.* Project Report. Department of Psychology, Iowa State University, Ames, Iowa.

Salvia, J. & Ysseldyke, J. (1981). *Assessment in Special and remedial education* (2nd Ed.) Boston: Houghton-Mifflin.

Sattler, J. M. (1982). *Assessment of children's intelligence and special abilities (2nd Ed.).* Boston: Allyn & Bacon.

Taylor, R. (1983). *Florida Norms for SOMPA.* Project Report, Title 6B Grant, Florida State Department of Education, Tallahassee, Florida.

ANNOTATED BIBLIOGRAPHY

Coulter, W. A., & Morrow, H. W. (Eds.) (1978). *Adaptive behavior: Concepts and measurements.* New York: Grune & Stratton.
This edited volume includes original chapters by leading figures such as Jane Mercer, Nadine Lambert, Henry Leland, and Kazuo Nihira. The differences among conceptions of adaptive behavior are presented effectively, but the previous literature on social competence was largely ignored. The content will soon be out of date.

Grossman, H. J. (Ed.) (1983). *Classification in mental retardation.* Washington, DC: American Association on Mental Deficiency.
This is the most authoritative source on the construct of adaptive behavior and on conceptions of mental retardation. This is essential reading for school psychologists involved with mental retardation classification/placement decisions.

Meyers, C. E., Nihira, K., & Zetlin, A. (1979). The measurement of adaptive behavior. In N. R. Ellis (Ed.) *Handbook of mental deficiency, psychological theory and research 2nd Ed.* Hillsdale, NJ: Lawrence Erlbaum.
This is a comprehensive, scholarly treatment of the theory and research pertaining to adaptive behavior measurement.

Reschly, D. J. (1982). Assessing mild mental retardation: The influence of adaptive behavior, sociocultural status and prospects for nonbiased assessment. In C. Reynolds & T. Gutkin (Eds.) *The Handbook of School Psychology.* New York: Wiley Interscience.
This chapter includes further discussion of the placement bias litigation as well as commentary on adaptive behavior theory, research, and measurement.

BEST PRACTICES IN ASSESSMENT OF VISUALLY HANDICAPPED STUDENTS

Greg A. Robinson
Iowa Braille and Sight-Saving School

OVERVIEW

School psychologists are constantly called upon to demonstrate their expertise with children and adolescents of all ages. Generally, student's needs are met through use of skills which school psychologists have acquired through their pre-service training program, on-the-job training, or continuing education.

Most school psychologists have had little training or experience with low incidence populations such as the visually impaired. Misconceptions and lack of information about visually handicapped individuals can negatively influence school psychologists. Goldman and Duda (1980) state that testing a partially sighted or blind child is a fascinating but bewildering experience for uninitiated school psychologists.

The purpose of this chapter is to make evaluation of a visually handicapped student less bewildering and more intriguing. The intent is to provide information for specific use in dealing with this population. The reader will be pleasantly surprised with the similarities of the assessment tools used. Issues regarding the use of standardized administrative test procedures as well as the adaption of assessment instruments are discussed. Background preparation, consideration of areas/materials/equipment, and efficient interpretation of data are the focus of the chapter.

History. Bauman (1972) wrote that early attempts at intellectual evaluation of the visually handicapped were initiated because several schools for the blind wanted to identify students who were mentally retarded. To assist with this task, Robert Irwin adapted the Goodard-Binet in 1914 for use with blind children.

In 1915, Haines developed the Paint Scale for the Blind. Through the administration of his test, he was able to demonstrate not only that blind children compared well with sighted children, but also that they needed tactual and social experiences. From this point forward, wheels were set in motion to adapt or create intellectual measures for this population.

Definition. The National Medical Foundation for Eye Care (1959) elucidates the following functions of the eyes:

1. *Central vision* is the perception and discrimination of object forms;

2. *Accommodation* is adjustment of focus for distant and near vision;

3. *Binocular vision* is the coordination of the two eyes so that a single object is perceived;

4. *Peripheral vision* is reception of small amounts of light in the outer part of the visual field; and

5. *Color vision* is the perception of color.

Barraga (1983) states that as far back as the early 1800s, professionals from various disciplines fueled the existing confusion and imprecise use of terminology associated with visual handicaps. In 1934, the American Medical Association proposed a medically oriented definition of a *legally blind person* as one who has visual acuity of 20/200 or less in the better eye with correction (e.g., lenses) or whose field of vision is narrowed so that the widest diameter of the person's visual field subtends an angular distance no greater than 20 degrees (*National Society for Prevention of Blindness Fact Book,* 1966, p. 10).

Normal vision acuity is 20/20. The 20/200 ratio indicates that a person with 20/200 acuity sees at 20 feet what a person with normal vision sees at 200 feet. Field of vision refers to the total visual area seen at any one time. This is usually at an angle of 60 to 70 degrees. When a person has a limited visual field, it is similar to looking through a tunnel, thus the term *tunnel vision.* For this chapter, the first part of this definition is referred to as the student's *central visual acuity.* When referring to the student's visual field, the term *peripheral vision* is used.

Also included in the medically oriented definition are those persons who are *partially sighted.* Their visual acuity ranges between 20/70 and 20/200. Educators view the sole use of this definition as inadequate. Though informative to a degree, it does not speak to the individual's residual level of vision (how much vision remains) or visual efficiency (how well a person uses the remaining vision).

Implying that people who are blind do not see anything is another myth. In a study of over 26,000 legally blind students, Willis (1976) found only 18% were totally blind. Large or regular print books were used by 52% of the sample. Large print and Braille were used by 3%, while 21% used only Braille, and 24% used tapes or records.

The medically oriented definition allows those who meet the legal criteria certain special services or benefits including tax deductions, materials and devices to assist them with their daily routines, supplementary income, vocational rehabilitation, library and mailing privileges, and so forth (DeMott, 1982; Hallahan and Kauffman, 1982).

Barraga (1983) states that from 1977 to the present there has been a gradual shift to terms such as *blind* and *low vision.* Previously mentioned terms are fading from the literature. The term *visually impaired* is giving way to the term *visually handicapped.* Barraga describes it as being used widely to "denote the total group of children who have impairments in the structure or functioning of the visual sense organ — the eye — irrespective of the nature and extent of the impairment (p. 21)."

For an educational definition, we again look to Barraga (1983):

A visually handicapped child is one whose visual impairment interferes with his optimal learning and achievement, unless adaptations are made in the methods of presenting learning experiences, the nature of the materials used, and/or in the learning environment (p. 25).

Included in this definition are those who are *blind.* DeMott (1982) describes this group as individuals who are completely without vision or who have light perception only. They usually learn through the "use of braille or related media without the aid of vision, even though they may be able to perceive light and use it for orientation or movement (p. 272)."

Individuals with *low vision* are also included under this definition. These children use their vision for some school related activities, possibly some reading. Others need tactual adaptations or materials including braille to assist them with their learning (Barraga, 1983). DeMott (1982) also states that low vision students frequently rely on their other senses to solicit information from their environment since they can see only what is close to them.

The final term under this definition are those children who are *visually limited.* This includes children who have difficulty with their vision under average circumstances. "They may have difficulty seeing learning materials without special lighting, or they may be unable to see distant objects unless the objects are moving, or they may need to wear prescriptive lenses or use optical aides and special materials to function visually (Barraga, 1983, p. 23)."

Prevalence. Kirchner and Peterson (1979) indicate that 1,391,000 individuals were listed as having severe visual impairments in a Health Interview Survey conducted by the National Center for Health Statistics. Rostetter, Kowalski, and Hunter (1984) reported information from the Data Analysis System of the Department of Education, Office of Special Education which stated the number of children ages 3-21 years who were served under PL 89-313 and PL 94-142 during the school year of 1980-81. They found 33,004 children identified as visually handicapped and 2,929 were deaf and blind. This means that visually handicapped students would make up 0.8% of the total population served by the two public laws (0.1% for deaf/blind and 0.9% for the total).

BASIC CONSIDERATIONS

School psychologists have similar goals in the evaluation process of visually handicapped students. Through the presentation of many tasks/activities across varying situations and environments, school psychologists sample behavior. The requirements of individuals conducting the evaluation are also similar. They must have training and experience that is psychologically-based and contains the necessary elements of measurement (Vander Kolk, 1981). Appropriately trained school psychologists are capable, therefore, of successfully meeting the challenge of evaluating visually impaired students.

The school psychologist can make

this an easier task by beginning with understanding the population. Many visual handicaps in children are caused by hereditary or congenital defects (Mandel and Fiscus, 1981) as well as by postnatal accidents, injury, trauma, or disease.

Examples of conditions (DeMott, 1982) are those which:

1. Impair central vision
   A. myopia
   B. hyperopia
   C. cataracts
   D. astigmatism
2. Impair binocular vision
   A. strabismus
   B. nystagmus
   C. amblyopia
3. Are caused by biological factors
   A. diabetes
   B. retrolental fibroplasia
   C. glaucoma
   D. albinism

Research also indicates that a large majority of visually handicapped students have additional handicaps. These include mental retardation, cerebral palsy, and hearing impairments (Graham, 1968; Freedman, 1978).

What is it like to be without vision? For infants, the distortion of early visual stimulation causes delays in reaching developmental milestones (Chase, 1977). Visually handicapped children most likely experience delays in movements, conceptual understanding, and self-awareness (DeMott, 1982). Situations must be created for the child to experience tactually what sighted children experience visually. Chase (1977) has observed that language development occurs at an initially slower rate with visually handicapped children. After initial words are picked up, however, the progress is faster than that of the sighted child. Language is a valuable tool to a visually handicapped individual. As they learn about their environments, they begin the process of matching words to concepts or objects that they cannot visualize. Difficulties in this area result in the use of "verbalisms" (Cutsforth, 1951; Harley, 1963; DeMott, 1966), in which the individual unsuccessfully or inconsistently matches language with what they are experiencing in their environment through other senses. Absences of opportunities for incidental learning also cause problems for visually handicapped students especially when tasks involve abstract thinking.

The last basic consideration that school psychologists should ponder is how to handle the issue of standardization. A major difficulty in evaluating visually handicapped students, especially if there is more than one handicapping condition, is the lack of reliable and valid diagnostic instruments (Swallow, 1977). Few school psychologists, until they are faced with the aspect of evaluating visually handicapped students, realize just how many of their assessment tools require vision (Bauman and Kropf, 1979).

Basic questions revolve around the issues of validity, reliability, norms, quantification, and standardization. Professionals have lined up on both sides of these spirited issues. In the end, school psychologists must consider the individual student being evaluated. Barraga (1983) lists a variety of questions for school psychologists to consider before starting the evaluation. What is the purpose of the evaluation? Is it to exclude from or to make the student eligible for programs? Are norms or age-level equivalents needed, and if so, are they in comparison to sighted or to blind children? How is functioning below what is expected, interpreted? Does it reflect a vision problem, lack of cognitive abilities, limited experiences, and so forth? When evaluating a visually handicapped student, school psychologists should be more concerned about determining strategies that are beneficial in maximizing the student's potential rather than predicting success

in relation to a norm group (Swallow, 1977).

The general goal is to measure what the student can do. Pushing the child into an unfamiliar standardized and rigid setting results in a performance that does not reflect true abilities. If a student uses learning aids in the classroom, these aids are not disallowed during an evaluation. Flexibility is needed. Yet so is accuracy. If assessment instruments are adapted, the adaptations must be noted.

BEST PRACTICES

The following approach does not represent any particular method, rather it is a combination of ideas suggested by those who work with visually handicapped students.

Gathering background information. Prior to any evaluation, background information is gathered. Vision information is important, but it does not answer all questions. When reviewing this information for the first time, school psychologists are often confused unless they are familiar with various terms including ophthalmologist, optometrist, visual acuity, visual perception, visual functioning, and visual efficiency.

This information directs school psychologists what to evaluate and how to do it. Information such as the etiology and prognosis of the visual handicap are beneficial not only in selecting techniques/instruments for a given student based on current levels of functioning, but also for arranging appropriate environmental conditions such as lighting or media form based on vision status.

When the student lost vision is another important consideration. Was it at or before birth (congenital) or after birth (adventitous)? This effects visual memory abilities. If a child had vision for the first three to five years of life, some visual memories such as environmental facts, colors, shapes, distance, or proportions were established although they may be altered by time or the quality of vision (Vander Kolk, 1981; Morse, 1975). If the vision was lost prior to this time period, visual memory abilities were most likely not established. Morse also suggests determining level of current vision; amount of residual vision; field of vision, learning modes such as regular print, large print, braille, or aural method; the amount of time that the student needs to complete a given task; and the lighting in which the student works best.

In addition, what learning aids is the student presently using? If none, are there some that might benefit the student?

Corn and Martinez (undated) describe a variety of aids, including:

1. Visual
   A. bookstands
   B. felt-tip pens
   C. acetate laid over paper to darken print and reduce glare large type books
2. Tactual
   A. Braillewriter
   B. slate and stylus
   C. templates
3. Auditory
   A. cassette
   B. Talking Book
   C. speech compressors
4. Electronic aids
   A. talking calculator
   B. Optacon
   C. closed circuit television

Optical aids such as glasses, bifocals, contact lenses, tinted lenses; magnifiers, and telescopic aids might also benefit the student.

Conference with teacher or other support personnel. As stated before, not all of the questions are answered by data in the cumulative file. Information relat-

ing to the individual student are gathered through interviews with other school personnel.

Parent interview or completion of a parent inventory. Parents are an untapped resource for information covering the four basic life skill domain areas of domestic, recreation/leisure, community involvement, and vocational. Their input is valuable in assessment and writing educational goals. If students can respond to questions pertaining to home responsibilities, use of free time, work interests, and so forth, their comments are then compared with those of their parents and teachers.

Observation of students. Observations are a valuable component in the evaluation process. School psychologists should begin to hypothesize about how they are going to answer referral questions. Observing students' work and study habits, their interactions with their peers and teachers, and their level of independence in accomplishing tasks are all valuable pieces of information. What reinforces students? What are their best modalities for learning? Do they problem solve by trial and error or systematically. Are there inappropriate behaviors that interfere with their learning? If so, are they attention seeking and/or frustration oriented? The more observations made across varied environmental settings, the better are pictures of students formulated.

Meeting students and preparing for evaluations. Evaluations should be enjoyable. Yet there is a tendency to be overly cautious in approaching the visually impaired population. Genshaft, Dare, and O'Malley (1980) offer the following helpful hints: (a) speak to the students as you approach so they know where you are, (b) offer your arm to assist them ("sighted guide") to the assessment area, (c) speak in a normal tone of voice unless there is a hearing loss (if there is, see how the loss is handled, i.e., with aids, etc.), (d) do not feel uncomfortable about using sight-oriented word, (e) explain what you are going to do, the instruments, purpose of testing and the situation, and (f) frequently use tactile and verbal reinforcements.

For younger children, a quick tour of the evaluation area helps eliminate questions about where they are or what is in the immediate area. This time is also used to "interview" students with regard to what lighting conditions (natural vs. artificial) they do their best work, what aids they use, and how they like their learning materials positioned (bookstand, on table, etc.). By now the examiner should be fairly sure about whether to use print or braille. If students state they read print, ask them to read prior to the start of the evaluation (Bauman, 1974). By placing students at ease, school psychologists can informally begin the evaluation through interview type questions which will hopefully spark conversation. Observing how students interact and handle the questions and how they manage their body position clues school psychologists when to move on to the more formal aspects of the evaluation.

Selection of instruments and adaptations. Vander Kolk (1981) breaks assessment instruments down into five areas:

1. those devised and based on norms for the visually impaired;

2. those originally standardized on the general populations with updated norms for the visually impaired;

3. those adapted in some form such as braille or large print;

4. those examiners can adapt for use with exceptional children by selecting items or subtests;

5. those to be used in a standard manner (pp. 39-40).

In an attempt to form a comprehensive picture of students, it becomes clear that a battery of measures is used in the evaluation process (Chase, 1977).

Should modifications/adaptations be made? Even if the chosen instrument has been normed on the visually handicapped, questions still arise due to the heterogeneous make up of this population (e.g., additional handicapping conditions, visually handicapped in residential schools, age of onset, degree of visually handicapped). Therefore, some modifications are necessary. Vander Kolk (1981) suggests that the administration of tests be adapted to the circumstances of the children being evaluated. If they want to walk around but still attend, let them. Note all deviations from standardized administrative procedures, and interpret the findings in light of the student's behavioral reactions to the changes.

Many assessment tools are available in large print or braille. A listing of these instruments is found in the *Central Catalog* (American Printing House, 1983), or by contacting the American Foundation for the Blind. Information can also be obtained by contacting the Test Division in the Research Department at the American Printing House. Some school psychologists employed by state schools for the visually handicapped, in conjunction with their excellent media departments, have made adaptations to assessment tools not available from the previous sources. If large print is used, the general rule is to allow one-and-a-half times longer on timed tasks, and double the regular time limits for braille readers (Swallow, 1981).

Selected instruments in key areas are briefly reviewed. For more information, read Vander Kolk (1981); Swallow (1981); Bauman and Kropf (1979); Genshaft, Dare and O'Malley, (1980); Scholl and Schnur (1976); and Langley (1980).

Vision. The *Program to Develop Efficiency in Visual Functioning: Diagnostic Assessment Procedure* (Barrage and Morris, 1980) measures the visual efficiency of children with low vision. It comes with a kit which assists in the programming to improve a student's residual vision. The *Visual Functioning Assessment Tool* (Costello, Pinkney, & Scheffers, 1980) is an informal instrument that is used primarily to provide supplemental information on students' visual functioning.

Intelligence. Bauman and Kropf (1979) surveyed school psychologists working with visually handicapped students to find what instruments they used. In both surveys, the Verbal Scales of the Wechsler tests were the most popular. A majority of the school psychologists rated them good, while the others rated them adequate. The Wechsler Preschool Scale was sometimes questioned. For these younger children, consideration might be given to the *McCarthy Scales of Children's Abilities* (McCarthy, 1972). Through a prorating technique developed by Kaufman and Kaufman (1977), Verbal and Quantitative Indexes can be derived. Modified versions of the Stanford-Binet have also been used.

In viewing performance measures, the Performance subtests on the Wechslers can be given to students with low vision, for qualitative reasons more so to obtain a score. A great deal of hope in evaluating performance abilities centered on the Perkins-Binet Tests of Intelligence for the Blind (Davis, 1980). This instrument is available in two forms for usable and non-usable vision. After being on the market for several years, questions were raised over several aspects of the tests. These concerns involve the manual, administration procedures, standard deviations, and so forth (Genshaft and Ward, 1982; Teare and Thompson, 1982).

Recently, over 400 protocols were collected from school psychologists who used the Perkins-Binet to gather correlative data. The manual was also reviewed and the use of the intelligence quotient was discussed. It is hoped that the Perkins-Binet will eventually become more of a diagnostic tool for qualitative use rather than just a score-rendering instrument (J. L. Morse, personal communication, February 15, 1984). This would be a great step, as the Perkins-Binet does have many qualitative benefits.

Work has also been initiated on the *Tactile Assessment of Performance* by Dr. Joan B. Chase. When finished, the six performance subtests will be given alternately with verbal tests from the Wechsler Scales.

The *Blind Learning Aptitude Test* (BLAT) (Newland, 1971, 1979) is intended to assess the learning aptitude of blind children. Six different functions are measured through the presentation of test items in bas-relief form. Although standardized on individuals between the age of 6 and 20 years, it is recommended for students between the ages of 6 and 12 years (Salvia and Ysseldyke, 1981).

For students over the age of sixteen years, two performance subtests are the *Haptic Intelligence Scale* (HIS) (Shurrager and Shurrager, 1964) and the *Stanford-Kohs Block Design Test* (Suinn and Dauterman, 1966). The HIS consists of six subtests intended to supplement the Wechsler Adult Intelligence Scale Verbal Scale. Drawbacks are that if students have vision, they need to wear a blindfold, and Streitfeld and Avery (1968) found a high correlation between the HIS and the WAIS Verbal Scale indicating they both measured the same construct. The question regarding the block arranging format of the Stanford-Kohs pertains to the predictive value of the test. The Stanford-Kohs does give qualitative insights.

Achievement. Bauman and Kropf (1979) report that the *Stanford Achieve-*

ment Test (1984 norms) *PIAT, PPVT,* and the *WRAT* are the most popular achievement instruments used with visually handicapped students. Because of their criterion referenced format the Brigance inventories are also getting more use as is the Key Math. As in the past (Ozias, 1975), most of the achievement measures have been modified either in format or administration.

Other. For smaller children the *Uzqiris-Hunt Ordinal Scales of Psychological Development* (Uzqiris and Hunt, 1975) is a conceptually based test which assesses the effects of blindness on early development (from birth to two years). Other tests for this level are the *Development Activities Screening Inventor* (DASI) (DuBose and Langley, 1977), the *Bayley Scales of Infant Development* (Bayley, 1969), the Hawaii Early Learning Profile (Furuno, O'Reilly, Hosaka, Inatsuka, Allman, and Zeisloft, 1979), and the *Oregon Project for Visually Impaired and Blind Preschool Children Skills Inventory* (Brown, Simmons, and Methvin, 1979).

Adaptive behavior and observational scales include the *Social Maturity Scale for Blind Preschool Children* (Maxfield and Buchholz, 1957), the *Vineland Adaptive Behavior Scale* (Sparrow, Balla, and Cicchetti, 1984), the *Wisconsin Behavior Rating Scale* which have normative data on visually handicapped (Song and Jones, 1980) and the *Peabody Mobility Program* which covers a variety of skills for blind and low vision students (Harley, Wood and Merbler, 1978).

SUMMARY

Human nature dictates that individuals act somewhat confused about what they are unfamiliar with or unable to initially understand. School psychologists can ⦁display this tendency when faced with evaluation of students who have low incidence handicapping conditions. Included in this group, are students with visual handicaps.

To assist school psychologists who find themselves in this predicament, background information was presented in reference to defining the population, its prevalence, and a brief history. Basic considerations were offered which dealt with the etiology of the vision loss, the development of visually handicapped students and the purpose for evaluating these students.

Finally, a best practice approach was discussed. Included were the analysis of formal and informal vision information, use of learning aides, meetings with parents and staff, observation and meeting students, and selecting appropriate evaluation measures. With regard to the latter point, examples of selected instruments as well as modification/adaptations of instruments were discussed.

REFERENCES

Barraga, N. C. & Morris, J. E. (1980). *Program to Develop Efficiency in Visual Functioning: Diagnostic Assessment Procedure.* Louisville, KY: American Printing House for the Blind, Inc.

Barraga, N. C. (1983). *Visual handicaps & lerning* (rev. ed.). Austin, TX: Exceptional Resources.

Bauman, M. K. (1972). Psychological testing and blindness — a retrospect. *Blindness.* Washington, DC: American Association of Workers for the Blind.

Bauman, M. K. (1974). Blind and partially sighted. In M. V. Wisland (Ed.), *Psychoeducational diagnosis of exceptional children.* Springfield, IL: Charles C. Thomas.

Bauman, M. K. & Kropf, C. A. (1979). Psychological tests used with blind and visually handicapped persons. *School Psychology Digest, 8*(3), 257-270.

Bayley, M. (1969). *Bayley Scales for Infant Development.* New York, NY: Psychological Corporation.

Brown, D., Simmons, V., & Methvin, J. (1979). *The Oregon Project for Visually Impaired & Blind Preschool Children: Skills Inventory* (rev. ed.). Medford, OR: Jackson County Education Service District.

Chase, J. B. (1977). Psychological implications of visual and related impairments. In J. Grotsky et al. (Eds.), *Individualized program planning for the visually impaired and multi-handicapped.* Blackwood, NJ: Potential Publishers.

Costello, K. B., Pinkley, P., & Scheffers, W. (1980). *Visual Functioning Assessment Tool.* Chicago, IL: Stoelting Company.

Corn, A. L. & Martinez, I. (1981). *When you have a visually handicapped child in your classroom: Suggestions for teachers.* New York, NY: American Foundation for the Blind.

Cutsforth, T. D. (1951). *The blind in school and society.* New York, NY: American Foundation for the Blind.

Davis, C. (1980). *Perkins-Binet Tests of Intelligence for the Blind.* Watertown, MA: Perkins School for the Blind.

DeMott, R. M. (1966). *Verbalism and affective meaning for blind, partially blind, and normally sighted school age children.* Vinton, IA: Iowa Braille and Sight Saving School.

DeMott, R. M. (1982). Visual impairments. In N. G. Haring (Ed.), *Exceptional children and youth* (3rd ed.). Columbus, OH: Merrill Publishing Company.

DuBose, R. F. & Langley, M. B. (1977). *Developmental Activities Screening Inventory.* New York, NY: Teaching Resources.

Freedman, S. (1978). Support services and alternatives to institutionalization for deaf-blind children. *Journal of Visual Impairment and Blindness, 72*(1), 249-254.

Furuno, S., O'Reilly, K. A., Hosaka, C. M., Inatsuka, T. T., Allman, T. L., & Zeisloft, B. (1979). *Hawaii Early Learning Profile.* Palo Alto, CA: VORT Corporation.

Genshaft, J. L., Dare, N. L. & O'Malley, P. L. (1980). Assessing the visually impaired child: A school psychology view. *Journal of Visual Impairment and Blindness, 74*(9), 344-350.

Genshaft, J. L., & Ward, M. E. (1982). A review of the Perkins-Binet Tests of Intelligence for the Blind with suggestions for administration. *School Psychology Review, 11*(3), 338-341.

Goldman, F. H., & Duda, D. (1980). Psychological assessment of the visually impaired child. In R. K. Mulliken & M. Evans (Eds.), *Assessment of children with low incidence handicaps.* Stratford, CT: The National Association of School Psychologists.

Graham, M. D. (1968). *Multiply impaired blind children: A national problem.* New York, NY: American Foundtion for the Blind.

Hallahan, D. P., & Kauffman, J. M. (1982). *Exceptional children: An introduction to special education.* Englewood Cliffs, NJ: Prentice Hall.

Harley, R. K. (1963). *Verbalism among blind children.* New York, NY: American Foundation for the Blind.

Harley, R. K., Wood, T., & Merbler, J. (1978). *Peabody Mobility Programs.* Chicago, IL: Stoelting Company.

Kaufman, A. S. & Kaufman, N. L. (1977). *Clinical evaluation of young children with the McCarthy scales.* New York, NY: Grune & Stratton, Inc.

Kirchner, C., & Peterson, R. (1979). The latest data on visual disability from NCHS. *Journal of Visual Impairment and Blindness, 73*(4), 151-153.

Langley, M. B. (1980). Assessment of multihandicapped visually impaired learners. *Peabody Model Vision Project.* Chicago, IL: Stoelting Company.

Lappin, C. W. (1983). *Central catalog* (14th ed.). Louisville, KY: American Printing House for the Blind.

Mandell, C. J., & Fiscus, E. (1981). *Understanding exceptional people.* New York, NY: West Publishing Company.

Maxfield, K. E., & Bucholz, S. (1957). *A Social Maturity Scale for Blind Preschool Children.* New York, NY: American Foundation for the Blind.

McCarthy, D. (1972). *manual for the McCarthy Scales of Children's Abilities.* New York, NY: The Psychological Corporation.

Morse, J. L. (1975). Answering the questions of the psychologist assessing the visually handicapped child. *The New Outlook, 69*(8), 350-353.

National Medical Foundation for Eye Care. (1959). *Identification of school children requiring eye care.* Washington, DC: American Association of Opthalmology.

Newland, T. E. (1971). *Manual for the Blind Learning Aptitude Test.* Urbana, IL: Instructional Materials Reference Center, American Printing House for the Blind.

Newland, T. E. (1979). The Blind Learning Aptitude Test. *Journal of Visual Impairment and Blindness, 73*(4), 134-139.

Ozias, D. K. (1975). Achievement assessment of the visually handicapped. *Education of the Visually Handicapped, 7*(3), 76-83.

Rostetter, D., Kowalski, R., & Hunter, D. (1984). Implementing the integration principle of PL 94-142. In N. Certo, N. Haring, & R. York (Eds.), *Public school integration of severely handicapped students: Rational issues and alternatives.* Baltimore, MD: Brookes Publishing Company.

Salvia, J., & Ysseldyke, J. E. (1981). *Assessment in special and remedial education* (2nd Ed.). Boston, MA: Houghton Mifflin Company.

Scholl, G., & Schnur, R. (1976). *Measures of psychological, vocational, educational functioning in the blind and partially and visually handicapped.* New York, NY: American Foundation for the Blind.

Shurrager, H. C., & Shurrager, P. S. (1964). *Manual for the Haptic Intelligence Scale for the Blind.* Chicago, IL: Psychology Research Technology Center, Illinois Institute of Technology.

Song, A. Y., & Jones, S. E. (Eds.). (1980). *Wisconsin Behavior Rating Scale.* Madison, WI: Department of Health and Social Services, Division of Community Services.

Sparrow, S. S., Balla, D. A., & Cicchetti, D. V. (1984). *Vineland Adaptive Behavior Scales.* Circle Pines, MN: American Guidance Service.

Streitfield, J. W., & Avery, C. D. (1968). The WAIS and HIS tests as predictors of academic achievement in the residential school for the Blind. *International Journal for the Education of the Blind, 18,* 73-77.

Suinn, R. M., & Dauterman, W. L. (1966). *A manual for the Stanford-Kohs Block Design Test for the Blind.* Washington, DC: Vocational Rehabilitation Administration.

Swallow, R. M. (1977). Assessment for visually handicapped children and youth. *AFB Practice Report.* New York, NY: American Foundation for the Blind.

Swallow, R. M. (1981). Fifty assessment instruments commonly used with blind and partially seeing individuals. *Journal of Visual Impairment and Blindness, 75*(2), 65-72.

Teare, J. F., & Thompson, R. W. (1982). Concurrent validity of the Perkins-Binet Test of Intelligence for the Blind. *Journal of Visual Impairment and Blindness, 76*(7), 279-280.

Uzgiris, I. C., & Hunt, J. McV. (1975). *Assessment in infancy: Ordinal scales of psychological development.* Urbana, IL: University of Illinois Press.

Vander Kolk, C. J. (1981). *Assessment and planning with the visually impaired.* Baltimore, MD: University Park Press.

Willis, D. H. (1976). *A study of the relationship between visual acuity, reading mode, and school systems for blind students - 1976.* Louisville, KY: American Printing House for the Blind.

ANNOTATED BIBLIOGRAPHY

Barraga, N. C. (1983). *Visual handicaps & learning* (rev. ed.). Austin, TX: Exceptional Resources. Educational oriented book by well known specialist in the area of vision. Chapters deal with terminology, development, movement, modes for learning, assessment and evaluation, and programming, as well as other pertinent issues. The book is very informative and easy to understand.

DeMott, R. M. (1982). Visual impairments. In N. G. Haring (Ed.), *Exceptional children and youth* (3rd ed.). Columbus, OH: Merrill Publishing Company.
A very good introduction chapter in the area of vision. Concisely written, the content is disseminated in such a way that the novice, as well as the specialist, will find it to be an informative overview of the different facets which make up this low incidence population. As a whole, the entire book is an excellent introduction to the different populations which make up exceptional children.

Jastrzembska, Z. S. (1982). *Model for a workshop on assessment of blind and visually impaired students.* New York, NY: American Foundation for the Blind.
Collection of articles, reports, and other papers pertaining to the assessment of visually handicapped students. These chapters are a result of the workshops sponsored by the American Foundation for the Blind for psychologists and psychometrists.

Vander Kolk, C. J. (1981). *Assessment and planning with the visually impaired.* Baltimore, MD: University Park Press.
A complete text book for school psychologists who work with visually handicapped students. Chapters include history, children and youth, intelligence, vocational skills, career development, personality, and assessment report and planning. It is easy to read and answers many questions.

Vaughan, D. & Asbury, T. (1980). *General Ophthalmology* (9th ed.). Los Altos, CA: Lange Medical Publications.
A medically oriented text which deals with the physiology of the eye. Is used in many vision programs as the text for that course. Although somewhat difficult to understand, it enables understanding of terminology and visual conditions which are unfamiliar to most school personnel.

BEST PRACTICES IN REPORT WRITING

Gary Ross-Reynolds
Nicholls State University

OVERVIEW

"Doug is an attractive, well-groomed, blond-haired, blue-eyed ten year old who accompanied the examiner willingly to the testing room." "During a 15 minute observation period using a 10 second time sample, Allyson was found to be on task 100% of the intervals compared with 86% for a peer. However, she is highly distractible." "Dwayne claims he has a good appetite and likes white beans, fruit, and spaghetti." "On his drawing of the female figure Jason drew breasts and genitals suggesting deviant or inappropriate sexual interest." "Nathan approaches new situations with a paranoid ego structure that on balance is preponderantly self defeating. However, this preferential initial approach to novel environments is gradually tempered as trust and confidence builds at which point he begins to amuse himself and gain control of situations through Machiavellian tactics." "Using the Fox-Burdette method 30 minutes per day David learned only two new sight words in two weeks.... It is recommended that David receive individual instruction in reading using the Fox-Burdette method."

Seemingly impossible to write well, merely difficult to write poorly, psychological reports constitute the gnawing ground of every school psychologist's existence. As static products of a dynamic process, they linger long after they might better be forgotten. Although the long-standing criticisms and short comings are familiar to most, boiling down to being a waste of time to write and read, there has been little change in the form and substance in reports through the years (Grimes & Ross-Reynolds, 1983; Lacks, Horton, & Owen, 1969).

It is essential that reports be given a purpose and context. To this end, a small, non-representative sample of school psychologists were asked why they wrote reports and for whom they wrote them. Responses are classified under the following categories: (a) documentation of psychological services/accountability; (b) district, federal, and state requirement; (c) documentation that a child is handicapped and/or in need of special services; and (d) assistance to the child and teacher. When asked for whom their reports were written, responses ranged from employers and the file to parents, teachers, and other professionals. Subjects' stammering in response to these queries suggested that most had never stopped to consider such basic questions.

The fundamental purpose of the psychologist's report is communication (Grimes, 1981). The extent to which a report clearly communicates useful information about a child is the extent to which the purpose of the report is being realized. If the information is not useful, or not presented clearly, then the report fails to fulfill its intended mission psychologists waste their time, and children are ill-served.

Communication, by definition, necessitates an interchange between the sender, in this case, the psychologist, and the receiver. But who is the receiver? The file? The director of special education? Teachers? Parents? Other professionals? The child? No one and everyone? It is an important question. Most psychologists recognize the multiple uses reports serve and the diverse audiences they reach. In trying to satisfy multiple consumers, psychologists risk having their efforts judged unsatisfactory by all. Although needs for data among groups are disparate, Hartlage and Merck (1971) found significant agreement within groups concerning what they considered to be valuable in a report. They concluded that psychologists can make their reports more relevant when they familiarize themselves with the uses that are made of the reports.

"Four attempts were made to obtain background information from Michael's parents. The principal and school psychologist then went to the home to interview Michael's step-father. Since home conditions were not conducive to conducting the interview, the step-father accompanied the principal and psychologist to the school where the interview was conducted."

When queried about the communicative intent of these statements, the writer explained, "There was no way I was going to the housing projects alone. When the principal and I got there, the step-father answered the door drunk with a bottle of whiskey in his hand so he followed us back to school for the interview." Clearly what was written in the report failed to communicate the writer's intent. Since the author was unwilling to enter such information in a report, perhaps the segment would best be deleted.

The problem of communication was documented by Cuadra and Albaugh (1956) who provided various professionals with copies of psychological reports and a multiple choice questionnaire. Raters were asked to answer each question based on the information in the written report. For all professional groups, the correspondence between their ratings and those of the report authors was only 53%. Shively and Smith (1967) investigated teachers', counselors' and student teachers' understanding of 30 terms commonly used in psychological reports and found that their subjects could identify only 54% of them.

Communication is the primary function of a report, and while it is problematic, the reader is not to assume that poor psychological reports do not communicate. All reports communicate, some just do so better than others. "Better" is a function of the degree of concordance between the information the writer intends to relay and the information the reader receives. If in reading the report the consumer's interpretation or understanding of the content is consistent with the writer's communicative intent, then the report has served its communicative function well. On the other hand if the reader's understanding differs from the psychologist's communicative intent, the report does a poor job of communicating.

The dimension of communication is not the only one considered in psychological report writing; value is a second critical component. Reports may communicate well but be of little perceived value. Conversely, reports that communicate poorly may be assigned high value by the reader.

Several research studies provide clues both to consumers' perceived value of psychological reports and to the variables which contribute to a report's being valued. Ownby, Wallbrown, and Brown (1982) asked special education teachers to rate the frequency with which certain types of information appeared in reports and to indicate how useful the reports were. High probability content included descriptions of the referral problem, lists of tests administered, IQ measures, achievement in grade equivalents, and statements concerning special education availability. Low probability content included lists of specific referral questions, playground behavior, prior classroom interventions, observations of antecedent behaviors, and estimates of expected progress. Teachers generally rated reports as only somewhat important in helping them manage classroom behavior and develop specific instructional strategies. In contrast parents reported a high degree of satisfaction with the psychoeducational evaluation reports generated at a university clinic with 66% being extremely satisfied with the report and 55% indicating they would make no changes in the report (Tidwell & Wetter, 1978).

Numerous variables enhance or detract from the value of a report. Speed enhances a report's value (Rogers, 1977). Teachers prefer an immediate brief report to a delayed formal and comprehensive report (though they would like both) (Mussman, 1964). Reports that were too brief, lacking in form and organization and whose recommendations were either vague, short, unrealistic, or not related to referral concerns were least valued (Brandt & Giebink, 1968; Rucker, 1967). Consumers placed highest value on recommendations and lowest value on IQ scores and projective test data (Isett & Roszkowski, 1979; Tidwell & Wetter, 1978).

The remainder of this chapter highlights the characteristics of effective and ineffective reports followed by specific practices.

BASIC CONSIDERATIONS

The chapter opened with several quotations from actual psychological reports. Each contains one or more basic flaws which have the effect of interfering with communication or decreasing the value of the report. The "Doug sentence" suffers from being trite, hackneyed, and irrelevant. It is likely that the primary reader of the report already knows what Doug looks like, and rarely is the purpose of the report to provide descriptive data so that someone will recognize Doug on sight. And how many students don't

"accompany the examiner willingly to the testing room"? Psychologists don't report that a subject has two arms and two legs, though they may note the absence of one or more limbs. Similarly they may note lack of willingness to accompany the examiner as in "Doug pulled a knife on the examiner who preceded him to the testing room," but statements of that which is generally taken for granted are best avoided.

Allyson is handicapped by a flaw of logic. The interpretation "she is highly distractible" simply is not consistent with the data reported. The psychologist needs to either change the interpretation in keeping with the data presented, or present additional data supporting this interpretation. Unless Dwayne's food preferences are to be used as reinforcers in a behavioral program, or he was referred for an eating disorder, the information is irrelevant and is better deleted from a report. Jason suffers more from a problem of the misapplication of psychological science and interpretation than he does from deviant sexual interest. In the absence of any other corroborating data such as high frequency of lewd comments, obsessive sexual thoughts or compulsive sexual acts, Jason's HFD production is probably best left as an unreported curiosity in light of the poor reliability and validity of the procedure.

Nathan gets lost in jargon and ponderous writing. The information is both ambiguous and inappropriately technical leaving the reader confused or with the illusion of understanding. Better treatment would be, "Nathan approaches new situations cautiously and suspiciously. However, once he becomes comfortable he actively attempts to exercise control over his environment by manipulating those around him." Finally, the psychologist recommends a teaching strategy that for David has clearly proven ineffective. Here is another problem of logic more starkly apparent in the example than would be the case in a report where the two sentences may be separated by several paragraphs.

Sattler (1982), Shellenberger (1982) and Tallent (1983) have clearly articulated the basic characteristics of effective psychological reports. Shellenberger's comprehensive literature review suggested that effective reports are those which (a) specifically answer referral questions; (b) describe behavior rather than present abstractions or psychological constructs; (c) describe the uniqueness of the individual; (d) are written clearly and precisely; (e) integrate, synthesize, and interpret information; (f) provide explicit, specific, and implementable recommendations; and (g) are timely.

Tallent (1983) summarizes the fundamentals of effective report writing in a quality checklist against which writers can evaluate their reports. In addition to those characteristics noted by Shellenberger, Tallent characterizes effective psychological reports as those which (a) do not unnecessarily duplicate the content of other reports; (b) provide illustrative material on which interpretations are based; (c) contain relevant and significant content; (d) contain data-based conclusions with limited and clearly identified speculations; (e) are client oriented rather than test oriented; (f) avoid theoretical or abstract concepts; (g) are logically and effectively organized; and (h) are adequately persuasive. With these fundamentals in mind, various report alternatives are presented in the following section.

BEST PRACTICES

The purpose of psychological reports as well as the characteristics of effective reports, briefly reviewed in previous sections of this paper, provide the basis from which best practices in report writing emerges. In this section, a variety of practices ranging from traditional to innovative (some might say radical) are discussed. Adopting any of the approaches presented here without carefully integrating them with basic principles of effective reporting results in a product that falls short of effectively fulfilling its fundamental purpose.

Traditional Report

Sattler (1982) and Shellenberger (1982) address report writing from a traditional point of view in terms of content and organization. Both the organization and content of the traditional report (Identifying Information, Reason for Referral, Background Information, Appearance and Observations, Test Behavior, Test Results and Interpretations, Summary, and Recommendations) is by now too familiar to practicing school psychologists. Nevertheless, a careful review of the Shellenberger and Sattler chapters is recommended for practitioners who conceptualize their role to be primarily that of test giver and who wish to hone their report writing effectiveness. Practitioners who are dissatisfied with the traditional reporting format and testing role it reflects could benefit from the sound review of general reporting principles both authors provide.

Psychological Report — Revised Format

Ross-Reynolds and Grimes (1983) proposed an alternative to the traditional psychological report epitomized by Shellenberger (1982) and Sattler (1982). Called the Psychological Report — Revised Format (PRRF), it is structured to provide a document which reflects a consultative, intervention-oriented assessment approach rather than the norm-referenced test-based approach closely associated with the traditional model. In the PRRF, assessment and intervention data are organized under the following headings: *Summary of Request for Conference, Purpose and Scope of the Psychologist's Investigation, Relevant History and Current Data, Discussion, Actions and Outcomes,* and *Follow-up.*

Differences between the PRRF and the traditional report format are more than cosmetic. Whereas the PRRF's "Summary of Request for Conference" is similar to "Reason for Referral," the former reflects the fact that a psychologist's involvement with a client begins with a conference with a concerned person who referred the child. By doing so psychologists more easily avoid the problems inherent in assessing clients in the absence of knowledge about the variables that need to be addressed (Hartlage, Freeman, Horine, & Walton, 1968).

Whereas the "Summary of Request for Conference" presents a brief statement of the salient concerns of the person requesting the assistance of a school psychologist, the "Purpose and Scope of the Psychologist's Investigation" explicitly narrows and defines the behaviors and critical variables which constitute the focus of the investigation. Since the focus is collaboratively developed with the referring party, the risk that psychologists' reports fail to relevantly address referral concerns is minimized. In contrast, assessment reports that convey the same information (WISC-R, WRAT, Bender, DAP) regardless of referral reason run a high risk of being viewed as irrelevant.

The content of the report under "Relevant History and Current Data" addresses each of the identified issues in turn, generally with a paragraph devoted to each area investigated. Psychologists commonly report different types of data in different sections of the report with test data separated from observational data which is distinct from historical data and interview data. In the PRRF, data from interviews, observations, rating scales, diagnostic teaching, curriculum-based assessment, intervention strategies, norm-referenced and criterion-referenced testing, work samples, environmental analysis, and review of records, all of which bear upon the specified concern are integrated and synthesized into a coherent whole. Data not directly relevant to the defined scope and purpose are not reported.

In the "Discussion" section the problems targeted for investigation are again mentioned to maintain the reader's focus. For each area of concern, a priority for action and accompanying rationale is presented based on an interpretation of the results synthesized in the previous section. For each problem listed in the "Purpose and Scope," the psychologist outlines a plan of action to remediate it. This is included in the section under "Proposed Actions and Outcomes" along with a statement of the anticipated effects of each intervention. The PRRF is concluded with specific information concerning follow-up including when, how, and under what circumstances the psychologist should be contacted, and when the case will be reviewed by the psychologist failing any prior request for case follow-up by concerned parties.

While the PRRF may appear cumbersome, with little practice it can be completed in two-to-four pages. It is one way to write a concise, relevant report which highlights outcomes and changes that make a difference in students' school-related functioning.

Letter and Memo Formats

Since the primary purpose of the psychological report is communication, letter and memo report formats were designed to enhance the contact between the psychologist and the referring person (McBeath, 1976; Ross-Reynolds & Grimes, 1983). The content of the letter format report is similar to that found in the PRRF, the difference being the personal focus of the former and the less formal though still professional style. Copies of the letter addressed to the referring person are sent to other relevant parties and to the file for documentation purposes. Psychologists who feel that letters or memos are too informal substitutes for a formal initial evaluation report may choose to reserve these formats to document and communicate the outcomes of other kinds of involvement. These include curriculum or class management consultation, counseling, and confirmations and reminders of agreed upon actions developed in case conferences. The memo format (McBeath, 1976) is an especially effective method for recording, communicating, and confirming an ongoing consultation interaction. While formal data are not available, teacher reaction to letters and memos has been positive both for communicating initial evaluation data and for follow-up of single or ongoing consultation.

Referral Oriented, Consultative Assessment Report

Recognizing the need to develop reports that improve communication between psychologists and other professionals (Hendler, Gerston, & Hendler, 1965; Tallent, 1983), Batsche (1983) developed a report writing model designed both to increase the value of the report as a relevant document and enhance the collaborative and communicative process between the psychologist and referring person. Called the Referral Oriented, Consultative Assessment Report (ROCAR), it is based on four principles articulated

by Hudgins and Schultz (1978). First, the psychologist enters the referral agents' frame of reference to clear confusion about the concern and emerge with a mutual understanding of the referral question. Evaluation procedures are then individualized to answer relevant referral questions. Next, the report focuses on the child's behavior. Finally, referral questions are addressed.

The ROCAR reflects a six-step assessment process. First, upon receiving a referral school psychologists review all existing data available on the student in order that they may be informed and intelligent participants in the initial interview with the referral agent. Second, an interview with the referring agent is conducted to explicitly articulate the concern and to develop a list of referral questions which will serve as focal points for the report. In addition the interview is designed to increase the referral agent's ownership and involvement in the evaluation process.

The third step, developing specific referral questions is critical to this model. Batsche (1983) notes that questions must be definable and measurable, and they must be agreed upon by the psychologist and referring agent. Questions that simply cue assessment procedures (What are the results of intellectual assessment? Is a psychiatric evaluation feasible?) are avoided in favor of those that target a specific problem area. "How" and "what" questions are preferable to "why" questions since the latter are less likely to result in problem remediation.

Once specific assessment questions are formulated, assessment procedures designed to answer each question are selected. Typically the procedures are listed in the report under the referral question. Information gathered from a single procedure may be used to answer more than one question. As in the PRRF, the fifth step is to integrate all data under the appropriate referral question with observation, test, interview, and review data blended to answer each referral question. The final step is to develop specific and realistic recommendations which address each problem reflected in the referral questions with the interventions arising logically from the assessment data collected.

"Translated" Report

Handler, Gerston, and Handler (1965) observed that the value of psychological reports would be enhanced "if the results were translated into possible problems in educational planning, and particular problems in academic functioning" (p. 77). Bagnato (1980) developed a "translated" report focusing on children's performance relative to the specific objectives of their preschool curriculum. Bagnato found that teachers who were given translated reports "were significantly more accurate, productive, and homogeneous in linking developmental diagnostic results to curriculum goals than teachers making judgments on the basis of traditional psychoeducational reports" (p. 555). To facilitate Individualized Educational Plan (IEP) development Bagnato recommended that reports (a) be organized by developmental or functional domains rather than by tests given; (b) describe strengths and skill deficits in behavioral terms with strengths and weaknesses linked to specific curriculum objectives, not norm-referenced test items; (c) emphasize data relevant to the child's learning strategy such as attention, learning rate, problem solving strategies, and reward preferences; (d) list functional levels, skill sequences and instructional needs facilitating assessment-curriculum linkages and IEP construction; and (e) detail specific recommendations for behavioral and instructional management.

Graphs in reports

Given that the purpose of any psychological report is to communicate data about a child and that the discipline of psychology prefers to market itself as a science, it is curious that the time-honored method of scientific data presentation, the graph, is rarely included in a report. A well-chosen graph vividly and concisely provides information concerning a child's performance that is only communicated tediously and fuzzily in writing. For example: "Tim's Iowa Test of Basic Skills scores in reading increased slightly from the 1.5 grade level in second grade to the 3.7 grade level in eighth grade. Math scores increased from the 2.3 grade level to the 9.0 grade level, while spelling and language scores increased from 1.5 to 5.0 and from 1.7 to 3.2 respectively."

While the above sentences give the reader the salient data concerning Tim's ITBS progress, they are more forcefully communicated by Figure 1. The choice of a particular graph depends upon the nature of the data to be presented and the point the psychologist wishes to highlight. Whereas Figure 1 depicts Tim's progress over time, Figure 2 highlights the discrepancy between ITBS scores and grade placement. It more cogently makes the point that in the area of language arts and reading Tim has fallen progressively further behind. When using graphs in a report, the psychologist is cautioned against simply presenting a graph and describing what is presented. The reader is better served when the psychologist interprets the data presented in the graph by highlighting trends and focusing on its implications (Grimes, 1984). To learn more about the use and construction of graphs refer to Thomas (in press).

Computer-assisted Reports

Psychological reports have not es-

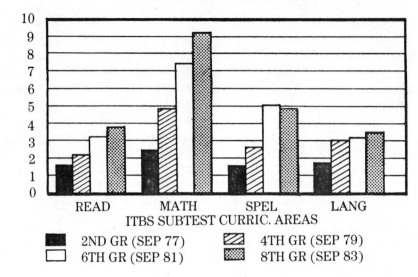

FIGURE 1
Tim's ITBS Scores Over 6 Years

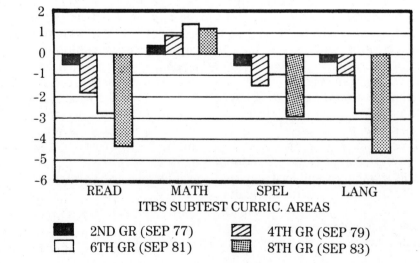

FIGURE 2
Tim's ITBS Scores Over 6 Years

caped the impact of the computer or word processor with mixed results. At the most rudimentary level is the form report characterized by standard, repetitive, and consistent text with no attempt to individualize the information to a specific reader (Grimes, 1983). Individual child differences are addressed by a simple fill-in-the-blank format. The narrative of every form-formatted report is identical to the narrative of every other form-formatted report with children's test scores the only variation. Since specific interpretation is impossible, the report content is preponderantly descriptive and general, focusing primarily on what various tests are thought to measure. Readers draw their own conclusions about the child based on the specific scores presented and the information concerning the general meaning, content, and purpose of the test. Relevance is sacrificed for efficiency.

Standard text format represents a slight improvement over the form format. It is possible to customize the report by inserting specific data such as the child's name, teacher's name, referral concern, and test scores, at specific points in the standard text. This is a familiar practice to any one receiving mailed sweepstakes notices or computer-generated narratives of MMPI results. The extent of customization varies from the insertion of a name or selection of a phrase within a standard block of text to the selection of entire blocks of standard text contingent upon assessment results as is done with computer-generated MMPI or Rorschach reports. The greater the extent of customization, the more individualized and relevant the report is; however, test data more easily lends itself to pre-packaged interpretive paragraphs than do the data which the school psychologist synthesizes and integrates into a report. Therefore, applicability is limited.

Grimes (1983) developed a more professionally viable alternative to computer-assisted report writing than that possible with either the form report or the standard text report. Called "starter text," it permits a degree of individualization by providing initial paragraph stems to which the psychologist can attach individually relevant data. Starter text consists of a series of frequently used blocks of text which can be included, as appropriate, in the report. The quality of the report is dependent upon the kind of information cued by the starter text. Starter text which cues descriptive data only results in a less valuable report than one that includes both descriptive and interpretive stems.

Grimes developed representative starter text for referral concerns, background information, educational history, achievement, personal-social functioning, vocational considerations, cognitive processes and learning style, medical and health concerns, behavior, diagnostic conclusions, and interventions. An example of a starter text for diagnostic conclusions highlights this approach.

"In considering all the information available I consider the most important areas for improvement to be ??" "With reference to special education programming, the data available support the conclusion that this student ?? The information that most readily supports this position is ??" (Grimes, 1983).

Having selected a given stem for inclusion in a report, the psychologist enters the relevant data at the locations cued by the double question marks. While starter text sacrifices the ease of the form report or standard-text format by requiring more input from the psychologist, it has the advantage of increased flexibility, thereby permitting the inclusion of relevant and highly individualized data. Computer-assisted reports are a relatively new phenomenon and new developments and refinements in the area can be expected in the future.

SUMMARY

Psychological reports represent the permanent product of a school psychologist's assessments, and no where is the dictum "garbage in, garbage out" more applicable. For if the assessment on which the report is predicated is poorly planned and executed, no report, regardless of how well written is adequate. Unfortunately the converse is not necessarily true. Thoughtful, thorough, and brilliantly conducted assessments are judged harshly if the report is poorly organized or poorly written.

There is strong consensus among writers on the characteristics of effective reports. Referral questions are specific and explicit, and reports are tailored to clearly and concisely answer these questions. The writer discusses the individual in behavioral terms, avoids abstractions, and highlights that which makes the individual unique. Writing is clear, fluid, precise, and straightforward. Information is synthesized and integrated rather than reported by test or other assessment technique. Recommendations that relate to the referral concerns are explicit, specific, and realistic.

The traditional psychological report is primarily test based and features such sections as "Reason for Referral," "Background and Observations," "Test Results and Interpretations," and "Summary and Recommendations." Although its place is well established in psychological practice by custom and training, consumer reaction has been mixed. Numerous alternatives to the traditional report have been proposed including brief written reports, letters and memos, outlines, and consultation-based reports. Most of these alternatives were designed to increase communication between the psychologist and the consumer, to save time, or increase utility of the report. Their effectiveness has yet to be evaluated. A variety of computer-assisted reports are appearing. Some are quite primitive, presenting only test scores; others are highly sophisticated and provide starter text which lends structure, form, and organization to the report while allowing the entry of individualized data.

REFERENCES

Bagnato, S. J. (1980). The efficacy of diagnostic reports as individualized guides to prescriptive goal planning. *Exceptional Children, 46,* 554-557.

Batsche, G. M. (1983). The referral oriented, consultative assessment report writing model. In J. Grimes (Ed.), *Communicating psychological information in writing* (pp. 29-43). Des Moines, IA: Iowa Department of Public Instruction.

Brandt, H. M. & Giebink, J. W. (1968). Concreteness and congruence in psychologists' reports to teachers. *Psychology in the Schools, 5,* 87-89.

Cuadra, C. A., & Albaugh, W. P. (1956). Sources of ambiguity in psychological reports. *Journal of Clinical Psychology, 12,* 109-115.

Grimes, J. (1981). Shaping the future of school psychology. *School Psychology Review, 10,* 206-231.

Grimes, J. (1983, October). *Micro uses in the macro world of school psychology.* Paper presented at the meeting of the Colorado Society of School Psychologists, Denver, CO.

Grimes, J. (1984, April). *Graphically speaking.* Paper presented at the meeting of the National Association of School Psychologists, Philadelphia, PA.

Grimes, J., & Ross-Reynolds, G. (1983). On skinning cats, choking dogs, and leaving lovers. In J. Grimes (Ed.), *Communicating psychological information in writing* (pp. 3-7). Des Moines, IA: Iowa Department of Public Instruction.

Handler, L., Gerston, A., & Handler, B. (1965). Suggestions for improved psychologist-teacher communication. *Psychology in the Schools, 2,* 77-81.

Hartlage, L., Freeman, W., Horine, L., & Walton, C. (1968). Decision utility of psychological reports. *Journal of Clinical Psychology, 24,* 481-483.

Hartlage, L. C., & Merck, K. H. (1971). Increasing the relevance of psychological reports. *Journal of Clinical Psychology, 27,* 459-460.

Hudgins, A. L. & Shultz, J. L. (1978). On observing: The use of the Carkhuff HRD model in writing psychological reports. *Journal of School Psychology, 16,* 56-63.

Isett, R., & Roszkowski, M. (1979). Consumer preferences for psychological report contents in a residential school and center for the mentally retarded. *Psychology in the Schools, 16,* 402-407.

Lacks, P. B., Horton, M. M., & Owen, J. D. (1969). A more meaningful and practical approach to psychological reports. *Journal of Clinical Psychology, 25,* 383-386.

McBeath, M. (1976). Memos to a teacher. In J. D. Krumboltz & C. E. Thorensen (Eds.), *Counseling methods* (pp. 445-451). New York: Holt, Rinehart & Winston.

Mussman, M. C. (1964). Teachers' evaluations of psychological reports. *Journal of School Psychology, 3,* 35-37.

Ownby, R. L., Wallbrown, F. H., & Brown, D. Y. (1982). Special education teachers' perceptions of reports written by school psychologists. *Perceptual and Motor Skills, 55,* 955-961.

Rogers, G. W., Jr. (1977). Maximizing the practical contributions of psychological reports. *Journal of School Health, 47,* 104-105.

Ross-Reynolds, G., & Grimes, J. (1983). Three counterproposals to the traditional psychological report. In J. Grimes (Ed.), *Communicating psychological information in writing* (pp. 11-25). Des Moines, IA: Iowa Department of Public Instruction.

Rucker, C. N. (1967). Report writing in school psychology: A critical investigation. *Journal of School Psychology, 5,* 101-108.

Sattler, J. (1982). *Assessment of children's intelligence and special abilities* (2nd ed.). Boston: Allyn & Bacon.

Shellenberger, S. (1983). Presentation and interpretation of psychological data in educational settings. In C. R. Reynolds & T. B. Gutkin (Eds.), *The handbook of school psychology* (pp. 51-81). New York: John Wiley.

Shively, J. J., & Smith, A. E. (1969). Understanding the psychological report. *Psychology in the Schools, 6,* 272-273.

Tallent, N. (1983). *Psychological report writing* (2nd ed.). Englewood Cliffs, NJ: Prentice-Hall.

Thomas, A. (in press). *Using graphs to facilitate communication.* Des Moines, IA: Iowa Department of Public Instruction.

Tidwell, R., & Wetter, J. (1978). Parental evaluations of psychoeducational reports: A case study. *Psychology in the Schools, 15,* 209-215.

ANNOTATED BIBLIOGRAPHY

Grimes, J. (Ed.). (1983). *Communicating psychological information in writing.* Des Moines, IA: Iowa Department of Public Instruction.
Presents a brief overview of current practice and provides sample reports using alternative formats (modified traditional, memo, and letter). Includes discussions and examples of multitrait/multimethod assessment, referral oriented, consultative assessment report writing, and 3 year re-evaluation reports.

Sattler, J. M. (1982). *Assessment of children's intelligence and special abilities* (2nd ed.). Boston: Allyn & Bacon, Chapter 24.
Delineates a traditional approach to report writing and includes many examples of correct and incorrect practice. Describes a suggested report outline and highlights common pitfalls and major considerations. A good introduction for beginners and worthwhile review for experienced psychologists.

Shellenberger, S. (1982). Presentation and interpretation of psychological data in educational settings. In C. R. Reynolds & T. B. Gutkin (Eds.), *The handbook of school psychology* (pp. 51-81). New York: John Wiley & Sons.
Presents a complete and well-written literature review on report writing highlighting characteristics of effective reports, consumer preferences and criticisms, and alternative approaches to traditional content and formats. Considerations for gathering and presenting psychological assessment data are presented as well as an example of a traditional psychological report.

Tallent, N. (1983). *Psychological report writing* (2nd ed.). Englewood Cliffs, NJ: Prentice-Hall.
Is the most thorough treatment of report writing extant. Although slanted to practice in clinic settings, Tallent's insights into problems, purposes, and effective practice in report writing make this the single best reference in the area.

BEST PRACTICES IN COUNSELING SENIOR HIGH SCHOOL STUDENTS

Marcia B. Shaffer
Steuben-Allegany B.O.C.E.S., Bath, New York

OVERVIEW

There are several reasons for school psychologists' apparent lack of interest in counseling secondary school students:

1. High school teachers see large numbers of students each day, are unlikely to know individuals well, and may miss any but the most egregious of problems. This means that a major source of referrals to school psychologists is not operating at full capacity.

2. High schools offer more guidance services than do elementary schools, and therefore the need for psychological services is decreased. It may also be the case that guidance counselors do not wish to share concerns with school psychologists.

3. School psychologists are not always drawn to high school students. Although intrepid when, armed with their WISC-R kits, they approach children shorter than themselves, they may contract a peculiar form of timidity when faced with the intensity of semi-adults who tacitly demand emotional commitment.

4. Perhaps the most encompassing reason why school psychologists confine their work to elementary schools is the belief which prevails among educators to the effect that, if the problems of small children are solved, there will be no problem children in the upper grades. Therefore, efforts concentrated on primary grades are felt to be more valuable than work with older students. There is evidence to support this belief (see Primary Mental Health Project, 1983, annotated bibliography).

Even if the dilemmas of small school-goers *are* smoothed out, however, new problems occur to *different* children at later stages of growth. Accidents happen: a child may suffer neurological damage in a car crash; illness may result in impairment of vision or hearing. Family circumstances may change; parents may die or be divorced. Currently, drugs, including alcohol, may so attract youngsters as to disrupt their entire lives. Perhaps most important, at least in terms of the number of difficulties engendered, is human development itself. It is not one steady trip up the road to maturity: human growth inherently goes through periods of tumult. Sometimes a child takes one step forward and two steps back. School psychologists often hear parents say, "He did so well until he got to seventh grade," or, "She never acted like this until she started middle school." Perfectly capable, well-behaved youngsters may suddenly fail or become truant or who knows what else, in the regressive period of pre-adolescence (Redl.) We do not arrange school structures and schedules suitably for this developmental stage, so natural struggles are exacerbated. Likewise, the period of adolescence, even if it's "storm and strife" is culturally derived (Stone and Church, 1968), it exists. Most young people are convinced that they should be in control of their own lives, but are vague about the responsibility involved. Society adds to their confusion. Laws permit them to assume such "adult" functions as driving, smoking, and drinking alcoholic beverages at different ages in different states. The teen years are an uneasy, intense time of life. The very vehemence of the adolescent's idolatry and love and loyalty cause personal and social upheavel.

There is insufficient research on the

efficacy of counseling either to disdain it or to tout its results with any certainty, but for those who work with secondary school students, the exigencies of development offer sufficient reason to continue.

BASIC CONSIDERATIONS

Who Should Counsel?

Forty years ago, there were two kinds of school psychologists. One group consisted of teachers who had taken enough courses to become "testers," and who rarely thought beyond their tests (and their increased prestige and salary). The others were clinical psychologists, schooled in therapeutic techniques and eager to use them. This later group brought counseling to schools. Currently, with changes in training, one cannot assume that counseling courses and practica have been included in a school psychologist's preparation for practice.

Some seasoned school psychologists feel very strongly about the necessity for in-depth training in counseling. They vigorously support academically-based knowledge and supervised practical experience in both individual and group counseling, which they feel require quite disparate skills. The most strictly ethical also believe that certain personal characteristics are requisite for the school psychologist who counsels: pervasive empathy, trustworthiness, tolerance of many varieties of language and life-style.

All of us subscribe to the ethical principle that school psychologists should do only what they have been trained to do. But over the past quarter century they have been forced by lack of training resources and the needs of their school populations to learn much on their own. Consequently, it is difficult to be dogmatic about what constitutes adequate qualifications for counseling, and how to acquire them. It is one of the questions on which professional organizations could provide guidelines.

Referrals

Once school psychologists have made it known that they will offer counseling, referrals come from predictable sources. On occasion, teachers *do* see emotional distress and report it. More often, they mention annoying or, by their standards, immoral behavior. Administrators may also send adolescents to school psychologists, for example, the high school sophomore who had confiscated the entire treasury of a school club; part of his punishment was to "see Mrs. Shaffer." Parents may ask for assistance. The ambiance of a school at a given time may suggest the need for counseling, especially of groups. Current laws and regulations regarding the handicapped have added a new dimension to the school psychologist's responsibilities for counseling.

The most interesting and seemingly the most numerous are self-referrals. They arrive by a number of routes, usually in desperation. Some have friends who have found the school psychologist helpful. Others have read about psychologists in popular magazines. Still others have heard the school psychologist speak to a health class. School psychologists who make themselves known to a portion of the student body are almost certain to find clients knocking at their doors.

Rarely, students refer themselves as a hoax, to see what the "shrink" is all about. The hoax tends to backfire, the jokesters discovering that, after all, they have some concerns to discuss.

Although it is not a unanimous conviction among school psychologists, there are those who believe that some referrals should not be accepted. Severely disturbed young people, such as the psychotic or drug-dependent, cannot be handled in the school setting. It has been suggested elsewhere (Shaffer, 1982) that there is personal or family information to which school psychologists should not be privy. Furthermore, the school is an unsuitable site for the plumbing of emotional depths that severe disturbances require. A student cannot tear his soul apart during one period and sit calmly in science class the next. It is well to remember that schools are not mental health clinics, but places to dispense learning.

Having decided that the school cannot provide an analyst's couch, is one's duty done? Not in the opinion of most "old hands." Students suffering from severe emotional distress should, if possible, be routed to an appropriate social agency or individual therapist. It may take time to persuade the student and his parents that treatment outside the school is advisable, and to help them find a satisfactory therapeutic situation. Even when that task is accomplished, the school psychologist should maintain communication with the agency and make provision for the student's educational programming.

Confidentiality

Whether counseling is group or individual, voluntary or forced, the question of confidentiality arises. Students who refer themselves often request that their parents not be told. The most widely held school of thought appears to be that unless parents are informed the student cannot be accepted for counseling. Those who espouse this opinion often spend a few sessions trying to convince the student that he should assume the responsibility of advising his parents. Another course of action is to offer to talk with the parents on the student's behalf.

Much of what a student tells a school psychologist can be kept between them. The student must be forewarned, however,

that revelations regarding such unlawful acts as drug use, the sale of drugs, or acts of violence will be reported to legal authorities.

Those rules seem unequivocal: tell parents; report illegal activities. Actual situations tend to be more complicated. Young people who have dredged up enough trust to present themselves voluntarily are already troubled by the approach of adulthood, the outcropping of unfamiliar impulses, the remnants of childish feelings, and, usually, the perceived perfidy of the adults with whom they are acquainted. A 16-year-old, after all, can be an emancipated minor, or a parent, or, in some localities, a felon. Should one disregard his privacy? As for the law, where, on a continuum of consequential crimes, does one place the information that a kid illegally purchased a six-pack of beer and drank two cans on the way to school? Conflict about confidentiality is a recurrent problem for the school psychologist who works with adolescents, conflict between the rules which school administrators expect one to uphold, and the advocacy of adolescents.

BEST PRACTICES

Individual Counseling

There are school psychologists who feel that individual counseling is not suitable for high school students, that it may be discomfiting for the counselee and frustrating for the school psychologist. These people may opt for group counseling.

If, however, one does believe in working with individuals; if a theory of counseling has been decided upon; if the significant ethical questions have been satisfactorily answered; if students are banging at the door — what next?

First, consider when the student will

be seen. Study hall periods are agreeable to school staff; if that time is otherwise inconvenient, vary the time from week to week, so that the same class is not missed regularly. No teacher will then feel put out except the one who thinks that psychologists are crazy anyway. It is important to be obliging but not obsequious. The students in counseling will gain as much from 45 minutes with the school psychologist as from 45 minutes in any class.

Now the student has arrived in the psychologist's office. No matter what theory is espoused, from Rogers to Freud, the first three steps in counseling are the same:

1. Listen.
2. Listen.
3. Listen.

Listening cannot be overemphasized. Even if it were the only response ever given, respectful attention would be helpful. It also assures that the school psychologist does not leap into action before the problem is made clear.

Somewhere between the second and third listens, one should ask a few straightforward questions, touching on such topics as with whom the student lives; sex and age of siblings; sources of family income; school achievement. This mundane information is necessary to complete one's grasp of the situation. In addition, it will bring a talkative and/or hysterical client to a halt and help him to gain control of himself; or induce a shy client to talk.

Once one has listened, various paths are open. One may focus on the student's relationship to the school environment; on his goals and how his behavior affects their achievement; on what alternative behavior is possible to him. Alternatives are in fact important in the philosophies of many school psychologist counselors. It is perfectly safe for the psychologist to lead the discussion, but wise not to be too rigid in controlling it. Given a little leeway, almost any adolescent will reveal his major problems in almost any context.

Techniques of counseling may be enhanced by the imagination of the counselor. The counselee may be assigned tasks which alleviate some aspect of the problem, as "Try walking away when your sister screams at you; let me know, next week, what happens." The student may be asked to pretend that he is a psychologist dealing with his parents; or some informal psychodrama may be used. Many adolescents are uncomfortable in talking with adults, so it may be useful to rehearse encounters with parents or teachers, as "Mr. Pauling, I'm sorry that my book report is late," etc.

Like many school psychologists of clinical background, I was trained in the years when Carl Rogers was king in the world of psychotherapy. I do not ordinarily set goals for individuals; the student uses me for his purposes. I tend to follow the student's lead at the expense of orderly procedures. I hear the same stories over and over, because I believe in the value of catharsis. In other aspects of counseling, I am probably more directive than most of my colleagues. Because so many troubled young people have no clear standards by which to live, I risk telling them my own values and standards. They are under no obligation to believe or act as I do, but they may be saved from excessive trial and error behavior in an emotional vacuum and a hostile world. Other school psychologists who work with teenagers will have developed procedures congruent with their theoretical biases.

Kids who run away from home and ones who threaten suicide may involve a school psychologist in unexpected crises. How to respond may be a very personal matter. This is what I do: every student who is in counseling with me has my home phone number. Calling me at home at any time is allowed. A potential runaway is not told to stay at home. He is asked not to leave until he is sure he has somewhere to go, to tell me where he will be (shades of confidentiality!), and to phone me at intervals, or I will call him. In addition, I give orders like "Wash your hair (or grease your car, or some other everyday chore) and come to see me in the morning." The "rules" in both cases are to give the student something specific to do and to anticipate, to keep him in contact with his own real world; to assure him, by my words and my actions, that he is a valuable person and that I, personally, do not wish to lose him. I am not a do-gooder, but the thought of kids missing or dead disturbs my sleep.

With individual students, two criteria are useful for deciding when their counseling should be terminated, at least temporarily. If appointments are frequently broken by the student, it is most likely a sign that his interest in the counseling relationship is ebbing and often that his problems are diminishing. It is true that broken appointments may have other meanings, such as a conflict in transference or an evasion of dilemmas. The healthy refusal to keep appointments has an open quality which distinguishes it from the unhealthy — "I like you, Mrs. S., but I'd rather play volleyball."

The other criterion is a relinquishment of egocentricity. When a student begins to show concern about the counselor, ("Is your cold better?" "How is your husband?") before launching into an account of his own experiences, it is a sign that he is emerging from himself, beginning to mature. Counseling may not be terminated immediately, but its intensity will start to wane.

Group Counseling

School psychologists offer a number of reasons for choosing group over individual counseling, not the least of which is that the psychologist's time is limited. Some believe that adolescents respond more readily in a group than alone with a counselor. Others see the formation of groups as a way to get to the root of conditions which may be bothersome to a school staff, such as defiance or truancy or to deal with problems of the times, such as drug use or teenage suicide. Assembling a group is also an excellent way to learn the mores of a community or of a school gang.

There are groups which are highly structured as to topics. In the belief that adolescents are troubled chiefly by social/moral questions, some schools set up what may most accurately be described as group discussions, inviting specified students to participate. Conversation is stimulated by showing a filmstrip about a contemporary issue, e.g., relationships with authority, peer pressure.

One writer who currently exerts considerable influence on group work with young people is Lawrence Kohlberg (1981). Kohlberg's ideas have to do with what he calls "Moral Reasoning." Briefly, he presents a method of values clarification as it occurs and matures in groups, moving from egocentric, divisive opinions to decisions which take into account the good of the group. The counselor acts as facilitator, not searching for one correct answer, but eliciting alternatives.

Carl Rogers' non-directive, client-centered approach works with groups as well as with individuals. Students' most personal attitudes surface quite rapidly in an atmosphere which is not rigidly controlled by a leader. The interactions among group members are gradually divulged, defined, and discussed. Counseling can home in on the aspects of their lives which really distress the students. The disadvantage of this arrangement is that it is difficult to keep the group in line. Conversations are likely to go off on tangents; the leader may be left out of the discourse entirely. A school psychologist who cannot bear disorder should shun group techniques which permit students to choose their own routes to self-discovery.

A few practical matters should be

considered before one plunges into group counseling:

1. Groups seem more manageable if the number of sessions is established at the initial session.

2. An administrator can usually find a place for a group to meet. Time for meeting may be more troublesome. One solution which is not too offensive to teachers is a staggered schedule, i.e., Feb. 10, period 1; Feb. 17, period 2; Feb. 24, period 3, and so on. Every administrator and teacher in the building should have a copy of the schedule.

3. In spite of what textbooks may say, if the counselees are at all antisocial, *six* is the maximum number a counselor can endure without danger of breakdown.

4. It is absolutely essential to announce a few rules at the outset. Minimally, no physical assault on another person should be permitted, nor property destroyed. Rules should be set on the basis of the psychologist's intimate knowledge of himself and the behavior which he can tolerate.

5. Offering individual counseling to group members, on request, adds to the efficacy of the group process.

6. Even non-directive leaders sometimes need to take control of the group. Socially maladjusted adolescents, in particular, tend to have no standards of behavior or belief. The school psychologist may have to suggest what is "good" behavior or a decent attitude, simply because no such thoughts occur to the group. A whole generation of high school kids in Williamsville, New York, said, "We don't say 'nigger' in here," like a catechism, thanks to the unyielding ways of their school psychologist!

7. The loyalty which may be engendered among group members will surprise the novice group leader. It is one of the signs that a group is maturing.

8. Be aware of the likelihood that counselees will need a buffer between themselves and adults. This is true for individual counselees, too, but there is a more conspicuous, public quality to the interference which must be run for group members.

9. Set simple goals. For several years, I worked with groups of acting-out students of average ability and both sexes, for whom there was only one aim: to keep them from being invited out of high school before they were graduated. The success rate was 80%.

In Conclusion

Schools have changed in the past 30 years. A wider variety of courses and "tracks" offers suitable programs for many students, and decreases the number who are academically misplaced. Social agencies come into schools to help the socially befuddled. PL94-142 and its corollary "spin-offs" have resulted in the prevention of some problems which accrue to high school students. No matter how altered the school environment, however, the course of life itself and the pressure of social change will leave a few troubled teenagers confronting the school psychologist in search of succor.

When they arrive, bear in mind a few homespun guidelines, some of which have already been mentioned here, but are important enough to be repeated.

1. No drastic changes will occur in the lives of students who are counseled. Be satisfied with achievable goals, germane to their school careers.

2. There are some personal qualities of the school psychologist which contribute to the success of counseling:

dependability, which means, for example, that one is where one has promised to be, and that, if it is necessary to break an appointment, students will be so informed.

honesty, which may extend to reacting with anger to patently stupid or destructive behavior.

empathy, which is the ability to pretend to be someone other than oneself.

3. When the school psychologist acts as a liaison between students and adults, each side must know that he will not plead for a relinquishment of penalties, nor promise perfection thereafter. What will be done is to explain extenuating circumstances and to try to arrange a really fair deal.

4. Never forget for a moment that the purpose of counseling is to support emotional/social maturation. The school psychologist is not an evangelist nor a scout leader. He is not there to convert students to a particular moral viewpoint, but to help them live fulfilling lives according to their own standards.

5. Remember that each counselee, although not always lovable, is an important person worthy of respect.

6. LISTEN!

SUMMARY

Most school psychologists have evinced little interest in counseling senior high school students, chiefly because of the widespread belief in the efficacy of early intervention. Problems do arise in older children, however, as a part of the process of growing up.

Clients are referred by teachers, administrators, parents; self-referrals are frequent. Severely disturbed students should be sent to an outside agency or therapist, with the school psychologist maintaining contact.

Potential runaways and suicides may confront the school psychologist on an emergency basis. Methods for dealing with these problems are idiosyncratic, and should be planned ahead of time. Confidentiality is an equivocal ethical problem, with parent involvement a major issue.

The school psychologist who counsels should be dependable, honest, and empathic. Ideally, he should have training in theories of counseling plus supervised experience. Any preferred counseling theory may be adopted; listening is always the vital ingredient.

Groups in counseling vary from highly structured to client-directed. Even the latter need a few limits, e.g., no physical attacks allowed. It is important to settle practical matters such as time and place of meetings and number of sessions before counseling begins. Try to adapt to the wishes of teachers and administrators.

To preserve the morale of the school psychologist, simple, achievable goals should be set. It is unrealistic to expect radical personal changes as a result of either group or individual counseling, but if aims are sensibly planned, counseling is rewarding.

REFERENCES

Kohlberg, Lawrence (1981), *The Philosophy of Moral Development: Essays in Moral Development* (vol. 1). New York: Harper Row.

Psychological Services in the High School (1982). *School Psychology Review*, 11 (4).

Shaffer, M. (1969). Group Counseling in a Senior High School. *The School Counselor*, 1969, 22-25.

Shaffer, M. (1982). Helping Children Cope with Parental Problems. In J. Grimes (Ed.), *Psychological Approaches to Problems of Children and Adolescents* (pp. 43-45). Des Moines, Iowa: Iowa Department of Public Instruction.

Stone, L. J. & Church, J. (1968). *Childhood & Adolescence* (2nd ed.). New York: Random House.

Redl, F. Pre-adolescents: What makes them tick? Source unknown.

BIBLIOGRAPHY

Claiborn, C. D., & Strong, S. R. (1982). Group Counseling in the Schools. In C. R. Reynolds and T. B. Gutkin (Eds.), *The Handbook of School Psychology* (pp. 530-553). New York: John Wiley & Sons.

The style is academic and the reader must translate ideas into practical procedures, but the chapter provides an excellent overview of theories of group counseling.

Fine, M. (1982). Issues in Adolescent Counseling. *School Psychology Review*, 11 (4), 391-398.
This useful article reflects Dr. Fine's considerable experience with children and families and his theoretical biases in working with them.

The Primary Mental Health Project is a successful program for helping primary grade children who are at risk for school adjustment problems. Further information and a bibliography are available from PMHP, 575 Mr. Hope Avenue, Rochester, New York 14520.

Thompson, C. L., & Rudolph, L. B. (1983). *Counseling Children*. Monterey, California: Brooks/Cole Publishing Company.
This is an exceptionally informative volume, dealing with (1) several theories of counseling, their advantages and disadvantages, and (2) step-by-step suggestions for responding to common problems of school age children.

AUTHOR NOTES

Contributing School Psychologists

Morton Brooks, Public Schools, North Tonawanda, New York.

Bradford Doane, Hastings-on-Hudson, New York.

Stanley Eaton, Sweet Home Public Schools, Amherst/Tonawanda, New York.

Helga Karker, Central School District, Averill Park, New York.

Robert Stewart, Rush-Henrietta Public Schools, Henrietta, New York.

BEST PRACTICES IN CRISIS INTERVENTION

Valerie S. Smead
Western Illinois University

Frequently in the literature on crisis intervention, crises are characterized not only as times of danger but also of opportunity. Therefore, many of the assumptions of crisis theory and practice are useful to school psychologists who certainly are not strangers to situations which evoke either possibility. Very recently, in a chapter on crisis intervention in the schools, the case was made that school psychologists along with other personnel should receive training in handling crises (Nelson & Slaikeu, 1984). However, to date there appear to be few reports of school psychologists using these approaches. The intent of this chapter is to review some of the major premises of crisis theory and practice. Areas of potential applicability are highlighted as are possible cautions and limitations.

OVERVIEW

The foundations of crisis theory and practice were established in large part by Erich Lindemann (Lindemann, 1944, 1979) and Gerald Caplan (Caplan, 1961, 1964). A "critical event" was a crisis situation, the tragic fire in Boston's Coconut Grove nightclub in 1943 (Korchin, 1976). Based upon his work with relatives of the deceased as well as others in threatening situations, Lindemann documented predictable stages of grief and possible means of intervention. In 1948 Lindemann and Caplan established the Wellesley Human Relations Service, a community mental health program where they implemented their formulations (Darbonne, 1967).

Crisis intervention received ready acceptance in the mental health field which previously had focused only on those with long-term illnesses (Farberow, 1978). It became an attractive alternative to psychotherapy for persons in immediate distress. Suicide prevention/crisis intervention centers and telephone hotlines multiplied. The idea that some crises might be anticipated and prepared for also suggested possibilities for prevention (Caplan, 1964).

Generally, from the perspective of crisis intervention theory, a *crisis* is seen as a period of psychological disequilibrium in the face of a hazardous event which can neither be escaped nor solved with customary problem-solving resources (Caplan, 1964). Students unable to cope with parental divorce, a failing grade, entering a new school, or losing a boyfriend may be referred to the school psychologist in a crisis state. Perhaps even more frequently, children referred for learning problems are having such difficulties due to crises related to hazards at home or at school.

Crisis reaction refers to the state of upset persons in crisis are undergoing. Typically, they experience feelings of helplessness, inadequacy, confusion, anxiety, and tiredness as well as disorganization in work and interpersonal relationships (Halpern, 1973). Lowered self-esteem and depression also have been documented (Lewis, Gottesman, and Gutstein, 1979). It's not difficult to see how school learning is disrupted.

Crisis intervention is designed to restore psychological equilibrium by improving coping skills and offering new alternatives for dealing with the troubling situation and the stress it is creating. Crisis reactions are not necessarily signs of pathology or emotional disturbance (Golan, 1978), but in many cases are short-term normal responses. Though antecedent factors such as individual personality or experience might "...load the dice in favor of a good or bad outcome," emotional disequilibrium is to be expected when faced with an important and insoluable problem (Caplan, 1964, p. 53). Therefore, crisis intervention is not usually directed towards the restructuring of basic personality as is seen in psychotherapy, but towards resolution of present problems and emotional conflicts (Auerbach & Kilmann, 1977).

Crises are times of increased vulnerability, however. Puryear (1979) notes that the individual in crisis "... is at the end of his rope, having tried everything he knows and can think of. He has finally succumbed" (p. 41). In such a state, people are quite susceptible to outside assistance. Caplan warns that such vulnerability not only provides the opportunity for growth but also threatens deterioration in personality and life situation (Caplan, 1964). Thus, a poorly resolved crisis does not bode well for future mental health. Conversely, timely intervention not only aids in alleviating immediate distress, but also in promoting positive mental health.

Implications for the school psychologist are multiple. First, in our mobile, highly industrialized society where knowledge and technology continue to increase at an explosive rate (Adams, 1980; Toffler, 1971), most people, by definition, seem to be susceptible to crises. Possibly, " . . . as never before in history, individuals are faced with the task of adapting to frequent and often abrupt life changes" (Felner, et al., 1983, p. 199). If crises states are not ipso facto signs of mental illness, and if intervention does not necessitate long-term psychotherapy, then highly specialized mental health professionals are not always required to aid those in crisis. As Korchin (1976) points out, "Crisis is universal and crisis intervention is everybody's business" (p. 502). Probably in the school situation it is the school psycholo-

gist's business.

Knowledge in this area should aid in recognizing, responding to, and, in some cases, alleviating individual and family crises. More global crisis situations which affect many members of the school also can be anticipated. Provisions are made for potential hazards such as redistricting, teacher lay-offs and sudden teacher or student death. Such knowledge also sensitizes school psychologists to how much is left to be learned about how people handle and adjust to hazardous events. Caplan (1976) admonishes, "Fundamental questions about the efficacy of crisis intervention have not been answered . . . we do not know whether such intervention is in fact successful in the short or long run . . . " (p. xxiii). Even more recently, lack of evaluative data was cited as a major deficiency in the literature on crisis intervention in the schools (Nelson & Slaikeu, 1984).

BASIC CONSIDERATIONS

In this section, information in three overlapping areas is presented. First, knowledge which can be brought to bear in *recognizing crisis situations* is reviewed. Current formulations concerning crises, types of crisis situations and variations in crisis reactions are discussed. Such information is useful to the diagnostician when assessing learning, behavioral, or emotional difficulties. Crisis states can be documented and possible contaminatory effects on test results recognized. Times when diagnosis itself promotes crisis also are suggested. Having one's child diagnosed as mentally retarded or learning disabled, for instance, constitutes a hazardous event for which some parents may have no coping strategies or resources.

Second, knowledge and skills which are useful in *responding to crisis situations* are presented. Building on the preceding information, this area addresses basic approaches to crisis intervention and then tailors them to particular roles the school psychologist plays. Possibilities for consultant-liaison work, crisis counseling and system-wide intervention in emergencies are targeted.

Finally, time is devoted to *planning for crises* of the future. Possibilities for prevention and in-service education are highlighted.

Recognizing Crisis Situations

Often recognizing crisis situations is not as cut and dried as we think. As a construct, crisis does not have an established meaning or formal theoretical base (Auerbach & Klimann, 1977). Generally, presence of a hazardous event coupled with evidence that the individual has been unable to adapt to its occurrence is a good starting point.

Crises are often subdivided into those which are accidental or situational and those which are maturational or developmental. Predictability of the hazardous event for groups of people is largely at issue. Some hazards and associated crises are purely accidental. They befall individuals or groups. Sudden death of a family member, a serious car accident, or devastation of the school by a hurricane fall at the accidental end of the continuum. Other situational crises do not come as a complete surprise, however. Not being promoted to the next grade, getting one's first C, or teacher lay-offs constitute not entirely unexpected hazards.

Maturational or developmental crises, on the other hand, are more predictable on a group-wide basis. Most children are exposed to the potential hazards of starting school, making the move from elementary to junior high school, and adjusting to the socio-emotional and physical consequences of puberty. Both developmental life stages and times of transition from one condition to another (Golan, 1978) are considered areas for these more predict-able hazards.

Crisis reactions are elicited by a range of stressful life events (Auerbach & Kilmann, 1977). Familiarity with Holmes and Rahe's (1967) Social Readjustment Rating Scale and Yeaworth et al. (1980) Adolescent Life Change Scale are helpful in sensitizing the school psychologist to some of the common stressors and their relative ratings on a group basis (also see Wise, in press).

Presence of a potentially hazardous event is not by itself evidence of crisis however. First, individuals must perceive the event as important and threatening and, second, they must be unable to deal with it. Knowledge concerning the individual's life goals and feelings about the event is essential, as is knowledge about their current life situation and coping resources. For instance, starting a new school late in the year probably constitutes a hazardous event for many students. One or two, however, see it as a very positive occurrence. For many of the rest, though, it is perceived as hazardous, they find that they can cope given their existing strategies for dealing with stress and fitting into new situations.

Puryear (1979) discusses various instances where people find that they cannot cope. Sometimes the problem is just too overwhelming, such as death of a family member. Other times several small problems over a short period of time have depleted the individual's ability to cope. In these cases there is not one hallmark hazardous event. For example, a first-year teacher who gets married and relocates finally goes into crisis when asked to do extra coaching after school. In still other instances, existing coping mechanisms are blocked. Moving is more likely to trigger crisis for a child who has always turned to a particular parent for support if it coincides with repeated absences on that parent's part. Situations also induce crises if they involve new and unique problems for which appropriate coping mechanisms have not been developed.

In addition, symbolic links to similar problems in the past which were not appropriately resolved have an effect (Caplan, 1964; Golan, 1978; Lukton, 1982). For instance, in the case of the accidental death of a fourth grader reported by Keith and Ellis (1978) his teacher's inability to aid her class in responding appeared to be based on such links (Nelson & Slaikeu, 1984). She had experienced several painful deaths in the past and this death '. . . stirred up repressed feelings about the loss of other important persons . . ." (Nelson & Slaikeu, 1984, p. 252).

Further evidence that an individual is in crisis comes from indications of the psychological disequilibrium associated with crisis reactions. Often people feel as out of control of their emotions as of the practical effects of the hazardous event. If an individual who previously has been functioning adequately begins manifesting anxiety, helplessness, lowered self esteem and depression, then additional evidence for an inability to cope has been secured.

However, individual variations in the intensity of these reactions have been documented (Halpern, 1973). In another instance, different emotions were found to develop at different times (Lewis, et. al., 1979). Patients learning that they had cancer experienced anxiety and helplessness almost immediately, while depression and lowered self-esteem did not develop until several weeks later. Difficulty in recognition also occurs with those individuals who do have more long-term emotional difficulties. While crisis reactions are not of necessity signs of pathology, those with previous pathology are not immune to them.

Often in the literature, the short-term nature of crisis reactions is highlighted as a further diagnostic indicator. Originally, both Caplan and Lindemann saw crisis reactions as being time-limited. The belief

was that within four to six weeks, emotional equilibrium was re-established whether the crisis was resolved well or not. More recently, this issue like the determination of a hazardous event, appears less clear. Though some hazards are of sufficient impact that a state of active crisis is immediately precipitated, usually they bring out predictable efforts to cope (Golan, 1978). Tension rises to a peak only when neither customary nor newly initiated problem-solving mechanisms have helped. As Golan (1978) suggests, finally a turning point is reached, often triggered by some precipitating event or series of small precipitants and the state of active crisis entered. Thus, time between hazardous event and crisis reaction varies. In some cases symptoms associated with active crisis last considerably longer than six weeks as well (Lewis et. al., 1979). Several have suggested that the initial crisis state is followed by a prolonged period of adjustment (Caplan, 1976; Lukton, 1982; Felner, et. al., 1983).

Summarizing this information on crises and reactions to them, several suggestions emerge for recognizing crisis situations. Look for an event or series of events which are important to the individual and perceived as hazardous. Look for evidence that he or she has been unable to cope using either traditional or newly initiated strategies. Look for signs of emotional disequilibrium. A short-term time-frame provides further evidence. However, timing between hazardous event and the turning point to active crisis varies as does the duration of emotional disequilibrium.

The following flow chart may be useful:

1.) Potentially Hazardous Event(s):
   ↓   Accidental-sudden death
       Situational-suspended from
         school
       Maturational-starting
         kindergarten
       Developmental-puberty

2.) Individual Perception of the
Event as Threatening:
↓ Important challenge to personal satisfaction or goals

3.) Individual Inability to Cope:
↓ Neither traditional nor newly-initiated strategies aid in avoiding or adjusting to the hazard. Inability to cope may be due to: trauma of hazardous event, many small problems depleting ability to cope, existing coping mechanisms blocked, novelty of hazardous event, or symbolic linkages with unresolved problems.

4.) Crisis Reaction:
↓ anxiety, helplessness, confusion, depression, lowered self-esteem, disorganization in work and interpersonal life.

Responding to Crisis Situations

What follows is an attempt at targeting common practices in crisis intervention so that the school psychologist has some immediate direction. Though there is much consistency in terms of the distinguishing characteristics of intervention efforts (Slaikeu, 1984), ". . . techniques are loosely organized and cover various procedures" (Auerbach & Kilmann, 1977). See the last section of this article for several variations.

The hallmarks of crisis intervention efforts are immediacy and flexibility. The thought is that persons in crisis need help and they need it without delay. As in most situations the psychologist encounters, efforts are made to establish rapport first. Often this is aided by allowing the individuals involved plenty of time to ventilate feelings of distress and helplessness. Active listening or empathic responding are useful in establishing a supportive relationship while allowing people room to express themselves (see Eddy, Lawson & Stilson, 1983 for descriptions of this technique). Once rapport has been established, probes for further indications of a crisis state and particular individual needs are employed. Often indications of dangerousness to self and others must be considered. Individuals who are stuck, feeling unable to cope with an important and threatening situation, may become suicidal or violent (see Eddy, et. al., 1983, and Slaikeu, 1984, for information on assessing lethality).

After initial information has been collected and a supportive relationship established, then attention shifts to providing assistance in handling and resolving the crisis situation. Generally, advice and information are given. However, efforts are made to discourage undue dependence (Korchin, 1976). One area of information useful with adolescents and adults is what this author calls translating normality; that is, sharing some of the preceding information on crises and what to expect. The idea that these are normal, perhaps time-limited responses can make their own experience more comprehensible and less threatening (also see Smith, 1976, last section).

Immediate efforts to mobilize resources are critical. The intervenor is actively involved in obtaining human and agency resources which facilitate clients' readjustment (Auerbach & Kilmann, 1977). Such efforts are familiar to the school psychologist who is used to coordinating between child, parent, teacher and whatever resources are necessary to alleviate the problem at hand. Balancing such active intervention with the need not to foster undue dependency can be tricky. Generally, individuals are made aware of resources and encouraged to do that which they can for themselves. The intervenor assists with that which is too overwhelming for the moment (see Puryear, 1979, last section).

Individuals are also assisted in considering different ways they, themselves, can approach and attempt to resolve the crisis situation. A frequent theme in crisis intervention is an emphasis on client competence, mastery, and capacity for autonomy (see Bloom, 1977; Korchin, 1976). Active involvement of the client is encouraged in considering options for dealing with the hazardous event and the stress it is engendering. If new more adaptive coping strategies are identified and the seemingly insurmountable conquered, then not only may immediate distress dissipate, but future growth occur.

Because schemes for conceptualizing and evaluating coping differ, the psychologist and crisis client need to consider a variety of options. Caplan (1964) suggested that strategies be reality-based and not rest on inappropriate defense mechanisms, or involve a retreat from life. A generic approach to crisis intervention based on his work and Lindemann's stages of grieving is sometimes employed. As summarized by Lukton (1982), clients are aided through a denial stage and led past periods of anger, confusion, guilt, or depression to cognitive exploration of the situation and of possible coping strategies (see Lindemann 1944 for more on stages of grieving). Tasks which are thought to be necessary in confronting particular developmental or situational crises are used in such a generic approach (see Lukton, 1982; Smith, 1976).

One general scheme for organizing coping strategies comes from work by Pearlin and Schooler (1978). They found that persons attempted to combat various life stresses using strategies within three areas. Some strategies involved direct change of the situation. Others addressed the meaning of the situation, and still others were directed towards the stress engendered by the situation. Using this format, strategies the client has already attempted in each area are elicited first, then new alternatives are generated.

For instance, in working with a teenager in crisis over an unwanted pregnancy, various changes in the situation are possible. She may only perceive the two options of marriage or abortion. Others such as single parenthood, adoption, or raising the child within her extended family would be raised and considered. The meaning she gives to the situation is another change point. As discussed, individual perception is important in documenting that an event is harzardous. Changes in perception may remove an event from this category and/or cut down on stress. If this teenager is seeing herself as a failure or her life as ruined, then alternative meanings may reduce disequilibrium independent of changes in the situation. Finally, her typical methods of coping with stress are reviewed and applied to this new situation. She might consider spending more time with friends and sharing her troubles with one or two confidants. New possibilities for stress reduction are also raised.

Research in the areas of life events, stress, and coping offers a variety of possible strategies to be considered when exploring alternatives in each category (see Antonovsky, 1979 and Kobasa, 1979 in addition to those cited below). Such research also suggests that caution be taken when attempting to identify the most adaptive options. As yet, a widely accepted taxonomy of coping does not exist (Roskies & Lazarus, 1980). Methodological difficulties make existing studies of coping efficiency problematical (Murgatroyd, 1982). One area, the importance of social support as a buffer against stress, has received repeated endorsements. Other areas, such as the necessity for immediately action-oriented, reality-based approaches are less clear. For instance, Roskies & Lazarus (1980) speculate that temporarily accepting helplessness and reducing distress however possible, even using denial, may be helpful. Elsewhere, women's success in adjusting to breast cancer appeared to rest "...fundamentally upon the ability to form and maintain a set of illusions" (Taylor, 1983, p. 1161). For instance, these women persisted in believing that they had control over the cancer despite little evidence of such. They also enhanced self-esteem through comparing themselves to others worse off even when such persons had to be created.

Others emphasize the importance of coping not only with the time of active crisis but also with the more long-term period of adjustment which follows (see Felner, et. al., 1983). Coping with any major threat often involves an amalgam of many diverse coping acts performed over time and in multiple contexts (Roskies & Lazarus, 1980, p. 48).

Thus, the crisis client and psychologist, of necessity, explore various options for changing the situation, its meaning, and handling stress. The author finds that the realization that options exist is useful in combating the feeling of being trapped and changing the meaning of the situation. Continuing to generate new alternatives in a tight situation also bodes well for mental health in the future. Once options have been identified, the client is in a position to make choices and take action. The degree of continued involvement of the helper varies. At this point roles the school psychologist assumes are discussed.

All involve recognizing crises and responding to them, through active listening, support, and perhaps some explanation of what is transpiring. If there is no indication of danger to self or others, and no wish for further assistance on the clients' part, the psychologist withdraws. Taylor (1983) argues, based on several research reports, that most persons sustaining severe personal tragedies readjusted well and achieved "...a quality of life or level of happiness equivalent to or even exceeding their prior level of satisfaction" (p. 1151).

What is more, most did so without the aid of professional assistance (Taylor, 1983).

However, if in the judgment of those involved more assistance is needed, help is provided by mobilizing resources and/or generating alternative coping strategies. These activities are approached from a consultant-liaison role alone or supplemented by individual or family crisis counseling.

In identifying necessary resources, both emergency provisions for day-to-day existence (food stamps, baby sitters, tutors, etc.) and sources of social support (forgotten relatives, old friends, support groups) are considered. Mental health and crisis intervention specialists also are important resources. Though ethical standards have rarely been raised in discussing crisis intervention (Golan, 1978), often professional training or access to mental health specialists is assumed. Indications of danger to self and others, of more long-standing difficulties, and of repeated life crises often point in this direction. In such cases school psychologists serve as liaisons between crisis agency or mental health specialist and the school. They also assist in coordinating with the family and other community agencies and generating and implementing alternative strategies for resolving the crisis.

In cases where time, training, and interest allow, the psychologist goes beyond liaison and consultant efforts to more extensive crisis counseling with the child or family (in addition to the last section of this article see Ewing, 1978; Golan, 1978; and Murgatroyd, 1982 for different approaches). Group work with students or teachers undergoing similar crises is also a possibility. In the counselor role more time is spent on generating and testing alternative strategies. Personal meanings and individual differences in life situation (see Lukton, 1982) are explored in more detail. Possible symbolic linkages to earlier events are addressed, and when appropriate, the grieving process facilitated. Student crises often benefit from direct exploration and coordination efforts with teachers and parents. When appropriate, their aid is elicited in restructuring the situation, altering meanings, and reducing stress. They prove an important source of social support as well.

Finally, this information offers suggestions for dealing with school-wide emergency situations such as sudden death of a student or devastation by storm. First, it is useful to distinguish between emergencies and crises as the term is used here. Though emergencies may often trigger crises, the two are not synonymous. For some, the particular emergency is not threatening given their situation and goals; others find that they are able to cope. Emergencies, therefore, are seen as potentially hazardous events for some, but not all persons.

A major order of business, then, becomes precluding unnecessary crises. Attention is immediately directed toward defusing the potential hazard and/or helping people to cope with it. Appropriate physical and interpersonal resources are mobilized quickly. Attempts are made to foster social support and accurate communication among members of the school body. Information about the particular hazard and about potential coping strategies aids in influencing the meanings persons are attaching to the event and in coping with its effects.

Many of these efforts are made on a group-wide basis working with teachers and students. However, individual differences are kept in mind. At one extreme, efforts are made to identify those already in crisis or at high risk in order to extend special attention. At the other, the psychologist is sensitive to those who, for whatever reason, do not respond well to group discussions or unsolicited attention (see Parad, Resnik, and Parad, 1976 for information on emergency and disaster management).

Planning for Crises of the Future

Rather than waiting and "putting out fires," it is tempting to think in terms of prevention and crisis-proofing students and teachers. This possibility of "anticipatory guidance" or "emotional inoculation" was conceived early in the development of crisis theory (Caplan, 1964). He suggested that preventive programs anticipate hazardous events which could be expected to trigger crises in a significant portion of the target population. In individual or small group discussions, the preventor attempts to evolve a vivid anticipation of the event and associated negative feelings. Next, ways of solving the problem, including mastering negative affects, are explored. Thus, "... the hazards will be attenuated because they have been made familiar by being anticipated, and the individuals will already have been set on the path of healthy coping responses" (Caplan, 1964, p. 84).

The notion of anticipatory crisis intervention is not essentially new; many organizations run orientation programs for new members (Korchin, 1976). In fact, "... all of education has been called, more or less accurately, 'preparation for life' " (Korchin, 1976, p. 508). Information from previous sections adds to what could be attempted, as does the increasing data base on preventative mental health (Felner, Jason, Moritsugu, & Farber, 1983). For instance, social support networks within the schools might be identified and made more accessible. Previous cautions are also applicable. See Lukton (1982) for others.

BEST PRACTICES

This section might more appropriately be subtitled, "Possible Practices." As yet, the point has not been reached where "tried and true" strategies can be summarized (Slaikeu, 1984, p. 77). Selections have been chosen which relate to issues raised previously. In summarizing these efforts, much has been de-emphasized. The reader is referred to these sources for nuance and complexity, as well as a firm grasp of major points.

Smith (1976), building upon the work of others, offers one fairly traditional approach to working with individuals. Treatment is time-limited. However, it continues until the crisis is resolved whether this takes six to eight weeks or beyond. The initial contact, which may take two to three hours, is directed toward six tasks. First, the worker must determine if the client is in a crisis state. Next, the client is encouraged to express and ventilate feelings. Such expression he feels allows necessary emotional catharsis as well as facilitates building a therapeutic relationship. Then the intervenor begins exploring how the client has approached the problem and why he or she is failing. Of interest is which problem-solving and coping strategies have been used and who besides the client is involved in the crisis. Assessment is also directed toward risk of suicide and homicide and whether there is a need for emergency hospitalization.

At this point the client is helped to understand why the crisis is occurring. Understanding is directed not only toward the precipitants, but toward understanding why solutions have not been reached. As the reaction becomes more comprehensible, the client usually feels less confused and out of control. Smith believes that when appropriate, the intervenor should explain that ". . . most people faced with similar problems would be reacting in the same way" (p. 204). The intervenor also attempts to instill hope. A good starting place is often where the client is struggling the most. Alternatives are explored, and efforts are made to show that help is on the way.

In subsequent sessions, additional tasks and problem-solving strategies are explored. Communication skills are used. Smith uses generic strategies when they are available but makes adjustments in accord with individual client needs. Intervention is ended when equilibrium in social functioning has been established, and the client has completed the psychological tasks associated with particular crises. Anticipatory guidance is used at this point. Successful strategies are reviewed in anticipation of future hazardous situations. If "underlying pathological malfunctioning" is suspected, need for referral and other treatment is discussed. Finally, the client is encouraged to return for further help if the need arises.

Puryear (1979) presents a family-oriented approach to crisis intervention. As described in the introductory chapters, it involves eight intervention principles derived from work with individuals, but applying to families, and ". . . working with a family is usually the best way to approach crisis intervention" (p. 2). Crisis intervention is not seen as psychotherapy. Puryear emphasizes the distinction and cautions that counselors or therapists sometimes erroneously slip into doing therapy when intending to do crisis intervention.

Puryear's approach which is derived from systems theory, personality theory, and crisis theory is designed to promote successful crisis resolution in one to six sessions which are supplemented by telephone calls. His principles involve immediate action-oriented intervention with limited goals. Over all, intervention seeks to restore equilibrium, ". . . hopefully with some growth also occurring" (p. 21). Its minimal goal is averting catastrophe. Puryear lists permanent disintegration of the family as one possible disastrous ending. He is referring to those situations where communication and acknowledged emotional ties with one family member are severed.

In seeking to restore equilibrium, his intent is neither direct personality change nor change in the basic pattern of precrisis family functioning. For instance, a crisis situation revolving around loss of a job or a wife's pregnancy might occur in a family whose typical pattern of functioning includes an alcoholic husband who becomes drunk every weekend. Attempting to stop the father's drinking is not considered an appropriate goal for intervention. Instead, the thrust of Puryear's approach is in defining the immediate problem and then resolving it through focused problem-solving.

The crisis intervenor is active. He or she listens enough so that the clients feel attended to and understood, but formulating a clear statement of the problem and developing a specific, concrete plan of action are key. Generally, feelings are dealt with only as much as necessary. Some ventilation and exploration are encouraged initially but as soon as possible feelings are related to the problem at hand. Problem definitions which facilitate problem-solving are chosen. For instance, " 'the family hasn't yet adjusted to Mother's death,' " is preferred to " 'Mother died' " (p. 36). In cases involving delayed grief responses where unexpressed feelings are primary, the emotions are brought into the problem-solving framework. The problem becomes, " 'the client has not yet dealt with his feeling about something' " (p. 38). In such special cases, Puryear feels intervention sometimes comes closest to resembling therapy.

Crisis clients are also active, working as a team with the intervenor in defining the problem and planning its solution. Puryear points out that most clients are not stupid. If easy, simple solutions were available, they usually would not ask for help. Intervenors do not present themselves as experts at solving others' problems, but as people with expertise in the process of problem-solving who will work with them. As well as attempting to foster hope and the expectation that the problem can be solved, attempts are also made to improve self-image and promote self-reliance through the focused problem-solving process. Puryear feels that it is important that clients leave the first meeting with a task they can accomplish. Over the course of intervention, things are not done for clients if they can do them on their own. Intervenors convey the attitude that ". . . the client is a capable, decent person who has been temporarily overwhelmed by extreme stresses, and who will use your help to cope with these stresses and get back on the track" (p. 43).

Nelson and Slaikeu (1984) offer suggestions tailored specifically to the schools. They point out that because of the regular amount of time students spend there, school personnel have a unique opportunity to recognize and respond to crises. Because at times of crisis, children are vulnerable to new ideas, methods, and ways of conceptualizing, crisis intervention is not seen as an extra duty. Instead, it is very compatible with the goal of ". . . growth and development based on learning" (p. 247). Knowledge gained in crisis ". . . might be very difficult, if not impossible, to achieve when things are more 'normal' " (p. 247). In fact, almost a guarantee that the classroom teacher has the classes' undivided attention occurs during crisis situations such as death and illness of other school members.

In tailoring crisis intervention to school settings, administrative support is important. They should include crisis services in the job descriptions of all personnel from secretaries and administrators to teachers and counselors. Agreement is secured ahead of time so that, when crises occur, the regular curriculum is modified sufficiently that class discussions or individual conferences are devoted to resolving and learning from the crisis. Parents and community agencies must be involved as well. In crisis situations where many students are affected, ". . . meetings which include parents, school personnel, social service workers, police and the like, should be the rule rather than the exception." (p. 256).

Two techniques which school personnel use in responding to crises are presented. Both methods, psychological first aid and crisis therapy, are described by Slaikeu (1984). Nelson and Slaikeu feel that virtually all school personnel should be trained in psychological first aid which involves immediate assistance, lasting from minutes to hours, but usually taking only one session. Its goals are to provide support, reduce lethality, and connect the person in crisis with other helping resources.

Crisis first aid is designed to reestablish immediate coping, not to finalize psychological resolution of the crisis. In addition, school psychologists, counselors, or social workers provide therapy as part of their counseling activities. This technique, designed for those with formal training in short-term therapy, seeks to finalize resolution by working through the crisis ". . . so that the event becomes integrated into the fabric of life" (Slaikeu, 1984, p. 82). Such therapy, which may last from weeks to months, builds upon the work of Lazarus (1976, 1981) and examines behavioral, affective, interpersonal, somatic and cognitive aspects of the crisis. Its four major tasks address physical survival, expression of feelings, cognitive mastery and behavioral/interpersonal adjustment.

Nelson and Slaikeu offer many suggestions for implementing both methods in the schools. They emphasize the wealth of information that is available through daily contact with the classroom teacher. As have others in regards to adults, they warn that children should be involved as much as possible in solving their own problems. Mastery is fostered as the child is aided in generating their own alternatives,

weighing pros and cons, and choosing next steps.

REFERENCES

Adams, J. F. *Understanding adolescence: Current developments in adolescent psychology.* Boston: Allyn & Bacon, 1980.

Antonovsky, A. *Health, stress, and coping.* San Francisco: Jossey-Bass, 1979.

Auerbach, S. M., & Kilmann, P. R. Crisis intervention: A review of outcome research. *Psychological Bulletin,* 1977, *84,* 1189-1217.

Bloom, B. L. *Community mental health: A general introduction.* Monterey, CA: Brooks/Cole, 1977.

Caplan, G. (Ed.) *Prevention of mental disorders in children: Initial explorations.* New York: Basic Books, 1961.

Caplan, G. *Principles of preventive psychiatry.* New York: Basic Books, 1964.

Caplan, G. Foreword. In H. J. Parad, H. L. P. Resnik, & L. C. Parad (Eds.). *Emergency and disaster management: A mental health sourcebook.* Bowie, MD: Charles Press, 1976.

Darbonne, A. R. Crisis: A review of theory, practice, and research. *Psychotherapy: Theory, Research and Practice,* 1967, *4,* 49-56.

Eddy, J. P., Lawson, Jr., D. M., & Stilson, D. C. *Crisis intervention. A manual for education and action.* Lanham, MD: University Press of America, 1983.

Ewing, C. P.: *Crisis intervention as psychotherapy.* New York: Oxford University Press, 1978.

Farberow, N. L. Foreword. In L. A. Hoff, *People in crisis: Understanding and helping.* Menlo Park: Addison-Wesley, 1978.

Felner, R. D., Farber, S. S., & Primavera, J. Transitions and stressful life events: A model for primary prevention. In R. D. Felner, L. A. Jason, J. N. Moritsugu, and S. S. Farber (Eds.). *Preventive Psychology: Theory, Research and Practice.* New York: Pergamon, 1983.

Felner, R. D., Jason, L. A., Moritsugu, J. N., & Farber, S. S. (Eds.). *Preventive psychology: Theory, research, and practice.* New York: Pergamon Press, 1983.

Golan, N. *Treatment in crisis situations.* New York: Free Press, 1978.

Halpern, H. A. Crisis theory: A definitional study. *Community Mental Health Journal,* 1973, *9,* 342-349.

Holmes, T. H. and Rahe, R. H. "The Social Readjust-ment Rating Scale," *Journal of Psychosomatic Research,* 1967, 11:213-18.

Kobasa, S. C. Stressful life events, personality, and health: An inquiry into hardiness. Journal of Personality and Social Psychology, 1979, *37,* 1-11.

Keith, C. R., & Ellis, D. Reactions of pupils and teachers to death in a classroom. *School Coun-selor,* 1978, *25,* 228-234.

Korchin, S. J. *Modern clinical psychology: Principles of intervention in the clinic and community.* New York: Basic Books, 1976.

Lazarus, A. A. *The practice of multimodal therapy.* New York: McGraw-Hill, 1981.

Lazarus, A. A. (Ed.). *Multimodal behavior therapy.* New York: Springer Publishing, 1976.

Lewis, M. S., Gottesman, D., & Gutstein, S. The course and duration of crisis. *Journal of Consulting and Clinical Psychology,* 1979, *47,* 128-134.

Lindemann, E. Symptomatology and management of acute grief. *American Journal of Psychiatry,* 1944, *101,* 141-148.

Lindemann, E. *Beyond grief: Studies in crisis inter-vention.* New York: Aronson, 1979.

Lukton, R. C. Myths and realities of crisis interven-tion. *Social Casework: The Journal of Con-temporary Social Work,* 1982, *63,* 276-285.

Murgatroyd, S. Coping and the crisis counselor. *Brit-ish Journal of Guidance and Counseling,* 1982, *10,* 151-166.

Nelson, E. R., & Slaikeu, K. A. Crisis intervention in the schools. In K. A. Slaikeu, *Crisis intervention: A handbook for practice and research.* Boston: Allyn & Bacon, 1984.

Parad, H. J., Resnik, H. L. P., & Parad, L. G. *Emergency and disaster management: A mental health sourcebook.* Bowie, MD: Charles Press, 1976.

Pearlin, L. I., & Schooler, C. The structure of coping. *Journal of Health and Social Behavior,* 1978, *19,* 2-21.

Phillips, E. L. *Stress, health and psychological prob-lems in the major professions.* Washington, DC: University Press of America, 1982.

Puryear, D. A. *Helping people in crisis.* San Fran-cisco: Jossey-Bass, 1979.

Roskies, E., & Lazarus, R. S. Coping theory and the teaching of coping skills. In P. O. Davidson & S. M. Davidson (Eds.), *Behavioral medicine: Changing health lifestyles.* New York: Brunner/ Mazel, 1980.

Slaikeu, K. A. *Crisis intervention: A handbook for practice and research.* Boston: Allyn & Bacon, 1984.

Smith, L. L. *Crisis intervention theory and practice: A source book.* Washington: University Press of America, 1976.

Taylor, S. E. Adjustment to threatening events: A theory of cognitive adaption. *American Psy-chologist,* 1983, *38,* 1161-1173.

Toffler, A. *Future shock.* New York: Bantam, 1971.

Wise, P. S. School psychologists' ratings of stressful events. *Journal of School Psychology,* in press.

Yeaworth, R. C., York, J., Hussey, M. A., Ingle, M. E. and Goodwin, T. The development of an adolescent life change event scale. *Adolescence,* 1980, *15,* 91-97.

ANNOTATED BIBLIOGRAPHY

Felner, R. D., Farber, S. S., & Primavera, J. Transitions and stressful life events: A model for primary prevention. In R. D. Felner, L. A. Jason, J. N. Moritsugu, and S. S. Farber (Eds.). *Preventive Psychology: Theory, Research and Practice.* New York: Pergamon, 1983.
This article addresses research on life events and coping. Long-term adjustments to life events are discussed. Useful additional infor-mation is provided in terms of prevention and also coping resources and strategies.

Korchin, S. J. Crisis intervention. In *Modern clinical psychology: Principles of intervention in the clinic and community.* New York: Basic Books, 1976, p. 501-510.
Brief overview of crisis theory and practice. Discusses the concept of crisis, necessary con-ditions for crisis intervention programs, tech-niques of intervention and anticipatory crisis intervention.

Lukton, R. C. Myths and realities of crisis interven-tion. *Social Casework: The Journal of Con-temporary Social Work,* 1982, *63,* 276-285.
Critical review of several assumptions upon which crisis practice is based. Recommends a holistic, phenomenological approach for theory and practice which takes into account the unique ecological matrix of each individ-ual in crisis.

Murgatroyd, S. Coping and the crisis counselor. *Brit-ish Journal of Guidance and Counseling,* 1982, *10,* 151-166.
Reviews the available literature on coping which has relevance to crisis counseling. Dis-cusses strategies for anticipatory coping, as well as coping with the effects of crisis.

Slaikeu, K. A. *Crisis intervention: A handbook for practice and research.* Boston: Allyn and Bacon, 1984.

Current review of theory, research and practice. Includes a comprehensive model for crisis intervention. Discusses psychological first aid (Chapter 6) and crisis therapy (Chapter 8) and gives case examples of each (Chapters 7 and 9). Includes chapter by Nelson and Slaikeu on crisis intervention in the schools (Chapter 16).

BEST PRACTICES IN INTERPRETING PSYCHOLOGICAL ASSESSMENT DATA TO PARENTS

Hedwig Teglasi
University of Maryland

OVERVIEW

Interpreting the results of psychological and educational tests to parents in the context of other relevant information such as interviews, behavioral observations, background material, history of the problem, medical records and reports from teachers and other professionals is the logical culmination of the assessment process. An effective interpretation influences the educational and social adjustment of the child and enhances the family interactions. However, sometimes parents do not comprehend explanations of their child's problem(s). If they do, they do not always act positively on the information. Parents are likely to feel apprehensive or at a disadvantage when they come to school for a conference with the school psychologist and may leave the interview with mixed feelings of frustration, confusion, bewilderment, denial and guilt (Searl, 1978; Waisbren, 1980; Wright, 1976). Accompanying these feelings are incomplete, misunderstood, or selectively perceived information (Dirks, Bushkuhl & Marzano, 1983; Hoff, Fenton, Yoshida & Kaufman, 1978). Well-prepared and well-conducted parent interviews are an important part of the functioning of the school psychologist and play an important role in promoting the welfare of children and families. This chapter reviews the current literature on parent conferences to describe general principles contributing to the effective interpretive interview. The emphasis is on the process of interaction with parents and on various approaches to conveying information. The assumption is made that the school psychologist is thoroughly familiar with the content to be imparted.

BASIC CONSIDERATIONS

Goals

Philosophically, the professional is not merely a conveyor of information but a change agent as well. The basic goal of the parent conference is to encourage parents to perceive their child realistically and to use their problem-solving skills on behalf of their child (Gilmore, 1974). The basic goals of the parent conference and skills needed to accomplish these goals are similar across settings. The need for home-school collaboration is an ongoing issue (Gottesman, 1980; Hobbs, 1975), and federal laws such as PL 94-142 mandate this collaboration. Whether the assessment takes place in an outside agency or in the schools, it must be acknowledged that a large proportion of a student's life is spent in school. Obtaining information about a child's adjustment in terms of educational progress, peer and teacher relationships is essential. Knoff (1982), working at an independent psychodiagnostic clinic, but also working closely with the local school system, asked parents and the school representative of the *same* child to identify presenting problem(s) from among 17 listed possibilities. School and parent consultees of a private clinic agreed only 57% of the time on the reasons for the referral.

A large discrepancy in the perception of the problem between school and parents prior to the psychoeducational assessment disrupts the entire process. Hayes and Oats (1978) found that differences in perception between parents' and professional's assessment of a child exists even after the parent conference. They suggest that it is important to discover parents' perceptions of their child's problem to bridge the gap.

In summary, interpreting assessment information to parents has the following goals: (a) The psychologist promotes a clear understanding of the child's problem and eliminates uncertainty (Shellenberger, 1982). The parent conference provides a thorough presentation of the child's condition including etiology, severity, and prognosis. The understanding involves an acceptance of the problem and its implications for the child and the family. New information results in an attitude change which alters expectations or promotes viewing a child's behavior in a different light. For example, by attributing the child's behavior to different causes such as conflict with the teacher as a smokescreen for the child's inadequacy in the subject matter, parents (and professionals) change their reaction and manner of relating to the child. By influencing the perceptions that others have of the child, subsequent interactions with that child are improved. Sometimes a professional reinforces and elaborates upon perceptions already held. (b) It is necessary to assist the parent in the emotional adjustment to the assessment information (Shea & Sauer, 1981). Interpretations are individualized according to the family's situation and needs. Resistance or denial by the parent is handled appropriately. Two-way communication between the parents and the professional is encouraged so that the interpreter is sure about parental assumptions and ideas; addresses parental concerns; and, thus, ascertains whether assessment information was understood and accepted. (c) Assessment information is of little use

unless it is interpreted and communicated so that it facilitates decision-making (Salvia & Ysseldyke, 1978). Recommendations are based on what parents can realistically do. Recognizing and dealing with the personal problems of parents as they affect the child or as they are exacerbated by the child's condition are important factors to consider (Sarason, 1959). It is important to convey to parents that recommendations are subject to modifications if they do not produce the desired results. The groundwork is laid for follow-up and future contact.

Training and Background Needed by School Psychologists

Effective interpretation of psychoeducational test results to parents involves a formidable and wide variety of skills including interviewing, sensitivity to parental responses, and grasp of diagnostic findings and their implications. The school psychologist deals with cognitive, emotional, and behavioral issues and is trained in diverse areas related to the psychological and educational development of children. Since assessment is implicitly tied to intervention, familiarity with therapeutic approaches is basic to assessment. There are several areas of competency needed by school psychologists.

1. Understanding the Concepts of Tests and Measurements: Selecting the most relevant tests, given the nature of the referral problem, is of utmost importance. The school psychologist knows the types of decisions that are made with particular types of test data. To accomplish this, technical knowledge of tests and measurements, expertise in specific tests as well as an understanding of the relationship of test scores and patterns of scores to real life variables are necessary. In-depth knowledge of specific tests is important so that the psychologist knows

the meaning and limits of its interpretation.

2. Background in Therapy: In many instances, test interpretation becomes a part of broader counseling (Gessell & Armatruda, 1974) that deals with feelings and emotions as well as facts to assure understanding and acceptance of the information conveyed. There is a continuing need to listen and respond to the family's expectations and questions. Simply telling parents the facts of an evaluation does not guarantee that they hear, understand, or are able to alleviate the child's problem (Buscaglia, 1975; Richman, 1967). Whenever parents hear information about their child that is discrepant from their expectations, there is a sense of loss, disappointment, anger, guilt, or denial (Dirks, Bushkuhl & Marzano, 1983; Shea & Saur, 1981).

The psychologist needs to understand the child's emotional functioning to give the parents insight which they can use. Obviously because of the link between assessment and intervention, the psychologist also understands remedial strategies to recommend those that would be most appropriate (Nagle, 1983).

3. Background in the Referral Issue at Hand: One cannot convey test interpretation to parents in a supportive manner without an indepth understanding of the problem and its implication for the child and family. Only when the professional has knowledge of the problem does he or she convey the message that "we understand children like yours and will do everything we can to help" (Shea & Saur, 1981). This gives the parents a feeling of not being alone. In addition, parents want reading materials which help them understand their child (Dembinski & Mauser, 1977). The school psychologist should have the titles and authors of books related to the primary issues or concerns readily available. Furthermore, the school psychologist should be acquainted with community resources and support groups available to parents.

4. Awareness of Ethical, Legal, and Professional Guidelines: Legal issues are increasingly dominating the practice of school psychology, particularly since the passage of two significant pieces of legislation — Education for All Handicapped Children Act (PL 94-142) and Family Educational Rights and Privacy Act (Buckley Amendment or PL 93-380). A school psychologist needs to be familiar with the details of these laws as well as with local, state, and federal guidelines for eligibility and placement. The legal mandate for parents to be participants in placement decisions and their right to due process hearings when they do not accept the decision should be an opportunity to establish a closer working relationship among parents, teachers, and school psychologists rather than lead to low risk taking and formalized procedures. Similarly, the legal mandate of access to school records is a vehicle to greater communication and involvement with parents to the ultimate benefit of the child (Bersoff, 1982; Hoff, Fenton, Yoshida, & Kaufman, 1978; Pryzwansky & Bersoff, 1978; Kirp & Kirp, 1976;).

5. Personal Insight: The professional's reactions to parents contribute to the climate of the interchange. To work successfully with parents, professionals understand and learn to control their unusual reactions and are aware of their philosophical orientations and biases (Losen & Diament, 1978). For example, if parental hostility evokes defensiveness and anger, perhaps even sarcasm or possibly more subtle reactions such as changes in tone of voice, posture or facial expressions, it is imperative that the professional learns alternative responses. Personal styles such as being stiff or serious, expressing too much affect, or being too lighthearted influence the reaction of parents to the interpretive conference.

Other behaviors such as too much self-disclosure, not focusing on the task, excessive talking, or interrupting parents are detrimental to the goals of the parent conference. Adverse reactions when others do not agree or disapprove, tendencies to take things personally, and an inordinate need to be liked or approved of must be recognized and addressed.

Setting in Which a Parent Conference Occurs: Team versus Individual

Both individually held parent conferences and interpretive meetings conducted by a team have advantages. Many parents prefer to meet with a team of consultants rather than a single professional to compare opinions and check information (Barclay, Goulet & Holtgrewe, 1962).

In a school setting parents are more likely to contact a recommended agency when two or three school personnel have made the decision for referral (Conti, 1975). Compliance with the recommendation is also more likely when two or more interpretive conferences are held with both parents.

There are times when communicating test results to parents in a team setting is inappropriate because of the emotional nature of the material to be conveyed and/or because sensitive family issues need to be discussed. Parents are not inclined to ask questions and interact when confronted by several professionals in a large, formal interview (Dembinski & Mauser, 1977; Stephens, 1969). A series of meetings combines the advantages afforded by the team with benefits of individual discussion where sensitive issues are best handled. An exploratory meeting with the school psychologist for the purpose of clarifying the referral for the parents and obtaining background information is helpful in setting the stage for parent-school cooperation. The psychologist holds a feedback session with parents before the formal team conference (Nagle, 1983). When parent conferences with the school psychologist are held prior to a placement or IEP meeting, parents assume a constructive role in the team meetings (Turnbull & Leonard, 1981). The task-oriented nature of the team meeting is emphasized at the outset so that work better done at other times with the child's parents is not attempted during the staff meeting. Parents are encouraged to meet with the school psychologist at another time if they have concerns other than those to be discussed during the team meeting.

General Principles for Conducting Effective Parent Conferences

The first ingredient of a successful interview is the communication of genuine interest in the people and problems involved. Sincerity, personal conviction, and feeling is not lost on parents who are likely to follow recommendations made by professionals whom they perceive as caring.

Professionals help parents retain and use information (Jones & Caldwell, 1981; Marshall & Goldstein, 1979). Parents are selective in the information they recall about the child. Positive facts are more likely to be recalled than negative information (Dirks, et al. 1983; Hopper, 1977). At times parents do not recall or understand test results very well because too many subtest scores are given to them (Hopper, 1977). Presenting composite scores and explaining patterns of scores provide a more integrated approach to test interpretation. When parents lack a conceptual framework, they do not have the opportunity to organize relevant information. When complex information is conveyed, parents have difficulty grasping the total picture. For example, when several alternatives for special education placement are considered, parents are confused about a final decision (Hoff, Fenton, Yoshida, & Kaufman, 1978).

Svarstad and Lipton (1977) found a significant relationship between professional communication regarding mental retardation and the subsequent acceptance of the child's handicap. Frankness facilitated trust in the professional, and detailed information was more comprehensible to parents who were unfamiliar with professional jargon. An explanation of the concept of retardation, including characteristics and expectations for future educational or occupational attainment was helpful. Parents had misconceptions about the meaning of retardation and their observation of their child was discrepant from their understanding.

The following suggestions are helpful (Biggs & Keller, 1982; Hooper, 1977; Richman, 1967; Shea & Suar, 1981): (a) translate technical concepts into everyday terminology. For example, one explains defenses of rationalization and projection by saying something like, "When Johnny feels in danger of looking bad, he makes excuses and blames others;" (b) provide unifying concepts and principles that bridge the gap between what the parent knows and still needs to understand. Explain the significance of the pattern that is emerging and emphasize the positive as well as problematic aspects; (c) forge links among scores on various subtests and between one test and another in relation to the referral problem; (d) sequence the test data with logic and organization that relates back to the referral issues; (e) give composite scores whenever these fit with the logical presentation of results; (f) use the parents' past experiences and current expectations as an anchor; (g) point out, explore and reconcile contradictions between results of testing and parent perceptions; (h) give groundwork and provide a mean-

ingful context for the information to be presented. For example, give academic information in the context of personality and intelligence; (i) encourage parental questions and respond to parental feelings; (j) provide a written summary to parents.

Enhancing Parental Compliance with Recommendations

As stated previously, a primary goal of the interpretive conference is to motivate parents to alter their perceptions of and/or interactions with the child and to follow through on recommendations. The following factors are associated with greater likelihood that parents carry out recommendations (Conti, 1975; Davidson & Schrag, 1969; Dembinski & Mauser, 1977; Dirks, et al., 1983; Hayes & Oates, 1978; Jones & Caldwell, 1981):

1. Parents who perceive their child's problem in a manner that is similar to the professional's are far more apt to accept the recommendation than if they disagree with the problem statement. Identifying the parents' attitude toward the child's problem and trying to change that attitude is time consuming, though worthwhile. On the other hand, there are times when the professional does not try to alter parental perceptions or attitudes but makes recommendations that are in keeping with parental resources and understandings.

2. The likelihood of following through on the recommendations is enhanced when both parents attend the conference, particularly if there are two or more conferences. An explanation of the referral if initiated by the school and dealing with the problems and resistances of both parents significantly increases the likelihood of acceptance of recommendations.

3. Precise communication or clarity of interpretive material is important. Par-

ents who do not comply with recommendations are confused by the interpretation of the findings. Those who followed through on recommendations report that the information was conveyed in a "specific and clearly stated manner."

4. Families are more likely to act on a recommendation from professionals whom they perceive as caring.

5. A family is more likely to follow through on a referral if a number of professionals are involved in making that referral.

6. The likelihood of contacting a counseling resource is greatly enhanced when a specific name is provided. The family is even more likely to contact the counseling resource when the psychologist expresses confidence in the recommended resource.

7. Other factors associated with the likelihood of follow through on recommendations which are less under the control of the professional are the family's socioeconomic status (high SES more lilely to follow through) and whether or not the family was previously referred (a family not previously referred is more likely to follow through).

BEST PRACTICES

Though each parent conference is unique and tailored individually in terms of content, there is a logical progression within each conference. The outline below represents an integration of the aproaches of several authors (Diament & Losen, 1978; Rheingold, 1945; Rockowitz & Davidson, 1979; Sarason, 1959; Sattler, 1982; Shea & Saur, 1981).

I. Exploratory Phase

Prior to the evaluation, it is helpful to meet with the parents to obtain their perceptions of the child, the history of the problem, and to discuss the reasons for the evaluation. During the exploratory conference, parents and professionals arrive at a mutual understanding of the goals and possible outcomes of assessment. If parents have misconceptions or unrealistic expectations about the testing, it is important to deal with them at this time (Biggs & Keller, 1982). Background information is gathered, and the reasons for the referral are clarified and formulated in a manner that can be addressed by the evaluation. Written permission to observe a child, speak to a teacher, or to obtain reports of previous evaluations is obtained at this time.

To evaluate how realistic parents are about the present problem, the psychologist encourages parents to talk about their expectations and aspirations for their child. The exploratory sessions set the tone for future interactions; parents are made comfortable and are encouraged to ask questions and talk freely. Their ideas about the problem are discussed fully, and frustrations or hardships that are faced by the parents are recognized. The information obtained from parents during the exploratory session clarifies the purpose of the evaluation and provides a basis for data gathering geared toward answering the referral question. However, other issues which emerge during the evaluation process are also pursued, and the psychologist should anticipate questions that may arise later.

II. Feedback Session

The purpose of the feedback session is to communicate interpretation of data from a variety of sources. The session has several phases.

1. Introduction: This phase is particularly important if the conference is to be conducted by a team. The person in charge of the conference introduces staff and reiterates the nature of the meeting particularly if the specific purpose is to arrive at a placement decision (Shea & Saur, 1981).

2. Review of Problem: Usually some time has elapsed between the exploratory session and the feedback conference so it is helpful to review the problem and ask if there are any changes in concerns. Restating the problem from the parents' viewpoint gives assurance to them that their concerns are being addressed and that their feelings are important. At the same time, such a review conveys the professional's recognition that parents are concerned about the child and sets the stage for cooperation.

3. Structuring the Feedback Session: Prior to the data interpretation, the professional conveys to parents the attitude that questions are not only encouraged throughout the presentation but are also expected. The parents are told that this conference is not the only time they have to discuss the child's problem. In addition, parents are prepared for hearing any conflict-arousing information.

4. Communication of Content: The interpreter begins by mentioning briefly the child's reactions to the tasks. A brief overview of how the psychologist will proceed and major points to be covered are helpful to parents. Then data interpretation is introduced incrementally, dealing with reactions and questions of parents as well as clarifying misconceptions.

Denial is one of the most common defense mechanisms which parents use to deal with the anxieties aroused by the recognition that their child is handicapped or somehow falls short of their expectations (Ross, 1964). Instead of becoming impatient with denials, the interpreter recognizes that parents need the defense at this time. Arguing with a parent's distorted perception is of no avail; the psychologist gives a statement of reality. By providing a framework of a supportive relationship, the psychologist diminishes parental anxiety enough to allow some confrontation by the parent with the reality of the child's problem.

Material that is unpalatable and/or most likely to result in parents' inability to hear other relevant information is embedded or sandwiched in the appropriate context to promote greater acceptance. The capacity of the informant to express positive feelings about the child as a person helps the parents to view the youngster in a new perspective.

Most parents want honesty in an interpretive session and resent ambiguous assurances. However, parents need to understand their child's abilities and assets as well as disabilities and deficiencies. What the child *can* do is far more important than what the child cannot do, and parents are encouraged to focus on the child's strengths (Graham, 1975).

Interpreters keep pace with the parents' progress on grasping the implications of the problem, avoid giving more information than is assimilated at one time, and deal with inconsistencies in the data.

5. Problem Solving and Recommendations: Moving from the data interpretation to the problem-solving and recommendation phase is done at the parents' pace and not the professional's (Shea & Saur, 1981). Parents neither hear nor accept specific recommendations while they are still reacting emotionally to unexpected test results or if they do not have a clear understanding and acceptance of the child's difficulty. If, as a result of the interpretive conference(s), parents acquire a different understanding of their child, a change in the way they interact with the child is likely to occur even without behavioral recommendations. On the other hand, specific and detailed recommendations given to parents which is not founded on a basic change in parental perception and understanding of the child are not likely to be implemented.

To discover where parents can and cannot effectively intervene, the psychologist identifies the parents' situation and previous efforts at managing the problem. For example, one should not recommend that a parent tutor the child if previous experience has shown that this has been ineffective. It is important to commend parents on any successful handling of their child. However, parents must not be given the idea that they must extend themselves constantly on behalf of their child. Recommendations are realistic, mindful of the resources of the parents, school, and community. Parents are not expected to meet all the needs of their child and, at times, the thrust of the recommendations is to allow the parent(s) to have more time to themselves or devote more energy to siblings.

Recommendations are specific and goal oriented. For example, exhorting a parent to set firm limits is not adequate without specific guidelines.

Both long and short range goals are considered when making recommendations (Dembinski & Mauser, 1977; Roos, 1978). One must also convey to parents that recommendations are evaluated and modified if any part of the plan does not work (Des Jardens, Gorham, Page, & Schreiber, 1975).

A recommendation such as placing a child in a special class is painful to parents. Therefore, the psychologist allows for parent reactions to the recommendation and informs them of legal rights.

6. Plans for sharing Results with the Child: The recommendations are not complete until the interpreter and both parents reach a decision about what will be communicated to the child, who will do it, and when it will be done (Jones & Caldwell, 1981; Rockowitz & Davidson, 1979). Parents' wishes and the cognitive and emotional development of the child are important in this decision. The examiner, having previously established rapport, is in a good position to interpret test findings and explain recommendations to the child. In addition to highlighting test results and explaining recommendations, the psychologist discusses with the child what (s)he hoped to get out of the evaluation and helps clear up any misconceptions.

7. Summary and Follow-Up: To help parents organize and recall the information presented, the psychologist gives a conceptual summary. Parents are asked to ask any remaining questions. Planning for future contact to follow up on the child's progress and evaluate the efficacy of the recommendations is an integral part of the conference. In dealing with a problem such as a child who is chronically handicapped and whose functioning is impaired in one or more areas, a single discussion seldom suffices to answer all of the family's concerns or to deal with all of the complexities of the situation (Arnold, 1978). If all of the goals have not been achieved or if parents desire further discussion, the psychologist schedules another conference.

When parents do not accept the interpretive information, it is useless to try to convince them of the validity of test results. At such times the most helpful responses are reflections or restatements of parents' feelings in a calm and accepting way and an offer to resume the discussion in the future. Should the parents feel that they want another opinion, a list of agencies or professionals who are competent to make such an evaluation is provided (Sarason, 1959; Sattler, 1982).

Parents request copies of written reports (Dembinski & Mauser, 1977), and professionals view the written report as helping to recall the information presented during the conference (Gorham, 1975; Sattler, 1982; Dirks, et al., 1983). At the end of the interpretive conference, the agency's policy about sending a written report to parents is explained.

Presenting Test Results

Test results are a place to begin to

understand the child and formulate goals. This attitude fosters a non-judgmental approach to communicating test results. Findings are simply stated, and then their meaning and implications for the child are shared. Giving parents a visual profile along with verbal interpretations helps them grasp results more easily. For example, explaining where their child falls relative to peers by drawing a normal curve helps some parents accept an average IQ score more readily when they can see that "most people are like most people." As another visual aid, parents are shown the WISC-R face sheet so that variability of subtest scores can be seen at a glance. It is important not to dwell on minutiae that confuse rather than clarify the parents' understanding. When several tests have been administered, one formulates a conceptual summary based on conveying informtion from several tests rather than presenting conclusions on a test by test basis.

In order to impart genuine knowledge and understanding rather than the illusion of information, one pays careful attention to the content, language, and audience. For example, conveying information to parents with limited intellectual capacity necessitates even more care in translation of technical material to everyday terms. Interpreting that a child is intellectually borderline to similarly functioning parents requires the use of concrete terms and metaphors.

Technical language is avoided by translating key concepts into everyday language. Thus, one does not refer to subtests of an intelligence test by name only. Similarly, concepts of achievement versus ability are explained clearly including possible discrepancies between school achievement and performance on standardized achievement tests. Since parents hear references to age level activities frequently in school such a way of describing observations provides an easy method

for them to undertand their child's difficulties (Greenspan, 1981).

One way to avoid too much emphasis on the IQ score itself is to point out to parents before the actual testing occurs that real life achievement is dependent upon a variety of factors besides IQ scores, that single test scores may not be wholly reliable, and that giftedness and retardation are in turn dependent upon more than IQ scores (Dirks, et al., 1983). Statements regarding ability scores in isolation serve no constructive purpose (Psychological Corporation, 1959). One must compare ability scores with achievement or point out subtest patterns in relation to the referral issue.

Reporting qualitative as well as quantitative descriptions of a child's performance such as cognitive style and approach to tasks allows the examiner to make statements that reflect the uniqueness of the child (Nagle, 1983). Too objective a discussion of the child, including the use of jargon, suggests a distant, rejecting stance. As a result, the parents attempt to assert the bond between themselves and their child, enumerate the child's strengths and emphasize bits of behavior that they see as incompatible with the psychologist's assessment (Rheingold, 1959). Parents need to view their child in human terms and reporting to parents that the responses on the Rorschach indicated severely disturbed thinking and perception is not as helpful as the following explanation: "When pressures and strains are great enough, then Joey can't think straight or tell the difference between what is or isn't real" (Richman, 1967). Observations of behavior during testing often help in understanding and interpreting of test results as well as in formulating recommendations. It is helpful to point out how much encouragement the child required to stay on task, how the child approached various types of tasks, reaction to failure or frustration, degree of spontaneity, and relatedness to the examiner. The examiner's observations frequently serve as vehicles to integrate parental perceptions and reports received from teachers or others with the test results.

Caution must be used not to draw general conclusions about a child's behavior on the basis of observtions in the testing situation. A distractible, learning disabled child does not attend to tasks in the classroom as well as he/she might in a one-to-one testing situation. A child experiencing difficulty relating to peers may seem more confident and interactive in a highly structured therapeutic activity group. Observations across various situations are integrated into a systematic observational study of the child which includes comparison of the child's behavior with another child (or children) across various situations. Whenever a psychologist observes a child it is helpful to ask the teacher if the behavior manifested was typical.

Presenting examples of a child's work is a powerful tool in helping parents understand results. However, it is also fraught with many potential problems. While the examiner typically bases interpretations on data converging from a number of sources, parents are not aware of the other sources of information and may feel that the example described by the examiner constitutes questionable evidence for the conclusions. Furthermore, parents may have alternative interpretations for the behavior that the psychologist is describing. Many parents do not openly express their doubts adout the examiner's interpretation of their child's behavior but remain silent and simply devalue the test interpretations and recommendations.

When projective test results are interpreted, the presentation should be in logical order, organized into sections which are easily understood, and related to the presenting concerns. The intent is not to present a global and comprehensive picture of the child's personality but to help parents understand the child's perceptions as these are relevant to the presenting concerns. Beyond the content of a projective instrument such as the Thematic Apperception Test, one evaluates how a child reacts to novel or ambiguous stimuli. For example, a bright child's failing performance in an open-unstructured class is consistent with inability to handle the lack of structure inherent in the projective tests.

Sometimes interpretations are best prefaced by statements that defuse parents' resistance and guilt. The psychologist reminds the parents that the interpretations reflect the child's perceptions of "reality" and are not necessarily consistent with the way things actually are. It is pointed out, for example, that a child may be very sensitive and perceive the slightest hint of preoccupation on the part of the parent as rejection. The psychologist points out that the child did not deliberately reveal certain attitudes and values, but that the interpreter made inferences on the basis of stories told by the child.

Explaining major areas of concern or conflict which are creating tension and anxiety helps the parents understand their child's view. Furthermore, parents are helped to understand how the child's perceptions create a cycle which leads to the anticipated reactions from others.

An understanding of the child's emotional functioning is especially important if the parents are stressing the academic progress to the detriment of the child's social, emotional, and cognitive development. Projective data are used to suggest different possible perspectives on the referral issues. Understanding the dominant behavioral characteristics and/or aspects of personality style which are relevant to the child's adjustment and to the referral problem often motivate others to alter their manner of relating with the child.

Climate of the Feedback Session

While it is important to be sensitive to parental reactions, the psychologist does not come across as seeking parental approval or confirmation of his or her conclusions. There is a vast difference between approval seeking and perception checking. Give parents a rationale before probing into areas that parents perceive as personal and stress that parental responses are confidential. Timing and sensitivity during the feedback session play an important role in conveying respect and setting the tone. Spend time getting a grasp of the problem and respond to the needs presented by the family. Sometimes, an immediate answer to a problem, even if appropriate, minimizes the situation and insults the parents' sensibility. If there is a severe disability, the psychologist does not offer easy and immediate solutions.

Role of Parents and Children in the Interpretive Conference

Parents differ in the way they understand the problem and in their attitude toward the child. Therefore, the psychologist involves *both* parents by making eye contact, drawing out the less verbal parent, or even asking one parent to wait while the other's concerns are addressed. Psychologists directly acknowledge discrepancies in parents' interpretation.

There is a wide range of opinion regarding the involvement of the child in the interpretive conferences. The parents only may be given the test interpretations. In this case the psychologist pursues with the parents their thoughts about how they might discuss the evaluation results and recommendations with their child. Separate interpretive conferences may be held or a joint conference can be held with parents and child. A conference may be held with the parents with the child being brought in at the end. Finally separate conferences can be held with parents and the child followed by a joint conference where the results are reviewed on the child's level.

The last option has several advantages. A frank discussion is held with the parents without the presence of the child (Ross, 1964), while the right of the child to know is respected and information is provided in ways that are understandable and helpful (Colley, 1973). The child is not overpowered by the presence of parents and other adults (if team meeting) (Adams, 1982).

Older children are provided with the test interpretation routinely though indications and contraindications are weighed in each case. Sometimes the child's fantasies about him/herself are far worse than is warranted, and honest discussion and clarification are immensely helpful.

Children and adolescents often decline to hear the results if they are offered the choice primarily because they fear and anticipate the worst. If the examiner feels strongly that an interpretation is helpful, only a choice of format is provided. The person doing the testing interprets results to the child as the testing procedure establishes a bond which makes the child particularly ready to benefit from the interpretation (Richman, 1967).

What to Say and What not to Say in the Presence of a Child

Sometimes parents have concerns that interpreting test results to their child may have an adverse effect. These concerns need to be discussed. Arnold (1978) has two axioms regarding what to tell parents in front of their child. (a) *Be the Heavy* — the idea is that the professional is expendable to the child, and the relationship between parent and child which is permanent is fostered. Thus, it is permissible to tell parents in front of the child to crack down or to deprive the child of junk food or excessive TV. The psychologist is the heavy, and the parents are off the hook; (b) *Be Santa's Secret Helper* —it is best to advise parents privately when suggesting something the child will probably find pleasant such as removing restrictions, spending more time or giving a desired object so that the child doesn't attribute the parental behavior merely to compliance with authority as opposed to a sign of love. An exception to the second axiom is the case of the parent who is so unreasonable that it is necessary for the child to see that another adult thinks the parents' strictures are unreasonable.

Parental Questions and Advice

Sometimes it is difficult not to get sidetracked by parents' questions. If the focus is kept clear, the discussion is not likely to get into the intricacies of the parents' personality, history, and so on. For example, when a parent raises the issue of similarity with the child, it is helpful to focus the session back on the child and at the same time address the parents' question by asking the parent to describe how his/her experiences over the years can now help the child.

When the parent feels imposed upon by the child, any advice or recommendation seems like an additional imposition. For such a parent, it is more helpful to emphasize the parent's own right to have something for himself including therapy rather than devoting all resources to the child. Advice is only given if parents can use it. A parent who helplessly says, "I just can't set limits on my 4-year-old" is not necessarily asking for advice on the most efficacious way to set limits; rather, she is asking for support and understanding.

Advice is given cautiously. Any rule must be flexibly applied when interacting with children. Simply telling parents to be firm may result in excessive physical punishment. Suggesting that parents ease up may result in no limits whatsoever. Any major change in parental behavior requires the opportunity for feedback and readjustment. Consequently, the change is not likely to be accomplished successfully on the basis of advice received during just one session. Rather, emphasizing parental insight and understanding of their possible role in the problem and motivating them to contact a referral source or to return for a series of sessions is preferred.

Hidden Agenda

A parent may request that a child be evaluated to accomplish a specific goal which the parent does not share with the evaluator. What the parent has in mind is the "hidden agenda." For example, a parent may really want help for himself, but is embarrassed to seek it directly. In all cases where the parent has a specific purpose in mind, the psychologist cannot just give a factual interpretation but must deal openly with the parental agenda.

Pitfalls to Avoid During Parent Conferences

Avoid Blaming Parents

Professionals resist the temptation to criticize parental attitudes or actions so as not to stifle expression of feelings or reinforce feelings of guilt and worthlessness. The professional discusses with the parents how they've handled the problem and whether their way of dealing with it was functional. Intent is separated from impact by recognizing that what the parents had been doing, however ineffective, was based on "good intentions." The psychologist works with the inclinations of the parents and helps them view suggestions as consistent with their priorities rather than as representing a different approach.

Avoid Passive Avoidance

Fear of contention results in minimizing a child's problem, not bringing up sensitive topics, failing to refer a child who needs counseling, and conveying false expectations. A psychologist may avoid challenging parents who are denying their child's problem. Parental denial is devastating because the child's problem has to escalate before it is acknowledged. If there is parental resistance to hearing the interpretive information or the recommendations, the interpreter should focus on the resistance. By skipping over it, the psychologist is just talking to finish a process (Greenspan, 1981).

Avoid a Tendency Toward Comforting

Sometimes problems do not have immediate or easy solutions and parents need to deal with the painful aspects of the information they've just received. The most common mistakes among beginning professionals result from their wanting to offer immediate comfort and solace to parents who are upset (Shea & Saur, 1981). Psychologists must fight the tendency to "make nice," to solve the problem, and to give advice too easily without considering all of the alternatives or parents' readiness to accept the advice.

Avoid Authoritarian Dogmatism

An absolutely certain manner of communication inhibits discussion because parents are reluctant to disagree and results in parental hostility. A dogmatic presentation of the material does not allow for complexity such as real limitations of particular tests nor are parental perceptions acknowledged. Even if parental agreement is obtained in the moment, the motivation to do what's best for the child does not persist.

SUMMARY

The role of the school psychologist in the interpretive conference is conceptualized as that of a change agent rather than merely a conveyor of information. It is assumed that the primary goal of the parent conference is to influence parents' perceptions of their child in ways that enable them to make decisions and/or change their interactions so that the development of the child and the welfare of the family are promoted. Given this goal the major emphasis of this chapter was on the psychologist's role in enhancing parental understanding and acceptance of the interpretive material including assisting parents with emotional responses. Literature was reviewed relating to parent understanding and retention of diagnostic information as well as follow-through on recommendations. The style of communication and the process of parent-professional interaction were emphasized rather than the content to be conveyed.

REFERENCES

Adams, G. L. (1982). Referral advice given by physicians, *20*, 16-20.

Arnold, L. E. (1978). Strategies and tactics of parent guidance in *Helping parents Help their Children*, Brunner Mazel: New York.

Barclay, A., Goulet, L. R., Holtgrewe, M. M., & Sharp, A. R. (1962). Parental evaluations of clinical services for retarded children, *American Journal of Mental Deficiency, 67*, 232-237.

Bersoff, D. N. (1982). The legal regulation of school psychology in C. Reynolds & T. Gutkin (Eds.) *The Handbook of School Psychology*, New York City: Wiley.

Biggs, D. A. & Keller, K. E. (1982). A cognitive approach to using tests in counseling. *Personnel and Guidance Journal*, May, 528-532.

Buscaglia, L. (1975). The Disabled and their Parents: A Counseling Challenge. Thorofare: New Jersey.

Colley, T. E. (1973). Interpretation of psychological test data to children, *Mental Retardation, 11*, 28-30.

Conti (1975). Variables related to contacting/not contacting counseling services recommended by school psychologists. *Journal of School Psychology, 13*, 41-50.

Davidson, P. O. & Schrag, A. R. (1969). Factors affecting the outcome of child psychiatric recommendations. *Am. J. of Orthopsychiatry, 39*, 774-778.

Dembinski, R. J. & Mauser, A. J. (1977). What parents of the learning disabled really want to know from professionals, *J. of Learning Disabilities, 10*, 578-584.

Dirks, J., Bushkuhl, J. & Marzano, P. (1983). Parents reactions to finding out that their children have average or above average IQ scores. *Journal of School Psychology, 21*, 23-30.

Gessell, A. & Armatruda, C. (1974). Parent counseling in developmental disabilities. In H. Knobloch, B., Pasamanich (Eds.). *Developmental Diagnosis*, Hagerstown, MD: Harper & Row.

Gilmore, G. E. (1974). Parent contact: An alternative model. *Psychology in the Schools, 11*, 170-174.

Gorham, K. A. (1975). A lost generation of parents. *Exceptional Children, 41*, 521-525.

Gorham, K. A., Des Jardens, C., Page, R. & Scheiber, B. (1975). Effect on parents, in N. Hobbs (Ed.) *Issues in the Classification of Children* Vol. 2, San Francisco: Jossey-Bass, 154-188.

Gottesman, R. L. (1980). Clinic, school and parents working together. *Journal of Learning Disabilities, 11*, 167-171.

Greenspan, S. I. (1981). The Clinical Interview of the Child, New York: McGraw Hill.

Hayes, S. & Oates, R. K. (1978). Parental and professional assessment of developmental handicaps in children. *Australian Journal of Mental Retardation, 5*, 133-137.

Hobbs, N. (1975). *The Futures of Children*, San Francisco: Jossey-Bass.

Hoff, M. K., Fenton, K. S., Yoshida, R. K. & Kaufman, M. J., (1978), *Journal of School Psychology, 16*, 265-273.

Hopper, G. (1977). Parental understanding of their child's test results as interpreted by elementry school teachers, *Measurement and Evaluation in Guidance, 10*, 84-88.

Jones, F. A. & Caldwell, H. S. (1981). Factors affecting patient compliance with diagnostic recommendations. *Amer. J. of Orthopsychiatry, 51*, 700-709.

Kirp, D. E. & Kirp, L. M. (1976). The legalization of the school psychologists world, *Journal of School Psychology, 14*, 83-89.

Knoff, H. M. (1982). Evaluating consultation service delivery at an independent psychodiagnostic clinic. *Professional Psychology, 13*, 699-705.

Knonick, D. (1981). *Social Development of Learning Disabled Persons*, San Francisco: Jossey-Bass.

Losen, S. M. & Diament, B. (1978). *Parent Conferences in the Schools: Procedures for Developing Effective Partnership*. Allyn & Bacon: Boston, Mass.

Marshall, N. & Goldstein, S. (1970). Effects of three consultation procedures on maternal understanding of diagnostic information. *Am. Journal of Mental Deficiency, 74*, 479-482.

Matuszek, P., & Oakland, T. (1979). Factors influencing teachers' and psychologists' recommendations regarding special class placement. *Journal of School Psychology, 17*, 116-125.

Morgan, S. B. (1973). Team interpretation of mental retardation to parents. *Mental Retardation*, June, 10-13.

Mosak, H. H. & Gushurst, R. S. (1972). Some therapeutic uses of psychologic testing, *Am. J. of Psychotherapy, 26*, 539-546.

Nagle, R. J. (1983). Psychoeducational assessment: Cognitive domain, in Hynd, G. W. (Ed.). *The School Psychologist: An Introduction*, Syracuse, NY: Syracuse Univ. Press.

Osman, B. (1982). No One to Play With: The Social Side of Learning Disabilities. Random House: New York.

Pryzwansky, W. B. & Bersoff, D. N. (1978). Parental consent for psychological evaluations: Legal, ethical and practical considerations. *Journal of School Psychology, 16*, 274-281.

Rheingold, H. (1945). Interpreting mental retardation to parents. *Journal of Consulting Psychology, 9*, 142-148.

Richman, J. (1967). Reporting diagnostic test results to patients and their families. *J. of Projective Techniques and Personality Assessment, 31*, 62-70.

Rockowitz, R. J. & Davidson, P. W. (1979). Discussing diagnostic findings with parents. *Journal of Learning Disabilities, 12*, 2-7.

Roos, P. (1978). Parents of mentally retarded children — misunderstood and mistreated. In Turnbull, A. & Turnbull, H. (Eds.) *Parents Speak Out; Views from the other side of the two-way mirror.* Charles E. Merrill; Columbus, Ohio.

Ross, A. O. (1964). *The Exceptional Child in the Family: Helping Parents of Exceptional Children,* New York: Grune & Stratton.

Salvia, J. & Ysseldyke, J. E. (1978). *Assessment in Special and Remedial Education.* Boston: Houghton Mifflin.

Sarason, S. B. (1959). Interpretation of mental deficiency to parents. Reprinted in W. Wolfenberger & P. Kurtz (Eds.) *Management of the Family of the Mentally Retarded,* 1969, 167-177.

Sattler, J. M. (1982). Assessment of Children's Intelligence and Special Abilities, 2nd Ed. Boston, Mass.: Allyn & Bacon.

Searl, S. J. (1978). Stages of parent reaction. *Exceptional Parent, 8,* 3-7.

Shea, V. & Saur, W. (1981). Interpreting developmental handicaps to parents: A guide for professionals. *Catalog of Selected Documents in Psychology, 11,* ms. 2210.

Shellenberger, S. (1982). Presenttion and interpretation of psychological data in educational settings. In C. R. Reynolds & T. B. Gutkin (Eds.) *The Handbook of School Psychology,* New York: Wiley.

Stephens, W. E. (1969). Interpreting mental retardation to parents in a multi-discipline diagnostic clinic. *Mental Retardation, 7,* 57-59.

Svarstad, B. L. & Lipton, H. L. (1977). Informing parents about mental retardation: A study of professional communication and parent acceptance. *Soc. Sci. & Med., 11,* 645-651.

Turnbull, A. P. & Leonard, J. (1981). Parent involvement in special education: Emerging advocacy roles. *School Psychology Review, 10,* 37-44.

Waisbren, S. E. (1980). Parents' reactions after the birth of a developmentally disabled child. *Amer. J. of Mental Deficiency, 84,* 345-351.

Wright, L. S. (1976). Chronic grief: The anguish of being an exceptional parent. *The Exceptional Child, 23,* 160-169.

ANNOTATED BIBLIOGRAPHY

Colley, T. Interpretation of psychological test data to children (1973). *Mental Retardation, 11,* 28-30.
The author describes a format for giving test results to children having mental ages of six and above.

Losen, S. M. & Diament, B. (1978). *Parent Conferences In the Schools: Procedures for Developing Effective Partnership,* Boston, Mass.: Allyn and Bacon, Inc.
This comprehensive book presents specific guidelines for working with parents in the public schools and is appropriate for school psychologists, counselors, special education teachers and social workers.

Shea, V. & Saur, W. (1981). Interpreting developmental handicaps to parents: A guide for professionals. *Catalog of Selected Documents in Psychology, 11,* Ms. 2210.
The authors present a comprehensive model for interpreting developmental disabilities to families. A variety of specific techniques concerning the structure, process and content of an interpretive are provided.

Shellenberger, S. (1982). Presentation and interpretation of psychological data in educational settings. In C. R. Reynolds & T. B. Gutkin (Eds.). *The Handbook of School Psychology,* New York: Wiley.
This chapter focuses on presentation of the content of assessment information both in a written report and orally to parents and children.

Wolfensberger, W. & Kurtz, P. (Eds.) (1969). *Management of the Family of the Mentally Retarded.* Follett Ed. Corp. Section C, Feedback Phase.
The chapter on the feedback phase consists of reprints of classic articles by authors such as Rheingold (1945), Sarason (1959) and others who offer practical suggestions from their own experiences on how to convey disheartening information to parents.

BEST PRACTICES IN REDUCING ERROR IN LEARNING DISABILITY QUALIFICATION

Cathy F. Telzrow
Cuyahoga Special Education Service Center
Cleveland, Ohio

OVERVIEW

The field of Learning Disabilities has experienced growth disproportionate to other handicapping conditions since Samuel Kirk, generally considered to be one of the major architects of the profession, so christened it 20 years ago. When P.L. 94-142 was signed into being in 1975, the federal definition highlighted the processing disorders associated with the condition:

"Specific learning disability" means a disorder in one or more of the basic psychological processes involved in understanding or in using language, spoken or written, which may manifest itself in an imperfect ability to listen, think, speak, read, write, spell, or to do mathematical calculations. The term includes such conditions as perceptual handicaps, brain injury, minimal brain disfunction, dyslexia, and developmental asphasia. The term does not include children who have learning problems which are primarily the result of visual, hearing, or motor handicaps, of mental retardation, of emotional disturbance, or of environmental, cultural, or economic disadvantage. (Procedures for Evaluating Specific Learning Disabilities, 1977, p. 65083)

The practical problem of how to identify a specific learning disability on the basis of this definition was addressed only indirectly in a subsequent section of the federal regulations. While the regulations state that a "severe discrepancy between achievement and intellectual ability" (Procedures for Evaluating Specific Learning Disabilities, 1977, p. 65083) must be demonstrated, criteria for defining a severe discrepancy were not provided. As a result, individual states were free to apply creative solutions to the problem. Nearly as many approaches as states were applied during the next six years with the result of creating an enormously complex justification system for rather arbitrary decisions about students (Divoky, 1974; Epps, Ysseldyke, & Algozzine, 1983; Shepard, 1983).

BASIC CONSIDERATIONS

Criteria in Common Use

By far the most common method of documenting the presence of a severe discrepancy between intellectual ability and achievement in the identification of children with specific learning disabilities employs some version of a discrepancy formula. In the firmly held notion that *in numeris veritas* [in numbers there is truth], most states have adopted a means of quantifying students' academic difficulties to determine whether these represent a "severe discrepancy." Several excellent publications (Berk, 1983; Reynolds, 1981; Shepard, 1980) have summarized and critiqued the major types of discrepancy formulas employed today. In general these are:

1. Grade level deviation scores;
2. Expectancy formulas based on IQ/ MA/CA, years in school, or some combination;

3. Ability-achievement discrepancy scores using standard scores: (a) z-score discrepancy method (e.g., Elliott, 1981; Erickson, 1975) (b) z-score discrepancy correcting for test reliability (e.g., Reynolds, 1981) (c) Regression discrepancy method (e.g., McLeod, 1981; Shepard, 1980).

While there is general agreement among measurement experts (Berk, 1982; Reynolds, 1981; Shepard, 1980) that this heirarchy of procedures is ranked from bad to somewhat better, all these procedures have inherent difficulties when applied to the identification of learning disabilities in children. A brief summary of the flaws associated with each of the discrepancy formula approaches follow:

Limitations to Major Discrepancy Score Formulas

Grade Level Deviation Scores

1. This approach relies on grade-equivalent scores which are notoriously inaccurate (Berk, 1981; Reynolds, 1981).
2. Normal variability in the population is ignored. Within any given elementary classroom expected achievement levels may well cover a three-year, or more, span.
3. If used with a specified cutoff point such as 50% below grade level or two years below grade level, this formula results in the identification of increasing numbers of students at upper grade levels because of larger standard deviation units (Reynolds, 1981; Shepard, 1980).

Expectancy Formulas Using Some Combination of IQ/MA/CA, Years in School

1. Individual formulas of this type vary widely and yield dramatically different results (Berk, 1982).

2. These approaches do not control for regression to the mean artifact and may overidentify high-IQ children and under-identify low-IQ children.
3. Expectancy formulas commit major statistical errors including one or more of the following: (a) Treating IQ scores as ratio scales; (b) Interpreting MA scores as accurate representations of developmental levels; (c) Employing grade equivalent (GE) scores as the index of achievement (see above for limitations of GE scores).

Z-Score Discrepancy Method

1. This approach does not correct for test reliability or unreliability. Hence, the derived discrepancy score is likely to be unacceptably low in reliability (Berk, 1982).
2. The correlation between the two measures (IQ test and achievement test) is not taken into account. The reliability of the derived discrepancy score is to some extent a function of the inter-test correlation coefficient (Salvia & Ysseldyke, 1981).
3. This formula does not correct for regression to the mean. This results in overidentification of bright children and vice versa (Cone & Wilson, 1983).

Z-Score Discrepancy, Correcting for Test Reliability

1. While this approach helps to determine whether there is a *real* difference between test scores by correcting for errors of measuremnt, it does not indicate whether this difference is *severe* as is required to identify a specific learning disability.
2. This approach does not correct for regression to the mean effect (see previous section).
3. The correlation between the two tests is not considered (see previous section).

Regression Discrepancy Method

1. While it does correct for two limitations of other approaches, regression toward the mean phenomenon and test intercorrelation, this approach does not take into account the reliability of the measures used (Berk, 1982; Shepard, 1980).

2. This approach, as all other approaches, requires that a cut-off score be established for the identification of what constitutes a "severe" discrepancy. Regardless of what method is used, some implicit decision regarding numbers of children to be identified must be made (McLeod, 1981).

In addition to these specific limitations to the five most commonly used discrepancy formulas there are other more general and pervasive criticisms associated with the use of formulas. Such difficulties enumerated by Shepard (1983) among others, include the unacceptably low reliability and validity coefficients of some of the most widely used measures incorporated into these formulas (Thurlow & Ysseldyke, 1979); the practice of comparing as "equivalent" two tests using widely discrepant normative samples; and the dubious practice of playing the "numbers game." This involves selecting measures known to inflate IQ scores or deflate achievement scores to "qualify" a child in order to get (even "a little extra") help.

Other, Non-Measurement Variables Affecting LD Identification

School psychologists function in a political context, and perhaps no issue is so politically ripe as the identification of children with learning disabilities. While the factors which are discussed below are not taken into consideration by any of the discrepancy formulas just described, they are perhaps among the most important variables in determining whether or not the LD designation is applied.

Teacher Pressure to Identify

During the decade of the 1970's, the period of feast in the feast-or-famine cycle, there was a great movement to "find" LD children and "fill" the special classes that were funded. Throughout the "find and fill" campaign in LD, school psychologists and others encouraged teachers to refer large numbers of children who weren't achieving up to grade level. Many ignored the fact that the regular class norm was becoming increasingly circumscribed, and that some, perhaps many, of these children represented normal variability rather than a handicapped population. The teachers learned well. Now, when federal and state education agencies have put the brakes on the flow of dollars, puzzled teachers suddenly are asked to "keep and teach" children who were once recruited to fill LD classes.

Teacher pressure to identify "problem" children as learning disabled is enormous (Shepard, 1983). School psychologists often experience similar pressure from other school personnel such as department heads, principals, LD supervisors, or curriculum specialists who, in a version of the displacement phenomenon, are experiencing residuals of the classroom teacher's frustration. The potency of the classroom teacher's influence on the identification process is reflected by the Ysseldyke and Algozzine (1983) finding that the most consistent single predictor of LD identification is the teacher referral.

Belief in Lack of Alternatives to Special Education Placement

Some school psychologists report they are troubled by the apparent lack of alternatives to LD service for children in academic difficulty. Their attitude is re-

flected by the belief that choices for referred children are limited to "help" (LD
service) or "nothing" (continuation in the
regular education program). School psychologists who agree that this dichotomy
of outcomes describes the total range of
possibilities may feel that declaring the
child ineligible for special education results in denial of any assistance whatsoever.

Parent as Politician

Since LD children are purported to be
of average or above average intelligence,
the LD label has taken on a remarkably
positive valence for many parents. Without
the stigma associated with the mentally
retarded or slow learner categories, identification of a child as learning disabled
helps to explain a variety of deficits without direct blame on anyone from parent,
to teacher, to even the child. Rather than
being lazy/bad/slow, the child has a learning disability.

In some regions, pressure from parents on school districts to apply the LD
label is a veritable grim reaper which
threatens the life blood of effective school
psychological practice. Parents may engage advocates; request repeated second-
opinion evaluations; solicit letters of support from neurologists, psychiatrists, and
others; and dictate that specific measures
be administered in an effort to derive
scores that "work" in the formula. Calls
and visits to school superintendends may
occur. Depending upon the political influence of the respective parent or the stead-
fastness of a given administrator, school
psychologists may receive subtle or not-
so-subtle pressure to identify a given
youngster as learning disabled.

Unilateral Decision-Making
Disguised as Consensus

In an issue of the *School Psychologye-
view* (12, 2), several articles were devoted to the practice of multidisciplinary
teams, and the decision-making processes
associated with special education placement. While much more detailed information pertaining to this topic is available in
that volume, brief mention seems appropriate in the context of non-measurement
variables which affect LD identification.

Federal regulations require that identification of learning disabilities be made
by a multidisciplinary team of qualified
professionals. The personalities of individual members of the decision-making
team, as well as the interaction of these
separate personalities, often place additional burdens on the decision-making effort (Ysseldyke & Algozzine, 1979). The
degree to which the respective members of
the team are knowledgeable about and
demonstrate respect for the professional
opinions of their colleagues may be as significant to the outcome as any of the data
collected at so high an investment of time
and money (Abelson & Woodman, 1983).

BEST PRACTICES

Several caveats were implied in the
preceding sections. The identification of
LD children is complicated by statistical
imprecision, conceptual vagueness, and
political undercurrents. In the face of
such pitfalls, recommending a best practice for school psychologists may appear
brash or naive. However, the suggestions
that follow are offered in an attempt to
effect the best school psychological response under a difficult set of circumstances.

The best practices are summarized in
six steps outlined in Table 1. In addition to
the recommended action, a rationale for
each practice is provided as well as a brief
description of the procedure to be followed to implement the action. Readings
of relevance to the theoretical or practical
aspects of implementation are listed for
each section

TABLE 1

Best Practices for School Psychologists for Reducing Error in Learning Disabilities Qualification

Recommended Action	Rationale	Procedure	Relevant Readings
1. Established differentiated referral procedure to respond to teachers' concerns without initiating evaluation for suspected learning disability.	Teacher referral for LD evaluation seems to lead almost inevitably to identification of the student as learning disabled. Hence, a differentiated referral system, whereby a building level response to teacher or parent concerns is made in lieu of evaluation may eliminate subsequent inappropriate placements. While an alternative response would be a gate-keeping mechanism to reject "frivolous" referrals, such a practice is not recommended because it is a potential violation of P.L. 94-142 and it ignores the very real plight of concerned, conscientious teachers and parents who	Differentiated referral procedures are best implemented within a district-wide structure, but with building specific characteristics. All approaches should offer a *support mechanism* for teachers having difficulty meeting the individual learning needs of children. One such mechanism utilizes *building level teams*, comprising teachers and support personnel. The purposes of the support mechanism (i.e., building level instructional assistance team) are to (1) convey the message that normal variability is to be expected within the regu-	Chalfant, VanDusen Psych, & Moultrie, 1979 *Ohio Guidelines*, 1983 Pryzwansky & Rzepski, 1983

Recommended Action	Rationale	Procedure	Relevant Readings
	(continued) have recognized and are trying to respond to children's needs.	(continued) lar classroom; (2) convince teachers that such variations in achievement may require educational adjustments, but most do not warrant the "handicap" label; (3) establish a mechanism for providing support and practical assistance to teachers in the management of normal variability within the regular classroom and school building. Only in cases when building level mechanisms are not effective in meeting the needs of individual students is a referral for a suspected handicap initiated.	
2. Implement required evaluations for stu-	All states have state rules prescribing LD eligibility	School psychologists must be cognizant of the very	APA, 1974 Berk, 1982

Recommended Action	Rationale	Procedure	Relevant Readings
(continued) dents referred for suspected handicap (LD). Identify major limitations to these procedures for other school personnel and parents.	(continued) requirements. School psychologists must comply with these standards. Careful knowledge about and attention to the limitations of these procedures is part of good professional practice.	(continued) real limitations to some of the measures they may choose or be required to use, as well as the measurement errors and artifacts inherent in the evaluation process, including various discrepancy formulas. *No state may rely solely on the discrepancy formula for identification,* since it violates federal regulations. Hence, school psychologists must point out statistical and conceptual limitations to the discrepancy formula they apply, and use these data within the context of other clinical findings.	(continued) Reynolds, 1981 Salvia & Ysseldyke, 1981 Shepard, 1980, 1983
3. Consider qualitative indicators of specific learning disabilities.	The identification of specific learning disabilities, like many disorders	This procedure requires the consideration of data in several categories:	Cone & Wilson, 1983 Hartlage, 1973, 1981 Kaufman, 1979, 1981

Recommended Action	Rationale	Procedure	Relevant Readings
	(continued) in the practice of psychology, requires the application of sound clinical skills. School psychologists who continue to apply discrepancy formulas in a slavish manner not only are showing disregard for the statistical imprecision of these procedures and federal regulations which prohibit sole use of a discrepancy formula, but also are reducing themselves to the level of a number-crunching technician.	(continued) medical history; developmental history; family history of learning problems; classroom behavior and work samples; qualitative test interpretation; demographic factors such as age, sex, ethnic group, socio-economic background; educational history relative to transfers and attendance; previous interventions attempted, and so forth. Data collection in these areas presumes familiarity with a wide range of research findings describing those characteristics which have been associated with learning disabilities in children and *those that have not.*	(continued) Obrzut, Hynd & Obrzut, 1983 Pirozzolo, 1979, 1981 Sattler, 1982 Selz, 1981
4. Evaluate indicators	A specific learning dis-	When considering the	Gresham, 1983

Recommended Action	Rationale	Procedure	Relevant Readings
(continued) and contraindicators of specific learning disabilities in light of relavance and consistency of the data and severity of the need.	(continued) ability is a *handicapping* condition. Considering it in those terms may help us remember that identification necessarily must be limited to those children with the most *extreme* conditions. Shepard's (1983) suggestion that state educational agencies should establish a ceiling specifying the percentage of children who may be identified is one way of making explicit the implied restriction to serve only the most severely handicapped in LD programs. School psychologists who don't have such imposed limitations are encouraged to impose their own since this practice rightfully restricts identification as learning	(continued) qualitative data, school psychologists may wish to categorize their indicators as positive (characteristic of learning disabilities), neutral, or negative (contraindicators of specific learning disabilities). Evaluation of the data will require clinical sorting since the factors will not have equal weight. For example, a negative health history might fly in the face of a 33-point V<P discrepancy for a 10-year old child unable to write any words other than a first name. Determination of eligibility requires consideration of (1) *the relevance of the data:* do several factors point to the same conclusion? (2) *the consistency of the data:* is	(continued) Helton, Workman, & Matuszek, 1983 *Ohio Guidelines,* 1983 Sattler, 1982 Shepard, 1983 Weller, 1980

Recommended Action	Rationale	Procedure	Relevant Readings
	(continued) disabled to those children with the most severe conditions.	(continued) there evidence across several data sources that the youngster is/is not learning disabled?; (3) *the severity of the condition: does it warrant identification as a handicap?*	Mercer & Lewis, 1978 *Ohio Guidelines*, 1983 *School Psychology Review*, 1983
5. Examine exclusionary criteria to determine whether a severe discrepancy may be attributed to a specific sensory or motor handicap, mental retardation, emotional disturbance, or environmental, cultural, or economic disadvantage.	Federal regulations prohibit identification as learning disabled children whose severe discrepancies between intellectual ability and achievement are caused by one or more of these conditions.	If there is evidence to suggest the presence of another handicapping condition, all required assessments relative to the suspected handicapping condition must be conducted as required by federal and state regulations. Thus in differentiating between LD and MR placements, the student's performance on a measure of adaptive behavior would be an essential factor in the decision. Similarly, in	

Recommended Action	Rationale	Procedure	Relevant Readings
		(continued) separating emotional disturbance from specific learning disabilities, the school psychologist would need to examine patterns of performance on measures of personality and behavior and interpret these with regard to the onset, duration, and intensity of the observed problems. Determination of cultural, economic, or environmental disadvantage requires careful judgment on the part of the school psychologist, who must evaluate the child's circumstance in relation to the sociocultural context of the school district. Hence, what constitutes cultural disadvantages in a suburban region may be the	

Recommended Action	Rationale	Procedure	Relevant Readings
		(continued) norm in certain rural areas.	
6. Provide alternatives to special education for ineligible children.	There is something between the rock of regular education and the hard spot of LD services. All school districts are capable of generating alternative solutions, regardless of size, federal funds received, and pupil-teacher ratio. Teachers and parents will find the decision that a child is not eligible for LD services considerably more palatable if other, non-special education responses to the child's problem are offered.	The alternatives which can be provided will be district, and often building-specific. The *mechanism* for identifying and effecting these alternatives might rest with the building-level support vehicle identified in Step 1, above. Alternatives which might be considered include peer tutoring; cross-age grouping; use of volunteers such as retired persons as tutors; remedial programs such as Chapter I; adding two children to each teacher's classroom, thus "freeing" up one teacher to serve as a floating resource teacher; and the	Corbett, 1982 Cummings & Nelson, 1982 *Ohio Guidelines*, 1983 Pryzwansky & Rzepski, 1983 Robinson, 1982

Recommended Action	Rationale	Procedure	Relevant Readings
		(continued) Alternative Education Program, described by Cummings & Nelson, (1982).	

SUMMARY

Unlike other handicapping categories such as hearing impairment or even mental retardation, the features associated with specific learning disabilities are too nebulous and difficult to quantify to permit precision in the identification process. Direction from federal and state education agencies has been slow in coming. When such help has arrived, it has taken the form of discrepancy formulas which may be no more than false idols promising truth which doesn't exist.

School psychological practice designed to minimize error in the identification of specific learning disabilities must adopt a systems intervention approach to address the problems of teacher and parent pressure to identify poor achievers as learning disabled and the dichotomy of LD versus regular class as the only possible solutions for children in academic difficulty. The mechanism suggested is the establishment of a differentiated referral procedure which incorporates a building-level support system to treat problems of many children. As a result, referral for LD identification is not necessary and alternative education approaches for children who are referred for evaluation and found not to qualify are effected and managed.

A second major phase of best practice requires that school psychologists be knowledgeable of and communicate to others the major limitations inherent in our measurement approaches. Such actions necessitate adherence to the APA guidelines for the selection and interpretation of tests and familiarity with the measurement artifacts in the discrepancy formulas required by state special education standards. Finally, school psychologists must use sound clinical judgment in the interpretation of a variety of qualitative data and make a diagnosis based on relevance and consistency of the data in light of what is reported in the literature, and with consideration of an implied ceiling which includes only those with the most severe conditions.

REFERENCES

Abelson, M. A., & Woodman, R. W. (1983). Review of research on team effectiveness: Implications for teams in schools. *School Psychology Review, 7*, 125- 136.

American Psychological Association (1974). *Standards for educational and psychological tests* (rev. ed.). Washington, D.C.: American Psychological Association.

Berk, R. A. (1982). Effectiveness of discrepancy score methods for screening children with learning disabilities. *Learning Disabilities, 1*, 11-24.

Chalfant, J. C., Van Dusen, M. & Moultrie, R. (1979). Teacher assistance teams: A model for within-building problem solving. *Learning Disability Quarterly, 2*, 85-96.

Cone, T., & Wilson, L. (1983, August). *The Iowa learning disabilities evaluation project* (final report). Des Moines, Iowa: Special Education Division Iowa Department of Public Instruction.

Corbett, H. D. (1982). Principal's contributions to maintaining change. *The Phi Delta Kappan, 64*, 190-192.

Cummings, J. A. & Nelson, R. B. (1982). The alternative educational plan (AEP). *School Psychology Review. 11*, 336-337.

Divoky, D. (1974). Education's latest victim: The "LD" kid. *Learning, 3*, 20-25.

Elliott, M. (1981). Quantitative evelution procedures for learning disabilities. *Journal of Learning Disabilities, 14*, 84-87.

Epps, S., Ysseldyke, J. E., & Algozzine, B. (1983). Impact of different definitions of learning disabilities on the number of students identified. *Journal of Psychoeducational Assessment, 1*, 341-352.

Erickson, M. T. (1975). The z-score discrepancy method for identifying reading-disabled children. *Journal of Learning Disabilities, 8*, 308-312.

Gresham, F. M. (1983). Multitrait-Multimethod approach to multifactored assessment: Theoretical rationale and practical application. *School Psychology Review, 7*, 26-34.

Hartlage, L. C. (1973). Diagnostic profiles of four types of learning disabled children. *Journal of Clinical Psychology, 29*, 458-463.

Hartlage, L. C. (1981). Neuropsychological assessment techniques. In C. R. Reynolds & T. Gutkin (Eds.) *Handbook of school psychology.* New York: Wiley.

Helton, G. B., Workman, E. A., & Matuszek, P. A. (1982). *Psychoeducational assessment.* New York: Grune & Stratton.

Kaufman, A. S. (1979). *Intelligent testing with the WISC-R.* New York: John Wiley & Sons.

Kaufman, A. S. (1981). The WISC-R and learning disabilities assessment: State of the art. *Journal of Learning Disabilities, 14,* 520-526.

McLeod, J. (1981). *Psychometric identification of children with learning disabilities* 2nd edition - revised. Unpublished manuscript, University of Saskatchewan.

Mercer, J. R., & Lewis, J. F. (1978). *Manual for the System of Multicultural, Pluralistic Assessment (SOMPA).* New York: Psychological Corporation.

Obrzut, J. E., Hynd, G. W., & Obrzut, A. (1983). Neuropsychological assessment of learning disabilities: A discriminant analysis. *Journal of Experimental Child Psychology, 35,* 46-55.

Ohio guidelines for the identification of children with specific learning disabilities (including differentiated referral procedures). (1983). Columbus, Ohio: Department of Education.

Pirozzolo, F. J. (1981). Language and brain: Neuropsychological aspects of developmental reading disability. *School psychology Review, 3,* 350-355.

Pirozzolo, F. J. (1979). *The neuropsychology of developmental reading disorders.* New York: Praeger Publishers.

Procedures for evaluating specific learning disabilities. *Federal Register,* December 29, 1977, Part III.

Pryzwansky, W. B., & Rzepski, B. (1983). School-based teams: An untapped resource for consultation and technical assistance. *School Psychology Review, 7,* 174-179.

Reynolds, C. R. (1981). The fallacy of "two years below grade level for age" as a diagnostic criterion for reading disorders. *Journal of School psychology, 19,* 250-258.

Robinson, D. (1982). The IEP: Meaningful individualized education in Utah. *The Phi Delta Kappan, 64,* 205-206.

Salvia, J., & Ysseldyke, J. E. (1981). *Assessment in special and remedial education.* Boston: Houghton Mifflin Co.

School Psychology Review, 12 (3), 1983.

Selz, M. (1981). Halstead-Reitan Neuropsychological Test Batteries for Children. In G. W. Hynd & J. E. Obrzut (Eds.), *Neuropsychological assessment and the school-age child.* New York: Grune & Stratton.

Shepard, L. A. (1980). An evaluation of the regression discrepancy method for identifying children with learning disabilities. *The Journal of Special Education, 14,* 79-91.

Shepard, L. A. (1983). The role of measurement in educational policy: Lessons from the identification of learning disabilities. *Educational Measurement: Issues and Practice, 2* (3), 4-8.

Sattler, J. M. (1982). *Assessment of children's intelligence and special abilities.* Boston: Allyn & Bacon.

Thurlow, M. L., & Ysseldyke, J. E. (1979). Current assessment and decision-making practices in model LD programs. *Learning Disability Quarterly, 2,* 15-24.

Weller, C. (1980). Discrepancy and severity in the learning disabled: A consolidated perspective. *Learning Disability Quarterly, 3,* 84-90.

Ysseldyke, J. E., & Algozzine, B. (1979). Perspective on assessment of learning disabled students. *Learning Disability Quarterly, 2,* 3-13.

Ysseldyke, J. E., & Algozzine, B. (1983). LD or not LD: That's not the question! *Journal of Learning Disabilities, 16,* 29-31.

ANNOTATED BIBLIOGRAPHY

Berk, R. A. (1982). Effectiveness of discrepancy score methods for screening children with learning disabilities. *Learning Disabilities, 1,* 11-24.
This article provides a comprehensive, well-documented critique of the most commonly used discrepancy formulas. A discussion of WISC-R profile analysis as a procedure for diagnosing learning disabilities also is included.

Cone, T., & Wilson, L. (1983, August). *The Iowa learning disabilities evaluation project* (Final report). Des Moines, Iowa: Special Education Division Iowa Department of Public Instruction.
This manuscript is a scholarly presentation of the Iowa effort to identify characteristics of learning disabled children and to evaluate methods of quantifying a severe discrepancy between achievement and ability. The publication includes a thorough review of the literature, and is an excellent summary of the pertinent issues in LD assessment and identification.

Ohio guidelines for the identification of children with specific learning disabilities (including differentiated referral procedures). Columbus, Ohio: Department of Education, 1983.
This document includes valuable sections on implementing a differentiated referral system and developing educational alternatives for low-achieving children who are not eligible for learning disabilities programs. The publication includes useful teacher checklists and observation strategies as well as suggestions for teachers for modifying the regular classroom demands.

Shepard, L. A. (1983). The role of measurement in educational policy: Lessons from the identification of learning disabilities. *Educational Measurement: Issues and Practice, 2* (3), 4-8.
This resource is the most recent in the author's series of cogent, sensible publications regarding the problem of LD identifications. Measurement limitations and human foibles are addressed within the interacting context of parents, kids, and school personnel. This is a "must read" for school psychologists concerned about the identification of LD children.

BEST PRACTICES IN COUNSELING ELEMENTARY STUDENTS

Deborah Tharinger
The University of Texas at Austin

Historically the role of the school psychologist has been defined by psycho-educational assessment, and more recently, consultation (Meyers, Parsons & Martin, 1979). Another function of the school psychologist is that of a direct service provider. This role, which takes various forms, is currently receiving more attention. This chapter discusses the role of school psychologists in counseling with individual children. The target children are those whose behavioral, cognitive, emotional and/or interpersonal functioning cause them or others distress and interferes with development and learning. Because they work in the child's natural environment, school psychologists are in a unique position to observe children experiencing behavioral and emotional problems, to intervene with them in their natural context, to evaluate their progress and to consider additional or alternative intervention.

Direct intervention through individual counseling is familiar ground for many school psychologists, uncharted ground for others and a place unknown to still others. Before proceeding, a caveat is necessary. Counseling is a serious intervention with children. It is undertaken only after formal knowledge of theory and research in child development, child psychopathology and treatment of psychological problems in children is acquired. It follows supervised training experiences with children. In addition, counseling is conducted only after a thorough assessment of the needs of the child and a variety of interventions are considered. Furthermore, counseling must be subject to constant evaluation of its appropriateness and efficacy. Psychological interventions can have side effects and incidental by-products that, while seldom studied, are nonetheless present and deserving of consideration (Barkley, 1983). The following is intended to provide a useful map that illustrates the difficult terrain and yet encourages exploration which leads to the provision of competent counseling services to children in the schools.

OVERVIEW

This chapter is divided into three sections. The first describes school-based counseling and the children typically referred for intervention. The second reviews the knowledge, training, and experience necessary for counseling. The third provides a step-by-step framework for selecting counseling as an appropriate intervention and preparing for counseling, a six stage model for describing the counseling process and suggestions for evaluating effectiveness. The six stage framework is generic in the sense that most counseling approaches can be used within this structure. As with applied psychology in general, each psychologist must determine what constitutes "best practice" for a given child in a particular situation.

Definition of Counseling

Not surprisingly, agreeing on an acceptable definition of counseling is a difficult task due to the diversity of theoretical models of psychopathology and change. The term "counseling" rather than therapy is used throughout this chapter because it is the term used in PL 94-142, the Education for All Handicapped Children Act. However, a distinction between counseling and therapy with children is not made. After an examination of many definitions of counseling with children, the following one, put forth by the Group for the Advancement of Psychiatry (1982), is offered.

> All forms of therapy for children attempt to influence the youngsters to make changes in three areas — cognition, emotion, and overt behavior. These are the essential ingredients common to all. Some emphasize one much more than others: the dynamic insight therapist, concerned primarily with cognitive and emotional spheres, expects that behavior will change as a consequence of changes in these; the behavior therapist believes that influencing behavior is primary, that attitudes and feelings will change as a result of the behavioral emphasis. (p. 47-48).

Unique Aspects of Counseling with Children

There are unique aspects of counseling with children (Clarizio & McCoy, 1983). First, children are unlikely to voluntarily seek help or initiate entry into counseling. The decision is usually made by an adult in the child's environment and is met with varying degree of acceptance, compliance, or resistance from the child. The "involuntary" nature of the child as client may result in little or no motivation on the youngster's part to engage in a relationship with the counselor and/or no admission that change is necessary. Second, children lack an explicit understanding of counseling, the purpose and goals of treatment and the role they are to assume. The first two points imply that it is the psychologist's task to form a relationship with the children and to educate them about the process. Third, children's verbal and cognitive abilities are limited

and their personalities are relatively unformed. Developmental considerations and the match between the developmental status of the child and the expectations of the environment must be taken into account when deciding whether to counsel the child and if so, by what methods. Fourth, children are dependent on their environment and are affected greatly by it. They have relatively little power to eliminate or prevent environmental changes or causes of stress. Consequently, significant people in the child's environment need to be involved in treatment.

Unique Aspects of School-Based Counseling

Counseling in the school occurs in a natural setting for children. Although the psychologist's office is unfamiliar to most children, it is less foreign than a mental health clinic or hospital setting. This is also true for their parents. The school setting enables observation of children's day-to-day functioning in a variety of situations. Information and feedback from significant others are readily available. Furthermore, the school setting allows for counseling concurrent with other interventions such as a classroom behavior management plan, affective education groups in the classroom, a change in class schedule or placement, and consultation with teachers, specialists, and parents.

Nevertheless, counseling with an individual child may be short term because of the pressure to provide service to many children. Effective methods of brief counseling with children are needed as are ways of identifying which children most need ongoing therapy. In addition, there is pressure to provide quick changes in overt behavior. The task of school psychologists is to help others understand the often slow and difficult nature of change and to engage them in the process.

Practical considerations for counseling in the school setting include working out a schedule of meeting times that fit both the child's and the psychologist's variable schedule. In addition, the work space is a problem for many who use the same area as an office, testing room, or a play room.

Children in Need of Intervention

Children referred for counseling are usually experiencing difficulties in their thoughts, emotions, behaviors or interpersonal relationships, that cause marked distress to themselves or others. Several classification systems have described childhood disorders or child behavior problems. Examples include the clinically derived Diagnostic and Statistical Manual of Mental Disorders III (American Psychiatric Association, 1980) and the empirically-derived systems of Achenbach (1982) and Quay (1979). The various classification schemes of childhood disorders are not reviewed here, but a framework for categorizing emotional and behavioral disorders most likely seen by school psychologists is presented. Rare and severe disorders such as early infantile autism or childhood schizophrenia are not covered as they are seldom encountered by school psychologists.

A useful dichotomy for conceptualizing children's manifestations of their psychological distress is the internalizing-externalizing dimension identified by Achenbach (1982). Internalizers are also referred to as neurotic, over-controlled, and anxious-withdrawn children and are characterized as anxious, fearful, tense, shy-timid, bashful, withdrawn, seclusive, friendless, depressed, sad, hypersensitive and easily hurt by others (Quay, 1979). They may show compulsive behavior or somatic complaints. Prevalence rates of

the internalizing disorders vary from two to eight percent with most estimates on the lower end. Although research suggests that most emotional disorders of this type do not persist into adulthood (Robins, 1966, 1979), these children need intervention to relieve the distress they and others are feeling and to prevent further impairment of normal developmental processes (Weiner, 1982).

Externalizers are also referred to as under-controlled, socially aggressive, and conduct disordered children. They differ from internalizers in that they are more likely to be boys, show reading difficulties, family discord, poorer response to short term treatment, and less favorable prognosis in adolescence (Rutter & Garmezy, 1983). Characteristics of "externalizers" include fighting, hitting, and assaultive behavior; temper tantrums; disobedient and defiant behavior; destructiveness of property; and uncooperative, resistant, and inconsiderate behavior (Quay, 1979). Children manifesting a conduct disorder are the most frequent referrals to outpatient clinics (Robins, 1979; Atkenson & Forehand, 1981). Prevalence figures are estimated to be at least 4% (Yule, 1981). Although interventions with externalizers are not always successful, treatment improves the prognosis. Educational intervention to remediate reading difficulties, behavioral interventions to change overt aggressive behavior, family interventions to alter disruptive patterns, and individual counseling to change emotion, cognition and behavior are all appropriate and perhaps necessary.

The syndrome referred to either as "hyperactivity" or an "attention deficit disorder" in DSM III is often included under "externalizing" disorders. This syndrome is characterized by inattention, impulsivity, short attention span, overactivity and restlessness (Barkley, 1983). The prevalence is estimated at 3% to 5% of the school age population. Poor peer relationships, aggression, disinhibition, and a poor response to discipline may accompany this disorder (Rutter & Garmezy, 1983). Attention deficit disorder has been found to be related to conduct disorders and learning disabilities (Rutter & Garmezy, 1983). School-based interventions help children with this syndrome to control their behavior, focus on learning tasks, and understand their difficulties. Intervention designed to help parents understand, manage and emotionally support children with attention deficit disorders is also effective.

In addition to describing the internalizing-externalizing dimension of children's problem behavior, it is useful to identify environmental stressors such as death of a parent or sibling, parental separation or divorce, an accident or an illness that is primarily responsible for a child's distress. The child is then said to have mild adjustment difficulties or an "adjustment disorder." A mild adjustment difficulty is a fairly normal and expected reaction to an environmental stressor, whereas an adjustment disorder is a maladaptive response to identifiable environmental stressor which results in impaired functioning in excess of the normal and expected reaction to the stressor. School-based counseling may be indicated if the adjustment problems interferes with school learning and/or social and emotional functioning.

Children who have other handicaps such as learning disabilities, physical disabilities, or language disabilities are often referred for counseling. They show both externalizing and internalizing behaviors, as well as manifest behaviors particular to adjusting to their handicap. Interventions beyond special educational programs may be needed to help these children and their families understand and cope with the disabilities and any distressing emotions and behaviors that accompany the handicapping conditions.

In summary, most children referred to school psychologists for counseling show behaviors that fit along the internalizing-externalizing continuum. For some, the emotional or behavior disturbance is the primary handicap interferring with their learning and development; whereas for others, it accompanies another exceptionality. The disturbing behavior of some children is traceable to a specific environmental stressor. For others it stems from a complex interaction of both internal and external factors.

All of the children described above may be evaluated to be in need of school-based counseling intervention to change their overt behavior and to help them understand themselves. It is difficult to propose firm guidelines to prioritize children. The selection of children to receive individual counseling is a professional judgment based on training and experience. School psychologists must examine the underlying assumptions they use to recommend children for counseling services to ensure that their decisions are ethical and a wise use of limited resources.

BASIC CONSIDERATIONS

This section highlights the background knowledge and training necessary to effectively counsel children. References are included for the reader who wants additional information.

Educational and Training in Child Development

Knowledge of theory and research findings in child development is essential. Understanding normal development is pre-requisite to the assessment and treatment of children experiencing distress. There is no single theory of child development, but a variety of conceptualizations that typically address one major aspect. In addition, there are accumulative research findings on children's emotional development, gender differences, aggression, and socialization which have lead to new theories or revisions of existing ones. The four volumes of *Handbook of Child Psychology*, Fourth Edition (Mussen, 1983) are an excellent source for reviews of theory and research in child development. In addition, books by Salkind (1981) Miller (1983) and Cowan (1978) contain summaries of major developmental theories.

Education and Training in Psychopathology and Treatment

Knowledge of theory, research and clinical findings in developmental psychopathology is important. An understanding of the continuum of normal-abnormal development, guidelines for differentiating normal from abnormal development, and the characteristics and course of major childhood disorders help guide the assessment and treatment of individual children. Useful references in this area include works by Achenbach (1982), Weiner (1982), and Rutter and Garmezy (1983).

In addition, knowledge of the various theories or approaches to counseling children is prerequisite. The major approaches include psychoanalytically-oriented or psychodynamic therapy, behavior therapy, cognitive-behavior therapy, person-centered therapy, and, although it is more a medium than a theory-based approach, play therapy. An understanding of the theoretical basis and the assumptions of each approach about the nature of psychopathology, behavior change and the processes and techniques for counseling are needed to choose an effective approach for a particular child in a particular situa-

tion. *Counseling and Psychotherapy with Children and Adolescents: Theory and Practice for School and Clinical Settings* (Prout & Brown, 1983) is an excellent resource in this area as is the *Handbook of Play Therapy* (Schaefer & O'Connor, 1983). Although formal knowledge of developmental psychopathology and counseling approaches is necessary, it is not insufficient for effective practice. This knowledge needs to be integrated with a variety of supervised experiences counseling distressed children.

Education and Training in Psychological Assessment

In addition, education and training in the assessment of children's psychological functioning is necessary to make appropriate intervention decisions and to set goals for counseling. One is trained and supervised in assessing: (a) behavioral, emotional, interpersonal, intellectual and academic functioning; (b) the child's contexts such as home and school; and (c) the interactions among them. Hypotheses about the causes of the child's behavior problems, the child's current needs, and the best intervention follow from an analysis of the assessment data. For further information, see Greenspan (1982), Koppitz (1982), Palmer (1983), and the *School Psychology Review* (Knoff, 1983a).

Education and Training Regarding Systems

School psychologists work within a system and are affected by other members of the system and the policies they set. Children exist in two major systems: the family and the school. Reciprocal influences exist between the child and each system and between the two systems. An

understanding of the potential and limitations for change in systems is necessary
when counseling children because of the
complexity of influences affecting both
the psychologist's and the child's behaviors (Apter, 1982; Bronfenbrenner, 1979;
and Knoff, 1983b).

Education and Training Regarding
One's Self

Although the education, training and
experience of school psychologists are
directed at assessment and intervention
planning for children, another critical
area is knowledge of one's self. Awareness
of oneself as a practicing psychologist
includes awareness of interpersonal skills,
the implicit theories of development and
change that one holds, personal strengths
and weaknesses, limitations of expertise,
the effects of the school system on personal functioning, and how these factors
influence one's style as a clinician. This
type of knowledge comes from supervision, personal therapy, peer collaboration, consultation, and self-reflection and
evaluation. Effective practice is conceived
of as an integration of formal education
and training, extensive experience and
self-awareness.

BEST PRACTICES

This section specifies step-by-step
guidelines. These make the inexperienced
school psychologist aware of the total
process in choosing, implementing and
completing a counseling intervention with
a child and serve as a refresher for experienced practitioners.

Examine the Referral

Children in elementary school are
usually referred for counseling by their
classroom teacher or their parent(s). Information is gathered through a carefully
designed referral form or through a brief
interview with the referral person to
determine: (a) the needs of the referring
person; (b) the specific problems as well
as when they appear, how often, for how
long, and in what setting; (c) the reason
that the child was referred at this time;
(d) interventions already tried to relieve
the child's distress, alter the behavior
and/or environment, or effect change in
significant others in the child's life, and
the success of these interventions, and (e)
the people who have a significant impact
on the child.

It is important to gather information
from teachers and parents. A comparison
of home with school views aids in determining if the child has similar problems in
both settings, and how the school and
home are handling or contributing to the
problem. It allows for a more complete
picture of the child's environment.

The final step in examining the referral information is an assessment of the
validity of the referral for school-based
counseling. Perhaps directing information
to the referral source is all that is needed.
For example, the child's behavior may be
normal for his or her age. Perhaps consultation with the parent(s) or teacher is the
preferred intervention. Or if the problem
is not affecting the child at school, a referral to an outside agency is more appropriate. If the problem effects the child at
school and a school-based intervention is
warranted, additional information may
be needed to determine that individual
counseling is the intervention of choice.

Conduct an Assessment to Arrive at
Hypotheses and to Select an Intervention
Program

The next step involves deciding what

additional information is necessary to further understand the nature of the referral problem and to decide on an intervention program. Data are obtained by using selected assessment methods that allow for the formulation of hypotheses in the following areas: Determine:

• the nature and severity of the child's problem by examining the type of problem as well as its frequency, pattern, intensity and duration.

• if the child's behavior is age appropriate and consistent with his or her developmental level;

• what internal and external factors are maintaining the child's problem;

• what internal and external factors hinder the child's normal development?

• if recent psychosocial stressors are present;

• the child's strengths and weaknesses;

• the environment's strengths and weaknesses;

• the match between the child and the environment;

• who in the child's environment is distressed and how they show and cope with it; and

• the motivation of the child, teachers and parents to become involved in an intervention, particularly counseling.

It is important to obtain information from the child, teachers, and parents using direct observation, interviews, behavior checklists or rating scales, self report and projective measures, and psychoeducational measures. The goal of the assessment is to determine the nature of the child's problem, the factors in the child and the environment that are contributing to the child's difficulties, and the best intervention program to change behavior and promote normal development.

In planning the intervention program, a variety of interventions are considered such as a change in placement or classroom, a classroom management program, consultation with the teacher, consideration for special education assistance, recommendation for membership in peer activities, referral for group counseling, referral for parent education, referral for family counseling, referral for medical examination and consultation, or individual counseling with the child. The interventions recommended are chosen after considering the hypotheses derived from the assessment data, the availability of resources, and what is most effective for the child.

Select Individual Counseling

Individual school-based counseling is considered as part of the intervention program for a child if the following conditions are met.

1. The goals for the child can be partially met through a therapeutic relationship where the school psychologist attempts to influence the child to make changes.

2. The child has the motivation for participating in a therapeutic relationship.

3. The child's parent(s) are supportive of participation and give permission. They are willing to participate in some sort of contact with the school psychologist to consider and understand their own part in the child's difficulties and/or to learn new ways of interacting with the child.

4. The child's case falls within the school psychologist's area of expertise. If this is not the case and counseling is indicated, supervision is obtained or a referral is made.

5. The school psychologist can commit the time and energy demanded by the case. In addition to direct work with the child, this also involves parent contact and teacher consultation to deal with the environment's contribution and reaction to the child's difficulties.

Specify Goals of Counseling

The overall need of every child is growth and development toward functioning as a unique, independent individual. The justification for counseling is intervention with the child and the environment to promote such growth. Rutter (1983) states that the goals of treatment with children include: symptom reduction, promotion of normal development, fostering autonomy and self-reliance, generalization of behavior gains, persistence of improvement and changes in the child's environment. Tuma and Sobotka (1983) cite two general goals: increased self-understanding and behavior change. Specific goals for an individual child address these areas and are constructed from the results of the assessment. The goals are optimistic yet reasonable and respect the complexity of the change process.

Choose a Counseling Approach

Children's specific needs and goals in counseling differ and what approach and methods works well with one child may not work with another child. As mentioned previously, the major counseling approaches include psychoanalytically-oriented or psychodynamic, behavioral, cognitive-behavioral, and person-centered, each of which proposes specific methods and techniques designed to promote behavior changes and/or self-understanding.

There are two major positions in the psychotherapy research literature regarding differential treatment. The first is the prescriptive approach (Schaffer & Millman, 1977) which suggests that one match the therapeutic approach and techniques to the specific emotional or behavioral disorder of the child. The long term goal of this approach is to refine therapeutic methods so that one eventually says what technique is best given a particular situation. The skillful application of the prescriptive approach involves the development of expertise in a wide variety of therapeutic methods. The trend toward selectively applying different methods reflects the belief that no one therapeutic approach is equally effective with all types of problems or people. There is a paucity of research evidence to indicate that one type of treatment is better for problem "X" than another (Casey, 1984). Perhaps further, better designed research studies will support this point of view.

The second position suggests that counseling is better than no treatment but one type is not consistently better than another (Casey, 1984). It is most important to examine the commonalities among approaches. Such factors as warmth, empathy and expectations of the therapist; attention and reinforcement; expectations from the client, and the opportunity for emotional and behavioral experience lead to change and not specific techniques generated from the major approaches. This implies that it is not the particular approach used, but factors common to most approaches that make counseling successful. Perhaps it is best to consider the above commonalities as necessary but not sufficient conditions. With the addition of selectively chosen therapeutic techniques, effective counseling is more likely to occur.

Proceed with the Course of Counseling

A sequence of stages is presented which describes the general process of school-based counseling.

Stage one: Preparing the child. This takes a variety of forms but includes setting up meeting times, describing the purpose of the meetings, discussing goals, taking into account the child's input, explaining confidentiality issues, agreeing on limits and consequences of behaviors and setting up a specific contract.

Stage two: Establishing the working relationship. For some children this is easy; for others it is a long, difficult process. Methods to use during this phase include showing an interest in the child through listening, reinforcement and participation in games and activities, being consistent and reliable, showing positive expectations, allowing the child to express emotions and behavior within set limits, and being persistent in the desire to understand the child. The choise of methods depends on the approach chosen, the goals of the intervention, and the response of the child. The goal of this stage is to establish trust, motivation, and positive expectations for change on the part of the child.

Stage three: Implementing the plan for change. The plan builds on the relationship established with the child and is structured by the approach and methods chosen to reach the goals. The plan makes use of methods from classical or operant conditioning such as systematic desensitization, shaping or reinforcement or from social learning theory such as modeling. Methods from the cognitive behavioral approach include the practice of self-control messages, social skills training, or challenging irrational beliefs. A plan guided by the psychodynamic approach includes verbal discussion or play with the focus on interpretation of the connection among the child's thoughts, feelings and behavior. Therapeutic techniques from the humanistic, person-oriented approach entail reflecting feelings, active listening, and the communicating of empathy and respect through discussions and/or play therapy. A specific plan for change involves one method or a combination. For guidelines in these specific techniques refer to Reisman (1972), Millman, Schaefer and Cohen (1980), Morris and Kratochwill (1983), Schaeffer and O'Connor (1983), and Prout and Brown (1983).

Stage four: Involving significant others. The fourth stage, which occurs concurrent with stages two and three, involves significant others in the child's life in the intervention. This takes many forms but most likely includes parental education, parental counseling, or family counseling and/or the teachers in consultation to establish strategies to facilitate peer interactions. The importance of this step is the practical awareness that the child is only one point in the systems in which she or he depends. Promoting positive change in the child's behavior and normal development necessitates intervening with the people who have the most influence on the child's life.

Stage five: Continuing the plan for change. The fifth stage includes a review of the child's progress toward the counseling goals. Data for this review come from the child's behavior in the therapeutic relationship and in school and at home. It is gathered through observation and self-report, as well as reports from teachers and parents. If the child is making adequate progress, a continuation of the present plan is appropriate. However, if little progress is made, the practitioner must choose among persisting with the present plan, making changes in the approach and methods or selecting a different intervention. In making this decision, it is helpful to review the case with a colleague to get an objective view on what is not working and why.

Stage six: Termination. The next and final stage is the preparation for termination. In theory, it is time to end counseling when the goals have been met and the child is functioning better. In practice, the decision to end counseling is seldom simple or ideally planned. The child may have only partially met the goals; parents or school personnel may not cooperate; new problems may surface due to environmental stressors; the child may move; the psychologist may leave the setting; or the school year may end. In addition, some goals such as persistence of change and generalization of behavior gains are only measurable following the cessation of treatment.

Through counseling, the school psychologist has attempted to reduce the child's behavior difficulties and psychological distress, effect change in the child's environment, increase self-understanding, and set the stage for normal development. The practitioner has used the relationship with the child, specific therapeutic techniques and strategies for change with significant others as tools for change. If all goals are met and the child is functioning well, the decision to end counseling is easy. If few goals were met and the child is not functioning well, the decision to end is difficult. In the latter case, it is apparent that another type of intervention would be more effective and should be implemented. Perhaps more intensive counseling than can be provided at school is required. Even if the goals have only partially been met, the child may have progressed enough that significant others can now interact more therapeutically with the child and continued progress can be expected.

If it appears that the goals have been sufficiently met that continued progress is expected, termination of the counseling relationship is begun. For some children, the end of the relationship is difficult and may stir up problems associated with earlier separations and losses. Although psychodynamic theory speaks of the importance and difficulty of the termination phase of therapy, these dynamics are not always apparent. However, the school psychologist should be sensitive to the significant relationship that may have been formed with the child and gradually

terminate it. Techniques such as seeing the child only twice a month and then once a month before final termination or seeing the child for only ten to twenty minutes toward the end or visiting with the child at recesses following the last meeting facilitates acceptance of termination. The school psychologist is in the position of working daily in the child's environment and thus has the chance to visit with the child and observe her. If needed, more systematic follow up is conducted to assess the stability, persistence and generalization of the behavior change and the reduction in psychological distress.

When the practitioner ends the direct counseling intervention with the child, he or she may not choose to end the intervention(s) with the parents and/or school. A school psychologist may continue to consult with the child's teacher regarding continued progress and may continue contacts with the parents. If these interventions also end, the others involved are prepared for the termination of service. Follow up with parents and/or teachers is conducted to trace the child's adjustment and progress.

Evaluate the Effectiveness of Counseling

To improve school-based counseling methods and outcomes it is important for school psychologists to systematically evaluate the effectiveness of their counseling interventions. This is accomplished by determining if any or all of goals were met, which methods were most effective, and how the child functioned at a follow-up time. In addition, noting concurrent interventions and environmental changes are useful in understanding the child's progress. Notes kept on each case, as well as pre- and post-assessment data, can be evaluated. If possible, measures of the child's behavior in natural contexts which correspond to the goals of the counseling intervention are obtained.

In addition to each school psychologist evaluating his or her counseling interventions, meetings held with colleagues to discuss particular cases or methods of counseling also improve the practice of school-based counseling. The awareness one obtains from reviewing cases and results with other professionals is part of one's development as an effective counselor.

evaluating the effectiveness of counseling interventions was also stressed.

Two additional aims of the chapter were to impress upon the reader the serious nature of undertaking a counseling intervention with a child and the importance of incorporating an ecological orientation. It is hoped that the formulations proposed in this chapter are of use to practicing school psychologists and will lead to improved competence in the practice of school-based counseling..

SUMMARY

This chapter was designed to serve as a resource to school psychologists unfamiliar with the area of counseling with children and as a refresher to experienced practitioners. No single best practice for counseling in the schools was proposed; rather a variety of issues and approaches within a generic framework were addressed. The three main purposes were: (a) to describe school-based counseling and the children typically referred for counseling; (b) to highlight the education, training and experience necessary for school psychologists to practice child counseling; and (c) to propose a step-by-step model for the practice of school-based counseling. The model included the following steps leading up to the actual counseling sessions with a child: examine the referral, conduct an assessment to arrive at hypotheses and to select an intervention program, select individual counseling if certain conditions are met, specify the goals of counseling, and choose a counseling approach and methods. Six stages were presented to describe the actual process of counseling: (a) preparing the child, (b) establishing the working relationship, (c) implementing the plan for change, (d) involving significant others, (e) continuing the plan for change, and (f) termination. The importance of

REFERENCES

Achenbach, T. M. (1982). *Developmental psychopathology.* New York: John Wiley.

American Psychiatric Association (1980). *Diagnostic and statistical manual of mental disorders — DSM III.* (3rd ed.). Washington, DC: American Psychiatric Association.

Apter, S. J. (1982). *Troubled children: Troubled systems.* New York: Pergamon Press.

Atkenson, B. M. & Forehand, R. (1981). Conduct disorders. In Mash, E. J. & Terdal, L. G. (Eds.), *Behavioral assessment of childhood disorders.* pp. 185-219. New York: Gilford Press.

Barkley, R. A. (1983). Hyperactivity. In Morris, R. J., & Kratochwill, T. P. (Eds.), *The practice of child therapy,* pp. 87-112. New York: Pergamon Press.

Bronfenbrenner, U. (1979). *The ecology of human development.* Cambridge: Harvard University Press.

Casey, R. (1984). The efficacy of child psychotherapy: A quantitative review of research. Unpublished manuscript. The University of Texas at Austin.

Clarizio, H. F. & McCoy, G. F. (1983). *Behavior disorders in children.* (3rd ed.). New York: Harper and Row.

Cowan, P. A. (1978). *Piaget with feeling.* New York: Holt, Rinehart and Winston.

Greenspan, S. I. (1981). *The clinical interview of the child.* New York: McGraw-Hill.

Group for the Advancement of Psychiatry (1982). *The process of child therapy.* New York: Brunner/Mazel.

Knoff, H. M. (1983a). Personality assessment in the schools: Issues and procedures for school psychologists. *School Psychology Review, 12,* 391-398.

Knoff, H. M. (Ed.) (1983b). Projective personality assessment in the schools. *School Psychology Review, 12,* 4.

Koppitz, E. M. (1982). Personality assessment in the schools. In Reynolds, C. R., & Gutkin, T. B. (Eds.), *Handbook of School Psychology.* pp. 273-295. New York: John Wiley.

Meyers, J., Parsons, R. D. & Martin, R. (1979). *Mental health consultation in schools.* San Francisco: Jossey-Bass.

Miller, P. H. (1983). *Theories of developmental psychology.* San Francisco: Freeman.

Morris, R. J. & Kratochwill, T. P. (Eds.). (1983). *The practice of child therapy.* New York: Pergamon Press.

Mussen, P. (Ed.). (1983). *Handbook of child psychology.* (4th ed.) Vol. I, II, III & IV. New York: John Wiley.

Prout, H. T. & Brown, D. T. (1983). *Counseling and psychotherapy with children and adolescents: Theory and practice for school and clinic setting.* Tampa: Mariner.

Quay, H. C. (1979). Classification. In Quay, H. C. & Werry, J. S. (Eds.), *Psychological disorders of childhood.* (2nd ed.). pp. 1-42. New York: John Wiley.

Reisman, J. M. (1973). *Principles of psychotherapy with children.* New York: John Wiley.

Robins, L. N, (1979). Follow-up studies. In Quay, H. C. & Werry, J. S. (Eds.), *Psychopathological disorders of childhood.* (2nd ed.). pp. 483-513. New York: John Wiley.

Rutter, M. (1983). Psychological therapies: Issues and prospects. In Guze, S. B., Earls, F. J., & Barrett, J. E. (Eds.). *Childhood psychopathology and development.* pp. 139-164. New York: Raven.

Rutter, M. & Garmezy, N. (1983). Developmental psychopathology. In Hetherington, E. M. (Ed.). *Handbook of child psychology.* (4th ed.). (Vol. 4): *Social and personality development.* pp. 775-911. New York: John Wiley.

Salkind, N. J. (1981). *Theories of human development.* New York: D. Van Nostrand.

Schaefer, C. E. & Millman, H. L. (1979). *Therapies for children.* San Francisco: Jossey Bass.

Schaefer, C. E. & O'Connor, K. J. (1983). *Handbook of play therapy.* New York: John Wiley.

Tuma, S. M. & Sobotka, G. F. (1982). Traditional therapies with children. In Wolman, B. B. & Stricker, G. (Eds.), *Handbook of developmental psychopathology.* New Jersey: Prentice-Hall.

Weiner, I. B. (1982). *Child and adolescent psychopathology.* New York: John Wiley.

Yule, W. (1981). The epidemiology of child psychopathology. In Lahey, B. B. & Kazdin, A. E. (Eds.), *Advances in clinical child psychology.* (Vol. 4). pp. 1-51. New York: Plenum Press.

ANNOTATED BIBLIOGRAPHY

Morris, R. J. & Kratochwill, T. P. (Eds.) (1983). *The practice of child therapy.* New York: Pergamon Press.
This is a treatment-oriented reference volume for practitioners working in the area of behavior disorders. It covers such areas as obsessive-compulsive disorders, childhood depression, fears and problems, hyperactivity, conduct disorders, and reading and academic problems. The general orientation is behavioral and the focus is on intervention strategies to change identified problem behaviors.

Prout, H. T. & Brown, D. T. (1983). *Counseling and psychotherapy with children and adolescents: Theory and practice for school and clinic settings.* Tampa: Mariner.
This book is a comprehensive overview of six major approaches to counseling/therapy with children. It includes coverage of behavioral approaches, rational-emotive approaches, reality therapy approaches, person centered approaches, Adlerian approaches, and psychoanalytic approaches. The theory, view of psychopathology and treatment guidelines for each approach are described and illustrated.

Reisman, J. M. (1973). *Principles of psychotherapy with children.* New York: John Wiley.
This book aims to make clear the practice of psychotherapy with children and their parents. It surveys the literature and arrives at seven principles that guide the conduct of psychotherapy with both children and adults and then illustrates the working of these principles in actual cases. The orientation is psychodynamic and humanistic.

Schaefer, C. E. & O'Connor, K. J. (1983). *Handbook of play therapy*. New York: John Wiley.
This book reviews the major approaches to play therapy and describes special play therapy techniques for particular settings including the elementary school setting. Also suggested are methods of play therapy for specific childhood disorders such as victims of child abuse, children of divorced parents, aggressive children, learning disabled children and physically handicapped children.

Walsh, W. M. (1975). *Counseling children and adolescents: An anthology of contemporary techniques*. Berkeley: McCutchan.
This book reviews major approaches in the counseling literature. It covers behavioral counseling, client-oriented counseling, eclectic counseling, existential counseling, developmental counseling, play therapy, rational-emotive therapy and reality therapy. The wide variety of techniques proposed may be useful to the beginning counselor/therapist.

BEST PRACTICES IN POLITICAL AWARENESS

Gilbert M. Trachtman
New York University

Each of us possesses a sense of either power or powerlessness which differentiates us from our fellows. Sometimes called sense of efficacy or locus of control, it is relatively independent of current external circumstances. However its roots may be traced, at least in part, to events much earlier in one's history. In the most benign environmental circumstances, where we might be largely in charge of our own lives, there are some who passively allow the wind to take charge and never manipulate sail or rudder. In the most invasive or controlled settings there are others who fight back and who strive to maintain control over part of their lives.

School psychology today often functions in a noxious setting and is surrounded by critics and enemies. Some of this we allowed to happen; some is beyond our control, but we individually bear responsibility for how we deal with our current situations. While we moan that our profession is controlled by others, that we are not permitted to function as we were trained and that we are whipping boys (or girls) of the courts, parents, administrators and teachers, school psychology abounds with exceptions to these generalizations.

Many journal issues include articles about exciting programs implemented by school psychologists. Most major conferences give fresh evidence that school psychologists serve children and parents in innovative and constructive ways. This book provides further evidence of how rewarding a profession school psychology is. Yet many of us work in increasingly restrictive settings and try to fulfill increasingly impossible job demands. The many exceptions we read about or hear of only tantalize us and frustrate us further. Sometimes these exceptions are the result of luck — individuals who find themselves in unusually benevolent circumstances — but often they are the result of individual initiative and assertiveness.

It would be of great vaue to our profession to systematically study selected school psychologists who, in these troubled times, function effectively and productively and to define the personal, behavioral and situational factors leading to their successes. When completed, that study would lead to a Best Practices chapter for the next edition of this manual. Absent such empirical data, this chapter offers subjective musings on the topic.

OVERVIEW

Having accepted an assignment to write a chapter on political awareness, I found myself making notes about political activism and concluded that these topics were inextricably intertwined. After reviewing a dozen different dictionary definitions of *politics* I found myself most comfortable with broad descriptions such as "competition between interest groups or individuals for power or leadership" or "the total complex of relations between individuals in society." The first rule of awareness for all of us, then, is that we are always political whether or not we perceive ourselves to be activists. Even when we do nothing but "our job" we present school psychology to the public. Each of us is either helpful, neutral, or harmful. Each of us leaves behind an impression with children, parents, teachers, specialists, and administrators. The impressions we create generalize to attitudes which become the context within which people vote for budgets, support legislation, or communicate to colleagues and neighbors. Each consumer who experiences a school psychologist as helpful or caring becomes a potential advocate for us. Each consumer who experiences us as harmful, unhelpful, ineffective, or uncaring contributes to the circumscription or rejection of our services.

Political activism occurs at many levels from on-the-job interventions within a single school building to attempts to influence federal legislation. The emerging themes from both the Spring Hill and Olympia Conferences were the need for school psychology to be proactive rather than reactive and to play some role in our own destiny. However, before we productively debate the issue of reactive versus proactive behavior, we must first diminish the massive inactive component in our professional ranks. For one reason or another the great majority of us are not politically active. Even this majority, however, should be politically aware, should recognize the political implications of our day to day activities, and should realize that some of the guidelines for political activism presented in this chapter are useful reminders that everything we do has political implications.

So, this chapter is for everyone. If you are not politically active, read further and consider why not. Then read a bit further and consider whether even in your apolitical professional functioning you might not benefit from being a bit more politically sensitive. If you're not an activist but would like to be, perhaps this chapter will help you get started. If you are an activist, see if you can learn from what follows and consider whether you can contribute some of your experience and wisdom towards a richer and more useful chapter in some future edition of this manual.

BASIC CONSIDERATIONS

Why Activism?

Active is better than passive. This statement is made not as a value judgment but as a fact of life and a basic assumption of this chapter. Support for the theorem that active is better than passive is garnered from the diverse disciplines of political science, philosophy, mental health, religion, ethics, sports, military science and the game of Monopoly. At the most basic level we are active to have some control over our lives. Activism in school psychology attempts to effect change in external circumstances. Laws, regulations, job descriptions, peoples' attitudes and perceptions are examples of some which exert control over what school psychologists do. Activism also involves establishing a climate for future political change. Altruistically our activism is directed at effecting change that enhances the welfare of our clients and allows us to provide more effective or valuable services. Pragmatically our activism makes our working conditions or our role more personally rewarding or supports the guild interests of school psychology. The pragmatic and the altruistic frequently coincide or, failing to do so, are at least not in conflict. In rare cases when our guild interests are detrimental to client welfare, ethical considerations must favor the interests of our clientele.

Some of us have urged for many years that we establish a political base by building alliances with parent groups, child advocacy groups, and other professional associations and by working cooperatively with these groups on political activity in the public interest (Trachtman, 1967). Primarily, political advocacy in the public interest on behalf of children benefits children, one of our major goals. As a secondary gain legislation and regulations which are beneficial to children sometimes involve constructive roles for school psychologists and, ultimately, increased recognition of the contributions school psychologists make to children, schools, and families. A tertiary benefit is that active advocacy efforts shoulder to shoulder with consumer and other professional groups and the eventual recognitions of our shared interests lead to the development of potential support from these groups when we are involved in more narrowly defined political action of a guild nature.

However, until quite recently school psychologists were not visible, either as individuals or through their major professional associations, at public debate on federal education policies or the federal education budget. Other professional groups are highly visible in the public record of these hearings. School psychologists also did not participate in educational policy debates at state or local levels except for vested interest issues such as licensure and certification (Abramowitz, 1981). This has not been a failing only of *school* psychologists. Speaking of psychologists in general, American Psychological Association (APA) President Bill Bevan stated, "they either have refused to concern themselves with policy questions for fear of contamination or, when they chose to engage themselves, they have been almost *totally* preoccupied with primarily self-serving, narrowly focused guild issues." (Bevan, 1981). A major outcome of the Spring Hill Symposium on the Future of Psychology in the Schools (Ysseldyke, J. and Weinberg, R., 1981) was the theme of proactivity. Many speakers and workshops focused on the need for a proactive stance and on the theme of social consciousness, viewing professional practice in the context of larger issues such as the state of the economy, sexism, and racism (Rosenfield, 1981). Over and over again we reminded ourselves of the need for school psychologists to develop

an internal locus of control, and self-directedness, and to become politically active in public policy areas with other professional associations, and with parent and community groups.

In the brief time that has elapsed since Spring Hill, the *Journal of School Psychology* published a series of reminiscences by some of our elder statespersons. Most included some mention of political action in their commentary. Mullen (1981) is not certain that school psychologists are able to be aggressive advocates of children's rights or fight for changes in state guidelines or federal legislation when they interfere with child welfare. Bardon (1981) discusses the need for school psychology and the rest of psychology to influence legislation at state and national levels. Meacham (1983) reminds us that "we can become more politically active at the state and local levels." Tindall (1983) refers to political battles around certification issues and the impact of federal legislation upon school psychological practice and Crissey (1983) reiterates "that school psychologists must have an influence on the statutory developments that will affect their work." Finally Sarason (1983) argues as he has for years on the need for psychology to relate to the larger society. With general consensus on the need for activism, the next task is to select the proper arena.

Where Can Activism Occur?

It has already been pointed out that even when we perceive ourselves as inactive, "just doing our defined job and nothing more," our day to day actions have political importance that affect people's perceptions of school psychology. It is also true that one's daily behavior beyond the job has unplanned or accidental political significance. When my raucous cheering for the visiting team offends a hometown spectator at a football game, the resulting altercation is often a funny footnote to the afternoon to share with friends that evening. When it turns out on Monday that the angry football fan is chair of the state legislature's education committee with whom several of us are meeting to discuss pending legislation, my treasonable behavior at the stadium proves costly to school psychology.

However, such fortuitous events just as often prove serendipitous, and, in any case, since they are difficult to plan they are not further considered here. For purposes of this chapter, political activism refers to beyond-the-job planned behavior focused either directly or indirectly on improving the welfare of our clientele or ourselves or both. This does not include day to day activities such as assessment, consultation and counseling, although such activities are obviously conducted on behalf of clients and do have political impact. Less traditional activities of school psychologists such as systems consultation for more effective school organization (Maher & Illbeck, 1982) are a step closer to political activism although routine practice for some school psychologists. While we maintain political awareness every moment of our waking life political activism refers here to activities outside of one's work as a school psychologist.

Given, then, that as working school psychologists we were motivated to become politically active and to invest energy in bringing about constructive change in the practice of school psychology, where should we contribute our efforts? The answer is almost anywhere, as long as we get involved somewhere. School psychology exists as a microcosmic component of the complex system called education which is, itself, a relatively minor component of the infinitely more complex political and social systems making up our society. A small hint of this

complexity is evident when one considers the many forces impinging on accreditation and credentialing in school psychology. Tom Fagan portrays this visually and vividly in his travelling road show and in an earlier chapter here (Fagan, 1985) when he diagrams sources of power and authority affecting school psychology. At the state level he alerts us to the influence of professional associations, certification boards and licensing boards; and at the national level to the influence of psychological associations, trainers organizations and accrediting agencies. His chart only scratches the surface, however, when we consider all the additional forces which affect our day to day practice. At the local, county or municipal level, practice is additionally regulated by educational agencies, legislatures or courts. At the state and federal level educational agencies, legislatures and courts also further enhance or inhibit our functioning either by regulatory action or by providing or withholding funding. Impacting on all these governmental agencies are our own psychological associations, other professional associations, and various parent and citizens groups. All are concerned about the same issues and attempt to influence who delivers what services to whom. Additionally, competing interests direct the attention of the legislature to other issues considered more important than ours. Futurists predicting how school psychologists will function tomorrow find it necessary to consider the impact of disparate forces such as economic, geopolitical, and ideological factors (Ogilvy, 1982) and to project various scenarios and alternate possibilities (Cardon, 1982). Activists attempting to affect how school psychologists will function tomorrow might aim their efforts at any of these contributing factors.

Were we to decide that the time had come for us to be politically active the problem is not to locate an outlet for our energy but rather to select the proper channels for our investment of effort. Individual efforts at political action are always possible. Getting a letter to the editor published in a major newspaper, testifying before a legislative committee, speaking directly to one's congressman, or protesting to a board of education or an education official about certain regulations always leaves one with a sense of accomplishment. A California state senator has acknowledged voting a particular way on legislation because of a single letter of support or opposition (Carpenter, 1983).

Generally, however, political action is more effective as a group endeavor over time and activist effort is more effectively expended by contributing to selected group activity. Most organizations deal with multiple issues. Most issues are attended to by many groups. Upon becoming an organization activist one could commit time fully to one organization, thereby supporting that organization's efforts on many issues. Alternatively, one might be so committed to a single issue that one becomes active in several organizations, focusing in each organization on activity devoted to the particular issue.

The machinery for political action by psychologists already exists. In recent years psychology has become active politically and quite recently, school psychology has begun to be more active. However, there is insufficient money and personpower available to do what needs to be done, unless many more of us become involved. Psychology in general is represented by the American Psychological Association, by affiliated state associations and by many local associations affiliated with the state groups. In 1974 APA organized the Association for the Advancement of Psychology. AAP was incorporated as a national lobbying organization to advance the science and profession of psychology and has been quite active on the national scene.

The National Association of School Psychologists was organized as an alternative national organization to APA when APA established a doctoral entry level for the definition of a practicing psychologist and for full membership. NASP has grown rapidly and has become a strong and articulate voice for school psychology. It is supported by affiliated state associations and by many local associations of school psychologists.

Organized psychology and organized school psychology now maintain parallel political structures. Most school psychologists who became active join their local, state and national school psychology organizations, although a distressing number of school psychologists fail to join anything. Some school psychologists also join psychology associations and most of those organizations contain school psychology divisions or sections. Often these organizations work cooperatively and are usually able to take similar stands on political issues involving consumer welfare. Even on some guild issues involving professional self-interest it has been possible to work cooperatively. However, APA, AAP and most state psychology associations are committed to the doctoral entry level and to the primary interests of clinical psychology vis-a-vis medicine. When these interests conflict with those of school psychology, clinical psychology interests take precedence even in organizations where school psychology is also represented.

The individual school psychologist needs first to make a financial commitment by joining several appropriate organizations. Political awareness entails recognition of the many societal forces impinging on the practice of school psychology. Strong local and national organizations are capable of maintaining ongoing political activity to have some role in the shaping of school psychology. Political activism begins by joining these organizations. Thus adding funds to their operating budget and numbers to their membership rolls increases their political clout. Too many school psychologists never take this first step but remain all too ready to complain about their lot. However, having joined an organization, many assume that responsibility ends with payment of dues and occasional participation at a convention. As a result, all of our professional organizations are insufficiently monitored by and insufficiently responsive to their membership. Most professional organizations are run by a small group of hard working individuals who frequently make and implement policy. Although most are responsible and serve their membership well, it is easy to lose touch with the priorities and needs of a silent constituency. In many organizations an attempt is made to communicate regularly with the membership via bulletins, newsletters, minutes of board meetings, drafts of policy statements, and so forth, but, typically membership response or commentary is virtually non-existent. Most organizations report few members participating in the nomination and election process. So, the second stage of activism is to be a *responsible* member. Read your newsletters, attend membership meetings, express opinions, send notes to officers or committee chairs, and participate in referendums or elections.

Having taken these baby steps toward activism we are now ready for real action. Now that we are informed citizens about the organization(s) we have joined, about their structure, focus, and activities, we are ready to become active in a particular arena. We may either join an existing committee or suggest the establishment of a new one. In most organizations the door is wide open for anyone interested in working. An expression of interest is enough to get involved. In some organizations it proves difficult to join an existing

committee or to get a new one started. While there occasionally is reasonable explanation for this, this should be of grave concern to the membership. There is no shortage of battles to be joined and causes to be advocated. For starters, if our organization is not already involved in activities to which we feel a strong commitment, consider the implications for public policy advocacy suggested by Hobbs & Robinson (1982) in their review of previous federal policy on compensatory education for disadvantaged children and recent research on the reversibility of early cognitive deficits. Consider also the policy implications for children, youth and families in a series of articles by key policy makers and psychologists comprising a special section of the American Psychologist (Takanishi, De Leon and Pallak 1983a). Or consider still another special section devoted to policy implications in a review of some of psychology's contributions to education (Takanishi, et al., 1983b). If these broad policy issues, primarily consumer oriented and relating to federal legislation, are too broad or too abstract to catch our immediate interest, consider instead the need for systematic organization and advocacy at the state level, more often related to guild issues. For an excellent overview of these issues as they relate to state psychological associations and doctoral licensing and practice, but with great potential relevance to school psychology's political issues, see Ginsberg, Kilburg, and Buklad (1983) and the articles which follow in the same journal issue.

Most of the above discussion has focused on activism within professional organizations. The suggestion has been made that our psychology asociations should more regularly join with consumer groups and other professional groups in public policy advocacy. For school psychologists who enjoy writing, a further contribution in this vein is publishing articles in the magazines or journals which consumers and other professionals read. Doing this often enough establishes school psychology in the consciousness of those whose support we seek. I did some of this years ago and the positive feedback was most rewarding (Salten, Elkin, & Trachtman, 1956; Trachtman, 1960a; 1961a; 1961b; 1962; 1967-68; 1970).

BEST PRACTICES

This section should cite a number of case histories or detailed published accounts of examples where political awareness and political activism led to attainment of political goals. Here and there a state association has provided insight into a successful political effort. Based on extensive experience with the California legislature, Dorken provided a general account of successful political process which, although it reflects the parochial interests of clinical psychology vis-a-vis professional psychology, serves as a valuable primer for school psychologists (Dorken, 1981). Forman and O'Malley (1984) describe an innovative field experience in the state legislature for school psychology graduate students which seems quite promising for the promotion of activism. Generally, however, while successful political endeavor does occur, detailed accounts of the political process are rare. Therefore, borrowing freely from Dorken's suggested steps, Bevan's (1981) precepts and Alinsky's (1971) rules and mixing them all with a dash of personal experience, here are Gil's Guidelines for effective political practice:

1. *Listen to others.* We are skilled listeners yet we often fail to take these skills with us into the political arena. Manifest content is not always what it seems to be; people do not always mean what they say. Be alert to the hidden agenda which others may be hiding from you or the uncons-

cious motivations of which others may be unaware. Be sensitive to previous history, to unpaid debts, to covert alliances, to secret enmities, to unobtrusive opinion molders and leaders, and to shifting alliances.

2. *Know yourself.* Keep in touch with your own need systems, motivations, values and attitudes which lead to perceptual distortion. An intimate and open relationship with peers who provide honest feedback is invaluable.

3. *Reach your audience.* At times your audience may be professional colleagues whom you are recruiting or rousing to action. Other times it may be skeptics, opponents or strangers whom you are attempting to proselytize. The name of the game is effective communication, and speaking loudly and clearly is not enough. It is vital that you speak to others in both their linguistic and affective language. This refers in part to elemental components of empathy. Sensing the experience background of another, speaking from some body of shared experience, and seeking out a shared value or interest serve to establish some level of rapport. This is one of the most complex and difficult of all the ground rules to observe and is hardly attainable by cognitive means alone. It encompasses rules 1 and 2 above and includes also such elements as basic respect for others and establishment of trust. Cognitively it requires that you communicate psychological concepts in plain English and that you know who your audience is and how it functions. If you want your voice to be heard you need to know who the key politicians or bureaucrats are, which staff members are vital links to which officials, how the legislature or bureaucracy functions, how budgetary factors affect policy-making, and what the timetables are.

4. *Establish credibility.* Another prior contribution to effective communication is the respect you have already earned by

advocating actively on behalf of children, educational programs, and the psychological welfare of families, or by providing consultation where your advice is perceived as educational, knowledgeable and nonpartisan.

5. *Be prepared for the vagaries of decision-making.* While all your efforts are directed toward logical and persuasive support for your cause do not expect policy decisions to always be made on rational bases. Remember the angry football fan who turns out to be chair of the legislature's education committee. Recall the state senator whose vote was based on a single letter (Carpenter 1983). A state licensing bill for psychologists laboriously shepherded through both houses of the legislature was vetoed by a governor responding to personal advice from his family physician. Budding or broken romances can have more influence on a policy decision than all the logic and persuasion we can muster, and yet we must continue to provide the logic and persuasion.

6. *Be patient and be persistent.* Change comes slowly and the work is tedious. Two childhood memories keep me going. Before the days of refrigeration a man with a horse and wagon came to sell us a nickel's worth of ice. He scratched a line in his huge cake of ice and then pecked along that line with his ice pick, seemingly to no avail for several moments. Suddenly, from the cumulative effect of all his previous picks, the ice cleaved cleanly at the line he had drawn. Another image which serves me well is sitting in the bleachers watching my heroes, the great baseball players of the New York Giants. I realize now that even the greatest of the great failed to hit safely more often than not. And so I have learned to keep swinging for the fences, to be undismayed when I strike out, and to be rewarded by a respectable batting average and an occasional home run. Successful politicking requires frustration

tolerance, delay of gratification, and a realistic level of aspiration.

7. *Maintain a sense of humor.* Humor is vital for maintaining one's balance and avoiding despair. Used aggressively, humor can convey truths which might not otherwise be accepted. At appropriate times in political battle, it can be converted to powerful weapons against the opposition who may be more vulnerable to satire and ridicule than to direct assault.

8. *Maintain flexibility.* Today's tactics do not work tomorrow, today's alliances dissolve tomorrow, today's major issues are preempted tomorrow.

9. *Know your bottom line.* Some issues are matters of such profound principle that no compromise is morally feasible and we must live or die by the stand we have taken. Most issues are not of such philosophical import and the art of compromise is a cornerstone of a democratic system in which many needs and many interests compete for recognition. This guideline for political activism is quite consistent with an affirmative but flexible professional style where you know the ideal recommendation for a particular child, but the administration, your team members or the parents disagree. You must enter the situation willing to find some balance between what you want and what others want but also knowing your bottom line. You do not impose your views unilaterally but also do not sell out your position without expressing it clearly.

10. *Acknowledge power issues.* Power is a key component of all political action. It is a factor in the assumption of leadership within a group and in that group's political program. Yet we find little open discussion about power issues, power strategies, or power needs. Our psychology textbooks devote little attention to power as a motivating force. Carpenter (1983) suggests that power is not a socially acceptable human motive and even more pointedly that those with

power tend not to talk about it.

11. *Embrace conflict appropriately.* The idea of conflict or controversy, although frowned upon in polite society, is vital to the democratic process. Conflict leads to victory or defeat or compromise and is therefore an essential component of change. Without conflict we would have status-quo obviously favorable to the "ins." The "in" group naturally finds confrontation distasteful or uncouth and, when its power is sufficient, often prefers to remain aloof and distant from the "outs." When their power is not sufficiently absolute the "ins" are delighted to avoid conflict by negotiating endlessly, by establishing joint task forces or study groups, by co-opting "out" leaders into the slow moving deliberative process, by clouding the issues or by introducing less salient issues. Conflict for the sake of conflict is not desirable. Energetic but polite activism or negotiation in the true spirit of mutual accomodation is preferable but confrontation and direct conflict is sometimes necessary to bring an issue to the surface. At times an issue has become so blurred that it needs to be dramatized, exaggerated, even polarized to the point of no imminent compromise. In the words of an early activist, "He that is not with me is against me" (Luke 11:23).

12. *Acknowledge self-interest.* We like to surround ourselves with the cloak of altruism when it is frequently obvious that our concern is not so much for the welfare of the child as for the comfort of the psychologist (Trachtman, 1960b); not so much for the protection of the public as for the protection of psychology (Trachtman, 1972). Pure altruism is quite rare and even when we are truly active on behalf of the public, have secondary self interest (see #4). Sometimes self-interest and the public interest coincide. What's good for school psychology is good for the people, and our political activism is still supported on the highest moral grounds.

However, most administrators and legislators are pragmatists and are more ready than we are to acknowledge the role of self-interest in policy-making. They consider our cause seriously if it is not inimical to the public interest, if we have established credibility and if we have demonstrated power. They respect us more if we deal with the self-interest openly.

13. *Establish networks.* Networks have always existed in society, have often evolved naturally and served the purposes of support or communication and have sometimes been used intuitively and productively by community organizers. It remained for Sarason (1976) to pioneer the formal concept of networking as a planned professional activity and to elaborate it further to cope with scarcity of human resources (Sarason 1977, 1979). At Spring Hill and Olympia, with the focus on school psychology's need for a proactive stance the importance of networking for political purposes was repeatedly affirmed. Networking with other groups is important for establishing a broader power base and credibility. A legislative network of psychologists (Dorken, 1981) is a vital mobilization tool at moments of political crisis.

14. *Work on several issues.* Individuals may choose to focus on a single issue as their prime passion even to the extent of finding several organizations within which to carry the same issue forward. Organizations and groups are well advised to develop an agenda of several issues. A single issue agenda is likely to attract a narrow constituency which is attached to the issue rather than the organization. An organization with a multi-issue agenda attracts a wider spectrum of members which provides more power and leverage for each of its campaigns. Membership remains stable as particular issues flare up or die but the general thrust of the group continues.

15. *Learn from your experiences.*

Feuerstein's (1979) concept of mediated learning, while initially applied to interactional processes between developing children and intentional adults, is equally applicable to all of us. Feuerstein describes the adult who "mediates the world to the child by framing, selecting, focusing and feeding back environmental experiences" so as to produce the appropriate learning. This is also how a good supervisor works with an intern, and how we need to mediate our own life experience if we expect to grow from experience instead of merely living through series of events. Political activism is a constant learning experience. No two situations are ever alike, no successful tactic is guaranteed to succeed again, and unsuccessful strategies may work next time around if we do not abandon them precipitously. It is therefore necessary to accompany each experience with reflection, analysis and interpretation if it is to become a learning experience.

SUMMARY

This chapter portrays political awareness and political activism as related concepts and reviews the need for both in the field of school psychology. It was noted that many psychologists are not actively involved but no attempt was made here to explain this inactivity.

Our developing awareness of the need for proactive behavior was described, followed by a review of possible arenas for action, from on-the-job behavior to more formal activism at all political levels. Further discussion considered individual activism versus organizational involvement, participation in psychological organizations and methods for the monitoring of these organizations, and the range of possible issues with which to become involved. Finally, fifteen ground rules for political activism were presented and dis-

cussed, borrowing heavily from the work of Saul Alinsky and several others.

It should be noted in closing that political awareness and political activism are indeed intertwined. To be neither aware nor active is to yield all responsibility for one's future to others. To be aware without being active seems a waste. To be active without being aware is futile and dangerous. To be aware and active is our only hope.

REFERENCES

Abramowitz, E. A. (1981). School psychology: a historical perspective. _School Psychology Review_, _10_, 121-126.

Bardon, J. I. (1981). A personalized account of the development and status of school psychology. _Journal of School Psychology_, _19_, 199-210.

Bevan, W. (1981). On coming of age among the professions, _School Psychology Review_, _10_, 127-137.

Cardon, B. W. (1982). Synthesis of the scenarios. The future: a context for present planning. _School Psychology Review_, _XI_, 151-160.

Carpenter, P. B. (1983). The personal insights of a legislator/psychologist. _American Psychologist_, _38_, 1216-1219.

Crissey, M. S. (1983). School psychology: reminiscences of earlier times. _Journal of School Psychology_, _21_, 163-177.

Dorken, H. (1981). Coming of age legislatively: In 21 steps. _American Psychologist_, _36_, 165-173.

Fagan, T. (1985). Best practices in the training of school psychologists. In A. Thomas & J. Grimes (Eds.), _Best Practices in School Psychology_. Kent, Ohio: National Association of School Psychologists.

Feuerstein, R. (1979). _The dynamic assessment of retarded performers_. Baltimore: University Park Press.

Forman, S. G. and O'Malley, P. L. (1984). A legislative field experience for psychology graduate students, _Professional Psychology_, _15_, 324-332.

Ginsberg, M. R., Kilburg, R. R. and Buklad, W. (1983). State-level legislative and public advocacy. _American Psychologist_, _38_, 1206-1209.

Hobbs, N. and Robinson, S. (1982). Adolescent development and public policy. *American Psychologist, 37*, 212-223.

Maher, C. A. and Illback, R. J. (1982). Organizational school psychology: issues and considerations. *Journal of School Psychology, 20*, 244-253.

Meacham, M. L. (1983). The development of school psychology in the state of Washington: a personal perspective. *Journal of School Psychology, 21*, 1-7.

Mullen, F. A. (1981). School psychology in the U.S.A.: reminiscences of its origin. *Journal of School Psychology, 19*, 103-119.

Ogilvy, J. (1982). The forces shaping the 1980's. *School Psychology Review, XI*, 112-126.

Rosenfield, S. (1981). Small group synthesis, group A. *School Psychology Review, 10*, 285-289.

Salten, D. G., Elkin, V. B. and Trachtman, G. M. (1956). Public school psychological services: recent growth and further potential, parts I & II. *Educational Administrtion and Supervision, 42*, 100-107 and 162-169.

Sarason, S. B. (1983). School psychology: an autobiographical fragment. *Journal of School Psychology, 21*, 285-295.

Sarason, S. B. (1976). Community psychology, networks and Mr. Everyman. *American Psychologist, 31*, 317-328.

Sarason, S. B., Carroll, C., Maton, K., Cohen, S., & Lorentz, E. (1972). *Human services and resource networks*. San Francisco: Jossey Bass.

Sarason, S. B. and Lorentz, E. (1979). *The challenge of the resource exchange network*. San Francisco: Jossey Bass.

Takanishi, R., DeLeon, P. H. and Pallak. M. S. (1983a). Psychology and public policy affecting children, youth and families. *American Psychologist, 38*, 67-69.

Takanishi, R., DeLeon, P. H. and Pallak, M. S. (1983b). Psychology and education: continuing, productive partnership. *American Psychologist, 38*, 996-1000.

Tindall, R. H. (1983). I didn't aspire to be a school psychologist: reflections. *Journal of School Psychology, 21*, 79-89.

Trachtman, G. M. (1970). Evils of educational research. *Phi Delta Kappan, L11*, 123-125.

Trachtman, G. M. (Nov., 1967). The school psychologist and legislation: a position paper. *New York State Psychological Association School Psychologists Division Newsletter*, 3-5.

Trachtman, G. M. (1967-68). Educational innovation and the school psychologist. *Education Synopsis, XIII*, 1.

Trachtman, G. M. (1962). Should parents know the results of intelligence tests? *PTA Magazine, 56*, 4-6.

Trachtman, G. M. (1961a). Role of an in-service program in establishing a new plan of elementary school organization. *Journal of Educational Sociology, 34*, 349-354.

Trachtman, G. M. (1961b). New directions for school psychology. *Exceptional Children, 28*, 159-163.

Trachtman, G. M. (1960a). The K-3 school evaluated by the K-3 principal. *American School Board Journal, 140*, 55.

Trachtman, G. M. (1960b). From the pen of the president, *Nassau County Psychological Association Newsletter, 8*, 4-5.

ANNOTATED BIBLIOGRAPHY

Alinsky, S. *Rules for Radicals.* New York: Random House, 1971.
Alinsky is our foremost purveyor of organizational know-how, and much of this chapter comes from Alinsky's thinking. I read Alinsky's earlier works 35 years ago and last read this book, which he subtitles "a pragmatic primer for realistic radicals" more than 10 years ago. In reviewing it for this chapter I was stunned to see how much of his writing I had absorbed as my own thinking.

Bevan, W. On coming of age among the professions. *School Psychology Review,* 1981, *X* (2), 127-137.
This was the keynote address at the Spring Hill Symposium, by the then President-Elect of APA. Bevan paints a lucid portrait of our complex society, issues of public policy, the role of professionals in this society with particular reference to school psychology issues, and closes with some simple rules of thumb about advocacy roles for professionals.

De Leon, P. H., O'Keefe, A. M., Vanden Bos, G. R. & Kraut, A. G. How to influence public policy: a blue print for activism. *American Psychologist,* 1982, *37* (5), 476-485.
This article reviews the importance of public interest advocacy and political activism for the guild interests of psychology, with particular focus on national health policy.

Dorken, H. Advocacy and the legislative process. *American Psychologist,* 1983, *38* (11), 1210-1215.

Dorken, H. Coming of age legislatively: In 21 steps.
    American Psychologist, 1981, *36* (2), 165-
    173.
    These articles focus on the legislative process.
    The earlier focuses on the organizational pro-
    cess for achieving legislative objectives and
    describes the necessary sequence of steps.
    The later article describes legislative activism
    as a systems problem and documents the
    need for ongoing and sustained advocacy.

BEST PRACTICES IN THE ASSESSMENT OF HEARING IMPAIRED CHILDREN

Susan M. Vess
Northeast Louisiana University

Laura S. Gregory
Ouachita Parish Schools

OVERVIEW

The hearing-impaired (HI) population in the United States numbers about 14 million persons (Boughman & Shaver, 1982). Of these, approximately two million are deaf, i.e., individuals who are unable to understand and learn through speech and/or audition even when using amplification devices (Liben, 1978; Schein & Delk, 1974).

HI youngsters whose loss exceeds 90 decibels are classified as profoundly deaf. Among the school-aged, about 90% have a congenital hearing loss and another 5% were deafened by two years (Schein & Delk, 1974). These children are virtually unaware of the existence of sounds, have not developed listening skills, do not recognize audition's contribution to communication, and have not acquired adequate speech or language skills.

Children deafened after two years of age, the adventitiously deaf, have varying degrees of sound awareness and may even understand sound's importance to communication. They have an ongoing struggle to maintain whatever speech and language developed prior to deafness. Subsequent communication skills are acquired through vision and other channels. Adventitiously deaf children also must resolve any adjustment problems arising from their new deafness. Concurrently, their parents grapple with problems in communicating with, teaching, and managing them as well as resolving their own feelings of shock, anger, denial, and depression.

Deaf children whose deaf parents are established in a deaf community are often more fortunate than other profoundly hearing handicapped children in adjustment, language acquisition, and educational achievement (Vernon & Koh, 1971; Schlesinger & Meadow, 1972). Usually, they are exposed to gesture in infancy which facilitates the acquisition of language and manual communication. Hence, these youngsters have had their need to interact, to be accepted, and to learn satisfied from an early age (Schlesinger & Meadow, 1972). Hearing family members such as grandparents or siblings often serve as intermediaries to the hearing community. Unfortunately, 90% of deaf children are born to hearing parents who know little about the implications of their child's disability (Furth, 1973; Schein & Delk, 1974; Liben, 1978).

Deaf children are difficult to educate and present a major evaluation challenge to the school psychologist. They use amplification devices, primarily, to register environmental sounds and do not rely on hearing for communication. Less than one-fourth of their speech is rated as intelligible by their teachers (Jensema, Karchmer, & Trybus, 1978), and only about 17% of these deaf children are involved in any form of mainstreaming (Karchmer, Milone, & Wolk, 1979). Profoundly deaf youngsters comprise the largest grouping among HI children in special education and account for an increasing percentage of special class enrollment as they grow older (Karchmer, Milone, & Wolk, 1979).

Children with a hearing impairment of less than 70 decibels have different needs. They enter special education classes at an older age, are frequently mainstreamed, and leave special education younger than their deaf counterparts.

Those students with a 40 decibel or less loss are least likely to use amplification (Karchmer, Milone, & Wolk, 1979). They have sufficient hearing to acquire language and speech. According to Jensema, Karchmer, and Trybus (1978), 60% communicate through speech alone and their speech is rated as intelligible by their teachers.

Mild-moderate HI youngsters are often multi-handicapped (Karchmer, Milone, & Wolk, 1979). Associated handicapping conditions include: mental retardation, epilepsy, cerebral palsy, uncorrected visual impairments, brain damage, and behavior problems (Vernon, 1969b; Sullivan & Vernon, 1979; Demographic Profile, 1977-78; Jensen & Mullins, 1974). The incidence of multiply handicapping conditions among the HI population appears to be increasing (Schildroth, 1980).

The etiology of the hearing impairment is an important determiner of the likelihood of concomitant handicaps. Maternal rubella, meningitis, complications from the Rh factor, and prematurity all increase the risk of additional handicaps (Vernon, 1969a), and, therefore, the possibility of other more severe learning problems. Although genetically deaf children have fewer other handicaps (Boughman & Shaver, 1982), about one-fourth to one-third of these HI youngsters have multiple problems (Schein & Delk, 1974). These additional handicaps not only impede the children's ability to learn and interact with their world, but also compound their educational and assessment problems.

Hearing impaired children are expected to attend school in order to master skills deemed necessary to succeed in mainstream society. Consequently, they are periodically evaluated by the schools to measure their progress in achieving this goal. The question, then, is how to conduct the most effective evaluations for both the children and the schools.

The psychological evaluation of HI children shares some of the dilemmas of assessing bilingual-bicultural youngsters. Their variable ownership of language is a primary issue since the examiner and children often do not share a common language base. Misdiagnosis occurs when it is assumed that the hearing loss can be ignored or by-passed through the use of non-verbal tests and/or communicating through writing, pantomine, etc. Dispelling some of the common misconceptions about deafness is, perhaps, the best way to prepare school psychologists to evaluate HI children.

The hearing impaired do not always learn and communicate through lip (speech) reading (Spragins & Cokely, 1980). Only about 40 to 60% of English sounds are distinguishable on the lips (Vernon, 1969b), and those visible sounds may be blocked by pencils, cigarettes, mustaches, hands near the face, etc. Assuming that the speech pattern of the speaker is clearly distinct, the message can be lost because oral language moves rapidly and is gone forever once uttered. Finally, many English words are very difficult to discern by someone with little opportunity to associate sounds, visual images, and context. The best lipreaders may understand one-fourth of spoken language (Sullivan & Vernon, 1979), and the average deaf child accurately lipreads only about 5% of what is being said (Vernon & Koh, 1970). Learning to lipread could be compared to learning a foreign language from the television with the sound turned off.

Visual acuity does not automatically become heightened in the HI. When these persons appear to "see better," it means that the skill has been carefully nurtured and trained. Actually, visual problems are commonly found in HI persons (Caccamise, Meath-Lang, Johnson, 1981). Additionally, eye strain and fatigue often occur as a result of sustained use of vision to help understand communication.

Hearing aids do not necessarily provide compensation either. Amplification devices equally intensify all sounds, from the human voice to the class passing in the hall. Moreover, some deaf children wear aids only to increase their awareness of environmental sounds rather than to amplify speech. Thus, while it enables some use of a deficient sense, amplification, unlike the ear, does not selectively increase the volume of the human voice or accentuate crucial sounds.

BASIC CONSIDERATIONS

Best practices in the assessment of HI children require basic minimum competencies. According to Levine (1981), the school psychologists must initially meet the standards and qualifications of their training programs and credentialing boards. Additionally, they need at least one course that considers both normal development and pathology in speech and language. Psychologists should have the sensitivity to recognize and respond to behavioral cues and the imagination and flexibility to modify the assessment situation to the child's unique needs. A sense of whimsy and creativity are important assets adapting the environment and contents of test kits for auditorily impaired children. On a personal-competency dimension, psychologists who like and respect children and who are liked and respected in return are most likely to be effective evaluators of HI children. This is important as these youngsters are extremely sensitive to the nonverbal facial and body cues that often reveal the psychologist's genuine feelings.

Preliminary to the evaluation of HI children, it is vital to review medical and audiological histories as well as prior evaluation reports. Depending on etiology, HI children may have intermittent losses due to conditions such as otitis media, and/or be at risk of further decline in hearing or visual acuity caused by disorders like Usher's Syndrome. Since it is reasonable to evaluate only when they are at peak hearing efficiency, youngsters who display symptoms of a hearing or respiratory illness or who are recovering from one should not be tested until the symptoms clear. Otitis media, an inflammation of the middle ear, recurs and may have a negative impact on the conductive HI children's speech, language, and learning (Reichman & Healy, 1983). Usher's Syndrome impairs both hearing and vision and affects all ranges of hearing loss (Vernon, Boughman, & Annala, 1982). Concomitant interfering symptoms in Usher's include eye fatigue, night blindness, clumsiness, and limited peripheral vision. Since it is difficult to diagnose, children who are suspected of being "at risk" for this genetic disorder may need to be examined by more than one physician.

Although the information it provides indicates only what they cannot hear, it is imperative to review the children's audiograms. Hearing impaired children are unable to perceive sounds below their threshold (decibel) level. Aside from volume, sounds vary in pitch. Thus, a higher pitched sound may need greater volume to be heard. While some HI children hear consonants better than the high-pitched vowels, others may have more awareness of low frequency environmental sounds. One syllable words such as *is* and *if;* sounds such as *sh, th, ch, p, t, f,* and *k;* plurals and ending sounds can all be poorly heard. Thus, HI children may lose key words and directions and err even when intellectually capable of responding correctly.

The configuration of volume of loss (decibels) across frequencies (pitch) tells what and how the children hear. Residual hearing is also very important because some children with a greater magnitude of loss have more access to their remaining hearing acuity. As Levine (1981) noted, deaf children who are academically and socially successful are often elevated to hard-of-hearing status despite no improvement in their audiograms. Because hearing loss can alter both sound perception and discrimination, it is important to know the degree of loss, the amount of residual hearing, and the threshold configurations before conducting the evaluation.

Classroom observation of HI children is crucial. Pretest or prior observation reveals how children communicate with persons in their home and schools; how messages are transmitted to them; and how their gestures, postures, and facial expressions contribute to meaning. Some children use conventional communication methods such as cued speech or typically, some form of signs. Others employ very idiosyncratic styles. Nevertheless, in so far as possible, their typical communication style should be used during the evaluation. As style changes from program to program, be cautious to review prior educational records to determine which communication mode has been most prevalent in the child's background.

Since there are few test norms for deaf children, each child becomes his or her own comparison group. Test results may be considered more reliable if they are similar to those previously obtained using the same instruments. Differences may occur because of a change in rate of progress, alternative tests, and/or modifications in test format, communication method, examiners, etc. Problems in replication of findings occur when standardization was violated, but not reported.

Several general rules can be made about test selection and their administration with HI children.

1. Recognize that tests and techniques that are invalid for hearing bilingual and/or bicultural children are invalid even when communication is apparently facilitated for the HI. For example, non-verbal tests such as human-figure drawings are unidimensional, poor predictors of school success, and culture bound in any population.

2. Check the norms. Some tests such as the Leiter are recommended for use with HI children but were not standardized on this population.

3. Select a test with a sufficient age range so that already tenuous test scores need not be extrapolated up or down.

4. Choose a test that can be validly communicated. Oral tests such as the Stanford-Binet or the Slosson are always inappropriate because they are language oriented.

5. Know that deaf students often take tests designed for younger students. For example, although the Stanford Achievement Test has normative data for all ages of youngsters, high-school aged students may continue to require a primary level test since their reading level may be at a second or third grade level.

6. Use multiple measures on the same dimension as a reliability check.

7. Schedule several short evaluation periods instead of one marathon testing session. Fatigue and communication problems of both the examiner and children lengthen evaluation time and reduce reliability.

8. Avoid the tendency to conduct extraneous conversations in front of the HI children. Many youngsters can pick up on comments that they supposedly cannot hear.

9. Recognize that hearing impairments are not a unitary disorder with performance differences primarily dependent on severity of loss. Charts that correlate magnitude of loss with language, academic and/or social skills are more applicable to the group than to the individual child.

The available tests and norms may not be the most useful or appropriate means of evaluating HI children, particularly the younger pupils. Critical to educational planning is an understanding of how information is learned, processed, sequenced, conserved, and manipulated. Hence, criterion referenced instruments such as the Brigance tests, Piagetian tasks, and a test-teach-test paradigm provide more relevant information. Although the Binet, itself, and other instruments are inappropriate, they contain a treasure of manipulatives. Criterion-referenced testing and behavioral observations are invaluable indicators of the child's skills and abilities, approach to problem-solving, ease in grasping task demands, need for reassurance, and quality of responses.

BEST PRACTICES

Establishing rapport and providing a conducive test environment are both essential aspects of the evaluation of HI children. It is conventional and polite to greet the children, ask for their names, and inquire as to how they are. Although they may not hear this message, even very young children are familiar with and expect these amenities and are accustomed to replying. However, be ever mindful that polite smiles and nods of the head do not necessarily indicate complete understanding of the message. HI students often reply with pleasant looks and knowing smiles to conceal their inability to communicate adequately. Finally, to prevent the appearance of "attacking," the examiner should refrain from exaggerated mouth movements, large dramatic gestures, and screaming at the children. Try to exhibit as normal a manner as possible.

The children should be seated so that light falls on the work table and their backs should be to any windows in the room. The work area should be cleared of all materials or objects which may be visually distracting to the children.

If a hearing aid is typically used, the examiner should check to insure that it is worn during the evaluation and is in working order. Aids that are dutifully worn but whose batteries are not operating might as well be left at home. Feedback or noise from the aid may indicate a need to postpone testing. Students of elementary age and older should be sufficiently familiar with the care and maintenance of their aids and know if it is not working properly. Non-functioning aids should be repaired before proceeding with the testing session. If prescribed, corrective eyewear should also be worn.

The psychological evaluation is an interactive process between examiner and child. Even with the HI child, it is necessary to establish a communication link. Although the child's speech is intelligible to the teacher, it may be very alien to the examiner. Thus, it is necessary to encourage speech to informally assess language skills and determine the amount of mutual understanding between the psychologist and the child. The psychologist should listen to the child in order to develop a sensitivity to the youngster's particular articulation style. Many HI children are very self-conscious about their speech and may give only minimal oral responses. Through the initial use of parallel play activities, the examiner may be able to "break the ice" and establish rapport as well as provide a vehicle for eliciting speech.

Always consider the use of an interpreter who is certified through the Registry of Interpreters for the Deaf when the student has a severe to profound loss. If professional interpreters are not available, the next best choice may be the child's teacher. Using members of the child's family is not recommended because their presence may inhibit the child's performance rather than improve it. Children may become preoccupied with whether their performance is pleasing the family member. The interpreter should sit beside and slightly behind the examiner. The interpreter's purpose is to help convey the psychologist's message to the student and vice versa, not to supercede or subvert the examiner-child relationship.

The examiner should address the student in short declarative sentences and avoid abstract words, clauses, lengthy, involved speeches, and fill-in-the-blank questions. Repeat the verbatim question or statement only once. If the child does not understand, it will be necessary to rephrase the message. Being attuned to the child's facial and body language can aid in understanding the response. Add demonstrations or visual clues when possible.

Increasing difficulty in comprehension can be an indicator of fatigue. When the tasks become more complex and the child indicates an increased need for repetitions, a break in testing may be helpful. If the child appears to become bored, tired, restless, or begins to handle his aid, it is time to stop (Levine, 1976).

Academic tasks provide a good starting point for the formal assessment. Since HI children are familiar with school-related activities, they will readily understand the task demand and feel most comfortable. If the children are able to read, they should be asked to read from their textbooks. This provides the examiner with another opportunity to compare the children's speech to a known stimulus. Deaf children read at the peak of their language competence, i.e. unlike other handicapped youngsters, deaf children's reading is not based on a broader foundation of spoken language (Levine, 1981). They should be expected to read below their grade placement. Indeed, at 16 years, only about 10% of the HI have 5th grade or better reading skills and have

generally shown less than a year's progress in the last four to five years (Mindel & Vernon, 1971). Trybus and Karchmer (1977) report that nationally only 10%, at the most, of HI 18 year olds can read at or above the eighth grade level. In fact, the average 18 to 20 year old deaf student reads at about the fourth grade level (Moores, 1982; Trybus & Karchmer, 1977; Furth, 1973). Thirty percent of deaf adults are considered to be illiterates (Vernon, 1969b). Direction for the children's remediation and identification of the student's academic strengths and weaknesses are best provided by criterion-referenced tests such as those which accompany a reading series.

Hearing impaired children perform best in technical scholastic areas such as spelling and arithmetic computation (Moores, 1982). Nevertheless, deaf students are generally three to five years behind their hearing peers academically (Levine, 1981; Moores, 1982; Skyer, 1982; Furth, 1966). Children with lesser degrees of loss are also expected to be behind grade placement, but with variable skill levels across subject areas. Although some HI children are also considered to be learning disabled, it is not uncommon to find severe discrepancies in "normal" HI children. A learning disability is more likely a factor to be considered if the etiology of the hearing impairment is also known to be linked with brain damage. Mentally retarded HI children are severely deficient across all academic areas and are lacking in most adaptive behavior skills. Gifted HI children share the zeal, enthusiasm, curiosity, and sense of humor that non-HI gifted youngsters display but they perform at grade level or only slightly above academically. These students should score in the above average or better range of measured intelligence on a non-verbal test (Whiting, Anderson, & Ward, 1980).

The assessment of the intellectual abilities of Hi children has a long history.

In the earlier part of this century, Pintner and others devised tests to assess the ability of the HI. Interest waned until the advent of PL 94-142 with its emphasis on appropriateness of evaluation instruments and non-discriminatory assessment practices. The presence of a hearing impairment has historically been linked with a lack of abstract thought and even mental retardation. However, research has indicated that the HI population demonstrates a normal range of intelligence (Vernon, 1968; Moores, 1982). Although thought patterns may be different, abstract thinking is present (Vernon, 1968; Furth, 1966).

In the evaluation of hearing students, verbal test results are considered to be the best predictor of academic success in general education (Furth, 1973). However, verbal test scores are, at best, of dubious reliability with deaf students. Most results are confounded by the variables of language and communication. Non-verbal activities are the preferred choice for the assessment of cognitive abilities (Vernon, 1967; Furth, 1973). Non-verbal tests do present the same difficulty in prediction with the HI as with the hearing. They may actually be less valid because of the lack of appropriate norms, the use of language in directions, and the problems of communication between the examiner and the child. If a student earns a low score, no specific conclusions can be drawn. If the child's performance indicates a high level of attainment, it may actually reflect an underestimation of the child's ability.

The following suggestions are made for use of standardized intelligence tests with the HI.

1. Test directions should be modified and repeated as needed.

2. Total communication results in higher test scores than either pantomime or visual displays (Sullivan & Vernon, 1979). In other words, any mode of communication that contributes to the child's understanding of the task demand should be used including pantomime, eye contact, natural gestures, demonstration, and writing.

3. Modify subtest order as needed by mixing boring and/or difficult subtests with easier and/or interesting ones (Levine, 1976).

4. Be cautious of the extent to which stop watches or timing devices distract the HI child from the task.

5. Use a test-teach-test format and report the number, kind, and difficulty of modifying a task for successful performance.

6. Encourage genuine effort but be cautious not to overly praise successes. It is important not to give the impression that the examiner is satisfied only with complete success or is surprised by the HI child's skill. Again, HI children understand through facial and body gestures without overdramatization.

7. Although conventional, norm-referenced tests are used, standardization will be broken. Scores, when reported, should be followed by an explanation of any modifications or breaks from standardization. Subsequent examiners will have a frame of reference for comparison of results because the child becomes his or her own reference group. Using conventional tests as criterion-referenced tools is a more productive way for teachers and professionals to translate the child's performance into classroom remediation.

The Wechsler is the intelligence test most frequently used in the assessment of school-aged HI children (Levine, 1976). Norms for deaf children (Anderson & Sisco, 1977) and suggestions for adapting the test are available (Ray & Ulissi, 1982).

Assessment of the psychosocial development of HI youngsters presents some very basic problems. The children do differ in communication styles but might approach normal age expectations in adaptive behaviors such as self help skills. On the other hand, while physically a part of the hearing world, HI children respond to an altered environment (Levine, 1981). The students typically look bright and eager because their handicap is virtually invisible. However, they may be confronted by an unreasonable parental expectation to meet the demands of the hearing society around them. Or, conversely, parental restraints and protectiveness resulting from their struggle to resolve their own guilt or fears may inhibit the children from maximizing their adaptive potential.

In addition to the confusing signals the children receive from their parents and other significant persons in their surroundings, the adaptive efforts of HI children may be impeded by the presence of somewhat aberrant behaviors. These behaviors may reflect the children's frustrations related to ineffective attempts to make their wants and feelings known or to fully understand the events in their environment. The behaviors may possibly indicate significant emotional difficulties. The literature is replete with articles describing the HI as maladjusted or emotionally disturbed (Schlesinger & Meadow, 1972; Vernon, 1969b; Jensema & Trybus, 1975). Descriptors commonly associated with deaf students include egocentricity, immaturity, dependency, impulsivity, irritability, and inattentiveness (Schlesinger & Meadow, 1972; Vernon, 1969b).

The psycho-social evaluation of the HI children should center around their behaviors at home and at school. The actions of these children may often signify poor management and/or inappropriate expectations and understanding by people around them rather than indicate individual pathology. Observations of the children and their interactions with adults and peers provide the best evaluation of their adjustment. If a HI child does not establish and/or maintain satisfactory peer relations, then there is an increased likelihood of a classifiable behavior disorder.

It is appropriate to use behavior rating scales and adaptive behavior inventories. The results must be evaluated in light of the children's opportunities to acquire the requisite skills, with close scrutiny of all possible intervening variables. Specific deficits may relate primarily to the adult's inability to communicate the adaptive standard to the child. Individual pathology or a massive breakdown in management are indicated by comprehensive deficient performances.

Verbal tests such as the Rorschach and incomplete sentence form tests are totally inappropriate for HI students, unless the examiner possesses a fluent command of the child's particular communication modality. Projective techniques provide only screening information about HI children. This information can be obtained more readily and more reliably through direct observtion and the use of checklists.

It should be remembered that variable test performance is the rule rather than the exception for HI children. Multiple instruments of the same construct, observations, and prior evaluation information provide a "check and balance" system for current findings. Impressions of the classroom teacher and members of the multidisciplinary assessment team are also resources for evaluating the validity of assessment findings. Parents, although providing invaluable information, may be more subjective in their views.

SUMMARY

Although the majority of school psychologists providing services to HI students lack training specific to the implications of dysfunctional auditory input, a basic knowledge of the dynamics of deafness coupled with a keen perception can provide a foundation for making appropriate decisions regarding the ongoing needs of the hearing impaired child. The psychologist should also be willing to refer hearing impaired students for further evaluation by professionals with expertise in the field of deafness.

The use of a multidisciplinary view of the HI student and input regarding all aspects of the child's environment can provide the necessary information for making quality professional judgments regarding the most appropriate types of programs and habilitative services to meet the child's unique educational and psycho-social needs.

REFERENCES

Anderson, R. J., & Sisco, F. H. (1977). *Standardization of the WISC-R*. Series T, Number 1, Washington, DC: Gallaudet Collete, Office of Demographic Studies.

Boughman, J. A., & Shaver, K. A. (1982). Genetic aspects of deafness: Understanding the counseling process. *American Annals of the Deaf, 127,* 393-400.

Bragman, R. (1982). Review of research on test instruments for deaf children. *American Annals of the Deaf, 127,* 337-346.

Caccamise, F., Meath-Lang, B., & Johnson, D. (1981). Assessment and use of vision: Critical needs of hearing-impaired students. *American Annals of the Deaf, 126,* 361-369.

Cantor, D. W., & Spragins, A. (1977). Delivery of psychological services to the hearing impaired child in the elementary school. *American Annals of the Deaf, 122,* 330-336.

Demographic profile of hearing impaired students. (1977-78). Washington, DC: Gallaudet College, Office of Demographic Studies.

Furth, H. (1966). *Thinking without language: Psychological implications of deafness.* New York: Free Press.

Furth, H. (1973). *Deafness and learning: A psychological approach.* Belmont, CA: Wadsworth.

Gallaudet College. (1980). *Directions: Assessment of hearing impaired youth: Update on academic, professional, career & research activities, 1*(4).

Garrison, W. M., & Tesch, S. (1978). Self concept and deafness, a review of research literature. *Volta Review, 80,* 457-466.

Gerweck, S., & Ysseldyke, J. E. (1975). Limitations of current psychological practices for the intellectual assessment of the hearing impaired: A response to the Levine study. *Volta Review, 77,* 243-248.

Jensema, C. J., Karchmer, M. A., & Trybus, R. J. (1978). *The rated speech intelligibility of hearing impaired children: Basic relationships and a detailed analysis.* Series R., No. 6, Washington, DC: Gallaudet College, Office of Demographic Studies.

Jensema, C. J., & Mullins, J. (1974). Onset cause and additional handicaps in hearing impaired children. *American Annals of the Deaf, 119,* 701-705.

Jensema, C. J., & Trybus, R. J. (1975). *Reported emotional/behavioral problems among hearing impaired children in special education programs: United States, 1972-73.* Series R., No. 1, Washington, DC: Gallaudet College, Office of Demographic Studies.

Jensema, C. J., & Trybus, R. J. (1978). *Communication patterns and educational achievement of hearing impaired students.* Series T., No. 2, Washington, DC: Gallaudet College, Office of Demographic Studies.

Karchmer, M. A., Milone, M. N., Jr., & Wolk, S. (1979). Educational significance of hearing loss at three levels of severity. *American Annals of the Deaf, 124,* 97-108.

Levine, E. S. (1960). *The psychology of deafness: Techniques of appraisal for rehabilitation.* New York: Columbia University Press.

Levine, E. S. (1963). Studies in psychological evaluation of the deaf. *Volta Review, 65,* 496-511.

Levine, E. S. (1971). Mental assessment of the deaf child. *Volta Review, 73,* 80-105.

Levine, E. S. (1974). Psychological tests and practices with the deaf. *Volta Review, 76,* 298-319.

Levine, E. S. (1976). Psychoeducational determinants in personality development. *Volta Review, 78,* 258-267.

Levine, E. S. (1981). *The ecology of early deafness: Guides for fashioning environments and psychological assessments.* New York: Columbia University Press.

Liben, L. S. (Ed.) (1978). *Deaf children: Developmental perspectives.* New York: Academic Press.

McQuaid, M. F., & Alovisetti, M. (1981). School psychological services for hearing impaired children in the New York and New England area. *American Annals of the Deaf, 126,* 37-42.

Mindel, E., & Vernon, M. (1971). *They grow in silence: The deaf child and his family.* Silver Springs, MD: National Association of the Deaf.

Moores, D. (1982). *Educating the deaf: Psychology, principles and practices.* 2nd ed. Boston, MA: Houghton-Mifflin.

Norden, K. (1981). Learning processes and personality development in deaf children. *American Annals of the Deaf, 126,* 404-410.

Ray, S., & Ulissi, S. (1982). *An adaptation of the "Wechsler Preschool and Primary Scale of Intelligence" for deaf children.* Natchitoches, LA: Northwestern State University.

Reichman, J., & Healey, H. C. (1983). Learning disabilities and conductive hearing loss involving otitis media. *Journal of Learning Disabilities, 16,* 272-278.

Sachs, B. (1977). *Psychological assessment of the deaf person: Mental health in deafness.* Washington, DC: U.S. Government Printing Office

Salvia, J., & Ysseldyke, J. (1981). *Assessment in special and remedial education.* 2nd ed. Boston, MA: Houghton-Mifflin.

Schein, D., & Delk, M. (1974). *The deaf population of the United States.* Silver Springs, MD: National Association of the Deaf.

Schildroth, A. (1980). Public residential schools for deaf students in the United States, 1970-1978. *American Annals of the Deaf, 125,* 80-91.

Schlesinger, H., & Meadow, K. (1972). *Sound & sign: Childhood deafness and mental health.* Berkeley CA: University of California Press.

Shepard, N. T., Gorga, M. T., Davis, J. M., & Stelmachowicz, P. G. (1981). Characteristics of hearing impaired children in the public schools. *Journal of Speech & Hearing Disorders, 46,* 123-137.

Skyer, S. C. (1982). Psycho-social aspects of deafness course as a counseling tool for the hearing impaired. *American Annals of the Deaf, 127,* 349-355.

Spragins, A. (1980). Psychological assessment of the school-aged hearing impaired child. In Milliken, R., & Evans, M. (Eds.), *Assessment of children with low incidence handicaps.* National Association of School Psychologists (pp. 58-66).

Spragins, A., & Cokely, D. (1980). Assisting communication skills. Gallaudet College: *Directions: Assessment of Hearing Impaired Youth: Update on Academic, Professional Career & Research Activities.*

Sullivan, P. M. (1982). Administration modifications on the WISC-R performance scale with different categories of deaf children. *American Annals of the Deaf, 127,* 780-788.

Sullivan, P. U., & Vernon, M. (1979). Psychological assessment of hearing impaired children. *The School Psychology Digest, 8,* 271-290.

Trybus, R. J. & Karchmer, M. (1977). School achievement scores of hearing impaired children: National data on achievement status and growth patterns. *American Annals of the Deaf, 122,* 62-69.

Vernon, M. (1967). Guide for the psychological evaluation of deaf and severely hard of hearing adults. *The Deaf American, 19,* 15-18.

Vernon, M. (1968). Fifty years research or the intelligence of deaf and hard of hearing children. *Journal of Rehabilitation of the Def, 1,* 1-12.

Vernon, M. (1969a). *Multi-handicapped deaf children: Medical, educational and psychological considerations.* Washington, DC: Council for Exceptional Children.

Vernon, M. (1969b). Sociological and psychological factors associated with hearing loss. *Journal of Speech and Hearing Research, 12,* 541-563.

Vernon, M., Boughman, J., & Annala, L. (1982). Considerations in diagnosing Usher's syndrome: R. P. and hearing loss. *Visual Impairment and Blindness, 76,* 258-261.

Vernon, M., & Koh, S. D. (1970). Effects of manual communication on deaf children's educational achievement, linguistic competence, oral skills, and psychological adjustment. *American Annals of the Deaf, 115,* 527-536.

Whiting, S. A., Anderson, L., & Ward, J. (1980). Identification of the mentally gifted minor deaf child in the public school system. *American Annals of the Deaf, 125,* 27-33.

ANNOTATED BIBLIOGRAPHY

Gallaudet College. 1980. *Directions: Assessment of Hearing Impaired Youth. Update on Academic, Professional, Career and Research Activities.*
This publication contains an overview of appropriate procedures for classroom assess-

ment and audiological, vocational, medical, psychological, and educational evaluations. Additionally, it has a chapter on the use of criterion-referenced tests that are appropriate for regular education and special education settings. This is one publication in a fine quarterly series produced by Gallaudet.

Schlesinger, H. S., & Meadow, K. P. 1972. *Sound and Sign: Childhood Deafness and Mental Health.* Berkeley: University of California Press.
This book discusses child development, manual communication and family and mental health issues in childhood deafness. It considers deafness in light of Erikson's developmental theory and investigates problems of childrearing such as toilet training and safety. *Sound and Sign* is a very practical contribution to understanding the young deaf child.

Moores, D. 1982. *Educating the Deaf: Psychology, Principles, and Practices.* 2nd ed. Boston: Houghton Mifflin.
This book presents very basic overview of hearing impairments and issues related to deafness. It is a good beginning in learning about hearing impairments, etiology of deafness, historical trends in education of deaf children, family relationships, etc. This briefly tells the reader "everything they ever wanted to know about deafness" — almost.

Liben, L. S. (Ed.) (1978). *Deaf Children: Developmental Perspectives.* New York: Academic Press.
This is an intermediate level book on deafness that includes a brief discussion of terminology, information, etiology, etc. It has four major divisions: Introduction, Linguistic Issues, Social Development and Educational and Cultural Contexts. Each division includes several chapters on some aspect of the larger topic. Liben's book contains contributions by the 'experts' in deafness.

Levine, E. S. (Ed.) 1981. *The Ecology of Early Deafness: Guide to Fashioning Environments and Psychological Assessments.* New York: Columbia University Press.
This book contains the best discussion of the impact of deafness on child development, personality, intelligence, and education. Her perspective is that deaf children are normal youngsters who are forced to adapt to an atypical environment. It includes "examination guides" for the psychological assessment of deaf persons of all ages. If you have any background in deafness and can buy only one book in the area, Levine is strongly recommended.

BEST PRACTICES IN IMPROVING SCHOOL CLIMATE

Milton Wilson
California State Department of Education

OVERVIEW

Since the earliest days of the profession, school psychologists have been aware of the effects of school climate on student behavior and the need to do something about it. In May, 1950, Dr. Eli Bower made the following statement in a keynote address at the first annual conference of the California Association of School Psychologists:

"Schools are beginning to recognize the need for meeting emotional needs of children and preventing malformed personalities. Prevention of emotional maladjustment in children is our biggest frontier. With an increased emphasis on total personality and the emotional life of children, prevention of distorted, unhealthy personalities can be more readily accomplished. When schools can purge themselves of practices aiding or causing pupil maladjustment and can make education a positive, constructive experience for all children, our biggest frontier will have been crossed." (Bower, 1950).

Definitions of School Climate

School climate is defined as those qualities of the school that affect how people feel while they are there. These qualities affect everyone — students, teachers, staff, administrators, parents, visitors, and school psychologists. They include such positive factors as respect, trust, morale, opportunities, input, growth, cohesiveness, renewal, and caring.

School climate is also defined as those factors in school life that influence behavior. These include: how people work together to solve problems or make decisions about how the school operates; how authority and status are distributed; the degree to which students feel they belong; how rules are stated, understood, and enforced; the formal curriculum and style of instruction; how personal problems are handled; relationships with parents and the community; and the appearance, organization, and use of the buildings and grounds.

Characteristics of Good School Climate

Schools with positive climate are places where even low-achieving students are respected. Teachers treat pupils as persons, and parents are seen as important partners. Teachers of one subject area or grade level respect those from others, and teachers are proud to be teachers.

In most schools with good climates, students feel that teachers are "on their side," and people share their concerns openly with each other even though they don't always agree. The principal represents the needs and interests of the school to the superintendent and school board. Students count on teachers to listen and be fair, and teachers trust students to use good judgment.

Positive-climate schools have students who are enthusiastic about learning and miss school only for good reasons, teachers who are proud of their school and its students, parents who rise to defend the school's program, and people who like working there.

In most schools with positive climate, important decisions are made by a governing council representing students, teach-

[485]

ers, administrators, and staff. People feel their ideas are heard and used. Before important program decisions are made, people hear about them and are involved in some of the discussion. People feel they have input into most decisions and that they "really count."

Background

Serious study of school environment began in the early 1950s. It was based primarily on research in business and industrial psychology. Charles F. Kettering and others developed methods to improve school climate using specialized sociometric surveys and needs assessment instruments.

In recent years there has been renewed interest at state, regional, and local levels in improving classroom learning environments. Many current practices are reminiscent of the earlier movements to promote positive mental health in students as noted in the 1950 quotation.

Case Studies of Schools with Positive Climates

School officials are discovering that as school climate improves, academic achievement improves. Many symptoms of student alienation diminish as well. Following are brief summaries of the results of climate improvement efforts in three schools. These case studies are representative of hundreds that could be presented.

Cleveland High School, Seattle. Cleveland High School is the smallest high school in Seattle. Before the improvement began, the school was noted for its racial tension, cliques, and gangs among its seven major ethnic groups. There was a high incidence of violence and discipline problems. School spirit was low at athletic events, especially football games; the football team had won only three games

in seven years! The absentee rate was 35%; the dropout rate was 40%. Academic achievement was low, and the failure rate was high.

Under the leadership of the principal, the school staff initiated an improvement project that included several interventions: Ethnic groups were recognized through spotlight performances and an International Day. A simplified discipline code was developed and active learning in most courses increased. Alternative grading systems were established to eliminate failing grades. New courses were offered in parenting, problem-solving, outdoor education, and careers. "School pride" activities were provided with high student involvement. These resulted in a student information center, projects to improve the school facilities, bulletin boards to recognize student accomplishments, and murals.

After the program was implemented fights between students were eliminated and discipline problems decreased sharply. Security officers were transferred to other schools where their services were in greater demand. School athletic teams began to win more games. Student requests to transfer to Cleveland High School increased. Attendance rose from 65% to 94% and use of the library increased 30%. Student achievement scores increased considerably.

Carmody Junior High School, Jefferson County, Colorado. Before the school climate improvement program started, achievement test results were low, the number of failing grades was high, and there was vandalism and graffiti, plus a high incidence of discipline referrals, absenteeism, and tardiness.

The school staff initiated a creative combination of various improvement activities which included an extensive in-school staff development project, frequent observation of classes, immediate feedback and teacher dialogue, school-wide emphasis on positive reinforcement methods, and extensive student involvement.

As a result of this program, the percentage of 8th grade students achieving at or above grade level increased in all eight areas measured by the Comprehensive Tests of Basic Skills. The number of failing grades decreased 75%, although standards and expectations were raised. Discipline referrals decreased 90% and incidents of vandalism and graffiti declined. Rates of absenteeism and tardiness were greatly reduced.

Eisenhower Middle School, Carlsbad, New Mexico. Carlsbad is a small city in southern New Mexico. Eisenhower School, which serves a large number of low-income Spanish-speaking families, was a pilot school for a state-wide improvement project that grew to include 23 schools. Before the project began, the school was characterized by low staff morale, graffiti, vandalism, truancy, absenteeism, a high percentage of failing grades, few students on the Honor Roll, and low academic achievement.

Using practices described in this chapter, the school staff formed two task forces — one to focus on the school plant and one to provide more varied learning environments. They redesigned the playground, renovated the school building, painted murals, established flexible activity periods, involved parents, set up new interdepartmental classes, expanded staff inservice training, and strengthened student advisor programs.

After one year, staff morale improved, graffiti and vandalism were reduced, the truancy rate decreased by 70%, attendance improved, the percentage of students receiving low grades was reduced, the number of students on the Honor Roll increased by 142%, and the students in the new programs showed documented academic gains.

How to Use this Chapter

The purpose of this chapter is to outline ways in which school psychologists can contribute to the improvement of the entire school program. Without a great deal of extra time and effort, they can help bring about many indirect benefits to students, including better achievement, improved behavior, greater attendance, higher self-esteem, more positive attitudes, greater self-discipline, and increased motivation.

This chapter presents basic ideas for consideration, describes best practices that have been used successfully to improve school climate and school discipline, and challenges school psychologists to become involved as a catalyst for school climate improvement. It is hoped that school psychologists will apply the information to help schools exhibiting characteristics of a negative climate to develop more positive indications of a good one.

BASIC CONSIDERATIONS

Leaders in the field of school climate improvement noted that schools with positive climates are characterized by beliefs, values, policies, procedures, rules, and regulations that are people-centered. They are "student-advocates." Their major goal is to help students grow and develop. On the other hand, schools with negative climates tend to be more institution-centered. They are "system-advocates." The major mission of these schools is to tell people what to do (Howard, 1981).

There are several reasons why school psychologists should become involved in the improvement of school climate: The professional background of the school psychologists makes that person ideally suited for this endeavor. No additional training or experience is required. No equipment is needed other than the basic action research skills that school psychologists already possess.

Many psychologists consider the task of improving school climate an exhilarating challenge, but find the odds against their planting a student-centered oasis in the middle of a system-centered desert to be too overwhelming. All that is needed to become involved in school climate improvement — aside from unbridled enthusiasm — is some basic information about available resources, effective program approaches, successful assessment methods, related materials, and some step-by-step approaches. This information is provided in the following section.

BEST PRACTICES

Many approaches to the improvement of school climate have been successful. There is no single "best" practice. Each individual can choose from several models or psychologists can design their own based upon the needs of their schools or their own interests. School psychologists can be as flexible as they want in the choice of areas to assess, factors to emphasize, and what to do with the results.

This section focuses on two general approaches that combine many of the best practices in improving school climate. One emphasizes school climate in general; the other focuses on school discipline.

Emphasis on School Climate

Program. One of the best improvement programs available is described in detail in the booklet *School Climate Improvement: A Challenge for the School*

Administrator, published by Phi Delta Kappa (1974). This handbook discusses the climate of the school, the improvement process, school climate leadership, selected activities, a school profile, climate determinants, developing indicators for the school, and why to do it.

Assessment Method. The assessment method used in this program is based on the *CFK Ltd. School Climate Profile,* developed by the Kettering Foundation. This profile can be used by students, teachers, parents, administrators, secretaries, custodians, and other staff members. It consists of four parts — General Climate Factors, Program Determinants, Process Determinants, and Material Determinants. On each part, the respondent compares his or her perception of *what is* with *what should be,* using a four-point frequency rating ranging from "almost never" to "almost always." There are five items to rate under each factor or determinant.

The eight General Climate Factors include such areas as trust, morale, cohesiveness, and caring. The description of schools with a positive climate previously cited are based on these profile factors. The seven Program Determinants focus on expectations, varied environments, support and structure appropriate to the learner, and rewards. The eight Process Determinants assess school goals, conflict management, decision-making, and effective teaching strategies, among others. The three Material factors are limited to resources, logistics, and the school plant.

The data provided by this profile can be analyzed in many interesting ways. Directions are included for summarizing the results and plotting the scores.

Most of the factors comprising this assessment form are closely related to the traditional functions of the school psychologist — improving services to students, to parents, to teachers, to administrators, and to the community.

Additional Materials. The Charles F.

Kettering Foundation was reorganized in 1974 and renamed CADRE — the Collegial Association for the Development and Renewal of Educators. CADRE members are involved in identifying elements of school climate, providing inservice training, and developing publications to improve interpersonal skills, classroom discipline, and school climate in general. In addition to publications, CADRE offers a research and bibliography service that provides condensed abstracts and reference lists rarely mentioned in other information retrieval systems.

Another useful publication is *Something More Than Survival*. This booklet is the outcome of a special project developed in Contra Costa County, California. Based on the assessment instruments of CFK and CADRE, the project involved students, teachers, and parents of five high schools.

Process. One of the best ways to use the CFK and CADRE materials is the eight-step process developed in Colorado by Eugene Howard (1981). His process has been used successfully by many schools in various states. This same approach may be adapted for use with other materials and assessment instruments. The following is a summary of his eight-step process.

Step 1. Form a School Climate Improvement Committee (SCIC). A committee is formed at the school to manage the program and provide leadership and support for specific task forces. A school psychologist could form the SCIC.

Step 2. Collect baseline data. General data are collected to answer two basic questions: (a) to what extent does the school now have a positive or negative climate? (b) what symptoms of a negative climate are most apparent in the school?

Step 3. Raise the awareness level of the faculty, students, and parents. The faculty, staff, students, and parents are provided with information on the importance of school climate, the improvement

process, and the rationale for starting an improvement project.

Step 4. Assess the school's climate. An assessment instrument is used that identifies strong and weak determinants and suggests improvement activities, programs, and projects that could have a positive impact on the school's climate.

Step 5. Brainstorm and prioritize. At a special workshop organized for this purpose, the information collected is shared. The school staff, parents, and student leaders brainstorm ideas for improving the school's climate. The group then chooses from one to five high-priority areas for future emphasis.

Step 6. Form task forces. The SCIC forms from one to five task forces, each related to one of the climate determinants (for example, "Active Learning") selected for emphasis. Each task force is given the charge to initiate appropriate activities, projects, and programs designed to make a positive impact in that area of school life.

Step 7. Manage the task forces. The SCIC and school principal support and facilitate the efforts of each task force. The task force leaders report regularly on their progress to the SCIC, principal, faculty, and key student and parent organizations and groups.

Step 8. Evaluate the results. The SCIC collects, interprets, and reports the data on the extent to which the school's climate has been improved and the changes in symptoms of a negative environment. Instruments and procedures are the same as those used in Step 2 to collect baseline data.

According to Howard, "Evidence is accumulating that as the climate of a school improves many symptoms of alienation tend to disappear. We now know how to measure climate, how to change it, and how to report what happens. Our school improvement efforts can now be focused on the causes rather than the

symptoms of student and staff alienation."
(p. 6, 1981)

In 1981 the Association for Supervision and Curriculum Development published a staff development kit which contains all the instruments, materials, and instructions necessary for implementing this eight-step process in a school.

Focus on School Discipline

Program. A highly effective approach to school climate improvement is presented in another Phi Delta Kappa publication, the *Handbook for Developing Schools with Good Discipline* (1982). This program is based on the research of the PDK Commission on Discipline. The PDK *Handbook* suggests that these two sentences be engraved on the wall of every teachers' lounge, administrator's office, and teacher-education classroom:

DISCIPLINE IS LEARNED.
BEHAVIOR IS CAUSED.

School psychologists know that when students misbehave, the misbehavior is caused. If students are expected to behave appropriately, ways must be found for them to learn the new behavior. This program emphasizes goal-directed behavior.

The *Handbook* contains a wealth of research data and information on the characteristics of well-disciplined schools. Goals and specific activities for improving school discipline are included as well as details on how to get a school started on an improvement program.

Assessment Method. The instrument featured in the PDK *Handbook* is Wayson's *Discipline Context Inventory* (1979). Despite its title, this survey is a comprehensive device for measuring positive school climate. It is based on the eight factors in school life that influence behavior noted earlier. Developed by William

Wayson in 1977, this *Inventory* outlines the major components in a system for improving school climate, based on research into the causes of desirable and undesirable student behavior.

Wayson's research indicated that in schools with positive climates, conditions and practices cause students to behave properly and to accept responsibility even when no one makes them do it. He also found that many common school practices cause much undesirable behavior.

Through the use of this *Inventory*, many school staffs have consciously changed their school climate and taught students self-discipline and responsibility. As Wayson points out:

These eight factors make up the living curriculum of the school; they convey to everyone in the school "how we behave around here." They show how an individual fits into the school every minute of the day, how he or she will be rewarded, and how to behave to receive those rewards. Improving discipline in a school can best be achieved by examining these eight factors and by acting to make them cause the behavior desired. (1979)

This *Inventory* is neither a "score card" nor an objective test. It is a working guide for use by school personnel, students, and parents to analyze programs and to identify problem areas on which they wish to work to reduce disruption and to improve discipline in their schools. A copy of the entire *Discipline Context Inventory* is included in the PDK *Handbook.*

Additional Materials. Current literature abounds with publications designed to improve student discipline. One of the most useful is the American Association of School Administrators report on *Student Discipline: Problems and Solutions.*

Process. The *Inventory* is designed to identify school problems and establish goals for solving them. The *Handbook* suggests the following procedure, which can be adopted to suit individual needs.

Step 1. Start with one area. The psychologist selects one of the eight factors on the survey on which to rate the school. This is best accomplished by having the entire staff rank the eight areas according to which one needs the most attention, or which one they would most like to see improved by their own efforts.

Step 2. Involve the staff from the beginning. Before any formal meetings, the *Inventory* is discussed and ideas for needed improvements are obtained from the faculty. Input is requested on major causes of school problems, such as high suspension rates, low test scores, or classroom disruption.

Step 3. Call a special meeting. One staff meeting is devoted entirely to a review of one of the eight sections of the survey. No attempt is made to deal with the entire *Inventory* at once. The staff could be overwhelmed if they are bombarded with too much data.

Step 4. Divide into groups. The staff is organized into small groups, which represent factions of the staff. Groups may represent departments, status levels, grade levels, racial and ethnic groups, and men and women. Customary procedures are used. Groups are arranged into circles to facilitate direct eye contact and communication.

Step 5. Pass out materials. Each group is provided with such materials as sheets of chart paper, marking pens, and tape.

Step 6. Get individual ratings. Each person is asked to rate the school on all of the items in the section selected on the *Inventory*. This rating could be done beforehand, at the start of the meeting, or at this time. Each rating is made individually, with no discussion from the group.

Step 7. Discuss the rationale. The group reads together and discusses the purpose of the survey. The leader makes sure that everyone understands the next steps and why they are doing them. Each member is given a chance to clarify ideas and express any disagreements. Everyone is encouraged to participate in the discussion.

Step 8. Have small group discussions. Each small group is asked to discuss their individual ratings. Then they each list on a chart the three or four items that have the highest positive ratings and the three or four that have the lowest ratings (negative climate) in the group.

Step 9. Compile a school list. The whole staff reviews the group charts showing the strongest and weakest items, as rated. From these, a list is developed of the items that need the most attention from the whole school. These items are selected through consensus, not by a majority vote.

Step 10. Classify the items. Using the school list from Step 9, each person is asked to classify each item into one of three categories, as follows: (a) items they think they cannot do anything about; (b) items they do not want to do anything about; and (c) items they think they *can* do something about and *want* to do something about.

Step 11. Assign committees. First, the items classified as category (a) or (b) are discarded. Then, using only the items in category (c), committees are assigned to work on one item each, with the intention of improving that area. Each committee is asked to prepare a work plan to submit to the next meeting, showing what will be done, who will do it, and when. A useful resource for participants is the PDK *Handbook*, which lists 8 goals, 70 related objectives, and 124 suggested activities for developing a well-disciplined school.

Step 12. Report on progress. Each committee reports on their progress at each faculty or special meeting. The leader continues to offer suggestions and help as they go along, and discusses each group's progress informally between meetings.

Following these suggestions, using these materials, and adopting this process to suit individual needs usually produces good results.

SUMMARY

School climate is defined as the qualities of school life that affect how people feel while they are there, or the factors in school life that influence behavior. They affect everyone. There is a renewed interest in enhancing the positive aspects of the learning environment. Many schools have shown great improvement as a result of these programs. School psychologists are ideally suited to act as leaders in school climate improvement. The best practices are readily available at very little cost. Efforts usually involve interesting surveys and involvement of students, parents, and staff. This program gives the school psychologist a chance to engage in some preventive rather than remedial activities, to contribute to the entire school program, and to help bring about better student achievement, behavior, self-esteem, attendance, discipline, and motivation.

REFERENCES

Bower, E. (1950). *Proceeedings of the Annual Conference of the California Association of School Psychologists and Psychometrists.* p. 15.

Fox, R. et. al. (1974). *School Climate Improvement: A Challenge for the School Administrator.* Bloomington: Phi Delta Kappa.

Howard, E. (1981). School Climate Improvement-Rationale and Process. *Illinois School Research and Development,* Illinois Association for Supervision and Curriculum Development, p. 2.

Phi Delta Kappa. (1982). *Handbook for Developing Schools with Good Discipline.* Bloomington: Phi Delta Kappa.

ANNOTATED BIBLIOGRAPHY

American Association of School Administrators. *Student Discipline: Problems and Solutions.* Critical Issues Report Series. Arlington, Virginia: AASA, 1980.
This timely publication is the result of a nationwide survey of 2000 school administrators. It offers valuable advice on discipline policies, codes of conduct, control measures, and more. Order from AASA, 1801 No. Moore St., Arlington, VA 22209. Price: $10.95 plus $1.50 postage.

Collegial Association for the Development and Renewal of Educators (CADRE). *Publications for Improving School Climate.* Tulsa, Oklahoma: CADRE, 1984.
This brochure describes current CADRE publications on such topics as discipline problems, parents' rights, secondary school programs, evaluation, implementation, and self-assessment, as well as a practitioner's guide, an annotated bibliography, and two adaptations of the CFK *School Climate Profile.* A complete set of fourteen publications is available at a cost of about $102 (1984 prices). Order from CADRE, College of Education, 600 South College, University of Tulsa, OK 74104.

Fox, Robert and others. *Something More Than Survival.* Walnut Creek, California: Center for Human Development, 1978.
This handbook describes in detail the complete process for initiating a school improvement program in an individual school, including chapters on making plans, bringing people together, training volunteers, conducting the survey, preparing reports, sharing results, and reviewing resources. It comes with a packet of printed materials to reproduce, with the necessary forms, flyers, and survey instruments. These materials are available from the Center for Human Development, 1852 Bonanza Street, Walnut Creek, CA 94596.

Howard, Eugene R. *Improving School Climate: A Total Staff Development Kit.* Alexandria, Virginia: Association for Supervision and Curriculum Development, 1981.
This kit includes three sound filmstrips, two mini-audits (one-day surveys), and a leader's guide. Materials include directions for preparing a school-wide climate improvement plan. Order from ASCD, 225 N. Washington St., Alexandria, VA 22314. Price: $95 for ASCD members, $125 for nonmembers.

BEST PRACTICES FOR IMPROVING SCHOOL PSYCHOLOGY THROUGH ACCOUNTABILITY

Joseph E. Zins[1]
University of Cincinnati

OVERVIEW

In a move designed to save the taxpayers of the Chestnut Hills Public Schools over twenty thousand dollars each year, the Board of Education last night voted not to renew the contracts of the district's three school psychologists. The decision followed a lengthy debate on the issue with the Board finally deciding that they could contract for the same services at a lower cost from Behavioral Consultants, a group of private practice psychologists.

Superintendent Dr. Mary Reynolds noted that the Board had accepted her recommendation regarding the lay-offs "with regret." She added, "We all feel saddened by the decision that had to be made. I know the school psychologists personally, and I regret the hardship that this action will cause for them and their families. Nevertheless, in the interest of fiscal responsibility, the district had no other choice. The people from Behavioral Consultants have assured me that they can provide the same services, that is, testing for special education placements, as our staff. Moreover, they can administer these tests for a much lower cost per student."

Preposterous you say? Well, look around. An increasing number of our colleagues are being replaced by contractual services. Others are being layed-off as the enrollments in their districts shrink. Some are having their contracts cut from eleven months to nine. These changes are occurring in Illinois, in Oregon, in Pennsylvania, in West Virginia, in New Jersey, and elsewhere. But it can't happen to me you say. Or can it?

While the above scenario is fictitious, the events depicted are taking place throughout the country. Therefore, one purpose of this chapter is to share ideas which will minimize the possibility of the scenario occurring. In addition, and of far greater importance, it is hoped that the ideas presented will lead to an increase in the quality of services provided by school psychologists.

Furthermore, the chapter is intended to encourage school psychologists to institute accountability procedures into their practice and to provide practical suggestions and ideas regarding how accountability data are obtained and used. A framework for determining the most appropriate method to collect the data is presented, and finally, references and sources of additional information are provided.

BASIC CONSIDERATIONS

Why Be Accountable?

The public is relatively uninformed about how their tax dollars are spent in the schools. A common image of school personnel is that they are overpaid and inefficient. "They only work nine months and are off every day at three!" In addition, recent national reports on the quality of education, such as *A Nation at*

Risk and *The Paideia Proposal*, have been catalysts for an increased interest in accountability in all aspects of education. Proposition 13 in California and Proposition 2.5 in Massachusetts significantly reduced taxes and thus funds available to state agencies including schools. The passage of taxpayer proposals such as these gives a clear message to all school personnel. We cannot expect the public's opinion about education to change until relevant data are provided. As part of the educational system, school psychologists must be concerned with documenting the effectiveness of their services.

There are many reasons why school psychologists have chosen to incorporate accountability procedures into their practice. These include: (a) clarifying school psychology program strengths and needs and suggesting areas of modification; (b) determining the impact of services through the assessment of outcome variables; (c) obtaining information regarding consumer satisfaction; (d) aiding in professional development; (e) determining patterns of use of services and indicating possible changes in staff assignments; and (f) charting progress toward goals (Curtis & Zins, in press; Zins & Curtis, 1984). Other reasons include demonstrating the importance or diversity of psychological services to consumers and promoting the development and refinement of the profession (Fairchild, Zins, & Grimes, 1983).

Accountability: What is It?

In this chapter, the term *accountability* is broadly defined as an

evaluative effort designed to gather systematically information relevant to the performance assessment of school psychologists. It enables them to demon-strate the effectiveness of their services to others, and it provides an evaluation of how well they have met their performance objectives. It is concerned with both quantitative and qualitative aspects of practice and addresses both individuals and groups. It is particularly useful in improving service delivery and in enhancing professional development. (Zins, 1984, p. 58)

In the next few pages, salient aspects of this definition are discussed.

First, accountability refers to *systematic* efforts to obtain information. We need a well-thought out plan of action for gathering these data rather than using a haphazard approach or hastily collecting evaluative data when our jobs are in jeopardy. Both formative and summative information are helpful. Too often, we only think of evaluating our services at the end of the year. By that time, it is too late to make changes in the way we provide services. However, if we periodically evaluate our efforts, we have more opportunity to make any necessary alterations and increase the probability of providing quality services.

Second, information should be collected about *specific* areas of performance rather than more global and general activities. For example, instead of asking, "Is the psychologist a good consultant?" it may be more helpful to obtain information about how s/he listens, clarifies problems, establishes a collaborative rather than authoritarian relationship, expresses interest, and helps to identify useful resources. Likewise, questions which elicit "yes/no" responses are typically not as helpful as are open-ended ones or those using a rating scale.

The related issues of *quantity* and *quality* of services deserve particular attention. Many of us routinely obtain quantitative data about our performance. We keep logs of when referrals are received and completed and can therefore determine average amounts of time it takes to complete a case. From a log we also can determine how many assessments were completed during the month or year. While quantitative information certainly is important with respect to accountability, it does not address qualitative aspects of service.

Qualitative information is obtained to document the outcomes of and consumer satisfaction with psychological services. Questions which are answered include not only what or how much was done, but also how effective and efficient the service was. Examples include asking parents how well the psychologist communicated with them or assessing how effective an intervention was.

The focus of the above examples is on obtaining qualitative information that has implications for the practice of school psychology. The central issue is the "need for the development and recognition of performance standards...that reflect the attachment of greater value to the *effectiveness* of services than is typically the case when performance is judged almost exclusively by the numbers of cases processed (commonly found in the individual child study model)" (Curtis & Zins, 1981, p. 291). Both quantitative *and* qualitative data are important and they complement one another.

Another aspect of accountability is that school psychologists need to be assertive and proactive regarding such efforts for the results to be meaningful and of help in improving services. Too often, we are subjected to performance evaluations which are not relevant to our work. For example, many districts have two formal, well-developed, comprehensive, behaviorally-oriented evaluation systems: one for administrators and one for teachers. However, as is readily apparent, neither of these systems specifically pertains to school psychologists. Compound-

ing this observation is the fact that the school psychologist's supervisor is frequently neither a school psychologist nor someone with sufficient knowledge about the field. As a result, the information obtained from such evaluations frequently is irrelevant to school psychology practice and of little value in improving effectiveness (Zins, 1984). Therefore, it is imperative that school psychologists regularly establish accountability procedures themselves to obtain useful data and to avoid inappropriate evaluations. Taking a proactive rather than a reactive stance helps insure the usefulness of performance evaluations.

CURRENT PRACTICES

Several surveys have been conducted to collect data about the accountability practices of school psychologists. The NASP Accountability Subcommittee of the Professional Standards and Employment Relations Committee contacted the presidents of each state school psychology organization requesting that they submit three examples of accountability procedures or instruments being used in their state (Zins, Grimes, Illback, Barnett, Ponti, McEvoy, & Wright, 1982). Responses were received from 30 states. Forty percent of the respondents indicated that they were unaware of accountability efforts in their states.

Another survey was conducted of state consultants or contact persons for school psychology to determine whether accountability data were collected systematically on a state level (Guthrie, 1982). A total of 34 (68%) responses were obtained, with only seven states indicating that they collected accountability data. All seven reported obtaining quantitative information such as the number of special education evaluations and placements completed. Two states indicated that they also obtained qualitative data, four collected service plans, and one a detailed job description.

doing so. These included inadequate knowledge of accountability techniques, lack of administrative sanction, and limited time and personnel.

Table 1.

Accountability Dimensions and Approaches

Consumers
 Students
 Teachers
 Administrators
 Parents

Services
 Consultation
 Assessment
 Intervention
 Program Planning and Evaluation
 Research
 Supervision

Measures of Effectiveness
 Enumerative
 Process
 Outcome

Recently, Zins and Fairchild (1984) conducted a national survey to determine the accountability practices of individual school psychologists. They found that approximately 40% of the respondents were not collecting accountability data.

In each of these surveys, a large number of the respondents indicated that they thought that the collection of accountability data was important and noted that they were interested in obtaining further information on the topic. Several persons indicated that while they desired to obtain these data, there were constraints which prevented them from

BEST PRACTICES

Obtaining Accountability Data

In discussing how accountability data are collected, several dimensions are relevant and should be considered. These dimensions include: (a) the consumers who are recipients of the services, (b) the types of services which school psychologists deliver, and (c) how effectiveness is measured (Fairchild et al., 1983).

Consumers. We provide services to a wide range of consumer populations including students, teachers, administrators, and parents. Each of these groups is a potential source of evaluative data which we should consider. In addition, school psychology colleagues can provide helpful feedback through a "peer review process" as they often have first-hand knowledge of our performance.

Services. A second aspect of accountability to consider is the various services which we provide. School psychological services typically include consultation, assessment, counseling, program planning, inservice training, research, and so forth. We can collect accountability information about any or all of these.

However, for accountability data to be representative and valid, they should be obtained both from several consumer groups and in relation to different services. Our performance may vary with different clients or from one service to another. For example, we may work well with students but not as effectively with teachers, or we may be skilled researchers but not as strong in consultation. A later section of the chapter discusses a process for determining specific populations and services to address.

Measures of Effectiveness. Numerous strategies are used to measure effectiveness depending upon the practitioner's and the consumers' needs and the particular services being addressed. These include enumerative, process, and outcome (Fairchild et al., 1983). Most approaches to measuring effectiveness in accountability are included within these general categories.

Enumerative or accounting data include information about how many times an activity was performed, the percent of time spent on a task, or efficiency in completing a job. The number of students counseled or consultation sessions held are examples. This information may be related to efficiency of practice. We determine the amount of time it takes between a referral being made and when it is acted upon. Likewise, calculating the amount of time spent in travel, direct service, administrative duties, and so forth, is helpful in structuring the work day, or in determining staffing requirements for secretarial support or geographic assignment. We may learn that inordinate amounts of time are spent providing direct services with little devoted to prevention and health promotion (e.g., Zins, Wagner, & Maher, in press).

Enumerative information frequently is gathered through a daily log. Many practitioners code service activities in various categories so that the data are easily analyzed by computer and monthly activity reports provided to each school psychologist as well as to supervisory personnel.

A second method of measuring effectiveness is to gather *process* data. In this approach, we are concerned with the effectiveness and/or quality of services rather than focusing on quantity issues. Attitudinal information about how well

the psychologist performed her/his job is usually included in this category. Such information is obtained through questionnaires or rating scales which are given to consumers. Does the psychologist respect the opinions of parents? Are the psychologist's recommendations realistic? Explained in an understandable manner, free of jargon? These instruments usually are constructed so that feedback is solicited on several services at one time. The relative ease in obtaining such information as well as its potential usefulness and validity account for the popularity of these accountability procedures.

Outcome or product data measure effectiveness by ascertaining whether actual behavioral change occurred as a result of an intervention. An example is deciding whether the use of a contingency contract which was developed during consultation was related to an increase in the completion of homework assignments. In this case, data are obtained regarding actual behavior change. Such information is obviously much more difficult and cumbersome to collect, but it is also extremely powerful. With most interventions, however, it is usually difficult to determine actual cause and effect relationships.

Since outcome approaches are potentially valuable and less frequently implemented than other procedures, two more detailed examples follow. The first was used in the state of Iowa by school psychologists as part of the *Psychologist's Data Management System* (PDMS) developed by the Department of Public Instruction (Grimes & Ross-Reynolds, 1981). The authors have outlined these procedures in considerable detail in the reference cited. The major components are shown in Table 2. Among them are: (a) specification of the target behavior; (b) procedures for measuring the behavior; (c) direction of the behavior change; (d) baseline level; (e) anticipated criterion level; (f) intervention

Table 2. Psychologist's Data Management System

	Whose Behavior	Direction of Change	Entry Level	Criterion Level	Imple- mentor	Inter- vention Method		Case Review Date
Behavior —————— Measurement ———								 Yr. Mo.
Behavior —————— Measurement ———								 Yr. Mo.

Note. From "Some thoughts on writing psychological interventions" by J. Grimes and G. Ross-Reynolds, 1981, unpublished manuscript, Iowa Department of Public Instruction. Adapted by permission.

method or procedures; and (g) case review date. A coding system for numerous categories facilitates the entry of information into the PDMS. By collecting such data, the psychologist not only insures that a well-thought out and developed plan is designed, but also the PDMS is helpful in organizing intervention efforts. Use of this system provides the psychologist with a relatively efficient method for monitoring the effectiveness of interventions. Since the information on the plan is organized to facilitate entry into a computer, summary information is available and reminders of review dates to encourage and facilitate follow-up are provided automatically. The system has been widely adopted throughout he state and it is one of the few "state-wide" accountability programs.

Another example of an outcome approach to performance evaluation is *Goal Attainment Scaling* (GAS) (Kiresuk & Lund, 1977; Kiresuk & Sherman, 1968). While this method has been widely discussed in the community mental health literature, it virtually has been ignored in school psychology, particularly with regard to accountability. GAS is a system for identifying problems of a student (client), assigning weights to those problems in terms of their importance, estimating the goals or expected outcomes for each problem, and collecting follow-up information (scores) on outcomes in each area. An attempt is made to predict outcomes (goals) or levels of attainment for each problem according to a five point scale. Points on the scale range from "much less than the expected level of outcome" to "much more than the expected level of outcome." As stated by the authors, the expected level focuses on what is *most likely* to occur rather than on what would be most desirable, and an emphasis is placed on making the goals realistic.

GAS has potential utility as a method to use in school psychology accountability. It could help in establishing realistic goals for intervention plans and in determining the effectiveness of various procedures.

Issues in the Selection of Accountability Procedures

There are numerous instruments, procedures, and systems used in assessing the performance of school psychologists, although there is no *single* best method. Furthermore, it is unrealistic to expect school psychologists to incorporate *all* of the dimensions discussed above in their accountability program. Therefore, a systematic procedure for selecting and developing an accountability program is presented in this section. Portions of this discussion are adapted from Fairchild et al. (1983) and Zins (1984).

In developing an accountability program, it is not necessary to operate in isolation. After obtaining sanction from the employing organization to implement the procedures, professional colleagues are helpful in determining techniques and areas to be addressed. Supervisors and the district may have specific informational needs which should be addressed in the evaluation procedures. By working collaboratively with supervisory personnel, psychologists take an active role in the development of performance standards which are appropriate and meaningful. Thus, there is less chance of being evaluated solely with instruments and procedures developed for teachers or other non-psychologist personnel.

Although there are many accountability instruments (see Zins et al., 1982), these are usually modified to meet local needs. There also are other areas of service in which instruments are unavailable. In such instances, the advantages of working with school psychology colleagues to develop relevant procedures is evident.

A logical place to start in determining accountability procedures is the job description. Unfortunately, many psychologists do not have job descriptions or have very brief, limited ones that do not fully describe the vast array of services which they provide. One is expected to meet the performance standards described in the job description; however, not all areas in the job description are evaluated at once. To select appropriate areas for evaluation and the approaches to use, it is suggested that a problem solving approach be used. The approach is based on the premise that "effective accountability practices can be enhanced through the use of the behavioral problem-solving approach" (Zins, 1984, p. 59). Extensive discussions of the problem-solving approach are contained elsewhere (Comtois & Clark, 1976; D'Zurilla & Goldfried, 1971; Goldfried & Davison, 1976; Maher, 1981).

Table 3 contains a brief outline of the problem-solving stages which are followed. Rather than discrete events, they are interrelated in that what happens at one stage influences what occurs at subsequent points in the process.

Problem Definition and Formulation

One reason why many school psychologists do not implement accountabil-

Table 3.

Stages in Problem Solving

Problem Definition and Formulation

Generation of Alternatives

Decision-Making

Implementation and Outcome Evaluation

Dissemination of Results

Meta-Evaluation

ity procedures is because they do not know where to begin. However, to develop an effective accountability program, goals must be clearly identified. Meeting the information needs of the district is, of course, important. Examination of the job description is an additional way of clarifying and prioritizing activities to assess.

Generation of Alternatives

Once the area(s) to be assessed have been identified, one determines the procedures to follow in the evaluation. Possible dimensions to consider were discussed earlier. Input from a broad sample of consumers and our school psychology colleagues, as well as data about a number of different services, are obtained. In addition, information is collected at several points during the year.

Whether to use enumerative, process, or outcome methods must be determined. Depending upon individual needs, some combination is probably most appropriate

as each provides valuable information.

Of particular assistance in generating alternatives and in decision-making is the list of accountability references contained in the *Improving School Psychology Through Accountability* (Fairchild et al., 1983) package. These are categorized according to the type of information which is discussed, that is, by consumer respondent(s) including administrators, teachers, parents, students, school psychologists and by type of data collected such as enumerative, process, and outcome. By reviewing some of these articles, ideas about possible approaches may be generated.

Decision-Making

If the reasons for collecting accountability data and the specific areas of focus have been thoroughly clarified in the Problem Definition and Formulation stage, decision-making is greatly facilitated. Each potential approach to collecting accountability data has advantages and limitations which are carefully weighed before a decision is made. The methods vary in terms of time, expense, personnel requirements, ease of obtaining the information, and potential personal or interpersonal effects of implementing the plan.

Implementation and Outcome Evaluation

After the decisions regarding procedures to use are made, the accountability plan is implemented. If unmanageable problems emerge, it is necessary to alter the procedures or return to an earlier point in the problem solving process to reformulate the plan. During implementation it is important to evaluate systematically if the accountability procedures are meeting information needs and then to determine implications for practice. Alterations in practice may be suggested by the results, or consumers may indicate satisfaction with current approaches. For example, a school psychologist may learn that teachers do not believe that the findings from evaluations are communicated in a reasonable amount of time. Or, one may find that parents highly value services. It is important to remember that *one cannot be successful in every case. Our goal is to establish a winning percentage* (Grimes, 1983).

Dissemination of Results

Once the data have been collected and analyzed, decisions are made regarding dissemination. "Marketing strategies" are used to increase consumers' acceptance of school psychological services and to demonstrate the importance of the services. Benefits of school psychological services are shared with consumers and educational decision-makers (Fairchild et al., 1983; Zins, 1981; Zins & Curtis, 1984; Zins & Hopkins, 1981). Unless such information is disseminated, much of its value is lost. The time has come to stop telling consumers that school psychological services are important; the need to *demonstrate* their importance has arrived.

Meta-Evaluation

After the evaluation process has been completed, the school psychologist reviews the events which have taken place. A determination is made about the effectiveness of the evaluation process, and whether it was worth its expense in terms of the resources required. If the results are merely "interesting," perhaps the reasons for conducting the performance evaluation were not clarified in the problem identification phase.

If self-evaluation and professional development are to become important components of our job, then an examination of the accountability process is very valuable. Thus, one's approach to self-assessment can be improved in a systematic manner.

SUMMARY

Gathering accountability data is a wasted effort unless the results are used to improve services. The scenario presented at the beginning of this chapter provides a good context for examining our use of accountability information. It implied that the school psychologists who were about to lose their jobs only engaged in assessment activities. This perception may be accurate or it may reflect a misconception of the psychologists' role. However, had the psychologists obtained accountability information and shared it with appropriate persons, the scenario may have been different.

Not only can accountability data be used to *inform* consumers of the services which are provided by school psychologists, but they can also be helpful in *expanding* practitioner roles or the amount of psychological services requested by schools. The data can be used to demonstrate that psychological services are *valued* by consumers. Furthermore, the information may indicate that consumers *benefitted* from the services in terms of solving problems and professional growth (e.g., Zins, 1981).

It is clear that accountability efforts must become an essential component of practice for all school psychologists. Furthermore, effective accountability programs are established on a proactive basis. They are responsive to consumer and practitioner needs, and they are carefully planned and initiated. The slogan of the Olympia Conference on the Future of School Psychology was, "School Psychology can make a difference in the future." Through the effective implementation and use of accountability procedures, this motto can be expanded and practically realized: School psychologists can also *demonstrate* that they make a difference!

REFERENCES

Bennett, R. E. (1980). Methods for evaluating the performance of school psychologists. *School Psychology Monograph, 4,* 45-59.

Carter, R. K. (1983). *The accountable agency.* Beverly Hills, CA: Sage.

Comtois, R. J., & Clark, W. D. (1976). A framework for scientific practice and practitioner training. JSAS *Catalog of Selected Documents in Psychology, 6,* 74. (Ms. No. 1301)

Curtis, M. J., & Zins, J. E. (Ed.). (1981). *The theory and practice of school consultation.* Springfield, IL: Charles C Thomas.

Curtis, M. J., & Zins, J. E. (in press). The organization and structure of school psychological services. In S. N. Elliott & J. C. Witt (Eds.), *The delivery of psychological services in schools: Concepts, processes, and issues.* Hillsdale, NJ: Erlbaum.

D'Zurilla, T. J., & Goldfried, M. R. (1971). Problem solving and behavior modification. *Journal of Abnormal Psychology, 78,* 107-126.

Fairchild, T. N., Zins, J. E., & Grimes, J. (1983). *Improving school psychology through accountability* (filmstrip and booklet). Washington, DC: National Association of School Psychologists.

Goldfried, M. R., & Davison, G. C. (1976). *Clinical behavior therapy.* New York: Holt, Rinehart & Winston.

Grimes, J. (1983, February). *Improving school psychology through accountability.* Presentation at the Ohio Department of Education School Psychology Intern Conference, Columbus, OH.

Grimes, J., & Ross-Reynolds, G. (1981). *Some thoughts on writing psychological interventions.* Unpublished manuscript, Iowa Department of Public Instruction.

Guthrie, P. (1982). *Survey of state consultants regarding accountability practices.* Unpublished report, National Association of School Psychologists.

Kiresuk, T. J., & Lund, S. H. (1977). Goal attainment scaling: Research, evaluation, and utilization. In H. C. Schulberg & F. Baker (Eds.), *Program evaluation in the health fields* (Vol. 2, pp. 214-237). New York: Human Sciences Press.

Kiresuk, T. J., & Sherman, R. E. (1968). Goal attainment scaling: A general method for evaluating comprehensive community mental health programs. *Community Mental Health Journal, 4,* 443-453.

Maher, C. A. (1981). Program evaluation and school psychology: Perspectives, principles, procedures. *School Psychology Monograph, 4,* 1-24.

Zins, J. E. (1981). Using data-based evaluation in developing school consultation services. In M. J. Curtis & J. E. Zins (Eds.), *The theory and practice of school consultation* (pp. 261-268). Springfield, IL: Charles C Thomas.

Zins, J. E. (1984). A scientific problem-solving approach to developing accountability procedures for school psychologists. *Professional Psychology: Research and Practice, 15,* 56-66.

Zins, J. E., & Curtis, M. J. (1984). Building consultation into the educational service delivery system. In C. A. Maher, R. J. Illback, & J. E. Zins (Eds.), *Organizational psychology in the schools: A handbook for professionals* (pp. 213-242). Springfield, IL: Charles C Thomas.

Zins, J. E., & Fairchild, T. N. (1984, August). *Accountability practices of school psychologists: A national survey.* Paper presented at the annual meeting of the American Psychological Association, Toronto, Ontario.

Zins, J. E., Grimes, J., Illback, R. J., Barnett, D. W., Ponti, C. R., McEvoy, M. L., & Wright, C. V. (1982). *Accountability for school psychologists: Developing trends.* Washington, DC: National Association of School Psychologists.

Zins, J. E., & Hopkins, R. A. (1981). Referring out: Increasing the number of kept appointments. *School Psychology Review, 10,* 107-111.

Zins, J. E., Wagner, D. I., & Maher, C. A. (Eds.). (in press). *Health promotion in schools: Innovative approaches to facilitating physical and emotional well-being.* New York: Haworth Press.

ANNOTATED BIBLIOGRAPHY

Improving School Psychology Through Accountability.
This unique package of printed and visual media was developed by T. N. Fairchild, J. E. Zins, and J. Grimes to stimulate discussion about accountability and to provide direction for school psychologists regarding specific procedures. It is suitable for use in inservice training as well as for university classes. It contains:

(1) Filmstrip and Cassette Tape: IMPROVING SCHOOL PSYCHOLOGY THROUGH ACCOUNTABILITY (color, 80 frames, 25 minutes)

(2) Booklet to accompany filmstrip (contains suggestions for use, tape narrative, and accompanying bibliography; 27 pages)

(3) Booklet: ACCOUNTABILITY FOR SCHOOL PSYCHOLOGISTS: DEVELOPING TRENDS (contains examples of accountability instruments and a bibliography; 100 pages) Available from: NASP Publications, 10 Overland Drive, Stratford, CT 06497

Planning and Evaluating Special Education Services.

This book, written by C. A. Maher and R. E. Bennett (1984), presents a comprehensive overview of how to evaluate a wide range of service delivery programs for exceptional children and youth. It encompasses all special education programs — assessment, instruction, related services, staff development, and administration. The practical methods and procedures described encourage a systematic, data-based approach to decision-making for each program area. Available from: Prentice-hall, Inc., Englewood Cliffs, NJ 07632

Accountability for School Psychologists: Selected Readings.

This informative book was edited by T. N. Fairchild (1977). It is the only book on accountability specifically for school psychologists. It contains a number of original and reprinted articles which provide practical suggestions and helpful examples of accountability efforts. Available from: University Press of America, Washington, DC

Professional practice standards of the National Association of School Psychologists and the American Psychological Association also make reference to accountability issues.

National Association of School Psychologists. (1984). *Standards for the provision of school psychological services.* Washington, DC: Author.

American Psychological Association. (1981). Specialty guidelines for the provision of services by school psychologists. *American Psychologist, 36,* 670-681. Available from: The NASP and APA organizations.

―――――――――
[1]Appreciation is extended to Charlene R. Ponti for her helpful comments on an earlier draft of this chapter.

Appendix I

NATIONAL ASSOCIATION OF SCHOOL PSYCHOLOGISTS
STANDARDS FOR THE PROVISION OF SCHOOL PSYCHOLOGICAL SERVICES

Approved April, 1984

1.0 Definitions

1.1 A *School Psychologist* is a professional psychologist who has met all requirements for credentialing as stipulated in the appropriate NASP standards. The credential is based upon the completion of a school psychology training program which meets the criteria specified in the NASP *Standards for Training and Field Placement Programs in School Psychology.*

1.2 A *Supervising School Psychologist* is a professional psychologist who has met all NASP requirements for credentialing, has completed three years of successful supervised experience as a school psychologist, and who has been designated by an employing agency as a supervisor responsible for school psychological services in the agency.

1.3 *Parent(s)*, as used in these *Standards*, include both biological parent(s) and/or legal guardian(s).

2.0 Standards for Administrative Agencies

The purpose of this section of the standards is to provide guidance to federal and state administrative agencies in regard to administrative organization, possible legal issues, and regulations as they pertain to the provision of school psychological services.

2.1 Federal Level Administrative Agency

2.1.1 Organization

The federal education agency should employ a supervising school psychologist in order to accomplish the following objectives:

2.1.1.1 To provide professional leadership and assistance to the federal education agencies, and the school psychology profession in regard to standards, policies, and procedures for program delivery, and for utilization, funding, education and training, and inservice education of school psychological services personnel.

2.1.1.2 To participate in the administration of federal programs providing funding for school psychological services in state, intermediate, and local education agencies, and for the eduction and training of school psychologists.

2.1.1.3 To encourage and assist in evaluation, research, and dissemination activities; to determine the effectiveness of school psychological education, training, and service programs; to determine needed changes; and to identify and communicate exemplary practices to training and service units.

2.1.1.4 To assure that consistent communication is established and maintained among professional organizations, federal, state, and local education agencies, and university training programs involved in providing and developing school psychlogical services.

2.1.2 Laws

2.1.2.1 The Congress of the United States should ensure that the rights of all parents and children are protected by the creation and modification of laws which provide for the services of school psychologists. These services include, but are not limited to, consultation, assessment, and intervention for individuals, groups, and systems. These services are. available to all children, their families, and school personnel.

2.1.2.2 The Congress should ensure that school psychological services are provided in a free and appropriate manner to all children, their families, and school personnel in need of such services.

2.1.2.3 The Congress should ensure that federal laws recognize the appropriate involvement of school psychologists in educational programs and that adequate federal funding is made available for the education, training, services, and continuing professional development of school psychologists in order to guarantee appropriate and effective services.

2 1.2.4 The Congress should create no laws which effectively prohibit the credentialed school psychologist from the ethical and legal practice of his/her profession in the public or private sector, or which would be in violation of these standards.

2.1.3 Regulations

2.1.3.1 All federal agencies should utilize the services of the federal educational agency school psychologist in developing and implementing regulations pursuant to all relevant federal laws.

2.1.3.2 All federal agencies should seek the advice and consultation of the National Association of School Psychologists prior to the adoption of regulations pursuant to any federal law which involves or should reasonably involve the profession of school psychology.

2.1.3.3 Federal agencies should promulgate regulations consistent with the principles set forth in these *Standards* and the NASP *Principles for Professional Ethics.*

2.2 State Level Administrative Agencies

2.2.1 Organization

Each state educational agency (SEA) should employ at least one full-time supervising school psychologist for each 500 (or fewer) school psychologists within the state. An equivalent ratio should be maintained if there are more than 500 school psychologists. It is recognized that this ratio may vary based upon administrative structures, available resources, and types of programs served. Appropriate objectives to be accomplished by the SEA school psychologist(s) include the following:

2.2.1.1 To provide professional leadership assistance to the SEA, local educational agencies, and the profession with regard to standards, policies, and procedures for school psychology program delivery.

2.2.1.2 To support the utilization, funding, education, training, and inservice education of school psychologists.

2.2.1.3 To participate in the administration of state and federal programs providing funding for school psychological services in intermediate and local educational agencies, and for the education and training of school psychologists.

2.2.1.4 To encourage and assist in evaluation, research, and dissemination activities to determine the effectiveness of school psychological education, training, and service programs; to determine needed changes; and to identify and communicate exemplary practices to training and service units.

2.2.1.5 To maintain communication with and assure the input of state school psychological associations into the policy making of the SEA.

2.2.1.6 To communicate with the federal education agency school psychologist to ensure recognition of state issues and to facilitate input into federal policy.

2.2.2 Laws

2.2.2.1 All state legislative bodies should ensure that the rights of parents and children are protected by the creation and modification of laws which provide for the services of school psychologists. These services include, but are not limited to, consultation for individuals, groups, and systems, assessment, and intervention. These services are available to all children, their families, and school personnel.

2.2.2.2 The state legislature should ensure that school psychological services are provided in a free and appropriate way to all children, their families, and school personnel in need of such services.

2.2.2.3 The state legislature should ensure that state laws recognize the appropriate involvement of school psychologists in educational programs.

2.2.2.4 The state legislature should ensure that adequate funding is made available for the education, training, services, and continuing professional development of school psychologists in order to guarantee appropriate and effective services.

2.2.2.5 The state legislature should ensure that state laws provide for the credentialing of school psychologists consistent with NASP standards.

2.2.2.6 The state legislature should create no laws which prohibit the school psychologist from the ethical and legal practice of his/her profession in the public or private sector, or that prevent the school psychologist from practicing in a manner consistent with these *Standards.*

2.2.2.7   The state legislature should ensure that there are sufficient numbers of adequately prepared and credentialed school psychologists to provide services consistent with these *Standards.* In most settings, this will require at least one full-time school psychologist for each 1,000 children served by the LEA, with a maximum of four schools served by one school psychologist. It is recognized that this ratio may vary based upon the needs of children served, the type of program served, available resources, distance between schools, and other unique characteristics.

2.2.3   Regulations

2.2.3.1   All state agencies should utilize the services of the SEA school psychologist(s) in developing and implementing administrative rules pursuant to all relevant state laws, federal laws, and regulations.

2.2.3.2   All state agencies should seek the advice and consultation of the state school psychologists' professional association prior to the adoption of rules pursuant to any state law, federal law, or regulation which involves or should reasonably involve the profession of school psychology.

2.2.3.3   All state education agencies should utilize the services of the SEA school psychologist(s) in the SEA review and approval of school psychology training programs.

2.2.3.4   All state education agencies should utilize the services of the SEA school psychologist(s) in developing and implementing administrative rules for credentialing school psychologists. Such rules shall be consistent with NASP *Credentialing Standards.*

2.2.3.5   State education agencies should promulgate regulations consistent with the principles set forth in these *Standards* and the NASP *Principles for Professional Ethics.*

3.0   Standards for Employing Agencies

The purpose of these standards is to provide employing agencies with specific guidance regarding the organization, policies, and practices needed to assure the provision of adequate school psychological services.

3.1   Comprehensive Continuum of Services

Employing agencies assure that school psychological services are provided in a coordinated, organized fashion, and are deployed in a manner which ensures the provision of a comprehensive continuum of services as outlined in Section 4.0 of these *Standards.* Such services are available to all students served by the agency and are available to an extent sufficient to meet the needs of the populations served.

3.2 Professional Evaluation, Supervision, and Development

3.2.1 Supervision

Employing agencies assure that an effective program of supervision and evaluation of school psychological services exists. School psychologists are responsible for the overall development, implementation, and professional supervision of school psychological service programs, and are responsible for articulating those programs to others in the employing agency and to the agency's constituent groups.

3.2.2 Supervisor(s).

The school psychological services program is supervised by a designated school psychologist who meets the requirements for a supervising school psychologist (Section 1.2) and who demonstrates competencies needed for effective supervision.

3.2.3 Availability of Supervision

Supervision is available to all school psychologists to an extent sufficient to ensure the provision of effective and accountable services (see Section 4.6 for specific requirements). In most cases, one supervising school psychologist should be employed for every ten school psychologists to be supervised (an equivalent ratio should be maintained for part-time supervisors). It is recognized that this ratio may vary based upon the type of program served, staff needs, and other unique characteristics.

3.2.4 Intern Supervision.

A credentialed school psychologist meeting the requirements of a supervising school psychologist, with at least one year of experience at the employing agency, supervises no more than two school psychology interns at any given time (consistent with the NASP *Standards for Training and Field Placement Programs in School Psychology*).

3.2.5 Peer Review.

After attaining independent practice status (See Section 4.5), school psychologists continue to receive appropriate supervision. The independent practitioner should also engage in peer review with other school psychologists. Peer review involves mutual assistance with self-examination of services and the development of plans to continue professional growth and development. Employing agencies assure that school psychologists are given appropriate time and support for peer review activities.

3.2.6 Accountability and Program Evaluation.

Employing agencies assure that school psychologists develop a coordinated plan for accountability and evaluation of all services provided in order to maintain and improve the effectiveness of services. Such plans include specific, measurable objectives pertaining to the planned effects of services on all relevant elements of the system. Evaluation and revision of these plans occurs on a regular basis.

3.2.7 Continuing Professional Development.

Employing agencies recognize that school psychologists are obligated to continue their professional training and development through participation in a recognized Continuing Professional Development (CPD) program (see Section 4.6). Employing agencies provide release time and financial support for such activities. They recognize documented continuing professional development activities in the evaluation and advancement of school psychologists. Private practitioners who contract to provide services are responsible for their own CPD program, and these activities should also be encouraged by employing agencies.

3.3 Conditions for Effective Service Delivery

In order to assure that employment conditions enable school psychologists to provide effective services, employing agencies adopt policies and practices ensuring that Sections 3.3.1 through 3.3.4 are met.

3.3.1   School psychologists are not subjected to administrative constraints which prevent them from providing services in full accordance with these *Standards* and the NASP *Principles for Professional Ethics.* When administrative policies conflict with these *Standards* or the NASP *Ethics,* the principles outlined in the *Standards* or *Ethics* take precedence in determining appropriate practices of the school psychologist.

3.3.2   School psychologists have appropriate input into the general policy making of the employing agency and the development of programs affecting the staff, students, and families they serve.

3.3.3   School psychologists have appropriate professional autonomy in determining the nature, extent, and duration of services they provide. Specific activities are defined within the profession, although school psychologists frequently collaborate and seek input from others in determining appropriate service delivery. Legal, ethical, and professional standards and guidelines are considered by the practitioner in making decisions regarding practice (see Section 4.4).

3.3.4   School psychologists have access to adequate clerical assistance, appropriate professional work materials, sufficient office and work space, and general working conditions that enhance the delivery of effective services. Included are test materials, access to a private telephone and office, secretarial services, therapeutic aids, professional literature (books, journals), and so forth.

3.4 Contractual Services

It is recognized that employing agencies may obtain school psychological services on a contractual basis in order to ensure the provision of adequate services to all children. However, each student within the educational system must be assured the full range of school psychological services necessary to maximize his/her success and adjustment in school. When an employing agency utilizes contractual services, the following standards are observed.

3.4.1   Contractual school psychological services encompass the same comprehensive continuum of services as that provided by regularly employed school psychologists. Overall, psychological services are not limited to any specific type of service and include opportunities for follow-up and continuing consultation appropriate to the needs of the student. Individual contracts for services may be limited as long as comprehensive services are provided overall.

3.4.2 Persons providing contractual psychological services are fully credentialed school psychologists as defined by these *Standards.* In specific instances, however, services by psychologists in other specialty areas (e.g., clinical, industrial/organizational) might be used to supplement school psychological services.

3.4.3 Contractual school psychological services are not to be utilized as a means to decrease the amount and quality of school psychological services provided by an employing agency. They may be used to augment programs but not to supplant them.

3.4.4 School psychologists providing contractual services are given appropriate access and information. They are familiar with the instructional resources of the employing agency to ensure that students they serve have the same opportunities as those served by regularly employed school psychologists.

3.4.5 Contractual school psychological services are provided in a manner which protects the due process rights of students and their parents as defined by state and federal laws and regulations.

3.4.6 Contracting for services is not to be used as a means to avoid legitimate employee rights, wages, or fringe benefits.

3.4.7 Psychologists providing contractual school psychological services provide those services in a manner consistent with these *Standards,* NASP *Principles for Professional Ethics,* and other relevant professional guidelines and standards.

3.5 Non-Biased Assessment and Program Planning

Employing agencies should adopt policies and practices in accordance with the following standards:

3.5.1 General Principles

3.5.1.1 School psychologists use assessment techniques to provide information which is helpful in maximizing student achievement and eductional success.

3.5.1.2 School psychologists have autonomous decision-making responsibility (as defined in Section 4.4) to determine the type, nature, and extent of assessment techniques they use in student evaluation.

3.5.1.3 School psychologists have autonomy (as defined in Section 4.4) in determining the content and nature of reports.

3.5.1.4 School psychologists use assessment techniques and instruments which have established validity and reliability for the purpose and populations for which they are intended.

3.5.1.5 School psychologists use, develop, and encourage assessment practices which increase the likelihood of the development of effective educational interventions and follow-up.

3.5.2 Professional Involvement

3.5.2.1 A multidisciplinary team is involved in assessment, program decision-making, and evaluation. The team conducts periodic evaluations of its performance to ensure continued effectiveness.

3.5.2.2 The multidisciplinary team includes a fully trained and certified school psychologist.

3.5.2.3 The school psychologist communicates a minority position to all involved when in disagreement with the multidisciplinary team position.

3.5.3 Non-Biased Assessment Techniques

3.5.3.1 Assessment procedures and program recommendations are chosen to maximize the student's opportunities to be successful in the general culture, while respecting the student's ethnic background.

3.5.3.2 Multifaceted assessment batteries are used which include a focus on the student's strengths.

3.5.3.3 Communications are held in the client's dominant spoken language or alternative communication system. All student information is interpreted in the context of the student's socio-cultural background and the setting in which s/he is functioning.

3.5.3.4 Assessment techniques (including computerized techniques) are used only by personnel professionally trained in their use and in a manner consistent with these *Standards*.

3.5.3.5 School psychologists promote the development of objective, valid, and reliable assessment techniques.

3.5.3.6 Interpretation of assessment results is based upon empirically validated research.

3.5.4 Parent/Student Involvement

3.5.4.1 Informed written consent of parent(s) and/or student (if the student has reached the age of majority) is obtained before assessment and special program implementation.

3.5.4.2 The parent(s) and/or student is fully informed of all essential information considered and its relevancy to decision-making.

3.5.4.3 The parent(s) and/or student is invited to participate in decision-making meetings.

3.5.4.4 The parent(s) and/or student is routinely notified that an advocate can participate in conferences focusing on assessment results and program recommendations.

3.5.4.5 A record of meetings regarding assessment results and program recommendations is available to all directly concerned.

3.5.5 Educational Programming and Follow-Through

3.5.5.1 School psychologists are involved in determining options and revisions of educational programs to ensure that they are adaptive to the needs of students.

3.5.5.2 The contributions of diverse cultural backgrounds should be emphasized in educational programs.

3.5.5.3 School psychologists follow-up on the efficacy of their recommendations.

3.5.5.4 Student needs are given priority in determining educational programs.

3.5.5.5 Specific educational prescriptions result from the assessment team's actions.

3.5.5.6 Where a clear determination of the student's needs does not result from initial assessment, a diagnostic teaching program is offered as part of additional assessment procedures.

3.5.5.7 Regular, systematic review of the student's program is conducted and includes program modifications as necessary.

3.6 School Psychological Records

3.6.1 The employing agency's policy on student records is consistent with state and federal rules and laws, and ensures the protection of the confidentiality of the student and his/her family. The policy specifies the types of data developed by the school psychologist which are classified as school or pupil records.

3.6.2 Parents may inspect and review any personally identifiable data relating to their child which were collected, maintained, or used in his/her evaluation. Although test protocols are part of the student's record, school psychologists protect test security and observe copyright restrictions.

3.6.3 Access to psychological records is restricted to those permitted by law who have legitimate educational interest in the records.

3.6.4 School psychologists interpret school psychological records to nonpsychologists who qualify for access.

3.6.5 School psychological records are only created and maintained when the information is necessary and relevant to legitimate educational program needs and when parents (or student if age of majority has been attained) have given their informed consent for the creation of such a record. This consent is based upon full knowledge of the purposes for which information is sought, and the personnel who will have access to it. The school psychologist assumes responsibility for assuring the accuracy and relevancy of the information recorded.

3.6.6 School psychological records are systematically reviewed, and when necessary purged, in keeping with relevant federal and state laws in order to protect children from decisions based on incorrect, misleading, or out-of-date information.

4.0 Standards for the Delivery of Comprehensive School Psychological Services

The purpose of these standards is to ensure the delivery of comprehensive services by school psychologists.

4.1 Organization of School Psychological Services

4.1.1 School psychological services are planned, organized, directed, and reviewed by school psychologists.

4.1.2 School psychologists participate in determining the recipients and the type of school psychological services offered.

4.1.3 The goals and objectives of school psychological services are available in written form.

4.1.4   A written set of procedural guidelines for the delivery of school psychological services is followed and made available upon request.

4.1.5   A clearly stated referral system is in writing and is communicated to parents, staff members, students, and other referral agents.

4.1.6   The organization of school psychological services is in written form and includes lines of responsibility, supervisory, and administrative relationships.

4.1.7   Where two or more school psychologists are employed, a coordinated system of school psychological services is in effect within that unit.

4.1.8   Units providing school psychological services include sufficient professional and support personnel to achieve their goals and objectives.

4.2   Relationship to Other Units and Professionals

4.2.1   The school psychological services unit is responsive to the needs of the population that it serves. Psychological services are periodically and systematically reviewed to ensure their conformity with the needs of the population served.

4.2.2   School psychologists establish and maintain relationships with other professionals (e.g., pediatricians, bilingual specialists, audiologists) who provide services to children and families. They collaborate with these professionals in prevention, assessment, and intervention efforts as necessary. They also cooperate with advocates representing children and their families.

4.2.3   Providers of school psychological services maintain a cooperative relationship with colleagues and co-workers in the best mutual interests of clients, in a manner consistent with the goals of the employing agency. Conflicts should be resolved in a professional manner.

4.2.4   School psychologists develop plans for the delivery of services in accordance with best professional practices.

4.2.5   School psychologists employed within a school setting coordinate the services of mental health providers from other agencies (such as community mental health centers, child guidance clinics, or private practitioners) to ensure a continuum of services.

4.2.6   School psychologists are knowledgeable about community agencies and resources. They provide liaison and consulting services to the community and agencies regarding psychological, mental health, and educational issues.

4.2.6.1   School psychologists communicate as needed with state and community agencies and professionals (e.g., child guidance clinics, community mental health centers, private practitioners) regarding services for children, families, and school personnel. They refer clients to these agencies and professionals as appropriate.

4.2.6.2   School psychologists are informed of and have the opportunity to participate in community agency staffings of cases involving their clients.

4.2.6.3   Community agency personnel are invited to participate in school system conferences concerning their clients (with written parental permission).

4.3 Comprehensive School Psychological Service Delivery

School psychologists provide a range of services to their clients. These consist of direct and indirect services which require involvement with the entire educational system: (a) the students, teachers, administrators, and other school personnel; (b) the families, surrogate caretakers, and other community and regional agencies, and resources which support the educational process; (c) the organizational, physical, temporal, and curricular variables which play major roles within the system; and (d) a variety of other factors which may be important on an individual basis.

The intent of these services is to promote mental health and facilitate learning. Comprehensive school psychological services are comprised of diverse activities. These activities compliment one another and therefore are most accurately viewed as being integrated and coordinated rather than discrete services. However, for descriptive purposes, they will be listed and described separately. The following are the services that comprise the delivery system.

4.3.1 Consultation

4.3.1.1 School psychologists consult and collaborate with parents, school, and outside personnel regarding mental health, behavioral, and educational concerns.

4.3.1.2 School psychologists design and develop procedures for preventing disorders, promoting mental health and learning, and improving educational systems.

4.3.1.3 School psychologists provide inservice and other skill enhancement activities to school personnel, parents, and others in the community, regarding issues of human learning, development, and behavior.

4.3.1.4 School psychologists develop collaborative relationships with their clients and involve them in the assessment, intervention, and program evaluation procedures.

4.3.2 Psychological and Psychoeducational Assessment

4.3.2.1 School psychologists conduct multifactored psychological and psychoeducational assessments of children and youth as appropriate.

4.3.2.2 Psychological and psychoeducational assessments include consideration as appropriate of the areas of personal-social adjustments, intelligence-scholastic aptitude, adaptive behavior, language and communication skills, academic achievement, sensory and perceptual-motor functioning, environmental-cultural influences, and vocational development, aptitude, and interests.

4.3.2.3 School psychologists utilize formal instruments, procedures, and techniques. Interviews, observations, and behavioral evaluations are included in these procedures.

4.3.2.4 When conducting psychological and psychoeducational assessments, school psychologists have explicit regard for the context and setting in which their assessments take place and will be used.

4.3.2.5   School psychologists adhere to the NASP resolutions regarding non-biased assessment and programming for all students (see Section 3.5.3). They also are familiar with and consider the *Standards for Educational and Psychological Tests* (developed by APA, AERA, and NCME) in the use of assessment techniques.

4.3.3   Intervention

4.3.3.1   School psychologists provide direct and indirect interventions to facilitate the functioning of individuals, groups, and/or organizations.

4.3.3.2   School psychologists design programs to enhance cognitive, affective, social, and vocational development.

4.3.3.3   School psychologists facilitate the delivery of services by assisting those who play major roles in the educational system (i.e., parents, school personnel, community agencies). Such interventions consist of, but are not limited to: inservice training, organiztion development, parent counseling, program planning and evaluation, vocational development, and parent education programs.

4.3.4   Supervision

School psychologists provide and/or engage in supervision and continuing professional development as specified in Sections 3.2 and 4.6.

4.3.5   Research

4.3.5.1   School psychologists design, conduct, report, and utilize the results of research of a psychological and educational nature. All research conducted is in accordance with relevant ethical guidelines of the profession (e.g., APA *Ethical Principles in the Conduct of Research with Human Participants*).

Applied and/or basic research should be pursued, focusing on:

(a) Psychological functioning of human beings;

(b) Psycho-educational Assessment tools and procedures;

(c) Educational programs and techniques applied to individual cases and groups of various sizes;

(d) Educational processes;

(e) Social system interactions and organizational factors associated with school communities; and

(f) Psychological treatments and techniques applied to individual cases or groups.

4.3.5.2   School psychologists' involvement in research can range from support or advisory services to having direct responsibility for one or more major components of a research project. These components may include planning, data collecting, data analyzing, disseminating, and translating research into practical applications within the school community.

4.3.6 Program Planning and Evaluation

4.3.6.1 School psychologists provide program planning and evaluation services to assist in decision-making activities.

4.3.6.2 School psychologists serve on committees responsible for developing and planning educational and educationally-related activities.

4.4 Autonomous Functioning

School psychologists have professional autonomy in determining the nature, scope, and extent of their specific services. These activities are defined within the profession, although school psychologists frequently collaborate with and seek input from others in determining appropriate service delivery. Legal, ethical, and professional standards and guidelines are considered by the practitioner in making decisions regarding practice. All practice is restricted to those areas in which the school psychologist has received formal training and supervised experience.

4.4.1 Professional Responsibility and Best Practices

Professional autonomy is associated with professional responsibility. The ultimate responsibility for providing appropriate comprehensive school psychological services rests with the individual practitioner. While being cognizant of the fact that there often are not explicit guidelines to follow in providing comprehensive school psychological services, the individual practitioner has a responsibility to adhere to the best available and most appropriate standards of practice. There is no substitute for sensitive, sound, professional judgment in the determination of what constitutes best practice. Active involvement in supervision and other continuing professional development activities will assist the practitioner in adhering to best professional practices.

4.5 Independent Practice

A credentialed school psychologist who has completed a school psychology training program which meets the criteria specified in the NASP *Standards for Training and Field Placement Programs in School Psychology* and three years of satisfactory supervised experience is considered qualified for independent practice, regardless of work setting.

4.6 Continuing Professional Development

The practice of school psychology has and will continue to undergo significant changes as new knowledge and technological advances are introduced. The development of new intervention techniques, assessment procedures, computerized assistance, and so forth, will require that practitioners keep abreast of these innovations as well as obtain appropriate professional education and training in these areas. All school psychologists actively participate and engage in activities designed to continue, enhance, and upgrade their professional training and skills and to help ensure quality service provision. These efforts are documented by participation in the NASP or other formal Continuing Professional Development (CPD) programs, although they are not limited to such activities. Memberships in professional organizations, reading of professional journals and books, discussions of professional issues with colleagues, and so forth, are also an integral component of a school psychologist's overall CPD activities.

4.6.1.   Participation in CPD activities and the maintenance of high professional standards and practice are continuing obligations of the school psychologist. These obligations are assumed when one initially engages in the practice of school psychology and should be required for continued credentialing.

4.6.2   School psychologists receive supervision by a supervising school psychologist for the first three years of full-time employment (or the equivalent) as a school psychologist. The supervisor shares professional responsibility and accountability for the services provided. While the level and extent of supervision may vary, the supervisor maintains a sufficiently close relationship to meet this standard. Individual face-to-face supervision is engaged in for a minimum of one hour per week or the equivalent (e.g., two hours bi-weekly). Standards for intern supervision are contained in the NASP *Standards for Training and Field Placement Programs in School Psychology*.

4.6.3   After completion of the first three years of supervision, all school psychologists continue to engage in supervision and/or peer review on a regular basis, and further their professional development by actively participating in CPD activities. The level and extent of these activities may vary depending on the needs, interests, and goals of the school psychologist, with more comprehensive service delivery requiring more extensive related professional exchanges. At a minimum, however, these activities are at the level required for successful participation in an appropriate CPD program.

4.6.4   School psychologists, who after three years no longer have supervision available, engage in peer review activities. These may include discussions of cases and professional issues designed to assist with problem solving, decision-making, and appropriate practice.

4.6.5   School psychologists readily seek additional consultation with supervisors, peers, or colleagues with particularly complex or difficult cases, and/or when expanding their services into new areas or those in which they infrequently practice (e.g., low incidence assessment).

4.7   Accountability

4.7.1   School psychologists perform their duties in an accountable manner by keeping records of these efforts, evaluating their effectiveness, and modifying their practices and/or expanding their services as needed.

4.7.2   School psychologists devise systems of accountability and outcome evaluation which aid in documenting the effectiveness of intervention efforts and other services they provide.

4.7.3   Within their service delivery plan, school psychologists include a regular evaluation of their progress in achieving goals. This evaluation should include considertion of the cost effectiveness of school psychological services in terms of time, money, and resources, as well as the availability of professional and support personnel. Evaluation of the school psychological delivery system is conducted internally, and when possible, externally as well (e.g., through state educational agency review, peer review). This evaluation includes an assessment of effectiveness, efficiency, continuity, availability, and adequacy of services.

4.7.4 School psychologists are accountable for their services. They should make information available about their services, and provide consumers with the opportunity to participate in decision-making concerning such issues as initiation, termination, continuation, modification, and evaluation of their services. Rights of the consumer should be taken into account when performing these activities.

4.8 Private Practice

4.8.1 School psychologists practicing in the private sector provide comprehensive services and adhere to the same standards and guidelines as those providing services in the public sector.

4.8.2 School psychologists document that they have formal training, supervised experience, licensure and/or certification, and demonstrated competence, in any areas of service they intend to deliver to clients within the private sector. They also have a responsibility to actively engage in CPD activities.

4.8.3 School psychologists in private practice adhere to the NASP *Principles for Professional Ethics*, and practice only within their areas of competence. If the services needed by clients fall outside the school psychologist's areas of competence, they are referred elsewhere for assistance.

4.8.4 It is the responsibility of the school psychologist engaging in private practice to inform the client that school psychological services are available without charge from the client's local school district.

4.8.5 School psychologists do not provide services on a private basis to students residing within their employing district who would be eligible to receive the services without charge. This includes students who are attending non-public schools located in the district.

4.8.6 School psychologists offering school psychological services in the private sector ensure that, prior to the commencement of treatment/services, the client fully understands any and all fees associated with the services, and any potential financial assistance that may be available (i.e., third-party reimbursement).

4.8.7 Parents must be informed by the school psychologist that if a private school psychological evaluation is to be completed, this evaluation constitutes only one portion of a multidisciplinary team evaluation. Private services must be equally comprehensive to those described in Section 4.3.

4.8.8 School psychologists in private practice provide and maintain written records in a manner consistent with Section 3.6.

4.9 Professional Ethics and Guidelines

Each chool psychologist practices in full accordance with the NASP *Principles for Professional Ethics*, and these *Standards*.

Appendix II

NATIONAL ASSOCIATION OF SCHOOL PSYCHOLOGISTS
PRINCIPLES FOR PROFESSIONAL ETHICS

Approved April, 1984

I. Introduction

Standards for professional conduct, usually referred to as ethics, recognize the obligation of professional persons to provide services and to conduct themselves so as to place the highest esteem on human rights and individual dignity. A code of ethics is an additional professional technique which seeks to ensure that each person served will receive the highest quality of service. Even though ethical behavior involves interactions between the professional, the person served and employing institutions, responsibility for ethical conduct must rest with the professional.

School psychologists are a specialized segment within a larger group of professional psychologists. The school psychologist works in situations where circumstances may develop which are not clearly dealt with in other ethical guidelines. This possibility is heightened by intense concern for such issues as due process, protection of individual rights, record keeping, accountability and equal access to opportunity.

The most basic ethical principle is that of the responsibility to perform only those services for which that person has acquired a recognized level of competency. Recognition must be made of the uncertainties associated with delivery of psychological services in a situation where rights of the student, the parent, the school and society may conflict.

The intent of these guidelines is to supply clarification which will facilitate the delivery of high quality psychological services in the school or community. Thus they acknowledge the fluid and expanding functions of the school and community. In addition to these ethical standards, there is the ever present necessity to differentiate between legal mandate and ethical responsibility. The school psychologist is urged to become familiar with applicable legal requirements.

The ethical standards in this guide are organized into several sections representing the multifaceted concerns with which school psychologists must deal. The grouping arrangement is a matter of convenience, and principles discussed in one section may also apply to other areas and situations. The school psychologist should consult with other experienced psychologists and seek advice from the appropriate professional organization when a situation is encountered for which there is no clearly indicated course of action.

[521]

II. Professional Competency

A. General

1. The school psychologist's role mandates a mastery of skills in both education and psychology. In the interest of children and adults served in both the public and private sector, school psychologists strive to maintain high standards of competence. School psychologists recognize the strengths, as well as limitations, of their training and experience, and only provide services in areas of competence. They must be professional in the ongoing pursuit of knowledge, training and research with the welfare of children, families and other individuals in mind.

2. School psychologists offer only those services which are within their individual area of training and experience. Competence levels, education, training and experience are accurately represented to schools and clients in a professional manner. School psychologists do not use affiliations with other professional persons or with institutions to imply a level of professional competence which exceeds that which has actually been achieved.

3. School psychologists are aware of their limitations and enlist the assistance of other specialists in supervisory, consultative or referral role as appropriate in providing services competently.

4. School psychologists recognize the need for continuing professional development and pursue opportunities to learn new procedures, become current with new research and technology, and advance with changes that benefit children and families.

5. School psychologists refrain from involvement in any activity in which their personal problems or conflicts may interfere with professional effectiveness. Competent professional assistance is sought to alleviate such problems and conflicts in professional relationships.

III Professional Relationships and Responsibilities

A. General

1. School psychologists take responsibility for their actions in a multitude of areas of service, and in so doing, maintain the highest standards of their profession. They are committed to the application of professional expertise for promoting improvement in the quality of life available to the student, family, school, and community. This objective is pursued in ways that protect the dignity and rights of those served. School psychologists accept responsibility for the consequences of their acts and ensure that professional skills, position and influence are applied only for purposes which are consistent with these values.

2. School psychologists respect each person with whom they are working and deal justly and impartially with each regardless of his/her physical, mental, emotional, political, economic, social, cultural, racial or religious characteristics.

3. School psychologists apply influence, position and professional skills in ways that protect the dignity and rights of those served. They promote the improvement of the quality of education and of life in general when determining assessment, counseling and intervention.

4. School psychologists define the direction and the nature of personal loyalties, objectives and competencies, and advise and inform all persons concerned of these commitments.

5. School psychologists working in both public schools and private settings maintain professional relationships with students, parents, the school and community. They understand the importance of informing students/clients of all aspects of the potential professional relationship prior to beginning psychological services of any type. School psychologists recognize the need for parental involvement and the significant influence the parent has on the student/client's growth.

6. In a situation where there are divided or conflicting interests (as between parents, school, student, supervisor, trainer) school psychologists are responsible for attempting to work out a plan of action which protects the rights and encourages mutual benefit and protection of rights.

7. School psychologists do not exploit their professional relationships with students, employees, clients or research participants sexually or otherwise. School psychologists do not engage in nor condone deliberate comments, gestures or physical contacts of a sexual nature.

B. Students

1. School psychologists are guided by an awareness of the intimate nature of the examination of personal aspects of an individual. School psychologists use an approach which reflects a humanistic concern for dignity and personal integrity.

2. School psychologists inform the student/client about important aspects of their relationship in a manner that is undertood by the student. The explanation includes the uses to be made of information, persons who will receive specific information and possible implications of results.

3. School psychologists recognize the obligation to the student/client and respect the student's/client's right of choice to enter, or to participate in services voluntarily.

4. School psychologists inform the student/client of the outcomes of assessment, counseling or other services. Contemplated changes in program, plans for further services and other pertinent information are discussed with the student as a result of services. An account of alternatives available to the student/client is included.

5. The student/client is informed by the school psychologist of those who will receive information regarding the services and the type of information that they will receive. The sharing of information is formulated to fit the age and maturity of the student/client and the nature of the information.

C. Parents

1. School psychologists confer with parents regarding assessment, counseling and intervention plans in language understandable to the parent. They strive to establish a set of alternatives and suggestions which match the values and skills of each parent.

2. School psychologists recognize the importance of parental support and seek to obtain this by assuring that there is direct parent contact prior to seeing the student/client. They secure continuing parental involvement by a frank and prompt reporting to the parent of findings and progress.

3. School psychologists continue to maintain contact with the parent even though the parent objects to having their child receive services. Alternatives are described which will enable the student to get needed help.

4. School psychologists discuss recommendations and plans for assisting the student/client with the parent. The discussion includes alternatives associated with each set of plans. The parents are advised as to sources of help available at school and in the community.

5. School psychologists inform parents of the nature of records made of parent conferences and evaluations of the student/client. Rights of confidentiality and content of reports are shared.

D. School/Organizational

1. School psychologists employed by school districts prepare by becoming knowledgeable of the organization, philosophy, goals, objectives and methodology of the school.

2. School psychologists recognize that a working understanding of the goals, processes and legal requirements of the educational system is essential for an effective relationship with the school.

3. Familiarization with organization, instructional materials and teaching

strategies of the school are basic to enable school psychologists to contribute to the common objective for fostering maximum self development opportunities for each student/client.

4. School psychologists accept the responsibility of being members of the staff of those schools. They recognize the need to establish an integral role within the school system and familiarize themselves with the system and community.

E. Community

1. Although enjoying professional identity as a school psychologist, school psychologists are also citizens, thereby, accepting the same responsibilities and duties expected of all members of society. School psychologists are free to pursue individual interests, except to the degree that these may compromise fulfillment of their professional responsibilities and have negative impact on the profession. Awareness of such impact guides public behavior.

2. As citizens, school psychologists may exercise their constitutional rights as the basis for procedures and practices designed to bring about social change. Such activities are conducted as involved citizens and not as representatives of school psychologists.

3. As employees or employers, in public or private domains, school psychologists do not engage in or condone practices based on race, handicap, age, gender, sexual preference, religion or national origin.

4. School psychologists avoid any action that could violate or diminish civil and legal rights of clients.

5. School psychologists in public and private practice have the responsibility of adhering to federal, state and local laws and ordinances governing their practice. If such laws are in conflict with existing ethical guidelines, school psychologists proceed toward resolution of such conflict through positive, respected and legal channels.

F. Related Professions

1. School psychologists respect and understand the areas of competence of other professions. They work in full cooperation with other professional disciplines in a relationship based on mutual respect and recognition of the multidisciplinary service needed to meet the needs of students and clients. They recognize the role and obligation of the institution or agency with which other professionals are associated.

2. School psychologists recognize the areas of competence of related professions and other professionals in the field of school psychology. They

encourage and support use of all the resources that best serve the interests of their students/clients. They are obligated to have prior knowledge of the competency and qualifications of a referral source. Professional services, as well as technical and administrative resources are sought in the effort of providing the best possible professional service.

3. School psychologists working within the school system explain their professional competencies to other professionals including role descriptions, assignment of services and the working relationships among varied professionals within the system.

4. School psychologists cooperate with other professionals and agencies with the rights and needs of their student/client in mind. If a student/-client is receiving similar services from another professional, school psychologists assure coordination of services. Private practice school psychologists do not offer their own services to those already receiving services. As school psychologists working within the school system, a need to serve a student may arise as dictated by the student's special program. In this case, consultation with another professional serving the student takes place to assure coordination of services for the welfare of the student.

5. When school psychologists suspect the existence of detrimental or unethical practices, the appropriate professional organization is contacted for assistance and procedures established for questioning ethical practice are followed.

G. Other School Psychologists

1. School psychologists who employ, supervise and train other professionals accept the obligation of providing experiences to further their professional development. Appropriate working conditions, fair and timely evaluation and constructive consultation are provided.

2. School psychologists acting as supervisors to interns, review and evaluate assessment results, conferences, counseling strategies and documents. They assure the profession that training in the field is supervised adequately.

3. When school psychologists are aware of a possible ethical violation by another school psychologist, they attempt to resolve the issue on an informal level. If such informal efforts are not productive and a violation appears to be enacted, steps for filing an ethical complaint as outlined by the appropriate professional association are followed.

IV. Professional Practices — Public Settings

A. Advocacy

1. School psychologists consider the pupils/clients to be their primary responsibility and act as advocates of their rights and welfare. Course of action takes into account the rights of the student, rights of the parent, the responsibilities of the school personnel, and the expanding self-independence and mature status of the student.

2. School psychologists outline and interpret services to be provided. Their concern for protecting the interests and rights of students is communicated to the school administration and staff. Human advocacy is the number one priority.

B. Assessment and Intervention

1. School psychologists strive to maintain the highest standard of service by an objective collecting of appropriate data and information necessary to effectively work with students. In conducting a psychoeducational evaluation or counseling/consultation services, due consideration is given to individual integrity and individual differences. School psychologists recognize differences in age, sex, socioeconomic and ethnic backgrounds and strive to select and use appropriate procedures, techniques and strategies relevant to such differences.

2. School psychologists insist on collecting relevant data for an evaluation that includes the use of valid and reliable instruments and techniques that are applicable and appropriate for the student.

3. School psychologists combine observations, background information, multidisciplinary results and other pertinent data to present the most comprehensive and valid picture possible of the student. School psychologists utilize assessment, counseling procedures, consultation techniques and other intervention methods that are consistent with responsible practice, recent research and professional judgment.

4. School psychologists do not promote the use of psychoeducational assessment techniques by inappropriately trained or otherwise unqualified persons through teaching, sponsorship or supervision.

5. School psychologists develop interventions which are appropriate to the presenting problems of the referred student/client, and which are consistent with the data collected during the assessment of the referral situation.

6. The student/client is referred to another professional for services when a condition is identified which is outside the treatment competencies or scope of the school psychologist.

7. When transferring the intervention responsibility for a student/client to another professional, school psychologists ensure that all relevant and

appropriate individuals, including the student/client when appropriate, are notified of the change and reasons for the change.

C. Use of Materials and Computers

1. School psychologists are responsible for maintaining security of psychological tests which might be rendered useless by revealing the underlying principles or specific content. Every attempt is made by school psychologists to protect test security and copyright restructions.

2. Copyright laws are adhered to regarding reproduction of tests or any parts thereof. Permission is obtained from authors of non-copyrighted published instruments.

3. School psychologists who utilize student/client information in lectures or publications, either obtain prior consent in writing or remove all identifying data.

4. When publishing, school psychologists acknowledge the sources of their ideas and materials. Credit is given to those who have contributed.

5. School psychologists do not promote or encourage inappropriate use of computer generated test analysis or reports.

6. School psychologists maintain full responsibility for computerized or any other technological services used by them for diagnostic, consultative or information management purposes. Such services, if used, should be regarded as tools to be used judiciously without abdication of any responsibility of the psychologist to the tool or to the people who make its operation possible.

7. In the utilization of technological data management services, school psychologists apply the same ethical standards for use, interpretation and maintenance of data as for any other information. They are assured that the computer programs are accurate in all areas of information produced prior to using the results.

D. School-Based Research and Evaluation

1. School psychologists continually assess the impact of any treatment/ intervention/counseling plan and terminate or modify the plan when the data indicates that the plan is not achieving the desired goals.

2. In performing research, school psychologists accept responsibility for selection of topics and research methodology to be used in subject selection, data gathering, analysis and reporting. In publishing reports of their research, they provide discussion of limitations of their data and acknowledge existence of confirming data, as well as alternate hypo-

theses and explanations of their findings.

E. Reporting Data and Conferencing Results

1. School psychologists ascertain that student/client information reaches responsible and authorized persons and is adequately interpreted for their use in helping the student/client. This involves establishing procedures which safeguard the personal and confidential interests of those concerned.

2. School psychologists communicate findings and recommendations in language readily understood by the school staff. These communications describe possible favorable and unfavorable consequences associated with the alternative proposals.

3. When reporting data which are to be representative of a student/client, school psychologists take the responsibility for preparing information that is written in terms that are understandable to all involved. It is made certain that information is in such form and style as to assure that the recipient of the report will be able to give maximum assistance to the individual. The emphasis is on the interpretations and recommendations rather than the simple passing along of test scores, and will include an appraisal of the degree of reliance and confidence which can be placed on the information.

4. School psychologists ensure the accuracy of their reports, letters and other written documents through reviewing and signing such.

5. School psychologists comply with all laws, regulations and policies pertaining to the adequate storage and disposal of records to maintain appropriate confidentiality of information.

V. Professional Practices — Private Settings

A. Relationships with School Districts

1. Many school psychologists are employed in both the public and private sector, and in so doing, create a possible conflict of services if they do not adhere to standards of professional ethics. School psychologists operating in both sectors recognize the importance of separation of roles and the necessity of adherance to all ethical standards.

2. School psychologists engaged in employment in a public school setting and in private practice, may not accept a fee, or any other form of remuneration, for professional work with clients who are entitled to such service through the schools where the school psychologists are currently assigned.

3. School psychologists in private practice have an obligation to inform parents of free and/or mandated services available from the public school system before providing services for pay.

4. School psychologists engaged in employment in a public, as well as private practice setting, maintain such practice outside the hours of contracted employment in their school district.

5. School psychologists engaged in private practice do not utilize tests, materials or services belonging to the school district without authorization.

6. School psychologists carefully evaluate the appropriateness of the use of public school facilities for part-time private practice. Such use can be confusing to the client and may be criticized as improper. Before the facility is utilized, school psychologists enter into a rental agreement with the school district and clearly define limits of use to the district and the client.

B. Service — Delivery

1. School psychologists clarify financial arrangements in advance of services to insure to the best of their ability that they are clearly understood by the client. They neither give nor receive any renumeration for referring clients for professional services.

2. School psychologists in private practice adhere to the conditions of a contract with the school district, other agency, or individual until service thereunder has been performed, the contract has been terminated by mutual consent, or the contract has otherwise been legally terminated. They have responsibility to follow up a completed contract to assure that conclusions are understood, interpreted and utilized effectively.

3. School psychologists in private practice guard against any misunderstanding occurring from recommendations, advice or information given a parent or child which a school may not be prepared to carry out, or which is in conflict with what the district is doing for the child. Such conflicts are not avoided where the best interests of those served require consideration of different opinion. Direct consultation between the school psychologist in private practice and the school psychologist assigned to the case at the school level may avoid confusing parents by resolving at the professional level any difference of interpretation of clinical data.

4. School psychologists provide individual diagnostic and therapeutic services only within the context of a professional psychological relationship. Personal diagnosis and therapy are not given by means of public lectures, newspaper columns, magazine articles, radio and television programs or mail. Any information shared through such media activities is general in

nature and utilizes only current and relevant data and professional judgement.

C. Announcements/Advertising

1. Considerations of appropriate announcement of services, advertising and public media statements are necessary in the role of the school psychologist in private practice. Such activities are necessary in assisting the public to make appropriate and knowledgeable decisions and choices regarding services. Accurate representation of training, experience, services provided and affiliation are made by school psychologists. Public statements must be based on sound and accepted theory, research and practice.

2. Individual, agency or clinical listings in telephone directories are limited to the following: name/names, highest relevant degree, certification status, address, telephone number, brief identification of major areas of practice, office hours, appropriate fee information, foreign languages spoken, policy with regard to third party payments and license number.

3. Announcements of services by school psychologists in private practice, agency or clinic are made in a formal, professional manner limited to the same information as is included in a telephone listing. Clear statements of purposes with clear descriptions of the experiences to be provided are given. The education, training and experience of the staff members are appropriately specified.

4. School psychologists in private practice may utilize brochures in the announcement of services. The brochures may be sent to professional persons, schools, business firms, governmental agencies and other similar organizations.

5. Announcements and advertisements of the availability of publications, products and services for sale are presented in a professional, scientific and factual manner. Information may be communicated by means of periodical, book, list, directory, television, radio or motion picture and must not include any false, misleading or comparative statements.

6. School psychologists in private practice do not directly solicit clients for individual diagnosis or therapy.

7. School psychologists do not compensate in any manner a representative of the press, radio or television in return for personal professional publicity in a news item.

8. School psychologists do not participate for personal gain in commercial announcements or advertisements recommending to the public the purchase or use of products or services.

Appendix III

PROCEDURAL GUIDELINES FOR THE ADJUDICATION OF ETHICAL COMPLAINTS

I. Responsibility and Function

The Ethics and Professional Conduct Committee shall be responsible for developing and maintaining a clearly defined position of the Association regarding the ethical and professional conduct principles to be adhered to by its members. The major area of particular ethical concern for the Committee will be that of the protection and general well-being of individuals served by school psychologists, in schools, in private practice, and in other institutions or agencies. The Committee is further charged to study and make recommendations to the Executive Board when it is alleged that a member has failed to follow the ethical principles of the Association.

Members of the Ethics and Professional Conduct Committee must recognize that their role is an extremely important one, involving the rights of many individuals, the reputation of the profession and the careers of individual professionals. They bear a heavy responsibility because their recommendations may alter the lives of others. Therefore, they must be alert to personal, social, organizational, financial or political situations or pressures that might lead to misuse of their influence. The Ethics and Professional Conduct Committee shall assure the responsible use of all information obtained in the course of an inquiry or investigation. The objective with regard to the individual shall, whenever possible, be constructive and educative, rather than punitive in character.

The function of the Committee in investigating complaints of alleged ethical misconduct involves obtaining a thorough and impartial account of the behaviors or incidents in order to be able to evaluate the character of the behaviors in question. When responding to complaints, members of the Ethics and Professional Conduct Committee have the responsibility to consider the competency of the complainant, to act in an unbiased manner, to work expeditiously, and to safeguard the confidentiality of the Committee's activities. Any committees involved in investigating and hearing issues relevant to any ethical complaint as outlined in the following procedures shall have members sign an oath of confidentiality prior to participation on the committees. Committee members and their designees have the added responsibility to follow procedures which safeguard the rights of all individuals involved in the complaint process.

II. Scope and Authority

The Ethics and Professional Conduct Committee shall address issues of ethical misconduct in an investigatory, advisory, educative and/or remedial role. What constitutes ethical misconduct shall be determined on the basis of the provisions of the NASP Principles for Professional Ethics and any published advisory opinions that from time to time are developed by the Ethics and Professional Conduct Committee. In applying the Principles, the authorized opinions of those charged by NASP with the administration and interpretation of the ethical principle shall be binding on all members and on the members of state associations affiliated with NASP.

When investigating and/or responding to a complaint or inquiry, the Ethics and Professional Conduct Committee shall conduct itself in a manner consistent with the Bylaws of the Association and with the NASP *Principles for Professional Ethics* and shall endeavor to settle cases informally, recommend disciplinary action when unethical conduct has occurred, report regularly to the Delegate Assembly on its activities, and shall revise and amend (subject to ratification by the Delegate Assembly), the NASP Principles and these procedures in a timely manner. The Association may, at the recommendation of the Ethics and Professional Conduct Committee, and in accordance with the Bylaws of the Association, expel a NASP member.

When a complaint is received about a non-member, the Ethics and Professional Conduct Committee shall respond only in an advisory or educative fashion and shall have no authority to investigate the case or to discipline the individual in question. However, the Ethics and Professional Conduct Committee may cooperate with other agencies and associations who do have authority in the matter, by sharing relevant and factual information or by referring the complainant to a more appropriate resource.

Complaints that address concerns about professional standards, organizations, employers and the like, shall be referred to the Professional Standards and Employment Relations Committee. Nevertheless, it should be recognized that in situations where an individual psychologist is being coerced to behave unethically, he/she bears certain ethical responsibilities and to fail to take appropriate action, e.g., refusing to behave unethically, could eventuate charges of misconduct against the individual psychologist involved. However, as a rule, such "standards" concerns would not fall under the purview of this complaint process.

III. Receipt and Acknowledgment of Complaints and Inquiries

A. The Ethics and Professional Conduct Committee shall recognize and respond to all complaints and inquiries from any responsible individual or group of individuals in accordance with these procedures. The individual who petitions the Committee (hereinafter referred to as the *complainant*), need not be a member of NASP or the affiliated state association. Anonymous letters and phone calls will not be recognized.

B. An oral complaint or inquiry may be formally handled, referred elsewhere when appropriate, or an Ethics and Professional Conduct Committee chairperson may request that the complaint be formally submitted in writing. Only written statements expressing the details of the alleged misconduct will be accepted for action. Such written statements shall be signed by the complainant and should state in as much detail as practicable, the facts upon which the complaint is based. All the correspondence, records and activities of the Ethics and Professional Conduct Committee shall remain confidential.

C. Within 15 days of receipt of a written statement outlining the details of the alleged misconduct, the chairpersons of the Ethics and Professional Conduct Committee shall do the following:

1. Notify the individual against whom the complaint is made (hereinafter referred to as the respondent) that a formal complaint has been filed against him/her. A copy of the PROCEDURAL GUIDELINES FOR THE ADJUDICATION OF ETHICAL COMPLAINTS shall be sent to both complainant and respondent. The notification to the respondent shall indicate that the respondent will receive information regarding status of the complaint as steps C 2-6 are followed.

2. Determine if the individual against whom the complaint is made (hereinafter referred to as the respondent), is a member of NASP. If the respondent is not a member of NASP, the complainant shall be so advised and when appropriate, referred to other agencies and/or associations who would have authority in the matter. The respondent shall receive notice of this action.

3. If the respondent is a member of NASP, the Ethics and Professional Conduct Committee chairpersons with any advisory opinions deemed necessary shall review the complaint. If it is determined that the alleged misconduct, even if true, would not constitute an actual violation of the NASP Principles a chairperson shall notify the complainant and respondent.

4. If the information obtained from the complainant is insufficient to make a determination regarding the alleged misconduct, the chairperson may send a written request to the complainant asking for clarification and/or additional information as would be needed to make such a determination.

5. If it is determined that the alleged misconduct, if substantiated, would constitute an actual violation of the NASP Principles, the Ethics and Professional Conduct Committee chairpersons shall direct a letter to and advise the complainant that the allegation will be investigated by the Committee. The complainant shall be asked to sign a release, authorizing that his/her name be revealed to the respondent.

6. If the complainant refuses to permit his/her identity to be made known to the respondent, such refusal may serve as a basis for forfeiting the complaint process. However, on its own volition when a member appears to have engaged in ethical misconduct that tends to injure the Association or to adversely affect its reputation, or that is clearly inconsistent with or

destructive of the goals and objectives of the Association, the Ethics and Professional Conduct Committee may proceed with the complaint process.

IV. Conduct of an Informal Inquiry

A. Within 15 days of receipt of the signed release, the Ethics and Professional Conduct Committee shall inform the respondent, in writing, with the envelope marked "confidential," of the details of the complaint filed against him/her. This letter shall describe the nature of the complaint, indicate the principle(s) which appear to have been violated, and request the respondent's cooperation in obtaining a full picture of the circumstances which led to the allegations. A copy of the NASP Principle of Ethics and any pertinent advisory opinions of the Ethics and Professional Conduct Committee shall also be enclosed. Ordinarily, the respondent shall be informed of the name of the complainant, when written permission to do so, has been obtained. (See Section III, C-5 above for Exception.)

B. The respondent shall be asked to provide a written statement outlining his/her view of the situation in order that the Committee may be cognizant of all relevant aspects of the case.

C. Whenever possible, the Ethics and Professional Conduct Committee shall attempt to resolve differences privately and informally through further correspondence with all parties involved. An attempt shall be made to bring about an adjustment through mediative efforts in the interest of correcting a general situation or settling the particular issues between the parties involved.

D. If the respondent does not respond to the original inquiry within 30 days, a follow-up letter shall be sent to the respondent by registered or certified mail, marked "confidential" return receipt requested.

E. If the respondent refuses to reply to the Committee's inquiry or otherwise cooperate with the Committee, the Committee may continue its investigations, noting in the record the circumstances of the respondent's failure to cooperate and shall also inform the respondent that his/her lack of cooperation may result in action which could eventuate his/her being dropped from membership in the Association.

F. As a rule, if the complainant wishes to withdraw the complaint, the inquiry is terminated, except in extreme cases where the Committee feels the issues in the case are of such importance as to warrant completing the investigation in its own right and in the interest of the public welfare or the Association. (See Section III, C-5).

G. The Association will not recognize a respondent's resignation from membership while there is a complaint pending before the Ethics and Professional Conduct Committee or before an ethics committee of a state association unless he/she submits an affidavit stating that:

1. The resignation is free and voluntary,

2. He/she is aware of a pending investigation into allegations of misconduct

3. He/she acknowledges that the material facts upon which the complaint is based are true, and

4. He/she submits the resignation because he/she knows that if charges are predicated on the misconduct under investigation, he/she could not defend him/herself successfully against them.

H. Within 30 days of receipt of the written statement from the respondent, or (in the event the respondent fails to reply or otherwise cooperate), within 30 days of receipt of the return receipt requested from the second notification by the Committee (Section IV, 4-5), the chairperson through advice of the Committee, shall determine if a violation may have occurred, and if so, what principles have potentially been violated.

I. If, in the opinion of the Committee, the complaint has a basis in fact but is considered likely to be corrected without further action, the chairperson shall so indicate in the record and shall so inform all parties involved.

J. If, in the opinion of the chairperson, the issues raised by the complaint would, if true, constitute a violation of the principles, and if it appears that the complaint cannot be resolved by less formal means, the chairperson shall, in coordination with the appropriate State Delegate, appoint two impartial NASP members from the State in which the respondent practices to form an Ad Hoc Committee, together with the chairperson of the Ethics and Professional Conduct Committee. The purpose of this Ad Hoc Committee is to investigate the case, to evaluate the character of the behavior(s) in question and to make recommendations to the Ethics and Professional Conduct Committee for final disposition of the case.

K. The Ethics and Professional Conduct Committee chairperson shall transmit to the members of the Ad Hoc Committee, by registered or certified mail, in envelopes marked "confidential" copies of the following:

1. The original complaint or material

2. The letter to the respondent apprising him/her of the nature of the alleged violation.

3. The response from the respondent, and

4. Any such further facts related to the case as the chairperson can assemble from sources of evident reliability.

L. The Ad Hoc Committee shall then determine whether:

1. The case shall be closed

2. Further investigation by correspondence is indicated

3. Further investigation by a Fact-Finding Committee is indicated, (See Section VI)

4. The respondent and/or complainant shall be asked to appear before the Ad Hoc Committee, or

5. Some other action or a combination thereof shall be taken.

V. Recommendations of the Ad Hoc Committee

A. When the Ad Hoc Committee has obtained sufficient information with which to reach a decision, or, in any event, in not more than 60 days from the formation of the Ad Hoc Committee, the Ethics and Professional Conduct Chairperson shall request that the Ad Hoc Committee vote on the disposition of the case.

B. If, in the unanimous opinion of the Ad Hoc Committee members, a violation of the NASP Principles has occurred and if, in the opinion of the Ad Hoc Committee, the unethical behavior can be terminated by action of the Committee itself, one of the following recommendations shall be made:

1. The Ad Hoc Committee shall request, in writing, that the respondent take corrective measures to modify or stop certain activities of practices.

2. The Ad Hoc Committee shall, in writing, censure or reprimand the respondent.

3. The Ad Hoc Committee shall require that the respondent provide restitution to or apologize, in writing, to an individual, group of individuals, or organization harmed by the respondent's unethical conduct or

4. The Ad Hoc Committee shall recommend that the respondent be placed under a period of probation of membership or surveillance under fixed terms agreed to by the respondent.

C. Within 5 days, the Ethics and Professional Conduct Chairperson shall inform the respondent of the Ad Hoc Committee's determination and recommendations. The respondent shall be notified that he/she may make a request for a hearing on the charges within 30 days from the receipt of a statement of the charges and the Committee's findings and recommendations. Such a request shall be in writing and directed to the President of the Association.

D. The Ethics and Professional Conduct Committee chairperson shall draft a report, summarizing the findings and recommendations of the Ad Hoc Committee, copies of which shall be distributed to the two other Ad Hoc Committee members, the respondent and, at the Committee's discretion, the complainant. This report shall be transmitted in envelopes marked "confidential" and in the case of the respondent, by registered or certified mail with a return receipt requested.

E. The unanimous decision of the Ad Hoc Committee shall be binding on the Association unless overturned by the Hearing Committee, Executive Board or Delegate Assembly in accordance with the procedures outlined herein. (See Section VIII

VI. Condict of a Formal Investigation

A. A formal investigation shall be undertaken if any one of the following circumstances prevails:

1. The Ad Hoc Committee finds that it lacks sufficient data with which to proceed,

2. The Ad Hoc Committee is unable to reach consensus,

3. The recommendations of the Ad Hoc Committee do not lead to resolution of the problem, or

4. The facts alleged in the complaint, if substantiated, would likely require action leading to termination of the respondent's membership in the Association.

B. When a formal investigation is warranted, under these procedures, the Ethics and Professional Conduct chairperson, in coordination with the President of the Association, shall appoint a Fact-Finding Committee which shall consist of not less than three, nor more than five members of the Association, for the specific purpose of more fully investigating the charges. The Fact Finding Committee shall appoint its own chairperson. No member previously involved in reviewing the case may continue on the Fact Finding Committee. The Ethics and Professional Conduct Chairperson shall serve on the Fact Finding Committee in ex-officio status in order to apprise the Fact Finding Committee of the procedures by which they are bound and to serve in an advisory capacity.

C. The Fact Finding Committee shall be bound by the same procedures and timelines as outlined in Sections III and IV of these procedures. In addition, the Fact Finding Committee may at the discretion of the Executive Board, retain a legal advisor as counsel to the committee while investigating its case.

D. The respondent may seek advice from any individual, including an attorney or another member of the Association at his own expense, for assistance in preparing and presenting documentary evidence requested by the Fact Finding Committee.

VII. Recommendations of the Fact Finding Committee

A. If the formal investigation was convened following a decision by consensus of the Ad Hoc Committee, and if the Fact Finding Committee unanimously concurs with the Ad Hoc Committee's findings and recommendations, all parties shall be so informed and this decision shall be binding of the Association unless overturned by the Hearing Committee, Executive Board or Delegate Assembly, in accordance with the procedures outlined herein.

B. If the case was not resolved at the Ad Hoc Committee level, the Fact Finding Committee must announce its findings and recommendations within the prescribed timelines. The Fact Finding Committee may exercise any of the recommendations open to the Ad Hoc Committee (Section V. B) and in addition, may also recommend that the respondent's membership in the Association be terminated.

C. Should the Fact Finding Committee so recommend, the chairperson of the Ethics and Professional Conduct Committee must present the findings and recommendations of the Fact Finding Committee to the NASP Executive Board and Delegate Assembly. A summary report shall be prepared, such that the confidentiality of all parties involved, i.e., identifying information of the informer, is strictly maintained. The case shall be reviewed in sufficient detail so as to allow the Executive Board and the Delegate Assembly members to vote to concur or overrule the decision of the Fact Finding Committee.

D. In accordance with NASP Bylaws, cases involving a recommendation for expulsion from the Association by the Ethics and Professional Conduct Committee shall be confirmed by a 2/3 vote of the Executive Board, with a majority ratification by the Delegate Assembly.

E. At the discretion of the Executive Board and Delegate Assembly, the respondent may be allowed to voluntarily resign his/her membership in the Association.

F. Within five days, the Ethics and Professional Conduct Committee chairpersons shall inform the respondent of the decision of the Executive Board and Delegate Asembly in the same manner as provided in Section V. C of these procedures.

G. If the Executive Board and/or the Delegate Assembly do not concur with the Committee's recommendation for expulsion from membership, the case shall be remanded back to the Fact Finding Committee for consideration of a lesser penalty.

VIII. Conduct of the Hearing Committee

A. Within 30 days of receipt of a statement of the charges against him/her and a statement of the Committee's findings and recommendations, the respondent has the right to request from the President of the Association, a hearing on the charges. This right shall be considered waived if such request is not made, in writing, within the 30 day period.

B. If the respondent does request a hearing, the President shall select a panel of ten members of the Association, none of whom shall be members of the Ethics and Professional Conduct Committee or have had any prior connection with the case. From the panel, the respondent shall have 30 days in which to choose a Hearing Committee of five members. If he/she does not make a selection, the President shall choose the five members to comprise the Hearing Committee.

C. The President shall select a chairperson of the Hearing Committee who shall conduct the hearing and assure that the procedures are properly observed. There shall be no communication between the members of the Hearing Committee and the Ethics and Professional Conduct Committee or any of its representatives prior to the hearing itself.

D. A date for the hearing shall be set by the President with the concurrence of the respondent. In no event shall the hearing take place later than 90 days from the date of the respondent's request for a hearing.

E. At least 30 days prior to the hearing, the respondent and the Hearing Committee members shall be provided with copies of all documents to be presented and the names of all witnesses that will be offered by the Ethics and Professional Conduct Committee in support of the charges.

F. Presentation of the case against the respondent shall be the responsibility of the Ethics and Professional Conduct Committee or such others as the Ethics and Professional Conduct Committee has designated to investigate the complaint. Legal counsel for the Association may participate fully in the presentation of the case.

G. All evidence that is relevant and reliable, as determined by the chairperson of the Hearing Committee, shall be admissible. Evidence of mitigating circumstances may be presented by the respondent.

H. The respondent shall have the right to counsel, to present witnesses and documents and to cross-examine the witnesses offered by the Ethics and Professional Conduct Committee.

I.   The hearing may be adjourned as necessary and the Ethics and Professional Conduct Committee may introduce rebuttal evidence.

J.   In the interest of obtaining a full and accurate record of the hearing, a tape recorder or other transcription device may be used, at the discretion of the Hearing Committee and the respondent.

IX. Recommendations of the Hearing Committee

A.   At the conclusion of the hearing, the Hearing Committee shall have 30 days in which to issue its report and recommendations.

B.   If the Hearing Committee recommends that the respondent be dropped from membership or that the respondent be permitted to resign, the matter shall be referred to the Executive Board. A recommendation that the respondent be expelled or be allowed to resign must be made by 4 of the 5 committee members. Other disciplinary measures may be recommended by a simple majority and would be decided upon per individual case.

C.   Only the disciplinary measures specified by the Ethics and Professional Conduct Committee in the formal statement of charges, or a lesser penalty, shall be recommended by the Hearing Committee. Although the Ethics and Professional Conduct Committee recommendations may be modified by the Hearing Committee, it may not increase the penalty recommended.

D.   The Hearing Committee shall submit its report and recommendations simultaneously to the Executive Board and to the respondent.

E.   The respondent shall have 15 days from receipt of the Hearing Committee's report in which to file a written statement with the Executive Board. The Ethics and Professional Conduct Committee shall then have 15 days in which to file a response.

F.   After consideration of the record, the recommendation of the Hearing Committee and any statements that may be filed, the Executive Board shall adopt the recommendations of the Hearing Committee unless it determines that:

1.   The NASP Principles and/or the procedures herein stated have been incorrectly applied,

2.   The findings of fact of the Hearing Committee as stated in the report are not supported by the evidence, or

3.   The procedures followed were in violation of the Bylaws of the Association.

**Procedural Guidelines for the
Adjudication of Ethical Complaints**

Written Complaint Received by EPC*
|

No Jurisdiction — . —— EPC Review ——————— Jurisdiction of another
Case closed   Agency/organization —

(membership principles   Refer complainant
violated)

(Complainant,
respondent)
|
Response of respondent
|

Informal resolution ——— EPC Review
|
Informal Inquiry

Ad Hoc Committee
|

Resolution ——————— EPC Review
|
Formal Investigation

Fact Finding Committee
|

Resolution ——————— EPC Review ——————— Hearing requested
| |
| Hearing Committee
| |
**EB/DA Decision ——————

* Ethics and Professional Conduct Committe

** Executive Board/Delegate Assembly

G. The Ethics and Professional Conduct Committee shall inform the respondent and, at its discretion, may inform the complainant of any final action taken by the Executive Board. The Ethics and Professional Conduct Committee shall report to the Delegate Assembly, at its next regularly scheduled meeting, in Executive Session, the names of those members who have been allowed to resign or who have been expelled from membership and the Ethical Principle(s) involved.

H. The Ethics and Professional Conduct Committee shall report annually and in confidence to the Delegate Assembly and executive Board in Executive Session the names of members who have been expelled from the Association and the ethical principle(s) involved.

I. In severe cases and when the welfare of the public are at stake, and when the Ethics and Professional Conduct Committee deems it necessary to maintain the principles of the Association and the profession, it may also notify affiliated state and regional associations and state and local licensing and certification boards of the final disposition of the case. Other interested parties may be notified of the final action when, in the opinion of the Ethics and Professional Conduct Committee, notification is necessary for the protection of the public.

APPENDIX IV

ORGANIZATIONS SERVING EXCEPTIONAL OR
HEALTH IMPAIRED PERSONS

Susan M. Vess
Northeast Louisiana University

This appendix lists organizations that offer a variety of services to handicapped or health impaired persons and their families. Although a comprehensive compilation of resources was the author's goal, it is recognized that some very important, even obvious, entries were omitted.

Adoption

Adoptee/Natural Parent Locators
18645 Sunburst Street
Northridge, CA 91324
(213) 886-3367

Aid to Adoption of Special Kids
3530 Grand Avenue
Oakland, CA 94610
(415) 451-2275

North American Council on Adoptable
  Children
1346 Connecticut Av., NW, Suite 229
Washington, DC 20036
(202) 466-7570

Pearl S. Buck Foundation (Amerasian)
Green Hills Farm
Perkasie, PA 18944
(800) 523-5328

Alcohol-Abuse

Al-Anon Family Group Headquarters
One Park Ave.
New York, NY 10016
(212) 683-1771

Alcoholics Anonymous
P.O. Box 459
Grand Central Station
New York, NY 10063
(212) 686-1100

Children of Alcoholics Foundation
540 Madison Avenue, 23rd Floor
New York, NY 10022
(212) 980-5860

Mothers Against Drunk Drivers
5330 Primrose, Suite 146
Fair Oaks, CA 95628
(916) 966-6233

National Clearinghouse for Alcohol
  Information
Box 2345
Rockville, MD 20852

Allergy/Asthma

Allergy and Asthma Foundation of
  America
9604 Wisconsin Avenue, Suite 100
Bethesda, MD 20814
(301) 493-6552

American Allergy Foundation
P.O. Box 7273
Menlo Park, CA 94025
(415) 322-1663

American Lung Association
1740 Broadway
New York, NY 10019
(212) 245-8000

Children's Asthma Research Institute
and Hospital
3800 E. Colfax Av.
Denver, CO 80206
(303) 388-4461

National **Amputation** Foundation
12-45 150th St.
White Stone, NY 11357
(212) 767-0596

Anorexia Nervosa

American Anorexia Nervosa Association
133 Cedar Lane
Teaneck, NJ 07666
(201) 836-1800

National Anorexic Aid Society
P.O. Box 29461
Columbus, OH 43229
(614) 846-6810

National Association of Anorexia
Nervosa and Associated Disorders
(Bulima)
Box 271
Highland Park, IL 60035
(312) 831-3438

Arthritis

Arthritis Foundation
1314 Spring St., NW
Atlanta, GA 30309
(404) 872-7100

Institute for Research of Rheumatic
Diseases
Box 955, Ansonia Station
New York, NY 10023
(212) 595-1368

Autism

National Society for Children and
Adults with Autism
1234 Massachusetts Ave., NW
Ste. 1017
Washington, DC 20005
(202) 783-0125

Ataxia

Friedreich's Ataxia Group in America
P.O. Box 11116
Oakland, CA 94611

National Ataxia Foundation
6681 Country Club Dr.
Minneapolis, MN 55427
(612) 546-6220

Birth Defects

Association of Birth Defect Children
3201 E. Crystal Lake Ave.
Orlando, FL 32806
(305) 898-5342

March of Dimes Birth Defects Foundation
1275 Mamaroneck Ave.
White Plains, NY 10605
(914) 428-7100

Parents of Premature and High Risk
    Infants
33 W. 42nd St.
Suite 1227
New York, NY 10036
(212) 840-1259

Know Problems of Hydrocephalus
Rt. 1, Box 210-A
River Rd.
Joliet, IL 60436
(815) 467-6548

Blood

Children's Blood Foundation
342 Madison Avenue
New York, NY 10173
(212) 687-1564

Cooley's Anemia Foundation
Graybar Bldg., Suite 1644
420 Lexington Avenue
New York, NY 10017
(212) 697-7750

National Hemophilia Foundation
19W 34th Street, Rm. 1204
New York, NY 10001
(212) 563-0211

Center for Sickle Cell Disease
2121 Georgia Av., NW
Washington, DC 20059
(202) 636-7930

National Association for Sickle Cell
    Disease
3460 Wilshire Blvd., Suite 1012
Los Angeles, CA 90010
(213) 731-1166

National Rare Blood Club
c/o Associated Health Foundation
164 Fifth Av.
New York, NY 10010
(212) 243-8037

Brittle Bones

American Brittle Bone Society
1256 Merrill Drive
Marshalton, PA 19380
(215) 692-9458

Osteogenesis Imperfecta Foundation
P.O. Box 428
Van Wert, OH 45891
(419) 238-9678

Burns

National Burn Victim Foundation
308 Main Street
Orange, NJ 07050
(201) 731-3112

International Society for Burn Injuries
Box 309 C
4200 East Ninth Avenue
Denver, CO 80262
(303) 394-8718

Cancer

American Cancer Society
777 Third Avenue
New York, NY 10017
(212) 371-2900

Association for Research on Childhood
   Cancer
3653 Harlem Road
Buffalo, NY 14215
(716) 838-4433

Candlelight Foundation
2025 Eye Street, NW
Suite 1011
Washington, DC 20006
(202) 659-5136

Leukemia Society of America
800 2nd Avenue
New York, NY 10017
(212) 573-8484

Make Today Count
P.O. Box 303
Burlington, IA 52601
(319) 753-6521

Catastrophic Diseases

City of Hope
208 West 8th Street
Los Angeles, CA 90014
(213) 626-4611

St. Judes Children's Research Hospital
505 North Parkway
Memphis, TN 38105
(901) 522-9733

United **Cerebral Palsy** Associations
66 East 34th Street
New York, NY 10016
(212) 481-6300

Child Abuse

Child Welfare League of America
67 Irving Place
New York, NY 10003
(212) 254-7410

Foundation for America's Sexually
   Exploited Children
P.O. Box 5370
Hacienda Heights, CA 91745
(213) 961-2796 or
(213) 633-5524 Hotline

International Society for the Prevention
   of Child Abuse and Neglect
1205 Oneida Street
Denver, CO 80220
(303) 394-7576

National Center on Child Abuse and
   Neglect
U.S. Children's Bureau
P.O. Box 1182
Washington, DC 20013

National Committee for Prevention of
   Child Abuse
332 Michigan Av., Suite 1250
Chicago, IL 60604
(312) 565-1100

Parents Anonymous
22330 Hawthorne Blvd.
Suite 208
Torrance, CA 90505
1-800-348-KIDS
(213) 371-3501

Parents United (Sex Abuse)
P.O. Box 952
San Jose, CA 95108
(405) 280-5055

Cleft Palate

American Cleft Palate
Administrative Office
331 Salk Hall
University of Pittsburgh
Pittsburgh, PA 15261
(412) 681-9620

Closer Look

National Information Center for
    Handicapped Children and Youth
P.O. Box 1492
Washington, DC 20013

Coma and Head Injury

International Coma Recovery Institute
133 Jericho Turnpike
Old Westbury, NY 11568
(516) 365-3433

National Head Injury Foundation
18A Vernon Street
Framingham, MA 01701
(617) 879-7473

Cornelia de Lange

Cornelia de Lange Syndrome Foundation
c/o Julie Mairano
60 Dyer Avenue
Collinsville, CT 06022
(203) 693-0159

Cystic Fibrosis

Cystic Fibrosis Foundation
6000 Executive Blvd.
Suite 309
Rockville, MD 20852
(301) 881-9130

Death and Dying

Bereaved Children's Program
Westchester Jewish Community Services
172 South Broadway
White Plains, NY 10605
(914) 949-6761

Make-a-Wish Foundation
4601 North 16th Street, Suite 206
Phoenix, AZ 85016
(602) 234-0960

Sunshine Foundation
2842 Normandy Drive
Philadelphia, PA 19154
(215) 743-2660

Deformities

Debbie Fox Foundation (facial)
P.O. Box 11082
Chattanooga, TN 37401
(615) 266-1632

Society for the Rehabilitation of the
    Facially Disfigured, Inc.
550 First Avenue
New York, NY 10016
(212) 340-5400

Dentistry

Academy of Dentistry for the
    Handicapped
1726 Champa, Suite 422
Denver, CO 80220
(303) 573-0624

Diabetes

American Diabetes Association
2 Park Avenue
New York, NY 10016
(212) 683-7444

Juvenile Diabetes Foundation
23 East 26th Street
New York, NY 10010
(212) 889-7575

Down Syndrome

Down Syndrome Congress
1640 W. Roosevelt Rd.
Chicago, IL 60608
(312) 226-0416

Parents of Down Syndrome Children
c/o Montgomery County Assn. for
    Retarded Citizens
11600 Nebel St.
Rockville, MD 20852
(301) 949-8140

Drug Abuse

National Clearinghouse for Drug Abuse
    Information
5600 Fishers Lane
Room 10 A 53
Rockville, MD 20852

Dystonia and Dysautonomia

Dysautonomia Foundation
370 Lexington Av., Suite 1504
New York, NY 10017
(212) 889-0300

Dystonia Medical Research Foundation
9615 Brighton Way, Suite 416
Beverly Hills, CA 90210
(213) 372-9880

Easter Seal

National Easter Seal Society for
    Crippled Children and Adults
2023 West Ogden Avenue
Chicago, IL 60612
(312) 243-8400

Epilepsy

Epilepsy Foundation of America
4351 Garden City Dr.
Landover, MD 20781
(301) 459-3700

Genetic Disorders

National Foundation for Jewish
    Genetic Disorders
250 Park Avenue, Suite 1000
New York, NY 10177
(212) 682-5550

National Genetics Foundation
250 W. 57th Street
New York, NY 10019
(212) 586-5800

Gifted

American Association for Gifted
    Children
15 Gramercy Park
New York, NY 10003
(212) 473-4266

Association for the Gifted
1920 Association Drive
Reston, VA 22091

National Association for Gifted Children
2070 County Rd. H
St. Paul, MN 55112
(612) 784-3475

Growth

Human Growth Foundation
P.O. Box 20253
Minneapolis, MN 55420
(612) 831-2780

Gluten Intolerance

Gluten Intolerance Group
P.O. Box 23053
Seattle, WA 98102
(206) 854-9606

Guillain-Barre

Guillain-Barre Syndrome Support Group
P.O. Box 262
Wynne Wood, PA 19096
(215) 649-7837

Hearing Impaired

Alexander Graham Bell Association
3417 Volta Place, NW
Washington, DC 20007
(202) 337-5520

Gallaudet College
7th and Florida Avenue, NE
Washington, DC 20002

International Association of Parents
   of the Deaf
814 Thayer Av.
Silver Springs, MD 20910
(301) 585-5400

John Tracy Clinic (Deaf, Deaf/Blind)
806 West Adams Blvd.
Los Angeles, CA 90007

National Association of the Deaf
814 Thayer Avenue
Silver Springs, MD 20910
(301) 587-1788

National Registry of Interpreters for the
   Deaf
814 Thayer Avenue
Silver Springs, MD 20910
(301) 588-2406

Heart Defects

American Heart Association
7320 Greenville Avenue
Dallas, TX 75231
(214) 750-5300

Mended Hearts
7320 Greenville Avenue
Dallas, TX 75231
(214) 750-5442

Herpes

Herpes Resource Center
Box 100
Palo Alto, CA 94302
(415) 321-5134

Huntington's Chorea

Committee to Combat Huntington's
   Disease
250 West 57th Street, Suite 2016
New York, NY 10107
(212) 757-0443

National Huntington's Disease
   Association
128 A East 74th Street
New York, NY 10021
(212) 744-0302

Ileitis/Colitis

National Foundation for Ileitis and
   Colitis
295 Madison Avenue
New York, NY 10017
(212) 685-3440

United Ostomy Association
2001 West Beverly Blvd.
Los Angeles, CA 90057
(213) 413-5510

Iron Overload

Iron Overload Diseases of America
5409 Harriet Place
West Palm Beach, FL 33407
(305) 689-6968

Joseph Disease

International Joseph Disease Association
P.O. Box 2550
Livermore, CA 94550
(415) 455-0706

Kidney

American Kidney Fund
7315 Wisconsin Avenue
Suite 203 East
Bethesda, MD 20814
(301) 985-1444

National Association of Patients on
    Hemodialysis and Transplantation
156 William Street
New York, NY 10038
(212) 619-2727

National Kidney Foundation, Inc.
2 Park Avenue
New York, NY 10016
(212) 889-2210

Laryngectomees

International Association of
    Laryngectomees
c/o American Cancer Society
777 Third Av.
New York, NY 10017
(212) 371-2900

Learning Disabilities

National Association for Children and
    Adults with Learning Disabilities
4156 Library Road
Pittsburgh, PA 15234
(412) 341-1515

Orton Dyslexia Society
724 York Rd.
Baltimore, MD 21204
(301) 296-0232

Leprosy

American Leprosy Missions
1262 Broad Street, Drawer A
Bloomfield, NY 07003
(201) 338-9197

Little People

Little People of America (dwarfs)
Box 126
Owatonna, MN 55060
(507) 451-1320

Liver

Children's Liver Foundation
28 Highland Avenue
Maplewood, NJ 07040
(201) 761-1111

Lou Gehrig Disease

Amyotrophic Lateral Sclerosis Society of
    America (ALS)
15300 Ventura, Blvd., Suite 315
Sherman Oaks, CA 91403
(213) 990-2151

National ALS Foundation
185 Madison Ave.
New York, NY 10016
(212) 679-4016

Lupus

Leanon
c/o Betty Hull
Box 10243
Corpus Christi, TX 78410

Lupus Foundation of America
1173 Holly Springs Drive
St. Louis, MO 63141
(314) 872-9036

Mental Deficiency

National Association for Retarded
  Citizens
2501 Ave. J
Arlington, TX 76011
(817) 261-0204

American Association on Mental
  Deficiency
Wisconsin Ave., NW
Washington, DC 20016
(202) 686-5400

Retarded Infants Services
386 Park Avenue, S.
New York, NY 10016
(212) 889-5464

Special Olympics
1701 K Street, NW
Suite 203
Washington, DC 20006
(202) 331-1346

Mental Health/Behavioral Disorders

National Alliance for the Mentally Ill
1234 Massachusetts Av., NW #721
Washington, DC 20005
(202) 783-6393

National Consortium on Child Mental
  Health Services
1424 15th Street, NW, Suite 201 A
Washington, DC 20036
(202) 462-3755

Council for Children with Behavioral
  Disorders
1920 Association Dr.
Reston, VA 22091
(703) 620-3660

Missing Children

Child Find
P.O. Box 277
New Paltz, NY 12561
(914) 255-1848
1-800-431-5005

National Runaway Switchboard
2210 North Halstead
Chicago, IL 60614
(312) 929-5854
Hotlines: (IL) 1-800-972-6004
  (U.S.) 1-800-621-4000

Mucopolysaccharidoses

MPS Society (Mucopolysaccharidoses)
552 Central Av.
Bethpage, NY 11714
(516) 433-4410

Multiple Sclerosis

National Multiple Sclerosis Society
205 East 42nd Street
New York, NY 10017
(212) 986-3240

Muscular Dystrophy

Muscular Dystrophy Association
810 Seventh Avenue
New York, NY 10019
(212) 661-0808

Myasthenia Gravis

Myasthenia Gravis Foundation, Inc.
15 E. 26th St., Suite 1603
New York, NY 10010
(212) 889-8157

Neurofibromatosis

National Neurofibromatosis Foundation
70 West 40th Street, 4th Floor
New York, NY 10018
(212) 869-9034

Pagets Disease

Pagets Disease Foundation
P.O. Box 2772
Brooklyn, NY 11202
(212) 596-1043

Parkinson's Disease

American Parkinson Disease Association
116 John St., Suite 417
New York, NY 10038
(212) 732-9550

Parkinson's Educational Program-USA
1800 Park Newport #302
Newport Beach, CA 92660
(714) 640-0218

Physically Handicapped

National Association of Physically
  Handicapped
76 Elm Street
London, OH 43140
(614) 852-1664

PKU

PKU Parents
518 Paco Drive
Los Altos, CA 94022
(415) 941-9799

Prader Willi

Prader Willi Syndrome Association
5515 Malibu Drive
Edina, MN 55436
(612) 933-0113

Psoriasis

National Psoriasis Foundation
6415 West Canyon Ct., Suite 200
Portland, OR 97221
(503) 297-1545

Red Cross

American National Red Cross
17 & D Street, NW
Washington, DC 20006
(202) 737-8300

Retinitis Pigmentosa

National Retinitis Pigmentosa
Rolling Park 131
8331 Mindale Circle
Baltimore, MD 21207
(301) 655-1011

Reyes Syndrome

American Reyes Syndrome
701 South Logan, Suite 203
Denver, CO 80209
(303) 777-2592

National Reyes Syndrome
P.O. Box RS
7045 Traverse Avenue
Benzonia, MI 49616
(616) 882-5521

National Reyes Syndrome Foundation
426 North Lewis
Bryan, OH 43506
(419) 636-2679

Scleroderma

United Scleroderma Foundation
P.O. Box 350
Watsonville, CA 95077
(408) 728-2202

Schizophrenia

American Schizophrenia Association
Huxley Institute
219 E. 31st St.
New York, NY 10016
(212) 683-9455

Scoliosis

National Scoliosis Foundation
48 Stone Road
Belmont, MA 02178
(617) 439-0888

Scoliosis Association
1 Penn Station
New York, NY 10001
(212) 845-1760

Severely Handicapped

Association for the Severely Handicapped
7010 Roosevelt Way, NE
Seattle, WA 98115
(206) 523-8446

Sibling

Sibling Information Network
Dept. of Ed. Psychology U64
University of Connecticut
Storrs, CT 06268
(204) 486-4034

Sleep Disturbances

American Narcolepsy Association
  (sleep apnea)
P.O. Box 5846
Stanford, CT 94305
(415) 591-7979

Narcolepsy & Cataplexy Foundation of
  America
1410 New York Avenue, Suite 2D
New York, NY 10021
(212) 628-6315

Spina Bifida

Spina Bifida Association of America
343 South Dearborn
Suite 319
Chicago, IL 60604
(312) 663-1562

Spinal Cord Injury

National Spinal Cord Injury Association
369 Elliott Street
Newton Upper Falls, MA 02164
(617) 964-0521

Stutterers

National Council of Stutterers
P.O. Box 8171
Grand Rapids, MI 49508
(616) 241-2372

Sudden Infant Death

National Sudden Infant Death Syndrome
    Foundation
Two Metro Plaza, Suite 205
8240 Professional Place
Landover, MD 20782
(301) 459-3388

Tay Sachs

National Tay Sachs & Allied Diseases
    Association
92 Washington Avenue
Cedarhurst, NY 11516
(516) 569-4300

Tinnitus

American Tinnitus Association
P.O. Box 5
Portland, OR 97207
(503) 248-9985

Tourette Syndrome

Tourette Syndrome Association
41-02 Bell Blvd.
Bayside, NY 11361
(212) 224-2999

Trisomy 18/13

Support Organization for Trisomy 18/13
c/o Kris Holladay
478 Terrace Lane
Tooele, UT 84074
(801) 882-6635

Tuberous Sclerosis

National Tuberous Sclerosis
P.O. Box 612
Winfield, IL 60190
(312) 668-0787

Twins

National Organization of Mothers of
    Twins
5405 Amberwood Lane
Rockville, MD 20853
(301) 460-9108

Visually Impaired

American Foundation for the Blind
15 West 16th Street
New York, NY 10011
(212) 620-2000

Association for Education of the
    Visually Handicapped
206 N. Washington St.
Alexandria, VA 22314
(703) 836-6060

Association for the Advancement of
    Blind and Retarded
164-09 Hillside Avenue
Jamaica, NY 11432
(212) 523-2222

Braille Institute of America
741 N. Vermont Avenue
Los Angeles, CA 90029
(213) 663-1111

Guidedog Foundation for the Blind
109-19 72nd Avenue
Forest Hills, NY 11375
(212) 263-4885

National Association for the
   Visually Handicapped
305 East 24th Street
New York, NY 10010
(212) 889-3141

National Federation of the Blind
1800 Johnson Street
Baltimore, MD 21230
(301) 659-9314

National Society to Prevent Blindness
79 Madison Avenue
New York, NY 10016
(212) 684-3505

Wilsons Disease

Foundation for the Study of Wilsons
   Disease
5447 Palisade Av.
Bronx, NY 10471
(212) 436-2091

Wilson's Disease Association
   (also Menkes' disease)
P.O. Box 489
Dumfries, VA 22026
(703) 221-5532

Appendix V

MEDICATIONS COMMONLY USED WITH SCHOOL CHILDREN

Susan M. Vess and Ira B. Goldberg, Pharm.D.
Northeast Louisiana University

School psychologists encounter many children with health problems that hinder the youngsters' abilities to profit from schooling. In addition, through their contacts with parents and through their review of school and health records, practitioners are confronted with the names of medications with which they are unfamiliar.

The following is a listing, by no means complete, of drugs used to control disturbances in behavior or to reduce the discomfort of arthritis and allergies. None of the medications eliminate the health problem, but all are expected to provide the child with sufficient relief of symptoms that he is able to learn.

The medications are listed in chart form for convenient access. More complete information about the disorder and medication should be sought from professionals such as physicians, pharmacists, and school nurses and from reference books including the Annual Physicians Desk Reference (PDR).

Disturbances in Behavior
Anxiety and Psychosis
"Tranquilizers (Psychotropic Drugs)"

TRADE NAME	GENERIC NAME	TREATMENT COMMENTS
Thorazine	chlorpromazine[1]	aggressive, very agitated behavior
Mellaril	thioridozine[1]	hyperkinesis
Stelazine	trifluoperazine[1]	
Phenergan	promethazine[1]	
Compazine	prochlorperazine[1]	
Haldol	haloperidol[2]	Childhood Schizophrenia, emotional tics Tourette Syndrome
Valium	diazepam[3]	ulcers, status epilepticus, reduce spasticity of Cerebral Palsy
Librium	chlordiazepoxide[3]	
Dalmane	flurazepam	
Equanil, Miltown	meprobamate[3]	
Lithane, Lithotabs	lithium[2]	manic-depressive, antipsychotic
Tofranil	imipramine[3]	anti-depressant, enuresis

Tranquilizers: sedation; decreased motor activity including hyperactivity and restlessness; reduce anxiety, aggression, combativeness

[1]phenothiazines: control aggressive and self-destructive behavior in psychotic children

[2]strong (major) tranquilizers: antipsychotics

[3]mild (minor) tranquilizers: control anxiety, sedation

Disturbances in Behavior

Seizure Disorders (Epileptics)
"Anticonvulsants"*

TRADE NAME	GENERIC NAME	*GM	*PM	*PM(TL)	TREATMENT COMMENTS
Luminal	phenobarbital	X		X	safest overall, first tried
Dilantin	phenytoin	X		X	little sedative effect
Mysoline	primidone	X		X	often combined with other medication, may act as sedative. Converted to phenobarbitol in the body
Zarontin	ethosuximide		X		choice drug for petit mal
Tegretol	carbamazine	X		X	best for psychomotor seizures
Clonopin	clonazepam		X		for epilepsy hard to treat with other drugs
Depakene	valproic acid	X	X	X	also for febrile convulsions
Mesantoin	mephenytoin	X		X	especially psychomotor seizures. Often reserved for resistant cases.
Mebaral	mephobarbital	X		X	barbituate; sedative effect
Tridione	trimethadione		X		effective but may be toxic
Paradione	paramethadione		X		effective but may be toxic
Celontin	methsuximide		X		mixed seizure types
Diamox	acetazolamide		X		supplemental in petit mal; diuretic for women several days before menstrual cycle with epilepsy associated with menstruation.

[* drug chosen by seizure type]   * GM = Grand Mal
     * PM = Petit Mal
     * PM(TL) = Psychomotor (Temporal Lobe) seizures

Status epilepticus: Valium (diazepam)
     Dilantin (phenytoin)
     Sodium phenobarbital
     Paraldehyde

Anticonvulsants reduce or control seizure activity.

Disturbances in Behavior
Attention Deficits Disorders (MBD, hyperactivity)
"Stimulants"

DRUG NAME	GENERIC NAME	TREATMENT COMMENTS
Ritalin	methylphenidate	Control the overt symptoms
Dexedrine	dextroamphetamine	but not the sole treatment;
Cylert	pemoline	learning improves as a consequence of increased attention span (of all drugs listed)

Stimulants: strengthen selective attention, reduce impulsivity, hyperactivity and restlessness in children of normal ability

Side Effects: insomnia and anorexia

Juvenile Rheumatoid Arthritis
"analgesics and anti-inflammatories"

DRUG NAME	GENERIC NAME	TREATMENT COMMENTS
Aspirin	acetylsalicylic acid	Reduce fever, and relieve
Ascriptin	acetylsalicylic acid, buffered	pain in order to restore
Tylenol	acetaminophen	and maintain joint motion
Tolectin	tolmetin	
Anaprox	naproxen	approved for children?
Butazolidin*	phenylbutazone	
Indocin*	indomethacin	
Motrin*	ibuprofen fenoprofen	
Corticosteroids	prednisone	Intermittent symptomatic treatment of inflammatory symptoms. May require stepwise discontinuation of therapy to prevent dangerous withdrawal symptoms.

* Not FDA approved for JRA but may be used by physicians

Goal: Enable normal physical and emotional functioning so that the child is sufficiently comfortable to attend school and learn.

Respiratory Illnesses
Allergies, Rhinitis, and "Colds"
"antihistamines, nasal decongestants, cough suppressants"

DRUG NAME	GENERIC NAME(s)	TREATMENT COMMENTS
Actidil	triprolidine[1]	All antihistamines below may be used for symptoms of hay fever, allergies, allergic rhinitis, allergic conjunctivitis
Chlor-Trimeton Histaspan Teldrin	chlorpheniramine[1]	
Dimetane Veltane Symptom 3	brompheniramine[1]	
Benadryl	diphenhydramine[1]	above plus frequently used for acute allergic reactions, skin rahs, etc., sedative effect
PBZ(Pyribenzamine)	tripelennamine[1]	also used for allergic skin reactions
Decapryn	doxylamine[1]	
Temaril	trimeprazine[1]	used primarily for itching, related to major tranquilizers structurally
Tacaryl	methdilazine[1]	same as Temaril
Atarax Vistaril	hydroxyzine[1]	mild tranquilizer with anti-histaminic effects, used frequently for itching and allergic rash, hives
Periactin	cyproheptadine[1]	itching, rash, hives; rarely used as "antihistamine"; may increase appetite and occasionally used for this purpose
Dramamine	dimenhydrinate[1]	antihistaminic used for nausea vomiting and dizziness, motion sickness
Bonine Antivert	meclizine[1]	as above
Marezine	cyclizine[1]	as above
Sudafed Novafed Afrinol Neosynephrol	pseudoephedrine[2]	nasal decongestant, stimulant side effects in some cases

(Respiratory Illnesses — allergies, rhinitis, and "colds" continued)

DRUG NAME	GENERIC NAME(s)	TREATMENT COMMENTS
Neosynephrine drops Alconefrin drops Isophrin	phenylephrine[2]	topical nasal decongestant
Afrin drops	oxymetazoline[2]	long acting product
Otrivin drops	xylometazoline[2]	long acting product
Dimetapp	brompheniramine[1] phenylephrine[2] phenylpropanolamine[2]	antihistamine nasal decongestant combination for head cold and allergy
Rondec	carbinoxamine[1] pseudoephedrine[2]	
Actifed	triprolidine[1] pseudoehpedrine[2]	
Co-Tylenol	chlorpheniramine[1] pseudoephedrine[2] dextromethorphan[3] acetaminophen	as above with Tylenol for fever, aches, pains, etc.
Novahistine products	chlorpheniramine[1] phenylpropanolamine[2] or pseudoephedrine[2] dextromethorphan[3] or	cough and cold combination of antihistamine with nasal decongestant, cough suppressant, and/or expectorant
Sudafed products	codeine[3] guaifensin[4]	Label of specific product should be consulted for specific combination
Robitussin products	same as above without antihistamine	
Triaminic products	pyrilamine[1] and pheniramine[1] or chlorpheniramine[1] phenylpropanolamine[2] dextromethorphan[3] or codeine[3] guaifensin[4]	
Actifed-C	triprolidine[1] pseudoephedrine[2] codeine[3] guaifensin[4]	cough and cold combination

(Respiratory Illnesses — allergies, rhinitis, and "colds" continued)

DRUG NAME	GENERIC NAME(s)	TREATMENT COMMENTS
Phenergan products	promethazine[1] ipecac fluidext[4] pot. guaicolsulfonate[4] citric acid[4] sodium citrate[4] dextromethorphan[3] or codeine[3]	
Naldecon products	phenyltoloxamine[1] chlorpheniramine[1] phenylephrine[2] phenylpropanolamine[2] dextromethorphan[3] or codeine[3] guaifensin[4]	

Treatment goal: relief of symptoms with minimum or no side-effects

[1]antihistamines: control itching, runny nose and sneezing of allergy, unknown potency, variable side-effects including drowsiness and drying of mouth, nose and throat.

[2]adrenergic agents, decongestants: improve airflow by causing constricted air passages to relax, reduce congestion by constriction of vessels of the nasal mucosa.

[3]cough suppressants: suppress the cough reflex, for non-productive dry cough.

[4]expectorants; liquefy phlegm and secretions to make easier to cough up.

Respiratory Illnesses
Asthma
"adrenergic agents, bronchodilators, steroids"

DRUG NAME	GENERIC NAME	TREATMENT COMMENTS
Theodur Slo-Phyllin Elixophyllin Aerolate Sustaire Theolair Theobid Theovent Somophyllin Slo-bid	theophylline[1]	bronchodilator, Long-acting products are used for prophylactic treatment of severe recurrent asthma. Nervousness, tremulousness, gastrointestinal upset (nausea and vomiting) and fast heart beat can be early signs of excessive blood levels of theophylline.

(Respiratory Illnesses — asthma continued)

DRUG NAME	GENERIC NAME	TREATMENT COMMENTS
Aminodur Aminophylline (var. mfg.)	aminophylline[1]	chemically related to and converted to theophylline in the body
Lufyllin Dilor Neothylline	diphylline[1]	theophylline analog
Choledyl	oxtriphylline[1]	theophylline analog
Bronkaid tablets Tedral tablets Primatene tablets Marax Brondecon Quibron Isuprel compd.	theophylline with: ephedrine[2], guaifensin[3] ephedrine[2], phenobarbital[4] ephedrine[2], phenobarbital[4] ephedrine[2], hydroxyzine[4] guaifensin[3] guaifensin[3] ephedrine[2], isoproterenol[2] phenobarbital[4], pot. iodide[3]	combination products used for asthma
Adrenalin Asthma Meter Medihaler-Epi Primatene Mist Bronkaid Mist AsthmaNefrin Vaponefrin AsthmaHaler	epinephrine[2]	inhalation for acute asthma attacks, adrenergic bronchodilator with short activity used by inhalation
Bronkosol	isoetharine[2]	adrenergic bronchodilator with longer duration of effect
Medihaler-Iso Isuprel Mistometer Norisodrine Inhaler	isoproterenol[2]	short-acting adrenergic bronchodilator used by inhalation
Proventil	albuterol[2]	longest acting (4-6 hrs.) inhalation bronchodilating adrenergics; may be used for prophylactic treatment by inhalation or as oral tablets.
Alupent Metaprel	metaproterenol[2]	adrenergic bronchodilator used either by inhalation or oral tablets. Inhalation may be used for acute attacks.
Bricanyl Bretnine	terbutaline[2]	primarily used to prevent asthma attacks.

(Respiratory Illnesses - asthma continued)

DRUG NAME	GENERIC NAME	TREATMENT COMMENTS
Intal Aarane	cromolyn[5]	used to de-trigger or prevent acute attacks of asthma as caused by cold or exercise but takes two weeks for full effect. Requires complicated technique for inhaling powder contents of capsule. Will worsen an acute attack due to irritation of airways if used then.
Beconase Vanceril	beclomethasone[6]	inhalation steroid used to decrease frequency of asthma attacks if used regularly; may be used for allergic rhinitis occasionally.

[1]theophylline: non-adrenergic bronchodilator. Use with adrenergic bronchodilators may give additive effects. Relaxes smooth muscle lining of the airways in bronchioles in lungs.

[2]adrenergic bronchodilators: same activity as theophylline but by a different mechanism or action. Frequent side effects are muscle tremors and nervousness sometimes seen even at normal dosages. May be stimulant in some patients.

[3]expectorants: Used to liquefy thick mucus secretions present in an acute asthma attack or often seen in bronchitis.

[4]sedatives: Thought to "calm" asthmatics and decrease the possibility of attacks triggered by nervous excitement. The value of these in asthma is questionable.

[5]cromolyn: product is thought to "stabilize" cells in the airway surface which might initiate an asthma attack in response to an allergic stimulation.

[6]steroids: anti-inflammatory agents felt to decrease the frequency and severity of asthma attacks due to allergic inflammatory stimuli.